D0881367

THE PAPERS OF
BENJAMIN FRANKLIN

SPONSORED BY

The American Philosophical Society

and Yale University

Benjamin Franklin

THE PAPERS OF

Benjamin Franklin

VOLUME 29 *March 1 through June 30, 1779*

BARBARA B. OBERG, *Editor*

DOROTHY W. BRIDGWATER, ELLEN R. COHN,

JONATHAN R. DULL,

AND CATHERINE M. PRELINGER, *Associate Editors*

MARILYN A. MORRIS, *Assistant Editor*

CLAUDE A. LOPEZ, *Consulting Editor*

New Haven and London YALE UNIVERSITY PRESS, 1992

Funds for editing this volume of The Papers of Benjamin Franklin *have been provided by the Andrew W. Mellon Foundation, the Pew Charitable Trusts, the American Philosophical Society, the National Historical Publications and Records Commission under the chairmanship of the Archivist of the United States, and the Kemper Educational and Charitable Fund. For all these sources of support the editors are most grateful.*

Publication of this volume was assisted by a grant from the National Historical Publications and Records Commission.

Library of Congress catalog card number: 59–12697
International standard book number: 0–300–05188–3

∞The paper in this book meets the guidelines for permanence and durability of the Committee on Production Guidelines for Book Longevity of the Council on Library Resources.

Printed in the U.S.A.

To

WHITFIELD J. BELL, JR.

Contents

French surnames and titles of nobility often run to great length. Our practice with an untitled person is to provide all the Christian names at the first appearance, and then drop them; a chevalier or noble is given the title used at the time, and details are provided in a footnote.

*Denotes a document referred to in annotation.

List of Illustrations

Contributors to Volume 29

The ownership of each manuscript, or the location of the particular copy used by the editors of each rare contemporary pamphlet or similar printed work, is indicated where the document appears in the text. The sponsors and editors are deeply grateful to the following institutions and individuals for permission to print or otherwise use in the present volume manuscripts and other materials which they own.

INSTITUTIONS

Algemeen Rijksarchief, The Hague
American Philosophical Society
Archives de l'Académie royale des sciences, Paris
Archives de la Marine, Vincennes
Archives du Ministère des affaires étrangères, Paris
Boston Public Library
Dartmouth College Library
Gemeente-Archief, Stadserf, Breda
Harvard University Library
Haverford College Library
Henry E. Huntington Library
Historical Society of Pennsylvania
Library of Congress
Massachusetts Archives
Massachusetts Historical Society
National Archives
New-York Historical Society
New York Public Library
Princeton University Library
Franklin D. Roosevelt Library, Hyde Park, New York
Royal Library, Windsor
United States Naval Academy Museum
University of Pennsylvania Library
University of Virginia Library
Virginia Historical Society
Yale University Library

INDIVIDUALS

Benjamin F. Bailar, Houston, Texas
Walter R. Benjamin Autographs, Inc., Hunter, New York
His Excellency M. Jacques Delarue Caron de Beaumarchais, Paris
S. Howard Goldman, Weston, Connecticut
Joseph Y. Jeanes, Jr., Wilmington, Delaware
Mrs. C. Phillip Miller, Chicago, Illinois
The 19th Century Shop, Baltimore, Maryland
M.H. Venables, Bristol, England

Statement of Methodology

Arrangement of Materials

The documents are printed in chronological sequence according to their dates when these are given, or according to the date of publication in cases of contemporary printed materials. Records such as diaries, journals, and account books that cover substantial periods of time appear according to the dates of their earliest entries. When no date appears on the document itself, one is editorially supplied and an explanation provided. When no day within a month is given, the document is placed at the end of all specifically dated documents of that month; those dated only by year are placed at the end of that year. If no date is given, we use internal and external evidence to assign one whenever possible, providing our explanation in annotation. Documents which cannot be assigned a date more definite than the entire length of Franklin's stay in France (1777–85) will be published at the end of this period. Those for which we are unable to provide even a tentative date will be published at the conclusion of the series.

When two or more documents have the same date, they are arranged in the following order:

1. Those by a group of which Franklin was a member (*e.g.*, the American Commissioners in Paris)
2. Those by Franklin individually
3. Those to a group of which Franklin was a member
4. Those to Franklin individually
5. "Third-party" and unaddressed miscellaneous writings by others than Franklin.

In the first two categories letters are arranged alphabetically by the name of the addressee; in the last three, by the name of the signatory. An exception to this practice occurs when a letter to Franklin and his answer were written on the same day: in such cases the first letter precedes the reply. The same rules apply to documents lacking precise dates printed together at the end of any month or year.

Form of Presentation

The document and its accompanying editorial apparatus are presented in the following order:

1. *Title.* Essays and formal papers are headed by their titles, except in the case of pamphlets with very long titles, when a short form is substituted. Where previous editors supplied a title to a piece that had none, and this title has become familiar, we use it; otherwise we devise a suitable one.

Letters written by Franklin individually are entitled "To" the person or body addressed, as: To John Adams; To John Adams and Arthur Lee; To the Royal Society.

Letters to Franklin individually are entitled "From" the person or body who wrote them, as: From John Adams; From John Adams and Arthur Lee; From the Committee of Secret Correspondence.

Letters of which Franklin was a joint author or joint recipient are titled with the names of all concerned, as: Franklin and Silas Deane to Arthur Lee; Arthur Lee to Franklin and Silas Deane. "Third-party" letters or those by or to a body of which Franklin was a member are titled with the names of both writers and addressees, as: Arthur Lee to John Adams; The American Commissioners to John Paul Jones. Documents not fitting into any of these categories are given brief descriptive headings, as: Extract from Franklin's Journal.

If the name in the title has been supplied from external evidence it appears in brackets, with a question mark when we are uncertain. If a letter is unsigned, or signed with initials or an alias, but is from a correspondent whose handwriting we know, the name appears without brackets.

2. *Source Identification.* This gives the nature of the printed or manuscript version of the document, and, in the case of a manuscript or a rare printed work, the ownership and location of the original.

Printed sources of three different classes are distinguished. First, a contemporary pamphlet, which is given its full title, place and date of publication, and the location of the copy the editors have used. Second, an essay or letter appearing originally in a *contemporary* publication, which is introduced by the words "Printed in," followed by the title, date, and inclusive page numbers, if necessary, of the publication. Third, a document, the manuscript or contemporary printed version of which is now lost, but which was printed at a later date, is identified by the words "Reprinted from," followed by the name of the work from which the editors have reproduced it. The following examples illustrate the distinction:

Printed in *The Pennsylvania Gazette,* October 2, 1729.

Reprinted from William Temple Franklin, ed., *Memoirs of the Life and Writings of Benjamin Franklin* . . . (3 vols., 4to, London, 1817–18), II, 244.

The Source Identification of a manuscript consists of a term or symbol (all of which are listed in the Short Title List) indicating the character of the manuscript version, followed by the name of the holder of the manuscript, as: ALS: American Philosophical Society. Since manuscripts belonging to individuals have a tendency to migrate, we indicate the year in which each private owner gave permission to publish, as: Morris Duane, Philadelphia, 1957. When two or more manuscript versions survive, the one listed first in the Source Identification is the one from which we print.

3. An editorial *Headnote* precedes some documents in this edition; it appears between the Source Identification and the actual text. Such a headnote is designed to supply the background of the composition of the document, its relation to events or other writings, and any other information which may be useful to the reader and is not obtainable from the document itself.

4. The *Text* of the document follows the Source Identification, or Headnote, if any. When multiple copies of a document are extant, the editors observe the following order of priority in determining which of the available versions to use in printing a text: ALS or ADS, LS or DS, AL, or AD, and copy. An AL (draft) normally takes precedence over a contemporary copy based on the recipient's copy. If we deviate from the or-

der set forth here, we explain our decision in the annotation. In those instances where multiple texts are available, the texts are collated, and significant variations reported in the annotation. In selecting the publication text from among several copies of official French correspondence (*e.g.*, from Vergennes or Sartine) we use the version which is written in the best French, on the presumption that the French ministers used standard eighteenth-century spelling, grammar, and punctuation.

The form of presentation of the texts of letters is as follows:

The place and date of composition are set at the top, regardless of their location in the original manuscript.

The signature, set in capitals and small capitals, is placed at the right of the last line of the text if there is room; if not, then on the line below.

Addresses, endorsements, and notations are so labelled and printed at the end of the letter. An endorsement is, to the best of our belief, by the recipient, and a notation by someone else. When the writer of the notation has misread the date or the signature of the correspondent, we let the error stand without comment. Line breaks in addresses are marked by slashes. Different notations are separated by slashes; when they are by different individuals, we so indicate.

5. *Footnotes* to the Heading, Source Identification, Headnote, and Text appear on the pages to which they pertain. References to documents not printed or to be printed in later volumes are by date and repository, as: Jan. 17, 1780, APS.

Method of Textual Reproduction

1. *Spelling* of all words, including proper names, is retained. If it is abnormal enough to obscure the meaning we follow the word immediately with the current spelling in brackets.

2. *Capitalization and Punctuation* are retained. There is such variety in the size of initial letters, often in the same manuscript, that it is sometimes unclear whether the writer intended an upper or lower case letter. In such cases we make a decision on the basis of the correspondent's customary usage. We supply a capital letter when an immediately preceding period, co-

lon, question mark, exclamation point, or dash indicates that a new sentence is intended. If a capital letter clearly indicates the beginning of a new thought, but no mark of punctuation precedes it, we supply a period. If neither punctuation nor capital letter indicates a sentence break, we do not create one unless their lack renders comprehension of the document nearly impossible. In that case we supply them and so indicate in a footnote.

Dashes were used for a variety of purposes in eighteenth-century personal and public letters. A dash within a sentence, used to indicate a break in thought, is represented as an em dash. A dash that follows a period or serves as a closing mark of punctuation for a sentence is represented as an em dash followed by a space. Occasionally correspondents used long dashes that continue to the end of a line and indicate a significant break in thought. We do not reproduce the dash, but treat it as indicating the start of a new paragraph.

When there is an initial quotation mark or parenthesis, but no closing one, we silently complete the pair.

3. *Contractions and abbreviations* are retained. Abbreviations such as "wd", "honble", "servt", "exclly", are used so frequently in Franklin's correspondence that they are readily comprehensible to the users of these volumes. Abbreviations, particularly of French words, that may be unclear are followed by an expanded version in brackets, as: nre [navire]. Superscript letters are brought down to the line. Where a period or colon is a part of the abbreviation, or indicates that letters were written above the line, we print it at the end of the word, as: 4th. for 4.th. In those few cases where superscript letters brought down to the line result in a confusing abbreviation ("Made" for "Mad^{e}"), we follow the abbreviation by an expanded version in brackets, as: Made [Madame].

The ampersand by itself and the "&c." are retained. Letters represented by the "y" are printed, as: "the" and "that". The tailed "p" is spelled out, as: "per", "pre", or "pro". Symbols of weights, measures, and money are converted to modern forms, as: *l.t.* instead of ₶ for *livres tournois.*

4. *Omissions, mutilations, and illegible words* are treated as follows:

If we are certain of the reading of letters missing in a word because of a torn or taped manuscript or tightly bound copybook, we supply the letters silently.

If we cannot be sure of the word, or of how the author spelled it, but we can make a reasonable guess, we supply the missing letters in brackets.

When the writer has omitted a word absolutely required for clarity, we insert it in italics within brackets.

5. *Interlineations* by the author are silently incorporated into the text. If they are significant enough to require comment a footnote is provided.

Textual Conventions

/	denotes line break in addresses and different hands in notations.
⟨roman⟩	denotes a résumé of a letter or document.
[*italic*]	editorial insertion explaining something about the manuscript, as: [*one line illegible*]; or supplying a word to make the meaning clear, as: [*to*].
[roman]	editorial insertion clarifying the immediately preceding word or abbreviation; supplies letters missing because of a mutilated manuscript.
(?)	indicates a questionable reading.

Abbreviations and Short Titles

AAE	Archives du Ministère des affaires étrangères.
AD	Autograph document.
Adams Papers	Robert J. Taylor, Richard L. Ryerson *et al.,* eds., *Papers of John Adams* (8 vols. to date, Cambridge, Mass., 1977–).
ADB	*Allgemeine Deutsche Biographie* (56 vols., Berlin, 1967–71).
ADS	Autograph document signed.
AL	Autograph letter.
Allen, *Mass. Privateers*	Gardner Weld Allen, ed., *Massachusetts Privateers of the Revolution* ([Cambridge, Mass.], 1927) (Massachusetts Historical Society *Collections,* LXXVII).
Almanach des marchands	*Almanach général des marchands, négocians, armateurs, et fabricans de France et de l'Europe et autres parties du monde . . .* (Paris, 1779).
Almanach royal	*Almanach royal* (91 vols., Paris, 1700–92). Cited by year.
Alphabetical List of Escaped Prisoners	Alphabetical List of the Americans who having escap'd from the Prisons of England, were furnish'd with Money by the Commissrs. of the U.S. at the Court of France, to return to America. A manuscript in the APS, dated 1784, and covering the period January, 1777, to November, 1784.
ALS	Autograph letter signed.
Amer.	American.
APS	American Philosophical Society.
Archaeol.	Archaeological.

Assn.	Association.
Auphan, "Communications"	P. Auphan, "Les communications entre la France et ses colonies d'Amérique pendant la guerre de l'indépendance Américaine," *Revue Maritime,* new series, no. LXIII and LXIV (1925), 331–48, 497–517.
Autobiog.	Leonard W. Labaree, Ralph L. Ketcham, Helen C. Boatfield, and Helene H. Fineman, eds., *The Autobiography of Benjamin Franklin* (New Haven, 1964).
Bachaumont, *Mémoires secrets*	[Louis Petit de Bachaumont *et al.*], *Mémoires secrets pour servir à l'histoire de la république des lettres en France, depuis MDCCLXII jusqu'à nos jours; ou, Journal d'un observateur* . . . (36 vols. in 12, London, 1784–89). Bachaumont died in 1771. The first six vols. (1762–71) are his; Mathieu-François Pridansat de Mairobert edited them and wrote the next nine (1771–79); the remainder (1779–87) are by ——— Mouffle d'Angerville.
Balch, *French in America*	Thomas Balch, *The French in America during the War of Independence of the United States, 1777–1783* (trans. by Thomas Willing Balch *et al.;* 2 vols., Philadelphia, 1891–95).
BF	Benjamin Franklin.
BF's accounts as commissioner	Those described above, XXIII, 20.
BFB	Benjamin Franklin Bache.
Bigelow, *Works*	John Bigelow, ed., *The Works of Benjamin Franklin* (12 vols., New York and London, 1904).

Biographie universelle	*Biographie universelle, ancienne et moderne, ou histoire, par ordre alphabétique, de la vie publique et privée de tous les hommes qui se sont fait remarquer* . . . (85 vols., Paris, 1811–62).
Bodinier	From information kindly furnished us by Cdt. Gilbert Bodinier, Section études, Service historique de l'Armée de Terre, Vincennes.
Bodinier, *Dictionnaire*	Gilbert Bodinier, *Dictionnaire des officiers de l'armée royale qui ont combattu aux Etats-Unis pendant la guerre d'Indépendance* (Château de Vincennes, 1982).
Bowler, *Logistics*	R. Arthur Bowler, *Logistics and the Failure of the British Army in America, 1775–1783* (Princeton, 1975).
Bradford, *Jones Papers*	James C. Bradford, ed., *The Microfilm Edition of the Papers of John Paul Jones, 1747–1792* (10 reels of microfilm, Alexandria, Va., 1986).
Burke's Peerage	Sir Bernard Burke, *Burke's Genealogical and Heraldic History of the Peerage Baronetage and Knightage with War Gazette and Corrigenda* (98th ed., London, 1940). References in exceptional cases to other editions are so indicated.
Burnett, *Continental Congress*	Edmund C. Burnett, *The Continental Congress* (New York, 1941).
Burnett, *Letters*	Edmund C. Burnett, ed., *Letters of Members of the Continental Congress* (8 vols., Washington, 1921–36).
Butterfield, *Adams Correspondence*	Lyman H. Butterfield *et al.*, eds., *Adams Family Correspondence* (4 vols. to date, Cambridge, Mass., 1963–).

Butterfield, *John Adams Diary*	Lyman H. Butterfield *et al.*, eds., *Diary and Autobiography of John Adams* (4 vols., Cambridge, Mass., 1961).
Case of Silas Deane	[Edward Ingraham, ed.,] *Papers in Relation to the Case of Silas Deane* (Philadelphia, 1855).
Chron.	*Chronicle.*
Claghorn, *Naval Officers*	Charles E. Claghorn, *Naval Officers of the American Revolution: a Concise Biographical Dictionary* (Metuchen, N.J. and London, 1988).
Clark, *Ben Franklin's Privateers*	William Bell Clark, *Ben Franklin's Privateers: a Naval Epic of the American Revolution* (Baton Rouge, 1956).
Clark, *Wickes*	William Bell Clark, *Lambert Wickes, Sea Raider and Diplomat: the Story of a Naval Captain of the Revolution* (New Haven and London, 1932).
Clowes, *Royal Navy*	William Laird Clowes, *The Royal Navy: a History from the Earliest Times to the Present* (7 vols., Boston and London, 1897–1903).
Cobbett, *Parliamentary History*	William Cobbett and Thomas C. Hansard, eds., *The Parliamentary History of England from the Earliest Period to 1803* (36 vols., London, 1806–20).
Col.	Column.
Coll.	*Collections.*
Commons Jours.	*Journals of the House of Commons* (233 vols. to date, [London,] 1803–); vols. I–LI are reprints.
Croÿ, *Journal*	Emmanuel, prince de Moeurs et de Solre et duc de Croÿ, *Journal inédit du duc de Croÿ, 1718–1784* (4 vols., Paris, 1906–07).

Cushing, *Writings of Samuel Adams*	Harry Alonzo Cushing, ed., *The Writings of Samuel Adams* . . . (4 vols., New York, 1904–08).
d.	*denier.*
D	Document unsigned.
DAB	*Dictionary of American Biography.*
DBF	*Dictionnaire de biographie française* (18 vols. to date, Paris, 1933–).
Deane Correspondence	*The Deane Papers; Correspondence between Silas Deane, His Brothers and Their Business and Political Associates, 1771–1795* (Connecticut Historical Society *Collections,* XXIII, Hartford, Conn., 1930).
Deane Papers	*The Deane Papers, 1774–90* (5 vols.; New-York Historical Society *Collections,* XIX–XXIII, New York, 1887–91).
DF	Deborah Franklin.
Dictionnaire de la noblesse	François-Alexandre Aubert de La Chesnaye-Dubois and M. Badier, *Dictionnaire de la noblesse contenant les généalogies, l'histoire & la chronologie des familles nobles de la France* . . . (3rd ed.; 19 vols., Paris, 1863–76).
Dictionnaire historique	*Dictionnaire historique, critique et bibliographique, contenant les vies des hommes illustres, célèbres ou fameux de tous les pays et de tous les siècles* . . . (30 vols., Paris, 1821–23).
Dictionnaire historique de la Suisse	*Dictionnaire historique & biographique de la Suisse* (7 vols. and supplement, Neuchatel, 1921–34).
DNB	*Dictionary of National Biography.*
Doniol, *Histoire*	Henri Doniol, *Histoire de la participation de la France à l'établissement des Etats-Unis d'Amérique. Correspondance diplomatique et documents* (5 vols., Paris, 1886–99).

DS	Document signed.
Duane, *Works*	William Duane, ed., *The Works of Dr. Benjamin Franklin* . . . (6 vols., Philadelphia, 1808–18). Title varies in the several volumes.
Dubourg, *Œuvres*	Jacques Barbeu-Dubourg, ed., *Œuvres de M. Franklin* . . . (2 vols., Paris, 1773).
Dull, *French Navy*	Jonathan R. Dull, *The French Navy and American Independence: a Study of Arms and Diplomacy, 1774–1787* (Princeton, 1975).
Ed.	Edition or editor.
Edler, *Dutch Republic*	Friedrich Edler, *The Dutch Republic and the American Revolution (Johns Hopkins University Studies in Historical and Political Science.* ser. XXIX, no. 2; Baltimore, 1911).
Elias and Finch, *Letters of Digges*	Robert H. Elias and Eugene D. Finch, eds., *Letters of Thomas Attwood Digges (1742–1821)* (Columbia, S.C., 1982).
Etat militaire	*Etat militaire de France, pour l'année* . . . (36 vols., Paris, 1758–93). Cited by year.
Exper. and Obser.	*Experiments and Observations on Electricity, made at Philadelphia in America, by Mr. Benjamin Franklin* . . . (London, 1751). Revised and enlarged editions were published in 1754, 1760, 1769, and 1774 with slightly varying titles. In each case the edition cited will be indicated, e.g., *Exper. and Obser.* (1751).
Fauchille, *Diplomatie française*	Paul Fauchille, *La Diplomatie française et la ligue des neutres de 1780 (1776–1783)* (Paris, 1893).
Ferguson, *Power of the Purse*	Elmer James Ferguson, *The Power of the Purse: a History of American Public Finance* . . . (Chapel Hill, N.C., 1961).

Fitzpatrick, *Writings of Washington*	John C. Fitzpatrick, ed., *The Writings of George Washington . . .* (39 vols., Washington, D.C., 1931–44).
Force, *Amer. Arch.*	Peter Force, ed., *American Archives: Consisting of a Collection of Authentic Records, State Papers, Debates, and Letters and Other Notices of Publick Affairs . . .*, fourth series, March 7, 1774 to July 4, 1776 (6 vols., [Washington, 1837–46]); fifth series, July 4, 1776 to September 3, 1783 (3 vols., [Washington, 1848–53]).
Ford, *Letters of William Lee*	Worthington Chauncey Ford, ed., *Letters of William Lee, 1766–1783* (3 vols., Brooklyn, N.Y., 1891).
Fortescue, *Correspondence of George Third*	Sir John William Fortescue, ed., *The Correspondence of King George the Third from 1760 to December 1783 . . .* (6 vols., London, 1927–28).
France ecclésiastique	*La France ecclésiastique pour l'année . . .* (15 vols., Paris, 1774–90). Cited by year.
Freeman, *Washington*	Douglas S. Freeman (completed by John A. Carroll and Mary W. Ashworth), *George Washington: a Biography* (7 vols., New York, 1948–57).
Gaz.	*Gazette.*
Gaz. de Leyde	*Nouvelles extraordinaires de divers endroits,* commonly known as *Gazette de Leyde.* Each issue is in two parts; we indicate the second as "sup."
Geneal.	*Genealogical.*
Gent. Mag.	*The Gentleman's Magazine, and Historical Chronicle.*
Gruber, *Howe Brothers*	Ira D. Gruber, *The Howe Brothers and the American Revolution* (New York, 1972).

Hayes, *Calendar*	I. Minis Hayes, *Calendar of the Papers of Benjamin Franklin in the Library of the American Philosophical Society* (5 vols., Philadelphia, 1908).
Heitman, *Register of Officers*	Francis B. Heitman, *Historical Register of Officers in the War of the Revolution . . .* (Washington, D.C., 1893).
Hillairet, *Rues de Paris*	Jacques Hillairet, pseud. of Auguste A. Coussillan, *Dictionnaire historique des rues de Paris* (2nd ed.; 2 vols., [Paris, 1964]).
Hist.	*Historic* or *Historical.*
Idzerda, *Lafayette Papers*	Stanley J. Idzerda *et al.,* eds., *Lafayette in the Age of the American Revolution: Selected Letters and Papers, 1776– 1790* (5 vols. to date, Ithaca, N.Y., and London, 1977–).
JA	John Adams.
JCC	Worthington C. Ford *et al.,* eds., *Journals of the Continental Congress, 1744–1789* (34 vols., Washington, 1904–37).
Jefferson Papers	Julian P. Boyd, Charles T. Cullen, John Catanzariti *et al.,* eds., *The Papers of Thomas Jefferson* (24 vols. to date, Princeton, 1950–).
Jour.	*Journal.*
JW	Jonathan Williams, Jr.
Kaminkow, *Mariners*	Marion and Jack Kaminkow, *Mariners of the American Revolution* (Baltimore, 1967).
L	Letter unsigned.
Larousse	Pierre Larousse, *Grand dictionnaire universel du XIXe siècle . . .* (17 vols., Paris, [n.d.]).

Lasseray, *Les Français*	André Lasseray, *Les Français sous les treize étoiles, 1775–1783* (2 vols., Paris, 1935).
Laurens Papers	Philip M. Hamer, George C. Rogers, Jr., David R. Chestnutt *et al.*, eds., *The Papers of Henry Laurens* (12 vols. to date, Columbia, S.C. 1968–).
Le Bihan, *Francs-maçons parisiens*	Alain Le Bihan, *Francs-maçons parisiens du Grand Orient de France* . . . (Commission d'histoire économique et sociale de la révolution française, *Mémoires et documents,* XIX, Paris, 1966).
Lee, *Life of Arthur Lee*	Richard Henry Lee, *Life of Arthur Lee, L.L.D., Joint Commissioner of the United States to the Court of France, and Sole Commissioner to the Courts of Spain and Prussia, during the Revolutionary War* . . . (2 vols., Boston, 1829).
Lee Family Papers	Paul P. Hoffman, ed., *The Lee Family Papers, 1742–1795* (University of Virginia *Microfilm Publication* No. 1; 8 reels, Charlottesville, Va., 1966).
Lewis, *Walpole Correspondence*	Wilmarth S. Lewis *et al.*, eds., *The Yale Edition of Horace Walpole's Correspondence* (48 vols., New Haven, 1939–83).
Lopez, *Mon Cher Papa*	Claude-Anne Lopez, *Mon Cher Papa: Franklin and the Ladies of Paris* (rev. ed., New Haven and London, 1990).
Lopez and Herbert, *The Private Franklin*	Claude-Anne Lopez and Eugenia W. Herbert, *The Private Franklin: the Man and His Family* (New York, 1975).
LS	Letter or letters signed.
l.t.	*livres tournois.*
Lüthy, *Banque protestante*	Herbert Lüthy, *La Banque protestante en France de la Révocation de l'Edit de*

Nantes à la Révolution (2 vols., Paris, 1959–61).

Mackesy, *War for America* — Piers Mackesy, *The War for America, 1775–1783* (Cambridge, Mass., 1965).

Mag. — *Magazine.*

Mass. Arch. — Massachusetts Archives, State House, Boston.

Mazas, *Ordre de Saint-Louis* — Alexandre Mazas and Théodore Anne, *Histoire de l'ordre royal et militaire de Saint-Louis depuis son institution en 1693 jusqu'en 1830* (2nd ed.; 3 vols., Paris, 1860–61).

Meng, *Despatches of Gérard* — John J. Meng, *Despatches and Instructions of Conrad Alexandre Gérard, 1778–1780 . . .* (Baltimore, 1939).

Meyer, *Armement nantais* — Jean Meyer, *L'Armement nantais dans la deuxième moitié du XVIIIe siècle* (Paris, 1969).

Meyer, *Noblesse bretonne* — Jean Meyer, *La Noblesse bretonne au XVIIIe siècle* (2 vols., Paris, 1966).

Morison, *Jones* — Samuel E. Morison, *John Paul Jones: a Sailor's Biography* (Boston & Toronto, 1959).

Morris Papers — E. James Ferguson, John Catanzariti, Elizabeth M. Nuxoll *et al.*, eds., *The Papers of Robert Morris, 1781–1784* (7 vols. to date, Pittsburgh, Pa., 1973–).

Morton, *Beaumarchais Correspondance* — Brian N. Morton and Donald C. Spinelli, eds., *Beaumarchais Correspondance* (4 vols. to date, Paris, 1969–).

MS, MSS — Manuscript, manuscripts.

Namier and Brooke, *House of Commons* — Sir Lewis Namier and John Brooke, *The History of Parliament. The House of Commons 1754–1790* (3 vols., London and New York, 1964).

Naval Docs.	William B. Clark, William J. Morgan *et al.*, eds., *Naval Documents of the American Revolution* (9 vols. to date, Washington, D.C., 1964–).
Neeser, *Conyngham*	Robert Walden Neeser, ed., *Letters and Papers Relating to the Cruises of Gustavus Conyngham, Captain of the Continental Navy 1777–1779* (New York, 1915).
NNBW	*Nieuw Nederlandsch Biografisch Woordenboek* (10 vols. and index, Amsterdam, 1974).
Nouvelle biographie	*Nouvelle biographie générale depuis les temps les plus reculés jusqu'à nos jours . . .* (46 vols., Paris, 1855–66).
Pa. Arch.	Samuel Hazard *et al.*, eds., *Pennsylvania Archives* (9 series, Philadelphia and Harrisburg, 1852–1935).
Pa. Col. Recs.	*Minutes of the Provincial Council of Pennsylvania . . .* (16 vols., Harrisburg, 1851–53). Volumes I–III are reprints published in Philadelphia, 1852. Title changes with Volume XI to *Supreme Executive Council.*
Palmer, *Loyalists*	Gregory Palmer, ed., *Biographical Sketches of Loyalists of the American Revolution* (Westport, Ct., 1984).
Patterson, *The Other Armada.*	A. Temple Patterson, *The Other Armada: the Franco-Spanish Attempt to Invade Britain in 1779* (Manchester, Eng., 1960)
Phil. Trans.	The Royal Society, *Philosophical Transactions.*
PMHB	*Pennsylvania Magazine of History and Biography.*
Price, *France and the Chesapeake*	Jacob M. Price, *France and the Chesapeake: a History of the French Tobacco Monopoly,*

	1674–1791, and of Its Relationship to the British and American Tobacco Trade (2 vols., Ann Arbor, Mich., 1973).
Proc.	*Proceedings.*
Pub.	*Publications.*
Quérard, *France littéraire*	Joseph Marie Quérard, *La France littéraire ou Dictionnaire bibliographique des savants, historiens, et gens de lettres de la France, ainsi que des littérateurs étrangers qui ont écrit en français, plus particulièrement pendant les XVIIIe et XIXe siècles* . . . (10 vols., Paris, 1827–64).
Rakove, *Beginnings of National Politics*	Jack N. Rakove, *The Beginnings of National Politics: an Interpretive History of the Continental Congress* (New York, 1979).
RB	Richard Bache.
Repertorium der diplomatischen Vertreter	Ludwig Bittner *et al.*, eds., *Repertorium der diplomatischen Vertreter aller Länder seit dem Westfälischen Frieden (1648)* (3 vols., Oldenburg, etc., 1936–65).
Rev.	*Review.*
s.	*sou.*
Sabine, *Loyalists*	Lorenzo Sabine, *Biographical Sketches of Loyalists of the American Revolution . . .* (2 vols., Boston, 1864).
Schelle, *Œuvres de Turgot*	Gustave Schelle, ed., *Œuvres de Turgot et documents le concernant* (5 vols., Paris, 1913–23).
Schulte Nordholt, *Dutch Republic*	J. W. Schulte Nordholt, *The Dutch Republic and American Independence* (trans. Herbert M. Rowen; Chapel Hill, N.C., 1982).
Sellers, *Franklin in Portraiture*	Charles C. Sellers, *Benjamin Franklin in Portraiture* (New Haven and London, 1962).

Sibley's Harvard Graduates	John L. Sibley, *Biographical Sketches of Graduates of Harvard University* (17 vols. to date, Cambridge, Mass., 1873–). Continued from Volume IV by Clifford K. Shipton.
Six, *Dictionnaire biographique*	Georges Six, *Dictionnaire biographique des généraux et amiraux français de la Révolution et de l'Empire (1792–1814)* (2 vols., Paris, 1934).
Smith, *Letters*	Paul H. Smith *et al.*, eds., *Letters of Delegates to Congress* (17 vols. to date, Washington, D.C., 1976–).
Smyth, *Writings*	Albert H. Smyth, ed., *The Writings of Benjamin Franklin* . . . (10 vols., New York, 1905–07).
Soc.	Society.
Sparks, *Works*	Jared Sparks, ed., *The Works of Benjamin Franklin* . . . (10 vols., Boston, 1836–40).
Stevens, *Facsimiles*	Benjamin F. Stevens, ed., *Facsimiles of Manuscripts in European Archives Relating to America, 1773–1783* (25 vols., London, 1889–98).
Taylor, *J. Q. Adams Diary*	Robert J. Taylor *et al.*, eds., *Diary of John Quincy Adams* (2 vols. to date, Cambridge, Mass., and London, 1981–).
Trans.	Translator or translated.
Trans.	*Transactions.*
Van Doren, *Franklin*	Carl Van Doren, *Benjamin Franklin* (New York, 1938).
Van Doren, *Franklin-Mecom*	Carl Van Doren, ed., *The Letters of Benjamin Franklin & Jane Mecom* (American Philosophical Society *Memoirs*, XXVII, Princeton, 1950).
Villiers, *Commerce colonial*	Patrick Villiers, *Le Commerce colonial atlantique et la guerre d'indépendance des*

	Etats-Unis d'Amérique, 1778–1783 (New York, 1977).
W&MQ	*William and Mary Quarterly,* first or third series as indicated.
Ward, *War of the Revolution*	Christopher Ward, *The War of the Revolution* (John R. Alden, ed.; 2 vols., New York, 1952).
Waste Book	BF's accounts described above, XXIII, 19.
WF	William Franklin.
Wharton, *Diplomatic Correspondence*	Francis Wharton, ed., *The Revolutionary Diplomatic Correspondence of the United States* (6 vols., Washington, D.C., 1889).
Willcox, *Portrait of a General*	William B. Willcox, *Portrait of a General: Sir Henry Clinton in the War of Independence* (New York, 1964).
WTF	William Temple Franklin.
WTF, *Memoirs*	William Temple Franklin, ed., *Memoirs of the Life and Writings of Benjamin Franklin, L.L.D., F.R.S., &c . . .* (3 vols., 4to, London, 1817–18).
WTF's accounts	Those described above, XXIII, 19.
Yela Utrilla, *España*	Juan F. Yela Utrilla, *España ante la Independencia de los Estados Unidos* (2nd ed.; 2 vols., Lérida, 1925).

Note by the Editors and the Administrative Board

As we noted in volume 23 (pp. xlvi–xlviii), the period of Franklin's mission to France brings with it roughly two and a half times as many documents as those for the remaining seventy years of his life. In the present volume once again we summarize a portion of his incoming correspondence in collective descriptions; they appear in the index under the following headings: commission seekers; emigrants, would-be; favor seekers and admirers; offerers of goods; and intelligence reports.

A revised statement of textual methodology appeared in volume 28 and appears again here. The original statement of method is found in the Introduction to the first volume, pp. xxiv–xlvii. The various developments in policy are explained in XV, xxiv; XXI, xxxiv; XXIII, xlvi–xlviii.

Four individuals have assisted the editors in the preparation of this volume. Karen Kauffman transcribed hundreds of documents with infinite care and good humor; Joanne Walroth, a National Historical Publications and Records Commission fellow, provided invaluable aid in research and annotation; Kate Ohno helped significantly during the final months of preparation; Karen Duval verified transcriptions at the American Philosophical Society and assisted materially in the last stages of preparing the manuscript for production. To each of them we offer thanks.

As this volume went to press we learned of the death of Jean-Claude David, our *chercheur* in Paris and Amiens. His mastery of French archives and eagerness to track down the most obscure reference greatly enriched the Franklin volumes, and we shall miss him.

Catherine M. Prelinger died in late summer, 1991. For two decades she was a mainstay of the Franklin project, bringing to us her knowledge, energy, laughter, and courage. We shall miss Kitty deeply.

One name has been associated with the Franklin edition since its inception: Whitfield J. Bell, Jr. In the early stages of the project Whit tirelessly searched for elusive Franklin documents in local and national historical societies, libraries, and private manuscript collections in the United States and England. Associate editor of the first five volumes, Whit reconstructed with care and elegance the story of Franklin's life in Philadelphia. With his profound knowledge of early American science, he laid the groundwork for understanding Franklin's contributions to science and technology. He served on the Administrative Board for twenty years, the last five of them as chairman. Whit has been the heart and soul of the Franklin edition. Like Franklin's, Whitfield Bell's enthusiasm for life and learning is boundless. We are greatly in his debt. In appreciation and admiration of his contributions to the Franklin edition, we dedicate volume 29 to him.

Introduction

This volume marks the first full months of Franklin's tenure as sole American minister to the Court of France. His former fellow commissioner John Adams doubted that Franklin could manage the post at all, and predicted that "the public Business, will suffer in a degree beyond Description."[1] On the contrary, as far as we can tell from the record, Franklin accomplished the official business of his mission smoothly, answering his correspondence, mastering the details of a proposed land-sea raid by Lafayette and John Paul Jones on the English coast, and taking steps to resolve the disputed accounts of his great-nephew, Jonathan Williams, Jr. Twenty-five years earlier Franklin had brought order and fiscal accountability to the postal service; now he applied a similar spirit and determination to the management of his *bureau* at Passy, even hiring the son of America's banker Ferdinand Grand to put the Commission's accounts in order for Congress.[2] Relieved from the necessity of having to work any longer with Adams and Arthur Lee, Franklin took charge of the American mission with newfound vigor.

He wrote on average fifty letters a month, sometimes in spurts of six or seven a day; this represents a solid increase in the outgoing post over the previous months. As before, William Temple Franklin served as secretary, generally preparing the most important letters for his grandfather's signature. Nicolas-Maurice Gellée continued in his post as amanuensis, copying some outgoing letters and occasional incoming materials. Just six weeks after Franklin received his appointment, Gellée remarked upon the heavier work load and hinted at the need for a raise.[3] None apparently was forthcoming. For the period of this volume, the fullest record of the correspondence is kept in letterbooks, possibly made several months later,

1. *Adams Papers,* VII, 256.
2. See BF's letter to the committee for foreign affairs, May 26.
3. See his letter of March 24.

now at the Library of Congress. These letterbooks, along with the substantial number of recipient's copies that are preserved in Franklin's papers at the American Philosophical Society, offer an unparalleled account of the issues, routine and significant, confronting America's first foreign mission.

In the absence of a network of American consuls in France (although there were agents and unofficial representatives in the ports), the business of receiving cargoes, fitting out ships, supervising the procurement of supplies, and tending to the interests of American citizens abroad fell to the minister plenipotentiary. Franklin urged Congress to use its authority to appoint consuls, who could better handle American commercial interests and would have the advantage over him of residing in the ports, but it did not act. The beleaguered minister complained over and over to those making requests that he lacked the power, the jurisdiction, the time, or the funds to answer their needs. For all those issues that he preferred not to deal with, he chanted his litany: "These are things totally out of my Sphere."[4]

The most serious problems with which Franklin grappled were financial. While currency finance had respectable colonial roots,[5] the staggering needs of a wartime economy and the inability of the Continental Congress to tax resulted in a depreciated currency and a mounting burden of individual and public debt. The fiscal crisis was both national and international; in 1779 much of the responsibility for dealing with it fell on Franklin's shoulders as bills of exchange were presented to him for payment. French commercial houses with American affiliations faced failure (one, Reculès de Basmarein & Raimbaux, had already gone bankrupt[6]); John Bondfield, American agent at Bordeaux, applied to Franklin for the temporary credit necessary to sustain his own financial standing, the weakening of which, he claimed, would also hurt America. The merchant John Ross was even more dramatic: unless afforded relief, he wrote, "ruin is immediate and unavoidable."[7]

4. To Pierre Landais, March 4.
5. Ferguson, *Power of the Purse,* p. 3.
6. XXVI, 677.
7. See Bondfield's letter of April 17 and Ross's of April 24.

Franklin, of course, had little relief to offer, unless he could negotiate a new loan from the French government, obtain private credit in Paris or Amsterdam, or accomplish both.[8] But he knew, as did everyone else—Foreign Minister Vergennes, the ever-vigilant reporter of events from the Netherlands Dumas, and the bankers Horneca, Fizeaux & Cie. and Jean de Neufville—that military setbacks in Georgia combined with large numbers of protested bills in Europe made America a bad risk. The "collateral" Franklin had to offer would make any respectable banker shudder. Nonetheless, Franklin, through Ferdinand Grand, did formally request additional credit, receiving a new loan of 1,000,000 *livres* and an understanding that Louis XVI would act as guarantor for the interest on a 3,000,000 *livres* loan to be floated in the Netherlands.[9] Heavy naval expenses and serious opposition by Finance Minister Necker prevented France from doing more.

The most important diplomatic event in the months covered by this volume was the entry of Spain into the war. The signing of the Convention of Aranjuez in April and the presentation of the Spanish rescript and departure from London of Spanish Minister Almodóvar in June signalled, at least in terms of plans and hopes, a new direction to the war. Certainly Spain had little interest in American independence, and her help to the U.S. would be indirect; nonetheless, article 2 of the Convention of Aranjuez specified that the combined French-Spanish fleets would undertake an invasion of Great Britain. Franklin's correspondents kept him informed of the public rumors regarding Spain's actions.[1]

This volume presents the relationship between Franklin and

8. When Vergennes wrote on March 13 that he could not reconcile the various loan attempts in process, BF replied on March 17 that even if all the loans succeeded they would not meet America's needs.

9. See Grand's memorandum of March 2 and BF to Vergennes of March 10 and 17. For the loan and the understanding see BF to the committee for foreign affairs, May 26, Vergennes to BF of March 18, and BF to Vergennes of June 1. The Dutch loan was never subscribed, so any French offer to act as surety was moot.

1. Described in Sartine's letter of April 27. Dumas' letter of June 9 predicted almost to the day when the Spanish rescript would be delivered, and

Adams in a new light, one upon which the editors of the *Papers of John Adams* have already remarked.[2] Turgot wrote on March 18 that Adams had left Paris, "ulcéré et jaloux à l'excès de Franklin," and Adams' *Diary* betrays some suspicion of Franklin.[3] In frequent correspondence during March and the first three weeks of April, however, Franklin and Adams were open and cordial with one another. Franklin was pleased to delegate to Adams the investigation of problems at Brest, Lorient, and Nantes.[4] The turning point in their harmonious working relationship came when Franklin's April 24 letter bitterly disappointed Adams by informing him that the *Alliance,* on which he soon hoped to sail home, was by order of Sartine to be held in France (for the proposed Lafayette-Jones expedition, though Adams was not told that). Franklin, sensing that the change in plans would surprise and anger Adams, had Sartine write a letter directing the alteration, so that this could be forwarded to Adams.[5]

Busy diplomat that he was, Franklin always had time for scientific pursuits, highlighted in this volume by the delivery (by Le Roy) of his paper on the aurora borealis to the Académie des sciences on April 14. He was complimented for taking time, in the midst of his diplomatic chores, to occupy himself with science.[6] As usual, he was asked to recommend individuals for scientific posts and to lend his name and prestige to the work of young scientists. Jean-Paul Marat sought to draw Franklin into a dispute with the French scientific community as he challenged conventional views on the nature of fire.[7]

Vaughan and Hartley, in their letters of June 17 and June 29, respectively, reported on British reaction to Spain's move.

2. *Adams Papers,* VII, xvi–xvii.

3. Schelle, *Œuvres de Turgot,* V, 588; Butterfield, *John Adams Diary,* II, 369–70.

4. See, for example, JA's letters of March 24 and April 13 and BF's of April 3.

5. For JA's suspicion that being sent on the *Sensible* was a plot against him see James H. Hutson, *John Adams and the Diplomacy of the American Revolution* (Lexington, Ky., 1980), p. 46.

6. From de Thury, on or after April 14.

7. See our headnote to Marat's letter printed before March 13.

What fascinated Franklin about the experiments was the ingenuity of a new instrument that Marat had built, the *microscope solaire.* The experiments several times had to be postponed, because of Franklin's busyness, his gout, or cloudy weather. But the American did attend, exposing his "tete chauve au foyer du microscope solaire,"[8] and greatly pleasing the ambitious Marat, who desperately wanted Franklin's imprimatur on his work. Franklin, however, as far as we know, never endorsed the theory the experiments were designed to prove.

Beyond the narrow world of belligerents in wartime, Franklin saw a universe that surpassed national boundaries, a scientific and humanitarian community whose work ought to go forward, despite the war. In this spirit, although he detested the behavior of the British (even going so far as to plan with Lafayette a series of prints to illustrate British cruelties), he exchanged ideas and writings with his old English scientific colleagues, requested volumes of the *Transactions* of the Royal Society, and promised to show his respect for that learned body by presenting them with a paper. Tangible signs of his vision of a world beyond the war were the passports he drafted for James Hutton to deliver supplies to a Moravian mission on the coast of Labrador and for the explorer Captain James Cook.[9]

Franklin had now been in France for over three years. He liked the French, "an amiable people," as he wrote to his sister on April 22. His circle of friends—the Brillons, the Chaumonts, the Le Veillards, the Le Roys—remained constant. Madame Brillon, despondent at the discovery of her husband's affair with the governess Mlle. Jupin, was particularly dependent on Franklin's ministrations in the spring of 1779. She poured out her feelings; he comforted her, urged her not to be too hard on herself, and declared her in the right.[1] In May the abbé Morellet, whom Franklin had met in 1772, reappeared in

8. [Auguste] Cabanès, *Marat inconnu: l'homme privé, le médecin, le savant,* (3rd ed.; Paris, n.d.), p. 175.

9. Hutton's passport is dated March 11 and Cook's April 10.

1. See her letter of May 11 and his reply, printed under the same date.

the Doctor's life. His entrance gives a hint of the vibrant, intellectual circle around Madame Helvétius at Auteuil that Franklin will be drawn into in 1780.

His correspondents and acquaintances ranged from the old to the very young. At his age he was bound to begin hearing of the deaths of friends, and he did.[2] But he took pleasure in his associations with the very young, entertaining Jonathan Williams, Jr.'s small son Josiah, wishing John Quincy Adams a good journey home and happy reunion with his "Mama," and passing on greetings from Benjamin Franklin Bache to his former schoolmates at Passy, Jesse Deane and Charles Cochran. As for nine-year-old Benny himself, Franklin in April sent him off in the company of Philibert Cramer to be enrolled in boarding school in Geneva. He did it so that his young grandson might be educated a Protestant and a republican. The child's first letter back to Passy, published here for the first time, reported a safe arrival, despite "quelques malheurs" on the way.[3] Although Franklin claimed that he hoped to visit his grandson, he never did make the trip.

As he had returned to earlier scientific interests with his work on the aurora borealis, so too did Franklin resume his earliest profession, avocation, and love: printing. He established a typefoundry at Passy, and had his press in operation by the late spring. In this volume is reproduced the first Passy imprint that can be dated with any certainty, the American minister's invitation to an Independence Day celebration. This document symbolizes a moment of personal triumph in his diplomatic career in France and adds a new dimension to his career as a printer.[4] When he plied his trade in the mercantile community of Philadelphia during the 1720's and 1730's, he took pleasure in the well-made, even elegant, page, whether legal or commercial form, psalter, newspaper, or political pamphlet; but he did it for profit. When he printed at Passy he

2. William Gordon, for example, reported on May 5 the death of John Winthrop.

3. From BFB, under April 20.

4. The story of BF's Passy press is discussed in our headnote to the Invitation to an Independence Day celebration, before June 24.

did it for himself; in his office as sole minister, for the amusement of his friends, and for his own pleasure. The invitation for the Fourth of July party was the first foray into the rebirth of B. Franklin, printer.

Also in the spring, Franklin wrote out one of his best-known bagatelles, "The Morals of Chess," for his Passy friends. A reformulation of an essay he had conceived over sixty years earlier, he would eventually print it for them on his Passy press.[5]

"Undoubtedly I grow older," Franklin wrote to his son-in-law Richard Bache, but he thought the last decade had made little difference in his health. He was, he said, "well and hearty."[6] In fact, he was a rejuvenated Franklin. As far as we can tell, he pursued his ministerial duties with energy and discipline; if the number of social notes and invitations is any indication, on top of his official duties, he also consolidated and extended his conquest of French society. He was honored by election as *Vénérable* of his masonic lodge, an act that probably signalled not simply respect for Franklin but a subtle attempt on the part of the Loge des Neuf Soeurs to use his prestige as a shield against the controversy that had clouded their reputation.[7]

To be sure, Franklin suffered a few episodes of the gout during these months, in particular a severe one in late February and early March that prevented the presentation of his credentials at Versailles until March 23. It died down, only to flare up later in the month (when Madame Brillon invited him to come for a visit, wearing his "souliérs de goutte").[8] But as Franklin wrote on more than one occasion, perhaps the gout was not a disease but a remedy, visited upon him so that he would mend his ways. And, as he wrote Montaudoüin, he was content in this world and far from eager to move on to the next.[9] All in all he was in excellent health, apparently thriving

5. See our headnote to "The Morals of Chess," before June 28.

6. To Richard Bache, June 2.

7. Discussed in our headnote to the Lodge's letter, before May 21.

8. She used the phrase in her March 20 letter.

9. See BF's letter to Jane Mecom of April 22 and to Montaudoüin of March 17.

on the confidence and new-found power that came with his elevation over Adams, Izard, and the Lees. We know one additional fact about his physical state: he purchased new spectacles.[1] A small complaint indeed in the eighteenth century for someone of seventy-three.

1. From H. Sykes, April 24.

Chronology

March 1 through June 30, 1779

March 1: French trade restrictions against Dutch go into effect.
Early March: BF, recovering from gout, suffers a relapse.
March 23: BF is received by the French court as minister plenipotentiary; thereafter has another relapse of gout.
April 1: JW reports the arrival at Nantes of the cartel ship *Milford* carrying American prisoners.
April 11–18: *Alliance* sails from Brest to St. Nazaire.
April 12: Signing of Franco-Spanish convention at Aranjuez.
April 14: BF attends session of Académie des sciences. Le Roy reads his paper on the aurora borealis.
April 15: BFB leaves for school in Geneva.
April 20: BF learns that La Luzerne will replace Gérard. Sartine asks BF to retain *Alliance* in Europe.
April 22: Congress votes not to recall BF. *Milford* embarks British prisoners.
c. April 28: Chaumont leaves for Lorient with new orders for John Paul Jones's squadron.
May 1: La Motte Picquet's convoy leaves Brest.
May 7–8: France closes coast to traffic with England.
May 10–12: *Alliance* sails from St. Nazaire to Lorient carrying John and John Quincy Adams on board.
May 13: Austro-Prussian peace agreement at Teschen.
May 21: BF elected *Vénérable* of the Loge des Neuf Soeurs.
May 22: French government cancels plans for joint Lafayette-Jones expedition.
May 26: BF describes his activities in a letter to the foreign affairs committee of Congress.
June 3: Admiral d'Orvilliers' fleet sails.
June 8: Congress votes to recall William Lee and Ralph Izard.
June 10: BF receives first installment of new 1,000,000 *l.t.* loan from French government.

June 11: Sir William Meredith moves in the House of Commons for peace with America.
June 12–23: Cruise of the privateer *Black Prince.*
June 16: Admiral Hardy's fleet sails. Ambassador Almadóvar delivers list of Spanish grievances to British government.
June 17: *Sensible* sails from Lorient.
June 18: Almodóvar leaves London.
June 19-July 1: Cruise of John Paul Jones's squadron.
June 25: *Milford* arrives at Portsmouth to receive second group of prisoners.
June 27: George III orders packet boat service between Dover and Calais halted.

THE PAPERS OF
BENJAMIN FRANKLIN

VOLUME 29

March 1 through June 30, 1779

Editorial Note on Franklin's Accounts

One new account begins during the period covered by this volume:[1]

XXIII. William Temple Franklin's Accounts, March 15, 1779, to February 12, 1782: American Philosophical Society, 56 pp.[2]

This is a running account in Temple's hand and is titled by him "Account of Family Expences, begun March 15th 1779." A variant copy, twenty-six pages in length, begins with the same entries but concludes on April 29, 1780. It is entitled "Account of Family Expences. 1779." and is also at the APS. Temple was given money to cover various household expenses.[3] His grandfather periodically reviewed and approved his expenditures; on two occasions (April 15 and June 11) during the months covered by this volume Franklin endorsed the document, "Examined the above Account & compared every Article with the Receipts, & found it right. B Franklin."

The account affords a glimpse of the Franklin *ménage,* which consisted then of a maître d'hôtel, Fremont, who took care of family expenses, postage, and miscellaneous bills, and two menservants, François and Arbelot.[4] Those two were not only paid their wages but reimbursed for the expense of buying their own dinner when Franklin or Temple dined out, the French custom being that each guest bring along a servant to serve at the dinner table. Madame St. Louis did the washing, and Cabaret furnished the stationery. Some outside help was used; the painter Roger is mentioned, as well as Le Clerc who papered the study, the mason F. Dupeux, an unnamed upholsterer whose furniture was rented for three months, and a blacksmith who installed and cleaned the stove in secretary Gellée's room. Le Veillard was reimbursed on May 3 for his purchase of Peruvian bark (used for treating fevers) furnished to John Adams.

1. The following accounts still apply: I, VI, and VII (XXIII, 19–21), XII and XIII (XXV, 3), XVI and XVII (XXVI, 3), XIX, XXI, and XXII (XXVIII, 3–4). An additional financial record, BF's purchase of china and earthenware, is published in full below, under May 20.

2. Similar in format to Account III (XXIII, 19), also kept by WTF.

3. For example, during the period covered by the present volume WTF received 2,400 *l.t.* on March 15, 1,200 *l.t.* on March 16, 1,200 *l.t.* on April 30, 1,200 *l.t.* on May 18, and 2,400 *l.t.* on June 11.

4. For Arbelot's later vicissitudes see Lopez, *Mon Cher Papa,* pp. 286–7.

To Jacques Leveux[5]

Copy: Library of Congress

Sir

Passy March 1 1779.

I have been uneasy that your Acct. of Disbursements for the Prisoners has been so long unpaid. As the whole Business here is now devolv'd on one Person, our Correspondence for the future may be more prompt & regular; and I should be glad to clear the past transactions immediately by paying off your Debt.[6] Be pleas'd therefore to draw on me for the Amount, & your Bill shall be duely honor'd. We have no Money in London; if in drawing on Paris, the Exchange is to your Disadvantage, charge me in your Acct. with the Difference.

There is a M. Rousseaux who has written to me from Calais;[7] and some Persons in your Prisons who say they are Americans & wish to return to our Service. I beg you would examine those Prisoners & obtain from them particular Accounts of the Province & Town they were born in, in what ships taken, by whom, where & how long Prisoners & by what means they came to be in the English Service? & of M. Rousseaux, I should be glad for such Particulars as you may have an Opportunity of Learning.

P.S. If any Letter should come to your Hands directed to M. Edward Bancroft, be pleas'd to send it directly to me.[8]

M. Leveux. Calais.

5. Agent for American affairs in Calais and responsible for former prisoners, he is identified in XXVI, 515n.

6. The commissioners on Nov. 9, 1778, had requested an account of Leveux's disbursements (XXVIII, 68). BF, who received news of his appointment as sole minister on Feb. 12, expected to handle correspondence more efficiently than the commissioners had done: XXVIII, 522.

7. Jean Rousseaux wrote from there on Feb. 12, and from Dunkirk on Feb. 28 (XXVIII, 514–15, 636–7), demanding prize money for his participation in the cruise of the *Lexington.*

8. BF was unaware that his friend was a British secret agent as well as a speculator on the London stock market: XXIII, 64n.

From the Duc de Croÿ[9]

AL: American Philosophical Society

[March 1, 1779]

Le Duc de Croÿ a fait resouvenir que dans la notte quil avoit donné Lannée passée pour que les vaisseaux du Roy menage et ayent tous les egards pour M Coock on navoit pas parlé des corsaires.

Sur sa remarque M de Sartinne vient de faire ecrire la lettre la plus forte et circulaire pour que tous nos corsaires soient avertis davoir les plus grands egards pour M Coock &c.[1]

Il seroit bon que les corsaires insurgents ayent le meme ordre M de Sarcefiel, a ma demende, doit deja en avoir parlé.[2]

Notations in different hands: Le Duc de Croy / sans date

From Charles-Guillaume-Frédéric Dumas

ALS: American Philosophical Society; AL (draft): Algemeen Rijksarchief

Monsieur Lahaie 1er. Mars 1779

Ma derniere étoit du 23–26 fevr. On s'est assemblé les deux derniers jours de la semaine passée, sans rien faire. Vendredi une Députation marchande de Rotterdam vint présenter des adresses aux Etats- Genx. & à ceux d'Hollde., pour se plaindre

9. Emmanuel, prince de Moeurs et de Solre, duc de Croÿ, is identified in XXV, 391. The duke was fascinated by natural history and navigation, and had taken upon himself the task of seeing that Capt. James Cook and the crew of the *Resolution* be allowed to voyage unmolested. According to his journal, the duke convinced Sartine in the summer of 1778 to issue such orders to all French navy warships, and in January, 1779, to all French privateers. Now he wanted BF to issue similar orders to American privateers. He visited Passy on March 1 and there, while waiting for the Doctor, drafted this document. See Croÿ, *Journal,* IV, 166–7, and his account of their meeting, under March 1, below.

1. Sartine's circular letter, dated Feb. 2, was printed in the *Gaz. de Leyde,* March 30, 1779.

2. We have no other record that Guy-Claude, comte de Sarsfield (XXIII, 231n) intervened, but BF did issue a letter to all American privateers: below, March 10.

du tort que leur fait l'arrêt publié en France.[3] Elle a eu audience aussi du Prince, &c.[4] Cette Adresse, & la derniere note de Mr l'Ambr. qui rend raison du refus d'accepter la réponse, ont fait nommer un Committé, pour besogner là-dessus avec l'Amirauté.[5] Depuis la publication du dit Arrêt, les assurances pour les vaisseaux hollandois, allant de Rotterdam en Angle-

3. The latest letter from the American agent in the Netherlands (XXVIII, 617–19) dealt with the reaction of the States General to a French trade ordinance which was to become effective on March 1. By this *arrêt* King Louis XVI revoked Dutch trade privileges and authorized privateers to seize English goods on Dutch merchant ships: Sir Francis Piggott and G.W.T. Omond, eds., *Documentary History of the Armed Neutralities 1780 and 1800* ... (London, 1919), pp. 108–9; Edler, *Dutch Republic,* pp. 122–3. France thereby hoped to pressure the States of the Province of Holland (the most important of the seven Dutch provinces) and the States General to provide convoy protection from the British Navy for ships carrying timber and other naval stores to France. Amsterdam and Haarlem, which supported the French position, were exempted from the French decree, adding to the pressure on such rival Dutch ports as Rotterdam and Dordrecht (Dort); for the outcry in Rotterdam see Fauchille, *Diplomatie française,* pp. 119–20. The Dutch dilemma is described in *Adams Papers,* VII, 34–5n.

4. William V of Orange, the stadholder or hereditary executive of the Netherlands, who was generally regarded as pro-British. Dumas sometimes calls him "le grand personnage," an example of the kind of shorthand references the American agent employed; another is "notre ami," for Engelbert François van Berckel, the pro-American Pensionary of Amsterdam (XXIV, 430n). For the French ambassador, the duc de La Vauguyon (XXIII, 215n), Dumas uses an actual code name, the "Grand Facteur" or "G—— F——." His most common practice, however, is abbreviating the names of people with whom he expected BF to be familiar: "Sir J—— Y——" for Sir Joseph Yorke, the British ambassador, "H—— F——" for the banking firm of Horneca, Fizeaux & Cie., "de N——" for the banker Jean de Neufville, "St——" for de Neufville's Swiss friend Johann Friedrich Stürler vom Altenberg, "le ch—— G——" for Sir ("chevalier") Georges Grand, "Baud——" for Sartine's secretary Baudouin, "le R—— de C——" for Jacques-Donatien Le Ray de Chaumont, the "G—— P——" (or other abbreviations) for the Grand Pensionary of Holland Pieter van Bleiswijk, and "LL.HH.PP." or "L.h.p." for "Leurs Hautes Puissances," *viz.* the States General of the Netherlands.

5. The Amsterdam Admiralty, the most important of the five Dutch admiralties (or "admiralty colleges") responsible for the Dutch Navy and hence the provision of convoys. For the Dutch system of naval administration see *Adams Papers,* VII, 188n.

terre, sont montées de 1 à 10 pct. La consternation est grande à Rotterdam; l'embarras croît ici. Notre ami pense, que ceux de Rottm. & de Dort accederont enfin tout de bon au sentiment d'Amsterdam & de Harlem. L'Epitre du Pce. aux Etats de Frise est si longue, que je n'ai pas le courage d'en entreprendre la traduction.[6] Le petit Imprimé ci-joint vous donnera une idée suffisante de son contenu. On m'a dit qu'il s'est débité 5000 Exemplaires de la dite Epitre: ce n'est pas qu'on la regarde comme un chef-d'oeuvre. Les Commentateurs veulent que les Lettres initiales, V. D. H, dans l'imprimé, désignent le Secretaire de l'Amirauté de la Meuse, qui s'appelle VanderHeim.[7]

Je suis avec le plus respectueux attachement, Monsieur Votre très-humble & très obéissant serviteur D

Passy à Son Exc. Mr. Franklin.

Addressed: à Son Excellence / Monsieur Franklin, Ministre / Plénipotentiaire des Etats-Unis / de l'Amérique / à *Passy*./.

Notation: Dumas 1er. Mars 1779.—

The Duc de Croÿ's Account of a Dinner with Franklin[8]

Reprinted from the vicomte de Grouchy and Paul Cottin, eds., *Journal inédit du duc de Croÿ, 1718–1784* . . . (4 vols., Paris, [1906–7]), IV, 167–9.

[March 1, 1779]

Le 1er mars, j'allai chez lui, à Chaillot, où il logeait à la petite maison du fond, ci-devant au prince de Monaco, où j'avais tant été dans ma jeunesse. M. de Chaumont occupait la grande et jolie maison, et ce petit réduit très modeste, mais commode, jouissant du superbe jardin et à proximité du Bois de Bou-

6. The letter of the stadholder to the States of the Dutch province of Friesland described above, XXVIII, 595n.

7. Jacob van der Heim (1727–99): *NNBW*, I, 1053–4.

8. Drawn from his informative journal, from which we previously published an extract: XXVI, 140–1.

logne, avait été prêté ou loué à M. Franklin.[9] On y arrive par Chaillot et une autre petite rue écartée où il n'était pas aisé de le trouver, et tout s'y ressentait de la modestie économique du philosophe.

Il n'était pas rentré. Je me promenai dans les beaux et immenses jardins de M. de Chaumont; ensuite, on me proposa d'entrer dans le bureau. J'y trouvai à l'ouvrage deux jeunes gens dont j'appris, ensuite, qu'un était son petit-fils.[1] J'y dressai mon mémoire pour M. Cook,[2] et nous y causâmes agréablement. Toutes les cartes entouraient la salle. Je remarquai que je les avais toutes, et j'étais bien aise d'être au centre des nouveaux Américains, pour l'Europe, car c'était là le bureau principal.

A deux heures, M. Franklin revint. Il me fit dire que je pouvais entrer, et il me donna toujours la main en ami, car nous étions bien ensemble. Je le priai de lire ma note pour M. Cook, et l'attention que tous les bâtiments insurgents devaient avoir pour lui. Il la lut avec grande attention, puis, avec son laconisme sublime, il me dit: "Cela sera fait!"[3]

Comme j'entamais pour M. Walker, ce député des Barbades établi à Calais, qu'il me dit bien connaître, et homme de mérite, on vint dire qu'on avait servi.[4] Il me dit: "Si vous voulez

9. For BF's residence at Passy and his landlord Jacques-Donatien Le Ray de Chaumont see XXIII, 244–6, and the illustration facing XXIV, 170. Chaumont's estate once had been owned by Prince Jacques I of Monaco: Meredith Martindale, "Benjamin Franklin's Residence in France: The Hôtel de Valentinois in Passy," *The Mag. Antiques,* CXII (1977), 266.

1. WTF's colleague was almost certainly BF's secretary Nicolas-Maurice Gellée (XXVI, 287n).

2. His letter of March 1, above.

3. A promise fulfilled on March 10, below.

4. George Walker had left his post as London agent for Barbados in 1778: XXV, 162n. His association with BF dates back to the latter's years in London; in 1774 and 1775 they both had lobbied against the restraint of American commerce by Britain. Walker was one of the two West India merchants who had testified before the House of Commons: see XXI, 489, and for Walker's testimony, R.C. Simmons and P.D.G. Thomas, eds., *Proceedings and Debates of the British Parliaments Respecting North America 1754–1783* (6 vols. to date, New York, 1982–), V, 555–65. In later years Walker acknowledged a personal debt to the duc de Croÿ: to BF, Dec. 1, 1782 (APS).

dîner, nous parlerons après!" Je crois réellement qu'il est quaker, à la manière de ces compliments dont la rigide simplicité a, pourtant, de la grandeur.

Je passai sans hésiter, et je fis, sans qu'on en fît de compliment, un dîner très frugal, où il y avait, cependant, le nécessaire. Il n'y avait qu'un service, et tout à la fois, sans soupe. Heureusement, je trouvai deux plats de poisson, un pudding excellent et de la pâtisserie, et j'en eus bien assez. Ils ne faisaient pourtant que ce repas. En effet, je n'étais pas attendu. Il n'y avait à table, outre lui et moi, que les deux jeunes gens du bureau, un enfant en pension, et un Anglais taciturne.[5] Je causai avec son petit-fils, qui était aimable.

M. Franklin sortait d'un grand accès de goutte pour lequel il venait de se baigner.[6] Il était changé et affaibli et tirait à sa fin. Il mangea de grosses viandes froides, but trois ou quatre rasades de bon vin, et fut tranquille et parla peu. Tout respirait, là, la simplicité et l'économie. Trois personnes faisaient tout le domestique. On lui prêtait un carrosse[7] quand il devait sortir, et, assurément, on ne pouvait pas moins coûter au Congrès. Cependant, il venait d'être accrédité ministre de l'Amérique à notre Cour, et il devait, dans peu de jours, aller, avec le corps diplomatique, les mardis, à l'audience du Roi. On l'en dissuadait, disant que les autres ambassadeurs et envoyés ne le reconnaîtraient pas, mais il comptait y aller, s'il pouvait marcher.[8]

Après ce dîner, qui fut remarquable, tout le monde s'é-

5. The taciturn Englishman may well have been the American Edward Bancroft, who was awaiting his departure for England to expedite the exchange of prisoners, a mission subsequently cancelled: XXVIII, 587–8. The "enfant en pension" was BFB, to be sent off to Geneva the following month.

6. In fact, the reason for BF's bathing was a worsening of his skin condition, as noted the previous day in the journal of his health (XXVII, 499). The attack of gout that had tormented him since Feb. 17 was subsiding at this point, and he enjoyed a brief respite between Feb. 28 and early March, when he suffered a relapse that lasted until March 22: see XXVII, 499, and his letter of March 22 to Saint-Lambert.

7. BF actually rented the carriage from Chaumont: XXVIII, 4n.

8. BF's gout prevented him from presenting his new diplomatic credentials as American minister plenipotentiary to Louis XVI until March 23: XXVIII, 565, 607.

chappa et je me retrouvai, comme devant, tête à tête avec lui dans son petit cabinet et je repris la conversation, comme si elle n'avait pas été interrompue.

Il me dit que je pouvais me fier à M. Walker. Voyant qu'il était difficile d'en tirer quelque chose pour lui faire voir comme je les avais bien aidés, il me vint à l'idée de lui faire lire le grand mémoire que j'avais donné à M. de Maurepas,[9] que je retrouvai dans ma poche.

Il le lut très posément, puis, me le rendant, il me dit, avec son ton sentencieux: "Ce ne sont pas là des mots mais des choses; vous y êtes; vous écrivez et pensez bien!" On pouvait un compliment plus long, mais non plus honnête.

Espérant l'avoir un peu échauffé, j'entrai en matière. Je dis: "Nous comptions sur l'Espagne!" Il me répondit: "Cela ne nous donnera pas bonne idée du Pacte de famille!" Il ajouta: "Elle devrait pourtant songer que nous pouvons être des voisins utiles, car, à présent, chez nous, tout homme est soldat!" C'était précisément ce qui pouvait donner à l'Espagne, avec raison, plus de crainte que d'espérance.[1]

Comme je le poussais, et ayant vu, par mon mémoire, que j'étais au fait, il lâcha le mot, en disant d'un ton ferme et noir: "Nous n'avons plus d'argent!"[2] Enfin, je vis très bien, comme je le savais d'ailleurs, qu'ils étaient tout à fait à bout, et mécontents. Il prétendit que les divisions, chez eux, n'étaient que

9. Jean-Frédéric Phelypeaux, comte de Maurepas, Louis XVI's chief minister. As mentioned at the end of this account, he was a fellow sufferer from gout.

1. The 1759 defensive alliance between France and Spain was known as the *Pacte de Famille* because its signers, Louis XV and Charles III, were cousins and fellow members of the House of Bourbon. Spain, lacking any interest in American independence, had not actively joined the war; French Foreign Minister Vergennes a few weeks earlier had authorized his ambassador in Madrid to sign whatever convention was necessary to win her cooperation: Dull, *French Navy,* p. 137. For a discussion of the Franco-Spanish negotiations see our annotation of BF's May 26 letter to the committee of foreign affairs.

2. BF could rightfully be complaining of his own financial difficulties as American minister; we believe, however, that both here and later in the paragraph he is speaking of Congress. See his May 26 letter to the committee of foreign affairs for an extended discussion of both matters.

personnelles, et non sur le fond. Il s'écria pourtant, et contre son caractère: "C'est une vilaine chose que ce monde!"

Je dis: "Je pense que tout en restera là; que les Anglais garderont les places qu'ils tiennent, et vous autres le reste, mais qu'ils vous bloqueront par mer." Il dit: "Ils devraient bien tout quitter! Comme vous dites, il faudrait de grands efforts!"

Voyant que je n'en tirerais rien de plus, je le quittai, mais je remarquai bien que tout baissait, de ce côté-là. Tout cela était d'autant plus curieux, qu'outre l'inventeur de l'électricité, le philosophe créateur d'une grande nation, c'était le moteur et le principal chef de la révolte.

En le quittant, je l'exhortai à presser. Il me dit: "Je tâcherai de voir M. de Maurepas, mais je crains son escalier!" Je vis que c'étaient deux goutteux embarrassés.

Intelligence from Amsterdam and Other Places

D: National Archives

The man who seems to have coordinated Franklin's receipt of maritime intelligence, the chevalier de Kéralio, was kept busy during the four months of this volume. Franklin received from him more than one hundred items of port news, generally arranged in chronological order by an unknown copyist; eventually Franklin forwarded this material to Congress.[3] The flow of information, however, would soon slow and then temporarily cease. On June 5, Kéralio informed

3. For Agathon Guynement, chevalier de Kéralio, see xxv, 413n, 469. Previous intelligence reports are published above: xxv, 469–72; xxvi, 71–3; xxvii, 211–14; xxviii, 98–110. All the present reports are in French (with the exception of the final report discussed) and are part of a collection at the National Archives entitled "Intelligence communicated to Dr. Franklin in France, and transmitted by him to Congress"; seven dated items (Nantes, March 11; Cadiz, March 23; Bilbao, March 31; Amsterdam, April 12; Dunkirk, April 15 and 16; and St. Malo, May 21) are in Kéralio's hand. A copy of the March 6 report from St. Eustatius in WTF's hand is at the University of Pa. Library. Although most of the items sent to Congress were arranged in roughly chronological order, BF also forwarded some items on loose scraps of paper, occasionally bearing neither date nor place of origin. One such item, in Kéralio's hand, dates from the period of the present volume, since it speculates on the course Admiral de Grasse will take to evade the British fleet in the West Indies. It must have been written prior to May 11,

William Temple Franklin of his impending departure on a five-month inspection trip of French military schools.[4] He promised to take measures for forwarding "les nouvelles maritimes," but the number of entries would dwindle to about ten per month in July and August and then cease for more than two months.

As in previous volumes, we print the earliest of these reports below, as a sample, and briefly summarize the remainder, arranged by port.

As might be expected, the huge naval base at Brest provides the largest number of items for our period, twenty-four entries detailing the arrival and departure of warships and convoys, the naming of captains for various vessels, and repairs and constructions in the port.[5] Since Kéralio and his correspondents are not privy to strategic decision-making, however, the news tends to be routine.

The second most frequent intelligence comes from St. Malo. The twenty-three reports (some of which are only a few sentences long) deal with a variety of subjects. Those of March 2 and 3, April 23, and May 21, discuss various privateers from nearby ports and other miscellaneous matters. The letters of April 3, 20, 21, 22, 23, 25,[6] 26, 27, 28, 29 and May 1, 2, and 11, narrate an unsuccessful French attack on the nearby British island of Jersey. The British sent a squadron which then destroyed part of the French escort that had returned to the port of Cancale, as reported on May 15 and 20.[7] The reports of May 18 and June 16, 19, and 22, are chiefly concerned with the chartering of ships and assembling of troops for an invasion attempt on England, for which St. Malo had been selected as one of the two embarkation points.[8]

Little of significance transpires in the small Breton port of Mor-

---

since on that date the *Courier de l'Europe* (v, [1779], p. 298) reported that de Grasse and four ships of the line had safely reached Martinique.

4. APS. Kéralio's inspection trips were a frequent occurrence: xxv, 413n.

5. March 1, 5, 8 (two reports on this day), 10, 11, 12, 13, 14, 15, 24, 25, 26 (two), 27, 29; April 12, 22, 25; May 5, 6, 17, 31; June 30.

6. With this report is also enclosed an extract of a Jan. 15 letter from the French-held island of Dominica, reporting that the French West Indian islands, although still awaiting reinforcements, were ready to repel any attack.

7. Sir William L. Clowes, *The Royal Navy: a History from the Earliest Times to the Present* (7 vols., Boston and London, 1897–1903), iv, 25.

8. See our annotation of Bondfield's letter of June 22 for St. Malo's selection. The report from St. Malo of that date noted that there were 96 trans-

laix, but fourteen days' events are noted, including troop movements in Brittany, occurrences in other ports (chiefly Brest), and the activities of various privateers.[9]

Dunkirk was a more important privateering center, as shown by items from there dated March 3, 6, and 9, and June 16. The visit of two navy cutters to the port provides material for entries of April 15, April 16, and May 1.[1]

A March 26 entry from Lorient concerns a privateer from La Rochelle, while a June 21 entry discusses the arrival of prizes and the departure of a small squadron commanded by John Paul Jones.[2]

Much of the news from Bayonne, near the border, deals with events in the Spanish ports or in Spanish waters. March 14 and May 1 entries report on various French privateers operating near Spain, while those of June 5 and June 8 relay news from the naval bases of Cadiz and Ferrol and from Madrid. On May 8 the correspondent recounts a battle between a French navy cargo ship ("gabarre du Roi") and a British privateer.

Intelligence from Toulon (March 9 and 25, April 20, and May 20) details the activities of that great Mediterranean naval base in constructing or overhauling various warships. Somewhat more variety appears in the items about the base at Rochefort: one of April 28 describes work in the port, one of May 13 concerns itself chiefly with the bad weather that detained nearby Admiral La Motte-Picquet's convoy (and wrecked two of its ships), and one of June 8 recounts the movement of the Rochefort squadron to Brest and details the success of the frigate *Hermione* in capturing British privateers.

A number of reports issue from commercial ports little used by the French Navy. April 10, April 26, and June 22 items from Bordeaux chiefly relay information from other ports (mostly about privateering), although one of June 12 passes on information received there from captains of incoming merchant ships.[3] A March 11 report

---

ports in the harbor and roadstead, a sufficient number for embarking 19,700 men and 456 horses.

9. March 4, 13, 14, 15, 27; April 5, 6, 23, 24; May 6, 8, 10, 11; June 23.

1. That of April 15 also mentioned that two Spanish couriers had left Calais for England.

2. See our annotation of Jones's June 18 letter.

3. The June 22 report is a translation of part of Bondfield's letter of that day.

from Nantes tells about local privateering and warship construction, while one of May 5 recounts news of London and America (the latter from an incoming ship), and one of June 17 describes the assembling of ships at St. Malo.

On May 15 Kéralio's Rouen correspondent relays news from Cadiz that the Spanish fleet has received sailing orders. On May 21 he notes ship construction, troop movements, and orders restraining British subjects presently in France and on June 23 and 26 he details preparations for the invasion of England; nearby Le Havre is one of the embarkation ports. The only direct news from Le Havre, however, is a brief item of May 8 about local merchants volunteering their ships for royal service.

From Marseilles come reports of May 13 and June 28, discussing the navy's activities at nearby Toulon and at Marseilles itself, where it was gathering supplies and expecting a shipment of Prussian wood. The intelligence from Paris (March 20 and April 26) actually comes mostly from the West Indies or India. From Calvi, a Corsican port, comes May 7 news about the cruise of the recently arrived frigate *Mignonne.*

Kéralio's most extensive foreign correspondence is from Spain. Five items (March 23 and 30, May 25 and 28, and June 25) report on the naval base at Cadiz and the huge Spanish fleet assembled there. Distant from such activities, the correspondent at the commercial port of Bilbao on March 3, 10, and 31, and May 15, discusses troop and ship movements elsewhere in Spain and speculates on their meaning. The person who writes from La Coruña apparently has his own network of correspondents; on June 2 he gives news from Toulon, Brest, Cadiz, and Calais and also from an incoming merchantman. Sometime after June 11 he has local news to report, as a squadron from the nearby naval base of Ferrol has arrived.[4] Finally, a June 26 item from Barcelona deals with the impending Spanish operations against Gibraltar.

The remaining intelligence discusses a variety of foreign locations. Four items about Amsterdam chiefly relate Dutch politics; we publish the first.[5] Attributed to the Dutch Caribbean colony of St. Eustatius are reports of March 6, June 18, and June 19, about the movements of the rival British and French fleets in the surrounding area. Two brief notes labeled London (March 30, April 22) do little

4. For this squadron see Dull, *French Navy,* p. 149, and our annotation of Bondfield's letter of June 22.

5. The others from Amsterdam are dated March 11, April 12 and 22, and are similar in content.

more than complain of the shortage of news. A June 1 entry from Lisbon relays erroneous news of the capture of H.M.S. *Chatham,* 50. Our final report may have been unconnected with Kéralio, but is located with the others at the National Archives. Written from Ostend in the Austrian Netherlands on March 7 and unsigned, it is in English and addressed directly to BF. It reports that a British courier is en route from Constantinople to London with news that war between Russia and Turkey is inevitable. How the correspondent ascertained the contents of the courier's dispatches is left unsaid.

Amsterdam le 1er. mars 1779.

Nous sommes bien instruits que les Etats Généraux accordent des Convois pour leurs navires. Cependant cela n'empéchera pas les Anglois de s'emparer de ceux qui auront des matures ou autres munitions de guerre et nous craignons qu'ils ne prennent aussi Ceux qui auront des marchandises pour compte Français, Surtout depuis la derniere ordonnance publiée en france qui permet d'arrêter nos Vaisseaux chargés pour compte Anglais.[6] Nous nous trouvons dans une position bien critique. Il parait que les Etats Généraux veulent soutenir leurs droits et que dorénavant tous nos navires Seront Sous bon Convoi. Peut être que les Anglais reconnaitront leurs torts et qu'ils laisseront à notre pavillon la liberté que les traités lui accordent.

Il parait que la Cour de Versailles est parvenüe à faire la paix en Allemagne.[7] Nous en avons eû la nouvelle hier, et Si elle se Confirme; Il n'y a pas a douter que la france ne pousse vigoureusement la guerre contre l'Angleterre.

6. See our annotation of Dumas' letter of March 1.

7. At the beginning of 1778, the new elector of Bavaria was bribed by Austria to transfer to it a sizeable portion of his principality. To protect the balance of power Frederick II of Prussia initiated hostilities against Austria. France and Russia offered their mediation, which was accepted that autumn. The threat that Catherine II of Russia would intervene on the side of Prussia forced Austria to back down; in March, 1779, a peace conference was assembling in the Silesian town of Teschen to arrange a return of most of the Bavarian territory: Isabel de Madariaga, *Britain, Russia, and the Armed Neutrality of 1780: Sir James Harris' Mission to St. Petersburg during the American Revolution* (New Haven, 1962), pp. 42–8; Paul P. Bernard, *Joseph II and Bavaria: Two Eighteenth Century Attempts at German Unification* (The Hague, 1965), pp. 130–1, and *passim.*

From the Marquis de Saint-Lambert[8]

ALS: American Philosophical Society

Monsieur. [after March 1, 1779?]

Vous n'aurés peutetre pas connu sous le nom de mäer, L'officier dont je Vous ai parlé, ce nom est celui de la famille, mais il porte chès Vous le nom du chevalier de Villepré, il est lieutenant colonel au service des *etats unis* il est actuellement a nante ou il doit s'embarquer incessamment pour boston. La grace que Mr. de Tressan Vous demande c'est que le neveu du cher. de Villepré puisse partir avec son oncle.[9] Ce neveu a de trés bons certificats du régiment ou il a servi.[1] Il paroit sage, et on pourroit en etre Content en amerique. Je Vous serai obligé, monsieur, si Vous Voulès bien me faire un mot de rèponse. Je souhaite que Votre santé soit meilleure et que nous Vous donnions Vaisseaux argent etc. et ladresse de meilleurs amiraux,[2] J'ai l'honneur d'etre avec toute la Veneration possible, Monsieur, Votre très obéissant serviteur St. Lambert

Notation: St. St Lambert

8. This is the first extant letter from a man who later became a familiar face to BF. Jean-François, marquis de Saint-Lambert (XXIV, 219–20n), had received a request dated March 1 from the comte de Tressan (discussed below), asking him to intercede with BF on behalf of one of de Tressan's friends, a certain Maër. Soon thereafter Saint-Lambert evidently visited Passy and spoke to BF; this letter is the follow-up to their conversation.

9. Louis-Elisabeth de La Vergne, comte de Tressan, was an old friend and neighbor of Saint-Lambert; he was also a colleague of BF at the Académie des sciences: Larousse; XXIV, 218–19, 331–2; XXVII, 476n. Rather than ask this favor of BF directly, however, he wrote a letter on March 1 to Saint-Lambert, then in Paris, asking him to urge BF to allow a young man named Febvet to accompany Maër, a relative, to America. Maër and Febvet, he stressed, belonged to an excellent Alsatian family. Saint-Lambert must have given this letter to BF when he called on him, as it is now among the Franklin Papers at the APS.

1. According to Tressan, Febvet had served six years in the Orléans dragoon regiment, "où mon cousin Genlis [XXVII, 422n] m'avait promis de l'avancer." Maër, a lieutenant-colonel with the *Insurgents,* hoped to make Febvet a lieutenant, maybe even a captain, once they reached America.

2. An ironic reference to d'Estaing, who had failed to recapture St. Lucia: XXVIII, 347–50, 598. A strong denunciation of d'Estaing's conduct appeared in François Métra, *Correspondance secrète, politique et littéraire* . . . (18 vols., 1787–90), VII, 313–18.

To the Comte de Vergennes

L (draft):[3] American Philosophical Society

Monsieur Le Comte. [before March 2, 1779][4]

J'ay eu L'honneur avec Messieurs les deputés des etats unis d'amerique de Representer a vostre excellence que le Retard des decisions en france sur Les Reprises faittes sur les anglais par les vaisseaux de guerre americains Les eloignoit des mers D'Europe, Nous avons ajoutté a Cette Consideration d'autres encore plus importantes. Il est de mon devoir, Monsieur Le Comte, d'informer le Congrès des etats unis d'amerique par mes premieres depesches et qui vont partir incessament des decisions finales sur plusicurs affaircs de ce genre dont La premiere me semble estre Celle du Cape. Maknil Commandant Le Corsaire americain Le general Mifflin.[5] Il me Repugne de mander que depuis Sept mois il n'a rien été arresté deffinitivement sur un objet aussi facil a decider, et je suplie instament Vostre Excellence, de me procurer du departement de la Marine unne decision ou les droits de la Nation americaine soyent traittés Comme ceux des propres Sujets de Sa Majesté.

Je suis avec Respect de vostre Excellence Monsieur le Comte V

M. Le Comte de Vergennes.

Projet de Lettres de M. franklin a M. le Comte de Vergennes.

3. In the hand of Chaumont, who had composed other letters in French for BF, *e.g.*, XXV, 678.

4. On March 12, below, Vergennes forwarded a response, dated March 2, from Sartine.

5. On Feb. 9 the American commissioners had written Vergennes about the lawsuit embarrassing Capt. Daniel McNeill of the privateer *General Mifflin:* XXVIII, 494.

To Francis Coffyn[6]

Copy: Library of Congress

Sir, Passy March 2d. 1779.

I received yours of the 17. past and thank you for your kind Congratulations. It will undoubtedly be best to forward all the Prisoners as fast as they arrive, to some Port used by American Ships, and this if possible by Sea, their Land Journies to Paris and thence to Nantes being very expensive. You will settle Mr Fitzgeralds Account according to Justice and draw upon me when you please for your Ballance.[7] If anything is afterwards recover'd from Samuel Woodberry you can give me Credit for it. Wishing heartily your Welfare, and being much obliged by your kind Care of our poor People, I have the honor to be &ca

Bn. Franklin

Mr Coffin—Dunkirk.

To Pierre Landais

Copy: Library of Congress

Sir, Passy March 2. 1779.

Your other Swedish Prize is retaken and carried into England, as we hear by the English News Papers. The other which is arrived, will I suppose be tried in the Court of Admiralty of the Port at which she is arrived, unless being unable to find Proofs that the Property of the Cargo is English, you should think fit to discharge her.[8]

Mr Adams will take his Passage in you, and I suppose writes to desire you to make Provision of Sea Stores for himself & Son, which you will do well to comply with.[9]

6. A friend of Chaumont's, he had helped the commissioners during the past year to aid escaped prisoners reaching Dunkirk, a common entry point into France: xxv, 495n. We have no further record of his Feb. 17 letter.

7. Fitzgerald had been assisting escaped prisoners: xxviii, 522.

8. Capt. Landais' ship, the American frigate *Alliance,* had captured two Swedish merchant vessels, the ship *Victoria* and the snow *Anna Louisa,* while en route to France. The former was sent into a French port with a prize crew, but the latter was reported missing, after becoming separated in a fog: xxviii, 488, 563.

9. Landais had been forewarned a week earlier that he might be asked to take BF's former colleague back to America: xxviii, 589. For details of JA's

I shall be glad to hear how your Refit goes on when you think you shall be ready, and whence you propose to meet the Merchant Ships from Nantes.[1]

I have the honor to be Sir &ca.— B FRANKLIN

Honble Capt. Landais.

To Antoine-Raymond-Gualbert-Gabriel de Sartine

Copy: Library of Congress

Sir, Passy March 2. 1779.

The Orders which your Excellency did me the honor to inform me (in your Letter of the 13. of January last)[2] were sent to all the Ports, for receiving into his Majesty's Prisons, the English Prisoners brought in by our Cruizers, have not it seems arriv'd at Brest. For I have just received a Letter from M. Schweighauser of Nantes, who has the Care of the Prisoners taken in the Drake by Capt. Jones, and which were put into the Brigt Patience lying in Brest Road, that the said Prisoners are still in the same suffering Situation of which he had the honor of informing your Excellency by his Letter of the 10. of Oct. last.[3] I therefore beg your Excellency would favor me with a Renewal of your Orders to the proper Officers at Brest to receive those Prisoners and keep them on Shore 'till they shall be exchanged, allowing them the same Provisions as are allowed to other English Prisoners, the Expence of

return voyage see our annotation to BF's certification for JA's shipment of books, March 2, below.

1. Landais had been ordered to convoy home fifteen American merchantmen stranded at Nantes: XXVIII, 589, 607. French Naval Minister Sartine had volunteered to let them accompany a French convoy to the West Indies: XXVIII, 476–7, 507.

2. See XXVIII, 375–6.

3. As American commercial agent, Jean-Daniel Schweighauser (XXII, 314–15n; XXVI, 62n) was responsible for caring for prisoners taken by American ships; see, for example, XXVII, 109. His letter to BF is missing, but see BF's to him of Feb. 25 and 28 (XXVIII, 602–3, 632–3). The difficulties of the prisoners aboard the *Patience* are detailed in XXVIII, 210–11.

which will be paid by the Congress. I have the honor to be with the greatest Respect Sir, &ca— B. FRANKLIN

M. De Sartine.

To Jean-Daniel Schweighauser

Copy: Library of Congress

Sir, Passy March 2. 1779.

The enclosed from Mr Adams I suppose acquaints you with his Intention of embarking at your Port for America. I am confident you will readily afford him all the Assistance in your Power, that he may be well accommodated at Nantes and in the Ship Alliance.

I have the honor to be Sir & B FRANKLIN

I write this Day to M. De Sartine about the Prisoners at Brest

M. Schweighauser.

To John Walsh[4] *et al.*

Copy: Library of Congress

Gentlemen, Passy March 2d. 1779.

I am sorry to understand by your Memorial of the 16. Past,[5] which came to hand but Yesterday, that you are still in that uncomfortable Situation on board the Brigantine in Brest Road, having understood that Orders had been long since given for taking you on Shore. I write again this Day to the Minister of the Marine, to obtain a Renewal of those Orders; and I hope in consequence that you will soon be better accommodated. I imagine the Delay has been in Part occasioned by the constant Expectations given us from England, of sending over a Cartel Ship with a Number of Americans to exchange for you.[6] The Passport for that Ship was sent from hence in September last: And we have been told from time to time these 3 Months past, that a Ship was actually taken up and

4. Who the previous fall had sent a memorial to John Paul Jones that was forwarded to the American commissioners: XXVIII, 210n.

5. See XXVIII, 554–6.

6. For the cartel see Hartley's letter of March 2, below.

victual'd for that Service; but as yet she has not appear'd.— I shall be glad to receive the Account you mention of the Provisions that have been afforded to you. It was always the Desire and Intention of the Commissioners here that you should be well treated.

I am, Gentlemen, Your very humble Sert. B. FRANKLIN

To Messrs. Walsh late Master of the Drake
Charles Artes Gunner
James Hay, Master at Arms,
and others, Prisoners on board
the Patience in Brest Road.

Certification of John Adams' Shipment of Books

DS:[7] Historical Society of Pennsylvania

Passy March 2. 1779

These certify, that the Box or Caise which accompanies this contains only a Quantity of Books belonging to the Honourable John Adams, one of the late Commissioners from the United States of America, and that they are intended for Nantes in their Way to America.—[8] All concerned are requested to permit them to pass.

B FRANKLIN
Minister Plenipotentiary
from the United States
to the Court of France.

Notation in Franklin's hand: Certificate for Mr Adams's Box of Books

7. In JA's hand.

8. BF's appointment as minister plenipotentiary left his former fellow commissioner JA without employment. (Former commissioner Arthur Lee was still commissioner-designate to the court of Spain.) JA told his wife, "The Congress I presume expect that I should come home, and I shall come accordingly"; to the president of Congress he reported that unless he received counterorders he would return via the first available frigate: Butterfield, *Adams Correspondence,* III, 175, 181n. On March 2, above, BF notified Landais that JA would be a passenger during his coming return voyage to America.

From Rodolphe-Ferdinand Grand: Memorandum[9]

AD: University of Pennsylvania Library

a Passy le deux Mars 1779

Le retour á protest des traittes du Congrés sur ses Comissionaires en france, seroit un malheur plus grand sans doutte, que la perte de la Georgie si elle est vraye,[1] parceque cette province peut etre reconquise & quil n'en est pas de meme du Credit & de la Confiance, dont La perte inevitable par la, entrainera necessairement celle de Lamerique, puisquelle ne trouvera plus chez Elle, ny en Europe, les memes ressources qui lont fait parvenir ou elle est, & Cella par une Suitte de l'Idée avantageuse que lon avoit conçüe de sa bonne foy & de son Exactitude.

Si Le Gouvernement avoit Jugé á propos de faire une reponce formelle au Memoire qui lui fut presenté á ce sujet dans le mois de 9bre. dernier[2] Les Comissionaires ne se seroyent pas Livrés á des Esperances que le Sillence de la Cour, L'Importance de Lobjet, & Linterret Commun rendoyent fondées & qui deviendroyent fatales aujourdhuy au Congrés envers Lequel ils se rendroyent responsables de L'Evenement sils ne faisoyent tout Ce qui est en eux pour L'Eviter. Cest en Consequence de Ce, que le soussigné ministre des Etats unis demande la permission de faire usage des promesses quil a fait Imprimer & de pouvoir proceder ainsy á L'Emprunt de deux million Sterling dont il est Chargé.[3]

9. We believe that Grand, BF's banker, drafted this memorandum for BF, "le soussigné ministre," to use in discussing with Vergennes the necessity of proceeding with a loan for the U.S. Apparently BF was so impressed with Grand's understanding of finances that he asked Vergennes to see Grand; see BF's March 10 and 17 letters to the French foreign minister.

1. A reference to the British capture of Savannah on Dec. 29, 1778: XXVIII, 250n. News of the event was reported in the Feb. 26 issue of the *Courier de l'Europe* (V, pp. 132–4).

2. It was actually on Dec. 7 that the commissioners had warned Vergennes that they might lack sufficient funds to meet all their obligations: XXVIII, 201–2.

3. A hitherto unaccomplished task which had been assigned the commissioners more than two years before: XXIII, 54–5. The promissory notes are presumably those printed for the abortive Dutch loan attempt of Horneca, Fizeaux & Cie. (XXVII, 322). On Feb. 19 BF had requested their return (XXVIII, 571), and he received the money on March 10: XXVIII, 271–2n.

Mais comme les traittes du Congrés arrivent successivement & vont Echoir dememe, il desireroit que le Gouvernement voulu bien venir á son secour á mesure de ses besoins & lui permetre de déposer au tresor royal des promesses pour la Valleur des sommes quil en retireroit & ce, en nantissement jusques á ce que le produit de son Emprunt le mette á meme de les retirer en les rembourçant successivement. Ce Service, tres Important pour Les Etats, ne sera qu'un pret momentané dont la durée dependra du succès de L'Emprunt & L'objet au plus de Deux millions dans le courant de Lannée.

Endorsed: Mr. Grand's Notes, about Money

From David Hartley

ALS: American Philosophical Society; transcript: Library of Congress

My Dear Sir London March 2 1779

Yours of 22d of february received.[4] I have been as much discontented with the delay respecting the Exchange of prisoners as you can have been, and before the receipt of yours, I had made an heavy complaint and remonstrance upon the Subject. I have now the Satisfaction to tell you, that the first Cartel ship has actually left Spithead, and is now upon her Passage to Plymouth, to take on board the first hundred. I have received this positive assurance from the Admiralty. The Cartel ship was got as far as Torbay upon her Passage, and was blown back, but they now presume that she must probably be arrived at Plymouth, by this time.[5] I have spoke to the Minister[6] upon your proposal of sending Dr Bancroft to ex-

4. See Letter I of that date: XXVIII, 587–8.

5. The prisoners received word on March 5 that the cartel had arrived at Plymouth and awaited orders from London before they could embark. On the 16th ninety-seven men were on board the cartel and waiting for a fair wind to sail: Charles Herbert, *A Relic of the Revolution* (Boston, 1847), pp. 225–7. The ship apparently left Plymouth on March 25; see Hartley's letter of March 30. For a discussion of the cartel and the prisoner exchange in the spring of 1779 see Catherine M. Prelinger, "Benjamin Franklin and the American Prisoners of War in England during the American Revolution," *W&MQ,* 3rd ser., XXXII (1975), 275–6.

6. Lord North, who had previously worked with Hartley on matters relating to prisoners: see XXV, 269, 350.

pedite the Exchange, as you state it. His answer to me was, that he thought it needless in so plain a business. He expressed surprize and displeasure at the delays, and assured me that he wd interfere to prevent any farther delays. I presume that Dr Bancroft will wait for your orders upon the Subject, however I shall apprize him by this Mail of the Ministers answer.[7] I will write to you again soon. I am Dear Sir Most affectely yours &c D HARTLEY

To Dr Franklin

Notation: D. hartley Londres 2. mars. 1779.

From Stephen Hills *et al.*[8]

LS:[9] University of Pennsylvania Library

Brest Harbour, Feby [*i.e.,* March][1] 2d 1779

May it please your Excellency,

Such is our unlimited confidence in your candour and generosity that we again presume to trouble you with a few lines respecting our present situation, and the manner in which things have been conducted, Vizt,

In America we were called upon by the Gentlemen who have the honour to compose the Navy-Board (Eastern Department) to exert ourselves with all possible diligence and attention for the better getting the Ship to Sea, which we are conscious we did to the utmost of our power, (and that with singular pleasure for so laudible a purpose) forgetting the prospect of a Cruize, and the great advantages which would

7. BF had proposed in a letter of Feb. 22 sending Bancroft. Hartley's March 2 letter to Bancroft is at the Library of Congress.

8. The first letter from the six commissioned officers of the *Alliance* had been written on Feb. 7, the day after their arrival in Brest: XXVIII, 478. BF replied, through Landais, that he would do what he could for them, and Landais claimed to have communicated the message. See XXVIII, 558, 635.

9. The letter is in the hand of Fitch Pool, clerk of the *Alliance.* He also wrote a letter for the warrant officers and the inferior officers the following day: from Benjamin Pierce *et al.*, below.

1. In another hand "March" is written above "Feby".

naturally arise.— We then represented to those Gentlemen the situation we should be in when in France and what we should expect while there.— For our better encouragement they promised us such supplies as would enable us to appear in the Character of Officers and Gentlemen from which we little suspected there was a necessity of a written Order for that purpose.—

We would inform your Excellency that all of us early took a part in the present Contest, and unfortunately have been captured, imprisoned for many months, on half allowance, one with the loss of a hand, and the others loss of property; add to this the insults of every mercenary Foot and private Soldier, as there was no distinction between Officers and Privates:— Our Families in want at home, and ourselves in distress abroad, naturally demanded the assistance of our friends and it has not been in our power to repay them again, our monthly Wages from the Continent (thirty Dollars) not being more than equal to a Guinea, the depreciation of Paper Currency being so great in America.—

We beg not to be understood as extravagant in our demands; all that is expected while here is sufficient to cloath ourselves as becomes the station of Officers, and this we are credibly informed has been granted to Captn Tucker of the Boston Frigate, his Officers and some of his Men, even the Ship Steward who is at present on board, assured us this day, that he was supplied with Money and Clothes to the amount of Four Hundred and fifty Livres, and the Officers to the amount of their Wages then due.—[2] We trust your Excellency has no disposition to grant favours to one, and deny them to others under like circumstances; it is no longer a secret from the present reserved behaviour of Captn Landais to his Officers, that very little can be expected from him— be that as it may, we are determined to act the part becoming our stations, and render every service in our power, for the welfare of America, and as the Ship is to return home, Convoy to those Vessels laden with stores for the Continent, embrace your Or-

2. The wages advanced to officers and new recruits amounted to 4,500 *l.t.:* XXVI, 538.

ders with pleasure, preferring the good of our Country to our own private emolument;—whatever answer your Excellency shall please to grant beg that it may be directed to one of your Petitioners, as there is not that Harmony subsisting between Captain Landais and ourselves that we wish for sincerely.—

It is with pain that we inform your Excellency of the general uneasiness which prevails on board, as every Officer is put to the same allowance of Provision and Liquors as the foremast Men, and that not equal to the allowance made by Congress;[3] but for the welfare of the Service hope the Observations made so justly upon the British, may not be applied to the American Navy, Vizt—"*Where the Captain is more intimate with the Purser, and makes him a greater Confidant than his principal Officers, very little happiness can be found.*—"[4] This is the case on board the Alliance.—

We are with all due defference your Excellency's Most Obedient and most humble Servants,

STEPHEN HILLS
JOSEPH ADAMS
JAMES DEGGE
JOHN BUCKLEY
THOS ELWOOD
M. PARKE

Benjamin Franklin Esqr Minister, Plenipotentiary, at Paris.

Addressed: His Excellency / Benjamin Franklin, Esquire / Minister and Plenipotentiary at the / Court of Versailles / Paris

Endorsed: Officers of the Alliance complaining of Capt Landais Cloathing 2d

Notation: Feb. 2. 1779—

3. For a discussion of the allowance see *Adams Papers,* III, 152–3.

4. Pursers, who were responsible for distribution of a ship's provisions and for a variety of other duties, were often an object of suspicion: N.A.M. Rodger, *The Wooden World: an Anatomy of the Georgian Navy* (London, 1986), pp. 87–98. The *Alliance*'s purser was Nathan Blodget; see his letter of March 3.

From Richard Bennett Lloyd[5]

ALS: American Philosophical Society

Dear Sir, London 2d. March—79—

The inclosed copy is from a letter which Mr. Hartley has received from the Office for sick & wounded seamen—[6] I would have sent you it by the last Mail but was prevented by a violent cold and inflammation in my eyes— I make no doubt if these people have been in earnest, but that you have heard from them before this time—. Mr. Hartley received me with much politeness and mentioned that should he get further information concerning the Prisoners, he wd. give you the earliest intelligence—. Whenever you have leisure it will give me particular pleasure to hear of your health— Mrs. Lloyd unites with me in best complts—and I am, Dear Sir, with very great respect your obedient humble Servant RICHARD BTT LLOYD

Our complts. to yr. Grandson I am anxiously waiting for a good conveyance to send him the books he desired—.[7]

R. B. Lloyd in Great George Street Hanover Square London—

Addressed: The Honourable / Benjamin Franklin / &c: &c: &c: / Passy

Notation: Richard B. Lloyd. Londres 2 mars 1779.

5. This Marylander who had been a captain in the Coldstream Guards (XXVI, 343n) and his wife, Joanna Leigh Lloyd from the Isle of Wight (*Md. Hist. Mag.*, XVII [1922], 29–30), had returned to England after an extended sojourn in France; he wrote from London to WTF on Jan. 8 (APS) and to BF in February (XXVIII, 574–5). He had previously carried a letter concerning prisoners from BF to Hartley: XXVIII, 420.

6. Possibly a letter of Feb. 5 from the Commission for Sick and Hurt Seamen informing Hartley that directions would be sent that night for the discharge of one hundred Americans confined at Mill Prison. APS.

7. XXVIII, 598.

From Jonathan Williams, Jr.

ALS: American Philosophical Society; copy: Yale University Library

Dear & hond Sir.— Nantes March 2. 1779—

Capt Collas is now ready to sail in a little Brig which Mr Johnson has given him & in which I have a small Share.— At His request I gave him the Privateer Commission which was made out for his intended Cruize last Spring in the Mediterranean, and in order to put the matter on a regular Footing I inclose you a new Bond in proper Form.—[8]

I am informed by Mr William Dennie[9] that "in his Letters to Mr Moylan & Myself jointly of the 1 & 12 of Decemr he inclosed Bills on the Commrs for 2318 Dollars." As I know one of the Vessells he wrote by is taken, and as I have never heard of these Bills, I shall be obliged to you if you will observe whether the Bills which may be presented to you endorsed by Wm Dennie to Mr Moylan or my order, are endorsed in turn by our genuine Signatures; I take this precaution because if the Letters were not Sunk, the Captor may, by counterfeiting Moylans or my Name, get the Bills paid.

I recvd the inclosed Letter from Doctor Cooper. I send it to you because if his Letters to you have miscarried you will see & be pleased at so good a mans remembrance of you.[1]

I hear you have had the Gout I hope you are now better &

8. BF's nephew-in-law Peter Collas had been given command of the brig *Franklin* the previous November: XXVIII, 78–9. A bond for that brig, signed by Joshua Johnson, JW, and Peter Collas, is at the APS. It is curiously antedated Dec. 14, 1777, and bears BF's notation, "Williams Johnson Collas / Privateer."

9. Dennie, a wealthy Boston merchant and ship owner, was active in that city's political and civic affairs. In 1773 he had been one of the most visible opponents of the British tea duties; he served on Boston's committee of correspondence from its organization in 1772 until 1776, as well as on various other committees whose concerns ranged from education to the maintenance of town property. Mass. Hist. Soc. *Proc.*, 2nd series, X (1895–6), 73, 80; XVI (1902), 92; *A Report of the Record Commissioners of the City of Boston* (Boston, 1887), XVIII, *passim;* Charles H. Lincoln, comp., *Naval Records of the American Revolution 1775–1778* (Washington, D.C., 1906), p. 400.

1. BF had received via Lafayette two letters from Samuel Cooper dated Jan. 4: XXVIII, 338–40.

will soon turn so troublesome a Companion out of Doors.— I have heard you intended to write to me about my accts which I anxiously wait for.—[2]

The Bergere a french Ship from America is arrived at Port Louis with 300 hhds Tobacco on acct of Congress. The proprietor Messr Colpron & Co sent to me to know if I had any orders about it, as they did not know who to deliver it to, having had no application— I refered to Mr Schweighauser.[3]

I am ever your most dutifully & affectionately

J WILLIAMS J

Dr Franklin

Addressed: A Monsieur / Monsieur Franklin / Ministre Plenipotentiaire / des Etats Unis / a Passy / pres Paris[4]

Notation: W. Dennie's Bills

William Bingham to the American Commissioners

Two ALS:[5] American Philosophical Society

Gentlemen, St: Pierre, Martinique, March 3d, 1779.

The arrival at this place of the Continental Frigate the Deane, & the armed Brigantine the General Gates, in order to be careened & refitted, & to procure a fresh Supply of Provisions, has greatly embarrassed me, not having sufficient Funds to answer their Demands.[6] I am therefore under the Necessity

2. See BF's reply of March 16.

3. The *Bergère* had sailed for Virginia the previous summer; see XXVI, 425–6, where the owners were named as "Corperon." They may have been the Nantais armateurs listed as "Corpron" in Villiers, *Commerce colonial,* pp. 193–4, and Meyer, *Armement nantais,* p. 265. BF had already sent the ship's invoices and bill of lading to Schweighauser on Feb. 25: XXVIII, 602–3.

4. Also on the envelope is a brief calculation in BF's hand of Dennie's bills which had come to hand and which were "accepted Feb. 19." They are the same figures that BF sent to Grand on March 16, totalling $1,494.

5. Both are duplicates made and sent by Bingham. The one from which we print also included his March 5 letter, printed below. The other is marked "Copy."

6. Bingham (XXII, 443n) was the congressional representative at Martinique. For the successful cruises of the *Deane* and *General Gates* see Gardner

of refusing them the necessary Supplies, or of furnishing myself with Funds for the Purpose by passing my Draughts upon you for the Amount of their Disbursments.[7]

These are cruel Alternatives, but I think it most proper & advisable to submit to the last. I shall therefore take the Liberty of drawing upon You for their Outfits, as soon as they are compleated.

Although I have no such Permission, in a direct Manner, from Congress, I have it by implication, for the Commanders of these Vessels have Instructions from the Navy Board to address themselves to me for all necessary Supplies, when, so far from having Funds belonging to the Public, for such Purposes, Congress is indebted to me, by their last Accot: Current, Livres 240,000, Currency of this Island.

It is with the greatest Difficulty that I can support the Weight of such heavy Advances, and I find it impossible to enter into any new Engagements, especially, as the Negotiation of Business, in this place, has taken an unfavorable Turn, since the Commencement of Hostilities; every Article being now sold for Cash only.

I shall do myself the Honor of transmitting you Copies of these Disbursments by the same Conveyances that carry my Draughts on you & of which I shall duly inform Congress.[8] I have no Doubt but both they & you will acquiesce in the Propriety of the Measure, being fully justified by the Necessity of the Case.

W. Allen, *A Naval History of the American Revolution* (2 vols., Boston and New York, 1913), II, 371–2. Capt. Nicholson of the *Deane* responded angrily to Bingham's reluctance to pay his ship's officers; Bingham eventually borrowed money for the ships from the government officials of Martinique: Robert C. Alberts, *The Golden Voyage: the Life and Times of William Bingham, 1752–1804* (Boston, 1969), pp. 72–3.

7. A year earlier Bingham had been authorized to draw on the American commissioners in France for 100,000 *l.t.,* but during 1778 he exhausted much, if not all, of this credit: XXVI, 300; XXVII, 217–8n.

8. Bingham wrote the committee for foreign affairs on April 13 that he was drawing on BF for another 100,000 *l.t.* in order to repay the loan he had contracted from the Martinique officials (National Archives); we have found neither the copies of the disbursements nor the drafts themselves.

I have the Honor to be, with due Respect, Gentlemen, your most obedient humble Servant. WM BINGHAM

Notation: Bingham March 3. 1779

From Nathan Blodget[9]

ALS: American Philosophical Society

May it please your Excellency Brest 3d. March 1779

I have many pressing affairs that urge me strongly to Paris. & pray your Excellency to give me leave to go for a short time. I am Purser on board the Alliance, my duty is very light at present, so, that I can safely assure your Exy. that the service I have the honor to be in, shall not suffer in the least. Capt. Landais says he would give me leave to go, but it is not in his power; & I must tarry with the Ship, till I have permission from You.

I go on my own account, that it will cost nobody a farthing & if you knew all the circumstances which relate to me, *for going* or *not going,* I'm sure You'd give leave. They are indeed *all* too trifling to write. I humbly ask your Positive answer as soon as Convenient, & am With the profoundest Respect Your Excellencies Most obedt. & Most humble Servant

NATHAN BLODGET

His Exy. Dr. Franklin.

Addressed: To his Excellency / Doctor Benja. Franklin / Minister plenipotentiary &c &c / Passy / near Paris

Notation: Nathan Blodged brest 3. mars 1779.

9. Blodget was a man whose company Landais preferred to that of the other officers of the *Alliance,* because, said Landais, "he behaved always with civility to me": Pierre Landais, *Memorial to Justify Peter Landai's Conduct during the Late War* (Boston, 1784), p. 17. The captain's partiality did not endear Blodget to the other officers; see their March 2 letter to BF.

From Dumas

ALS: American Philosophical Society; AL (draft): Algemeen Rijksarchief

Monsieur LaHaie 3e.[–9] Mars 1779

Je viens ce soir de chez notre Ami. Le Committé, dont j'ai parlé dans ma précédente, n'a rien fait encore. Notre Ami va demain à Amsterdam, où les Bourguemaîtres l'ont mandé pour conférer avec lui. Ce matin Sir J. Y., après avoir quelque temps paradé dans l'antichambre, ayant à la main une Lettre du Roi d'Angleterre pour le St——, l'a remise à celui-ci,[1] qui l'ayant lue, & Sir J. ayant ensuite conféré une demi-heure avec lui, a congédié incontinent tout le monde, s'est rétiré, trouvé mal, & n'a presque rien mangé à table, contre son ordinaire. Le Gd. Pre——,[2] après que Sir J. avoit été chez lui aussi, s'étoit rendu ensuite chez le St——

4e.

Le St—— a été vu ce matin bien portant, & de bonne humeur. Je n'ai pu savoir encore ce qui lui avoit causé du *spleen.*

6e.

Notre Ami est revenu. J'ai appris de lui, que le *Spleen* du 3e. a été occasionné par la déclaration que lui ont faite les Députés de Rottm., qu'il ne leur est plus possible de se refuser aux pressantes sollicitations de leur Ville, pour qu'elle se conforme à l'avis d'Amsterdam & de Harlem. L'avis de l'Amirauté est prêt: on le tient encore secret; mais je sais de très-bonne part, qu'il sera tel qu'Amstm. le desire, c'est-à-dire, de donner convoi aux vaisseaux de la Rep. selon toute l'étendue des Traités, sans exception des bois de construction.

1. On March 3 Sir Joseph Yorke, the British ambassador to the Netherlands, informed the States General of the birth of King George III and Queen Charlotte Sophia's thirteenth child, Octavius (1779–83), on Feb. 23: *Gaz. de Leyde,* March 9, 1779. Presumably the King's letter to the stadholder (St——) was a courtesy letter on the same subject. Yorke's subsequent conversation, as explained below, dealt with the more distressing topic of Dutch politics.

2. The Grand Pensionary of Holland, Pieter van Bleiswijk (XXIII, 381–2n), whose position entailed responsibility for Dutch foreign affairs.

Le jour de naissance du Prince, célébré hier, est cause qu'on n'a rien fait tous ces jours passés.[3] Si j'apprends quelque chose dans la journée je l'ajouterai.

Les Etats d'Hollande ne recommenceront que demain leurs séances. Je suis avec un très-grand respect, Monsieur Votre très-humble & très obéissant serviteur D

Passy à S.E.M. Franklin

Addressed: à Son Excellence / Monsieur Franklin Esqr. / Ministre Plénipotentiaire / des Etats-Unis de l'Amérique / à Passy.

Notation: Dumas March 3 1779

From ——— Duverger and Other People with Goods to Offer, with Franklin's Notes for Replies[4]

ALS: American Philosophical Society

Goodwill toward America and its representative kept flowing—sometimes at a price—from various sources. Some correspondents wanted to help the war effort, others to make known whatever interesting discoveries they had made.

On March 3 came the offer, printed below, of the Liège arms manufacturer Duverger. Writing from Pennautier, near Carcassonne, on March 20, the firm of Tarbouriech & Cie.[5] proposes high quality cloth for officers' uniforms and for those civilians who can afford it. The desired goods will be delivered in a French port but not shipped overseas. Franklin's note for a reply reads, "Thanks for his obliging Offers of Services to the U. States. It is now some time since their Ministers have made any Purchases of Goods for America; the Commerce being now open'd by Treaty between France &

3. The stadholder was celebrating his 31st birthday.

4. Unless otherwise mentioned, all letters discussed are written in French and deposited at the APS. BF drafted notes for replies to two of them (a practice which he began when he became sole minister: XXVIII, 583), those from Duverger and Tarbouriech. Copies of those replies, in French and in a letterbook, are at the Library of Congress.

5. The firm is mentioned in the *Almanach des Marchands,* p. 130.

America, those Affairs are left to private Merchants.— I will communicate his Letter to one of them Mr Jonathan Williams, at Nantes, who possibly may have Orders from time to time for the Articles proposed."[6] The chevalier de Forstner offers on March 28 a system of his own device for the safe loading of cannons, particularly at sea. His asking price: one thousand *louis,* plus travel expenses.

The following day Jacques Faynard, writing from Paris but a resident of London, extols the virtues of the powder he has invented to stop both internal and external bleeding.[7] Its efficacy is to be tested on April 3 by four commissioners of the Royal Academy of Surgery. Would Franklin honor that distinguished assembly with his presence? We do not know whether he obliged, but a report on the experiments carried out that day by Chenel, *maître en chirurgie,* is to be found among his papers. Dated May 21, it specifies that six dogs, submitted to various kinds of cuts, and treated with the powder, recovered well. Faynard also furnished Franklin with a printed list of the lords, diplomats, physicians, and other distinguished people who purchased his powder in England. King George, who graciously accepted the first box, after granting Faynard his patent in 1773, heads the list.

Another inventor, named Marche, describes, on April 27, the ingenious and very affordable machines he has designed in order to facilitate the various facets of agriculture and save labor, which must be in short supply in such a vast country as America. He has also planned convenient granaries and found a new, cheap way to produce saltpeter. All he asks in return is to be allowed to demonstrate his inventions and to eat at the servants' table. He has been robbed of all he possesses and is waiting at the door for an answer.

On May 30, the chevalier de Cointeval (Cointeral?), a captain of dragoons, offers for sale six hundred fifty barrels of Irish salt beef captured by a French privateer in which he has an interest, the price not to exceed thirty-five *l.t.* per hundred, should the Americans be interested. He lives at the Place Louis XV.

6. The actual reply was dated April 12.

7. Faynard is listed in G. Touchard and F. Roberge, *Dictionnaire chronologique et raisonné des découvertes . . . en France . . . de 1789 à la fin de 1820 . . .* (17 vols., Paris, 1822–25), XIV, 199–200, as having invented the hemostatic powder and obtained an exclusive right to it in 1790. For his dispute with Peter Fowler, who also claimed to have discovered it, see XXV, 267n. Faynard's letter is at the University of Pa. Library; the report and printed list are at the APS.

Monsieur, à Liége le 3. Mars 1779

Je suis françois, sujet fidele, et entiérement dévoué aux Etats unis de l'amérique et fort disposé à en donner des preuves dans toutes les occasions. On fait ici des fusils qui sont destinés pour la grande Bretagne sur lesquels sont les armes du Roi d'angleterre et le nom du s. Tower avec cette inscription (Georges Roy) Si vous desirez je vous en ferai passer un semblable. Le fusil avec sa Bayonnette pèse 13 Livres environ et est payé pris à Liége vingt deux livres dix sols argent de france. Si les Etats unis en avoient besoin et que vous voulussiez me charger de cette commission, je les ferai faire avec tout le soin et l'economie possible et je pourrai les fournir à 16 *l.t.* 10 *s.* argent de france sortant de Liége.[8] Vous ne feriez payer ces armes que lorsqu'on vous les livreroit dans telle ville de france que vous jugeriez à propos ou bien en hollande. Ces fusils seront à l'épreuve et ceux que vous ne trouverez pas de bonne qualité resteront à ma charge ainsi qu'à celle de mes associés. Au reste comme je vous ferai passer un modele aussitôt vos ordres, vous serez à portée non seulement d'en juger, mais encore de le faire faire soit plus court soit plus leger de Canon. Trop heureux, Monsieur, si je puis mériter en cette occasion votre confiance et donner des preuves de mon zele tant à ma patrie qu'aux Etats unis de l'amérique. Il est inutile de vous observer que ma discretion en tout genre est à toute épreuve.

Je suis avec un très profond respect Monsieur, Votre très humble et très obéissant serviteur DUVERGER

Négociant près la place
St. Paul
maison de M de france.

Endorsed:[9] That I am oblig'd to the Gentleman for his Offers to supply us with Arms, but have not at present any Orders of that kind to execute

Notation: Duverger. Liege March. 3. 1779

8. This was not the first offer of arms from Liège, a center of gun manufacture; see XXV, 465–6; XXVIII, 12. JW's arms repair operation at Nantes also had drawn workmen from there: XXVI, 206–7.

9. The actual reply was dated March 13.

From Landais

ALS: American Philosophical Society

May it Please your Excellency Brest March 3d 1779

Mr Windship arrived So late the 28th of february that I had no Time to answer the last article of Yours of the 22d.[1] I have no other orders or papers from the Hble Navy Board of Boston Promissing any one of the Ship Money but one of which herein is inclos'd a Copy;[2] Mr Cottentin adgent Commrs. here[3] had a translated one in french at my arrival here (of which I Suppose he Sent a Coppy to Mr Schweighausen adgent at Nantes) upon which order Mr Cottentin geve me the meney to pay the frenchmen but I have few more of the crew to whom the Same promisse was made.

I Shall be very glad to have the Hounble Adams a passanger beside the Honnour and Benefit of his company[4] I Shall have an Eye Witness for to justify my futur cunduct as my former has had.

I Am waiting for Your Positive order and cannot Proceed to do any thing till I have receiv'd them.

I am with the Greatest Respect Your Excellency's Most obeidient Most humble Servant P: Landais

Doctor B. Franklin Minister Plenipotentiary to the united States

Addressed: To His Excellency / Benjamin Franklin Esqr. / Passy / near Paris

Endorsed: Capt Landais March. 3. 1779 With Copy of a Letter from the Navy Board—

1. For BF's of Feb. 22, see XXVIII, 589. Amos Windship (XXVIII, 478n) was the *Alliance*'s surgeon, who had carried messages to Passy.

2. Probably their letter of Jan. 8, in which the Eastern Navy Board ordered Landais to pay a bounty of $20 per crewman either at Boston or upon the *Alliance*'s arrival in France. It also told him "to apply to the agent of the United States at any of the Ports in France that you shall arrive at for money & all the necessaries that you may want for your Ship." APS.

3. Berubé de Costentin, Schweighauser's agent at Brest, charged with dealing with American ships and prizes: XXVII, 293.

4. Landais told JA the same: *Adams Papers,* VIII, 7.

From Jean-Baptiste Le Roy

AL: American Philosophical Society

à onze heures trois quarts ce Mercredy matin
[March 3, 1779?][5]

Un oubli Mon Illustre Docteur m'oblige à vous récrire un mot c'est pour vous prévenir que pour arriver à tems à L'Académie françoise nous nous mettrons à Table à une heure au plus tard. J'espere toujours que vous ne nous ferez pas banqueroute et que vous ferez un effort en faveur de Mr D'arcy qui le mérite bien vous aurez un dîner de choses fort saines enfin si la goutte vous a tourmenté depuis votre dîner dhier j'espere qu'elle vous donnera du relache pour demain adieu mon Illustre Docteur voila une vilaine goutte qui prend bien mal son tems.

From Benjamin Pierce *et al.*[6]

ALS:[7] University of Pennsylvania Library

Brest Harbor, Alliance Frigate
March 3d. 1779.

May it please your Excellency,

The known goodness of your disposition and firm attachment to the Welfare of America has emboldned us to make application to your Excellency in this manner in preference to any other, being destitute of Friends in France, and ignorant of the method made use of for the redress of grievances. Some of us applied, upon our Arrival here to Captain Landais for

5. The date is based on our guess that the session of the Académie française which BF and Le Roy are planning to attend is that of March 4, in the course of which a reception was held in honor of Jean-François Ducis, successor to Voltaire's *fauteuil*: *Jour. de Paris,* March 5, p. 253. Le Roy's mention of d'Arcy may have been a slip of the pen for Ducis. The letter we published in XXVIII, 570, may well be the companion to this one.

6. The warrant officers and inferior officers of the *Alliance;* the ship's commissioned officers (Stephen Hills *et al.*) had written the previous day. For the different types of officers see N.A.M. Rodger, *The Wooden World: an Anatomy of the Georgian Navy* (London, 1986), pp. 16–29, and *Adams Papers,* III, 148.

7. In Fitch Pool's hand.

the Provision allowed us in other Frigates, and received his assurance that if we would give him an Obligation to pay for the same in Case the Navy Board at Boston did not allow it, that it should be granted; upon our complying with his request, received for answer that our complaisant Letter should be forwarded to your Excellency our Provision in many respects being shortned, demanded the Continental Allowance, and was denied, unless the foremast men would insist upon it.

Upon the Commencement of Hostilities in America it required the Serious attention of every friend to his Country, the love of Liberty and revenge for our injured brethren, induced us upon the first Establishment of a Navy to exert ourselves for the Public Welfare as well as our own honor, in this Service we have continued 'till the present time, many of us captur'd Stript of our Clothes, in Prison for many months, and upon our return order'd to France without the Benefit of a Cruize.

The depreciation of Paper Currency is so great in America at present; that our monthly wages (twelve or fifteen dollars) is not more than equal to Two Dollars here,—therefore beg your Excellency would be pleas'd to give orders to the Agent to pay us our Wages now due sufficient to cloath ourselves as becomes our Stations, and the Honors of the Country We Serve.

We have the Honor to be, your Excellency's most obedient and very huml Servants.

Benja Pierce Gunner
John Darling Boatswain
James Bragg Carpenter
Lewis Larchar Master's mate
Thomas FitzGerald . . . do:
James Hogan—Midshipman
Arthur Robertson . . . do. . . .
James Lynd. . . . do. . . .
Natha. Marston. . . . do. . . .
James Daly Surgeon's mate
Samuel Guild. . . . do. . . .
Fitch Pool . . . capts: Clerk

Addressed: His Excellency, / Benjamin Franklin Esqr. / Minister Plenipotentiary at the Court of / Versailles, / Paris

Endorsed: Warrant Officers of the Alliance. Provision—Cloathing / Officers of the Alliance March 3d. 1779 complaining of short Allowance

To All Commanders of Vessels of War[8]

ALS (draft): American Philosophical Society; copy: Library of Congress

[March 4, 1779]

To all Commanders of Vessels of War commission'd by the Congress of the United States of North America,

These are to certify you, that the Bearer M. *Riotto* is a Subject of his most Christian Majesty the King of France, appertaining to his Highness the Prince of Conti, *and that the Horses* and the *Dogs, or other Effects* that may be in his Possession in crossing these seas are the Property of the said illustrious Prince.[9] If therefore any English[1] Vessel in which he may pass should by the Fortune of War fall into your Hands, you will afford, to the said M. *Riotto,* & the Person or Persons attending him your full Protection for them and the Property under their Care, that they may be set at Liberty and as far as in you lies forwarded to the Place of their Destination. And I earnestly recommend it to you to give them all the Assistance due to good Friends, & which they may stand in need of. Given at Passy, this *4th Day of March* 1779

BF.—
M.P.

Notations:[2] Pass for the Prince de Conti / March. 4. 79

8. This passport, requested by the prince de Conti, was enclosed with BF's letter to him of the same date, immediately below. BF used this draft as a model for five more passports, issued in response to the prince's subsequent requests (see XXVIII, 633n). The dates of the additional passports were noted at the bottom of this draft: Nov. 30, 1779, Jan. 25, 1781, June 11, 1781, Feb. 2, 1782, and April 8, 1782. Riotto's full name, Augustin Badran, was interlined by a later hand.

9. The phrases "that may be" and "in crossing these seas" were added above the line.

1. He had first written simply "the Vessel".

2. The first is in BF's hand.

To the Prince de Conti[3]

Copy: Library of Congress

Monseigneur

Passy Le 4 Mars 1779

Je joins ici Le Passeport que votre Altesse serenissime ma demandé pour Le Sr. Riotto dans La Lettre qu'ill ma fait l'honneur de mécrire Le du mois dernier.[4]

J'ai l'honneur d'etre avec Le plus profond Respect, Monseigneur de votre altesse Serenissime Le tres h. & t. o. S.

BF

His Highn. the Prince de Conti.

To all Commanders of Vessels of War

To Landais

Copy: Library of Congress

Sir

Passy, March 4 1779

I receiv'd yours of the 26 past, relating to the Refitting of your Ship.[5]

Your Reasons for not mixing french seamen with the American seem to be good. On the Representations of Dr. Winship to the same Effect, who came from you and expressed your Mind to me, I laid aside the thought of applying to the Minister for a proper Number of them, to enable you to make a Cruize in these Seas; and the same Gentleman assuring me that the Ship had by this Voyage acquired such a Character for fast Sailing, & the Captain for good usage of his People that he was confident she would on her Return be immediately mann'd fully with Americans only, which I saw was impossible here, and that tho' she would not have Men enough left for a Cruize, because she could spare none to mann Prizes, yet there were enough to fight her; I resolv'd therefore to send her directly back; the rather as he told me she may be ready in

3. Louis-François-Joseph de Bourbon, comte de la Marche and prince de Conti, a leading French nobleman: XXVIII, 633n. On Feb. 28 he had requested a passport for his huntsman Riotto to bring hunting dogs and horses from England.

4. Riotto's passport is printed immediately above.

5. XXVIII, 619–22. The letter was carried by Amos Windship; see Landais' letter of March 3.

ten or twelve Days, and Mr. Adams my late Colleague wanted such an Opportunity of a Passage home. As to sheathing her with Copper, tho' your Reasons for doing it may be good, it is quite out of the question, as I have neither Orders for doing it, nor Money to pay for it. If the Congress had approv'd of doing it, they might have done it in America, as Copper & Nails were sent over Lately, & are, I believe, arriv'd, more than sufficient for Such Purpose. I think there is more of the same still lying at Nantes in the Hands of M. schweighauser, which you may take over with you; and then perhaps you may prevail to have it done. But I am now surprised to understand from you that So much Work & time is necessary to fit her again for the Sea. I am afraid you will contrive to make such an Expence, that being unable to pay, I shall be oblig'd to sell her.

As to the Gratification you speak of for your Voyage in the Flamand,[6] it is an Affair I know nothing of, having had no Concern in the Projecting of that Voyage. It is Pity you had not settled all such Demands when you were with M. Deane & the Congress in America. Nor have I anything to do with the Payment of the Wages you mention as due to you from this Ship.

These are things totally out of my Sphere. I have order'd such Repairs to be made as are absolutely necessary for your Return.[7] You & M. Schweighauser must judge whether these are best done where she is or at L'Orient. I mentionn'd the Latter Place only because I know they often fit Large India Men there, and that you cou'd not be admitted into Brest, it being contrary to a standing Law to admit in time of War any foreign Vessels into that Harbour. Besides, their Docks & Workmen are so full of Employ & so hurried at that time that they cannot be spar'd for us.[8] If these Repairs don't cost too much, I may possibly be able to afford some small necessary Advance in Money to you & your Officers before you go:

6. One of Roderigue Hortalez & Cie.'s ships, which Landais had commanded on a voyage to America: XXVIII, 622–3.

7. Orders that BF had sent to Schweighauser: XXVIII, 559, 602.

8. For the shortages in workers, matériel, sailors, and money that the dockyards were facing see Dull, *French Navy,* pp. 145–6.

otherwise it will be out of my Power, whatever may be my Inclination to serve & oblige you and them.

I have discours'd with the Minister on the Subject of your Mutineers.[9] The Result is that they cann't be tryed here by the Laws of this Country; and as you can't make up the Court Martial requir'd by those of the Congress;[1] it is advis'd that you do what I before proposed, deliver to the Admiralty at Brest to be kept as English Prisoners of War such as are least guilty, and carry home with you for tryal a few of the Ring-leaders.[2] I shall endeavour to send you herewith an Order to receive those you Leave here. I have the Honor to be &c.

Capt. Landais

From Jean-Gabriel Montaudoüin de La Touche[3]

ALS: American Philosophical Society

Monsieur Nantes 4 mars 79

Permettés moi de vous faire mon compliment sur le nouveau caractere dont vous venés d'être revetu, ou plutôt d'en feliciter le Congrès, et les Etats unis, et tous ceux qui s'interessent a la cause Ameriquaine qui au fond est la cause du genre humain. Malgré vôtre Modestie on aura le droit en vous parlant ou en vous ecrivant d'emploïer le mot *Vôtre Excellence.* Il y a bien long tems que ce mot vous est dû. Bien des membres du Corps Diplomatique ne doivent qu'a leurs places cette formule de l'etiquette, mais pour vous cette expression est due a vôtre personne. On peût même sans flaterie vous dire *Vos Excellences.* Vous êtes en effet excellent de bien des manieres. Vous L'etes en politique, en physique, dans les sci-

9. The minister presumably was Sartine. In his first letter from Brest, Landais had provided a full description of the mutiny: XXVIII, 486–9. According to JA's later testimony, the presence of nearly forty conspirators impeded preparation of the *Alliance: Adams Papers,* VIII, 103–4.

1. A court martial for the conspirators would have required at least three naval captains and three first lieutenants: *JCC,* III, 382–3.

2. BF also sent WTF to procure orders from Sartine for the Brest authorities to receive the conspirators; see BF's March 8 letter to Vergennes.

3. The Nantais merchant is identified in XXII, 332n.

ences en general, et dans les arts, dans La societé &c. J'ai apris, Monsieur, que la felicité dont vous Joüissés a été troublée par les persecutions de la goutte. Je desire fort que vous vous en soiés delivré promptement, et Je l'aprendrai avec Joie; ainsi que ma femme qui vous prie d'agréer ses felicitations. Elle vous dit mille choses honnêtes.

Nous sommes bien touchés des mauvais succés de M. Le Comte D'Estaing.[4] Il paroît qu'il n'est pas heureux.

Mr. David de Morlaix dans nôtre province m'a temoigné un grand desir de vous rendre ses hommages, et m'a prié de l'introduire auprès de vous. Je le fais avec d'autant plus de plaisir que c'est un fort honnete homme, et un de nos bons amis. Il aura L'honneur de vous remettre cette lettre.[5]

Adieu, Monsieur, portés vous bien. Je recite pour vous très devotement la priere d'horace pour Auguste:

> Serus in cœlum redeas, Diuque
> Lætus intersis.[6]

Je suis avec Respect Monsieur vôtre très humble très obeissant serviteur MONTAUDOIN

Addressed: A Monsieur / Monsieur Le Docteur Franklin / Ministre Plénipotentiaire des etats unis / en son hôtel / à Passy

Notation: Montaudoïn Nantes 4 mars 1779.

From Richard Oliver[7]

ALS: American Philosophical Society

Dear Sir London March 4th 1779

I shall very shortly embark for the West Indies where my affairs require my presence, and I shall depart with three or

4. See our annotation to Saint-Lambert's letter, printed after March 1.

5. David l'aîné is listed as a merchant in Morlaix in the *Almanac des Marchands,* p. 336. He left a note on March 29 saying he had come to pay his duties and bring Montaudoüin's compliments and thanks for BF's answer. APS.

6. Horace, *Odes,* I, 2, 45. "Late mayest thou return to the skies and long mayest thou be pleased to dwell [amid Quirinus' folk]."

7. Born in Antigua, the M.P. and former alderman of London (XXII, 13n) had withdrawn from politics at the end of 1778 and was returning to the

four select friends. If with propriety your name can be given to them and myself, to assure good personal treatment should the fate of War make us Prisoners, I shall deem my Convoy most sufficient under its sanction.

I do not desire either for my friends or myself any favour respecting property; for in war that of individuals should depend on general Laws, & I never desire that mine either in war or peace, should be favoured by partial exemption, altho' I shall always be happy to exercise & to receive the good offices of humanity.[8]

Our friend Benjamin Vaughan thinks my request is not improper:[9] I therefore desire to be obliged to you, and for no reason so much as because I am, with the most perfect esteem and all sincerity of respect, Dear Sir Your most Obedient and most Humble Servant RICHD OLIVER

Notation: Richar Oliver Londres 4 March 1779.

From Thomas Paine

ALS: American Philosophical Society

Dear Sir Philadelphia March 4th. 79

I wrote you twice from York Town in June 78, but have not received a line from you since yours of Octr. 7th 77 by Capt Folger.[1]

I have lately met with a turn, which, sooner or later, happens to all Men in popular Life, that is, I fell, all at once, from high credit to disgrace, and the worst word was thought to good for me. But so sudden is the Revolution of public opin-

West Indies to look after his estates: Namier and Brooke, *House of Commons,* III, 225.

8. BF's letter on behalf of Oliver, addressed to all American captains and commanders of warships, is below, March 11.

9. Vaughan had served as a go-between for Oliver and BF before. He had recently written WTF seeking information for Oliver on the brother of a friend fighting with Burgoyne: Feb. 2, 1779, APS.

1. Paine may be referring to his two letters of May 16, 1778: XXVI, 478–89. For BF's Oct. 7 letter and an identification of his distant relative John Folger see XXV, 45, 48–9.

ion, that the same Cause which produced the fall recovered me from it.

Mr. Deane is here. He is certainly not the Man you supposed him to be when you wrote your Recommendatory letters of him.[2] He published a most Inflammatory address in the news-papers of the 5th of Decr.[3] last, which, by the means of a party formed to support it, obtained such an ascendency over all Ranks of People, that the infatuation was surprising. He introduced it by saying that "*the Ears of the Representatives were shut against him*" This declaration, tho' very unjustly made, *gave pretence to the Publication.* The Clamor against Congress was violent. And as I saw no prospect of its abating, I gave, after ten days an answer to it;[4] hoping thereby to stay the rage of the Public till the matter could be calmly understood. I shared the same fate with Congress, and was set-down for a pensioned writer, and most furiously abused both in the news papers and every where else;[5] and what may perhaps appear extraordinary, I was at the same time attacked by Congress, as if they, or a Majority of them wished the Imposition to pass. I had suspicions of Mr. Deane which others had not. I compared his single letters with the joint letters of the Commissr. and other letters and found such a disagreement as could not be honestly accounted for. To support Mr. Deane the affair of the Supplies, from Mr. B——s,[6] was brought up

2. BF had written an unsolicited letter on Deane's behalf to Henry Laurens, president of Congress, on March 31, 1778 (XXVI, 203–4). For a summary of the Deane controversy to this point see XXVII, 584; XXVIII, 470–1, 517–18.

3. For Deane's "To the Free and Virtuous Citizens of America," which was first published in *The Pennsylvania Packet,* see XXVIII, 303n.

4. Paine's answer, signed "Common Sense," appeared in *The Pennsylvania Packet* for Dec. 15, 1778. Many of the documents pertaining to the controversy have been republished in *Deane Papers,* III, 66ff., and in Philip S. Foner, ed., *The Complete Writings of Thomas Paine* (2 vols., New York, 1945), II, 96–188, 1154–80.

5. See, for example, the final paragraphs in the article by "Plain Truth" [Matthew Clarkson?] in the Dec. 21, 1778, *Pennsylvania Packet.*

6. Pierre-Augustin Caron de Beaumarchais, for whose connection with Deane and the French supplies see XXII, 453–5; XXIII, 25–6. In answer to

and Mr Deane's Merit in procuring them was represented equal to that of the Savior of a Country. I had at the same time my suspicions concerning the loss of the dispatches, and the purpose for which they were lost, as you will fully see by the enclosed, to which no answer has been given; and the Torrent has taken a direct contrary turn.[7] The dispute has been a disagreeable one, but the Imposition had it passed would have been still worse. And it will serve to shew to the Enemy that the Congress are not the absolute leaders of America.

Mr. Deane and these who at first supported him, constantly endeavored to involve all his affairs with yours in such a Manner as to admit of no Separation. I, who have carefully read all the letters can best see where they meet and where they are distinct. His Agency before you arrived is one thing, and his joint Commission with you afterwards is quite another thing. Mr. Beache[8] exceedingly surprised me one day, by telling me, that he supposed I intended to attack you after I had done with Mr. Deane. From what he could draw such an inference I cannot conceive as I have constantly studied to keep Mr D—— agency distinct from the joint Commission.[9] I have always had my Eye to the issue, that turn out as it would, you might not be unjustly involved in it. Mr. Deane's connections shelter him under you for support—and there may be others, not your friends, for every Man has his Enemies, who would likewise tack you to him, to share any discredit that might fall on

"Plain Truth," Paine published a detailed account of U.S. diplomacy from the beginning of the war: *Pennsylvania Packet,* Dec. 31, 1778, and Jan. 2, 5, 7, and 9, 1779. Calling all of the publications "ill judged, premature and indiscreet," Congress objected strenuously to Paine's publicizing the charge that the supplies provided by Beaumarchais were intended as a gift, rather than a loan. When French Minister Gérard formally protested, Congress began debating whether to dismiss Paine from his post as secretary for the committee for foreign affairs. *JCC,* XIII, 31–8, 47–9, 54–5, and 75–7.

7. We have not found the enclosure. For the loss of the dispatches see XXV, 48–9; XXVI, 470n.

8. Richard Bache.

9. Paine's pieces in the *Pennsylvania Packet* of Dec. 15, 1778, and Jan. 26 and Feb. 16, 1779, support his assertion.

him. I have endeavored to keep you Clear from both these dangers— When I say that there may be others not your friends &c. I have no particular Authority for saying it; but it being the natural Consequence of Parties, I have endeavored to guard against the probability of any such Injury. I have never heard a Syllable of disrespect towards you from either of the Col Lee's, or any of Mr Izards connections. They know my attachment to you, and I have taken every Care to show by a Comparison of things dates and letters, that you were not privy to such parts of Mr. Deane's Conduct as may be found Censureable. I really believe he has made mischief, between friends to screen himself. I can account for the difference between the Commissioners upon no other plan. I have had a most exceeding rough Time of it; But the Scale of Affairs is now entirely turned as to the Public Sentiment.

I am Dr. Sir Your Affectione Friend and humble Servt.

THO PAINE

P.S. I sent in my Resignation of Secretary to the Com foreign affair Janry. 8th.—[1] My Compliments to your grandsons.

From Matthew Ridley

ALS: American Philosophical Society

Honorable Sir Nantes March the 4th: 1779

Being much taken up with preparations for my departure to America[2] has prevented me makeing you my congratulations, earlier, on your appointment as sole Commissioner from the United States of America, to the Court of Versailles— Tho' late, I trust you will not think me less sincere.— My Wishes are, that you may long live to enjoy your appointment; that you may live to see Peace, restored, and our Independance acknowledged by all Nations; and that after accumulated Honors in the service of our Country, the Evening of your days, if

1. *JCC,* XIII, 36. Paine's letter is in Foner, *Complete Writings,* II, 1159–60.
2. The Baltimore merchant (XXVI, 227) did not actually embark until the summer. JW also had believed Ridley would leave immediately and recommended him to BF as a courier: XXVIII, 557.

your desire, may be closed in the Land of America, destined I hope to be the retreat of the Virtuous & Free— I am with respect Honorable Sir Your most Obedient and most humble Servant MATT: RIDLEY

Addressed: His Excellency Benjn. Franklin Esq. / Plenipotentiary from the United / of America to the Court of Versailles / at Passy / près de Paris

Notation: Math Ridley Nantes march the 4e. 1779.

William Bingham to the American Commissioners

ALS:[3] American Philosophical Society

Gentlemen, March 5th, 1779.

By the eleventh Article of the Treaty of Commerce entered into betwixt His Most Christian Majesty & the United States of America, the Americans are exempted from the Payment of all Duties on the Article of Molasses, notwithstanding which the Duties have, until now, been constantly exacted & paid.[4] This has occasioned great Clamours on the Part of the Americans, which induced me to apply to the Intendant, in order to procure the Exemption which the said Article of the Treaty stipulates in their favor. He informs me that he will repay me the Amount of all Duties that have already been received on this Account at the Custom House if an Order can be procured from the Minister for so doing.

If this can be obtained through your Interest, you will thereby render an essential Service to a Number of the Americans, who have been compelled to pay the said Duties, contrary to the Express Letter of the said Treaty.

I have the Honor to be, with due Respect, Gentlemen, your most obedient humble Servant WM BINGHAM

3. Written on the same sheet as his letter of the 3rd.

4. In fact, this article (XXV, 605) had been deleted from the Treaty of Amity and Commerce by mutual consent of Congress and the French government: XXVI, 448, 462; XXVII, 128, 330–2.

Francis Hopkinson to the American Commissioners

Three ALS:[5] American Philosophical Society

Gentlemen, Philada. March 5th. 1779

Since my last of Feby. 20th. there have issued from my office, the following Loan Office Bills of Exchange[6]

To the State of New Hampshire

25 Setts	12 Dollars each	No. 1045—1069
25	18	1045—1069
25	24	1045—1069
13	30	1044—1056
13	36	1054—1066
13	60	523—535
13	120	774—786

To the State of New Jersey

12 Setts	60 Dollr. each	No. 536—547
10	120	787—796

To the State of Virginia

10 Setts	12 Dollr. each	No. 1070—1079
10	18	1070—1079
10	24	1070—1079
5	30	1057—1061
5	36	1067—1071
5	60	548—552

5. Marked "Original," "Duplicate," and "Triplicate."

6. The treasurer of loans had been reporting to the commissioners and to BF since September, 1778, on the distribution of bills of exchange to the state loan offices: XXVII, 417–18; XXVIII, 68–9. Hopkinson's subsequent letters during the period of the present volume informing the commissioners what bills of exchange had been emitted are dated March 20 ($5,040 to N.J.), May 7 ($13,200 to N.Y.), June 5 ($21,600 to Pa.), and June 19 ($7,800 to N.J.). All the letters are at the APS.

In another letter of March 20 Hopkinson wrote that he had issued several sets of loan office bills amounting to $1,026, the originals having been lost. APS.

I have the Honour to be Gentlemen, your very humble servt.
FRAS. HOPKINSON
Treasr. of Loans

(No. 7)

(Original)

Commrs. at Paris

Addressed: To / The Commissioner or Commissioners / of the United States of America / at / Paris / (Original) / (On public Service) (No. 7)[7]

From Christopher Baldwin

ALS: American Philosophical Society

Londo. 5 March 1779

Many thanks my dear Sir, for your kind letter of 26th. of Janry in answer to mine of 18th. Decr., for nothing could be more acceptable to me.[8] When I wrote to you, it was with a wish and hope, that my letter might get to you, tho at the time, I little expected it would do so; I am therefore the more pleased with my success and have no doubt of this letter reaching you, since I put into the hands of our worthy friend Mr. Bridgen,[9] who has promised to convey it to you upon Condition that I present his best compliments to you, which I now do.

Be assured I have read your letter more than once, and the Ladies of my fire side have done the like. You and our very worthy friend Mr. Small, are, & always have been, a frequent subject of conversation wth. us—that worthy amiable friend, is stil at Minorca. I wish he was here and you too—this wish

7. On the lower left corner of the envelope the treasurer gave his customary admonition: "To be sunk if in Danger of falling into the Hands of the Enemy."

8. For the letter of Dec. 18, 1778, from BF's old London friend see XXVIII, 243–5. Several of the persons and topics mentioned in the present letter are identified there: Alexander Small, Jane Baldwin, Mary Watkins, and Penelope Atkins Pitt, Lady Rivers. BF's letter of Jan. 26, 1779, is missing.

9. Edward Bridgen: XII, 422n. For his postal arrangements with BF see XXVI, 377.

contains multum in parvo, I would to God it was accomplished! Think for a moment of the pleasure we have had in smoothing the ruffled surface of the Pond on our Common, between me & neighbour Brown.[1] Oh! that I could join you in pouring oil on a more troubled surface! *Your* Liturgy, wch. has long been Mrs. Baldwins regular Sunday entertainment, admits of praying for Peace in *our days.* Most heartily *I* do so. A few days after the receipt of your letter, I had an opportunity of writing to my Son and informing him of your kind intention to forward to him recommendations to the Marqs. de Bouillé;[2] at the same time I desired him to address himself to Mr. Williams for such business as he might have at Nantes & also to recommend him to his friends. Some time after I wrote to my Son, we received accounts from the West Indies by which it seems probable, that Dominica may again be in the hands of the English—be that as it may, our obligations to you are the same, and I hope my Son will have the letters you sent him, to make use of in case of need.

The Profile I alluded to, is I am told, about 2 1/2 inches long, of the Royal manufactory of Sauve—[3] Miss Watkins promises to kiss it, the moment it comes to hand—so that your *Experiment* will certainly be tried.

I had a letter a few days ago from my friend Lady R from Nice, in wch. she tells me she was prevented calling on you, as she fully intended, by the shortness of the time she could stay at Paris.

Mrs. Baldwin and Miss Watkins desire to be very kindly rememberd to you and I beg you'l consider me my dear Sir as Your very sincre friend and humble Servant CHR. BALDWIN

Addressed: Dr. Franklyn / from yr. Humble servt. *Genet*[4]

Notation: Chtr. Baldwin Londres 5. mars 1779.

1. Henton Brown, the creator of Mount Pond, Clapham Common: XX, 466n.

2. François-Claude-Amour, marquis de Bouillé, governor of Martinique since 1777: XXIV, 60n.

3. BF had been presenting the medallions made at Sèvres as gifts; see XXVIII, 292n.

4. Edme-Jacques Genet (XXVI, 271n), who forwarded to BF letters, books and information from England.

From Pierre Bon de Corcelles and Other Applicants for Emigration, with Franklin's Notes for Replies[5]

ALS: American Philosophical Society

Of the nine people who applied to Franklin for his help in emigrating to America during the four months covered by this volume, three still believed that land in America was to be had for the asking.

Pierre Bon de Corcelles, whose letter is printed below, desires land for himself and some *soldats-agriculteurs.* So does Count Werzerÿ who, writing from Florence on March 25, explains under what conditions he and two companions, all three dissatisfied officers in the service of an unidentified Italian prince, would consider emigrating to America. Franklin is requested to observe the greatest discretion in his answer and to address it under cover to an Augustinian monk.

The conditions, written in Italian, are:
1. Freedom for all of them, including servants, to practice Catholicism.
2. To be granted a tract of fertile land, along with a furnished house, cattle, equipment, enough seed for two years and a number of Negroes or peasants to do the heavy work—this in lieu of an annual pension.
3. To be registered in some city chosen by Congress and be granted, for themselves and their posterity, all urban privileges.
One of the applicants has a mother, wife, and children, and it is hoped that the republic will show proper appreciation of such assets. All points, except the first one, are open to negotiation.

Gerard d'Auzéville also wants land. He came to see the Doctor on March 24 and hand-delivered an extremely long letter, full of nostalgia for life in the country and regret for having moved to Paris, on the advice of friends, only to find that there was no work for him in the capital—only hypocrisy and other vices, poverty and despair. But among the Americans, who have risen from the glorious ashes of the Greek and Roman republics, he will find a congenial climate. In a follow-up letter of April 9, the writer explains that he had found Franklin encouraging during his first visit, but

5. Unless otherwise noted, all the letters are in French and at the APS. On two of the letters—Bon de Corcelles' and Aubry's—BF drafted notes for replies. Copies of those replies, in French, are in a letterbook at the Library of Congress.

was warned that he would need funds for his passage, equipment, and maintenance until his first crop; land was not to be had for free in the New World. Discouraged, but as flowery as ever, he praises American virtues while remaining quite vague about his personal circumstances.

The other six applicants are professional people. Aubry, who writes on March 6, is a twenty-year-old physician, son of the doctor who runs the mineral waters establishment in Luxeüil.[6] He does not feel that his wish to go to America is a betrayal of his fatherland since the two are allied. Franklin sketched a reply: "That I am obliged to him for his Offers of Service, but have no Orders to send over any Physicians. That America is open to all French People who desire to settle there, but all Persons going hither must bear their own Expences—"[7]

A professor and mining engineer by the name of Anthonius Albertus Vergeel writes in German from St. Petersburg on March 27: he is a Dutchman, thirty-years-old, unmarried, who has worked in various parts of Germany and in Siberia, and now wishes to become a citizen of the United States. He understands Latin, Greek, Russian, Spanish, French, German, and Dutch.[8] Another Dutchman, Petrus Van Noemer, pens sixteen pages in Latin dated 9 Calend. Jun. A.C. 1779, which we interpret as May 24. After congratulating Franklin on a recent dispatch sent to Boston by the French king, promising his protection to the oppressed, he counts himself among those oppressed and tells his life story. Born in Zierikzee (Zeeland) to a middle-class family (his father was a senator and delegate to the provincial assembly), he was schooled in Greek and Latin, later acquired a medical degree in London, and then returned home to study philosophy and literature, while practicing medicine. To please his father, he became a senator in Middelburg and remained in that post for ten years. When the time came for a promotion, however, he was passed over in favor of a man with less seniority but better connections. After many discouraging episodes, he now thinks of "Libera America" as the solution to his difficulties. If Franklin could help him get there and recommend him to a patron,

6. Aubry's father, Jean-François Aubry (d. 1795), was the author of a commentary on Hippocrates: *DBF.* The thermal waters of Luxeuil, at the foot of the Vosges, had already been known to the Romans.

7. The actual reply was dated March 14.

8. A brief summary in English, in an unknown hand, is on the verso of his letter. His letter is dated March 16 old style.

perhaps a member of Congress, he could work as a librarian for a yearly salary. He asks many questions about the country and indicates a preference for Philadelphia or Charleston.

Unmarried, in his early thirties, a lawyer from Bannalec in Brittany declares on June 7 that he trusts the new republic to secure him a fitting position. As to his moral standards, he can produce the best certificates from ecclesiastics, magistrates and officers; he feels free to emigrate now that his beloved mother has died. His signature, almost illegible, looks like "Evén."

An accountant in the War Office in Vienna, named Bek, applies on June 10. He has studied philosophy and jurisprudence, served as secretary in Constantinople and now wants to devote himself to America. His references are minister Vergennes and count Zinzendorff, head of his current department.[9]

Overcoming his shyness on June 11, L. F. G. E. Gedike, an eighteen-year-old student at a seminary, begs in German to be allowed to fulfill his dream of living in America and of helping the country maintain its liberty in any humble way he can. "A burning passion may be able to accomplish what years cannot." The son of a preacher in Brandenburg, he is now an orphan, fast losing his zest for theology.

De Moudon au Canton de Berne le 5e. Mars 1779.

Monseigneur

Les lois constitutionelles de la nouvelle Republiq. des 13. Provinces unies d'ameriq. remplissent d'admiration tous ceux qui les connoissent et font desirer à tout homme, qui aime la liberté, de vivre dans un Paÿs où elle se trouve si bien conciliée avec l'ordre; quant à moi, non seulement je suis decidé à y aller finir ma Carriere, mais encore à employer mes petites facultés pour concourir à l'affermissement de la nouvelle constitution; ce sera ma Patrie d'adoption, la seule que je connoisse selon mes principes; dès là, il me semble que ce seroit une espèce de defection d'attendre que le grand ouvrage soit fini pour y aller habiter, qu'il y a de lhonneur et meme du devoir de partager les perils; mais simple particulier avec une fortune bien mediocre ma jonction seroit très peu de chose; n'importe nous ne devons que ce que nous pouvons.

9. Graf Karl Zinzendorf (1739–1813), for whom see Constant von Wurzbach, ed., *Biographisches Lexikon des Kaiserthums Oesterreich* (60 vols., Vienna, 1856–90), LX, 160–3.

Je puis avoir quelques soldats-agriculteurs robustes et braves qui passeroient chez vous sous ma conduite sils avoient l'assurance que là ils eussent du terrein à cultiver;

Pourriés vous donc Monseigneur me conceder à moi, au nom de vôtre Republiq. une certaine portion de Terre dans l'une des 13. Provinces (si possible dans celle de Pensilvanie) sous des conditions favorables?

Je me garderai bien, toutefois de presenter comme assuré un projet que plusieurs evenemens peuvent croiser, parceque je ne cherche pas à vous tromper, c'est pourquoy je consens que la concession prementionnée si elle est faisable soit conditionelle et quelle porte que j'aurai Cent acres de terre pour moi, *arrivé sur les lieux,* et en outre cinquante pour chaque personne de ma suite, où Tel nombre quil vous plaira de determiner pour le prix qui sera convenu sil netoit accordé gratis aux Charges et conditions de droit envers le gouvernement.

Autant eloigné des lieux que je le suis il peut arriver que je megare dans mon projet, peut être meme ce que je sollicite est-il impossible; en ce Cas puis-je me flatter Monseigneur d'avoir une notice en redressement & si la chose est faisable oserois-je vous prier de m'honnorer d'une Reponse? Je vous indiquerai incessamment à Paris une personne notable et connuë en Cour qui vous donnera des Temoignages suffisans de ma loyauté et de ma Candeur: Et dans l'un comme dans l'autre cas Votre Excellence daignera faire attention que ma resolution quoique bien juste seroit considerée par nos aristocrates Bernois comme un Crime d'Etat si elle leur etoit connuë: on nous dit libres et Cependant on nous puniroit duser de nôtre liberté en changeant de Patrie; Cest pourquoy je supplie instamment Vôtre Excellence de garder ce secret et de pardonner ma liberté en faveur de zèle qui manime et des sentimens de respect et de Confiance avec les quels je suis Monseigneur De vôtre Excellence Le trés humble et trés Obeïssant Serviteur PIERRE BON DE CORCELLES

Endorsed:[1] That I am obliged to him for his Good Will to America.—That the Lands in Pensilvania not yet granted, all

1. The actual reply was dated March 19.

belong to the Proprietary Mr Penn.[2] That he sells them for 5 £ Sterling the 100 Acres. A Price so low that probably the Gentlemen would chuse rather to purchase than accept them as a Gift. That no Lands are given to encourage Strangers to settle in that Province. A Good Climate, good Air, good Soil, good Government, good Laws & Liberty, have been found sufficient Encouragements, without hiring Inhabitants by other Gifts: and all those he will meet with, besides an honest virtuous People, who receive Strangers with a sincere Welcome, and will respect his Talents.

Notations in different hands: Bon de Corcelles Mars 5. 1779 / Pierre bon Da Corcellin Moudon 5. Mars 1779.

From Gourlade and Moylan[3]

ALS: American Philosophical Society

Honord Sir L'Orient 5 March 1779

The Captain of the Ship Bergere which arrived here about a fortnight since from Virginia, with three hundred Hhds of Tobacco for account of the United States of America, apply'd to us yesterday for an explination of the Bills of lading wch: he sign'd for their delivery and the method he shou'd take to have his vessel discharged of her cargo speedily. By those Bills of lading we perceiv'd that said Tobacco is to be deliverd to your order, we in consequence advised him to wait the receipt of it, and that we wou'd write you on the subject to prevent further delay & demurage.[4] The Farmers General Agent likewise informd us, that he had their directions to receive this

2. William Penn's grandson, John Penn (XIX, 337n). In 1771 he had inherited from his father, Richard Penn, the life use of one quarter of the proprietary rights in Pennsylvania. Under the Divestment Act of 1779 the state granted the former proprietors the retention of their private estates and a monetary compensation for lands taken by the state. *DAB.*

3. The commercial house recently formed by Jacques-Alexandre Gourlade and James Moylan: XXVIII, 209n. The letter is in Moylan's hand.

4. Demurrage is money owed to the owners of a detained vessel in compensation for its lost earnings.

Tobacco from those you might apoint here to deliver it to him,[5] we will therefore only add, that to prevent the expence of demurage, it will be necessary your instructions regarding this Tobacco shou'd be here as soon as possible and that they shou'd be accompany'd by the Bill of Lading indorsed by you. We have the Honor of remaining Honord Sir Your most obt hl St GOURLADE & MOYLAN

The Honorable Benj: Franklin Esqr—

Addressed: The Honorable / Benja: Franklin Esqr—

Notation: Gourlade et Moylan. L'orient 5 Mars 1779.

From the Chevalier de Laneuville[6]

ALS: American Philosophical Society

Monsieur, [before March 6, 1779][7]

Ayant eu l'honneur de servir Dans l'armee De la nation de la qu'elle vous êtes le Ministre plenipotentiaire, j'ai cru ne pouvoir et ne devoir pas me dispenser de mettre sous vos yeux les témoignages flatteurs que j'ai été assèz heureux pour mériter du Congres et de differents officiers généraux.[8] Nous sommes partis mon frere[9] et moi sans aucune convention pour

5. Part of the tobacco from the *Bergère* had been promised to the farmers general in fulfillment of the American commissioners' contract with them: XXIII, 514–17; XXVIII, 602–3, 613, 628.

6. Louis-Pierre Penot Lombart (or Lombard), chevalier de Laneuville, had served as Gates's inspector general before returning to France with Lafayette: XXIII, 500n; XXVIII, 490n.

7. When BF answered. Laneuville's letter could have been written any time after his arrival in Brest on Feb. 6.

8. One of these must have been Gen. Samuel Parsons' of June 28, 1778, as a copy in BF's hand is among his papers at the APS. Parsons described Laneuville and his brother (identified in the next footnote) as having manifested "in their agreable Manners a Decency and Modesty not often found in Gentlemen of so extensive Knowledge of Men & Manners in European Nations. . . . They have pursued the Duties of their Office with uncommon Assiduity & unremitted Application . . ." In granting leave to Laneuville Congress also testified to his fidelity and reputation: *JCC,* XII, 1187.

9. René-Hippolyte Penot Lombart de Noirmont, who served as Gates's deputy inspector general and remained in America: XXIII, 500n.

les grades, et quoique jouissant d'une fortune médiocre nous n'avons jamais demandé le moindre dédomagement, trop flattés d'avoir pu montrer notre zele dezintéréssé.

J'ai L'honneur d'être avec respect. Monsieur, Votre tres humble et tres obéissant serviteur LANEUVILLE
Brigadier gènéral
au service des Etats unis
de l'amèrique.

Aprês avoir lu les papiers cy joint jose vous prier de les remettre au porteur.

Notations in different hands: Laneuville / Laneuville. . . . .

To Landais

Copy: Library of Congress

Sir Passi March 6 1779

Since writing mine of the 4th, I have rec'd the Honor of yours dated the 28th. past.[1]

I am sorry to find that, after having settled every thing as I thought to your Mind with your Messenger Dr. Whinship, new Difficulties arise upon every Article. The great Distance occasions such Delay in Business if I am to be consulted on every Step to be taken, and afterwards to answer & remove all Objections, that I see no end, nor can I conjecture when you would in this Way be ready to sail.

The Carrying home a few of the most Guilty for Trial was suggested by Dr. Whinship, as the Example of their Punishment in America would have a better Effect than if transacted here. It was suppos'd that by your Court of Enquiry you had obtain'd a knowledge who were the most guilty, and who were the Evidences necessary to convict them. If this cannot be done, and since they cannot be tryed here, I see nothing left but to deliver them all as English Prisoners to the Commissary who has the Charge of Such Prisoners, or to the Person who shall be appointed by an Order from the Minister to re-

1. XXVIII, 634–6.

ceive them. We may perhaps in Time receive Americans from England in Exchange for them.

You are directed by the Navy Board, as they write me, to apply to the Commercial Agent for supplies & necessaries to get the Ship in Readiness for the Sea with the utmost Expedition.[2] He has undertaken to do it, & being better acquainted with such Business, I must leave it intirely to him. He will judge of the Place and best Manner of executing his Craft. I shall interfere no farther than absolutely to forbid the Copper sheathing, for the Reason before given; & to enjoin the utmost Frugality in the Rest, on acct. of the Lowness of our funds here.

You mention that the Raleigh was admitted to dock in Brest.[3] If so, it was not in Time of War. I made the Proposition again on thursday last & was told that absolutely it could not be. I hope to send the Order by next Post for receiving the Prisoners, & I wish you to proceed with all Diligence in refitting your Ship, under Direction of the Agent, in Order to your Return. I have the Honor to be &

Capt. Landais

To Laneuville

ALS (draft) and copy: Library of Congress

Sir, Passy, March 6. 1779

I have perused the Papers you communicatd to me[4] by which it appears that you have been so disinterestedly serviceable in the American Armies.—And it is with great Pleasure I have added my Certificate, that those Papers are genuine and authentic; hoping they may be of Service to you, where the Power of Advancing Merit is more extensive than with the poor young States of America.—I have the Honour to be,

2. XXVIII, 255–6.

3. In his Feb. 28 letter Landais actually had referred to the *Randolph* (which never visited Europe). Her sister frigate *Raleigh* spent some time in Lorient in 1777, but not in Brest; see the numerous references to her in vol. 25.

4. Which we print before March 6.

with much Esteem, Sir, Your most obedient & most humble Servant B FRANKLIN

Brigadier General de Laneuville

Notation: To Brigdr. Genl. De la Neufville 6. March 79 & to All Captains & Commanders relative to Cook 10. March 79.—[5]

From John Bondfield[6]

ALS: American Philosophical Society

Sir Bordeaux 6 March 1779

I am honor'd with your favor of the 25th Ulto.[7] and am much Obliged to you for forwarding the Letter of Marque &c agreable to my request. A Vessel Arrived at this port from Charles Town saild the 25 January. The Troops and Inhabitants of the Province were all in motion. Six Thousand men are United under Lincoln & Thompson and are perfectly secure from any attempt against the State of So Carolina.[8]

A Ship is arrived that left the Capes of Virginia the 16 Jany in Company with four Ships bound to Europe one of them is arrived at Nantes the other two at Sea or taken no publick Letters by her that is arrived and the few private contain no interesting intelligence.

They write me from Nantes our Ships are Loaded and will be ready to Sail at the Arrival of the Frigate expected to take them to the Isl d'Aix where a West India Convoy is to take

5. The letter for Cook begins immediately below BF's draft of his letter to Laneuville. We print it under March 10, below.

6. This merchant and American agent in Bordeaux (XXIV, 403n) was a frequent correspondent of the American commissioners and BF.

7. Above, XXVIII, 600–1.

8. Major Gen. Benjamin Lincoln (1733–1810), appointed commander of the Southern Department Sept. 25, 1778, reached Charleston too late in December to prevent the British capture of Savannah: *DAB.* William Thompson (1727–96) was colonel of the third S.C. regiment and, from November, 1778, state senator: John R. Alden, *The South in the Revolution 1763–1789* (Baton Rouge, 1957), pp. 204–5, 237; Heitman, *Register of Officers,* p. 398; *S.C. Hist. and Geneal. Mag.,* III (1902), 98–107.

them so far as the Steer the same Course.[9] I hope a Frigate will be order'd at the Seperation of the Fleets to accompany Our Ships to the Continent.

I have the honor to be with due Respect Sir Your most Obedient Humble Servant JOHN BONDFIELD

The Honble. Benj Franklin Esq

Addressed: The Honble. Benjamin Franklin / Plenipotentiary from Congress / a / Paris

Notation: John Bondfield Bordeaux 6 mars 1779.

From S. & J.-H. Delap[1]

ALS: American Philosophical Society

Sir Bordeaux 6th March 1779

Messrs. La Veuve Mathurin Cornic & Mn. fils of Morlaix advise us that our Privateer the Marchioness de la Fayette Commanded by P: Barry under American Colours had sent into their port a small Brig laden with Fish & Oil the Sale of which was stoped by the Judge of the Amiralty untill she was deemd a Legal Prize by you & the Conceil des Prizes;[2] she is an English Vessell that was taken by a French Privateer, retaken by a Jersey Man & afterwards recaptur'd by Captn. Barry, therefore dont Immagine that we shall meet any difficulty in getting her Condemned, but as fish is a Perishable article & this the Season[3] for placing same to advantage, we have to request your giving your decision on this affair as soon as will be convenient & with out Loss of time, as delay will not only prejudice the Sale of this Cargo but also make

9. For the West India convoy see our annotation of BF's March 2 letter to Landais.

1. For the Bordeaux firm see XXII, 445. Although Samuel Delap had been dead for seveal years (XXIII, 340n), the firm retained his name. The present letter is probably in the hand of Jean-Hans Delap.

2. The members of the Council of Prizes are listed in the *Almanach royal* for 1779, p. 196. The Morlaix firm had already reported to BF the arrival of Capt. Barry's prize, the *Papillon:* XXVIII, 456–7.

3. Lent.

the greater part thereof prove a total Loss. We take this opportunity of Rendering you an offer of our best Services at this Port & are with the greatest respect—sir Your most obedt, & most devoted humle. Servants— S & J H. DELAP

The Honourable Benjamin Franklin

Addressed: To / The Honourable Benjamin Franklin / Plenipotentiary to the United States / of America. / at the Court of / Versails

Notation: Delap. Bordeaux 6. mars 1779.

From Joshua Johnson

ALS: American Philosophical Society

Honble. Sir Nantes 6 Mar 79.

I have the honour to acknowledge the Receit of your polite and much esteemed favour of the 28 Ultimo[4] for which and your readiness in interfearing to releave me from the duties imposed by the Farmers General on my Furniture I beg you to accept of my gratefull thanks, at your request I forward you a List of those Articles on which they have charged the duty and have hopes, that through your interposition, that I shall be discharged from the payment of it.—

As an Individual who is established here in Trade, I take this method to return you my thanks for your great attention to it in the early appointment of the Alliance Frigate to Convoy our Ships to America, and notwithstanding what may be insinuated to the contrary I have not a doubt but you will inforce your Orders so as to have her here at or near the time you originally fixed.—[5] The La Bergere lately arrived from Mary'd at L.'Orient has three hundred Hhds Tobacco on board on Account of Congress, the Owner has made frequent applications to M. Williams & self to receive them, I have thought proper to mention thus much for fear you had not been in-

4. Above, XXVIII, 629.

5. The *Alliance* had been ordered to escort the Nantes merchantmen to America; see BF to Landais, March 2.

formed of her arrival & that you may be pleased to give your Orders accordingly.—[6] I remain on all occasions with the most sincere esteem & regard— Sir. Your most obliged & ready Hble Servant JOSHUA JOHNSON

His Excellency Benjamin Franklin Esqr. Passy.

Addressed: His Excellency / Benjamin Franklin Esqr: / Plenipotentiary / at the Court of / Versailles.

Notation: Joshua Johnson Nantes 6. Mars 1779

From John Paul Jones ALS: American Philosophical Society

Honored and dear Sir, L'Orient March 6th. 1779

The mystery which you so delicately mention in your much esteemed favor of the 24th. Ulto.—[7] it has been my intention for more than Twelve Months past to communicate to you; which however I have put off from time to time on reflecting that the Account must give you more pain than pleasure:—yet had I not, on my sudden departure from hence for Paris, inadvertently neglected to take with me the Original Paper whereof the inclosed is a Copy,[8] I certainly should then have put it into your hands.—The subject at the beginning of the War was communicated to sundry members of Congress among whom I may mention Mr. Hewes of No. Carolina and Mr. Morris of Philadelphia; and to various other persons in America before and since.—[9] It was the Advice of my friends, Govr. Young[1] among many others, when that great Misfortune of my Life happened, that I should retire Incog to the

6. Johnson was the commercial representative for Maryland (for which see XXVI, 227–8), as well as a private merchant at Nantes.

7. XXVIII, 599. If there was a postscript to that letter mentioning the mystery in question, it is no longer extant; see BF's March 14 response to the present letter.

8. Printed below Jones's signature to the present letter.

9. Joseph Hewes and Robert Morris had served with BF on the secret committee of the Continental Congress: XXII, 355.

1. William Young had been Lt. Gov. of Tobago in 1773, when the incident which Jones describes below occurred: Morison, *Jones,* p. 25.

continent of America, and remain there Until an Admiralty Commission should Arrive in the Island, and then return.— I had waited that event Eighteen Months before Swords were drawn and the Ports of the Continent were Shut. It had been my intention from the time of my misfortune to quit the Sea Service Altogether, and, after Standing Trial, as I had the means, to purchase some small tracts of Land on the Continent, which had been my favorite Country from the age of thirteen, when I first saw it.—[2] I had settled my future plan of retirement in "calm contemplation and Poetic ease".—[3] But the revolution in America deranged every thing— And the person with whom I had *in Trust* left a considerable part of my Effects in the West Indies, had, while the ports were open shewn very little inclination to make me proper Remittances.— Many of my friends had expressed their fears that he meant to abuse my confidence and take Advantage of my situation.[4] Among these I can mention a person whom I very much esteem, and who has always expressed great Obligation to you, I mean Doctor John K. Read of Goochland County Virginia.[5] I was not however Undeceived Until after the Ports were Shut.

I had made the Art of War by Sea in some degree my Study and been fond of a Navy from my boyish days up.— Knowing the perfidy and ingratitude of Dunmore, as soon as an expidition was adopted against him from Philadelphia by Sea, I had the honor to be appointed Senior Lieutenant in the Navy of the Colonies which was then established under Hopkins.—[6] I

2. In May, 1761, when the brig *Friendship* (on which he was a ship's boy) reached Virginia: *ibid.*, pp. 12–13.

3. James Thomson, "Autumn," *The Seasons* (James Sambrook, ed., Oxford, 1981), p. 198, line 1277. Morison, *Jones*, p. 29, claims this was Jones's favorite quotation from the poem.

4. Either Jones's former partner in Tobago, the merchant-planter Archibald Stuart, or his agent Stuart Mawey: Morison, *Jones*, pp. 22, 24.

5. Deborah Franklin's nephew, Dr. John Kearsley Read: x, 69n; for Jones's relationship with him see Morison, *Jones*, pp. 27–9.

6. On Dec. 7, 1775, Jones received a First Lieutenant's commission from Congress; Esek Hopkins had been commander-in-chief of the Continental Navy: Morison, *Jones*, pp. 31–2.

need not observe that as I had not then heard the doctrin of Independence even in a whisper, and that as the Pamphlet called common Sense did not Appear till a considerable time afterwards, I could have no Views of protection from a new Government; and therefore as I adhered to my first resolution of returning to the West Indies, to Stand Trial, and to Settle my affairs there as soon as peace should be restored to the Continent, it was the Advice of my friends that I should till that wish'd event might be brought about, remain Incog.— Within a few Months after my first Appointment, as a proof of the public Approbation of my conduct, I had the honor to receive a Captains Commission,[7] without my having either said or written a single word in my own favor to any person either in or out of Congress.— In the Character of an American Officer, I think you are convinced that Gain has not been the Object of my pursuit.— I shall say nothing either of my Abilities (if I have any) or of my Services.— It is the province of others to determin the merits of both.— I have received no pecuniary gratification whatsoever, not even the expences of my daily Dinner, from the publick Funds.— On the contrary I have disbursed for the publick Service, when our prospects were at the worst, considerable Sums of my private fortune, which has never yet been repaid.— But I have Always acknowlidged that Congress have far more than rewarded my poor endeavours; by the generous and Unsolicited Attentions, and by the Confidential preferences which I have so often had the honor to experience in their Appointments; and I hope, at least, never to tarnish the honor of the American Flag.

It may be said that I have been Unfortunate—but it cannot be made Appear that I have ever, even in the weakest Moments of my Life, been capable of a Base or a mean Action.— Nature has kindly given me a Heart that is heighly susceptible of the finer feelings—and I have endeavoured to watch over the happiness of my poor Relations *Unseen.*— For that purpose I sent several little remittances (Bills) from America *in Trust* to a very worthy friend of mine Captain Plaince of

7. On May 10, 1776: *ibid.,* p. 53.

Cork,[8] to be Applied for their Use without their having the pain of knowing whence:—But to my great Sorrow I find they have all miscarried the letters that contained them some of them having been Sunk, the rest taken on the passage.— I brought no funds with me to Europe and since my Arrival in it you know that my hands have been Tied.— My Will, now in the hands of Mr. Morris, will evince that I have not been Unmindful of the duties which I owe to Nature—And, were it equally in my power, I think Pope himself could not have taken more pleasure than I should "to Rock the Cradle of declining Age"—[9]

In short, however chequered my fortune may have been, I feel no Sentiment in my Breast that can ever make me wish to conceal Any event of my Life from persons of Candor and Ingenuity—therefore you are at perfect liberty to communicate my Story to whom you think proper, and particularly to Doctor Bancroft.— I am, and shall be always, ready to give you every explanation that you can require.

With respect to Lord Selkirks plate, it is my wish to restore it *to the Lady* from whom it was taken.—[1] When I wrote to her I expected that the plate had been of far more Value than it really is—But since you agree to restore the One half in the Name of the Continent—And as I feel myself above the Idea of receiving any profit from such a Pillage—I hope Lord Selkirk will gratify me so far as to Suffer the Plate to be restored.— I claim no merit in this, nor has it been my intention to Attract his notice either by my history or otherwise, except only as far as he might have been concerned in my Scheme of bringing about an Exchange of Prisoners.— If, however his delicacy will not suffer him to receive what he thinks an Obligation from me—it will be no difficult matter to point out to him, if he should be at a loss, how to discharge that Obligation.— How Lord Selkirk came to renew his correspondence

8. Probably the person praised in 1776 (following his capture) by prize agent John Langdon: *Naval Docs.,* VI, 1346.

9. Actually "reposing Age": "An Epistle from Mr. Pope, to Dr. Arbuthnot," *The Poems of Alexander Pope* (John Butt, ed., New Haven, 1963), p. 612, line 409.

1. See XXVIII, 500, 599.

with Mr. Alexander,[2] and on that particular Subject too, appears to me rather Surprising.— While I was at Passy in the Summer, Mr. Alexander asked me several questions about the landing on St. Mary's Isle—to gratify him I shewed him a Copy of my letter to the Countess.— He invited me to dine with him and said "he would keep the Copy among the Papers which he most esteemed"— I remember Also that in the course of the day he complained that Lord Selkirk had taken great offence at some freedom of Sentiment which had marked his letters, and that in consequence they had not corresponded for a great while past.— I remember too that he has frequently, by appearing to disclose his own Plans in some Measure, endeavoured to fish out mine.— Mrs. Amiel[3] has told me often that he is my Enemy.— Yet why he should be so I cannot imagin, as I never gave him Cause.— But this I know, that let them place round me as many Spies as they please—as I have no Confidants near me, and as I do not keep my intentions by me in Writing, they cannot betray my Councils—And I may yet appear in a quarter of the Globe which they little imagin.

The inclosed little correspondence between Mr. Schweighauser and myself on the Subject of the Plate I send you to Shew that he makes difficulties where there are none.— You will perhaps See fit to send him Orders in consequence, as I have not to this moment recd. payment of my claim to the Prizes which have been in his hands.

Mr. Williams did me the honor to shew me the first paragraph of your letter to him on the Subject of your Appointment as sole American Ambassador at the Court of Versailles.—[4] I believe that Appointment to have been Unsolicited on your part, and I am sure that you are Above writing any thing that could tend either to Magnify the Merit of your own Services or to diminish that of others.— In the fullness of my heart I congratulate you on your well merited Appoint-

2. The Scottish banker William Alexander: XIV, 75n. He was at Auteuil (near Passy) for much of 1778.

3. Charlotte Amiel, wife of Jones's friend Peter Amiel: XXVI, 221n, 492n; XXVII, 508–9; XXVIII, 116–17.

4. XXVIII, 522–3.

ment, and I trust you will believe me that I do now and ever shall rejoice in every circumstance that tends to the honor or happiness of a great and good Man, who has taught me as well as his Country to regard him with a Veneration and Affection which proceeds directly from the Heart, and that is due only to the best of Friends.

The outfit of the Poor Richard has engaged my whole Attention since I returned here.— I received this day 33 Seamen from Brest, and Volunteers for Soldiers enlist with me daily to Serve for three years or during the War.— I have found several, and hope soon to have a full set of Brave and deserving Men, for Officers.— Their Names &ca. I will send up to you.— I find myself under the necessity of taking a Journey to Bordeaux to give directions about the Set of Cannon that are to be made there for the Poor Richard.— I shall set out after to morrow, and as I return immediatly, may I hope to be favored with a letter from you to meet me at Nantes on my way Back.

I hope nothing will prevent Doctor Bancroft from going to England on the Exchange of Prisoners.[5]

I am with greatful and real Affection and respect Honored and dear Sir, Your very Obliged very Obedient very humble Servant JNO P JONES

His Excellency Doctor Franklin

The Master of a West Indea Ship from London[6] had occasion to ship sundry Seamen at the Island where he Loaded—one of whom in particular behaved himself very ill— He was a principal in Embezzling the Masters Liquors— He got frequently Drunk— He neglected and even refused his duty with much insolence.— He stirred up the rest of the Crew to act in the Same Manner and was their avowed Ringleader.

As the Masters engagements were of such a Nature that his all depended upon dispatch, he gave his Crew every reason-

5. Bancroft's mission had been cancelled; see Hartley's March 2 letter.

6. Jones himself (then using his name of birth, John Paul). At the time he was master of the merchant ship *Betsy:* Morison, *Jones,* pp. 21–3.

able Encouragement.— They had plenty of good Provision and were in other respects well Used.— Notwithstanding of which one forenoon when the Master came on Board that the Crew had formed or were then forming a plot to desert the Ship.— As the Master was walking aft the Ringleader rushed up from the Steerage and stopped him with the grosest Abuse that Vulgarism could dictate—because, as he pretended, the Master had sailed his Ship fourteen Months without paying Wages.— The fellow having some time before complained that he wanted Cloaths, the Master now gave him Frocks and Trowsers telling him to go about his duty and to inform himself better—for that what he had said was not so.— But mildness had no good effect, for while the Master was distributing Cloathing to some of the rest who were also in want, the first conveyed his things into the Boat and another of the Crew was following his example, till observing that the Master had an Eye upon their proceedings, they Sneaked back into the Ship.— They remained quiet for a short space— But the Ringleader soon broke out again with Oaths and insisted on having the Boat and quiting the Ship.— This the Master Refused, but offered to give up his agreement if a Man could be found to serve in his Room. The disturber Swore with horrid imprications that he would take away the Boat by force!— And for that purpose actually rushed over the Gangway, bidding the Master the most contemptuous defiance!— Upon the Masters stepping up to prevent this, the Man (having threw his strength) leapt into the Ship and forced him into the Cabin; Using at the time language and Attitudes too indecent to be mentioned, and charging him not to Shew his Nose upon Deck again till the Boat was gone at his Utmost Peril.— The Master searched the Cabin for a Stick, but not finding one, and his Sword, by chance being on the Table, he took it up in hopes that the sight of it would intimidate the Man into Submission.— The Man had by this time descended the Gangway within a Step of the Boat, so that it would have been impossible to prevent his Elopement had he persisted.— But he now reentered the Ship breathing Vengeance, and, totally regardless of the Sword, tho within its reach, turned his back towards the Master, ran on the Main Deck, Armed himself there with a Bludgeon with which he returned to the quarter Deck and Attacked the Master.— The Master was thunder Struck with Surprise, for he had considered the Mans ravings as the natural effect of disappointed Rage which would soon Subside of itself.— But now his sole expedient was to prevent bad consequences by returning again to the Cabin;— And this he endeavoured to do as fast as possible by retiring backwards in a posture of defence.— But alas! What is human foresight?—The After Hatchway was Uncovered and lay in a direct line between the Masters back and the Cabin door, but the Momentary duration of the Attack did not Admit of his recollecting that circumstance before his heel came in contact with the Hatchway, which obliged him to make a Sudden Stop.— Unhappily at that instant the Assailants Arm being heigh raised, he threw his Body forward to reach the Masters head with the descending Blow—the fatal and Unavoidable consequence of which was his rushing Upon the Swords Point.

After this melancholy Accident the Master went Publickly to a Justice of the Peace and Offered to Surrender as his Prisoner.— The Justice, who calld himself the Masters friend, persuaded him to withdraw and said it was Unnecessary to Surrender before the day of Trial.— And the rest of the Masters friends who were present forced him to mount his Horse.— Two weeks before this the Chief Mate had been for the first time in his Life Advanced to that Station—and yet Unworthy as his conduct had been in it he now openly Arrogated his Unblushing pretentions to the Command; and to Attain it Associated with the Crew. The Testimony of such a combination may easily be imagined, conscious as they were of having embezzled the Masters property they were not likely to dwell on any circumstance that manifested their own dastardly and Undutiful Conduct.— And as the Second Mate, a young Gentleman of worth lay Sick as well as all the inferiour Officers and best disposed of the Crew, in all human probability the Truth could not escape the grossest perversion.— Besides the Nature of the Case Subjected it to the cognizance of Court Martial—And there was no Admiralty Commission then in the

Government.— For these obvious reasons the masters friends constrained him for atime to leave the Country.

N.B. The foregoing has been written in great haste to save the Post.

Notation: P. Jones L'Orient 6. May. 1779.

From William MacCreery

ALS: American Philosophical Society

Sir Bordeaux 6 March 1779

I had the honor to address your Excellency some short time ago on the subject of Port Duties here chargeable on sundry goods shipp'd by the Subjects of the United States of America.[7] Since that time the Ship Buckskin is arrived at this Port, and will be ready in a very short time to take her Cargo on board; and least your Excellency shou'd not be able to procure the desired regulations on the Shipping of Salt &c. I wou'd beg of you to procure a permission from the Minister, for Saml. and John Hans Delap & William MacCreery, to load on the Ship Buckskin, Aquilla Johns Master,[8] Three Thousand Six Hundred Bushels, or one Hundred & fifty Tons of Salt, free of Duties.

This Ship carrys 22 Nine Pounders, will be well Man'd. Shou'd there be any Goods belonging to the States to go on Freight to Maryland, think she wou'd be an exceeding good & safe conveyance, as any that has yet offerd; as she Sails remarkably fast, having been constructed for Cruizing. She will have nothing to detain her here above a Month, provided the order for loading the Salt, be had in due time. I have the Honor to be, with the utmost respect, Your Excellency most Obedient and most Humble Servant WILL MACCREERY

7. The Maryland merchant, in Bordeaux since September, 1777, had written on this matter the previous month: XXVIII, 625–7.

8. Johns was a naval lieutenant from Baltimore: Claghorn, *Naval Officers*, p. 166. For the *Buckskin* see also Charles H. Lincoln, comp., *Naval Records of the American Revolution* (Washington, D.C., 1906), p. 243.

Addressed: His Excellency / Benjamin Franklin / Plenipotentiary from the U. S. of A. / Versailles

Notation: Will MacCreery Bordeaux 6. mars 1779.

From Jacques-Dominique de Roberdeau and Other Favor Seekers and Admirers

ALS: American Philosophical Society

A number of people asked Franklin for a favor during the spring of 1779. According to our custom, we publish a collective summary of their requests, grouped by topic: the forwarding of mail, financial advice or assistance, a position as commissary, and sheer admiration of Franklin.[9]

The favor most frequently applied for is that of forwarding mail to America. On March 6 Jacques-Dominique de Roberdeau, whose letter is printed in full below, renews a plea for Franklin to send on a letter to his relative, General Daniel Roberdeau. An unsigned letter written from Paris on April 27 urges the Doctor to insert into his dispatches for Boston, on three successive occasions, one of the three identical copies enclosed, in the hope that one of them will reach its destination. They are unsealed and contain nothing of a suspicious nature. Also unsealed is the letter that a man called Boÿer sends Franklin on May 16, from Paris, with a plea to seal and forward it. The widow Presle de Saintemarie thanks Franklin for having promised her, the previous Sunday, that he would forward a letter for her son in Guadeloupe and one for his protector, M. Boyer de l'Etang. Now, on May 19, she sends him the letter in question from the rue St. Louis in the Marais, in Paris. About to leave for Le Havre, a food commissioner named Duvivier asks Franklin on June 24 to show his usual benevolence to the bearer of his message, Lafosse, an honest man who has been trying in vain for twenty years to get in touch with his father, a very great distance away.

Grateful to Franklin for having transmitted a letter of hers to Salem in 1778, the baronne de Mahuet, who resides at the hôtel de Lambesc, rue du Jour, begs for an appointment.[1] She hopes he can

9. Unless otherwise indicated, the letters are in French and deposited at the APS.

1. She was born Catherine-Gabrielle de Rennel (b.1723): *Dictionnaire de la noblesse,* XII, 751. Her letter is dated April 1.

give her some news of a relative she has in that part of the world. Also eager for news is P. Jeanrenaud who writes from Geneva on May 21, wondering whether Franklin has heard of his son's safe arrival in Philadelphia. The Doctor will remember that in January he kindly gave the young man and three of his friends a letter of recommendation, as they were about to embark on the *Lantilus*.

Another category of favor seekers sought help in settling financial transactions that seemed to have gone awry. On March 10, an unsigned letter in the third person asks Franklin to accept the three enclosed bills of exchange, one of which says by mistake three thousand and five *l.t.* instead of three thousand and five hundred *l.t.* The following day, someone by the name of Sovalete said he would like Franklin to give his approval to the enclosed bill of exchange which he is not able to cash otherwise. A merchant called Guinot (or Gumont?) is in a similar predicament. He has a bill of exchange on Franklin originating from Nantes and amounting to 1,800 *l.t.* Unable to find Franklin's hotel in Paris, he takes the liberty of writing. His letter is dated June 30.[2]

2. BF not only helped individuals with problems raised by their bills of exchange, but also handled transactions for the U.S. government. On March 18 a set of three bills of exchange on the American Commissioners, signed by Francis Hopkinson, treasurer of loans, and countersigned by Nathaniel Appleton, commissioner of the continental loan-office in Massachusetts, gave instructions to pay to James Leighton one hundred and fifty *l.t.* ($30) for interest on the money he had lent the U.S. Two days later Appleton advised "the Commissioner or Commissioners" that a mistake had been made on March 3rd when two sets of bills of exchange for thirty-six dollars had been given the same number, 206. They were meant for two different people, Ichabod Smith and James Brackett Jr., who were both entitled to payment. BF endorsed it: "Two Papers are fixed to No. 206 for 36 Dol. in favour of Ichabod Smith." Both letters are at the APS.

Reminiscing years later about the hardships of his mission, BF singled out the bills of exchange as the most grievous aspect of his work. Writing to his old friend Charles Thomson, he included a "Sketch of Services" to the U.S., written in the third person, to be shown to the president of Congress, if Thomson saw fit. In it he complained that "the part of his service which was the most fatiguing and confining, was that of receiving and accepting, after a due and necessary examination, the bills of exchange drawn by Congress for interest money, to the amount of *two millions and a half of Livres annually;* multitudes of the bills very small, each of which, the smallest, gave as much trouble in examining, as the largest. And this careful examination was found absolutely necessary, from the constant frauds attempted by presenting *seconds* & *thirds* for payment, after the firsts had been discharged. As these bills were arriving more or less by every ship and

The case of Philip Wagner (or Wagener) is puzzling. His first letter, written in German on April 10, probably not in his own hand, was sent from Rotterdam—hence the Dutch used for his address. For reasons that he does not specify, he has run off to "accursed Holland," a country in which he has no friends and where "humanity has sunk to its lowest level." He has found an American ship to go home on but cannot sail for lack of funds. Would Franklin, whose kindness is well known, give him some help? Franklin obliged with ten *louis* and the advice to sail under the Dutch flag.[3] The man writes again on July 23, this time from Dunkirk, and using the services of a Frenchman. Having spent half the sum he received to buy himself food and clothing, he has only five *louis d'or* left and needs twenty more, which he will repay in gold, and with interest, within one week of his arrival in Philadelphia. He has met the captain of a Dutch vessel who is about to leave for St. Eustatius but, having no need of extra sailors, seeks ten louis for Wagner's passage. A third document comes from the man in whose house Wagner has been staying in Dunkirk, Conrad Georg Bauer, who addresses Franklin in German on August 16 to complain that Wagner has left without paying his bill. Could his Excellency give some "hard information" as to Wagner's plans, such as whether or not he intends to return? We also learn from Bauer that the young man, who claimed to be an American, hailed from Saarbrücken.

Also trying to obtain money was a Venetian woman, by the name of Felicie Françoise Francalanza, who sent two letters from Lisbon. In the first, dated April 20, she explains that her family name is a combination of the town of Franca and the lance that her ancestor was allowed to put into his coat of arms, because of his valor. Her father, who held the position of Venetian consul in Lisbon, told her that a male relative had emigrated to England, thence to America; his name had evolved to Franklin in the process, since Anglo-Saxons favor short names. Her family, along with other Italian ones, was ruined by the marquis de Pombál.[4] Her father emigrated to

every post, they required constant attendance. Mr. F. could make no journey for exercise, as had been annually his custom, and the confinement brought on a malady that is likely to afflict him while he lives." Smyth, *Letters,* IX, 697.

3. Dated July 1, three copies of a promissory note for ten louis (two in English and one in French) are signed in an almost illegible way by "fillib Wagner." APS.

4. The Portuguese minister Sebastião José de Carvalho e Melo, marquês de Pombal (1699–1782). In order to centralize all the Portuguese commerce

Cairo, where he died, and she had to move to a humble little house on the other side of town. She hopes that, since they are related, Franklin will help her in her present state of misery. She is not married, and her needs are small. And how good it will feel to pay back in kind those Englishmen in town who have mocked her alleged family tie to Franklin! She covers the same ground in a second letter, on May 4,[5] reveals that she is thirty-four years old, and indicates where the money should be sent in case Franklin decides to come to her rescue.

Also in need of money, but more blunt about it, is a young man named Boule. In a letter from Passy dated April 9, he tells his life story. Born in Nancy to a family of slender means, a mediocre student, he was sent to Nantes to learn about commerce, found work in Denmark as secretary to the French consul, hated the climate and the monotonous lifestyle there, came back to France and was hired by M. La Faye who runs the most elegant shops in Paris.[6] He went into debt in order to purchase decent clothing and is now pressed for repayment by various people. He admires truth and confesses that he ran away that very morning with only six *l.t.* in his pocket and a silver watch that does not belong to him. Having reached Versailles, he felt so disgusted with himself that he retraced his steps and while walking back, thinking that in his case suicide was justifiable, he was struck with the inspiration that Franklin, that *mortel vertueux*, might help him in his desperate "*phrénétique*" state. Another letter, dated April 8,[7] but certainly written after his first one, probably the following day, apologizes for the liberty he took in ignoring the vast social gap between Franklin and himself. He had decided meanwhile to go back to Paris and found some pretext to explain his absence. But the urgency of his debt remains, and the threat of losing his employ if it came to be known. Should Franklin decide to lend him the sum he needs (154 *l.t.*), he is certain to be able to pay it back within six months. He encloses a list (now missing) of the merchandise to be found in the shop, which also carries British goods and jewelry. How cruel his predicament! May it find a resolution!

in the hands of one company, to which he granted exorbitant privileges, he drove many other merchants into exile or deported them.

5. At the Harvard University Library.

6. A Lafaye, *parfumeur,* on the Pont-Neuf is listed in the *Almanach des marchands,* p. 394.

7. At the University of Pa. Library.

There is a whiff of threat in the letter sent on March 12 by a young man who signs Arondel (or Orondel?). His family, a branch of the illustrious English house of Arundel,[8] settled in France many years ago and seemed all but forgotten when a letter from Lord Arundel arrived for the writer, containing a recommendation for the comtesse de Guerchy.[9] Encouraged by his colonels, he immediately went to Paris but met with no success. Unless Franklin takes him under his protection, he will find himself constrained to go back to England, in order to enjoy the lord's protection. This he would do mostly for his father's sake, for on his simple soldier's pay he cannot help the elderly man who has lost his fortune. Father and son put all their hope in Franklin's kindness.

Other petitioners need financial help, and quickly. The three brothers de Laporte, who were part of de la Plaigne's unfortunate expedition of the previous year, tell their pitiful story in an undated memorandum addressed to the Representatives of the United States of America.[1] Lured by de la Plaigne who presented himself as the agent from Georgia, and spurred by their pro-American feelings, they abandoned good positions in Bordeaux in order to embark on the *d'Argentré* where they were the only ones, of the twenty-three people on board, to pay their own passage. Through the Captain's bumbling, they were captured by a Jersey privateer and forced to spend twenty-seven days in irons, lying on wet cables, because they had put up a spirited resistance. Then they had to endure a harsh captivity of nine and a half months, longer than the other passengers, since their intention to fight for the Americans was well known. They contracted debts in England, with the result that the third brother was kept hostage there to ensure repayment. They urgently need a "gratification" to provide for his subsistence. Franklin endorsed their plea, "Memoire of some of De la Plaigne's Officers."

Financial compensation for a loss endured in the American cause is requested by Montleger, mayor of Port Louis, in Brittany, in favor

8. The house had died out, and its title had passed to the dukes of Norfolk; the current holder was Charles Howard, Duke of Norfolk and 23rd Earl of Arundel (1720–86). G.E. Cokayne, *et al.*, eds., *The Complete Peerage* (13 vols.; London, 1910–40), I, 259; IX, 633.

9. Probably Gabrielle-Lydie d'Harcourt, widow of Claude-François Regnier, comte de Guerchy, who after a brilliant military career became France's ambassador to London from 1763 to 1767 and died soon after: *Dictionnaire de la noblesse,* XVI, 925.

1. Emmanuel-Pierre de la Plaigne is identified in XXIV, 83n.

of a widow named Mat (maiden name Rosnarho) whose son lost his life on the *Reprisal* where he served as an officer. Her pitiful situation was brought to Franklin's attention on March 8, he writes, and it would be an act of justice and charity to remedy it now.[2] Montleger's letter is dated June 25.

Peter Berail would like the position of commissary in Cette (Sète), in Languedoc. He explains to Franklin in English on June 15 that he has dealt with English captains and merchants for forty years, to their satisfaction. He has fulfilled the function of quay master, equivalent to captain of the harbor. His son, recently arrived from England where he spent several years improving his knowledge of the language, would inherit his present commission.[3]

The three people who desired nothing from Franklin but the privilege of telling him of their admiration chose to express themselves in verse. On March 13 the Neapolitan François Astori sends four pages of flowery French alternating with some Latin verse of his composition. He recalls Voltaire's exalted view of Franklin, often expressed in conversation, which high opinion only reflects that of all humankind. How does a poor, stupid man like himself dare submit his ridiculous verse to a Franklin? Because the gods themselves deign to accept man's feeble tribute.

Writing from Roissy-sur-Seine on May 22, someone called Bocheron, who claims to be known to the jurist Malesherbes and La Luzerne (Malesherbes' nephew), sends a poem which we have not been able to locate. It will show Franklin, he writes, that love of liberty has become a source of inspiration to the French.

And finally, at an unspecified date, a man named John Hallinan addresses himself jointly to Franklin and Lafayette. In a Latin quatrain he compares them—"*Graecia Franclinum, bellatrix Roma Fayetam*"—respectively to Solon, the Athenian sage and lawgiver, and to Camillus, the patrician military hero of Rome.[4]

2. The March 8 letter is missing. For the sinking of the *Reprisal* (the ship that had carried BF to France in 1776), see XXV, 205. While nobody named Mat appears on lists of the *Reprisal*'s crew, a seaman Rosnarho was among those lost: Clark, *Wickes,* p. 376.

3. The Berail family will send a new round of applications after the peace, in 1783.

4. Hallinan offered his own expanded translation, which concludes: "In Franklin Solon's Genius breathes as yet, and Europe views Camillus in Fayette." All we know about him is what he says in his covering letter: that he had recently been introduced to BF by Lafayette, to whom he refers as "Colonel of Dragoons." The letter and poem must, therefore, have been

Monsieur à haguenau en alsace ce 6 mars 1779

J'ai pris La Liberté au mois de fevrier passé de Vous addresser une Lettre pour la faire parvenir, au General daniel Roberdeau aujourd'hui membre du congré des Etats unis de l'amerique.[5] Comme je n'ai Receû aucune Reponce, il ÿ á apparence qu'elle ne lui est pas parvenuë et qu'elle á été intercepté. Il est connû, Monsieur, combien Vous est obligeant et bienfaisant. Faite moi la faveur, je Vous En Supli, de Lui faire tenir par Mr. franklin, Votre fils, ou une autre Voie Sûre une Seconde Lettre, par duplicata, que Mr. Le Baron de Kageneck, Vous Remettra de ma part pour lui.

Je me flatte qu'en faveur de M. daniel Roberdeau, Votre ami et du meme nom que je Porte, Vous Voudré bien me Rendre ce service, que je Vous demande avec instance, et en lui Ecrivant un mot En Recommendation, de me procurer une Reponse de lui. Je ne doute pas, que nous Sommes proches parents et meme Suivant mes papiers de famille, cousins Germains, jugé, Monsieur, du desir que j'ai d'etre allié avec un homme distingué de Vôtre continent, que j'admire ainsi que toute L'Europe!

Je Vous aurois un Surcroi d'obligation Si Vous Vouliés lui ajoutter cette Lettre á une de Recommadation de Votre part et attester que je Suis ainsi que ma famille consideré et distingué En france. Ma Reconnoissance sera conforme à la faveur, que Vous ferés, dans cette occassion á celui qui á Lhonneur d'etre avec tous les Sentimens d'un parfait attachement, Monsieur, Votre tres humble et tres obeissant Serviteur

JACQUE DE ROBERDEAU
colonel de La cavallerie de S.M. tres chrètienne

Addressed: A Monsieur / Monsieur Benjamin franklin / Ministre plenipotantiare des Etats / unis de L'amerique, á la cour / de france / á Passÿ / Près et á Paris

Notation: Jacques de Roberdeau 6e mars 1779.

---

composed after March 3, 1779, the day on which Lafayette purchased the command of the *dragons du Roi,* a cavalry regiment. See Idzerda, *Lafayette Papers,* II, 228n.

5. See XXV, 672; XXVI, 258.

Passport for John Adams, John Quincy Adams, and Servant[6]

DS:[7] Yale University Library

[March 7, 1779]

Nous Benjamin Franklin Ministre Plenipotentiaire des treize Etats Unis de l'Amerique septentrionale

Prions touts ceux qui sont a prier de vouloir bien laisser surement et librement passer l'honorable John Adams sujet des dits Etats allant a Nantes avec son fils et un Domestique sans leur donner ni permettre qu'il leur soit donné aucun Empechement, mais au contraire de leur donner toute sorte d'Aide et d'Assistance, comme nous ferions en pareil Cas pour ceux qui nous seroient recommandés.[8]

En foi de quoi nous leur avons delivré le present Passeport, valable pour trois mois, signé de notre Main, contresigné par l'un de nos Secretaires et au Bas duquel est le Cachet de nos Armes.[9]

Donné a Passy en notre Hotel, ce septieme Jour du Mois de Mars, Mil sept cent soixante dix neuf

Par son Excellence B FRANKLIN

N M GELLÉE

Gratis.

Endorsed by John Adams: Passport

6. The wording of this passport follows the French government's form, which the American commissioners had adopted (and BF now followed) for all their French-language passports. For an earlier example see XXVI, 440–1.

7. In the hand of BF's secretary Gellée, who also countersigned.

8. BF drew on his banker Ferdinand Grand to provide JA 7,200 *l.t.* for traveling expenses (Waste Book, entry of March 8). The Adams party left for Nantes on the same date. Arriving there four days later, however, they discovered the *Alliance* was still at Brest and began a series of journeys which took them to Brest, back to Nantes, and eventually to Lorient before they could embark for home: Butterfield, *Adams Correspondence,* III, 195; Butterfield, *John Adams Diary,* II, 356.

9. The seal is that of the Franklin arms (II, 229–30n and facing illustration).

From the Marquis de Lafayette

ALS: S. Howard Goldman, Weston, Connecticut (1989)

Dear Sir Sunday morning [March 7, 1779][1]

Inclos'd I have the honor to send a letter which I beg leave to Reccommend to your excellency that (if possible) Mr Blodget Might obtain the leave of Coming to Paris— I am just Going to Versailles, and if you have any Commands for me they shall ever be well Come.

With the highest Regard and sincerest affection I have the honor to be Dear Sir Your most obedient humble Servant

LAFAYETTE

Had you any interesting paper I'd thank you for 'em. I beg also you would let me know When you intend to write by the Alliance

From Sartine

Copy: Library of Congress

a Versailles ce 7. mars 1779.

J'ai reçu, Monsieur, la lettre que vous m'avez fait l'honneur de m'écrire relativement aux Prisonniers des Etats Unis, detenus dans la rade de Brest.[2] Je renouvelle les ordres que j'avois dejà donné pour faire transferer ces Prisonniers qui n'ont pu l'être plustôt parcequ'il regnoit des Maladies épidemiques à Dinan,[3] mais il seront incessamment conduits au Chateau de Fougéres.[4]

J'ai l'honneur d'être avec la Consideration la plus distinguée, Monsieur, Votre très humble et très obeissant Serviteur

(signé) DE SARTINE.

Mr. Franklin.

1. The Sunday following Blodget's March 3 request to BF for leave. Lafayette met Blodget during his recent passage to France aboard the *Alliance* (for which see XXVIII, 486–9).

2. Above, March 2.

3. A castle used to hold British prisoners (a number of whom claimed to be Americans): XXVII, 517. The epidemic there had broken out the previous month: XXVIII, lxiv.

4. A château northeast of Rennes with a medieval *donjon* altered in the 17th century: Larousse.

From Samuel W. Stockton[5]

ALS: American Philosophical Society

Frankfort on the Maine in Germany March 7th. 1779.

Sir.

Some few weeks since I received information from The Honble Wm. Lee Esqr. that he had not expectation of the continuance of supplies from The Honble The Commissioners at Paris, and therefore he advised my return to America.[6]

He sets out in a few hours for Paris and is kind enough to promise to forward this to Passy.

I intend myself to depart tomorrow from hence for Holland; where I expect to wait some time until I hear of a good conveyance for America, either from Holland or France. In the mean time I take the liberty of requesting your friendly advice.— You, Sir, are already acquainted with the principle of my coming & continuing in Germany— I am now about to return to America, unless you advise otherwise, or should be so obliging as to mention to me some situation wherein I could be of any service to my country, in Europe. If not I hope you may think proper to send by me the next dispatches that you may wish to have conveyed to Congress, and that you will do me the favor to acquaint me by a line, (when more important business does not engage you) of your pleasure in this respect, which I will attend, either by going to Paris or whatever else you advise. I would wish for these dispatches on more accounts than one, which besides the pleasure of having in charge any thing acceptable to my countrymen, I might perhaps have my passage free: and which I confess myself at present unable to pay for. Will you permit me, Sir, to congratulate on the approbation which Your conduct has met with

5. William Lee's secretary: XXII, 198n; XXVI, 582–3. American commissioner-designate to the Holy Roman Empire and Prussia, but welcome at neither, Lee was residing at Frankfurt am Main: XXVIII, 211n.

6. BF had already been told of Stockton's dismissal by their mutual friend Dumas: XXVIII, 551. A draft by Lee on the commissioners recently had been honored: XXVIII, 380. Lee dismissed Stockton, however, without paying him all his salary, asking Congress to make up the arrears: Ford, *Letters of William Lee,* II, 528–9.

from Congress, by their appointment of you to be their sole minister plenipotentiary at Paris?

I have the honor to be, with the highest respect & esteem Sir your most obliged & most faithful humble Servant

SAML. W. STOCKTON.

P.S. A line for me to the care of Mr. Dumas at the Hague will be recd.

His Excellency B. Franklin Esqre &c &c.

Addressed: His Excellency / Benjamin Franklin Esqre.

Notation: Sam. W. Stockton frankfort 7. Mars 1779.

From Vergennes

L (draft):[7] Archives du Ministère des affaires étrangères; copy: Library of Congress

A Versailles le 7. Mars 1779.

J'ai l'honneur de vous prèvenir M. que le Roi ne recevra pas les Ambassadrs. et Ministres étrangers mardy prochain;[8] au moyen de quoi votre presentation ne pourra avoir lieu que le mardy 16. de ce mois/.

M. franklin

To Vergennes

Copy: Library of Congress

Sir Passy, March 8 1779

I am much oblig'd to yr. Excy. for the Notice you were so good as to send me yesterday.

I send my Grandson to M. de Sartine, to procure from him two Orders to the proper Officers at Brest. The one to receive

7. In the hand of Joseph-Mathias Gérard de Rayneval (XXVI, 376n), a *premier commis* (undersecretary) of Vergennes.

8. At his weekly reception for foreign diplomats, during which BF hoped to present his new credentials as American minister plenipotentiary; see the duc de Croÿ's account of a dinner with BF, March 1.

the Prisoners brought in long since by Capt. Jones.[9] The other to receive the Mutineers from on Board the Alliance.[1] I beg you would be pleas'd to give a Line, if you think it proper, to Mr. de Sartine, that we may obtain more readily these Orders. I have the Honor to be &c

Ct. de Vergennes.

From Lafayette

ALS: Dartmouth College Library

Dear Sir Monday at five o'clock [March 8, 1779][2]

I Am very Sorry it was not in My power to wait on Your excellency this Morning but I was oblig'd to Ride with the Queen at a partie of pleasure in the Bois de Boulogne— I saw yesterday the first and other Ministers[3] and Spoke to them about the Necessity of Giving you Monney for fulfilling the engagements taken in Bills of exchange—that they Became pretty Sensible of, and I hope they will do what they Can— I want to see your excellency on several points and shall have the honor to call on you to morrow evening or to accept any Rendés-vous in paris you will be pleas'd to give.

With all the Sentiments of affection and Regard I have the honor to be Your excellency's Most obedient humble Servant

LAFAYETTE

9. See BF's March 2 letter to Sartine and Sartine's response of the 7th.

1. We have no record of the request, which may have been handled orally. Sartine had asked on Feb. 28 what to do about the crewmen who had mutinied aboard the *Alliance* (XXVIII, 637–8); on March 4 BF told Landais, above, that he had conversed on the subject with "the Minister," presumably Sartine, although possibly Vergennes, from whom BF had earlier sought advice about the mutineers: XXVIII, 536.

2. Idzerda, *Lafayette Papers,* II, 237, ascribes March 7 as the date of this document, but March 7, 1779, was a Sunday.

3. The first minister was Jean-Frédéric Phélypeaux, comte de Maurepas.

From John Bondfield

ALS: American Philosophical Society

Sir Bordeaux 9 Mar 1779

The vessel I advised you arrived at Rochelle proved to be a Ship belonging to some Merchants at Baltimore.[4]

By Letters yesterday from Bilboa we are advised of the Arrival of two American Vessels at that Port from New England one of them a Brig from Salem took on her Passage a homeward bound Jamaica man estimated at Twenty five Thousand Pounds. The prize I understand is safe arrived at Bilboa.

The French privateers from these Parts have not been successful not any of them as yet having taken to cover the amount of their Outfits.

A French Martinico Ship took and brought into this Port a Dutch Ship from St Sabastians for Bristol we are anxious to learn the dessition of the Admiralty if the claimants dont prove the property Spanish the Cargo its expected will be Condemnd and the Ship restored as is practiced in England.[5]

I have the honor to be with due respect Sr Your very hhb Servant JOHN BONDFIELD

The Honble Benj Franklin Esq

Addressed: To the Honble. Benj Franklin Esqr / Plenipotentiary from Congress / at / Paris

Notation: Jonh Bonfield Bordeaux 9 mars 1779.

From Jonathan Williams, Jr.

ALS: American Philosophical Society, copy: Yale University Library

Dear & honoured Sir.— Nantes March 9. 1779

I received a Letter from Billy per last Post in which he tells me you desire to know the general run of the Orders I have recvd from America. Bohea Tea composes much more than

4. Bondfield had informed the commissioners on Feb. 22 of the ship's arrival: XXVIII, 590.

5. Recent French prize law, unlike British, treated enemy property on neutral ships as *not* subject to confiscation: Samuel F. Bemis, *The Diplomacy*

half, and the remainder is assorted— The articles are too numerous to give an exact accot of them, but in general they run on what is called necessarys for Familys, and under this Head is ranged what relates to dress & appearance; I have Orders for some Boxes of Glass and some Copper for Stills.[6]

Mr Lee being here, I thought it my Duty to demand of him a justification of his assertions (if they could be justified) and pointed out the means, I have not yet received any answer, when I do, I will transmit it to you with a Copy of my Letter to him, in which I inclosed a Copy of the one I wrote to You and Mr Adams.[7]

I hope you have got rid of your troublesome Companion the Gout— The Captain of the Alliance has informed that he will not be able to sail these 3 Weeks for want of hands & many necessary Repairs—

I am ever with the greatest Respect Hond Sir Your dutifull & affectionate Kinsman JONA WILLIAMS

Notation: Jona. Williams. Nantes 9 mars 1779.

---

of the American Revolution (rev. ed., Bloomington, Ind., 1957), pp. 130–9. France, however, had suspended the privileges for Dutch ships except for those of Amsterdam and Haarlem; see Dumas' letter of March 1.

6. JW's letterbooks, beginning Feb. 20, 1779, and continuing through 1785, are in the Franklin Collection of the Yale University Library; they provide a record of JW's mercantile activities during the period of this volume. Thirteen chests of tea had been ordered by Boston merchants, and throughout the following months JW managed to place most of them (through Gourlade and Moylan) on the *General Washington,* Capt. John Young, and the rest on his own *Three Friends.* Seventy-seven casks of glassware were ordered by John Holker, who also requested twenty casks of Rouen ware, printed velvets and cottons, and two cases of ladies' caps for M. Gérard. The copper was ordered by Thomas Cushing, and proved to be unobtainable; the rest of his order, twenty ells of black silk, was shipped.

7. A copy of JW's letter to Lee, dated March 8, is at the APS. Its enclosure was JW's letter to BF and JA of Jan. 31, informing the commissioners of certain critical endorsements which Lee had secretly entered on his accounts and defending himself against Lee's charges (XXVIII, 443–6). JW also requested that an impartial committee of American merchants be formed to examine his accounts; his March 8 letter asked Lee to join him in this request.

To All Captains and Commanders of American Armed Ships

Three LS:[8] Yale University Library, American Philosophical Society, Joseph Y. Jeanes, Jr., Wilmington, Delaware (1955); AL (draft) and two copies: Library of Congress

Franklin issued this passport for Captain James Cook, the famed British explorer, at the suggestion of the duc de Croÿ, who had paid the American minister a visit to discuss the matter on March 1.[9] The pass was distributed to all American vessels in the ports of France and Spain, and Franklin also sent a copy to Holland for publication.[1]

The news that Cook was already dead, murdered by Sandwich Islanders on February 14, 1779, did not reach Europe until January, 1780. At that time the Royal Society decided to issue commemorative medals in gold, silver, and bronze, bearing Cook's image. In recognition of the humanitarian gesture of this passport Franklin was nominated to receive a gold medal. The gift was a long time in coming, however. Sir Joseph Banks, president of the Royal Society, first insisted on receiving proof that Franklin had indeed issued such a document,[2] and then found reasons for delaying the award until 1784. Four years later, Franklin was called upon to defend his issuing of the passport against false accusations that he had acted contrary to the wishes of Congress.[3]

Gentlemen, [March 10, 1779]

A Ship having been fitted out from England before the Commencement of this War, to make Discoveries of new Countries, in Unknown Seas, under the Conduct of that most celebrated Navigator and Discoverer Captain Cook; an Undertaking truely laudable in itself, as the Increase of Geographical Knowledge, facilitates the Communication between distant Nations, in the Exchange of useful Products and Man-

8. We print from the one in WTF's hand. The others were written by Gellée.

9. The duc de Croÿ's account of that meeting is above, under March 1.

1. BF to Digges, Feb. 15, 1780, Library of Congress. The passport, in French translation, was published in the *Gaz. de Leyde,* no. XL, supp., May 18, 1779.

2. Banks to BF, March 29, 1780. APS.

3. See William Bell Clark, "A Franklin Postscript to Captain Cook's Voyages," APS *Proc.,* XCVIII (1954), 400–5.

ufactures, and the Extension of Arts, whereby the common Enjoyments of human Life are multiplied and augmented, and Science of other kinds encreased to the Benifit of Mankind in general. This is therefore most earnestly to recommend to every one of you; that in case the said Ship which is now expected to be soon in the European Seas on her Return, should happen to fall into your Hands, you would not consider her as an Enemy, nor suffer any Plunder to be made of the Effects contained in her, nor obstruct her immediate Return to England, by detaining her or sending her into any other Part of Europe or to America; but that you would treat the said Captain Cook and his People with all Civility and Kindness, affording them as common Friends to Mankind, all the Assistance in your Power which they may happen to stand in need of. In so doing you will not only gratify the Generosity of your own Dispositions, but there is no doubt of your obtaining the Approbation of the Congress, and your other American Owners.

I have the honour to be Gentlemen, Your most obedient humble Servant

At Passy, near Paris, this 10th Day of March 1779.

B FRANKLIN
Minister Plenipotentiary from the Congress of the United States at the Court of France

To all Captains & Commanders of arm'd Ships acting by Commission from the Congress of the United States of America, now in War with Great Britain.

Notation: Dr. Franklins Requisition To The Commanders of Ships in the Service of Congress &c.

To Vergennes

LS:[4] Archives du Ministère des affaires étrangères; copy: Library of Congress

Sir, Passy, March 10. 1779.

It is with great Reluctance that I give your Excellency any farther Trouble on the Subject of a Loan of Money: But the Bearer Mr. Grand, who is much better acquainted with the Nature and Manner of such Operations than I am, being of Opinion that the Sum we want might with your Permission & Countenance be procured in France, I beg you would be so good as to hear him upon the Subject, both of the Necessity of obtaining such a Loan and of the Means of accomplishing it.[5]

I have the honor to be with the sincerest Esteem & Respect Your Excellency's most obedient and most humble Servant.

B. FRANKLIN

His Excellency Cte: De Vergennes.

Notations: M. de R.[6] / rep le 13 mars

From Louis-Adrien Prévost d'Arlincourt[7]

ALS: American Philosophical Society

Monsieur. Paris Ce 10 Mars 1779

J'ay Recu Dernierement une Lettre De change Tirée Par M Schweighausez de Nantes Pour La Somme de 3100 *l.t.* Paiable

4. In WTF's hand.

5. See Grand's memorandum of March 2. Grand also presented a personal memoir to Vergennes arguing that the French government had a moral obligation to assist BF. It warned of the consequences if BF's bills were to be protested and expressed the hope that he could make use of the promissory notes he had had printed. Bearing the notation "1779. Mars 10," the memoir is at the AAE. Vergennes himself was involved in finding bankers to handle an American loan: XXVIII, 571n.

6. Gérard de Rayneval, entrusted with drafting the response.

7. D'Arlincourt (1743–94) was a farmer general, as was his father, Charles-Adrien Prévost d'Arlincourt (1718–94). They were guillotined within a few days of each other: *DBF.*

sur Messieurs Les Ministres Plenipotentiaires des Etats unis de L'amérique. Ne Croiant pas que je fusse Dans Le Cas De Vous Troubler Pour en requerir Le Paiement L'on m'avoit Dit de m'adresser a M Grand Banquier Rue Montmartre. J'ay Donc eu L'honneur de Lui faire présenter Ce matin La Lettre De change en Le priant de me faire Scavoir Les formalités quil y avoit á remplir a Cet Egard. Il a eu L'honneteté de me marquer quil etoit nécessaire de La faire revetir de Votre *Visa*. Je Vous Serai Donc obligé, Monsieur, de Vouloir bien me faire Connoitre Le jour et L'heure de Votre Commodité que je Pourrai me présenter chez Vous Pour Satisfaire á Cette obligation, Etant bien aise de Profiter Par moi même de Cette occasion Pour avoir L'honneur De Vous Saluer.

Je Suis avec respect Monsieur Votre tres humble et tres obeissant Serviteur

DARLINCOURT FILS
fermier Général

From Anne-Louise Boivin d'Hardancourt Brillon de Jouy

AL: American Philosophical Society

ce mércredi 11 [*i.e.* 10][8] mars [1779] a passy

Aprés avoir passé trois semaines entiéres sans dormir, je crois mon chér papa que je vais dormir trois semaines de suitte; quand on me parle, on m'endort, et je réponds en dormant: hiér au soir je fus tiré de cet état languissant, par le son d'une voiture qui vous annonçoit; le plaisir d'imaginér que j'allois passér une heure avéc vous, me ranima tout a fait; mes yeux s'ouvrirent, je sonnai, je fis faire un grand feu, pour vous réchauffér, je me sentis présque guaye, j'allois au devant de vous, quand cétte voiture repartit et emporta mon éspérance et ma joye: je dis aussitôt; j'ai fait un joli songe mais il a été

8. The date is a puzzle. When BF's "daughter" had last written, in February (XXVIII, 599–600), she was in the throes of a physical and psychological malaise, which worsened over the following months. Only once during BF's stay in France did March 11 fall on a Wednesday and that was in 1778, at a time of high good spirits on the lady's part. We can only suggest that in her state of drowsiness, she wrote March 11 instead of 10 and that the year was 1779.

bien court; ne pourriés vous pas le réallisér mon chér papa en venant prendre le thé aujourd'hui ou demain avéc moi, il y a longtems que je ne vous ai vû; si vous ne pouvés pas venir, je prendrai le parti de dormir toujours, parcequ'au moins je pourrai resvér a vous:

Addressed: A Monsieur / Monsieur Franklin / [*in another hand*] A Passy

From Landais

LS: American Philosophical Society

May it please your Excelly. Brest 10. March 1779

Your Letter of the 2d. Instant, came safe to hand, yesterday, the first article of which, respecting the tryal or dismission of our Sweedish prize, I transmitt to Monsr. Pitot, coms. agent at Morlaix,[9] where she is; leaving it to him & [*to*] act as his wisdom shall direct, he having all her papers.

Your Exy. desires to hear, how my refitt goes on? I had the honor of addressing your Excellency the 26th. & 28th. February, and 3d. March, in the two former I laid before your Exy. the scituation of this Ship, & pointed out the obstacles to my proceeding to refitt &c this I have also done to Mr. Schweighauser, agent at Nantz; but I have not had the honor of a single word in answer. I beg leave to referr your Excellency to those, espicially that of the 28th. and to inform you that the same hindrances remain, & that nothing is done, or can be done, without your Excellency's positive orders: when they come, let them be what they will, they shall be strictly complied with, to the extent of my abillities.

When I am nearly ready for Sea, the merchant Ships at Nantz shall be duly notified, the rendezvous appointed &c:[1]

9. One of several merchants of that name at the Breton port: *Almanach des marchands,* p. 336. The rival house of Cornic, veuve Mathurin & fils had complained the previous July that Schweighauser had appointed an agent to replace them (XXVII, 113–14), but this is the first appearance of the apparent replacement.

1. The ships Landais had been ordered to convoy to America; see our annotation of BF's letter of the 2nd.

but it would be impossible for me in these circumstances, before I receive your Excellency's orders, to be clear'd of my prisoners, refitted & Man'd, to say when or where.

I shall with the greatest pleasure, do every thing in my power, that will contribute to the convenience of Mr. Adams & his Son, on board, and when I can fix upon a time, that I can think we shall be ready for Sea, acquaint him. I am with the greatest respect Your Excellency's most obedient and most humble Servant. P: LANDAIS

His Exy. Doctor Franklin &c &c &c.

Addressed: To / His Excellency Doctr. Franklin / Minister plinipotentiary &c &c &c / Passy / near Paris

Endorsed: Capt Landais March 10 1779—

From Stephen Sayre[2]

ALS: American Philosophical Society

Sir Copenhagen 10th Mar: 1779

I did myself the honor of acquainting your Excellency just before my departure that I should make a short visit to Stockholm. I am well pleased at the disposition of that Court, & have good reason to believe it will soon show itself freindly to our Cause. I not only had the honor of several conferences with the first Minister, but one with the King in person.[3] There are some objects to be offer'd, which, in my opinion, would bring forward most favourable changes—those are within our power, and by no means contrary to our Interest—perhaps I am warranted in supposing, that thro' Sweeden,

2. Arthur Lee's former secretary: XX, 308n; XXIV, 53–4.

3. Sayre had written in January about his plans to visit Stockholm: XXVIII, 377–9. According to the March 2 issue of the *Gaz. de Leyde* he arrived there in mid-February. We are suspicious of his claims of a conference with King Gustavus III; the French ambassador wrote in April, 1779, that the king had not shown himself favorable to the American cause: H.A. Barton, "Sweden and the War of American Independence," *W&MQ*, 3rd ser., XXIII (1966), 419. The Feb. 22 issue of the London *Public Advertiser* reported that, at the request of the British ambassador, Gustavus III had ordered Sayre expelled.

Russia might be wrought upon to change her conduct, with her opinions—

I wish I could be explicit; but you would condemn me were I to commit the subject matter to the hazzard of the post—

I am about taking my departure for Amsterdam; from thence mean to sail for St Eustatia, & for some part of America, by the first good opportunity—for I can no longer, in prudence, wait for any thing I have ask'd. If you are, as is supposed, the sole Representative of America now in Europe: and if you think yourself authorised to employ me in any manner consistent with what you think I merit, your Letters will meet me at Amsterdam. I shall be known to the Hope's[4]—I mean where I may lodge: for I am already acquainted with them.

I have hitherto had no fears as to our union in America: but the conduct of *a certain family*, may possibly sow the fatal Seeds of division there. I could say a great deal which came within my knowledge at B——[5] but hope there will be no occasion for it.

May I beseech your Excellency to honor me with a Line communicating, as far as may be prudent, the state of our affairs. I am extremely anxious to know what consequences have attended Mr Deane's Letters &c &c—

It is with great Respect I subscribe myself your Excellencys most obed Servt STEPHEN SAYRE

Addressed: A / Son Excellence / Benj: Franklin / Embassadour Extray. &c / de America. / Verseilles

Notation: St. Sayre 10. Mar 79

4. Thomas and Adrian Hope, Dutch bankers whom BF had met in 1761: IX, 367n.

5. Berlin, where in 1777 Sayre had accompanied Arthur Lee: XXIV, 53–4. Undoubtedly the family whose conduct Sayre is questioning is the Lees.

From ——— Taverne Demont Dhiver[6]

ALS: American Philosophical Society

Mylord, Dunkirk 10th. march 1779.

I am honoured with your letter of the 28. ulto.[7] by which I observe you desire to hear from the congress, before you grant my request, as I doubt not you shall have soon that satisfaction! I shall wait your pleisure, in hope you shall comply to my demand, since I gott a Cutter and a brig of 16 four pounders, ready to gett to sea, which I intend to give to some of your nationals to cruise together,—Inclos'd I transmitt you letters from them to which they beg you'll honour them of an answer.[8]

I have the honor to be respectfully your most humble & Obedient Servant Mylord, TAVERNE DEMONT DHIVER

Notation: Taverne de Mont Dhiver Dunkeque 10 march 1779.

From Jonathan Williams, Jr.

ALS: American Philosophical Society; copy: Yale University Library

Dear & hond Sir.— Nantes March 10. 1779

I mentioned in mine per last Post that I had written to Mr Lee, who was then here, & that I declined sending you a Copy of my Letter because I intended to send you a Copy of his answer at the same time; But as he has suddenly taken his Departure without giving me any answer I now inclose my above mentioned Letter,[9] and earnestly request you to record it with the one I wrote to Mr Adams & yourself, in the same

6. A Dunkirk merchant, who planned to outfit a privateer for the American captain Stephen Marchant: XXVIII, 591. For Marchant see XXVIII, 471n.

7. Which denied BF had the authority to grant commissions to Marchant and his second-in-command, Jonathan Arnold: XXVIII, 628. William Bell Clark, in his *Ben Franklin's Privateers,* pp. 16–17, speculates that BF was using this supposed lack of authority to avoid becoming involved in the privateering scheme.

8. Missing.

9. To Arthur Lee, March 8; for this, and the letter he next mentions, see JW's letter above, March 9.

File with my Accts, that at any Future Day (in whosever hands they may Fall,) the Wound and the Balm to my Reputation may appear together: What must we say of a man who so deliberately makes such heavy Charges & shrinks from every opportunity of supporting them.— His own Conscience is my advocate.—

I intend to send all these Papers to my good Friend Carmichael to be made use of if occasion requires, and with (your Consent) I will give him leave to publish them, but this I will not do without your Consent, because I think we should be cautious in bringing our Disputes before the World.—[1]

I am sorry to hear that Mr Beaumarchais and the late Commrs could not agree.[2] I hope for the Credit of our Country you will prevent the Extremitys, which were talked of.—

I am ever with the greatest Respect your dutifull and Affectionate Kinsman JONA WILLIAMS J

some of your late memorialists who were so lavish of their *Honours* as to give the Commrs 18 of 'em in one Letter, do not now seem inclined to answer your last Letter to them. If the Zeal of the *best* of them should succeed, I dare say you will not again be *6ly Honours* from the same quarter.[3]

Dr Franklin.—

Notation: Mr. Williams March 10. 79 enclosing Letter to Mr A Lee—

1. On March 24 JW did send William Carmichael copies of eleven letters that documented the controversy surrounding his accounts and the attempt to form a committee to examine them. He insisted that Carmichael refrain from publishing them unless given specific orders to the contrary. Yale University Library.

2. For the disagreement see our annotation of BF to Vergennes, March 17.

3. BF, who did not understand this postscript, asked on March 19 for a clarification. JW explained it in his answer of March 23.

To All Captains and Commanders of Vessels of War[4]

Copy: Library of Congress

Gentlemen. [March 11, 1779]

I do hereby certify to you that I have long & intimately known the Bearer Richd. Oliver Esq; Member of Parliament & late Alderman of London & have ever found him a sincere & hearty friend to the Cause of Liberty & of America; of which he has given many substantial Proofs on various Occasions. Therefore, if by the Chance of War he should in his Voyage from England to the West Indies, happen to fall into your Hands; I recommend him warmly, with the friends that may accompany him, to your best Civilities, requesting that you would afford your generous Protection to their Persons, & favour them with their Liberty when a suitable Opportunity shall offer. In this I am sure your Conduct will be approv'd by the Congress & your Employers, and you will much oblige (if that may be any Motive) Gentn. yr. mt. o & mt h. St. BF

at Passy near Paris this 11 Day of March 1779

To all Captains & Commanders of Vessels of War, Privateers and Letters of Marque belonging to the U. S. of America.

To François Bordot[5]

Copy: Library of Congress

Sir Passy March 11 1779

I receiv'd your favours of the 27th past[6] containing an Acct. of the taking of a strong English Privateer by the Courageuse. I am much oblig'd to you for the Information & have the honor to be &c.

M. Bordot at Rochelle

4. Enclosed with BF's letter to Oliver of March 14, below. He had requested the passport on March 4, above.

5. A former admiralty clerk at St. Pierre and Miquelon now interested in an American consulship: XXVIII, 44–5.

6. XXVIII, 625.

To Stephen Hills *et al.*

Copy: Library of Congress

Gentlemen Passy, March 11 1779

I received your Letter of the 7th. of february and 2d. of March. The Application to me either for Advance of Cash or Payment of Wages to Officers in the Continental Service is quite irregular; as I am neither furnish'd with Money nor Authority for such Purposes. And I believe it is the Constant Practice with all maritime Powers to pay the Ships in their Service at home on their Return, and not in foreign Countries. I am sensible however of Some Hardship in your present Circumstances relative to the high Prices of Cloathing in America; and as I respect your Zeal for your Country, and Readiness to engage in its Defence, and hope I shall on those Accts. be excus'd in doing it, I have this Day in a Letter to the Agent at Nantes given Leave to advance to each of you and also to the warrant-Officers, a decent Suit of Clothing, suitable to your respective Stations.[7] But I must recommend it to you, and I flatter myself, that you will not take it amiss, to be as frugal as possible for your own Sakes, and not make yourselves expensively fine, from a Notion that it is for the Honor of the States you serve. It seems not necessary that young & poor states, labouring as at Present, under the Distresses of a most burthensome War in Defence of their Liberties, should vie in the Dress of their Officers, with ancient and wealthy kingdoms who are in full Prosperity. The Honor of the States will be better supported, by the prudent Conduct of their Officers, their Harmony with each other, their ready Obedience to the Commands of superior Officers, their reasonable & kind Treatment of Inferiors, and above all their Bravery in fight & Humanity to those they conquer. I am confident that you, Gentlemen, have the same Sentiments. If it should be in my Power to do anything farther for you, before you go, it will give me Pleasure. But expecting daily a great Number of Prisoners in Exchange from England who will be in Want of every thing, and our funds here being low, I doubt it can be but little. The greater Advances made to the Officers of the

7. To Schweighauser, below. The warrant officers (Pierce *et al.*) had petitioned BF on March 3.

Boston at Bordeaux by the Agent, which you mention as an Example, were without Orders from the Commissioners here, and were much disapprov'd, when we saw the Accounts. I wish that something handsome may fall into your Hands on your Return and that you may have a happy sight of your Friends & Country. I am, Gentlemen y. m. o. h. S. BF.

M M. Hills, Parkes, Adams, Degge, Buckley, Elwood & Warren Offic. on Board the Alliance

To Landais

Copy: Library of Congress

Sir Passy. March 11 1779

I received your favour of the 3 inst. The Order of M. de Sartine was sent from Versailles on Monday last[8] for taking your Mutineers off your Hands, so that I hope you are free of them before this Time & employ'd in fitting your Ship for the sea; in which you will make all the Dispatch possible & follow the Directions of the Agent as to the Place of Rendezvous in Order to take under your Convoy our Ships for America. M. Adams is gone down to Nantes to wait there till you are ready to receive him on Board. I have the Honor to be &c

Capt. Landais.

To Schweighauser

Copy: Library of Congress

Sir Passy March 11th. 1779.

I have before me your favors of the 2d & 6th. inst.[9] Inclos'd is a Copy of a Letter I receiv'd from M. de Sartine relating to the Prisoners on Board the Patience.[1] His Excy.'s positive Orders to receive them on shore went on Monday Last, directed to M. Le Comte d'Orvilliers.[2] I have just received assurances

8. March 8. BF wrote Vergennes on that date, above, to expedite Sartine's order.

9. Missing.

1. Above, March 7.

2. Louis Guillouet, comte d'Orvilliers, commanded the French fleet at Brest: XXVI, 236n.

from England that a Vessel is actually gone to Plymouth to take on Board an hundred Americans & bring them to France for Exchange.[3] If this is true & she arrives, an equal Number of these Prisoners must be given for those brought; and some Care should be taken that they be as near as may be of equal Rank. The List of Articles ordered by the Navy Board which you mention as inclos'd, is not come to Hand, being probably omitted in making up your Letter. But it is immaterial, as I cannot Judge what Art. are most wanted, not knowing the Circumstances. I can only acquaint you that if they amount to much Money, it will not be in my Power to pay for them; and if you supply them, it will be well to write pressingly to the Navy Board to make you immediate Remittances. The Purser's Demand of Slops is also omitted.[4] But I am totally a Stranger to such Matters and can give no Orders about them. The Navy Board should have been explicit: I think however that you cannot be wrong in furnishing what is absolutely necessary for the Men; and in this, you will use that Discretion which your knowledge and Experience in such Business has afforded you, and which I doubt not will by the Board be found satisfactory. The Officers of the Alliance write me too that they are in Want of Cloaths.

I cannot but suppose it will be approv'd of, that they should be furnish'd each with a Decent Suit proper for his Station, whether Commission—or warrant-Officer; which therefore I would recommend to you to supply them with as soon as may be. M. Adams is probably with you before this time: where you are in Doubt on any Point, it will be well to take his Advice. I am with great Esteem Sir &c.

P.S. Capt. Landais in a Letter to me, makes several Claims of Money which he says is due to him from the Congress.[5] I have

3. From David Hartley, March 2.

4. The list of articles ordered by the Navy Board and Blodget's Feb. 27 request for clothing for the *Alliance* did eventually come to hand. Written on reverse sides of the same sheet of paper, the document was endorsed by BF, "Blodget Purser of the Alliance Articles furnishing at Brest." University of Pa. Library.

5. XXVIII, 622–3; BF's response is above, March 4.

answered him that I cannot judge of Such Claims & that he should have settled them when in America. I see by A Copy of a Letter to him from the Navy Board that he is directed to apply to You for Money & other Necessaries he may want for his ship.[6] You will be satisfied that what Money you supply him with is necessary for his Ship & not on Acct. of these old Claims. But as he may also want some Cloathing & Pocket Money, I should suppose an Advance of 50 Louis on his own private Acct. may be thought reasonable.

M. Schweighauser.

From Joseph Priestley

ALS: American Philosophical Society

Dear Sir London 11 March 1779

The bearer of this letter is Mr Hamilton a young gentleman of Ireland, travelling for his improvement.[7] I have had a good deal of his company both in Wiltshire and in London,[8] and think him to be a person who will not disgrace any little countenance that it may be convenient to you to give him. He is a friend of liberty, and a lover of science.

I often wish to have an opportunity of conversing, or even of writing with freedom, on the subject of a scheme you once had in my favour.[9] I was very happy to hear by a common friend, that you were in good health and spirits.

I am just printing off a volume of a new work of Experiments in various branches of Natural Philosophy, which I shall take the first opportunity of conveying to you.[1] I am,

6. Eastern Navy Board to Capt. Pierre Landais, December (?), 1778 (National Archives).

7. William Hamilton (1755–97), born in Londonderry, was a naturalist who founded a learned society that was the nucleus of the Royal Irish Academy. *DNB.*

8. Priestley, serving at this time as Lord Shelburne's librarian, divided his time between the London residence and the Bowood estate in Wiltshire: XIX, 299; XX, 420n.

9. BF had once inquired about an academic post for Priestley in America; see XX, 90–1n.

1. Priestley had indeed just finished his *Experiments and Observations Relating to Various Branches of Natural Philosophy; with a Continuation of the Observa-*

with the greatest respect and affection, Dear Sir, Yours most sincerely J PRIESTLEY

Addressed: To / D Franklin

Notations in different hands: Dr Priestley / Priestley 11 march 1779

To Dumas

LS:[2] Henry E. Huntington Library; copy: Library of Congress

Dear Sir, Passy March 12th. 1779.

I lately received yours of Oct. 18. recommending Mr Huet Du Plessis, He left it at my House when I was not at home; and having been these three Weeks past much confined by the Gout, I have not been able to look for him.—[3] I have also received yours of Feb. 23. 26 & March 1. The Informations they contain are very Satisfactory. Mr Deane is not arrived as had been told you, but is expected to be in Europe about the Beginning of May. The Difference you mention between him and Mr Lee is an unpleasant one; but will I hope not be attended with very ill Consequences.[4] I shall be glad to see the Plan of the Treaty as soon as you have copied it fair.[5] I wish also that you may be permitted to point out to me the false Friends you mention that I may be upon my Guard against

---

tions on Air (London, 1779). His preface to the work is dated March 1, 1779. By May, he had hit upon a means of conveying the work to Paris; see his letter of May 8.

BF's copy of this book, taken from his library and now in the Franklin Collection at Yale University, is inscribed "from the Author."

2. In WTF's hand.

3. For Dumas' letter recommending this doctor and old family friend see XXVII, 565; see also XXVIII, 22.

4. Dumas inquired about the return of former commissioner Silas Deane in the first of the three letters: XXVIII, 595. Deane himself was expecting to return momentarily to Europe once he had finished testifying before Congress about his former service there: *Deane Papers,* III, 403–4. For Dumas' concern about the dispute between former commissioners Arthur Lee and Deane see XXVIII, 618.

5. Dumas was either copying William Lee and the Amsterdam banker Jean de Neufville's draft American-Dutch commercial treaty or preparing a

them.[6] I thank you for the Copy of the little printed Pamphlet.[7]

Your Friend brings to my hand a little Memoir of your Services. I am not insensible of them, and shall keep the Memoir under my Eye.[8] The immence Expence necessarily incurred in this War, and the Difficulty of raising Money render this an unfavourable Time to propose Additions to Salaries; especially for Services in a Country, from whence I believe they begin in America not to expect the Advantage of much Friendship. The Times may change, our Affairs become more prosperous, and our Means greater. You will then not be forgotten. But it is not good to place much Dependance on future Contingencies. It seems to me that you lay out too much in News Papers, &c which I am sorry for as it lessens your support: but I consent that you draw for an additional 25 Louis on Account of such Expences, and I wish you to limit them accordingly.

Your Friend having reduced his Proposals, 'till they came within the Limits of my Instructions, I agreed to take of him the Sum of 1,500,000 Florins and give for it the Promises of the States when he should produce a Subscription amounting to that Sum: But I own I do not rely much upon it.[9]

I am ever, Dear Sir, Your affectionate Friend & humble Servant. B FRANKLIN

M. Dumas.

---

similar treaty of his own: XXVII, 344n; XXVIII, 551, 595; Ford, *Letters of William Lee,* II, 672.

6. Dumas' warnings are in his Feb. 26 letter: XXVIII, 618–19.

7. Sent with Dumas' letter of March 1.

8. The friend was probably de Neufville, whom Dumas had introduced to BF: XXVIII, 353. Dumas describes the memoir (now missing) in his March 23 letter, below. Hitherto the commissioners had provided him with 200 *louis* (4,800 *l.t.*) per annum: XXVII, 117, 128, 142.

9. De Neufville had originally proposed to raise two million guilders for the United States: XXVIII, 629–31. "Guilder" and "florin" are interchangeable terms; the guilder traded at slightly more than 10 per £1 sterling: John J. McCusker, *Money and Exchange in Europe and America, 1660–1775: A Handbook* (Chapel Hill, 1978), pp. 43–4, 60. BF later explained that he gave de Neufville a chance to find subscribers on the same terms as those offered

To Ferdinand Grand

Copy: Library of Congress

Dear Sir

Passy. March 12. 1779

Enclos'd is the propos'd Letter to the House in Holland, which you will send if you approve of it.[1] If I have not exprest rightly the Affair of Interest, please to keep it back, and I will correct it for next Post: what is mention'd of another House relates to the final Offer made me by M. Neufville.[2] I own I have not an Expectation of much farther Assistance from Holland at Present. But when the Offer was reduced so as to come within my Limits, you see I would not refuse it without making myself liable to this Reflection from M de Vergennes, that an Offer of the Sum for which he had engaged to guarantee the Interest,[3] had been made to me, and that I might probably have had the Money, but would not accept of it.

I observe an Error of 3600 florins in the Words of your Receipt upon the Acct.[4] but the figures rectify it.

I am ever, with sincere Esteem &c

Ferd. Grand.

To Horneca, Fizeaux & Cie.

Copy: Library of Congress

Gentlemen

Passy, March 12 1779

I received the Honour of your Letter dated the 4th inst.[5] together with the Bills for 34010. Ecus 41.6. which are ac-

---

to Horneca, Fizeaux & Cie.; this attempt also failed: Wharton, *Diplomatic Correspondence,* III, 361–2.

1. To Horneca, Fizeaux & Cie., which immediately follows. The Dutch banking firm had been attempting to raise a loan for Congress; see our annotation of Grand's March 2 memorandum.

2. The rival banker had offered to take over the loan on similar terms; see the immediately preceding letter.

3. For Vergennes' explanation of his guarantee see our annotation of his March 18 letter.

4. Presumably Account XI (XXIV, 3), Grand's recently-terminated account with the commissioners.

5. Both the letter and the bills it enclosed are missing, although a March 10 entry in BF's Wastebook acknowledges receiving the money and turning it over to Ferdinand Grand: XXVIII, 271n. An écu was worth three livres.

cepted. I am glad to understand that you think some more of the Promesses may be dispos'd of as they are signed:[6] I therefore recall the Direction I gave in a former Letter[7] to return the Book, and desire you to retain it for the Present, and dispose of the whole if you can. But this must be on the Condition first propos'd and agreed to between us, that the U.S. were not to pay more than 6 per cent, all Charges and Expences included.[8] This is what I am limited to, by my Instructions & cannot go beyond it. I apprehend your Account as you have stated it to be within that Rate of Interest and as such I approve of it.[9]

I ought to apprize you, that another House in Holland has offer'd to procure us a Loan of 1,500,000 florins on similar Terms.[1] But as I did not chuse even to appear to quit the House of friends without a Certainty of obtaining thereby what they had hitherto fail'd of supplying us with, I proposd to print and send you other Books, sign'd by my Name alone if you thought there was a Prospect of its being useful; and I refused to furnish Promises for Sale to any other. I have only agreed that, if a Subscription is produced to me, by which that whole Sum is engaged for, I will then give out the Promises; but not otherwise. I have the Honor to be &c

Horneca, fizeaux et Co.

6. *I.e.,* the subscription to the Dutch loan with which the firm was charged. The first book of promissory notes and interest coupons had been sent them on Aug. 31, 1778: XXVII, 322.

7. XXVIII, 571; see also XXVIII, 493.

8. XXVII, 484. Of this, five percent apparently was the interest on the loan, and one percent, Horneca, Fizeaux & Cie's commission: XXVII, 322.

9. This sentence is interlined in red ink above the following passage: "*I consider it therefore as an Error in your Acct the Charging 8 per cent for those Expences, as it Occasions an Exceeding of 1070 florins above the 6 per cent. I have desired M. F. Grand our Banker here to explain this to you, wch. I doubt not but he will do to your Satisfaction, & that you will correct the Acct. accordingly.*" A marginal note explains that "On farther consideration of the Acct: and a new Calculation being made, it was found just.— The part underlined of this Letter was omitted & what is wrote in red put in its Place."

1. Jean de Neufville & fils; see the two preceding letters.

From Thomas Mante[2]

ALS: American Philosophical Society

Sir 12 March 1779.

I hope that you will not think me importunate in soliciting an answer to the letter that I had the honour of writing to you some few days past.[3] Though I would wish to avoid asking of you pecuniary aid yet the distress of my situation orleaps the barrier of delicacy and again compels me to address myself to your humanity. A short time I hope will enable me to return the relief you afford me, and to thank you personally for your goodness.

I have the honour to be Sir, Your most obliged humble servant THOMAS MANTE

Addressed: A Monsieur / Monsieur Franklin / Ministre plenipotentiare des Etats / unis de L'Amerique / A Challot.

Notation: Thomas Mante 12 mars 1779.

From Vergennes

L (draft):[4] Archives du Ministère des affaires étrangères

A Vlles le 12 Mars 1779.

J'ai communiqué à M. de Sartine, M. la lettre que vous m'avez fait l'honneur de mècrire au sujet de l'affaire du S. MaCniel;[5] vous verrez par la rèponse ci jointe du 2. Mars de ce Ministre[6] qu'il se propose d'en faire incessamment le raport au Conseil royal des finances/.[7]

M franklin

2. A British writer who had been imprisoned as the result of a business dispute: XXVII, 348–9.

3. Requesting BF's help: XXVIII, 592–3. Mante also wished to dedicate his latest book to him.

4. In Gérard de Rayneval's hand.

5. Above, before March 2.

6. The enclosure, signed by Sartine, explains the procedural difficulties of the case. AAE. The phrase "du 2. mars" is written in the margin in another hand and its place in the text is marked by an asterisk.

7. For this council, which met weekly, see Marcel Marion, *Dictionnaire des institutions de la France aux XVIIe et XVIIIe siècles* (Paris, 1969 [reprint of 1923 ed.]), pp. 134–5. Its members are listed in the *Almanach Royal* for 1779, p. 187.

Jean-Paul Marat

From [Jean-Paul Marat] ALS: American Philosophical Society

On December 13, 1778, Franklin noted in his journal that he had received, from an unknown philosopher, a manuscript on elementary fire written in English "with a little tincture of French idiom," but he felt he could not pass judgment on it until he had seen the experiments.[8] The unknown philosopher turned out to be Jean-Paul Marat, and a number of letters in the early spring of 1779 deal with the experiments in question.

Franklin and Marat had a surprising link: they both held degrees from the University of St. Andrews in Scotland. Franklin's honorary one went back to 1759 and Marat's, a degree in medicine, to 1775.[9] After ten years in England and Ireland (1767–77), in the course of which he had published a book attacking Helvétius and Voltaire,[1] the future revolutionary, now in his mid-thirties, was back in Paris, where he occupied the prestigious position of physician to the *gardes-du-corps* of the comte d'Artois.

A restless, ambitious man, Marat set out to challenge the views of Lavoisier and other establishment scientists on the nature of fire. In order to prove that from fire there emanates a fluid, for which he used the term *fluide igné,* and that this fluid can be made visible, he devised a series of one hundred twenty experiments to be carried out in a dark room with the help of an instrument he had perfected, the *microscope solaire.*[2]

Those experiments were witnessed by a commission appointed by the Académie des sciences, consisting of Franklin's old friend Jean-Baptiste Le Roy, Sage, Maillebois, and de Montigny.[3] They were held first in the rue de Grenelle, and, as of early March, in the

8. See XXVIII, 226.

9. For BF's degree see VIII, 277–80; for Marat's see [Auguste] Cabanès, *Marat inconnu: l'homme privé, le médecin, le savant,* (3rd ed.; Paris, n.d.), pp. 63–6. According to Sidney L. Phipson, *Jean Paul Marat: his Career in England and France before the Revolution* (London, 1924), pp. 39–47, he merely purchased the diploma for ten guineas from an impoverished university.

1. *De l'Homme,* Amsterdam, 1775–6.

2. Cabanès, *Marat inconnu,* pp. 161–74.

3. For the mineralogist Balthazar-Georges Sage see XXV, 678. Yves-Marie Desmarets, comte de Maillebois, a military man (XXIII, 287n), served several times as president of the Académie des sciences. Etienne Mignot de Montigny, Voltaire's nephew, was *trésorier de France:* Larousse. All three men are listed in the *Index biographique des membres et correspondants de l'académie des sciences de 1666 à 1939* (Paris, 1939).

rue de Bourgogne at the hotel of the marquis de l'Aubepine.[4] Franklin's presence was much desired both by Marat, who, in a series of letters signed "the author's representative,"[5] begged him to come, and by Le Roy acting as a go-between.

After several missed appointments, possibly because of his gout, Franklin eventually joined in. Sage left a vivid account of the Doctor's participation: "M. Franklin, qui était témoin de ces expériences, ayant exposé sa tête chauve au foyer du microscope solaire, nous l'aperçûmes ceinte de vapeurs ondulantes, qui se terminaient en pointes torses; elles représentaient l'espèce de flamme que les peintres ont fait l'attribut de Génie."[6]

Le Roy, in his report to the Academy, related the same episode in more sober terms: "M. Francklin qui a assisté avec nous à plusieurs de ces expériences, ayant présenté sa tête, sa main à ces rayons, on en vit s'élever sur la toile des émanations on ne peut pas plus apparentes . . ." His review sounds somewhat embarrassed, as if he were torn between his wish to be fair to the novelty and ingenuity of the experiments and his doubt as to the validity of the theory they were meant to prove.[7] Marat, however, interpreted Le Roy's statement as an endorsement and used it as an introduction to the essay he published soon after under the title, *Découvertes sur le Feu, l'Electricité et la Lumière Constatées par une Suite d'Expériences Nouvelles qui Viennent d'Etre Vérifiées par MM. les Commissaires de l'Académie des Sciences.* He presented this work to the Academy on June 19.[8] But his next foray against the scientific establishment, an attack on Newton's theories of color—for which once again in August he sought Franklin's par-

4. The marquis' wife, once Marat's patient, had become his mistress. The marquise and the marquis are in the *Dictionnaire de la noblesse,* I, 907.

5. In a letter to a friend written in 1783, Marat explained that his desire for anonymity was based on his fear that some of the *philosophes,* whom he felt he had good reason to distrust, would plagiarize his works; thus he opened his heart only to Maillebois, who, on Dec. 5, 1778, filed on his behalf a "mémoire anonime sur le feu." See Charles Vellay, "Lettres inédites de Marat à Benjamin Franklin (1779–1783)," *Revue historique de la Révolution française et de l'Empire,* XI (1912), 353–61. Beginning in August, Marat's letters to BF bore his signature.

6. Sage, *Analyse chimique et concordance des trois règnes* (3 vols., Paris, 1786), I, 117, as quoted in Cabanès, *Marat inconnu,* p. 175.

7. Académie des sciences, *procès-verbaux,* XCVIII, fols. 97–100. The report was read on April 17. Marat is referred to throughout as *L'Auteur.*

8. *Ibid.,* XCVIII, fol. 200.

ticipation—was sharply rejected and intensified his hatred of all academies.

Sir. [before March 13, 1779][9]

The honour of your company at the repeating of the lately made discoveries on the igneous fluid is earnestly requested by the author. In an age where envy obstructs the way to the truth, ingenious and candid men are much wanted to support it.

New experiments on the electrical fluid will be performed.

The place of meeting is the hotel de M. le Marquis de l'Aubepine Rüe de grenelle F S.G.[1]

The day & hour are to be fixed by the gentlemen of the Commitee.

I am with the greatest respect Sir Your most obedient humble Servant. THE AUTHOR'S REPRESENTATIVE

Endorsed: Marquis d'Aubepine Rue Grenelle F.S.G. Place of Experimts.

To John Adams

ALS: Massachusetts Historical Society

Dear Sir, Passy, March 13. 1779

I hope you got well to Nantes with your Son.[2] We sent you two Letters by yesterday's Post, that had been deliver'd here for you since your Departure; the enclos'd came last Night.[3] By Captain Landais' Letters, I am afraid he will not be ready so soon as we were made to expect.—[4] I have the honour [*torn:* to] be, Sir, Your most obedient humble Servant

B FRANKLIN

Honble Mr Adams

9. We base this date on BF's reply, March 13, below.

1. Faubourg St. Germain.

2. For the Adamses' journey see our annotation of their passport, March 7.

3. For JA's recent correspondents see *Adams Papers,* VIII, 3–12, 395. On March 17 WTF forwarded the rest of JA's mail (Mass. Hist. Soc.).

4. See Landais' letters of March 3 and 10. The captain was still at Brest, whereas the Adams party was en route to Nantes where it expected to find the *Alliance.*

To the Gentlemen at Nantes[5]

Copy: Library of Congress

Gentlemen Passy. March. 13. 1779.

Great Objections having been made by the Honble. M. A. Lee to the Accts. of M. Jonathan Williams late Agent for the Commrs. at Nantes, which are therefore yet unsettled; and, as not being conversant in mercantile Business, I cannot well judge of them, and therefore, as well as for other Reasons I did not & I cannot undertake to examine them myself, and they may be better examin'd at Nantes where the Business was transacted than either here or in America, I beg the favor of you, Gentlemen, that you would for the Sake of Justice and of the public good, take that Trouble upon you; and make Report to me thereupon; which I do hereby agree shall be conclusive & final (subject only to the Revision of Congress) in Case M. Williams shall previously sign an Engagement to abide thereby; and Hoping you will comply with my Request, I have ordered him to lay his Accts. fully before you; and I have requested the Honble. M. A Lee who makes the Objections to furnish you with the Same; that by having the whole in View, you may be able to form an equitable Judgement. I have the Honor to be with great Respect &c

MMrs. W. Blake, D. Blake, J. Johnson, P. R Fendall, J. Wharton, M. Ridley, J. Ross ——— Lloyd ——— Ogilvie & J. D. Schweighauser. Merchants now at Nantes.

5. A group of American merchants who had joined together the previous fall to solicit protection for their ships; see XXVIII, 56–7. JW had suggested, at the end of January, that the gentlemen or a small committee of them be asked to examine his accounts in light of Arthur Lee's accusations: XXVIII, 443–6.

To Arthur Lee: Two Letters

(I) AL (draft):[6] Library of Congress; copies: Library of Congress, National Archives; transcript: National Archives; (II) LS:[7] Harvard University; copy: Library of Congress; transcript: National Archives

I.

Sir Passy March 13. 1779

A severe Fit of the Gout, with too much Business at the same time necessary to be done, have prevented till now my answering yours of the 21st past.[8]

I did not imagine there would have been any Difference of Sentiment between us concerning the Propriety of returning to me the Papers which you have at various times taken from this House. Where several Persons join'd in the same Commission are to act upon Papers, it seems necessary that they should be lodg'd in one Place where all the Parties may be sure of finding them, & under the Care of one Person who should be accountable for them. And if there were not some particular Reasons to influence another Choice, I should suppose the first Person named in the Commission might with great Proprety take charge of them. I am sure that if you had been that Person I should have made no Objection to it.— Mr Adams having a Room more convenient & more private than mine, and in which he lodg'd, I approv'd of his keeping the Papers: He has voluntarily return'd me all he had, without asking; and I thought Asking was only necessary to obtain the rest from you; for the whole Business which before was transacted by us jointly, being now devolved on me, and as there must be frequent Occasion to look back on Letters receiv'd, Memorials deliver'd, Accounts given in,[9] Contracts made, &c.

6. The draft indicates BF's substantial revisions, which we have incorporated; significant cancellations and alterations are discussed in our notes. The copies are virtually identical to the emended draft. That at the National Archives (in the hand of Arthur Lee's nephew, Ludwell Lee), is noted as being a "True Copy from the Original Letter."

7. In WTF's hand.

8. XXVIII, 585–6, in which Lee refused BF's request for the commission's public documents in his possession.

9. Replaces "Accounts settled".

&c. which if I cannot have the Opportunity of doing, I must be frequently at a Loss in future Transactions, I did not imagine I should have any Difficulty in obtaining them, nor had I the least Idea that my Asking for them would occasion any Dispute.[1]

I suppose that the Papers Mr Deane mentions to have taken and secur'd, were those only that related to his separate commercial Transactions for the Publick before his Appointment with us in the political Commission. If he took away any of the Papers we were jointly concern'd in, I conceive he was wrong in doing so, and that his doing wrong would not justify the rest of us[2] in following his Example. I can have no Desire to deprive you of any Paper that may be of Use to you in answering Mr. Deane's Accusations, having no Concern in them nor Interest in Supporting them. On the contrary, if any Papers remaining in my hands can be of such Use to you, you are welcome to have authenticated Copies of them, (which shall on request be made out for you), as well as of any others "evidencing our joint Transactions" which you may desire.— On the whole it seems to me that this Matter may be reasonably settled, by your keeping if you please all those Originals of which there are Duplicates at Passy;[3] retaining for a time such of the rest as you desire to copy, which Copies being compar'd by us with the Originals may be authenticated by our joint Signatures; and returning immediately all the others; docketed & catalogu'd as you please, so as that you may know what & where they are, & call for a Copy of any of them you

1. The following paragraph originally began with the phrase, "I know nothing of Mr Deane's having taken and secur'd such of the Public Papers as he chose;".

2. BF first wrote "me", and replaced it with "the rest of us".

3. BF originally ended the sentence here and followed it with three paragraphs, each containing a proposition. He deleted the first and third, and incorporated the second into his text. The deleted paragraphs read:

"1. That you cause to be made out and sent to me a List of all the Publick Papers in your Possession, on which a Receipt shall be signed when you deliver them.

That you be furnished with a List of those remaining here, and at any time with Copies of such as you may have occasion for."

may hereafter have Occasion for, wch shall always be given you.—

If these Propositions are agreed to, the Affair may soon be settled; if not I must wait the Orders of Congress; and in the mean time do as well as I can with their Business, which I think must often suffer by my want of the Knowledge those Papers might occasionally furnish me with. I have the honour to be, with great Respect, &c.—

Hon Ar. Lee Esqr

Notation: A. Lee. March 13. 1779[4]

II.

Sir, Passy March 13. 1779.

Finding by a Note of yours on the Back of Mr Williams's Accounts, dated October 6. but which I never saw 'till lately by Accident, expressing that you are "perfectly satisfyed from his own Accounts that Mr. Williams has now, and has long had in his hands upwards of an hundred thousand Livres belonging to the Publick, which have not been employed in the Publick Use. &ca—"[5] I have resolved to have those Accounts carefully examined by impartial Persons skilled in such Business; and if you have any other Objection to them than what appears in your Note, or any other Reasons than what appears upon the Face of his Accounts, for believing such a Sum in Mr Williams's Hands I beg you will furnish me with them, that I may communicate them to the Examiners. I wish Justice to be done and that you had shewn your Note either to Mr Adams or me when you made it; the Matter would not have been so long neglected. The Money if due ought to be recover'd immediately.

4. The draft also bears a reminder by BF: "write to Mr Williams to take Care and send the Types to Niles." For Niles and the types see XXVI, 547; XXVIII, 314n.

5. BF and JA were warned of this endorsement by JW, who denied the accusation and requested his accounts be independently audited: XXVIII, 443–6.

I have the honor to be, Sir, Your most obedient & most humble Servant. B FRANKLIN

Honble: Ar. Lee Esqr.

P.S. The Persons I have requested to examine the Accounts are the American Merchants now at Nantes, with our Deputed Commercial Agent, Mr. Schweighauser.[6]

Endorsed: March 13. 1779

Notation: Dr. Franklin

To Marat

ALS: The 19th Century Shop, Baltimore, Maryland (1991)

Sir Passy, March 13, 1779

I think my self much honour'd by the Invitation, and shall endeavour to be present at the farther Exhibition of those ingenious Experiments, when I am informed of the Day and Hour appointed by the Committee.[7] I am, with great Esteem Sir, Your most obedient humble Servant B FRANKLIN

To the Representative of the Author of Experiments on the igneous Fluid

From Louis-Marie Boyenval and Other Commission Seekers, with Franklin's Notes for Replies

ALS: American Philosophical Society

It is doubtful that any of the people who applied to Franklin for commissions in the American army during the spring of 1779 ever crossed the ocean. Franklin was under orders from Congress not to send over any more French officers and France, anyway, was at war. Still, some twelve candidates tried their luck. During the first weeks of his tenure as Minister Plenipotentiary, Franklin jotted down on the applications—ever more succinctly—the negative answers his French secretary was to compose. Eventually, Franklin's notations

6. See the preceding letter.

7. See Marat's letter inviting BF, printed above, before March 13.

cease, either because the applications did not seem to warrant the effort or because the secretary knew what to do. The following résumé of the appeals follows chronological order; unless otherwise noted, they are in French and at the American Philosophical Society.[8]

Writing from Bern on March 20, Samuel Marcel is so upset by his reversals of fortune that he feels justified in seeking death. Let it be death in fighting for a glorious cause. He can serve America in three capacities: in the army, in trade, in agriculture. In the first case, he feels entitled to the rank of officer since, for two years, he administered, in a secretarial capacity, a company in a Swiss regiment serving in Holland; in the second, his lifelong involvement in commerce and the mishaps he has just experienced give him a solid base for the future; as to agriculture, he has run a rather large estate for a few years. Personally, he would prefer the military. Adding that he is known to the banker Grand, he begs Franklin to send his answer to Rougemont & Comp. at Amsterdam where he is prepared to accept a commercial position, should his offer to fight for America be turned down. It was.

Franklin made the following notes on the last page of Marcel's letter: "That I am oblig'd to the Gentn. for his Good Will to America, & Desire of being serviceable to her. That our Armies are full, &c. That with a Capital he might follow Commerce with Success in America when Peace shall be made, at present it is much interrupted. That with a small Stock he might follow Agriculture there to Advantage, but his Voyage thither must be at his own Expence, and I am not authoris'd to promise any kind of Establishment, Office or Employment to Newcomers. They will find there a good Climate, good Soil, good Laws, good Government, and good People to live with, and Liberty both civil & religious: but we do not entice Strangers to come among us by particular Promises—"[9]

A Burgundian gentleman, formerly captain in the Soissonais regiment, Lanneau de Marcy, writes on March 22 enclosing a memoir in favor of his twenty-four-year-old son who wants desperately to obtain an officer's post in an infantry regiment fighting in America. The young man has served six years in Flanders with the gen-

8. The appeals of two candidates warrant their exchanges being printed in full: those of John Beckwith, a British general, and M. de Vatteville, personally recommended by Vergennes.

9. The answers were most likely sent in French. Copies in French of this one, dated April 1, and all others discussed below are in a letterbook at the Library of Congress.

darmes, then had to leave because of his health, but is quite fit at present. He wants to advance his career, which in France is impossible. Franklin jotted down the elements of a reply: "That I am oblig'd to the young Gentleman for his Good Will to America & his Desire of serving it, but cannot give him any Encouragement to go thither in Expectation of Employment, our Armies being full—"[1]

Neÿdecker, a captain in the Royal Deux-Ponts, a German regiment in the service of France, declares on March 28 that he has twenty-eight years of service behind him. He left his post in August, 1777, for family reasons but is now burning to rejoin active duty, provided, of course, he is granted a higher rank in America. He is well known to the maréchal de Broglie, and to the marquis de Castries. He asks Franklin to direct his answer to Mr. de Pachelbel, the French envoy to the duchy of Deux-Ponts. Franklin's notes for an answer: "Thanks for his Offers of Service &c—Armies full &c—cannot give him any Encouragement."[2]

An artillery officer named Lavalette says he experienced nothing but opposition from his parents when he talked about fighting in America. Now that they have finally relented, he wastes no time in informing Franklin, on April 17, that he served eight years as lieutenant of artillery in the regiment of Grenoble[3] and wishes for an equivalent position; if encouraged, he will send the relevant certificates. Far from encouraging him, Franklin jotted down in French, with his usual disregard for genders, the beginning of a reply: "Remerciemens Les Armées de l'Amérique sont pleins &ca &ca."[4]

On April 30, retired Captain Christian von Francken writes in German from Hildesheim to report that after twenty-four years of service to the Electorate of Hanover, he learned that a favorite of the English ministry had been chosen over him for the rank of major. So he quit that service and begs Franklin to grant him a company in the artillery or infantry of North America. If accepted, he could train a number of men in Lower Saxony and bring them along. He encloses five certificates from prominent people.

It is from Wesel, in Prussia, that Baron L. F. van Wynbergen sends his request on May 21. Born in the Netherlands he has, in

1. The outgoing answer was dated April 1.

2. The reply to Neÿdecker, dated April 12, is short and polite. Georg Wilhelm von Pachelbel is in the *Repertorium der diplomatischen Vertreter,* III, 306.

3. His regiment was stationed in Strasbourg: *Etat militaire* for 1779, where he is listed on p. 246.

4. We have found no trace of the actual letter.

family tradition, devoted himself to the military and risen to the rank of captain in the Orange Nassau regiment. A year ago, believing that the War of the Bavarian Succession would enhance his fortune, he enrolled under the Prussian flag but at present, with peace about to be concluded, discovers that this was a mistake. His heart, now republican, tells him that he should fight for the liberation of the United States of America. Only Franklin can help him achieve his goal. Please answer soon and he will rush to Paris.

On May 24, the comte de Beaufort announces, from Liège, that he is anxious to lead to America a corps of good Walloon troops, battle-hardened from having served in foreign countries such as France, Holland, Austria, and Spain. He also owns two foundries "*à l'angloise*" that turn out cannon balls ranging from one to twenty-four pounds. He is under pressure to enter the service of a foreign power but would rather contribute to the cause of liberty. A prompt answer is requested.

Lieutenant-Colonel de Petterelly, writing in German from Bregenz on June 1, pleads the cause of his twenty-four-year-old son who has distinguished himself in the imperial service but now feels "a noble desire to serve the American United States." The young man's superiors in the Harrach regiment are well satisfied with his performance.

The following day, a Frenchman sends in his application from Olmütz, in Bohemia. Captain Hyppolite de Verité has been serving the Empress of Hungary, in the capacity of engineer, for twenty-six years. The book that mentions him has certainly reached Franklin's hands; at any rate M. de la Condamine owns it.[5] He hopes not to be confused with the mass of Austrian officers who have no choice but to go abroad. He, on the contrary, is only following his inclination in this move and plans to bring along his wife and two children as guarantee of his commitment.

Monseigneur, Montreuil ce 13 mars 1779.

Animé par le Desir le plus Vif De consacrer mes jours au Service Des etats unis, Jay L'honneur De vous presenter le memoire cy joint. Je prie Votre excellence de vouloir bien jetter Les yeux Dessus, et D'accepter mes offres De service.

Daignez agréer le profond respect avec lequel j'ay L'hon-

5. *Dimensio graduum meridiani Viennensis et Hungarici* (Vienna, 1770), by the Jesuit Joseph Liesganig. The physician La Sablière de La Condamine would briefly correspond with BF in 1784.

neur d'etre, Monseigneur, De Votre excellence, Le tres humble et tres obeissant serviteur. BOYENVAL.

A Son excellence Monseigneur Franklin ministre plenipotentiaire Des etats unis de L'amerique près La cour De france.
presenté de montreuil sur mer le 13 mars 1779.

Monseigneur,

Louis marie Boyenval agé de vingt ans fils du sieur Boyenval Directeur Des aydes De montreuil sur mer, expose tres humblement a Votre excellence, qu'etant Dans L'age de prendre un parti, et se decidant pour celui Des armes, il Desireroit ardemment passer au service Des etats unis, et S'y attacher comme Sujet pour Le reste de ses jours. Il vous supplie de considerer quil est Determiné dans ce choix par L'honneur de concourir autant quil sera en lui au soutien de la Liberté de L'amerique, et de la justice de sa cause. Si vous daigniez acquiescer a sa Demande, il vous devra tout le bonheur dont il jouira. Une ame comme la votre, Monseigneur, sent combien il est doux de marquer tous les jours de sa vie par des bienfaits. Comme vous pourriez desirer quelques eclaircissemens sur ses moeurs et sa conduitte, il a L'honneur D'envoyer a Votre excellence Des certificats De Mrs. Les commandants Des villes et citadelle de montreuil, de Mr. Le lieutenant, juge De police, et de Mr. Le lieutenant général. Si vous L'honorez D'une commission pour le service des etats unis, il vous offrira l'hommage et le tribut le plus flatteur pour un coeur généreux, c'est la plus vive reconnoissance. Il tachera de prouver par son courage et son zele quil sent tout le prix de ce que vous aurez fait pour lui, et quil veut faire ses efforts pour meriter vos bontés. L'exposant vous supplie tres humblement De Vouloir bien lui faire connoitre vos intentions, et d'etre assuré, Monseigneur, quil ne cessera D'adresser ses voeux au ciel pour la conservation des jours precieux de Votre excellence.

BOYENVAL

Endorsed: Thank him kindly for the offer of his Services, but cannot accept them, being particularly instructed by Congress not to give the least encouragement to any Persons whatever desirous of serving in America as Officers. The Army there being full. And abundance of Foreigners in the Country who cannot find Employment.—[6]

Notations in different hands: March 13, 1779—Boyenval offering services ansd / Boyenval Montreuil sur Mer. Mar. 13, 1779

From Arthur Lee

AL: American Philosophical Society

Chaillot March 13th. 1779.

Mr. A. Lee has the honor of presenting his Compliments to Dr. Franklin— He receivd this Evening the two Letters dated this day, which Dr. Franklin has donc him the honor of writing to him. Being employd in moving to new Lodgings,[7] it will be some days before he can answer them.

Notation: Mr. A Lee. Chaillot 18 mars 1779.

From H. Sykes

ALS: American Philosophical Society

Sir Place du Palais Royal le 13 Mars 1779.

As you Seem'd desirous to know the Particulars Relatif to a Small Globe about Which I had the Honour of Writing to you Some time Ago,[8] I now take the Liberty of inclosing a Letter from Mr. Haywood Which will Explain the Whole Matter to you.[9]

I am Sir, with much Esteem Your Most Obedient and Most humble Servant H SYKES

P.S. I have in my Warehouse, Whatever is most curious in Opticks, and Mathematicks, made By Dollond, and Ramsden, of London—[1]

6. The actual reply was dated March 16.

7. In the Saint Germain district of Paris: Louis W. Potts, *Arthur Lee: a Virtuous Revolutionary* (Baton Rouge and London, 1981), p. 223. Potts speculates the move may have been connected with a romance.

8. Jan. 26, 1779: XXVIII, 430–1.

9. That letter, which BF returned on March 18 (below), is missing.

1. Peter Dollond and his brother-in-law Jesse Ramsden were preeminent London opticians. Dollond was carrying on the distinguished work of his

Addressed: A Monsieur / Monsieur Franklin, / Deputé des Etats Unies de / L'Amerique / á Passy

Notation: h Sykes Paris 13 mars 1779.

From Vergennes

L (draft):[2] Archives du Ministère des affaires étrangères

A Vlles. le 13. Mars 1779.

J'ai reçu, M, la lettre que vous m'avez fait l'honneur de m'ecrire le 10. de ce mois, et qui m'a été remise par M. Grand. Je ne puis combiner la commission dont vous l'avez chargé avec loperation dont s'occupe M. de Chaumont et je vous prie de vouloir bien m'expliquer confidemment cette enigme:[3]

J'avois lieu de croire que ce dernier etoit au moment deffectuer votre emprunt./

M. franklin

To John Paul Jones

Copy: Library of Congress

Dear Sir Passy March 14 1779

I yesterday recd. your favor of the 6th inst. I did not understand from M. Alexander that Lord Selkirk had any particular

father, the inventor of a refracting telescope with which BF was familiar: XI, 22. Ramsden, in addition to his optical work, was a brilliant inventor and instrument-maker. His work won him membership in the Royal Society and, in 1795, a Copley Medal. *DNB;* Charles Joseph Singer *et al., A History of Technology* (5 vols., Oxford, 1955–58), IV, 387–404, 603–4, plate 1; Maurice Daumas, *Les Instruments scientifiques aux XVIIe et XVIIIe siècles* (Paris, 1953), pp. 206, 315–20.

2. In the hand of Gérard de Rayneval.

3. At this point in the draft the following words were marked for deletion: "au surplus, M, vous vous rapellez certainement ce que j'ay eu l'honneur de vous dire concernant l'emprunt dont vous êtes occupé." Chaumont had been acting as an intermediary between BF and Vergennes in the search for bankers to handle an American loan; see BF's March 17 letter to Vergennes. For Chaumont's interest in American finances see also XXVIII, 316–20.

Objection to receiving the Plate from you. It was general, that tho' he might not refuse it if offer'd him by a public Body, as the Congress, he cou'd not accept it from any private Person whatever. I know nothing of M. Alexander's having any Enmity to you, nor can I imagine any Reason for it. But on the whole it seems to me not worth your while to give yourself any farther Trouble about Lord Selkirk. You have now the Disposal of what belongs to the Congress; and may give it with your own Share if you think fit, in little Encouragements to your Men on particular Occasions.

I thank you for your kind Congratulations on my particular Appointment. It will give me more Satisfaction if it enables me to be more useful.

We cou'd not obtain a Passport for Dr. Bancroft. We were told it was needless, as the Cartel ship was actually sail'd for Plymouth to take in the first 100 Americans to be brought to Nantes or l'Orient. Inclos'd is a Copy of a Letter from the Board to M. Hartley.[4] I wish they may be arriv'd, and that you may obtain such of them as you think proper. Possibly the Alliance which wants Hands, may endeavour to engage some. M. Adams goes over in her; and I must not interfere, but leave you to scramble for the Men. I think, however that if the Cartel comes to L'Orient you will have the best Chance.

I have look'd over the Copy of my Letter to you of Feby. 24,[5] not being able to imagine what Part of it could give you the Idea that I hinted at an Affair I never knew. Not finding any thing in the Letter, I suppose it must have been the Postscript of which I have no Copy; and which I know now that you could not understand.—tho' I did not when I wrote it. The Story I alluded to is this: L'Abbé Rochon[6] had just been telling me & Madame Chaumont that the old Gardiner & his Wife had complained to the Curate, of your having attack'd her in the Garden about 7 O'Clock the Evening before your

4. Possibly their Feb. 5 letter. See our annotation of Richard B. Lloyd's letter of March 2.

5. XXVIII, 599.

6. Alexis-Marie Rochon, an astronomer who had taken minor clerical orders: XXVI, 472n; Larousse.

Departure; and attempted to ravish her, relating all the Circumstances, some of which are not fit for me to write. The serious Part of it was that three of her Sons were determin'd to kill you, if you had not gone off; The Rest occasioned some Laughing: for the old Woman being one of the grossest, coarsest, dirtiest & ugliest that one may find in a thousand, Madame Chaumont said it gave a high Idea of the Strength of Appetite & Courage of the Americans.— A Day or two after, I learnt that it was the femme de Chambre of Mademoiselle Chaumont who had disguis'd herself in a Suit I think of your Cloaths, to divert herself under that Masquerade, as is customary the last evening of Carnival: and that meeting the old Woman in the Garden, She took it into her Head to try her Chastity, which it seems was found Proof.

As to the unhappy Affair of which you give me an Acct., There is no Doubt but the Facts being as you state 'em, the Person must have been acquitted if he had been tried, it being merely *se defendendo.*

I wish you all the imaginable Success in your present Undertaking; being ever with sincere Esteem &c.

Honble Capt. Jones.

To Stephen Marchant[7]

Copy: Library of Congress

Sir

Passy. March. 14. 1779

I recd. yours of the 27th of february requesting a Commission.[8] I had before written to M. Demont d'hyver,[9] that it was not in my Power to grant his Request untill I had recd. fresh Orders from Congress.

But as it is easy for that Gentleman now in Time of War to obtain a Commission for you from the Admiralty of France, I

7. A prospective privateer captain; see Taverne Demont Dhiver's letter of March 10.

8. XXVIII, 627.

9. On Feb. 28: XXVIII, 628.

wish you would explain to me why you desire rather an American one.[1] I am Sir, your humble servt. BF.

Capt. Steph. Marchant

To Richard Oliver

Copy: Library of Congress

Dear Sir Passy March 14 1779

It will always be a Pleasure to me to do what may be agreeable to you. Inclos'd is the Passport you desire.[2] I wish you & your Friends a prosperous Voyage; being ever with the sincerest Esteem Dear Sir &c

Richd. Oliver Esq;

To Vergennes

LS: Walter R. Benjamin Autographs, Inc., Hunter, New York (1982); copy: Library of Congress

Sir, Passy, March 14. 1779.

The Gout having again attacked me, and confined me to my Chair, I find I shall not be able to present myself at Versailles on Tuesday.[3] Your Excellency will have the Goodness to excuse me, and believe me ever, with the sincerest Esteem and Respect. Your most obedient & most humble Servant.

B FRANKLIN

His Exy. Count De Vergennes.

1. Such a commission could provide better protection for the crew if captured; Marchant eventually manned his privateer with a number of Irish smugglers, who could more easily pass as Americans than as Frenchmen: William B. Clark, *Ben Franklin's Privateers,* pp. 24, 28–9, 93–4.

2. Dated March 11, above. This letter and its enclosure were forwarded to London by Samuel Petrie (XXIV, 543n), who assured BF in an undated note that he had sent off the letter the day after receiving it. APS. (We conjecture below that Petrie's note was written on April 21; see the annotation of Margaret Stevenson's letter printed under March 16.)

3. March 16; see Vergennes' letter of the 7th arranging for BF to present his credentials as minister plenipotentiary.

From Abraham-Hyacinthe Anquetil-Duperron[4]

ALS: American Philosophical Society

Monsieur à Paris Le 14. mars. 1779.

Le Ministre du premier Etat libre de l'Amérique est un phénoméne fait pour paroître chez des françois. L'Ouvrage que j'ai l'honneur de présenter à vôtre Excellence, lui prouvera que nous étions dignes de l'honneur que nous ont fait les *Etats Unis de l'Amerique,* en s'adressant d'abord à la france. Nous avons des foiblesses; c'est le tribut de l'humanité: Mais la franchise, l'honneur, le courage qui forment notre carattere nationnal, sont des garants sur les quels l'Amerique peut compter. Dans mon particulier, Monsieur, je croirai avoir fait un Ouvrage utile, si le ton de la *Législation* Orientale, en vous décidant sur mon caractere, confirme dans vôtre esprit l'idée que vous vous êtes formée de celui de la nation. Daignez agréer cette foible marque du respect avec lequel j'ai l'honneur d'etre, Monsieur de vôtre Excellence le très humble et très obeissant Serviteur ANQUETIL DUPERRON

P.S. Comme j'entends assez bien mes interêts, j'ai voulu, Monsieur, que la main qui vous présenteroit mon ouvrage, pût au moins y donner quelque relief.[5] Je suis persuadé que vous m'aurez obligation du choix.

Notation: Anquetil du Perron

4. Anquetil-Duperron (1731–1805) was an orientalist and member of the Académie des belles-lettres. His *Législation orientale, ou le Despotisme considéré dans les trois états: la Turquie, la Perse et l'Indoustan* was published in Amsterdam in 1778: Quérard, *France littéraire.* BF had brought his work on the *Zend-Avesta* (Paris, 1771) to the attention of Ezra Stiles in January, 1772; see XIX, 30–1 and I. Bernard Cohen, "Anquetil-Duperron, Benjamin Franklin, and Ezra Stiles," *Isis,* XXXIII (1941), 17–23.

5. His friend was Jean Dusaulx; see the following document.

From Jean Dusaulx[6]

AL: American Philosophical Society

[*c.* March 14, 1779][7]

Dusaulx est venu pour avoir l'honneur de rendre ses devoirs à Monsieur Franklin, et pour lui présenter de la part de M. Anquetil Duperron son confrère, un Livre intitulé, *De La Législation Orientale &c.*

M. Anquetil Duperron, de l'Academie des Belles-Lettres, demeure Chausée d'Antin à peu près vis-à-vis l'Hôtel de Madame de Montesson.

Addressed: pour Monsieur / Franklin.

From Patience Wright

ALS: American Philosophical Society

Lysle Hous no 4 facing Leslefield
March 14th 1779

Dear Sir/

I have moved from Pall mall with the full Purpose of mind to settel my afair and get Ready for my Return to america—[8]

I shall take France in my way and call at Parris where I hope to have the Pleasur of seeing my old american Friend—: and take off some of your cappatall Bustos in Wax— England will very Soon be no longer a pattron for artists—the Ingeneous must flye to the Land of Peace & Liberty—as I Intend to make good Use of my time While I Stay at Parris I shall be hapy to meet with the Same Encouregment as I have meet with in England, (at my first Coming before the unfortunat war).

I shall be glad before I set out to have your opinion I beg

6. Dusaulx (1728–99) was a man of letters, translator of Juvenal, protégé of King Stanislas, and a popular figure who counted Rousseau, d'Alembert, and Le Roy among his many friends: Larousse.

7. Dated on the basis of the preceding document.

8. BF's old friend (XIX, 93n) had moved her home and waxwork studio from the fashionable Pall Mall near St. James's Palace to Leicester Square and then to Charing Cross. Her outspoken advocacy of American independence had angered the government leaders who formerly had flocked to her. Charles Coleman Sellers, *Patience Wright: American Artist and Spy in George III's London* (Middletown, 1976), pp. 53, 135, 138.

the favor of you to Recomend my Perfformens and as you Know my abillites in taking Likeness in Wax Work I am hapy to have the Pleasing Prospect of doing your Recomendation Honour by my Best performance. It is with the Right gratitod to my Friends and Perticurly to yoù I owe the grat Encoureg-ment my Jenei[9] meet in London, and now come to France Improved and in high Spirits with the most faithful and afec-tanat Servt to Comand I am Honered Sir yor old Friend

P: WRIGHT

"I long to See you and love you more then Ever if I dont write to you it is not for want of good will but for fear of being troubelson"[1]—would to God you would sind for me.— My Servises are worthy of the Planeypotenterey of amerrica

For My Gardien Spirit the great Philosphe and american Agent.

Addressed: For / Benja: Franklin / att Passey / ner Parris

Notation: D. Wrigt Mars 1779.

To Pierre-Augustin Caron de Beaumarchais

Copy: Library of Congress

Sir Passy March 15 1779

I know of no new Order being given relating to the Action against M. Peltier.[2] I never heard of any being commenced against you. I am at present confined by the Gout: but should be glad to see you when convenient to you, that I may better understand the Affairs between us. I have the Honor to be with much Esteem &c—

M. Beaumarchais

9. She had lately been credited "not with genius but with genii, and she herself was wearing the tag with satisfaction." *Ibid.*, p. 135.

1. Sellers speculates that the quotation marks were used to emphasize her distress at having had no reply to so many appeals: *ibid.,* p. 136.

2. Jean Peltier-Dudoyer was involved as Beaumarchais' agent in the dis-pute over the ownership of the cargo of the *Thérèse,* a ship which had been chartered by Beaumarchais' business firm, Roderigue Hortalez & Cie.: XXVIII, 523n.

From L. Bauchot

ALS: American Philosophical Society

Monsaigneur à Nantes ce 15 Mars 1779

L'ors que j'us Le Bonheur de vous presanté Les deux ameriquin que j'avais aidér à déserté de douvre a Calais, dans une petite enbarcation, La bonté avec Lequel vous nous Resute, me prouvat Combien votre, ame, Généreusse: Etai Suseptible de Soulagér Les Malheur. J'avais Subit Le meme Sort que Mr. Marchante que vous envoiate à donquerq pour Commendeé une fregade Et en Reconnoissance des petis Service que je Luy avait Rendûs il mavait promis Le poste de Segond Capitainne avec Luy—[3] je n'est Reçus aucunne nouvelle depüis. Et Comme vous faite Beaucoup darmement à Nantes, pour vos Colonnïes, puije me flatée, Monsaigneur, dune Lêtre de Recommendation pour Mer: peltie dudoyée, ou D'acostas frers:[4] Mes armasteurs j'atant tous de votre bienveillance, trop heureux de trouvér L'occasion De vous Marquér mon Zele:

Et Le profonde Respecte: avec Lequel J'ai L'honneur D'être Monsaigneur Votres humble Et tres obeisant Serviteur

L: Bauchot

Addressed: A Monseigneur / Monseigneur De Franclin / Ministre Plenipotentier Des Colonie / hunie De La Merique / A Paris

Endorsed: Bauchot

Notation: Bauchot 15 Mar 1779

From Dumas

ALS: American Philosophical Society; AL (draft): Algemeen Rijksarchief

Monsieur La Haie 15e. Mars *1779*

Les Etats d'Hollande se séparerent Samedi, sans avoir rien résolu du tout. Ils se rassembleront demain en huit.

3. Marchant was presently attempting to procure an American commission; see BF's March 14 letter to him.

4. He sought a letter of recommendation to either Jean Peltier-Dudoyer or D'Acosta frères, a Nantais merchant firm (XXVII, 343n).

J'ai eu le plaisir de voir arriver successivement Mr. Sturler de l'Altemberg & Mr. De Neufville.[5] L'un & l'autre m'ont appris les arrangemens pris avec ce dernier, tant de votre part, Monsieur, que de la part d'autres personnes respectables. J'ai, de mon côté, pris les miens avec Mr. De Neufville, pour tirer à l'avenir par lui, de 6 en 6 mois, les appointemens que je tirois ci-devant par Mrs. Grand; & dans l'espérance que vous l'approuverez, Monsieur, je tirerai à son ordre, à la fin de ce mois, une Lettre à Usance, de 100 Louis-d'or, pour la premiere moitié de cette année, qui sera échue en Juin prochain.[6]

Mr De Neufville vint ici d'Amst. Samedi matin. Il m'a dit qu'il étoit venu pour voir 3 personnes: Notre Ami, G—— F——, & votre serviteur. Il ne fut qu'un quart-d'heure avec chacun de ces deux, & me pria de lui tenir compagnie tout le reste de la journée. Nous fumes à la Comédie; ce que je n'avois pas fait depuis plusieurs années. Le Prince & la Princesse[7] y étoient, qui nous fixerent beaucoup. Je suis sensible, comme je le dois, à toutes les choses obligeantes que ces deux Messieurs m'ont dites de votre part. J'espere que la goute a cessé. Je ne suis pas trop bien non plus depuis plusieurs semaines: mais je me ménage présentement pour le temps où je desire de pouvoir enfin vous aller rendre mes devoirs en personne. J'ai mis en ordre le projet du futur Traité, que notre Ami m'avoit remis; & je le garde, pour avoir l'honneur de vous le présenter moi-même, quand vous me le permettrez.[8]

Ces deux Messieurs m'ont assuré que j'aurai bientôt de la besogne, dont personnne ne devra avoir connoissance, & que vous me donnerez vos instructions sur la maniere dont je devrai me conduire avec diverses personnes. Tant mieux car je suis souvent très-embarrassé; & les pas glissants, au lieu de diminuer, se multiplient.

5. Johann Friedrich Stürler vom Altenberg (XXVIII, 353–4n), who had accompanied de Neufville on his journey to Passy: XXVIII, 570n.

6. For the 200 *louis* per annum to which Dumas refers see our annotation of BF's March 12 letter.

7. Of Orange.

8. For the future treaty see BF's March 12 letter. This is our first indication Dumas was planning a trip to Passy.

Je suis avec un très-grand respect, Monsieur, Votre très-humble & très-obéissant serviteur DUMAS

Passy à Son Exc. Mr. Franklin

Ma derniere, du 3 au 9 Mars, étoit sous couvert de Mr. Grand.[9]

Addressed: à Son Excellence / Monsieur Franklin, Esqr. / Min. Plenip. des Etats-unis / de l'Amerique / à *Passy*./.

Notation: Dumas la haie, March. 15. 79

From the Comte Sutton de Clonard[1]

AL: American Philosophical Society

15 March 1779./.

M. de Clonard has the honour of presenting his best Compliments, & prays him to Send him per Bearer the two Passports, he left with him yesterday, & the needfull papers he was so kind as to Say he would add to 'em, & for which he returns his thanks.

He also prays that when a Cartel Ship will come for the Exchange of prisoners, He may think of ordering that *Thomas Wilkinson* formerly Pilot of the Drake Arm'd Ship, & now prisoner on his parole at St. Pol de Leon in Brittany may be comprehended in the first Exchange—[2]

Addressed: A Monsieur / Monsr. Franklin Ministre / Plenipotentiaire des Etats unis / de l'Amerique—/ à Passy./.

Endorsed: M. le Comte de Clonard[3] Thos Wilkinson to be one of the first Prisoners exchang'd—

Notations in different hands: Le Comte de 15. March 1779. / Clonard le Comte de 15. March 1779.

9. The Amsterdam banker Isaac-Jean-Georges-Jonas Grand (Georges Grand), brother of BF's banker Ferdinand Grand.

1. Jean, comte Sutton de Clonard, was formerly a colonel of the Walsh regiment in France's Irish Brigade: Richard Hayes, ed., *Biographical Dictionary of Irishmen in France* (Dublin, 1949), p. 292. In 1778 he had written on behalf of another prisoner: XXVI, 576–7n.

2. Wilkinson had been granted a parole for reasons of health: XXVII, 254.

3. "M. le Comte" has been deleted by a later hand.

William Lee's Account of a Conversation with Franklin

AD: Virginia Historical Society

Paris 15 March 1779.

Waited this day on the Honble. Doctor Benjamen Franklin Minister Plenipo. from the U. S. of America at the Court of Versailles, congratulated him on his apt.—gave him an account of the Political state of Germany & Hold.—[4] of the danger there was of G. B. geting a considerable number of Troops in Germany as soon as the peace between the Emp. & K. of P. shd. take place, as there wd. be 20,000 disbanded & there were a number of B. Agents now dispers'd over Germany waiting to ingage them.[5] That I wish'd him to aid me in an application to the F. Ministry, to get their influence & assistance, in the most effectual measures for preventing so heavy a blow on us. The Doctor replyed that he knew so little about the situation of affairs in the North, he cou'd not meddle in.

I then told him that I had strong reasons for beleiving as soon as the German peace was settled, the Courts of Vienna & Berlin or at least one of them wou'd acknowlege our independence provided the Court of Versailles wd. assist us in Negotiating this business,[6] which I tho't it probable the F. Ministry wd. do, if he wd. go with me to Count Vergennes that we might jointly urge this measure. The Doctr. replyed that it was a matter to be consider'd whether it was worth our while to ask any of the Courts of Europe to acknowlege our Independence. This I confess astonish'd me greatly, however I calmly replyed that I tho't it of infinite importance for many reasons, but particularly it appear'd to me the most probable

4. Holland. Lee, now residing at Frankfurt am Main, had recently arrived in Paris for a visit; see Stockton's letter of March 7.

5. The Holy Roman Emperor, Joseph II (who was also co-ruler of Austria with his mother the archduchess and widowed former empress Maria Theresa), and King Frederick II of Prussia were preparing to negotiate an end to their hostilities, which had been prompted by Austria's acquisition of a sizeable portion of Bavaria a year earlier; see the Amsterdam intelligence report of March 1.

6. A colossal delusion on Lee's part; neither power recognized the United States during the war.

way to bring G. B. to her senses & to make the K. & his Ministers, enter into a Peace, with us, for my first object & wish always had been & still was, to obtain Peace on honourable & independent terms. The Doctor said that I might apply myself to Count V. abt. it, but he was so ill that he cou'd not go to Versailles. I ask him then, if he wd. write a short letter by me to Count V. excuseing his not going with me in Person on acct. of his health, but that he had confer'd with me on the subject of my visit, which he much wish'd to be adopted. I farther urged that it was in some measure necessary, as it was the form in all the Courts of Europe, for the Public Minister of any Country residing at a foreign Court, to wait on the Ministers of that Court, to introduce any subject of his Nation especially if that Subject was in a public Capacity. That this mode of proceeding seem'd to me more necessary at this particular time as Congress had recommended confidence & harmony to all the representatives to the different Courts[7] & to show the Ministers here, that the public business wd. not be affected by the late extraordinary proceedings of Mr. Deane in America.[8] All that I cou'd urge had no effect, & the Doctor plainly refused either to go with me, or to write by me.

I observ'd to him, that as he had refused to accept or pay the dft I had some time ago drawn on the Comrs. in France for my expences agreeable to the order of Congress, it seem'd neacessary for me to know of him, whether he intended to pursue the same conduct in future, & whether I was to depend on him or not for supplies to support the expences of my Comn., that I might inform Congress accordingly,—[9] he replyed that he had no money & therefore wd. not engage to supply me, for no supplies came from America except Tobacco, which was deliver'd to the Fermers General, under the old Contract made by him & Mr. Deane.[1]

7. See XXVII, 655.

8. For the turmoil Deane caused see Paine's letter of March 4.

9. William Lee had already received 72,000 *l.t.* from BF and the commissioners to France; see our annotation of BF's letter of May 26 to the committee for foreign affairs. For Lee's acerbic comments on BF's refusal to provide more money see Ford, *Letters of William Lee,* II, 598.

1. In which the commissioners agreed to furnish five million pounds of tobacco to the farmers general: XXIII, 514–17.

To Ferdinand Grand

Copy: Library of Congress

Sir Passy March 16 1779

I find in my Bill Book, that I accepted on the 19 of february, the following Congress Bills drawn in favour of Wm. Dennie, Dollars 600, 12, 600, 30, 120, 12, 120. These Bills were probably Part of a Number sent by the said Dennie to Mess. J. Williams & ——— Moylan; and as one of the Vessels he wrote by is known to have been taken, it is suspected they have been presented on Acct. of the Captors who may have counterfeited the Indorsements of Williams or Moylan.[2] I request therefore that you will stop Payment of these Bills till I have had an Opportunity of examining such Indorsements. I have the Honor to be &c

M. Grand.

To Schweighauser

Copy: Library of Congress

Sir Passy March 16 1779

I understand that there is a Case of Goods in your Hands, which belongs to Mr. Simeon Deane, but was delivered to you on a Supposition of its belonging to Congress. Please to redeliver the said Case to M. Jona Williams, taking his Receipt for the same.[3] I have the Honor to be &c—

M. Schweighauser.

To Jonathan Williams, Jr.

Copy: Library of Congress

Dear Jonathan Passy March 16 1779

Agreeable to your Desire I have requested the American Gentlemen residing at Nantes to examine your Accounts. I have added M. Schweighauser, he having been appointed by

2. See JW's letter of March 2.

3. JW had first reported the mix-up more than three months earlier: XXVIII, 221–2. In mid-February the commissioners finally promised to order Schweighauser's delivery of the goods to JW, who in turn agreed to receive them: XXVIII, 495, 580.

my former Colleagues to manage our Affairs there, and may be supposed interested particularly to do Justice to the Congress. And the others, I imagine, can have no Interest in favouring you, as perhaps you may stand in their Way respecting Business. Inclos'd you have Copies of my Letter to the Gentlemen and of another on the same Business to Mr. Lee.[4] If I had known of his going to Nantes, I should have desired him to state his Objections to the Accts. there; But I did not hear of his being there till a Day or two before his Return. I have yet no Answer from him.

I show'd your Letter of Feby. 20[5] relating to M. Simeon Deane's Goods to M. Adams, who thought the Proposition reasonable. I send by this Opportunity an Order to M. Schweighauser to deliver you the Case which remains; And if you will send me the original Invoice, and the form of the Bills you propose, I shall sign & return them; if no Objection arises on signing them that does not at Present occur to me.

I suppose you settled the Affair yourself with Mercier's Agent, as he took the Papers from me, saying that he was going to Nantes: this was before I received yours of feby. 23 relating to that Business.[6]

I received the Bond for Collas's Commission.[7]

The following Bills drawn before the 12th of December in favour of William Dennie were presented & accepted on the 19 of febry. Last. viz: Dollars 600. 12. 600. 30. 120. 12. 120. in all 1494 Dollars. These may possibly be a Part of those you mention. I shall order Payment to be stopt till I have examined the Endorsements, tho' I am not sure that I can well refuse Payment after having accepted them. We shall strictly examine such Drafts in favour of Dennie as may appear hereafter, till you let us know farther.

I return Dr. Cooper's Letter, with Thanks to you for com-

4. Both dated March 13, above. The following notation appears at the bottom of the page: "NB. inclosed were sent BF's Letters to A Lee & to The Gentn at Nantes. March 13. 1779"; it has been lined through.

5. XXVIII, 580.

6. For JW's complicated relationship with Mercier, who had contracted to repair arms, see XXVIII, 497–9, 596–7.

7. This and the following three paragraphs answer JW's letter of March 2.

municating it. I am much obliged to that good Man for his kind Expressions of Regard to me.

The Tobacco which came in the Bergere, & all the Tobacco which comes to us from America, is to be delivered directly out of the Ships to the Agents of the Farmers General in the Ports where it arrives. I had sent Orders accordingly before the Receipt of your Notice of her Arrival.

I am ashamed of the Orders of my Countrymen for so much Tea, when necessaries are wanting for Cloathing and defending![8]

I have been long ill, and unfit to write or think of writing, which occasioned my omitting to answer before your Several Letters since the 16 of February. I omitted also answering a kind Letter from M. Ridley,[9] who, I suppose, is now gone. If not, present my Respects to him, & best Wishes of a prosperous Voyage & happy Sight of his Friends. I am getting better, and hope our Correspondence will now be more regular.

I am ever yr. affectionate Uncle. BF.

Jona Williams

From Arthur Lee

Copy:[1] University of Virginia Library; transcript: National Archives

Sir/ Paris March 16th. 1779

I had the honor of receiving yours of the 13th.[2] touching my endorsement on your Nephew's Accounts.

When Mr. Bondfield's Accounts were sent to the Commissioners I examind them with the Vouchers & endorsd upon them the observations which occurrd to me. I compard M. Schweighauser's Accounts with the original Vouchers & Receits which lay two months at Passy & were then returnd to

8. See JW's letter of March 9.

9. Dated March 4, above.

1. In Arthur Lee's hand.

2. Letter II of that date. Lee did not answer BF's first letter of March 13th until the 19th, below.

him as he desird. In these Accounts I found no Errors. Upon M. Montieu's giving in his demand, I objectd his not having producd a receit from our Agent to vouch the delivery of the Articles for which he demanded payment. It was agreed that this was proper, & he promisd to produce such a receit. What he some time afterwards sent us as such was dated a year after the alledgd delivery of the Goods, was in the form of a Letter from Mr. Williams & conceivd in such terms as coud neither satisfy us that the things chargd had been recievd nor render your nephew responsible for them to the Public. I gave in my objection to this as unsatisfactory.[3]

Upon examining the first accounts given in by your Nephew, which was six months after the goods had been shipt, I found a darkness & inaccuracy which I had never seen in Accounts before, & that they were not accompanied with either Bills of Loading, or reciets to elucidate & support them. I stated my objections in writing.[4] The Answers neither informd nor satisfyd me. It appears too that you—yourself, Sir, was convinc'd that these Accounts, as they stood coud not be passt, because tho you agreed to pay him the ballance he demanded, you stated in the order, that this payment was not to be considerd as any approbation of his Accounts, nor prevent Mr. Williams from being accountable to Congress, or the Commissioners for the expenditure of the Sums entrusted to him.[5] His Accounts from the first Livre he receivd to the last, which as far as I can trust my memory exceeds a million, & the time is more than two years, remain in the same unsettled State.

When your Nephew sent us his 2d. Account which was in Sepr. or Ocr. last I examind it also, & reported my opinion endorsd on the Account itself, on purpose that you might not examine it without seeing my observations. The Account so

3. XXVIII, 305–6, 329–30, 407–8. Jean-Joseph Carié de Montieu, a business associate of Beaumarchais' Roderigue Hortalez & Cie., had extensive business dealings with JW; he first appears in XXII, 464n.

4. Presumably XXV, 462. For Lee's continued criticism of JW's accounting practices see XXVI, 228n; XXVII, 117n; XXVIII, 407–8, 443–6.

5. XXVII, 68, a joint order to Ferdinand Grand.

endorsd, I returnd immediately to Passy. It is therefore singularly unfortunate that you shoud not have seen this endorsment, in the course of near six months, *'till lately & by accident,* as you inform me, & that I shoud have incurrd some degree of your censure as not having—"shewn it to you when made, & there by occasioning the matter to have been so long neglected."

In all this, Sir, I acted equally to all, from the irresistible motives of duty to the Public as a Commissioner; & have been unhappy enough to have seen it taken up personally, & subject me to the greatest ill-will & abuse. You must there fore excuse me, Sir, now that it is no longer my indispensible duty, from concerning myself with a business which is in much abler hands. If Congress shoud call upon me for farther reasons than those I have already given, it will then be my duty to act & I will obey— But as this has been made a personal matter, I shall expect, as an act of justice, to have a Copy of your Nephew's Accounts, as settled by the impartial persons, to whom you do me the favor to inform me, you mean to refer them.

The Honble. Dr. B. Franklin M. Plenipote.

Notation: L'orient 15th May 1780 Examined with the Letter book & found to be a true copy JOHN G FRAZER
JOSEPH BROWN JUN[6]

From Jean-Joseph Carié de Montieu[7]

LS: American Philosophical Society

Monsieur, a Rochefort 16 Mars 1779.

J'avais bien entendu dire que vous étiez Seul Ministre Plenipotentiaire des Treize Etats unis de l'Amérique, mais je craignais que cette nouvelle n'existât que par le desir de toutes

6. For an identical notation see XXVIII, 408.

7. Montieu's accounts were the subject of great controversy in the previous months; see the preceding letter.

les personnes qui ont l'honneur de vous Connaitre. Elle vient de m'etre confirmée par Mr. Williams, et je vous prie d'agréer a ce Sujet mon bien Sincère compliment.

J'ai L'honneur de vous remettre, Monsieur, Deux Etats visés et certifiés par Mr. Williams de la Maniére La plus Satisfaisante, et pour vous et pour moi. L'un de ces Etats est une Facture de divers objets montant a 69455.2.7. que J'ai payé uniquement par Service d'ami. L'autre est La notte des divers articles de ma fourniture, Sur laquelle vous trouverez quelques petites différences dont le resultat est cependant à mon avantage. Il ne Se trouve que 97100 *l.t.* cuivre rozette au lieu de 100 Milliers que J'ai passé dans ma facture. Le fait est que J'en ai bien payé Cent Milliers, et je ne comprends pas d'ou provient cette petite différence. D'un autre coté, vous trouverez 25949 *l.t.* de cuivre en planches et en cloux dont je ne reclamais que 22 Milliers.

A L'egard de L'Etain vous n'en trouverez que 16710 *l.t.* poids de marc, au lieu de 20 Milliers portés Sur ma Facture, et cette différence N'est opérée que par celle du poids anglais au poids français.

Il en resulte, Monsieur, que vous m'etes toujours debiteur a peu prés de la Somme de 143 M£. que Je reclame depuis Si long tems. Les affaires dont je Suis chargé, exigent toutes mes ressources et j'ai fait Sur vous pour 130 M£ de traittes payables moitié a une usance, et moitié a 2—que Je vous prie de vouloir bien accepter au Domicile de M. Grand—a qui J'en adresse directement pour 124,500. *l.t.* en ayant donné une de 5500. *l.t.* au Sieur chevallié Negociant de cette Ville.[8]

Au Moyen de cet arrangement vous me demeurerez debiteur d'environ 13 M£. que Je Laisse exprés en arriére tant pour payer Ce que Je vous dois pour quelques vieilles armes que M. Williams m'a cédé, que pour les avances qui ont été Faites a charlés Town au Capitaine de mon Navire la Thérèse. Ces deux objets réunis peuvent Se monter a 10 M£ Tournois de maniére que J'aurai encore un Solde a recevoir, que nous réglérons dés mon retour a Paris.

8. Pierre-François Chevallié: XXVIII, 126n.

J'ai l'honneur d'etre avec tous les Sentimens de la reconnaissance la plus vive et La plus respectueuse, Monsieur, Votre trés humble et trés obeissant Serviteur MONTIEU

M. franklin Ministre Plénipre—des états unis de l'amerique

Notation: Montieu Rochefort 16 may 1779.

From Margaret Stevenson

ALS: Historical Society of Pennsylvania

My Dear Sir Cheem March: 16[–April 11] 1779

I receved your kind Letter of Jany 25, verey good of you Indeed to grartfice a poor old woman but old as I am my filings of friendshipe and grattued will allways reemane, i own i was afread of your esteem lessing, and allthoe i never expecte to see you moere If i hear your weel it gives me Pleasuer, morer if you ware hapey for that you cannot be to Luese so many of your Dear friends by the Swoerd, and many say you Blew up all this mischive, that is hard Indeed, but thoe thay charge you, theay know you Better.

I shall endever to send the Pot, as for the Paces of Eliphants Tooth I never saw it, after Mr Williams sent your Books.[9] Whin I was at Margait(?), and soon as I could Lett the Hous I Packit all your things and carid them to Norththumbland Court with me— I soposs Jona W—— sent it with the goods to Philadilapy[1] when you see him I hope it will be heard of I shall be very sorey to be thougt ever to have neglicted the caire of aney thing that belonged to my worthy friend, I have

9. See XXVIII, 421n, where BF had asked for his copper roasting vessel and piece of elephant's tooth. Ingenhousz wrote on April 9 and May 25, both below, that he would send the roasting pot. Possibly it came with the parcel Ingenhousz brought to France in November, 1779; see his letter of Nov. 18 (APS), BF's reply of Nov. 22 (Library of Congress), and BF to Mary Hewson, Jan. 10, 1780 (APS).

1. JW had packed BF's possessions in London and sent them to Philadelphia in 1775: XXII, 128n, 197.

hear your aoeconemest the siver Milke Pott kip bright the chain I hartily wish it may be recover:d—[2]

2 Box: sparmoacity candles som knife Cep in a Box Left at Mrs Lechmers[3] 4 Shifled Stickes for Candlis your Silk Coat if you Rember Mrs Wright[4] had the Wast Coat & Breches thar may be more than I mention: but I am shuer the Toth is not, soo careful was to bring the wax for your Eletrelecole exsperment some small Glass Tubes in a long Box and papers which i am now writing one sum quickslver the wetherhous,[5] why shur, cold not, miss of so Large a thing as the Ivery. I rember it well and hope you find it— Mr Viny fichs me to his Hous in too or three days I shall then goe to Henley and in quire what his deands ar[6] I doe not Recolicat that ever he cam to me with aney Bill if had I should sertanly have Paid him as I dide every one excepet the Barber which Refusd be caus I de not know how your accot. stude— he sed verey well he should write to his Banker for you to Pay him— you diser to know my acconat stands—

I know not that you ar atall in my Debt, but have inclosd all that I have paid and J: Wll.—— you know I am not Equile Settell accot. you allways dide it for me—and when you have time Pleas to doe it Mrs Hewson has Coped the Bills for fear of acciedans.

When in Towen I will Endever to geat the Pot & heater sent, I wishs you had pointd out some way that mit be Lickly for it but I shall Triy for it lickwise the drawing, Poor Viny I hope he will doe weel he has maney freinds. I writ you Last

2. BF had referred to her as "my *Oeconome*," or housekeeper, in his last letter to Mary Hewson: XXVIII, 164. For the milk pot see Hewson's letter of May 30.

3. Charles Lechmere, her former landlord at Northumberland Court (XXII, 263n).

4. Patience Wright.

5. A hygrometer in the shape of a house. The level of humidity is indicated by toy figures attached to strings that contract in the presence of moisture.

6. John Viny, a wheelwright and long-time friend of BF, had recently gone bankrupt. For Viny and the linendraper William Henly, or Henley, see XXVIII, 422.

year when I was at Vinys to taker of the famliy as she Lain of Girll[7] poor Child he came out off time, but thay ar verey happey and she is a kind affectnat Wiff— Bess is in a bad state of health, I shal clows this when I am thear—

Now my Deast friend I thanck you for the faover of your friendly Letter, but I am apperhesive that you thought me in a Piy Crust thums as you youst to tell me sometimes, mayby I was a litell, but why becauss I had worght, and not anssred—by Mr. Petree write a longe letter to my Dear Temple, I did not wish to take up your time but Expectd him to say every thing to you in my behalf. Pray is he weel dos he know his Mother is dead— Please my Love to him—[8]

I hope he is verey, affectionat and Dutiful, I dont dout him you dont mention Mrs Beach what most she feill for her Dear father wheris Mr Beach? Combs I hear is in London and his wife is dead thines this arivel.[9]

It give me grat Plesuer that you tell me your happey and have nothing to complain of may you ever be so— I am shuer your genrous Thoung never speaks the thing your Hairet disprovs now I hope your Pleased with bad spealing.

I am Much obleged to my good friend for his kind Inquerey with Regard to my health, I thank god for haveing Nother Complant then shackings hands, which is ba enevef but I make Shifte sivest meall make Bread and Pasty &ct: take the caire Off all Domistak Sarviss so your to know I am yossful

7. As she was in childbed, and gave birth to a girl. Bess, mentioned immediately below, is the Vinys' child: XXVIII, 422.

8. Mrs. Stevenson had written to WTF *c.* January, 1778: XXVI, 90. Samuel Petrie had been the bearer of that letter and may also have forwarded this one from his residence in Paris. A note from Petrie to BF, dated only "Rue Ste. Anne. Wednesday 2 o'Clock," announces that he is forwarding a letter from London and will be happy to hear that BF "is perfectly recover'd from his late Indisposition." We therefore conjecture that the note was written on April 21, 1779, the earliest Wednesday that Petrie might reasonably have received this letter, and not long after BF had recovered from his recent attacks of the gout. APS. Elizabeth Downes Franklin had died on July 28, 1777: XXIV, 446–7.

9. For the career of Rev. Thomas Coombe, his marriage in 1773 to Sarah Badger, and her death five years later, see XIX, 56n; XX, 193n. His last extant letter to BF had been written from Philadelphia in 1774: XXI, 313–17.

yeet—but you ar miss stackin, we ar not in a Country Town it is only a small vilage & know Neighbours in Winter, however its as well: the Children ar Nois a Neufe(?) your godson was put to Scool the Day after your Brithday.[1] Dor. Papers was the health of the day and a Goudy Day te was: the Girle drewe your Houner. She was not a littl Prowed, now dont you tirey: noe pray dont I am a littel afraid, your to Poilit for me now your finshing yor Edigtion—[2] but good sceins will oblige you to Look back at your old-Landlady, and Reember— I can not forgit you, I most however Try to give a litle Rein for I know you have tender filings Mrs. Blunt gave us a Cow she was wissus,[3] and went to drive her from Eating the Cabbig shc Tost mc down, thar I laye my Daughter Children & maid, scraming the Creaetur stamping her head and foot tied I heald the Rope at arms Length that she cold not Treed on my Sthomak I Lay tell all most spent, but haply for me I was thrown upon Cabbges she found, a dillichous and powerfuly she pourd her froth on my Fass than My Poor arms and thiys wear Black & Blew for maney Days— our Boy Thomas is standing by bids tell you he all ways Nocke glass at your health, when Everr wee drink wine say In dede he is Pritey felow but verey small the Girll Tall & Lareg the mother humers them to much, she Teach them when thay will be taught but that not for you to know so i shal bed you Good Night, and will drinke your Health Satturday night—

I shal benig agane next weeke.

I have seen Henly he has noe Accot. for I pad him, but forgot Sent for him to know what your Deat was, he sed you ode him Nothing for I had Pad him in a month affter you was gone how came such a Report, to Be mad— he sed I spocke to 2 or 3 friend, Pray how wass thay—Dr Pristly & Price he sed; but told them he was pade every one he was, he was glad

1. In January. She was living with Mary Hewson and her children, for whom see XXVI, 360. William, the eldest, was BF's godson.

2. Hewson had kept in touch with Benjamin Vaughan, and presumably with the progress of his edition of BF's writings: XXVII, 202.

3. Dorothea Blunt, Mary Hewson's old friend, may have been inspired to generosity by an inheritance in 1776; see our annotation to her letter of March 18, below.

to hare you did not goe off in Debt, why, to be shuer you cold not Suspect it (he had heard so) will that is harde upon me for i pad Evrey won that had aney demads & he Left me Cash to discharg all I thike He is a poor Crauter and I am tired so you mak it out. He is pad, you will find it in Williams Acct. I in close all the Paper I have as you desird my acct. I do not know how to settile nor know that your aney in my Debt when you have time you will find Poly tells me she is in your debt 4:14:6 so if you find the Ballnes in faover of me Pleas to deucit that, charg it to me—

My Dear, I have bine Long writg this and now fill a shamd to send, but have Wait:d the Drawing you mention:d—[4] Mr Viny has had drawins but not to Plas so he got the out of the Magazine—I shall send the Book by Dr. Ingenhous he thinks to sait out sone & bring your Coper and I own I hope the Elfants Tooh is at Philad. sartenly W—— packit it up with the Books—

I hear you have ben unweel Latly, i pray God allmity for your health & Peacs all your frinds Love & Esteem you None More than Dear Sir Your most afft. and Most oblied frind for Ever and Ever Amen MARGT STEVENSON

from Mach 16 to April 11 Craven Street

Mrs Wrights Daughter[5] tells me her mother intends bring in all her family to franes dont be Surprisd if i packe my self up with her figers, and Pipe upon you.

To Isaac-Jean-Georges-Jonas Grand

Copy: Library of Congress

Sir, Passy March 17. 1779

As Americans, Prisoners in England sometimes escape from thence, and get to Holland; where they are without Money to proceed to a Port whence they might take Passage to America; I hereby request, that if any such should apply to you for

4. BF had asked for "a good Drawing, with the Proportions, of the little Carriage without Horses, which his [Viny's] Children came once in to see us" (XXVIII, 422).

5. Elizabeth, who had married Ebenezer Smith Platt in 1778 (XXIII, 322n).

Assistance, as they have heretofore done,[6] you would be so good as to furnish them with as much Money as may be necessary to carry them to some French Sea-Port, in the most frugal Way, according to the Circumstances, which shall be thankfully repaid by Sir Your most obedt. humble Servant

B. FRANKLIN

Sir George Grand.

To Joseph Gridley

Copy: Library of Congress

Sir

Passy March 17 1779

I duely received your Favor of the 25th past.[7] Continued Indisposition with too much Business have occasioned the Delay in answering it, which I hope you will excuse.

I think with you that an American Consul at Nantes might be useful in the Cases you mention. What Inconveniences or Expence might attend it, I am unacquainted with. The Congress have by the Treaty a Right to appoint Consuls in the several Ports:[8] But they have not yet thought fit to do it; nor have they given me any Authority for that Purpose. I suppose We have had not less than 50 Applications of the same kind from the different Ports of France;[9] none of which the Commissioners could comply with, having no Instructions on that Subject from Congress: nor can I venture upon it for the same Reason. I rather think it my Duty to leave the Matter open, that in Case they should determine to make such Appointments, their Choice might not be embarrassed by Appointments already made.

I was much pleas'd with the Report of that able Chemist M. Sage, upon your Ores.[1] He favoured me with a Copy of it.

6. Grand had provided help in 1778 for Lt. Philip Hancock, an escaped prisoner: XXVII, 283.

7. XXVIII, 608–9.

8. A right accorded by Article 31 of the Treaty of Amity and Commerce: XXV, 624.

9. See XXVI, 209–14; XXVII, 263–4, 326, 385, 470–1, 495, 583; XXVIII, 44–5, 51–2, 88, 397–8, 460–6.

1. For the mineral samples see Richard Gridley's letter of introduction for his son Joseph (XXVII, 658–9).

When you write, please to present my Respects to your good Father. I have the Honor to be &c

M. Gridley.

To Joshua Johnson

Copy: Library of Congress

Sir

Passy March 17 1779

I received the Honor of yours of the 6 inst. I took the first Opportunity of speaking to M. D'Arlincourt fils, one of the Farmers general in whose Department you reside, on the subjet of your Furniture, who told me very politely that as it was a Matter in which I interested myself, he would order the Duties, if they had been received to be returned. By our Treaty we are only entitled to such Advantage respecting Duties as is enjoyed by the most favor'd Nations: I have not yet been able to obtain a certain Knowledge of the Duties paid by other Nations in France, and I am told it is not easy to obtain, as they are very different in the Different Provinces, and there is not as in England a printed Book of them.[2] So not being enough informed at Present to claim your Exemption as a Right, I was obliged to accept it as a Favor. But these Sorts of Favours I shall find a Difficulty in asking hereafter; for the States being under great Obligations to the Farmers general who lent us Money in our Distress;[3] and having often Occasion to ask Aids from this Government; one can hardly with any Grace demand at the same Time in Favour of Particulars an Exemption from paying their Share of the Duties whence only the Ability of affording such Aids can arise.

I have ordered the Alliance to be got ready as soon as possible; the Execution depends on M. Schweighauser and the Captain. I thank you for your Information relating to the Ber-

2. America's most-favored-nation status was based on Article 2 of the Treaty of Amity and Commerce (XXV, 598). On Jan. 7, 1779, the American merchants at Nantes had asked the commissioners to ascertain and publicize American liabilities for French duties: XXVIII, 357.

3. The farmers general had advanced the commissioners 1,000,000 *l.t.* on the promise, unlikely of fulfillment, of repayment in tobacco: XXIII, 514–17.

gere. Orders had before been given relating to her Cargo.[4] With great esteem I have the Honor to be Sir y m o a m h S

BF

P.S. If you can by any Means obtain an Acct. of the Duties to be paid by different Nations in yr Port, I shall be obliged to you for it, and will pay any Expence necessary for Copying &c

M. Joshua Johnson

To Montaudoüin

Copy: Library of Congress

Dear Sir Passy March 17 1779

I received your favour of the 4th inst. by M. David with much Pleasure; as it informed me of the well fare of Friends I love, and who are indeed beloved by every Body. I thank you for your kind Congratulations, & for the Prayer you use in my Behalf. Tho' the Form is heathen, there is a good Christian Spirit in it: and I feel myself very well disposed to be content with this World, which I have found hitherto a tolerable good one, & to wait for Heaven (which will not be the worse for keeping) as long as God pleases. In short I should have no Objection to living with you & Mrs. Montaudoin in France another Century. I don't complain much even of the Gout, which has harrassed me ever since the Arrival of the Commission you so politely mention: There seems however some Incongruity in a *Pleni-potentiary* who can neither stand nor go. With the Sincerest Esteem, Respect & Affection, I am &c

M. Montaudoin

4. See JW's letter of March 2.

To Vergennes

LS:[5] Archives du Ministère des affaires étrangères; AL (draft) and copy: Library of Congress

Sir, Passy, March 17. 1779.

I received the Letter your Excellency did me the honor of writing to me the 13. Instant. I imagine that M. De Chaumont has been disappointed in the Expectations he had of finding Bankers here who would advance the Sum for which he sollicited your Excellency to guarantee the Interest. He at length brought to me a Merchant of Amsterdam, who has undertaken to procure a Loan of 1,500,000 Florins at 6 per Cent.[6] But by what I can learn & judge of that Person, I think there is little Dependance to be had upon his Success; especially as the English borrow there at a higher Rate, and the House of Hornica Fizeaux & Co. have been already engaged more than 6. Months in endeavouring to obtain such a Loan, and have succeeded only to the Amount of 51,000 Florins. In the mean time my Apprehensions of approaching Distress grow stronger, and give me a great deal of Anxiety.[7] And having more Hopes from Mr Grand's Endeavours to procure us a

5. In WTF's hand, as is the copy.

6. Jean de Neufville; see BF to Dumas, March 12.

7. At this point in the draft appears a lengthy passage that has been bracketed for deletion: "The Supplies sent from America, have either been taken by the Enemy, or if they arrive in Tobacco are deliver'd as justly due to the Farmers General, or they are seiz'd by Mr Beaumarchais, who threatens (as your Excellency will see by the enclos'd) to seize all our Cargoes that may arrive in France, if a Suit is not stopt, that was commenc'd by the Commissioners against a Mr Peltier of Nantes for selling without our Orders, a Cargo of Rice consign'd to us, and delivering by his Orders the Produce to him [Beaumarchais]. The Congress order'd us to settle his Accounts, but he has never produc'd them to us, tho' we earnestly desir'd & he promis'd it. He talks of immense Demands that he has against the States, but does not ascertain them by delivering an Account: We gave up to him one large Cargo of Rice at his Request; he has got Possession of another without our Consent by Means of Mr Peltier; and tho' I am dispos'd to do every thing in the Business that is just and honourable, I know not how to proceed with him, being ignorant of the Foundation as well as of the Extent of his Claims. I am sorry to give your Excellency so much Trouble with our Affairs, but I have great Need of your Counsel with regard to this Gentleman.—" The intended enclosure must have been Beau-

Supply, than from those of M. De Chaumont by the Dutch Merchant, I wish his Plan may be examined, and if found practicable encouraged.[8] For if both should succeed they will not be too much for our Occasions.

With sincere & great Respect I have the honor to be, Your Excellency's, most obedient & most humble Servant

B FRANKLIN

His Excy. Count De Vergennes.

Notation:[9] M. Francklin

From Landais

LS: American Philosophical Society

Sir Brest March 17th. 1779

I received your favours of the 4th. 6th. & 8th. Instants.[1] In answer to the first, Doctr. Windship has made you a plan for acting, out of his own head: telling you that we were enough to fight the Ship. I send you the list inclosed of the Ships company,[2] out of which number, three are missing; by which your Excellency will judge what I can do with so few Seamen.

I blush'd, when I read, that your Excellency is afraid I'll contrive to make such an Expence &c. But was surprised and humbled by the article which followed. If I had not been present when Mr. Deane read to your Excellency, all the papers he dispatch'd me with, told you my generous confidence in the Congress, what Mr. Monthieu had offer'd me at first, & heard your Excellency give your assent: I would never have offer'd

marchais' lengthy memoir of Feb. 13 (XXVIII, 523–31); for the controversy over the *Thérèse* see BF to Beaumarchais, March 15.

8. Grand wrote the foreign ministry on March 15 to report that BF was suffering from gout and to remind Vergennes of their conversation of the 10th (AAE); see our annotation of BF to Vergennes, March 10.

9. In Gérard de Rayneval's hand.

1. BF's latest extant letters to Landais are those of the 4th, 6th, and 11th. He may have enclosed with the last of these his letter of the 8th to Vergennes.

2. Possibly an undated list of the *Alliance*'s officers, seamen, and marines. A separate document lists her petty officers; both are at the University of Pa.

to write about it. And should not now, say a word if my delicacy had not been wounded.[3]

I am sorry after receiving yours of the 6th. to be compelled to trouble your Excellency again, in telling you that having rec'd. yours of the 8th. I went to see Count D'Orvilliers, & Monsieur La Porte, Intendt. about receiving the mutineers; the Last told me he should be ready to receive them in five or six days. He would then let me know of it. Yesterday, hearing nothing from that gentleman, I again waited on him, then he told me, he & Mr. de la Prevalay had wrote on Sunday to the Minister about it, & waited for his answer, so I must wait 'till then.[4]

I have been to Mr. Costentin, for to have very necessary things for the present, to rigg the Ship with, such as a topmast having but one, & that two feet too short, some blocks, & old Canvas his answer was, that Mr. Schweighauser had wrote to him, not to furnish any thing for the ship, but daily supplies, 'till he had himself, receiv'd your Excellency's orders, which he would send to Mr. Costentin. After this, your Excellency will Judge whither I can get ready or not. Mr. William's is here, and may tell your Excellency all the troubles I undergo in every respect.[5]

I have forty caulkers working on board, have obtain'd also to have the Iron work mended. I wish I could have enough to rigg the Ship once. I should, after the mutineers are ashore, try if the crew be strong enough to get under sail, & proceed where Mr. Schweighauser will write me to go, let the consequence be what it may.

I have also to acknowledge the receipt of your favour of the 11th. & your order respecting Capt. Cook.

3. See *Deane Papers,* II, 122–4, for Deane's use of Landais, who brought to America one of the ships chartered by Roderigue Hortalez & Cie. from Montieu. The commissioners mentioned the ship soon thereafter in a letter to the committee for foreign affairs: XXIV, 516.

4. *Chef d'escadre* Pierre-Bernardin de Thierry, marquis de la Prévalaye (XXVII, 294n), was Brest's acting port commandant and Arnauld de Laporte (XXVII, 238n) its *intendant,* or administrative head.

5. JW's uncle, John; JW wrote to him at Brest the following day (Yale University Library). The elder Williams had been in France since the preceding November: XXVIII, 136.

I am with the greatest respect Your Excellency's Most obedient humble Servant P: LANDAIS

His Excellency Doctor Franklin &c &c

Addressed: To his Excellency / Doctor Benja. Franklin / Minister plenipotentiary to the / United States / Passy / near Paris

Notation: P. Landais. Brest Mars. 17th 1779.

From Le Roy

AL: American Philosophical Society

mercredy matin [March 17, 1779?][6]

Mon Illustre Docteur nous envoyons Mde Le Roy et moi savoir de vos Nouvelles nous esperons que votre nouvel accès de goutte est bien diminué ou appaisé.

J'ai l'honneur de vous prévenir en même temps que sil fait beau demain jeudy le Monsr Inconnu ou anonyme fera des experiences sur le feu principe à Onze heures mais Je crains bien que vous ne puissiez pas être des nôtres recevez mon Illustre Docteur Mille sincères assurrances de mon attachement éternel pour vous. Avez vous recu des Nouvelles de L'Amèrique? L'anonyme ne fait plus ses experiences dans le même endroit. C'est actuellement ruë de Bourgogne faub. St Germain chez M Le Marquis de LAubespine.

Addressed: A Monsieur / Monsieur Franklin Ministre / Plenipotentiaire des Etats unis de / LAmèrique Septentrionale / a Passy

From Georgiana Shipley

ALS: American Philosophical Society

Bolton Street March 17th *1779*

It is long very long since I had the happiness of receiving a line from my dear Doctor Franklin; how often have I regreted

6. We assign this date on the basis of experiments that Marat was performing in March, first scheduled for the rue de Grenelle, then for the rue de Bourgogne. See Marat's letters of before March 13, above, and March 25, below.

the necessary interruption of a correspondence, from whence I derived so much *pleasure* & advantage; an opportunity now offers of conveying a letter to you which I have not *prudence* sufficient to resist,[7] particularly as I have lately heard of your being confin'd with the gout, I hope, my dear Sir, you take all imaginable care of yourself, indeed you ought, when you reflect, that the happiness of many depends upon the preservation of a life so valuable, nor shall I feel satisfyed till I receive an account of your perfect recovery for even your slightest indisposition must alarm a family by whom you are so sincerely respected & beloved, I believe a day seldom passes without our mentioning our excellent friend, & I may truely say I never am so well pleased as when I am in company with those who know & esteem you as much as we do.

We have left Jermyn Street some time, & my father has bought an house the corner of Bolton Street which belonged to the late Mr Howe, perhaps you may recollect it, if so you will be sensible we have changed much for the best in every respect. This Summer we propose spending at Twyford, never shall I forget the happy days we passed there, in happier times, when you were so good as to visit us:[8] I continue as fond of reading as I was when you knew me first, neither have I neglected my drawing, if I had an opportunity I would send you another, that you might yourself judge of my improvement. As for electricity I fear I have made no great progress now my Instructor has left me, however I have learnt some new experiments, & likewise performed some *wonderfull* cures. But now I must say something concerning the rest of my family, my father & mother are both remarkably well, & in no respect alterd since you saw them. Amelia continues my *only* married sister;[9] she has but one child, a sweet tempered lovely

7. Bishop Jonathan Shipley had warned his daughter, BF's favorite of the family (XVIII, 200n), that in the present state of affairs a continuation of her correspondence with their old American friend would be imprudent: XXIII, 304.

8. BF had stayed at the family's country house during the summer of 1771: XVIII, 137.

9. For Amelia, who in 1774 had married William Sloper, later an M.P., see XVIII, 200n.

little Girl, just three years old, whom all our family adore. My brother has married a Miss Yonge a very amiable pleasing young woman, & heiress to a large fortune.[1] They live entirely in Wales, & also have one child a fine little boy about four months old. I am sure you will be pleased with this account of your friends, indeed it was never more necessary than at this period to look for happiness at home & even there how rarely is it to be met with. Mr Vaughan is so obliging as to undertake to send this letter to you. & I wish you may be able to convey an answer through his hands. I cannot be so unreasonable as to expect you should write to me yourself who must have so much important business to transact. But if you will permit your Grand-son to send a few lines merely to assure us of your recovery, it will give the greatest satisfaction to a family who feel themselves warmly interested in your health & welfare.

Adieu my dear Sir, that every respect & blessing you so justly deserve may constantly attend you, is the sincere wish of yr much obliged & affectionate GEORGIANA SHIPLEY

Addressed: A Monsr. / Monsr. F. / a Passy / pres de Paris.

Notation: Georgiana Shipley Bolton 17. mars 1779.

Jean-Jacques Caffiéri to William Temple Franklin

ALS: American Philosophical Society

Monsieur Paris ce 17 mars 1779

J'ai fait encaisser Le Buste de M. franklin, vous pouve Monsieur qu'ant il vous plairat faire enlevée cette Caisse dans mon atelier du Louvres, j'ai fait Durcir ce buste avec de La Cire Comme vous Le Désiries, je Compte qu'il arrivera à bon port: Permettes que M. franklin trouve icy Les assurance de mon Respect.

1. Her only brother, William Davis Shipley, a churchman, married in 1777 Penelope Yonge, heiress of Sir John Conway, last baronet of Bodrhyddan. *DNB* under Shipley.

J'ai Lhonneur d'etres tres parfaitement Monsieur Votres trés humble et tres obeïssant Serviteur[2] CAFFIERI

Endorsed: M. Caffiery Paris 17. mars 1779.

To John Bondfield

Copy: Library of Congress

Sir Passy Mar. 18 1779

I received your favours of the 6 & 9 inst. & thank you for the Intelligence they Contain. I hope generals Clinton & Thomson will give a good Acct. of the Invaders of Georgia.[3] But if they should remain there till the end of the summer, a general fever at least will do a great Deal towards demolishing them. With much Esteem I am &ca

M. Bondfield.

To S. & J.-H. Delap

Copy: Library of Congress

Gentlemen Passy March. 18 1779

I duly received the Letter you did me the Honor of writing to me, the 6 inst. mentioning a Prize "the sale of which was stopt by the Judge of the Admiralty untill she was deemed a legal Prize by me & the Council of Prizes." and desiring my Decision "without Loss of Time." I was ill when I received your Letter, and have not yet been able to go out, or attend much to Business, otherwise I would have enquired at Ver-

2. Two days later, Caffiéri confirmed that the crate was ready to be picked up and enclosed instructions, to be forwarded to America, on the way to unpack it (APS). On June 16, the artist sent two more busts, made hard and shiny by a coat of wax dissolved in essence of turpentine. His bill amounted to 291 *l.t.,* plus the porter's expenses. BF paid it on June 16 (Account XVI, XXVI, 3). In a letter to WTF, probably written from Lorient in June, Chaumont *fils* relates having seen a BF bust, "grandeur naturel et tres ressemblant," already loaded. It must have been unloaded at some point, since Sally complained of having received the instructions but no bust. For its further misadventures see Sellers, *Franklin in Portraiture,* p. 201.

3. Surely BF wished for a good account from Benjamin Lincoln, not Sir Henry Clinton, and the copyist made an error.

sailles about it; for I never heard before of this Prize, nor have I any Concern in the Council of Prizes, or any Right to give any such Decision, if I was acquainted with the Case which I am not. I hope the Difficulty is removed before this Time; But if upon a fuller Explanation of the Nature of the Case, it should appear that any Interposition from me with the Ministry is necessary & proper, you may rely on my Readiness to do whatever may be useful to your Interests, being with much Esteem &c

Mess. S. & J. H. delap.

To Dumas

Copy: Library of Congress

Dear Sir Passy, March 18 1779

I received duly yours of the 3 inst. My Indisposition seems to be wearing off; and I hope will permit me to go abroad in a few Days.

Mr. Neufville's first Propositions were so much out of the Way, that I could not accept them. He required a fifth Part of the Loan to be sent over to him annually during the first 5 years in the Produce of America for Sale, & the Money to remain in his Hands as a Fund for paying off the Debt in the last 5 years. By this Means, he would have had the Use of our Money while we were paying Interest for it. He dropt this Demand on my Objecting to it, and undertook to procure a subscription on reasonable Terms. I wish him success, but as the English give at Present higher Interest than I am permitted to offer, I have little Dependance on that Subscription. Let me know what you hear of it from Time to Time.

M. Adams is gone to Nantes to take his Passage for America in one of our Frigates. Mr. A Lee has retired from Chaillot to Paris; And his Brother is come on a Visit from Francfort. He talks of a Congress to be held in Germany & seems to want me to advise his Attendance there incogn. I know nothing of it, or of any Use he can be of there, & therefore can give no Advice about it. He talks of 20,000 Men at Liberty by the German Peace to be hired by the English against us, and would be employd in preventing it—[4] What do you think or learn of these Circumstances?

The present Situation of Affairs in your Country is interesting. Unacquainted as I am with your Parties & Interests, I find it difficult to conceive how they will terminate. I am, Dear Sir &ca

M. Dumas.

To Gourlade & Moylan

Copy: Library of Congress

Gentlemen Passy Mar. 18 1779

I duly received the Letters you did me the Honor to write to me of Febry. 17 & Mar. 5.[5] A continued Indisposition for near five Weeks, occasioned the Delay in answering them, which I hope you will excuse. I am much obliged by your kind Congratulations. Please to accept my thankful Acknowledgements and best Wishes for your Prosperity. I know not how it happened that my Orders for delivering the Tobacco to the farmers general were so long in getting to Hand. I had sent them to M. Schweighauser at Nantes with the Bills of Lading as soon as I had Advice of the Arrival. I thank you for the Notice you so kindly gave me of the Delay. I am exceedingly sensible of the Services you have always so readily afforded us, and shall be glad of every Opportunity of demonstrating the Regard and esteem with which I have the Honor to be &c

Messrs. Gourlade & Moylan.

To Richard Bennett Lloyd

Copy: Library of Congress

Dear Sir, Passy Mar. 18 1779

I duly recd. your favours of feb. 19 & Mar. 2[6] inclosing a Copy of the Letter to M. Hartley from the Board who have

4. Lee warned about the troops in his March 15 conference with BF, above, and hinted at the possibility of attending the Austro-Prussian peace conference which was assembling at Teschen in Silesia, for which see our annotation of the Amsterdam intelligence report of March 1.

5. The former is in XXVIII, 563; the latter is above.

6. The former is in XXVIII, 574–5, and the latter is above.

the Care of sick & wounded Seamen, relating to the Exchange of Prisoners. Accept my Thanks for the Pains you have taken in Behalf of those poor unfortunate People. M. Hartley writes me that he thinks they will now be soon exchanged.[7] I hope your cold & the Inflammation in your Eyes have passed away without leaving any ill Consequences. Please to make my Respects acceptable to Ms. Lloyd, And If you have an Opportunity, be so good as to acquaint Mr. D.[8] that I have received and am much obliged to him for his Letters, and for his Attention to the Distresses of the Prisoners &c. I have not written to him because the most innocent Letters from me falling into some Hands may occasion Suspicions to his Prejudice. I shou'd hardly have ventured writing this to you, but that it relates to an allow'd Transaction & Correspondence with M. Hartley[9] with great esteem & Respect I have the Honor &c.

R. B. Lloyd Esq;

To William MacCreery

LS:[1] Historical Society of Pennsylvania; copy: Library of Congress

Sir, Passy Mar. 18. 1779.

I received your Favours of Feb. 27. and March 6.[2] Continued Illness, with want of Information on the Subject, have occasioned the Delay in answering them.

I have endeavour'd to learn what the Duties are that are payable by *the most favour'd Nation* on the Exportation of Salt from France: I am at length told that the Duties are very low; that they consist chiefly in what is paid for the Forms or Papers necessary in transacting the Business regularly, and that they are equal on all Foreign Nations, and paid equally by all. If so we also must pay them. But you seem to think we have a Right to load Salt at Bordeaux *free of Duty:* Perhaps you have

7. See Hartley's letter of March 2.
8. Thomas Digges, who is identified in XXVII, 420n.
9. Lord North had assured Hartley that any correspondence with BF which might forward peace would not be interrupted: XXV, 662, 691.
1. In WTF's hand.
2. The first is in XXVIII, 625–7, and the latter above.

heard that there is some favour'd Nation which is allow'd that Right. Be so good as to enquire and obtain a Certainty of this, and an Account what the Duties are, and of the different Duties paid by different Nations, if there is any difference. When I am well acquainted with the Facts, I shall know whether I can by any Application to the Ministry be of Service to you, and I shall exert myself with a great deal of Pleasure in ascertaining your Rights: But if our Shipping of Salt free of Duties be not a Right, and must be asked as a Favor for particular Persons, which I apprehend you mean with regard to the Lading of the Buckskin, I find a Difficulty in doing this: For as we are obliged to be frequently requesting Aids of Money from the Government for our *Public Uses,* one cannot at the same time with any good Grace, desire, for *private Persons,* an Exemption in the Payment of those general Duties from whence only the Ability of granting such Aids must arise. I thank you for the Offer of conveying Dispatches in that Vessel, which I may possibly make Use of.

I have the honor to be, Sir, Your most obedient humble Servant. B FRANKLIN

Mr McCreery Bordeaux.

To Jean de Neufville

Copy: Library of Congress

Sir Passy March 18 1779

I hope you got safe home & had a happy meeting with your Family & Friends; and that you will succeed in your Undertaking.[3]

I have considered the Memorial of the Person who calls himself Baron de Mons, & have made some Inquiries. I have since your Departure received a long Letter from Me. La Baronne de Mons.[4] Upon the whole I am of Opinion that their

3. To raise an American loan in the Netherlands.

4. Among BF's papers at the APS are two documents in French concerning a Samuel Stanley, Baron de Mons. One is a Sept. 18, 1778, memorandum from him to Congress reclaiming his property rights in Massachusetts and South Carolina and giving power of attorney to De Neufville & fils, Jean de Neufville's banking house. The memorandum also describes the

Story is all a Fiction, and that they are Imposters and have no such Estates in America. I give you this Information, that you may be careful in making farther Advances to them. She writes from Altona. I have the Honor to be &c.

M. Neufville

To ——— Ridou[5]

Copy: Library of Congress

Sir, Passy Mar. 18 1779

I should be very happy in being possessed of a Remedy for that terrible Distemper a Dropsy; for I would communicate it immediately to all the world. But I have not, nor ever had, or pretended to have any such Knowledge. A Report of the kind has, I know not by what means, been inserted in the News Papers; but it was totally without Foundation.[6] I regret therefore that I cannot enable you to afford that Relief to your Friend which your tender Regard for him prompts you to wish; and am with esteem for your Humanity

Sir y. m. ob. & h S. BF.

M. Ridou

---

properties in question, the former, near Boston, containing 100 acres, and the latter, near Charleston, 160 acres. The second document is a March 5, 1779, letter from the baroness de Mons reporting that they are at Altona (adjoining Hamburg) and that the baron is ill. She explains their claims, repeating much of the information from the earlier memorandum.

5. Written in response to Ridou's letter of March 12, in French, from the rue de Braque in Paris (APS). Ridou had just been informed that a friend was suffering from the dropsy and that the *Journal de Bouillon* had reported "que le Docteur francklin a guerri radicalement aux invalides deux hommes attaqués de cette maladie." He had gone to Les Invalides, to various infirmaries, and had looked in the *Journal* for BF's cure, all in vain. Would the Doctor consent to give him the remedy?

6. The rumor of BF's cure for dropsy had originated in England in 1777, and spread to France and the Netherlands. See XXV, 178–9n.

To Antonio Francesco Salucci et fils[7]

Copy: Library of Congress

Gentlemen Passy March 18 1779

I am honor'd with your Letter of the 5th. ult. and am glad to learn that you have ventured on an Expedition of Goods to America. I must heartily wish they may arrive safe and that the Returns may afford you an encouraging Profit. You may rely upon it that your Ship will meet with a most friendly Reception in any one of the U.S.; with all the facilities for your Commerce and all the Protection that well regulated & good Governments afford to Strangers with whom they are in Friendship. I have the honor to be &c

Mess. Ant. Bran. Salucci & freres (Livourne)

To Samuel Stockton

LS:[8] Yale University Library; copy: Library of Congress

Sir, Passy March 18. 1779.

I received yours of the 9th[9] per Mr Lee: I am told there is a Vessel at Rotterdam bound to N. America, but if you do not find a ready Passage from Holland, there are Vessels almost continually going from Nantes and Bordeaux. I do not at present think of any thing worth your while to stay in Europe for: and as Mr. Adams is returning & will go directly to Congress, I purpose to send my present Dispatches by him.

I thank you for your kind Congratulations on my Appointment; Should you pass this Way, you may rely on such friendly Offices as may be in the Power of, Sir, Your most obedient humble Servant. B FRANKLIN

Mr. Stockton.

7. For the commercial venture on the *Prosperité,* the first ever from the port of Leghorn to the U.S., of this Tuscan firm (whose name BF apparently misread as "frères") see XXVIII, 472–4.

8. In WTF's hand.

9. Actually the 7th.

Addressed: To / Mr Stocton. / at the Hague—

Endorsed: From Dr. Franklin March 18th. 1779.

To H. Sykes[1]

Copy:[2] Library of Congress

Sir, Passy March 18. 1779.

I return you enclosed Mr Haywoods Letter and am much obliged to you for communicating it, as it acquainted me of the Welfare of some Friends whom I much Esteem (Mr & Mrs Nairne)[3] and at the same time inform'd me of that most Ingenius Invention of Mr Haywoods for making Globes, which I much admire. Mr Whitechurch[4] never deliver'd that, He did me the Favor to design for me. Perhaps it was broke by some Accident, or lost. Please to present my thankful Acknowledgements however and assure Mr Haywood of my Respect. I have the honor to be, Sir, Your most obedt humble Servant

B FRANKLIN.

I shall take the Liberty of calling to see your Warehouse the first convenient Opportunity

P.S. If those Plaister Globes are heated hot in an Oven (after the Bread is taken out) and then washed over with melted *hot* white Wax, by means of a Soft Hair Brush, the Wax will penetrate 1/8 of an Inch, and so toughen the Surface may afterwards be polished: by rubbing it with a Silk handkerchief, will look like Marble; and may at any time be washed if Flies or Smoke &ca should dirty it. BF.

Mr. Sykes is requested to send this to Mr Haywood

Mr Sykes

1. In answer to his of March 13.
2. In WTF's hand.
3. Edward Nairne, English electrician and instrument maker: X, 171n.
4. The engraver, William Whitchurch: XXVI, 17.

To Jesse Taylor[5]

Copy: Library of Congress

Sir Passy Mar. 18 1779

I received but very lately your Letter & Memorial dated the 21 of Novr. last. If there be really a considerable number of Persons dispos'd to adventure upon the Voyage you mention, I will undertake to procure them all the security desired, You have only to send me a List of their names, expressing their Sex & Ages, and the names of the Vessels, Capt. &c. Sir E. N. has not been here to my knowledge.[6] I have the Honor to be &c

Capt. Jesse Taylor (Belfast)

From Dorothea Blunt

ALS: American Philosophical Society

Dear Sir Kensington March the 18th. 79

Our friend Saint Hutton[7] offers me a chance for getting a letter to you, which tho I have *long'd* a long while for, & have not had, or you w'd have stood a chance for one of my superiour epistles which I know you did not dislike because you always answer'd. Why did you come to my native country? Or continue so long time in it, and then so quarrel with *some,* that you may as well not love *others?* Now for these, and other reasons, if I had not loved you very much I sh'd now dislike you exceedingly— Even I, who am many years younger than you, find nothing more desirable than peace and the society of those I've long known, I wish I c'd believe that the benefits gain'd by our loss of you were either considerable to the Many or likely to be lasting to the few. I find it impossible to write to you, and not in a certain degree to blame you for not doing more than you had in your power rather than leave us—but I have done and will learn to submit to all evils, I thank God,

5. The Irish merchant who had requested protection for a group of Belfast Protestants desiring to emigrate: XXVIII, 147–8.

6. Sir Edward Newenham, according to Taylor, had promised to represent their cause to BF in person.

7. James Hutton, the Moravian leader (XVII, 223n), was going to visit BF; see his letter of April 11.

that I firmly believe His kind providence directs every Evil of Life, to some good to Man.

As Mr Hn: is not acquainted with my family I shall myself give you a little account of them. I lost my amiable Sister three years ago, who gave the strongest proof of being so in a patient resignation to a severe and lingering disorder, and to *Death,* notwithstanding her strong desire for *Life.* I was with her 7 months—never saw once out of temper, and tho except 600£—she bequeathd all she had to me, never once told me so,[8] I am by the addition enabled to command a little dwelling of my own and I think it would give you pleasure to see me in it because I am told that I appear as I am very Comfortable. I see but little of Mrs Hewson she finding herself perhaps equally so in a little Cottege or small house at Cheam in surry. My Bror: Cs— has 10 children 8 of them Girls. I can say nothing on this subject as it realy distresses me, my Bror: Harry a Widdower still resides near Bath, has long had bad health has 2 Sons likely to give him comfort. My Bror: Walter plump as a partridge is I hope happy—and has only at present 2 Sons and one daughter.[9] Mrs M: Barwell still a fine woman, and *more* pleasing because *less busy.* Henckell with her respectable Parents resides at Hampstead and works in her Garden. D: B: has a little Garden, and tho she does not work in it is mighty fond of it. May God bless you and yours. D: BLUNT

Mrs Hawkesworth the same, and comes to me tomorrow.[1] I see my friends often from my situation which as I live alone I like.

Addressed: Doctor Franklin

Notation: D. Blunt. Kensingten. [*torn*]oo 18. mars 1779.

8. For Catherine Blunt's long illness, and death in December, 1775, and Dolly's reluctance to accept her inheritance see XXII, 63n, 594.

9. Dolly's three brothers are discussed in XIX, 151n. Sir Charles (XIV, 93n) had no sons until the younger Charles Blunt was born in December, 1775: XXII, 301n.

1. Mary Barwell (XVII, 194–5n), Elizabeth Henckell (XIX, 152n), and Mrs. John Hawkesworth (IX, 265–6n; XXII, 595n) belonged to the circle of friends that Polly Hewson and Dolly had shared with BF during his years in London.

From Vergennes

L (draft):[2] Archives du Ministère des affaires étrangères; copy: Library of Congress

à Vlles. le 18. Mars. 1779.

J'ai reçu M la lettre[3] que vous m'avez fait l'honneur décrire ce matin. Je desire que M. grand reussise mieux que M. de Chaumont à vous procurer les fonds dont vous avez besoin; le Roi tiendra à son égard les mêmes promesses que j'avois faites en son nom à M. de Chaumont, et s'il veut bien se rendre ici, je les luy expliquerai.[4]

J'ai l'h d'être

M. franklin

From Jonathan Williams, Jr.

ALS: American Philosophical Society

Dear & hond Sir.— Nantes March 18. 1779

I have received your agreeable Favour of the 8th Instant per Mr Adams, who did me the Favour to send for me immediately—[5] I pressed him very much to accept a Bed at my house, which he declined, I however had the pleasure of his Company to dine with me the Day after his arrival with sev-

2. In Gérard de Rayneval's hand.

3. Of the 17th.

4. In February Vergennes had written Gérard, the French minister in Philadelphia, that the expenses of the war were too heavy to enable the King to continue a subsidy to the U.S. Vergennes told him, in confidence, that BF had found a firm of bankers to lend three million *l.t.* and that if Congress were unable to come up with the money to pay the interest on the loan, the King would supply it. In April, to clarify his earlier letter, the French minister reiterated that the King had guaranteed nothing; he had simply agreed to pay interest of 6% in the event that Congress could not reimburse it in time. Meng, *Despatches of Gérard*, pp. 538, 610–11. The arrangements apparently did not provide sufficient security; the loan was not subscribed.

5. JA arrived in Nantes on Friday, March 12, and recorded having seen JW; see Butterfield, *John Adams Diary*, II, 356. BF's letter of the 8th has not been found.

eral Gentlemen of this place. We went together on Sunday to Painbeuf, & passed two agreeable Days in seeing all the River and places on the Borders of it could afford us.— Yesterday morning he set out for Brest.

M de Fontevieux went passenger in the Ship Duchesse de Grammont which arrived at Portsmouth in new England last Summer, I have not heard anything of him since, his Friends may however be sure that (unless some personal accident happened to him) he is in america.[6]

When your leisure will permit I shall be glad of a Line relative to the Complexion of affairs, so far only as is *discreet* in me to ask, & in you to communicate.

Mr de Montieu now wants me to go in the Franklin Frigate of 36 Guns & to take her & one or two others to my address. I don't know what to determine, all that know me advise my Stay because (as they seem to think) Congress will order a return of my public affairs.— For my own Part, I have no great expectations, but I want to hear once more from america before I decide.

I have already [*torn:* written] to you about the general Run of my orders.—

I am ever with the greatest Respect Your dutifull & affectionate Kinsman JONA WILLIAMS J

I have shewn my Letter to Mr Lee (while here) to most of the Americans about to depart.[7] I thought this a duty I owed to my Character, for Lee would otherwise have said that I feared an Examination.

Addressed: a monsieur / Monsieur Franklin / Ministre Plenipotentiaire / des Etats Unis—/ en son Hotel a / Passy prés Paris

Notation: Jona Williams Mar. 18. 79—(Prie)

6. Jean-Baptiste-Georges, chevalier de Fontevieux, a nephew of the duchesse de Deux-Ponts, had gone to America as a volunteer in the army in the spring of 1778: XXV, 314n. The duchesse had been inquiring after him: XXVII, 274; XXVIII, 539.

7. JW's letter of March 8, which he had mentioned to BF on March 9 and 10, above.

From Stephen Lee

ALS: American Philosophical Society

Honoured Sir [before March 19, 1779][8]

The Brave Assistance most Wisely given by you, to Set the Gallant Americans at Liberty, Emboldens me a poor prisoner of War, to beseech your protection, and Aid, in gaining me my freedom; I have many friends in America, Defending their Rights, and Priviledges, and as my Wish and Intention was, the first Conveyance to go to them friends, I now Humbly beg your Honours Assistance in forwarding my Intention, which if I am so happy, as to Obtain I shall behave like a true American—

I am from the Province of Munster in Ireland. Ambition Lead me to Travel, having a beloved Brother who resides in Jamaica, whom I was determin'd to Visit, therefore Traveled to the City of Dublin, and Embarked on board the Eliza Letter of Marque Bound to Jamaica, with a heart Glowing with Expectation, of my soon seeing that dear Brother, (but Alas) the Brest fleet, frustrated all my hopes, for on the 6th. morning of Our Sailing was taken, and Brought into Brest—[9]

Being now in the 21st. year of my Age and having experienced better days, and better fortune, Humbly beseeches your Honour to take Compassion on my Sufferings and release a Guiltless Prisoner and Grant him his request, which shall always with Gratitude be Acknowledged by a Distressed Young Gentleman— Stephen Lee—

If these Uncouth Lines meet with Success, (which I am in hope they will from the Noble Character your Honour Support) By directing to the Governor of Dinan, and mentioning my Name and the ship I was on Board of It will be duly Attended to, I have Obtain'd Admittance in the Hospital where I am at present not, Confined by Sickness, but waiting for a

8. BF arranged for the young Irishman to enter on board the *Bonhomme Richard* on this date as secretary to John Paul Jones: Lee to BF, Feb. 1, 1780 (APS). He is listed on the ships's roster as "Stephen Lee Captains Clark." John S. Barnes, ed., *The Logs of the Serapis-Alliance-Ariel under the Command of John Paul Jones 1779–1780* (New York, 1911), p. 4.

9. The *Eliza,* 18, was captured in early November, 1778: *Courier de l'Europe* for Nov. 6 (IV [1778], 296).

Letter from my father having lost my Little all whereby I was rendered unable to afford a Parole which Was Offered me—

Addressed: To / John Franklin Esqr.—/ Ambassader from the United / States of America at the Court / of France—/ Paris—

Notation: Stephen Lee

To Nathan Blodget

Copy:[1] Library of Congress

Sir Passy Mar 19 1779

I lately received yours of the 3d inst. I conceive that it is with the Capt. alone to give his Officers Leave of Absence; and that If I had such a Power it would be very improper for me to exercise it, especially at this Distance, unacquainted as I must be with the Persons & Circumstances. For it might be attended with great Inconveniencies to the Service & would weaken that Subordination which is necessary to good Government in the Ship.[2] I have the Honor to be &c

Nathan. Blodget

To ——— Durif de Cazaneuve[3]

Copy:[4] Library of Congress

Sir Passy March 19 1779

It wou'd be a Pleasure to me if I could comply with your Request, and every other of the same Nature; But the great

1. This page of BF's copy book, containing letters of March 19 to Cazaneuve and March 20 to Sartine, in addition to the present letter, has been struck through. The actual letters, however, may well have been sent; see our annotation of BF to Sartine, March 20.

2. There is no record of a response by Blodget; he retained his position as the *Alliance*'s purser, signing in that capacity a certificate of *c.* Oct. 22, 1779, given by the ship's officers to Capt. Landais (University of Pa. Library).

3. A former ship captain and British prisoner, who had wished BF to advance him money on a disputed bill of exchange: XXVIII, 581–2.

4. Like the one to Blodget, immediately above, this letter was lined through.

Excess of Demands upon me for Advances of Money, above the Supplies I receive obliges me to refuse all that are not of absolute Necessity. As M. Adams is now at Nantes, who probably is acquainted with you, I imagine he has been good enough to furnish you. I am, Sir, y. m. o. h. S. BF

M. Cazenauve

To Daniel-Marc-Antoine Chardon[5]

Copy:[6] Library of Congress

Monsieur, Passy ce 19. Mars 1779.

J'ai lû avec Admiration votre requisitoire sur le Proces du Capitaine Mc Neil.[7] Heureux sont les Rois qui ont des Magistrats aussi scavants et aussi habiles que vous, Monsieur, pour eclairer leur justice. J'en sens tout le Bonheur pour la Nation Americaine que j ai l'honneur de representer en cette Cour: elle sçaura Monsieur qu'elle y est traittée en Frere, et que vous l'y deffendez en Ami. Agréez l'hommage de ma Reconnoissance et les Sentiments distingués avec les quels j ai L'honneur d'etre Monsieur, Votre tres humble et tres obeissant Serviteur,

B.F.

A Monsr. Chardon Mtre Des Requetes.

To Bernard Pées

Copy: Library of Congress

Sir Passy March 19 1779

I received yours with the Paper Money inclosed, (mostly of Georgia) which you desire me to change for you, abating for

5. Chardon (1731–1805), a former correspondent of Voltaire, was presently both *procureur général* of the *conseil des finances pour les prises en mer* and head of the *comité des pêches: DBF.*

6. In WTF's hand.

7. Ultimate jurisdiction over the case of McNeill's prize, the *Isabelle,* rested with the *conseil royal des finances,* which met directly with the king; see Vergennes to BF, March 12. It finally reached a decision on June 15. Two days later Chardon wrote BF that the council had ruled in McNeill's favor. Chardon himself was drawing up the decree, which he expected to present in a few days for Sartine's signature. APS.

the Difference of exchange.[8] As the value of that Money has been very variable, and I am totally ignorant of its present Situation, my appearing to set a certain Value on it here, by exchanging it at a particular Rate, might be attended with great Inconveniencies. I am therefore obliged to return it to you, as I do inclosed. You will easily find at Nantes Some Person going to America who will give you the worth of it. I am, Sir &c

M. Bernard Pees

To Schweighauser

Copy: Library of Congress

Sir

Passy March 19 1779

I have just received your favour of the 16 inst.[9] I think it right that those poor Prisoners who want necessary Clothing shou'd be supply'd. Humanity requires it.

I send you herewith Copies of several Letters written to Capt. Landais by which you will see that he has for some Time had the most positive Orders from me to take your Directions and make the greatest possible Dispatch in refitting his Ship, and that I have also sent the Order for taking his Mutineers off his Hands; So that nothing remains with me to do towards his Dispatch. I hope Mr. Adams's Going to him will have the good Effect you mention.

As to the Order of Goods from the navy Board,[1] Since Capt. Landais cannot take the Goods, and we have now no other Opportunity of sending them, it seems, as you say, needless to think more of them at Present.

I cannot Judge of any of the Art. that they are more necessary than the Rest, and so can give no Advice about them. It will be proper to keep the Invoice by you, that if hereafter we shou'd be in a situation to send those Goods, it may be done.

8. Pées's letter, dated March 12, was written from Nantes and recounted his story. A native of St. Pierre, Martinique, he had twice been captured by the British. The money which he entrusted BF to exchange was the sole resource he possessed to rejoin his wife and children. APS.

9. Missing.

1. Also discussed in BF's letter of March 11 to Schweighauser.

The Slops required by the Purser seem to be necessary. I have the Honor to be, Sir, your most o. h. S. BF.

P.S. I hereby desire you will suspend the Action against M. Peltier till farther Order.[2]

M. Schweighauser

To Jonathan Williams, Jr.

LS: Dartmouth College Library; copy: Library of Congress

Dear Nephew, Passy, March 19. 1779.

In your receipts for M. Monthieu's Copper there is mention made of *Copper Ore.* Explain this to me: For as we bought no Copper Ore of him and as it is not so valuable as Copper, it ought not to be given us instead of Copper.

Mr Lee has yet sent me no Ansr—to mine relating to your Accounts.[3] Let me know whether the Reference is accepted by the Referrees, and whether it goes on. I send you three Original Papers that may be of use to you, as they shew Mr Lee's great Skill in Accounts and Ability in objecting them. The *first* is a Proposition Mr Monthieu made to *obtain* a Contract. The *second* is the Contract actually made, differing from the Proposition. The *third* is Mr Lee's *Report;* wherein he took Mr Monthieu's Proposition of a Contract, to be an *Account of Charge* for the Execution of it; and comparing it with the Contract, he charges all the Differences he finds, as so many Errors in M. Monthieus Acct.[4] For Instance, M. Monthieu *proposed* to make 10,000 Suits; we agreed with him only for 6,000. Here Mr. Lee

2. For this action see BF's March 15 letter to Beaumarchais.

3. Lee's answer had been written on the 16th; see above.

4. The first two enclosures must have been the documents dated June 6 and Aug. 6, 1777, which appeared in vol. 24. There we published in full the earlier one, which BF here calls a "proposition," as the first contract with Montieu; see pp. 123–6. The second document, described on p. 123n, was evidently the only binding contract with the French merchant.

Arthur Lee, in his "report" (the third enclosure), quoted from the Aug. 6 contract and, as BF says, did compare its figures to those presented in the June 6 document. It would appear that BF did not see this report, dated

finds an *overcharge* of 4000 Suits. M. Monthieu proposed we should give him 38 Livres per Suit; we agreed for 37. Here Mr Lee finds an Overcharge of 10,000 Livres: And so of the Rest: When in fact M. Monthieu in his real Account had charged exactly according to the Agreement. You must take good Care of these Papers, say nothing how you came by them, and return them to me safely. I send you enclosed the Proposals of a Tin plate Manufacturer, which may some time or other be of use to you.

I shall dispose of your Letter to M. Lee as you desire. I would advise your avoiding the Publication you mention.

Explain to me what is meant in your Postscript, by *the Zeal of the best of them* &ca.[5]

I send an Order this Day to suspend the Action against Mr. Peltier. But surely he acted very irregularly to sell a Cargo consign'd to us, without our Order, and give the Produce to another. We ourselves never had any Dealings with Mr Beaumarchais, and he has never produced any Account to us, but says the States owe him a great deal of Money. Upon his Word only we gave him up the Cargo of the Amphitrite: He promised then to give us an Account, but has never done it: And now by means of M. Peltier he has seized another Cargo. I imagine there is no doubt but Mr Peltier would be obliged to pay us the Money, if the Action were continued. And methinks every Man who makes a Demand ought to deliver an Acct. For my own Part, I imagine[6] our Country has been really much obliged to Mr Beaumarchais; and it is probable that Mr Deane concerted with him several large Operations, for which he is not yet paid. They were before my Arrival and therefore I was not privy to them. Had I been alone when the Action was commenced perhaps I should have thought of some

Sept. 27, 1778, and entitled "Observations on M Montieu's Acct." (*Lee Family Papers,* reel 5, frames 342–3, 349–50), until his recent probe into Lee's endorsements on JW's accounts.

5. See JW's letter of March 10.

6. The MS is torn, and "imagine our" and "obliged to" have been supplied from the copy.

milder Proceeding; making Allowance for Mr B's not being bred a Merchant, But I think you cannot well justify Mr Peltier. I am ever Your affectionate Uncle B FRANKLIN

Jona. Williams Esqr—

Notation: Paris B. Franklin March. 19. 1779 Recd March 23. 1779 Answered March 23. 1779

From Arthur Lee

LS:[7] American Philosophical Society; copy and transcript: National Archives

Sir. Paris. March. 19th. 1779.

I receivd the letter you did me the honor to write me on the 13th. Relative to the few papers of our late joint Commission remaining in my hands. They are confounded among a multitude of other papers. I will examine the whole soon, and if I find any that relate to public Accounts remaining unpaid (which I do not believe I shall) I will inform you of it that Copies may be taken of them.

You are pleasd to say—that Mr. Adams gave you the papers unaskd. Mr. Adams gave you the general papers which no way related to him in particular, on your promise that you woud have them arranged and kept in order. Mr. Adams was not a calumniated person, nor were the papers he deliverd to you necessary to justify him, & prove the wickedness of his Accuser. In circumstances so totally different, I cannot imagine, Sir, that you can think we shoud act the same. Your pressing so earnestly to get from me a few original papers, which you only conjecture may be in some shape or other useful to you, after I have informd you, that they are absolutely necessary to my Vendication from an Impeachment, that touches even my Life, & honor, gives me great uneasiness. Whether you are concernd or not, in the Accusations, it is equally necessary for me to refute them. And I am sure, Sir, you know that Originals are better evidence than Copies, however authenticated.

7. In the hand of Lee's secretary Hezekiah Ford (XXVI, 685n); the copy is in Ludwell Lee's hand.

On the Contrary, Copies are as adequate to the purpose you mention as originals, &, I am most ready to give you Copies seald & authenticated of all, or any of the papers in my hands, as you may command.

I beg, Sir, that you will have the goodness to believe that when I give my reasons for my Conduct, I do not mean to enter into, or occasion, a dispute.

I have the honor to be with great respect. Sir Your Most obedt. Hble Servt. ARTHUR LEE

Hon. Dr. B. Franklin. M. Plenipotentiary.—

To Sartine

Copy:[8] Library of Congress

Monsieur A Passy Le 20 Mars 1779

Je prends la Liberté d'introduire aupres de votre Excellence le Commodore Gillon de la Caroline Meridionale. Cet Etat l'envoie en France pour y negocier une Affaire tres Importante.[9] Il desireroit soumettre quelques Propositions aux Lumieres de votre Excellence, & je me flatte qu'elle voudra bien lui accorder une Audience favorable. J'ai L'honneur d'etre avec beaucoup de Respect Monsieur de votre Excellence Le t. h. e. t. o. S. BF.

His Excy. M. de Sartine

From Madame Brillon

AL: American Philosophical Society

ce samedi 20 mars [1779]

J'envoye sçavoir de vos nouvélles mon bon papa, et vous demandér si vous viendrés ce soir prendre le thé je n'appuyerés pas sur le plaisir que vous nous ferés de peur de gesnér votre volonté; mais je vous observerés que vous trouverés un grand fauteuil, un tabourét pour reposér vos piéds; qu'il faudra venir

8. A line is drawn through this copy, found in BF's letterbook, but the letter must have been sent, as Sartine acknowledged it on March 22.

9. Alexander Gillon, Commodore of the S.C. Navy, had been sent to Europe to obtain three warships: XXVII, 47n. He arrived at Brest on Jan. 25: XXVIII, 423.

avéc vos souliérs de goutte, que nous n'aurons point d'étrangérs, que vous aurés de la musique, des échécs et de l'amitié tant que vous en voudrés:

Addressed: A Monsieur / Monsieur Franklin / [*in a different hand:*] a Passy

From Gioanni de Bernardi with Franklin's Note for a Reply

ALS: American Philosophical Society

⟨Turin, March 20, 1779, in Italian: The reputation acquired throughout Europe by the glorious thirteen American colonies, their success and wise legislation, have aroused in me a desire to see this new republic with my own eyes and offer it my services as a jurist. The best way I can think to accomplish this is to turn to you. I realize that you know nothing about my qualifications, but I trust in your acumen and your kindness. Should you give me some encouragement, I shall send you my credentials. I am a twenty-four-year-old lawyer and citizen of Milan, currently living in Turin.[1]⟩

Endorsed:[2] Thank the Gentleman for his Good will and Offers of Service to America in qualité of Jurisconsulte but that our Laws and Language being different from those he is acquainted with, I can neither advise nor encourage him to go thither—

1. The young lawyer sent an undated letter, in the same vein, the following year (when he gave his age as twenty-five). Library of Congress.

2. The actual reply, based on BF's note, was dated April 1. A copy in French is at the Library of Congress.

From the Duchesse de Deux-Ponts[3]

ALS: American Philosophical Society

20 Mars [1779]

Je Nait qun instent Mon respectable amis pour vous envoyér ce petit Memoir quon Ma bien priez de Vous recomandér[4] et pour Vous renouveller le plus tendre et le plus fidel homage de Mon Coeur

FORBACH DOUAIRIERE
DU DUC DE DEUXPONTS

Je part dans Le Moment pour Versaille dous je ne reviendres que pour Loger dans ma Nouvelle Maison ous jespere bien exelant home que vous me gagnerés quelques partie dechecs

Addressed in another hand: A Monsieur / Monsieur le Dr Franklin / Ministre Plenipotentiare / des Etats Unis de L'Amerique / a Passy

From Lafayette

ALS: American Philosophical Society

Dear Sir Paris Saturday Evening [March 20, 1779][5]

I am just Coming from Versailles where I went à hunting with the king, and I Do take this first opportunity of inquiring

3. Marianne Camasse, comtesse de Forbach (XXV, 313n), widow of the duc de Deux-Ponts, was a mutual friend of BF and the chevalier de Kéralio, the military inspector.

4. The "petit Memoir" must be that of the baron de Ried, on whose behalf BF had already received a recommendation the previous fall: XXVII, 104. In the present memoir the baron writes that he has a good knowledge of forges and the manufacture of tools, as well as firearms, and he offers to procure for America the best workmen in these activities. The comtesse adds to his statement that the man has received a good education, is strong in mathematics, speaks many languages, draws and paints admirably, and is unhappy with the inaction he now endures. He has the air of a robust man, about forty years old. APS.

Kéralio wrote WTF on April 12, gently inquiring into the status of the memoir in favor of the baron. Would BF be so kind as to make "une petite réponse ostensible qui prouve que la commission a été faite?" APS.

5. Possibly March 27, but more likely the 20th; Lafayette here requests a meeting for the following Monday, and we know BF and Lafayette did meet on Monday the 22nd: Idzerda, *Lafayette Papers,* II, 244; our annotation of BF to Lafayette, March 22, below.

for the state of your health— I hope you are free by this time from your troublesome Gout— I make no doubt but that you knew last Night of the Senegal being taken by our troops—[6] that Advantage I think is interesting[7] for the Allied powers, and will Most Certainly excite disputes among the good people of Both houses in London— I Remember I heard Complaints among the Southern Gentlemen of America about the Senegal being in the enemy's hands and preventing the Nigrò trade for that part of the United States—So that I Believe our Conquest will be pleasing to them and I wish to know your opinion Concerning that affair— there is An important one I want to Communicate to Your Excellency and I schall beg the favor of a Meeting at Passy Monday Morning where we Might Speack without disturbance— it is Relating to some ideas of ours we had Agreed upon in our last interview, and I wish it to be the Same with our Ministers.

With the highest Respect and tenderst affection I schall ever be My dear Sir Your excellency's Most obedient humble Servant LAFAYETTE

Addressed: To / his Excellency Benjamin Franklin / Esq. plenip. Minister of the Unit. / States of America at the Court / of Versailles / At Passy / the m de lafayette

Notation: Lafayette 79—

From Leveux

ALS: American Philosophical Society

Sir Calais March 20th 1779.

I have had the honour of writing to you the 8th of this month.[8] Since that time I have taken proper informations about the americans detained here as prisoners. Here inclosed

6. The March 30th issue of the *Courier de l'Europe* (v [1779], 201–2) reported the capture of the main British fort at Senegal on Jan. 31 by French troops commanded by the duc de Lauzun. The accompanying French naval squadron then proceeded to the West Indies: Dull, *French Navy,* pp. 125, 159n. Vergennes reported the news to Ambassador Montmorin in Spain on March 22 (AAE).

7. He first wrote "obvious".

8. Missing.

you will find a proper Note of their names, the places they are born in, the Ships they was taken upon & how they came to be in the English Service.[9] The Commissaire de la Marine[1] has sent such a Note to the Ministre de la Marine & as asked his orders about it. I believe those people are true americans, by their saying & by the other people saying. If you will ask for an order for them to be set at Liberty & send it to me I will make a proper use of it. I will glad to know, if I am to give those people any money & how much, for they are quite Naked.

As to Mr Rousseaux which has wrote to you;[2] such person is not to be found here & there is nobody of this name, so that I am not able to give you the wanted information on him.

I remain with Due respects Sir Your most obedient & very humble Servant
JES LEVEUX

From Woestyn frères[3]

ALS: American Philosophical Society

Son excéllence, Dunkerque Le 20 Mars 1779./.

Les vœux que toutte la france forme pour l'heureux accomplissement des soins qui vous occupent et le desir qui nous anime de contribuer en notre particulier et par nos foibles moiens à reduire nos énnemis Communs, nous à determiné de faire construire au havre de grace, une frégatte pour la Course de 24 canons de 8 *lb.* de balle et de Suplier Son Excéllence de nous accorder la faveur de le baptiser Sous son nom *Le franklin.* Ce nom cheri & répetté Continuellement dans le cœur des Francois, nous presage d'avance, le plus heureux avenir, et nous assure une double confiance de la part des personnes qui inclineront de sÿ intéresser, Il nous réste le 1/3. à remplir: Notre satisfaction Seroit Complette, si votre Excéllence daigneroit ÿ prendre un interest quel qu'il soit, nous Serons au comble de nos vœux. Nous prénons en Conséquence la con-

9. The enclosure is missing. BF had requested the information on March 1.

1. D'Anglemont, *ordonnateur* for Dunkirk and Calais. His correspondence with Sartine is in the Archives de la Marine, B³DCLX.

2. See BF's letter of the 1st.

3. The firm is listed in the *Almanach des marchands,* p. 193.

fiance de lui adresser inclus une de nos police pour lui faire connoittre la nature de cét armément;[4] nous nous règarderions doublément heureux Si independament du service que nous attendons de son Excéllence pour la grace que nous lui démandons, d'accorder son nom à ce Corsaire, elle voulut bien aussi proposer aux personnes qui ont le bonheur de l'approcher et de meriter sa confiance, d'y prendre quelque intérest, Ce seroit un grand rélief pour notre entréprise et qui accellereroit d'autant plutot son èxpedition.

Nous sommes encore occuppés à une autre éxpedition que nous faisons remplir à Marseille d'un Navire marchand de 180. tonneaux déstiné pour l'amerique Septentrionalle. Nous n'avons pas eté autrement heureux Jusqu'a present dans nos opérations avec le Continent, mais cela ne nous rébutte pas, et nous osons tout attendre de celle dont nous nous occupons aujourdhui, par les précautions redoublés et les moiens que nous nous sommes Procurés pour des expèditions masquées; on n'acquiert des connoissances que par l'experience, nous croions pouvoir nous flatter de conduire Cette entréprise à une heureuse fin. Nous prendrons la confiance de faire part en son tems à son éxcéllence, de son issû.

Dans l'ésperance d'une réponce favorable rélativement à notre Corsaire, Nous sommes avec le plus profond réspéct de son Excéllence Les très humbles et très obeissants Serviteurs

WOESTŸN FRERES[5]

Notation: Woestyn frs. 20. Mars 1779.

4. This printed three-page document provided information about the proposed crew (two hundred men), the launching date (June), and the time of the first cruise (August), as well as the estimated cost (about 210,000 *l.t.*) and financial modalities for the would-be backers. The ship was not the same *Franklin* as that mentioned in JW's letter of March 18.

5. Not hearing from BF, the firm sent a second request, couched in more or less the same terms, on April 16. On April 20, BF responded that he was not willing to participate in their scheme; see below. Not to be discouraged, they wrote again on April 25 to say that they would be content with only the use of his name, which was bound to stimulate financial participation in this venture. Backed up by Le Roy's plea in their favor, published under May 4, they addressed BF once again on May 11 and were rewarded by his positive letter of May 17, below. All three of the firm's follow-up letters are at the APS.

Edward Bancroft to William Temple Franklin

ALS: American Philosophical Society

Dr. Sir Chaillot 20th. March. 1779

Mrs. Bousie whose Husband is in London,[6] has sent to desire me to apply to Dr. Franklin for a Passport for a Vessell called the London Packet Capt Mariton of 70 Tons Burthen, with 6 men, bound from Calais to London. It seems the French & English Governments have consented to Let this Vessel carry a cargo of French Wines from Calais to England, & Mr. Sartine has given her a Passport, but to be quite safe They also want one from the American Minister. How far the Doctr. properly can or may chuse to Comply with this application I do not Know,[7] but beg you will be so Kind as to mention it & inform me of his Answer by the Bearer. I am Dr. Sir your most Obedt. Humble Servant EDWD. BANCROFT

Addressed: Monsieur / Monsr. Franklin Fils / a Passy

To David Hartley

LS:[8] M.H. Venables, Bristol, England (1976); copy and transcript: Library of Congress

Dear Sir, Passy, March 21. 1779.

I received duly yours of the 2d Inst. I am sorry you have had so much Trouble in the Affair of the Prisoners. You have

6. The husband is William Bousie (Bousic?), a merchant who supplied Silas Deane with 294 *l.t.* of wine between January and April, 1778: Deane to Bousie, APS. He also served as a cover for the British agent Isaac Van Zandt (alias George Lupton [XXV, 180n]) to receive mail in Paris: Stevens, *Facsimiles,* II, no. 179, p. 6. An unsigned note dated only "Saturday" links Bousie with some London acquaintances of BF. A Mr. Dumont, who had written BF in 1777 (XXIV, 61), carried a letter (now missing) and brought greetings from a Mr. Sargent and a Mr. Chambers. The former must have been BF's old friend John Sargent, and the latter his partner in the merchant firm of Sargent, Chambers, and Co.: VII, 322; XIII, 295.

7. The commissioners had granted such passports immediately at Sartine's request (XXVIII, 153, 174–5, 180), but BF apparently here proved more cautious; see Bancroft's next letter to WTF, printed under March 21.

8. In WTF's hand.

been deceived as well as we. No Cartel Ship has yet appear'd. And it is now evident that the Delays have been of Design, to give more Opportunity of seducing the Men by Promises and Hardships, to seek their Liberty in engaging against their Country. For we learn from those who have escaped, that there are Persons continually employed in cajoling & menacing them, representing to them that we neglect them, that your Government is willing to exchange them, and that it is our Fault it is not done:[9] That all the News from America is bad on their Side; we shall be conquer'd and they will be hang'd, if they do not accept the gracious Offer of being Pardon'd on Condition of serving the King, &c. A great Part of your Prisoners have been kept these Six Months on board a Ship in Brest Road, ready to be delivered; where I am afraid they were not so comfortably accommodated as they might have been in the french Prisons. They are now order'd on Shore.[1] Dr Bancroft has received your Letter here.[2] He did not go to Calais.

Knowing how earnestly and constantly you wish for Peace, I cannot end a Letter to you without dropping a Word on that Subject, to mark that my Wishes are still in Unison with yours. After the Barbarities your Nation has exercis'd against us, I am almost ashamed to own that I feel sometimes for her Misfortunes & her Insanities. Your Veins are open, and your best Blood continually running. You have now got a little Army into Georgia, and are triumphing in that Success. Do you expect ever to see that Army again?[3] I know not what Genl Lincoln or Genl. Thomson may be able to effect against

9. See, for example, XXVII, 491–2.

1. For the orders concerning English prisoners on the *Patience* see BF to Sartine, March 2; Sartine to BF, March 7; and BF to Schweighauser, March 11.

2. Dated March 2 (Library of Congress). See XXVIII, 588n.

3. In a letter to Lord North of March 31 Hartley quoted the second paragraph of the present letter up to this point. He was using the passage to persuade the English minister that there exists "no ill disposition towards this country in a certain quarter." Library of Congress. For further details about the letter to North see our annotation of Hartley's April 10 letter to BF.

them; but if they stay thro' the Summer in that Climate, there is a certain Genl. Fever that I apprehend will give a good Acct of most of them. Perhaps you comfort your selves that our Loss of Blood is as great as yours. But, as Physicians say, there is a great Difference in the Facility of repairing that Loss, between an old Body and a young one. America adds to her Numbers annually 150,000 Souls. She therefore grows faster than you can diminish her, and will outgrow all the Mischief you can do her.[4] Have you the same Prospects? But it is unnecessary for me to represent to you, or you to me, the Mischiefs each Nation is subjected to by this War; We all see clear enough the Nonsense of continuing it; the Difficulty is where to find Sense enough to put an End to it. Adieu, my Dear Friend & believe me ever, Yours most affectionately

B FRANKLIN

David Hartley Esqr—

To Montieu

Copy: Library of Congress

Sir

Passy March 21 1779

I received the Honor of yours of the 16 inst. and thank you for your kind Congratulations.

I have not Time at present to consider and adjust the Differences in the Accts. about the Copper & Tin. They may easily be settled when we meet, as well as the Advances at Charlestown. I shall immediately accept the Bills you have drawn upon me, except as many as amount to the Sum of £69,455. 2. 7. which sum for the Goods shipt per the Therese has been long Since paid, and which you have now charged again by Mistake. With great Regard I have the Honor to be Sir &c

M. Monthieu.

4. BF had warned the British in 1751 that the mother country could never keep pace with the growth of America's population, which would double itself every twenty years. See his "Observations Concerning the Increase of Mankind," IV, 225–34. See also his remarks after the British losses at Bunker Hill: XXII, 218.

From William Gardner and Joseph Bailey

ALS:[5] American Philosophical Society

Bayone march the 21 1779

Sur I make bold of being an american prisoner I make to present this humble pretition to your honour hopeing that your honour Will Lend a lissening Ear to my Calamity As I am Now In a lonesome prisoner Being Captivated by a french privateere In an English Bottom And to Let you know further my Name Is William Gardner Born upon the Iseland of Nantucket Sailed from there for South Carolina and from there In a briggenteene bound for Bourdox belonging to may & Crips Consind to one mr Rainbo In Bourdox[6] But unhappily falling In With the kings ship the mars Wass taken on the Ninetenth of october 1777[7] Jest In Sight of Cape finister Carried Into porthmouth and Condemd I was mate of the said vessel and Not haveing arms wass forsd on bord a man of War Where I continued until Last march When one meader An american Liveing In London[8] hove a partision to the Lords of Admiralty for myselfe and six prisoners more for to Goe In the Whale feshery Whitch being Granted we proseaded and fisht In the mouth of the streights of Gebralter and A soone as we ha Got money for our support We mad an atempt to Git Into the Spanish Lines but unfortunately my self and one more Wass taken up and sent back to England In Ions When the above Capt John meader heard of hove In another protion and Could be Got Clear under No other head but to prosead In the fishery again they or to be kept as there own subiects as being once protected by the English flag We Now Came out agien

5. In the hand of Gardner, who signed for Bailey as well.

6. The Charleston, S.C., mercantile house of Florian C. May and John Splatt Cripps suffered heavy losses in the 1778 fire that devastated that city: *S.C. Hist. and Geneal. Mag.,* LXIV (1963), 25–6; I (1900), 32n. The Bordeaux firm of Reculès de Basmarein & Raimbaux, who had an office in Charleston, had sent sixty ships to America in eighteen months, but was now bankrupt: XXVI, 472–3, XXVIII, 550.

7. On Oct. 25 news was received at the Admiralty Office that the *Mars* had captured the American brig *Charming Betsey* bound from Charleston to Bordeaux with a cargo of rice and oak staves: *Gent. Mag.,* XLVII (1777), 506.

8. For John Meader, another Nantucket whaleman, see XXVII, 515n, 660n.

and are taken and Imprisond hear the other man that Is hear In the same Condition With my selfe Is Joseph bailey there Likewise Is one Joseph tailer belongin to philadelphia taken In anther vessel I therefore Desire your honor Will Doe your Indeavour to take us out of prison and Convey us Where we may Git on bord of Some Continental vessel or merchant vessel so as to Goe to our one Country once more Whitch I make no Doupt but your honour Can Doe as Never being In arms against the Country I shall send you a tru Coppy of my Discharge on the tother side the paper So I shall Conclude hopeing that your honour Will Doe me all the service In your power And Deliver me out of this Lonesome prison As soone posible I shall Ever hold my selfe Your humble servant

William Gardner
Joseph Bailey[9]

A tru Coppy of my Discharge

These are to sertify the prinsible officers and Commsoners of his maiestyes Navy that William Gard an american prisoner on board of His maiestyes Ship Lenox Was this Day Dischargd and set free Be order of their Lords Commisoners of the Admiralty Given under my hand on bord the Lenox at Spithead 20th January 1779 Thomas Walton Lieute.[1]

Addressed: His Excellency—Franklin / for the United States of / America & / residing at / Paris

9. The pair wrote again on April 25, still from Bayonne. This time the writer was Bailey, who repeated the story of their capture. BF endorsed the letter, "Prisoners." APS.

Bailey subsequently petitioned John Bondfield; see Bondfield's letter of May 22.

1. Another copy of the discharge, in Gardner's hand, is at the APS. In that copy, his last name is spelled out in full.

From the Chevalier de Kéralio[2]

ALS: American Philosophical Society

Monsieur à L'Ecole Rle. mre. 21e. mars 1779.

Made. la comtesse de Forbach m'a chargé de vous faire passer la copie ci-jointe de la Lettre qu'elle a reçue de M. Le Marquis de la fayette,[3] et de vous assurer en même temps de toute son amitié. Je lui avois mandé que vous l'aimiés—toujours beaucoup; elle vous répond qu'elle en est tres flattée, qu'elle y est plus Sensible que personne au Monde, mais cela ne lui suffit pas, elle veut que vous le Lui écriviés;—autrement elle adoptera la religion de Made. Helvetius qui prétend que vous n'aimés Les gens que quand vous les voyés.[4]

Je vous envoie tout ce que j'ai de Nouvelles. D'après tout ce que je sais, ce que je vois et ce que j'entends, je suis toujours fondé a croire que la déclaration de l'Espagne n'est pas éloignée.

Je n'ai point encore de détails de L'Expédition de M. de Vaudreuil au Sénégal. M. le Duc de Lauzun qui est à Bord du *Fendant* en a appris la nouvelle à M. le Maréchal de Biron son oncle.[5]

Me permettrés vous de vous rappeller que vous m'avés promis une réponse pour Le Prince de Gallitzin.[6]

2. The inspector of the Ecole Royale Militaire, who provided BF with numerous intelligence reports, particularly from French ports: above, March 1. He and BF were both friends of the duchesse de Deux-Ponts; see our annotation of her March 20 letter.

3. A letter of March 5 about his efforts on behalf of the chevalier de Fontevieux (for whom see JW's letter of March 18, above): Idzerda, *Lafayette Papers,* II, 492. The enclosed copy, in Kéralio's hand, is at the APS.

4. Anne-Catherine de Ligniville d'Autricourt Helvétius (XXVI, 429n), widow of the *philosophe,* who was becoming the "aimable rivale" of Mme. Brillon in BF's affections: XXVIII, 315.

5. The marquis de Vaudreuil was the commander of the naval detachment sent to Senegal; the *Fendant,* 74, was one of his two ships of the line: Larousse; Dull, *French Navy,* p. 125. The duc de Lauzun commanded the troops which captured the colony; see Lafayette's letter of March 20. Louis-Antoine de Gontaut, duc de Biron, an elderly *maréchal de France,* was governor of Languedoc, but spent most of his time in Paris: *DBF.*

6. Prince Dmitrii Gallitzin (or in modern usage Golitsyn) was the Russian minister at The Hague (XXIII, 248n). On Jan. 19 Kéralio had forwarded

Rendés toujours justice, je vous en supplie, à la Tendre Vénération avec laquelle je suis, Monsieur Votre tres humble et très obeisst. Serviteur LE CHR. DE KERALIO

Notation: Cheve. de Keralio

From Stephen Sayre

ALS: American Philosophical Society

Sir Copenhagen 21 Mar: 1779

I did myself the honor of writing your Excellency a few Lines upon my return here from Stockholm;[7] expressing my belief, that a freindly disposition prevail'd at that Court, & might be cultivated to advantage: but that I could not, with propriety, risque a communication of my Ideas on this subject, by the common post—

I shall shortly be in Amsterdam—the place of my abode, while there, will be known, by application to Messrs Hopes. I request, earnestly to have the favour of a Letter which may meet me there, communicating your Excellency's opinion on my last, if thought of sufficient Import: but more *particularly on the matter here offer'd*—

In the course of last Summer, I employ'd my time, chiefly in Experiments, to know, & ascertain what shape or model of wood makes the quickest way thro' the water; preserving the shape necessary for Ships: and upon a variety of models, I found, clearly, that the mode, hitherto used in construction, is extremely erroneous. Some Americans, who came from England to carry on the Sperma Cœti whale fishery from hence, were here. And tho' they had their prejudices, as to the method in use, they were thoroughly & decidedly convinced, by various Experiments, that an astonishing improvement might be made; I mean in the Hull of the Ship: but still more as to the rigging—the complex mode of rigging, now in prac-

BF an inquiry of his about electricity: XXVIII, 399. On March 7 Kéralio had urged WTF to remind his grandfather of his promise to communicate his observations on Golitsyn's views (APS).

7. Above, March 10.

tice, when compared to a simple natural one, which I show'd them: struck them all with wonder.

The King's Draughtsman here, Capn Gardner, who knew your Excellency in England, has acknowledged his astonishment on its appearance, and tho' he had done a good deal towards such a simplicity, my Ideas had left him a great way behind. I remember to have mentioned his name to you on a former occasion, & indeed allow'd him the merit (whatever it may be) on this subject. Yet if appeal'd to he will—he must, acknowledge that the model I made surpasses any thing he had conceived.[8] Indeed our acquaintance took place in consequence of my having shown it to another Gentleman here. I mention this that I may not be robb'd of the honor, should the world hereafter come universally into the improvement—

Had your Excellency's answer to my proposition for sending a Ship to America come immediately, one of those Ships, lately built here, would most assuredly have been rigg'd & dispatch'd as hinted at—[9]

But perhaps 'tis best that no such improvement appears in Europe; for upon further contemplation & pursuit of this great Subject, I see not only the certainty of an infinite difference in point of sailing (under all possible circumstances)—not only less necessity for the same number of hands—less expence for outfit—less difficulty in repairs—less inconveniencies in battle &c &c. But, with half the bulk—half the number of guns—& half the number of men: she shall be sure, of victory. I will say more— *She cannot be taken by any Ship now in use, of any burden or denomination whatever—But shall with certainty ruin the first rate Ships in the world, in a very few moments*—nor is there the last probability of losing a single man in the Engagement— She shall not only sail faster, but be a better Sea Boat, in all weathers, & under all circumstances—In short, I can promise the immediate & utter ruin of all the British Navy, or will render it of no use; & this with

8. In his letter of Nov. 7 (XXVIII, 59–62), Sayre described, in terms similar to those he uses about his own ship in the present letter, an unsurpassable ship designed by Gardner (earlier called Gardiner).

9. XXVIII, 59–60, 279, 377–8.

a very few Ships. If then America can rise superior to G. Britain, in naval Strength, by obliging her to construct another I will say, if there is a hope of effecting this; I am confident your Excellency will immediately require some further evidence & communications on this Subject. I have not yet given the world any Instances of *Insanity*, therefore don't suspect me of it till you hear what I have to offer. I can easily make your Exy. perfectly sensible of its practicability. Nothing can be more simple, or decidedly clear. I am exceedingly sorry, that I have open'd myself rather too far, in order to get the approbation of some Gentlemen here: yet I hope nothing will be absolutely put in execution, soon enough to disappoint our reaping the first advantages, from it—

Luckily, I have reserved one capital point, as to ships of war, within my own breast—nor will I hereafter open my thoughts, but on the last occasion—

If your Excellency can put any confidence in my Understanding, you will probably think proper to desire my attendance at Paris: from whence too I can, with more safety, get into America, by a Ship of force: for if the thing is to be adopted, it must be there, & immediate. I ask only to have my expences borne to Paris— I rest all Events on its own merits: and I am sure you will lend your utmost aid, when convinced of its practicability—

If I have no call to come to Paris, I shall sail from Amsterdam to St Eustatia—from thence take a passage for America in the best Ship I may find: or go down to St Croix: there stay with my old acquaintances till a good Opportunity offers—

I feel it somewhat hard to be so long, & so strangely neglected by Congress. For if I am taken Prisoner I may expect to suffer all the miseries of War, perhaps unnoticed. I have been cruelly sacrifised to the Enemies of America: but have hitherto found no countenance from her freinds to encourage such a principle of conduct. I hope the ruin of a certain disagreeable family, which they have brought on their own heads, will leave me the hope of meeting Justice in future. I suppose we have the same Opinion of them. It was with infinite difficulty, that I restrain'd myself from an open rupture with one of them, while at Berlin.[1] I conceive he did us infinite prejudice there, tho' he might have done great, & essential Service. I found myself too weak to support an opposition to him & too delicately circumstanced, even to complain—

If you think the Ideas I have suggested above, too visionary to require my coming to you, I request the favour of a Letter of Recommendation to the Governor of Martineco, or Dominica: for I would go from St Eustatia, for a few days, in order to recover an Estate I had in Dominica. &c &c—

I hear some Report that the French have abandon'd Dominica— I don't beleive it: but pray give me your Opinion, whither you think they would put it under the protection of Sweeden. If so, it would not only gain that Power, but the Island would be, to all purposes of commerce, American—

I am now in Correspondence with the prime Minister of Sweeden, on a Subject somewhat of this nature. Perhaps this question leads to consequences of much more import than you will at first suppose—

If I can do any thing in Holland to promote our Interests, you may confide in me. I shall have such an acquaintance with the Hopes, as to secure their Influence, *if they are not totally anti american.*

I am with real respect & Esteem your Excellency's most obedient & most humble Servant STEPHEN SAYRE

P.S. If any Letters from America—pray convey them to me—

Notation: Stephen Sayee Copenhagen 21. mars 1779

1. Arthur Lee. See Sayre's March 10 letter.

Edward Bancroft to William Temple Franklin

ALS: American Philosophical Society

Dr. Sir [between March 21 and March 24, 1779][2]

I have recd. the inclosed Lettres from Mrs. Bousie respecting the Passport—[3] I have some Knowledge of Mr. Audibert Captain of the Port of Calais, & from his Letter have no doubt of Mr. Sartines having given the Pass port mention'd; however if the Doctor thinks it expedient he can make his Pass port conditional as suggested by Mrs. Bousie.[4] I am Dr. Sir truly Yours

EDWD BANCROFT

Addressed: A Monsieur / Monsr. Franklin / Le Fils / a Passy

To Lafayette

AL (draft): American Philosophical Society; copy:[5] Library of Congress

Dear Sir Passy, March 22. 79[6]

I admire much the Activity of your Genius, and the strong Desire you have of being continually employ'd against our Common Enemy.

2. Between the time Bancroft received Mrs. Bousie's letter and BF's issuance of the passport she wished; see the following notes.

3. Which she had requested Bancroft to procure for her; see his letter of March 20 to WTF. Apparently, BF was reluctant to issue the document until he had seen the passport that Mrs. Bousie claimed Sartine had granted. Bancroft must have written her the next morning because on a Sunday noon, undoubtedly of the 21st, she wrote to thank him for that morning's note. She explained that she could not send him the passport because it had gone directly to the ship's captain at Calais. In lieu of it she produced a letter she had received from Audibert l'aîné, captain of the port of Calais, acknowledging that the passport had arrived. Both of these letters are with BF's papers at the APS; the former bears WTF's notation, "Papers relating to a Pass port granted to a Vessell of Mr. Bousies."

4. For the passport see our annotation to Bancroft's letter printed under March 25.

5. BF made a single correction of a copyist's error in the first sentence, changing "desire" to "admire".

6. This letter was written in conjunction with a meeting that day between Lafayette and BF, which Lafayette described to the comte de Maurepas, the

It is certain that the Coasts of England & Scotland are extreamly open & defenceless. There are also many rich Towns near the Sea, which 4 or 5000 Men, landing unexpectedly, might easily surprize and destroy, or exact from them a heavy Contribution, taking a Part in ready Money and Hostages for the Rest.[7] I should suppose, for Example, that two Millions Sterling, or 48 Millions of Livres might be demanded of Bristol for the Town and Shipping; twelve Millions of Livres from Bath; Forty-eight Millions from Liverpoole; Six Millions from Lancaster, and twelve Millions from Whitehaven.— On the East Side, there are the Towns of NewCastle, Scarborough, Lynn, & Yarmouth;[8] from which very considerable Sums might be exacted: And if among the Troops there were a few Horsemen to make sudden Incursions at some little Distance from the Coast, it would spread Terror to much greater Distances and the whole would occasion Movements & Marches of Troops that must put the Enemy to a prodigious Expence, and harrass them exceedingly.— Their Militia will probably soon be drawn from the different Counties to one or two Places of Encampment; so that little or no Opposition can be made to such a Force, as is abovementioned, in the Places where they may land. But The Practicability of such an Operation, and the Means of facilitating & executing it, military

---

French chief minister (Idzerda, *Lafayette Papers,* II, 244–7). According to Lafayette, BF was enthusiastic about his plan to embark 1,500 French troops to "be sent along the coasts of England into the Irish Channel and be used to harass this area by sudden and unexpected raids." (The plan is described in an earlier letter to Maurepas: *ibid.*, pp. 238–41.) BF would provide Jones's *Duc de Duras* (*Bonhomme Richard*); he was reluctant, however, to suspend the *Alliance*'s departure for America, largely for fear of displeasing JA, who intended to embark on her. Lafayette hoped to change BF's mind. A biographer of Lafayette suggests that the idea for Lafayette's expedition originated from one of Jones's confidants: Louis Gottschalk, *Lafayette and the Close of the American Revolution* (Chicago, 1942), p. 9.

7. Lafayette had told Maurepas, "Contributions from the cities we would deign not to burn would completely pay the expenses of the enterprise": Idzerda, *Lafayette Papers,* II, 239.

8. In a letter of the 26th to Vergennes Lafayette explained his plans in detail and suggested attacks on Liverpool, Whitehaven, Lancaster, and Cork: *ibid.,* pp. 247–50.

People can best judge of. I have not enough of Knowledge in such Matters to presume upon Advising it; and I am so troublesome to the Ministers on other Accounts that I could hardly venture to sollicit it if I were ever so confident of its Success. Much will depend, on a prudent & brave Sea Commander who knows the Coasts, and on a Leader of the Troops who has the Affair at Heart who is naturally active & quick in his Enterprises, of a Disposition proper to conciliate the Goodwill & Affection of both the Corps, & by that Means to prevent or obviate such Misunderstandings as are apt to arise between them, & which are often pernicious to joint Expeditions.— On the whole it may be encouraging to reflect on the many Instances of History, which prove, that in War, Attempts thought to be impossible, do often for that very reason become possible & practicable; because nobody expects them, and no Precautions are taken to guard against them. And those are the kind of Undertakings of which the Success affords the most Glory to the Ministers who plan & to the Officers who execute them.— With the sincerest Esteem & Affection, I have the honour to be Sir &c

M. le Marquis de la Fayette

Letter to M. de la Fayette Mar. 22. 79

To Saint-Lambert

Copy: Library of Congress

a Passy le 22 Mars 1779

Je suis honteux, Monsieur, d'avoir été si longtems sans repondre a la Lettre que vous m'avez fait l'honneur de mécrire au sujet du jeune Homme[9] qui voudroit passer en Amerique. Deux Raisons ont occasionné ce Retard et m'excuseront aupres de vous. La premiere, est un nouvel Accés de Goutte qui ma repris le soir même du jour que j'eus L'honneur de vous voir. La seconde est que je n'avois jamais entendu parler du lieutenant Colonel Maeu ou le Chevalier de Ville-pré. Je n'en ai rien pu decouvrir et je ne connois pas non plus aucun

9. Febvet. See Saint-Lambert's letter, printed under March 1.

Officier au service des Etats Unis qui se dispose a partir pour Boston. S'il en est quelqu'un qui veuille emmener son Neveu avec lui, ma Permission est inutile et je n'ai pas Droit de m'y opposer. Toute l'Amerique est ouverte aux Francois et ceux qui y passent peuvent m[ener] avec eux qui bon leur semble. Je crois cependant devoir vous prevenir, Monsieur, que si le jeune homme auquel vous vous interessez passoit en Amerique dans le Des[sein] de servir dans notre Armée, il se trouveroit desagreable[ment] detrompé a son Arrivée. Touts nos Corps sont plus que complets et d'excellens Officiers sont repassés en Europe faute d'emploi. Mais il me semble quil y a du lou[che] dans cette Affaire et que M. de Tressan n'a pas été bien informé. J'ai l'honneur detre avec l'estime la plus vraie etc.

M. de st. Lambert

From Françoise-Antoinette-Jeanne Langlois du Bouchet, Comtesse Conway[1]

ALS: American Philosophical Society

[*c.* March 22, 1779][2]

Voila mon cher papa le billet que vous m'aviés acordé pour mr mullens[3] je n'en suis pas moins reconnoissante quoiquil n'en ait plus de besoin j'ai mon mari depuis 3 jours ce qui me fait grand plaisir après tant dinquietudes. Je lui ai dit que je vous aimois bien.

Adieu my dear father I am your most and Sincer *daughter*

FE CONWAY

1. This is the first time that the comtesse (XXIII, 582) addresses BF in French. With her husband's return, they had abandoned their plan to settle in the United States and she gave up her attempts to write in English.

2. Dated on the basis of her husband's letter, immediately below.

3. For Thomas Mullens, an aide to Gen. Conway, see XXIV, 397n. Taken by a privateer on his way back to France, he had lost all his belongings. For further details on the episode of the *billet* see BF's letter to the comtesse of March 25.

Mon mari proffitera du premier moment que je lui donnerai pour vous aller voir. Mandés moi si mon billet vous est parvenu.

From Thomas Conway

ALS: American Philosophical Society

Sir 22d March 1779

The inclos'd is from our common friend Mr richard peters.[4] I would have been the Bearer my self were it not for sudden and very pressing occupations. The Little tribulations I have met with are of a private Nature and did not alter my principles or opinion concerning the important cause which I Wish'd to Serve to the Best of my abilities. With Much regard I am, Sir your Excellency's Most obedt servt[5] THO. CONWAY

From Veuve Leleu & Cie.[6]

AL: American Philosophical Society

Ce 22 Mars 1779

MM Veuve Leleu et Coe. ont l'honneur d'adresser a Monsieur franklin Une Lettre qui Vient de leur parvenir par Voye de Londres.

4. In late 1777 Conway had been named inspector general of the continental army while Peters (XXIII, 274n) was named to the reorganized continental board of war headed by Horatio Gates. Conway's "little tribulations" were his resignation and the wounds he received in a duel, both the result of his supposed participation in the so-called "Conway cabal," for which see Freeman, *Washington,* IV, 555–63, 586–611. The enclosure, now missing, may have been Peters' letter of Nov. 4, 1778 (XXVIII, 33–4), recommending its bearer, Col. Mauduit du Plessis, and inquiring about Peters' father, with whom he had lost contact. Conway was still in Philadelphia at that date; five days later he wrote from there to Henry Laurens (National Archives).

5. On the verso of this letter is a sketch of four connected L-shaped figures.

6. Almost certainly the firm in Amiens listed in *Almanach des marchands,* p. 24, as Laleu. An N. Leleu, merchant, had written from that place in 1778 (XXVII, 27).

From James Lenox Napier *et al.*

ALS: American Philosophical Society

Sir Bayonne March 22d. 1779

Encouraged by your Universal Character for Charitable Excelence and humanity, Your love for the good & preservation of mankind in general, but the States of America in particular Permit me in the Names of the Subscribers hereto, to Subplicate Your Excellency, influance and Interest to Enter into the American Service, under whose Sanction & protection they Assure themselves Success, many of them being Natives, and the rest haveing families & Property there, wishing only for an Opportunity to Vendicate their much wronged, Injoured, & Oppress'd. Country.

The Chance of fortune throwing Many of them into the English power, in London, to Avoid the disagreeableness of being impressd Enterd on Board a privateer of London, was taken on the third of Jany Last by the Audatious of Bayonne—

Behold them Noble Sir imploreing for mercy at your feet as to the great daiety of heaven, Incline your ear to their Supplications, the french Court will Never deny the Request of a Nobleman repleat with knowledge, wisdom & understanding—Confirm, Your Greatness & Goodness by their Enlargment & their Posterety, & Country will have reason to Testifie with the Deepest Impression of gratitude your Emeniant & Excelent Goodness Conferd on them & Sir Your Most humble & Most Obedt. Servt. James Lenox Napier[7]

Addressed: To / The Hon: Benj Francklin Esqr / Secretary for America at / Paris

7. On a separate page are the following signatures: Lenox Napier, Jno. Green his Mark, Wm: Gates, Wm Lase, Rich Carnley, John Cannon, Wm Teewater, Elias Clarke, Thomas Morris, Hught Cantrey, Thos Oisant, Cors Fabian, Wm. Bugby, Daniel Thomas, Jno: Vicaroy, James Clegg.

Napier repeated his application on May 28. APS.

From Sartine

Copy: Library of Congress

Versailles 22. mars 1779.

J'ai reçu avec plaisir, Monsieur, le Commodore Gillon de la Caroline meridionale que vous m'avez annoncé[8] et j'espére qu'il aura été content de l'accueil que je lui ai fait.[9] Je serai fort aise de levoir pendant son Sejour ici et de conferer avec lui sur les Objets de sa Mission qui pourront concerner mon Departement.

J'ai l'honneur d'être avec une parfaite Consideration, Monsieur, votre très humble et très obeissant Serviteur—

(signé) De Sartine.

M. Franklin.

From Jacques-Donatien Le Ray de Chaumont

AL: American Philosophical Society

[before March 23, 1779?][1]

L'hotesse de L'hostel de Joui a versailles Rue des Recolets Reclame L'avantage qu'elle a eu de Loger M. franklin chez elle pour le Recevoir et ses Equipages quand il ira faire sa Cour.

C'est unne femme Estimée et Recommandée par les Bureaux de M. de Vergennes.

8. See BF's letter of March 20.

9. Gillon described an interview with Sartine in a June 15 letter to the S.C. congressional delegation. Sartine listened to his proposals and then asked for them in writing. Gillon responded by requesting a French loan or loan guarantee and, above all, the chance to purchase on credit three seaworthy French frigates. Gillon also explained to both BF and Sartine his plan to attack the British in Georgia either with the newly purchased frigates or with a French expeditionary force of three ships of the line, three frigates, two cutters, and six row galleys. Gillon volunteered his services to this force, provided France would sell South Carolina any ships, supplies, and ammunition she captured (a provision to which Sartine objected). "Letters from Commodore Alexander Gillon in 1778 and 1779," *S.C. Gen. and Hist. Mag.*, x (1909), 131–5.

1. The date BF was finally presented at the French court as the first American minister plenipotentiary. See our annotation of an account of the duc de Croÿ's dinner with BF under March 1, above, and, for a description of the presentation, BF to JA, April 3, below.

From Dumas

ALS: American Philosophical Society; AL (draft): Algemeen Rijksarchief

Monsieur, La Haie 23 Mars *1779.*

Mes deux dernieres étoient du 3–9, & du 15 Mars. La derniere étoit partie, quand on m'apporta l'honorée vôtre du 12.

On ne m'a point défendu de vous nommer ceux que l'on croit être de faux amis: c'est ma propre délicatesse qui m'a retenu. Je ne voudrois nuire à personne, encore moins à ceux qui n'ont eu que de bons procédés pour moi. Mais puisque vous souhaittez que je parle plus clair, je vous dirai, Monsieur, qu'on m'a averti, que les secrets ni les affaires des Américains ne devroient point être confiés au Chev. G. & que c'est le sentiment de vos amis en France les plus intimes, qui se défient très-fort de lui.[2] Par contre, on me dit constamment du bien de son frere, qui réside toujours en france. En général on se défie de toutes les *maisons Genevoises* établies tant en France qu'à Amsterdam. Ils sont tous, dit-on, partisans secrets de l'Angleterre, & trop interessés dans le Négoce des fonds Anglois, pour ne pas leur sacrifier l'Amérique s'ils pouvoient. Les Germany, Girardot, Tourton, Bour, Haller, *&c.&c.*[3] ne sont, dit-on, rien moins, que les amis des Américains, détruisent tant qu'ils peuvent leur crédit, épient & trahissent leurs secrets. Voilà pourquoi l'on a été bien aise de vous lier avec Mr. De Neufville, après avoir fait les perquisitions nécessaires, pour s'assurer qu'il n'étoit en liaison ni correspondance réglée avec aucune des maisons susdites, mais, au contraire, *ennemi déclaré des Anglois, & de leur parti en Hollande.*

2. Georges Grand had been named a chevalier of the Order of Vasa by King Gustavus III of Sweden for his help in the August, 1772, coup d'état which restored Swedish absolutism (a coup also assisted by Vergennes, then French ambassador in Stockholm): Lüthy, *Banque protestante,* II, 614. Dumas' caution may also have been related to BF's warnings not to cast aspersions on Grand: XXVIII, 506.

3. For BF's most recent contacts with the banking firms of Girardot, Haller & Cie. (formerly Germany, Girardot & Cie.) and Tourton & Baur see XXVIII, 32–3, 112n.

Pour revenir au Chev., j'ignore la force & la nature des preuves qu'on peut avoir, pour soupçonner sa fidélité & sa solidité: on m'assure que vous pourrez en apprendre davantage là-dessus de vos meilleurs Amis. Je sai seulement, que ce Colonel Prev——, qui vient d'envahir la Géorgie, est son gendre,[4] qu'il reçoit très familierement dans sa maison un Marchd. Anglois établi à Amsterdam nommé *Rich,* qui est l'Espion de Sir J. Y; qu'il a déjà fait faillite une fois à L——[5] en Suisse, où il étoit Banquier; & l'on dit que, s'il prenoit fantaisie à Mr. H——a de retirer tout de bon ses fonds, comme il en a quelquefois l'idée, il ne resteroit rien à lui ni à Mr. F——x.[6] Il m'a assuré lui-même, qu'il étoit en liaison intime avec le Minre. des affaires étrangeres; que vous-même, Monsieur, n'aviez rien de caché pour lui, & qu'entre autres il lisoit toutes mes Lettres à Passy.

Mr. De N—— ne se pressera pas quant à la souscription; & il a raison: le moment actuel n'est pas favorable. Les mauvaises manoeuvres du Comte d'Estaing, l'invasion de la Géorgie, &, tout récemment, la prise de Pondichery &c. aux grandes Indes, ont effrayé & refroidi les esprits pour un temps.[7] Il ne veut point risquer, comme d'autres ont fait, le crédit de l'Amérique. Mais comme il ne veut pas non plus manquer son coup, il m'assure qu'il prépare dès à présent ses opérations; & j'ai opinion qu'il réussira.

Mr. Sturler, témoin de mon zele ici pour le service non seulement de l'Amérique, mais aussi de la France, m'avoit pressé de lui raconter tout ce que j'avois fait depuis le commencement, & promis de me faire connoître à cet égard aux

4. Maj. Gen. Augustine Prevost, currently commanding British forces in Georgia, was married to Georges Grand's daughter Anne: *DNB* under Sir George Prevost (their son).

5. Lausanne.

6. Jean-Jacques Horneca and Henri Fizeaux were Georges Grand's banking partners: XXVIII, 271n.

7. D'Estaing had failed to dislodge the British from recently captured St. Lucia; see our annotation to St. Lambert's letter, after March 1. The British had also taken Savannah and Pondicherry, the major French trading post in India (*Gaz. de Leyde,* March 23–April 2, 1779).

Ministres, mieux que je ne pensois de l'être, par de petits mémoires qu'il dresseroit. Je ne savois, Monsieur, ni leur contenu, ni qu'il vous en remettroit un, encore moins qu'il insisteroit sur une augmentation de salaire pour moi dans ces circonstances: au contraire, je croyois lui avoir suffisamment fait connoître, avec ma situation, la discrétion que je me suis prescrite à cet égard. J'accepte cependant l'addition des 25 Louis par an, que son zele officieux me procure de votre part, avec d'autant plus de plaisir, qu'elle termine fort à propos, au gré de ma femme, un différent facheux survenu entre elle & moi: je la pressois de se transporter avec son ménage au fond d'une de nos provinces; ce qui la chagrinoit beaucoup, parce que certaine infirmité, & l'éducation de ma fille, lui rendent le séjour de cette ville préferable.[8] Du reste, je limiterai les dépenses comme vous le souhaitez; je ne solliciterai aucune augmentation ultérieure, & attendrai avec résignation les futurs contingents. Quant aux Papiers Anglois & François que j'envoie en Amérique, je ne fais que suivre les ordres du Committé.

J'avoue, Monsieur, que l'Amérique, non plus que la France, n'a guere lieu d'être contente de cette Rep. Permettez-moi seulement de vous faire remarquer, par la conduite de la France-même avec cet Etat, qu'il est important d'y avoir correspondance avec l'opposition, & de la soutenir & encourager tant que nous pourrons: car c'est réellement affoiblir vos ennemis. Quant à moi, si vous jugiez mes services plus utiles auprès de vous, ou par-tout ailleurs qu'ici, disposez-en selon votre gré & sagesse. Je ne plaindrai jamais ma peine ni mon temps, s'ils sont utiles à l'Amérique & à ma petite famille.[9]

Comme la copie du Projet est un peu trop volumineuse

8. For Dumas' wife Maria and his daughter Anna Jacoba (b. 1766) see Schulte Nordholt, *Dutch Republic,* p. 48.

9. At this location Dumas deleted the following paragraph from both the draft and the ALS: "Mr. William Stockton est arrivé ici de Francfort apres avoir été là & à Vienne Secretaire de Mr. W. Lee. Son intention est d'attendre ici réponse à la Lettre qu'il vous a ecrite de Francfort, pour savoir s'il s'arrêtera plus longtemps en Europe, ou si & par quelle voie(?) il pourra retourner en Amérique." The letter in question is Stockton's of March 7.

pour l'envoyer par la Poste, que cette affaire ne presse pas actuellement, & que je dois encore la montrer à notre Ami, qui a d'autres affaires plus pressantes pour tout le reste de ce mois, je la laisse reposer, pour le présent, dans mon pupitre.[1]

J'espere, Monsieur, d'apprendre que votre santé est parfaitement rétablie, & que vous avez reçu de bonnes nouvelles de l'Amérique. Je languis d'en avoir, pour rabattre l'insolente joie que les dernieres nouvelles donnent à vos ennemis ici.

Je suis avec un très respectueux attachement, Monsieur, Votre très-humble & très-obéissant serviteur D

Passy à S. Exc. M. Franklin

Notation: Dumas la haie, March. 23. 79

From Jonathan Williams, Jr.: Two Letters

(I) and (II) ALS: American Philosophical Society; copies: Yale University Library

I.

Dear & honoured Sir. Nantes March 23. 1779.

Before I recvd your Favour of the 16th Instant I saw yours to the American Gentlemen of the 13th, and as some of the Persons named were gone to Painbeuf, I sent an Express immediately with your Letter & one from myself of which No 1 is a Copy.— The next Day I was honoured with your above mentioned Favour and I immediately wrote a Letter to *all* the Gentlemen, of which No 2 is a Copy.— My Express returned on Saturday Evening, and Mr Wharton returned with him to offer in Person all in his Power for the Support of Justice and the Good of the Public. Mr William Blake sent an answer in the Style of an honest, independant Gentleman, of which No

1. The project was the draft commercial treaty on which Dumas was working; see BF to Dumas, March 12, and Dumas to BF, March 15. Dumas apparently brought a copy of the Lee-Neufville treaty with him to Paris in July, as there is a copy of a May 17 letter from Berckel to Dumas enclosing it; the letter bears Dumas' certification, dated Paris, July 13. APS.

3 is a Copy. The remainder of the Painbeuf Gentlemen did not condescend to answer either your Letter or mine.[2]

Your kind Intentions are thus frustrated, as the whole Number being appointed without mentioning that a Majority might Decide, no number short of the whole would be (in the opinion of the Gentlemen) competent.[3] I therefore request you will send down another order to the Gentlemen who remain, of whom you have inclosed a List No 4,—and please to impower any number of the said Gentlemen (not less than three) to decide, & if it should happen that the number remaining is an even Number, impower them to appoint another for a casting Vote if there should be occasion. I am thus particular because the Gentlemen, are, most of them, on the Eve of their Departure. Please at the same time to signify to Mr Lee that if his Objections are not furnished by the Time your new Order is received here the Gentlemen will go into the Accots on the ground of his accusations as they Stand, please to say also whether I may produce Billys Copy of the Indorsements on my accounts as an authentic Paper, if you do not choose Billys name should be thus brought forward, please to send me an attested Copy of these Indorsements that nothing may be wanting.—

2. Actually, both of JW's letters to the Gentlemen were dated March 20. The first letter entreated all those in Paimboeuf to return to Nantes to examine his accounts; the delay of the convoy would allow them sufficient time. The second letter, sent to Nantes, asks the group to name a time and place for the business. With only a few exceptions, the addressees were essentially the same. William Blake, Daniel Blake, Philip Fendall, John Lloyd, and Charles Ogilvie were named in both letters; Joseph Wharton, Jr., was among the Gentlemen in Paimboeuf, and Ross, Schweighauser, and Joshua Johnson were included among those in Nantes. William Blake's reply, dated March 20, expressed regret that his participation was impossible, since his ship was prepared to sail and all his clothing was already on board. He promised to do what he could for JW in America. Copies of all three letters are in the APS.

3. Philip Fendall's letter of March 21, mentioned in the postscript, used this as the primary argument for refusing JW's request. Since Schweighauser was ill, he wrote, then presumably the Gentlemen could not meet; if only the appointment had been to three, five, or seven of the men, he would have served. Moreover, the men from Carolina seemed to think the examination would take up to six weeks. APS.

I earnestly request also that this Letter, the Copies No 1. 2. 3. & 4 inclosed, my Letter to Mr Adams & yourself, Copies of your Letter to the American Gentlemen and of that to Mr Lee, may be all inclosed in the File of my accounts, and so annexed to those which have Mr Lees Indorsements on the Back as to be forever inseperable; so that your Successors may see, how cruely I have been treated & how industriously my accuser avoids any Explanation.—

I am ever with the greatest Respect Your dutifull & affectionate Kinsman JONA WILLIAMS J

Since writing the above I have received the inclosed Letter from Mr. Fendall which shows this Gentlemans Love of Justice & willingness to appear in support of it but for the Objections he mentions. It is No 5. and I request it may be put with the other Numbers.

Addressed: The Honourable / Doctor Franklin.

Notation: Mr Williams's Accts.

II.

Dear & Hond Sir. Nantes March 23. 1779

I have already answered your Favour of the 16th in mine of this date, but I confined that answer to the Subject of my accts, meaning the Letter to be a public one.

Mr Schweighausers ill Health has yet prevented my receiving the Case, when I do I will send you such Papers relative to Mr Simeon Deans Goods as appears to me in strict impartiality just.

I thank you for your attention to my Request about Bills in favr of Mr Dennie. I have written to Mr Moylan also on the same Subject, so as to have a ready Detection in Case there should appear to be a Fraud.[4]

I have this day received your Favour of the 19th Instant with the Papers inclosed, which shall be carefuly returned to you next Post,— Ignorance is the mother of Suspicion, & when added to a malignant Disposition, makes a Man equaly ridiculous & detestable.

4. A copy of that letter, dated March 20, is in the Yale University Library.

The words *Copper Ore* is probably a mistake in my Translation, the words in the original are *Cuivre en Rosette* which I supposed to be copper in unwrought Lumps, or Ore, but I find on Searching the Dictionary that it is *red Brass or molten Copper.* This Explanation I hope will put the matter right.

By *the Zeal of the best of them* &c I meant that Mr Wharton had endeavoured to get your Letter to the Memorialists answered, & had twice drafted one for that Purpose, the first was refused because it contained a congratulation on your appointment, and after modifying it all in his power to make it go down, it was declined *without a Reason,* thus, these forward complainers, and (after an attention to their Complaints) servile adulators, refuse you a single *Honour* tho' you will find 18 repetitions of this enchanting Word in the Letter written to the 3 Commrs. By these Gentn I mean the Painbeuf Gentlemen excepting Mr W. & Mr W B.—[5] One of these Gentn Mr L—— has it seems written to London to get Certificates from two or three members of Parliament that Mr Fox quoted the Treaty in the House from a Letter of yours,[6] this Mr Wharton tells me, and he has accordingly written to D Bancroft. I refer you to that Letter for the particulars.—

As I don't know the particulars of Mr Beaumarchais affairs, I can say nothing about it, nor is it of consequence to me whether I can justify Mr Peltier or not, but I am pretty certain that he acted only as he was *ordered,* & indeed being only a *Factor* in the Business He could not act otherwise.—

I am ever with the greatest Respect most dutifuly & affectionately Your J WILLIAMS J

The Hon. Doctor Franklin

Notation: Jona Williams Mar. 23. 1779 (Private)

5. Joseph Wharton, Jr., and William Blake. "Mr L——" in the following sentence is John Lloyd. The letter to the commissioners is the one we résumé in XXVIII, 406.

6. See XXV, 651–2n.

John S. Harmanson[7] to Franklin and Arthur Lee

ALS: American Philosophical Society

Northampton County Eastern Shore Virg. March 24. 1779

Gentlemen

Mr. George Kindall a Neighbour of mine, being bound to France, & not provided with Letters to Paris, I have taken the Liberty to request the favor of Your Civilities shoud he visit Paris—[8] I hope you'll excuse this Liberty, & also the Liberty to inform you that as I am situated on the Eastern Coast of Virginia oposite to Sandshoal [Island?] abt. 20 Miles North of Cape Charles, that If Any of Your Friends shou'd have Occasion for a Correspondent situated as I am, that I shall do all in my Power to serve them—Goods in general being in request & Tobacco abt £ 10 Virga. C.Y. [Currency] per Ct— I am with much Esteem Gentn. yr. Mo. Obt Srt

John S. Harmanson

P.S. I request my Compts to Mr. Franklin Junr.

Addressed: To / The right Honorable / Benj. Franklin & Arthur Lee Esqrs. / Ambassaders for the united States / of N. America. / at the Court of France: / Mr. Kindall

Notation: Harminson March 24. 79—

From John Adams

ALS: American Philosophical Society

Sir Brest. March 24. 1778 [*i.e.,* 1779]

I had the Honour of a Letter from, your Excellency at Nantes, but as I was setting off for this Place could not then acknowledge it.[9]

7. Harmanson had written once before, some fifteen months prior to the present letter, when he was detained at Bordeaux: xxv, 454–5.

8. On the verso of Harmanson's letter is one from Kindall, dated Morlaix, April 27 and stamped Morlaix. Having arrived on the 25th, he regrets that his short stay will prevent his visiting Paris in person. In five or six weeks he will return to America and is happy to be honored with commands. He is in a Virginia-built boat, the *Marmy,* Joshua Lunz, master.

9. The letter presumably is BF's of March 13, which JA must have received soon before his March 17 departure for Brest (for which see JW's letter of

I Staid, no longer at Nantes, than just to look about me, before I determined to see Captain Landais, that I might know, the state and Prospects of his Frigate.

As you was so good as to desire Mr schweighauser, to consult with me, and Mr Schweighauser wrote to Mr Berube du Costentin, to take my Advice, I have ventured to give him and Captain Landais, my opinion in Writing that it will be most for the public service, for Mr Costentin to apply to the Intendant of the Marine[1] for Such Materials and Workmen as are absolutely necessary to repair the ship, and after this shall be done and the Prisoners, put on shore, that he proceed for Nantes.

I have had the Honour twice to wait on the Intendant and this afternoon, he very politely promised to take the Prisoners on shore, and furnish the Necessaries forth with.

I must confess, that I am not very well pleased with putting all the Prisoners on shore— But the Captain is sanguine that the ship would not be safe with any of the Ring Leaders on Board.

With a very little alteration of our naval Code, three or four of these might have been punished, and the rest would have made the better Men. For I am inclined to think, that altho the Conspiracy was bad enough, it has been made more of than was necessary.

The Midshipmen and some other Petty officers, have been with me, to solicit the same favour which you have granted to the Commission and Warrant officers, a suit of Cloaths proportional to their stations.[2] And as these perhaps have more need of it than the others, and as I thought it not probable that

---

the 18th). The dateline contains an obvious slip of the pen: JA was still en route to France on March 24, 1778.

1. Arnauld de Laporte; see our annotation of Landais' March 17 letter. The naval intendants were charged with the administration of the navy's dockyards, of which Brest was the most important; a good summary of their work and importance is in James Pritchard, *Louis XV's Navy, 1748–1762: a Study of Organization and Administration* (Kingston and Montreal, 1987), pp. 37–54 and *passim*.

2. See BF's March 11 letter to Hills and the other officers of the *Alliance*.

it was your Intention to exclude them, I have promised them to interceed with your Excellency in their Behalf.

Congratulate you on the Capture of Senegal, which is all the News I have heard.[3] I return to Nantes, tomorrow, or next day—there to wait the Motions of the Frigate.

I have the Honour to be, Sir, your most obedient and most humble servant JOHN ADAMS

His Excellency Dr Franklin

Notation: Jonh Adams Brest 24 mars 1779.

From Chardon[4]

LS: American Philosophical Society

Monsieur, A Brest le 24. mars 1779.

Vous pouvez precher l'admiration; c'est un sentiment que vous inspirez; mais je me rends trop de justice pour croire mériter tout ce que vous voulez bien me marquer de flatteur sur mon requisitoire. J'ai fait parler le Langage de la vérité; c'est le devoir de tout magistrat, et je ferai parler celui de mon cœur, et je me joindrai à toute la france, quand j'exprimerai l'admiration pour la nation américaine et ma vénération pour votre Génie, vos vertus et vos talents.

Je suis avec Respect, Monsieur, Votre très humble et très obéissant serviteur CHARDON
procureur General Des prises

M. frankelin.

Notation: Chardon Brest 24 Mar 79

3. See Lafayette's letter of March 20.
4. In answer to BF's highly complimentary letter of the 19th.

From Dumas

ALS: American Philosophical Society; AL (draft): Algemeen Rijksarchief

Monsieur Lahaie 24[–25]e. Mars *1779*

La ci-joint d'hier étoit prête à partir, lorsque je me vis honoré de la vôtre du 18. J'ai remis à Mr. Stockton, qui dînoit chez moi, celle qui étoit pour lui.[5] Il me charge, avec ses respects, de vous en témoigner sa reconnoissance. Comptez, Monsieur, que je vous obéirai, & que vous serez informé du succès quelconque de la souscription de Mr. De Neufville. J'ai tout lieu de croire qu'il se fera un point d'honneur de la faire réussir: mais, je le répete, il faut laisser passer la mauvaise impression que viennent de faire ici d'Estaing, la Géorgie & Pondicheri. L'affaire qu'il a conclue avec vous, Monsieur, n'est ni l'unique ni la plus considérable qu'il ait faite dernierement en France. Quand j'aurai l'honneur de vous voir, je pourrai vous en dire davantage de bouche. Je prévois que sa Maison deviendra la maison de la F——ce & de l'Am——e à Amsterdm. Lui-même ignore que j'en sais tant.

Le Congrès Allemand, dont on vous a parlé, se tient depuis le 10 de ce mois à Tesschen dans la Haute-Silésie. On assure qu'il ne durera que 6 semaines, & qu'en attendant les Armées gardent leur position, pour recommencer à s'entretuer si l'on ne s'accommode pas.[6] Mr. Lee n'auroit donc guere le temps d'arriver avant sa séparation. Je ne vois pas non plus ce que sa présence pourroit produire là de bon. J'ignore d'ailleurs jusqu'à quel point il peut compter sur la solidité de ses liaisons avec les Ministres de Vienne & de Berlin. Ce qu'il dit des 20,000 mercenaires, que la paix d'Allemagne mettra les Anglois à même de prendre à leur solde contre nous, est trop vague & trop général. Je demanderai 1°. Sera-ce un nouveau

5. BF's letter of the same date.

6. For the Congress of Teschen see BF's letter to Dumas of the 18th. An agreement was signed on May 13 by which Austria relinquished most of her acquisitions in Bavaria; for details see Paul P. Bernard, *Joseph II and Bavaria: Two Eighteenth Century Attempts at German Unification* (The Hague, 1965), pp. 130–2.

Corps de troupes? 2°. qui le fournira? Hesse-Cassel, Hanau, Brunswick, Anspac, Waldeck & Anhalt Zerbst, ont assez de peine déjà à livrer les recrues pour les Corps déjà vendus. L'Empereur, ni le Roi de Prusse, ni la Saxe ne fourniront rien. Le Roi de Prusse, comme on sait, voit de très-mauvais oeil les Princes ses Alliés s'affoiblir par ces émigrations, & s'est déclaré ouvertement là-dessus avant la guerre d'Allemagne. Le Wurtemberg ne fournira rien; les Etats du pays s'y opposent; Bade, Deuxponts, Palatin, Hesse-Darmstad, ne fourniront rien; ils sont trop interessés à menager la France. Il n'y a que le Pays d'Hanover, d'où le Roi d'Angle. peut en tout temps, sans qu'on puisse l'en empêcher, faire partir 20,000 hommes qu'il y a. Le fera-t-il? dégarnira-t-il ainsi sa derniere ressource? Je l'ignore. On lui a fait faire déjà tant d'autres extravagances, que je ne saurois répondre de rien de sa part.[7]

Je demanderai 3°. quels sont les moyens qu'auroit Mr. Lee, s'il se trouvoit, contre toute apparence, quelque prince prêt à vendre de nouveaux Corps aux Anglois, *to prevent it?* Je ne puis en imaginer qu'un: ce seroit de pouvoir renchérir sur les Anglois à ce marché-là; mais Mr. Lee ne l'a pas; & si je l'avois, je voudrois l'employer mieux pour le bien de l'Amérique. La vertu, la constance, & la *concorde* des Etats-Unis, seront, j'espere, avec l'aide de Dieu, des moyens plus sûrs & plus honnêtes, qui les feront triompher des derniers efforts de la tyrannie, comme des premiers; &, grace à Dieu, ils sont en leur puissance mieux que l'argent ne l'est en celle de leurs ennemis. Mr. Stokton m'a dit, que Mr. Lee avoit su empêcher que le prince de Darmstad n'ait fourni des troupes à l'Angleterre. Les vraies causes qui l'ont empêché, sont 1°. le Roi de P——, à qui cela ne convient pas; 2°. les terres considérables que ce Prince de Darmstad possede en Alsace; 3°. son second fils, qui est au service de france dans le Regiment d'Anhalt.[8]

7. Dumas' analysis proved prescient. During 1779 the British obtained only 960 recruits for existing Hessian regiments and engaged no new military units: Rodney Atwood, *The Hessians: Mercenaries from Hessen-Kassel in the American Revolution* (Cambridge, Eng., and New York, 1980), p. 254.

8. The Prince d'Anhalt Goethen was *colonel propriétaire* of the regiment: *Etat militaire* for 1779, p. 233.

du 25e. Mars

Les Etats d'Hollande sont rassemblés depuis hier. Le dernier avis qu'un grand personnage avoit proposé à l'Assemblée précédente, porte en substance, de continuer d'exclure des convois les bois de Construction, jusqu'à-ce que la rep. se fût mise dans un état complet de défense, tant par terre que par mer, c'est-à-dire, jusqu'à-ce qu'elle eût sur pied une armée de 50 à 60 mille hommes, & 50 à 60 vaisseaux de Ligne. Amsterdam & son parti, au contraire, protestent de vouloir s'en tenir à l'Armement des 32 Vaisseaux résolu en Novembre dernier,[9] & à la résolution du 26 & 28 Janvier quant aux Convois;[1] & pour des troupes de terre, qu'on n'en a pas besoin. Notre Ami pense que cette fois la pluralité l'emportera sur l'avis ci-dessus du gd. personnage. Nous verrons.

La Chevalier Gd. vint hier au soir me faire une courte visite, revenant de Paris par Breda. Il m'a paru ignorer, ou faire semblant de ne rien savoir du tout de ce qui concerne Neufville. Nous ne nous sommes tenus de part & d'autre que des propos généraux. Je l'ai mis sur le chapitre de Mr. D'Estaing, pour lequel il paroît s'intéresser & vouloir le justifier en tout. "L'affaire, dit-il, de Pondicheri, on s'y attendoit en france depuis 3 mois, & elle ne signifie rien: celle de Géorgie est encore moins de conséquence: quant à l'emprunt en Hollande, il n'y a rien à faire; il ne faut point y penser présentement." De Mr. De Neufville, nous ne nous en sommes pas dit le mot l'un à l'autre. Il me quitta, pour aller passer le reste de la soirée chez Mr. l'Ambr. de France; & il est parti ce matin à 6 h. pour Amst.

Je ne suis point surpris, Monsieur, que vous trouviez la *situation* des affaires ici interessante. Elle l'est effectivement. Quant aux *Partis* dont vous parlez, & à leurs *Intérêts,* je ne puis vous en donner une idée plus claire que celle-ci— Il y a d'un côté le grand personnage, avec l'influence que lui donnent dans toutes les provinces & villes, excepté la Régence d'Amsterdam, la disposition qu'il a des emplois civils & mili-

9. Ambassador La Vauguyon lobbied for the prompt outfitting of these ships and the recall of all warships except those bound for the West Indies so that convoying could begin: Fauchille, *Diplomatie française,* pp. 122–5. The "grand personnage" working against him was the stadholder.

1. See XXVIII, 431.

taires, de l'Armée, des Amirautés, & de la Compe. des Indes. Ce parti est encore fortifié par tant de rentiers interessés dans les fonds Anglois; il est tout dévoué aux Anglois.— Le parti républicain, qui est en même temps celui du Commerce, est aujourd'hui concentré principalement à Amsterdam; & c'est ce parti qu'il importe à la France & à l'Amérique de ménager & encourager, parce qu'il empêchera l'autre de faire déclarer la rep. pour l'Angle. Le *Palladium* de ce parti, c'est l'unanimité requise pour que la Rep. fasse une telle démarche.

Je suis avec le respect & le zele qui vous sont connus, Monsieur Votre très humble & très obéissant serviteur D——

P.S. Ce que je dis concernant les voyages que Mr. Lee voudroit faire, &c. ne provient nullement de mauvaise volonté de ma part. Je lui souhaite sincerement toutes sortes de succès en Allemagne. Mais vous me demandez mon sentiment, Monsieur, & je le dis sincerement. A moins d'être bien sûr de réussir, il faut éviter, ce me semble, tout éclat, comme d'être tympanisé dans les gazettes; & là où il y a quelque chose à faire, s'adresser tant qu'on peut aux sources. Après l'éclat fait à Vienne,[2] il est impossible que Mr. Lee soit incognito au Congrès de Tesschen.

Passy à Son Exc. Mr. Franklin

Notation: Dumas la haie March. 24. 79

From Nicolas-Maurice Gellée

ALS: American Philosophical Society

Sir Passy March 24 1779

When you have been pleased to accept of my Services as Secretary, you did me the Honor to mention that, in Case I should after some Time be found fit, you would make a more particular Agreement.[3]

I thought it most proper, before reminding you of the Mat-

2. Where Lee had unsuccessfully attempted in 1778 to assume his post as commissioner to the Holy Roman Empire: XXVII, 139, 182n.

3. For Gellée's hiring see XXVI, 287n.

ter, to wait till the Affairs should be settled on a more firm Basis, as they are now, when your Correspondence likely to spread wider around, influenc'd by your one Genius, will afford me in many Respects more Occasions of proving to you my Zeal for your Person and your Cause.

With the utmost Respect and strongest Attachment I have the Honour to be Sir your most obedient and most humble Servant N M Gellée

His Excy. B Franklin

Notation: Gellé, Mar 24. 1779.

From Jonathan Williams, Jr.

ALS: American Philosophical Society

Dear & honoured Sir. Nantes March 24. 1779

This will be presented to you by Mr Samuel Bradford[4] a young Townsman of mine, warmly reccommended to me by my Friends, & by his deportment & agreeable Manners, he appears to deserve all they have said of him.

I take the Liberty to introduce him to your notice & am with the greatest Respect Your dutifull & affectionate Kinsman Jona Williams J

Addressed: The Honourable / Doctor Franklin / minister Plenipotentiary of / the United States—/ Passy

Notation: Jona. Williams 24 Mar 79.

To the Comtesse Conway

Copy: Library of Congress

Passy March 25 1779

I find, Ma chere fille, that you and I have been very unlucky in our Endeavours to oblige Mr. Mullens: for on the Contrary we have grievously offended him. I understood he had been taken Prisoner and stript by the English, and had not wherewith to

4. He was the son of John Bradford and would later marry JW's sister: XXVIII, 278n.

pay the Expence of his Journey to his Regiment. I sent him an Order on my Banker for ten Guineas.[5] He returns me the Order, and to make it & me & the Congress look ridiculous, he tells me "I sent it him as a Gratification" for his Services "in the name of the Honble. Congress." I had no such Idea. I had declared that I had no Authority to make Gratifications to Officers, nor any Money put into my Hands for such Purposes; and he could not but see that the real Intention of the Order was expressed in the face of it; whereby his Claim, if he has any, to a Gratification, is left open. If his intention was to obtain it from me, he was mistaken in the Application: He shou'd have apply'd to the Congress. They might know him & his Services. But I was totally unacquainted with both; I had only heard, as you may remember I told you that he spoke his sentiments very freely in Paris against the Congress and America, which however did not prevent my offering him the little Aid I thought he stood in need of. I am glad he has no Occasion for it.

I join heartily in your Joy on the Return of your Husband; as I was a Witness to your perpetual Anxiety for his Welfare during his Absence. I wish your Happiness together may not again be interrupted, but continue during your Lives—being ever your affectionate Father (as you do me the Honor to call me)

Madame Conway

To Thomas Conway

Copy: Library of Congress

Sir

Passy, March 25. 1779

I received the Letter you were so kind as to bring me from our Friend M. Peters.[6] I congratulate you on your safe Return to your amiable Family. It would have given me great Pleasure, if the Service in America had been made so agreeable to

5. Indeed, BF recorded in the Wastebook (Account I, XXIII, 19) that he had sent ten *louis* to Mullens in order to allow him to "return to his Regiment in Bretagne." He subsequently struck through the entry and wrote "return'd" in the margin.

6. See Conway's letter of March 22.

you as to induce you and yours to settle there. With much Esteem I am, Sir &c.

Genl. Conway.

From Edward Bancroft

AL: American Philosophical Society

Chaillot Thursday Evening [on or after March 25, 1779][7]

Dr. Bancroft presents his most respectful Compliments to Dr Franklin & sends him inclosed the desired Passport.[8]

Addressed: To the Hon'ble / Dr. Franklin / Passy

From Marat

AL: American Philosophical Society

Ce jeudy 25 Mars 79

Le répresentant de l'auteur des experiences nouvelles sur le feu, apprend avec bien de la mortification, Monsieur, que vous Soyes incomodé; et il fait des voeux pour que la goutte vous quitte au plutot: il espère avoir lhonneur de vous recevoir Samedy prochain, Rue Bourgogne hotel de M. le Marquis de lAubespine. MM. les Comissaires Sy rendront a neuf heures et demi du matin, pour profiter du Soleil.[9]

7. On March 24, a Wednesday, BF had issued an American passport for the vessel *London Packet.* See Bancroft's letters to WTF, one of March 20 and the second printed under March 21. The present letter must have been written shortly thereafter.

8. A draft of the passport in WTF's hand is at the APS, and a copy is at the Library of Congress. Addressed "To all Captains and Commanders of Vessels of War, Privateers and Letters of Marque belonging to the United States of America," the document states that Louis XVI had thought fit for reasons of state to issue his own passport to the vessel bound from Calais to London. Hence, the ship and its cargo of wine should be considered as the property of French subjects; American commanders should let the ship pass once she produced this French passport.

9. In order to use the *microscope solaire.* See our headnote to Marat's letter printed above, before March 13.

Franklin *et al.*: Report to the Académie Royale des Sciences[1]

ADS and copy:[2] Archives de l'Académie royale des sciences

[March 26, 1779]

M. Lavoisier ayant demandé à LAcadémie au nom des Regisseurs des poudres son avis sur la meilleure manière de reconstruire le magazin à poudre de L'Arsenal et La Compagnie nous ayant nomme M. Franklin M. D'arcy M. De Montigny M. Perronet[3] M. Lavoisier et moi Commissaires à ce sujet Nous allons lui faire part de nos observations sur cet objet important et de ce que nous croyons qu'il seroit le plus avantageux de faire pour le remplir.

Pour qu'un Magazin à Poudre soit le mieux construi, non seulement il faut le mettre autant qu'il est possible à l'abri des accidens extérieurs et intérieurs du feu et de l'eau, mais encore qu'il le soit de maniere que ces accidens arrivans, surtout par rapport au feu, il en résulte le moins de maux et de dommages possibles car on ne sait que trop, que malgré toute la prudence humaine, ces accidens arrivent.

Dirigés par ces vûes, après avoir conféré avec Messieurs les Regisseurs sur l'Endroit le plus propre à établir le nouveau Magazin nous étions convenus quil seroit bati en saillie sur le fossé de l'arsenal en dessus des plus hautes eaux comme on le voit dans le dessein, et qu'il seroit construit de la manière suivante:

D'une forme quarrée, chacun des côtés devoit avoir, pris intérieurement, 24 pieds; ses murs devoient avoir 12 pieds de hauteur du Rez de chaussée du jardin au dessus de l'entablement, leur epaisseur devoit être au moins de 7½ pieds; les paremens intérieurs de ces murs devoient être en ligne droite

1. For the request for this report see XXVII, 236–7n.

2. The ADS is in Le Roy's hand and signed by all the members of the committee. It is filed in a *pochette.* The official copy is bound in the *comptes-rendus, tome* XCVIII, folios 83–85.

3. Jean-Rodolphe Perronet (XXVII, 249n) was the leading engineer in France.

mais leur face inclinée à l'horizon en sorte que le magazin devint par là évasé ou plus large en haut qu'en bas dans une certaine proportion, afin de faciliter par cette forme d'entonnoir la sortie du fluide de la poudre en cas d'explosion. Au lieu d'être en ligne droite les paremens intérieurs de ces murs devoient être en ligne courbe. Sur le sens horizontal la concavité tournée en dehors ou bien en arc de cercle dont la corde seroit de 24 pieds ces murs elevés à plomb devoient être flanqués à chaque angle, par un corps quarré de maçonnerie de 14 pieds 2 pouces. Enfin comme dans un pareil magazin on n'a point à craindre les bombes, La couverture devoit être en ardoise et legere, afin qu'en cas d'accidens, le tout fut enlevé facilement, comme on sait que cela se pratique, dans les moulins à poudre. Tous ces détails sont sensibles dans le dessin des plans, et élevations de ce magazin qui sont sous les yeux de L'Académie.

Telle étoit la construction que nous nous proposions de lui donner et les différentes dimensions que nous avions reglé pour les épaisseurs de ses murs, d'aprés celles que M. De Vauban[4] a décidées autrefois et qu'on suit encore aujourdhui.

Mais lorsque nous avons cherché à approfondir ce qui avoit donné lieu à la détermination de ces dimensions, sur quoi elles étoient fondées; les Expériences que l'on avait faites sur la résistance des pierres, la force que la Poudre exerce dans son explosion Enfin les différents elemens sur lesquels il est nécéssaire d'avoir des apperçus déterminés jusqu'à un certain point pour fixer quelque chose de certain sur la forme des magazins à poudre, les dimensions de leurs murs etc. nous nous sommes bientôt apperçus que nous n'avions pas assez de données pour résoudre d'une manière convenable un problème de cette importance.

En effet Dans les dimensions que M. De Vauban a prescrites pour les magazins à Poudre, ce grand homme paroît n'avoir suivi que ce que son expérience et le bon sens lui dictoit à ce sujet et surtout par rapport aux effets de la bombe mais sans avoir pu se déterminer par la connoissance des données qui

4. Sébastien Le Prestre, marquis de Vauban (1633–1707), who under Louis XIV had carried the art of fortification to new heights: Larousse.

étoient requises necéssairement pour la solution de ce problème.

D'après ces considérations, et les diverses réflexions que nous avons faites à ce sujet, nous avons pensé que nous ne pouvions répondre dignement à la confiance que L'Académie nous a témoigné dans cette occasion, que nous n'ayons acquis de connoissances plus certaines et plus étendues sur les élemens dont nous avons parlé; Qu'il seroit à souhaiter en conséquence que le gouvernement ordonne qu'on fit les expériences necéssaires pour les acquérir; Qu'il en resulteroit un grand nombre de connoissances nouvelles et utiles dans un sujet entièrement nouveau sur lequel on n'a tenté jusqu'ici aucune expérience; Que les épreuves que l'on a faites pour mesurer la force de la poudre, et particulièrement l'un de nous, M. D'Arcy, donnoient lieu d'espérer de réussir dans ces recherches et qu'enfin la matière etoit d'une si grande Importance pour L'artillerie et pour La sureté du public par le grand nombre de magazins à poudre répandus dans le Royaume; Qu'il étoit de la plus grande Conséquence de déterminer par les faits Tout ce qui pouvoit mener à la solution du problème de la meilleure manière de construire les Magazins à poudre.

Fait dans L'Académie des Sciences le 26 mars 1779

Le Roy	Lavoisier	Le chev. d'Arcy
B Franklin	Perronet	De Montigny

To Sartine

Copy: Library of Congress

Monsieur A Passy Le 26 Mars 1779

Votre Excellence voudra bien recevoir mes Remerciemens pour La Reception favorable dont elle a honoré le Commodore Gillon qui en est on ne peut plus satisfait.

Il est echoué sur Les Cotes de France dans Le Mois de Janvier dernier un Vaisseau Anglois nommé l'Amphitrite.[5] Il y avoit a bord de ce Vaisseau trois Matelots Americains qui s'y etoient embarqués a Londres pour se soustraire a La Presse et

5. Not to be confused with Beaumarchais' ship of the same name (XXIII, 31n), this *Amphitrite* was wrecked at Dunkirk on Dec. 31, 1778: *Courier de l'Europe,* v (1779), 40 (issue of Jan. 15).

se rendre en Amerique.[6] Ils ont été mis dans Les Prisons de Calais et j'espere que V. Ex. ne me refusera pas la Grace de Les faire elargir. Ils serviroient sur le Vaisseau du Capitaine Jones.[7] J'ai L'honneur d'etre avec Le plus grand Respect et l'estime la plus parfaite de votre Excellence &c.

His Excy. M. de Sartine

From the Duc de La Roche-Guyon et de La Rochefoucauld

AL: Dartmouth College Library

Vendredi 26. Mars. [1779]

Le Duc de la Rochefoucauld ignoroit, en faisant à Monsieur franklyn des propositions de diner pour Mercredi que Me. sa mere envoioit ce jour là sa maison à la campagne; elle est bien fâchée d'être privée par ce contretems du plaisir et de l'honneur de recevoir Monsieur franklyn; elle espere être plus heureuse à son retour de la campagne;[8] le Duc de la Rochefoucauld le prie d'agréer ses excuses et ses regrets.

From Arthur Lee

AL: University of Pennsylvania Library

Paris March 26th. 1779

Mr. A Lee presents his Compliments to Dr Franklin, & has the honor of enclosing to him one of Mr Schweighauser's Accounts, which he has found among his Papers.[9]

6. The three seamen must have written BF for help (in a letter now missing) prior to this request to Sartine on their behalf. They wrote again on April 4; see James Longwell's letter of that date.

7. We do not find any of the three listed among the *Bonhomme Richard*'s crew.

8. Another note from La Rochefoucauld, dated "Mercredi matin" [Oct. 27, 1779?], invites BF to dinner, in his mother's name, for "Jeudi 28." The late October date would coincide with their return from the country. Dartmouth College Library.

9. On the same day Lee sent WTF a dinner invitation and a letter requested by JA. APS. WTF's acceptance (also dated March 26) is at the Yale University Library.

Addressed: The Honble. / Dr. B. Franklin / minister plenepotentiary / of the United States of / America / at / Passy

Notation: A Lee 26. March 1779.

From Le Roy

ALS: American Philosophical Society

Vendredy Matin [March 26, 1779]

Mon Illustre Docteur recevez mon Compliment. J'ai appris avec grand plaisir que la goutte vous ayant laissé plus tranquile vous etiez enfin allé à Versailles Mardy.[1] Je crois qu'actuellement malgré votre éloignement pour les complimens vous ne vous opposerez plus a ce que L Académie vous fasse une députation aussi Je compte bien qu'elle la décidera définitivement aujourdhui qu'elle se separe, pour ses vacances de paques.[2] Je ne vois pas les raisons qui pourroient vous engager a mettre opposition à son desir la dessus. Cependant marquez moi un petit mot de réponse sur cet objet pour me mettre plus en liberté vous savez combien je serois fâché de faire quelques choses qui vous fut désagréable.

Le temps étant si beau sil continuë de même demain samedy nous irons voir les Experiences du fluide igné à neuf heures et demie dix heures—ce n'est plus au gros Caillou mais ruë de Bourgogne maison de M. Le Marquis de L Aubespine au dessus du Corps de Garde des gardes françoises. J'imagine et j'espere bien que nous aurons lhonneur de vous y voir; M. De Maillebois le désire beaucoup, il compte même aller diner chez Mde De chaumont dimanche [*dans*] l'esperance de vous voir l'aprés Midy soit chez elle soit chez vous si vous y dinez.[3] Adieu Mon Illustre Docteur. On ne peut vous etre plus veritablement attaché que Moi

LE ROY

1. BF indeed had presented his letter of credence on March 23; see Chaumont's letter printed before March 23, above.

2. Le Roy had already proposed on Feb. 18 that the Académie extend formal congratulations to BF on his appointment as minister plenipotentiary; see XXVIII, 569. Easter fell on April 4 in 1779.

3. See our headnote to Marat's letter, published before March 13.

Addressed: A Monsieur / Monsieur Franklin / Ministre Plenipotentiaire des / Etats Unis de L'Amérique / en son hôtel / a Passy

From Rudolph Erich Raspe[4]

ALS: American Philosophical Society

Honourd Sir London. March. 26. 1779.

Mesrs Waiz V Eshen, nevews of the Minister of that name, whom Your Excellency was acquainted with at Cassell in Germany,[5] will have the honour to deliver those lines, in testimony of the profound esteem, which animates them for Your Excellency. They have travelled through the greater part of Germany, Sweden, Norway, and England in order to acquire usefull Knowledge in whatever relates to Mountains, Mines and Foundaries; and I am very happy to have an opportunity of assuring Your Excellency that I am with the truest and warmest and highest admiration and esteem Your Excellency's most obedient humble Servant R. E. Raspe.

At Mr. Lockyer David Bookseller Holbourn.

Notation: R. E. Raspe Londres 26 mars 1779.

4. For the writer, former librarian, and curator-turned-thief who had been in exile from Germany since 1775 see XIII, 345n.

5. The minister was Friedrich Siegmund von Waitz, Reichfreiherr von Eschen (1745–1808): Robert L. Kahn, "Some Unpublished Raspe-Franklin Letters," APS *Proc.*, XCIX (1955), 130n. The messieurs Waitz wrote BF on May 8, 1779, to inform him that the indisposition of one of them would prevent their waiting upon him the following day. In another brief note, undated, they ask to present their respects to BF "Vendredi prochain." Both documents are at the APS.

To ——— Gratien

Copy: Library of Congress

Monsieur A Passy ce 27 Mars 1779

J'ai recû La Lettre que vous avez ecrite le 19 de ce Mois aux Deputés des Etats Unis d'Amerique,[6] et j'ai l'honneur d'y repondre en ma qualité presente de Ministre Plenipotentiaire des dits Etats.

Les Papiers des deux Prises que vous auriez pû, Monsieur, conformement a L'Art. 11 du Reglement du 27 7bre. 1778,[7] m'adresser, ont été envoyés par M. De Grand Bourg secrétaire general de La Marine a M. de Sartine. Je demanderai, Monsieur, que ces Prises soient jugées suivant Les Loix de France, parcequ'il est ordonné par Le Congrés Americain aux Commandans des Vaisseaux des E. U. d'Amerique de suivre les Loix des Pays ou ils conduiront leurs Prises;[8] j'exposerai en même Tems combien il est necessaire de prononcer sur leur Sort le plutot possible, tant pour eviter leur Deperissement que pour faire cesser les Dommages et Interets de celles qui ne seroient pas jugées Bonnes. J'ai L'honneur d'etre &c.

B.F.

M. Gratien Lieut. Genl. de l'Amirauté de Morlaix.

To Landais

Copy: Library of Congress

Sir Passy March 27, 1779

I received your favour of the 17 inst.—with the List inclosed of your Ships Company. I am concerned to see the Number so small, But it is not in my Power to enlarge it; as

6. BF forwarded Gratien's letter to Vergennes on the same day, below. The prize cases it must have discussed are those of the *Papillon* and *Victoria*, both of which came under the jurisdiction of the Admiralty of Morlaix; see XXVIII, 563, 632, and Gratien's letter of April 23.

7. For the French navy's new regulations on prizes see XXVII, 178, 248–9, 260, 272, 562.

8. Among BF's papers at the APS is a blank printed commission signed by former President of Congress John Hancock on which is underlined a passage instructing the captain to direct any prizes to a neutral port where the courts can try them according to local custom. On the back of the document BF wrote, "Copy of Commission to American Privateers."

you do not chuse to have french Seamen, and Americans are not to be had; and If I shou'd procure a Permission for you to enlist Volunteers from among the British Prisoners in France, there is Danger of their Treachery, and that you may be as much embarrassed with them as with the Villains of the same Nation that shipt themselves at Boston.[9]

I had no Intention of offending you when I mentioned my having no Concern in projecting the Voyage of the Flamand. On my Arrival I found M. Deane in Possession of all that sort of Business which I left to be continued with him, because he best understood it.— As you say you remember the Transaction, I have no Doubt of his communicating to me what had passed between you & him on the Subject, and that, relying on his Judgment, I might say I approved of it. My not giving my Attention then to such Affairs, is I suppose the Reason of my having totally forgot it. But it is my Opinion that whatever Agreement he had made with you before my Arrival or even after it, as I made no Opposition ought to be honorably comply'd with, whether I approved of it or not; And I make no Doubt but the Congress when acquainted with the Circumstances, will do what is just & proper.[1]

I am glad to hear that you have got the Caulkers and Smiths at Work: I hope you will now soon be ready. M. Schweighauser has had for some Time all the Orders necessary from me. The sending to Paris for Orders in such Business is very inconvenient; it occasions great Loss of Time; and is the more perplexing to me, as I do not understand it. Merchants in the Ports are the only Men fit to manage it. The Navy Board di-

9. According to Landais the bulk of the *Alliance*'s crew when she sailed from Boston was English, Irish, or Scotch, thereby facilitating the conspiracy during her voyage to France: XXVIII, 486–7.

1. On March 6 Congress had voted Landais 12,000 *l.t.* in compensation for the dangers he had run and propriety he had shown in bringing the *Flammand* (formerly *Heureux*) to America; eleven days later it resolved that he should draw on BF for the money: *JCC,* XIII, 288, 323. The passage, which took from late September to the beginning of December, 1777, indeed had been a difficult one: Charles O. Paullin, "Admiral Pierre Landais," *Catholic Historical Review,* XVII (1931–32), 298.

rected very properly the Application to the Commercial Agent.

I hope the Delay of receiving the Mutineers is over and that you are at length clear of em. I have the Honor to be with great Regard, Sir, y. m. o. h. s. BF

If M. Adams is with you, please to present my Respects to him.

Honble. Capt. Landais

To Arthur Lee: Two Letters

(I) and (II) copies: Library of Congress

I.

Sir Passy, March 27. 1779.

"The offer you make of Sending me Copies Sealed and authenticated of all the Papers in your Hands"[2] is very satisfactory; and as you Say they are but few, I suppose it may Soon be done. I imagined when I desired you to Send me the Originals, that they were a great Many, and at present of no Importance to you; and therefore not worth copying. I assure you I had not the least intention of depriving you of anything you might think necessary for your Vindication. The suspicion is groundless and Injurious. In a former Letter, I offer'd you authenticated Copies of any remaining in my hands that you Should judge might be of Such Use to you;[3] and I now offer you the Originals if you had rather have them, and will content my Self with keeping Copies.

Mr. Adams did not as you insinuate exact any Promise of me to arrange and keep in Order, the Papers he Sent me. He knew Such a Promise unnecessary, for that I had always kept in order and by themselves the public Papers that were in my hands; without having them so "confunded among a multi-

2. Lee had made the offer in his letter of March 19.
3. In his first letter of March 13 to Lee.

tude of other Papers" that they could not be found when called for.[4]

I have the honour to be with great Respect Sir, &c.

Honble. M. Lee.

II.

Sir Passy, March 27. 1779.

I have not hitherto undertaken to justify Mr. William's accounts nor to Censure your Conduct in not passing them. To prevent any suspicion of Partiality towards him as my Nephew, I avoided having any thing to do with the examination of Them; but left it entirely to you and M. Adams: After that Examination, Mr. Adams drew up and sent me in for signing the Order you mention:[5] I considered the Expressions in it as only serving to Show that the accounts were not finally Settled; and I considered Mr. Adams's drawing up and Sending me the Order as Proof that in his Judgment who had with you examin'd the accounts, the Bills drawn on Mr. Grand, ought to be paid.— I therefore Sign'd it. I was not, as you Suppose "*convinc'd that the Accounts as they Stood could not be pass'd;*"[6] for having never examined them, I could form no such Opinion of Them.— It was not till lately, that being press'd by M. Monthieu for a Settlement of his Accounts and finding they had a reference to M. Williams I got those from M. Adams. They were put up in a paper Case which cover'd the note you had made upon them, and that Case was fastened with Wax. This prevented the Notes being before Seen either by My Self, or Mr. Adams among whose Papers you had left those Accounts. He was as much Surpriz'd at Seeing it as I was and as much dissatisfied with another you had made in the body of the Accounts, which taken, with the first, imports that notwithstanding it appeared from Mr. Williams's own Acct., that he has now and has long had in his hands upwards of an hun-

4. JA recollected in his *Autobiography,* however, that "It was utterly impossible to acquire any clear Idea of our Affairs": Butterfield, *John Adams Diary,* IV, 77.

5. A joint letter to Ferdinand Grand: XXVII, 68.

6. A quote from Lee's letter of the 16th.

dred Thousend livres belonging to the Public, that have not been applyed to the public Use, "B. franklin and John Adams, Esqrs. had given an Order on the Public Banquer for the payment of all Mr. Williams's Demands."[7] This being a Severe Reflection upon us both might be suspected, if I were dispos'd to be suspicious, as one Reason why it was shown to neither of us, but left conceal'd among the Papers to appear hereafter as a Charge, not controverted at the Time where by a future accusation might be confirmed. Mr. Adams Spoke in strong Terms of your having no right to enter Notes upon Papers without our Consent or knowledge, and talk'd of making a counter Entry, in which he would have shown that your assertion of our having given "an order for the Payment of all Mr. Williams's Demands," was not conformable to truth nor to the express Terms of The order, But his attention being taken up with what related to his departure, was probably the cause of his omitting to make that Entry.— On the whole I judg'd it now encumbent on me (for my own sake and Mr. Adam's, as well as for the Public Interest) to have those accounts fully examined as Soon as possible by Skilful and Impartial persons, of which I inform'd you in mine of the 13th. Instant, requesting you to aid the Enquiry by stating your Objections that they might be considered by those judges, which I am Sorry you do not think fit to comply with.— I have no desire to skreen Mr. Williams on acct. of his being my Nephew; if he is guilty of what you charge him with, I care not how soon he is deservedly punish'd, and the family purg'd of him; for I take it that a Rogue living in family is a greater Disgrace to it, than one *hang'd out* of it. If he is innocent, Justice requires that his Character should be Speedily clear'd from the heavy Charge with which it has been loaded.— I have the honour to be, &c.

H. A. Lee Esqe.

7. From Lee's first endorsement on JW's accounts: XXVIII, 443.

To Vergennes

LS:[8] American Philosophical Society; copy: Library of Congress

Monsieur Le Comte Passi ce 27 mars 1779.

J'ai l'honneur de remettre a votre Excellence une Lettre que jai recu de M. Gratien Lieutenant Gal. de L'amirauté de Morlaix avec une copie de la reponse que j'y ai faite, et un Exemplaire du reglement du 27. 7bre 1778 concernant les prises faittes par les corsaires Français et Americains, permettez moi de vous observer, Monsieur Le Comte, en ce qui concerne les corsaires Americains, que les Capitaines ont ordre dans leur commission de se conformer aux loix des pays ou ils conduiront leurs prises,[9] et en Consequence je prie votre Excellence d'obtenir de sa Majesté, que celles qui sont dans le cas d'etre jugées en France le soient comme celles faittes par des corsaires Francais, et sans aucuns retards, attendu le deperissement qui en resulte, et les domages qui en pourroient resulter, si les Vaisseaux amenes n'etaient pas de bonne prise. Je suis avec respect Monsieur Le Comte Votre tres humble et tres obeissant serviteur B FRANKLIN

a Son Excellence M. Le Comte de Vergennes.

Notation: M de Rayneval . . . [1]

From John Bondfield

ALS: American Philosophical Society

Sir Bordeaux 27 Mar 1779

I am honord with your favor of the 18th Inst. We have had no arrivals on this Coast from the United States since my last, a Brig arrived at Brest somedays past that left Edenton 5 feby. The intelligence she brought has not reachd this City.

8. In the hand of Chaumont's son Jacques (XXVIII, 239n). The elder Chaumont probably translated this letter from English as he did an earlier letter on the difficulties facing American captors: XXVIII, 494n.

9. BF's letter to Gratien discussing the regulations on prizes is above, March 27.

1. This notation, which has been lined through here, commonly appears on incoming AAE documents for which Gérard de Rayneval was expected to draft a response.

Captain Jones arrived here last Week in quest of Seamen and Cannon. The Ship Buckskin Capt. Johns took on her passage from Baltimore a Privateer having on board sixty hands that he set at liberty taking their parole which parole the Captain gave to Captain Jones and will entitle you to an equal Number in the Exchange or Cartel. I suppose he will transmit you the Parole per Post. He was not able to procure the Cannon the sizes he wanted as early as he desires—exprest great desire to have them[2] I have Casting by your order I expect he will apply to you for them agreable to your Instructions I shall duly attend.

I receivd yesterday from Ferol a Note of a quantity of Cannon lodged there for Sale. I inclose you the list and Conditions should you have occation for all or any part of them.[3]

I have the Honor to be with due respect Sir Your very hhb & Obedient Servant JOHN BONDFIELD

His Excellency Benj. Franklin Esq

Addressed: To / His Excellency B. Franklin / Esqr. / Plenipotentiary from Congress / a / Paris

Notation: John Bondfield 27. Mar. 1779.

From the Comtesse Conway[4]

ALS: American Philosophical Society

mon cher papa ce 27. mars 1779

Je ne puis vous exprimer Combien je suis fachée d'être La Cause innocente, du désagrement que vous èprouvés, pour avoir voulu m'obliger en La personne de mr mullens; ce n'est que d'aprés ses instances que je vous ai engagé à reparer Les pertes qu'il a faites dans sa traversée, et lorsque je lui ai remis

2. Writing to Bondfield from Angoulême on March 27, however, Jones reported an offer from the firm of Messrs. Louis Sazerac l'aîné et fils promising delivery of cannon for the *Bonhomme Richard* by the end of May: Bradford, *Jones Papers,* reel 3, no. 558.

3. The enclosure (described in XXV, 131n), in Bondfield's hand, is at the APS.

4. Answering BF's of March 25.

La petite lettre de change de votre part je lui ai dit *que ce n'etoit pas au nom du Congrés, mais de votre poche que partoit cette Legere somme pour L'aider et que vous L'aviés donnè purement pour moi* il m'en parrut trés Content, et je vous assure que ce n'est pas de son propre mouvement qu'il vous en a fait La remise, C'est par ordre de ses superieurs: Lorsqu'il m'en a parlé je lui ai dit que j'etois au désespoir de mettre meslée de ses affaires, et que je me broullerois avec lui s'il n'etoit pas un ami de mon mari, j'ai crû cher papa qu'il étoit moins malhonnette de vous rendre moi même votre billet que de vous Le Laisser renvoÿer par mr mullens. Mon mari m'a grondè, de m'être chargée de cette Commission ce n'est pas de son aveu que son ami vous a êcrit; et quand aux propos que vous croÿés que mr mullens a tenus, je puis vous jurer que ce n'est pas en ma présence, et que mon mari le désaprouveroit fort d'en tenir; il pense que pour des désagrements particuliers un officier ne doit jamais décrier la puissance qu'il a servie avec tant de zèle; à son premier moment libre, il aura L'honneur de vous voir, et moi mon cher papa j'irai bientôt déjeuner avec vous, et vous prier de me Conserver Le titre et L'amitié de pere que je mèritte par mes sentimens inviolables votre fille CONWAY

Addressed: Monsieur / Monsieur franklin ministre / plenipotentiaire des Etats unis de / l'amérique / A passi

Notation: Made Conway.

From Joshua Johnson

ALS: American Philosophical Society

Honble. Sir Nantes 27 Mar. 1779

I rece'd the Honour of your favour of the 17 Instant. I am particularly obliged to you for the trouble you have taken with Mr. D:Arlincourt about the Duties on my Furniture & for getting it exempted from the Payment of them, I would not have given you any trouble on this Account had I not been perswaided that it might fix a Precedent on those Americans that hereafter Settles in France, but Sr. depend on it I feel the favour in the strongest manner and you may rely on a gratefull remembrance of it.

I will do every thing in my Power to obtain the Duties charged on all Goods Imported & Exported at this Port tho I fear much of being able to succeed to your wishes. Inclosed I foward you a Letter from the Govenor of Maryland, a Resolution of the House of Delegates dated 28 November 1777 and an Order of Council dated 3d April 1778[5] by which you will observe they have directed me to procure Sundry Cloathing &ca. or a loan of Money sufficient to purchase this amo. all which I should long ere this lain before you had I not been two well convinced that it would have met with opposition from one of your late Colleagues,[6] but as that object is now happily removed I hope through your Interest and known goodness to your Country to be able to satisfy our States request, I shall be greatly obliged to you for your opinion & directions on this Business and if you think my attendance at Paris will by any means promote their desire I will immediately set out on my Journey, but in the meantime I have taken the liberty to request Dr. Bancroft and Mr. Jenings[7] to wait on you & to take of your hands any trouble they possibly can which may attend this Business. Hoping that you will honour me with an Answer I remain with the most sincere attachment and regard Sir. Your most Obedt. & most Hble St

JOSHUA JOHNSON

His Excellency Benjamin Franklin Esqr.

Addressed: His Excellency / Benjamin Franklin Esqr. / Paris

Notation: J. Johnson Mar 1779

5. The Order of Council is printed in XXVI, 229–30, the other documents discussed in XXVI, 230n.

6. Presumably Arthur Lee, who, with his brother William, was engaged in a rival effort to secure French aid for Virginia; see BF's April 8 reply to Johnson.

7. Edmund Jenings, a fellow Marylander: XXIII, 320n; XXVIII, 513n.

From George Washington

ALS: American Philosophical Society; copy: Library of Congress

Dear Sir, Camp at Middlebrook[8] March 27th. 1779.

This letter will be delivered to you by Mr. Mason, son to George Mason Esqr. of Virginia, a Gentn. of fortune and influence in that state—a zealous & able supporter of the liberties of this Country—and a particular friend of mine.[9]

The young Gentlemans bad health induces him to try some other clime, probably the air of Montpelier, while inclination may lead him to Paris, in which case, I take the liberty of recommending him to your friendly countenance & civilities; give me leave at the sametime to assure you, that with the greatest esteem & regard I have the honr. to be Dr Sir Yr. Most Obedt. Hble Servt Go: Washington

The Honble. Benjn Franklin Esqr.

From Jonathan Williams, Jr.

ALS: American Philosophical Society; copy: Yale University Library

Dear & honoured Sir. Nantes March 27. 1779

I send you enclosed Messrs Horneca Fitzeau & Cos Invoice with such an order on them as appears to me equitable on all Sides, if you think so, please to sign it & return it with the Invoice. It will be proper for you to keep Copies of both these Papers.[1]

8. In New Jersey, Washington's 1778–79 winter headquarters: Freeman, *Washington*, IV, 425.

9. To our knowledge, BF never corresponded directly with the Virginia revolutionary leader, George Mason, who had requested letters of introduction for his son, George, Jr. (1753–96), from Washington to both BF and Lafayette. See Robert A. Rutland, ed., *The Papers of George Mason, 1725–1792* (3 vols., Chapel Hill, N.C., 1970), II, 488–9. The younger Mason remained in Europe until the spring of 1783, when he requested a letter of introduction from BF to Robert Morris. George Mason, Jr., to WTF, April 12, 1783, APS.

1. BF had requested this invoice concerning Simeon Deane's goods on March 16. He may have kept as his own copy the order JW enclosed here,

I return you enclosed the papers you so kindly communicated to me.—[2] I shall observe your Directions about how I came by them, but I suppose you have no objection to my mentioning the Fact, where I may have occasion of showing the great Skill & ability of my Calomniator.—[3]

I am ever with the greatest Respect most dutifully & affectionately Yours JONA WILLIAMS J

My Love to Billy.

P.S. to assure yourself that these Goods were delivered by me to Mr Schweighauser, please to see the marks & numbers in sd Mr Schweighausers Receipt transmitted to the Commrs in my Letter dated Jan. 23. 1779.— JW

The Hon. Doctor Franklin

Notation: Jona Williams March 27. 1779—

From Dumas

ALS: American Philosophical Society; AL (draft): Algemeen Rijksarchief

Monsieur Lahaie 28e. Mars *1779*

Mes dernieres sont du 15, & du 23–25 de ce mois. Jeudi[4] l'assemblée d'Hollde. fut longue; & l'on ne put en venir à une Résolution. Des Villes d'Hollande les principales furent de

---

and used it as a draft of the letter he sent on April 20 to Horneca, Fizeaux & Co.; see our annotation to that letter.

2. Which were enclosed with BF's letter of March 19. They included a recently discovered report on Montieu's accounts made by Arthur Lee the previous September, and copies of Montieu's proposals and contract with the commissioners.

3. JW had, in fact, already mentioned those papers. BF's letter had arrived on the 23rd. On March 24 JW wrote to William Carmichael repeating, almost exactly as BF had written it, the description of how Lee had erred in evaluating Montieu's accounts. JW also enclosed copies of all correspondence relevant to his attempts to assemble a group of merchants to examine his own controversial accounts (eleven letters in all). Yale University Library.

4. March 25.

l'avis d'Amsterdam, ou en firent semblant: les autres, au nombre de 10, furent de celui du Prince. Il faut savoir, que l'Assemblée consiste en 19 Membres, savoir le Corps des Nobles, qui n'a qu'une voix, & 18 villes,[5] dont chacune a sa voix: or la voix de la moindre se compte comme celle de la plus grande. Le corps des nobles est de 8 têtes; le Stadhouder fait la 9e. Quatre de ces Nobles, savoir Mrs. Vanderduyn de Maasdam, Wassenaar Obdam, Wassenaar Sterrenburg, & Aarssen de Sommelsdyk, n'approuvent point la proposition. Les quatre autres, savoir les 2 Boetselaar, Nordwyk & Catwyk, opinent pour la proposition. J'ai dit à notre Ami, que je voulois parier qu'on ne résoudra rien: il n'a pas osé me prendre au mot. L'effet seul du Reglement françois[6] pourra amollir à la longue ces coeurs endurcis. Ils sont dans l'opinion, que la France n'est pas dans son sérieux, & qu'elle ne peut se passer d'eux. D'ailleurs ce qui vient de se passer aux Indes or. & occid. & en Géorgie, fait que tous les Anglomanes se rengorgent ici de nouveau. Je suis avec un grand respect, Monsieur

Votre très humble & tres obéissant Serviteur D——

Passy à S. E. M. Franklin

Addressed: à Son Excellence / Monsieur Franklin, Esqr., / Ministre Plenipotentiaire / des Etats-Unis de l'Amerique / à Passy./.

Notations in different hands: Dumas la haie. March. 28. 79 / Holland / Dumas

From Joseph Gellée[7]

ALS: American Philosophical Society

Monsieur Chaalons sur Marne 28 Mars 1779.

J'esperois de jour a autre pouvoir faire le voïage de paris, ou une affaire importante m'appelle. J'aurois eû l'honneur,

5. For their names see Dumas' letter of March 29.

6. For the French suspension of Dutch trading privileges see our annotation of Dumas' letter of March 1.

7. This distinguished physician was the father of BF's secretary, Nicolas-Maurice Gellée: XXVI, 401n.

Monsieur, en vous presentant mon respectüeux hommage, de vous faire de vive voix mon compliment sur votre nomination a la place de Ministre plenipotentiaire a la cour de françe. Abstraction de toutes autres raisons qui ont pû determiner le Congrés dans son choix, il en est une, Monsieur, que je regarde comme un trait de politique des plus adroits de sa part. "La premiere attention a faire dans le choix d'un Ambassadeur (dit Wiquefort) est qu'il soit agreable a la nation auprés de laquelle on l'envoit."[8] Vous emportez personellement, Monsieur, l'estime generale de la nation françoise; et cette estime generale des françois pour Monsieur franklin doit etre pour le Congrés un sûr garant du succès de votre Mission.

Puisse mon fils se rendre digne, Monsieur, de votre confiançe! J'ai remis en vos mains tous mes droits sur lui; et, ce qui sera a jamais pour moi un motif de la plus vive reconoissançe, vous eûtes la bonté de me dire que vous en prendriez soin. Jai L'honneur d'etre avec respect Monsieur Votre tres humble, et tres obeïssant serviteur GELLÉE

Notation: Gellée 28 Mars 1779.

From Landais

ALS: American Philosophical Society

Please Your Excellency Brest March 28th. 1779

I landed the day Before yesterday the Eight and thirty mutiners, I am getting Ready for to Sail for Nantes as fast as Possible and Expect to be ready in Eight days thence. I have had here all the Iron work repair'd and nothing but the most necessary things have been done or had. I shall wait for your orders at Nantes in a forteen night if the wind Permits.

I am with the Greateast Respect Your Excellencys Most Obeidaint humble Servant P: LANDAIS.

8. A paraphrase of L.M.P. [Abraham von Wicquefort], *Mémoires touchant les ambassadeurs et les ministres publics* (Cologne, 1677), p. 241. Wicquefort (1606–82) had been minister of Brandenburg-Prussia to the French court at the end of the Thirty Years' War: *Repertorium der diplomatischen Vertreter,* I, 36.

P.S. The Honnble John Adam is here I hope he will Go to Nantes in the Ship.[9]

To his Excellency Dr franklin

Notation: P. Landais 28. Mar. 79.

From Marat

ALS: American Philosophical Society

Ce Lundy 29 Mars 79.

Jesperois, Monsieur, que vous nous feries lhonneur d'assister aux dernieres Sceances de MM. les Commissaires, et M. le Roy m'en avoit flatté.

Comme les nouvelles experiences Sur lèlectricité ont étés imaginees par l'Auteur pour vous Seul, j'ai remis a les faire que nous eussions le plaisir de vous posseder. Je conte que vous voudres bien accepter la partie pour demain Sur les dix heures du matin. La chambre obscure est trés comode, l'apareil trés complet, et tous les instrumens jouent à volonté.

J'ai l'honneur detre avec les Sentimens les plus respectueux Monsieur Votre trés humble et tres obeissant serviteur

LE REPRESENTANT DE LAUTEUR

To [Marat]

ALS: American Philosophical Society

Sir Passy. Monday March 29.—79.

I am extreamly sorry that I could not be present at your curious Experiments on Saturday, and that indispensible Business will prevent my waiting on you to-morrow: I shall be at liberty the rest of the Week, if some other day may be convenient to you; and will then attend them with Pleasure, being very sensible of the honour done me in your obliging Invita-

9. JA had told BF on March 24 that he planned to return to Nantes by land to await the ship. On the same day he had told WTF that Landais expected to sail in eight days and that the *Alliance*'s stay in Nantes would be three or four weeks: *Adams Papers*, VIII, 16. JA was already back in Nantes on April 11, the day the *Alliance* finally sailed from Brest: Butterfield, *John Adams Diary*, II, 358n.

tion.— I am, with great Esteem, Sir, Your most obedient & most humble Servant B FRANKLIN

From Dumas

ALS: American Philosophical Society; AL (draft): Algemeen Rijksarchief

Monsieur, Lahaie 29[–31]e. Mars *1779*

Ma Lettre d'hier vous expose la division qu'il y a dans le Corps des Nobles de cette Province: voici celle des villes.

Pour la derniere proposition du Stadhr.[1] se sont déclarées les villes suivantes: Gouda, Brielle, Hoorn, Enkhuysen, Edam, Monnikendam, Medemblick, Purmerende.— Contre la Proposition: Dort, Harlem, Delft, Leide, Amsterdam, Rotterdam, Schiedam, Alcmar.— Les deux Villes de Gorcum & de Schoonhoven ont pris la chose ad referendum; & l'on croit qu'elles se rangeront du côté d'Amsterdam.— Les Députés de Rotterdam ont déclaré, non seulement au Stadhr., mais à l'Assemblée-même, que leurs Bourgeois commençoient à perdre patience, c'est-à-dire, qu'il y avoit des émeutes à craindre. Le Grand-Pensre., pour les tranquilliser, leur a dit Samedi dernier, que Mardi 30e. tout sera ajusté à leur gré. C'est ce que disent aussi certains Torys modérés. Notre Ami me l'a confirmé.

du 31e.

Enfin la derniere proposition du Stadhouder succomba hier à l'Assemblée provinciale d'Hollande, par une pluralité de 10 villes contre 7 à 8. Gouda & Gorcum se rangerent du côté d'Amsterdam. Schoonhoven se joignit aux 6 villes de la Nordhollande du côté du Stadhr. La Brielle biaisa. Le Corps des Nobles, partagé, ne pencha du côté du Stadhr. que pour autant qu'il en est le 9e. Membre. La résolution fut donc prise de convoyer incessamment tout ce qui n'est pas expressément déclaré contrebande par les Traités.[2] On essaya de faire faire une

1. To exclude timber from the convoys to be escorted: Dumas to BF, March 24–25, above.

2. Specifically the Anglo-Dutch maritime treaty of 1674 which provided that only contraband of war could be seized from a neutral vessel and did

protestation au Corps des Nobles contre cette résolution; mais comme il se trouvoit partagé également, il n'y eut pas moyen. Au défaut de cette protestation, qui ne peut plus avoir lieu, le Pce.[3] fera faire aujourdhui par la noblesse une nouvelle proposition: démarche inutile, qui ne pourra rien changer à la resolution, ni à son exécution. Cette résolution de la province d'hollde. devra être communiquée aux Etats-Généraux: ainsi il se passera encore quelque temps avant qu'on ait la résolution générale des provinces: mais on n'a pas besoin de l'attendre pour convoyer les vaisseaux. Ce qui augmente l'embarras de la Cour c'est que de toute la pétition pour l'état de guerre pour cette année,[4] les villes n'ont encore consenti qu'à la levée de l'impôt, au moyen du quel cet état de guerre des provinces sera entretenu, & nullement à l'application des deniers provenants de cet impot. Ainsi elles n'ont proprement pas encore consenti à la pétition de guerre pour l'an 1779.

Les Etats d'hollde. se separeront Samedi, pour se rassembler dans la quinzaine.

Je suis avec un grand respect, Monsieur Votre très humble & très obeissant servit. D

Passy à Son Exc. M. Franklin

Addressed: à Son Excellence / Monsieur Franklin, Esqr. / Ministre plenip. des Etats-Unis / de l'Amerique / à Passy./.

Notation: Dumas la haie March. 29. 80

---

not include naval stores and timber among the items listed as contraband: Samuel F. Bemis, *The Diplomacy of the American Revolution* (rev. ed.; Bloomington, Ind., 1957), p. 135; Daniel A. Miller, *Sir Joseph Yorke and Anglo-Dutch Relations, 1774–1780* (The Hague and Paris, 1970), pp. 69–70n. A French translation of the resolution is given in Fauchille, *Diplomatie française,* pp. 126–7.

3. The "Prince," or stadholder: Fauchille, *Diplomatie française,* p. 126.

4. *I.e.,* the military budget.

From William Lee

ALS: American Philosophical Society

Paris Hotel D'Espagne Rue Guenegaud March 30th 1779

Sir,

I had the Honor of writing the 23d. of Jany. last to the American Commissioners at the Court of Versailles[5] requesting that they wou'd, in consequence of the recommendation of Count De Vergennes, apply to the Prince De MontBarey for certain Artillery, Arms & Ammunition for the State of Virginia which I had authority to engage that State to pay for, as soon as it was practicable to send their Commdities to Europe for that purpose.[6]

To this Letter I have not recd. any answer, nor do I know whether any application on the business has been made to Prince De MontBarey or not: I am now therefore to request that you Sir, will be so good, as Minister Plenepotentiary here from Congress, to do this favor to the State of Virginia; in which case I will do myself the Honor of waiting on you any time tomorrow that you shall appoint, with a list of the Articles wanted;[7] the particulars of which, were annexed to my Letter above mention'd.

Those things that appear to me most necessary to be immediately dispatched are 20,000 Stand of Fusils & Bayonets compleat, 20 Tons best Canon Powder, 20 Tons best Fusil powder, & the more so as I apprehend Congress depends on each State for supplying these things for the Troops they raise for the General Service this Campaign.

I have the Honor to be with the Highest Consideration and Respect Sir Your most Obedient & most Humble Servant

W: LEE

P.S. The favor of an answer is requested by the Bearer

5. XXVIII, 413–14.

6. Lee had received his orders from Patrick Henry in the spring of 1778. Thereafter, the attempts to procure military supplies for Virginia became increasingly complicated; see, in particular, XXVII, 361–3.

7. BF gave Lee an appointment for that evening or the next day; see the following letter. The list Lee brought of artillery, arms, and ammunition needed by Virginia, dated March 31, 1779, is at the APS. It approximates the list Lee had sent the commissioners on Jan. 23; that list is published in *Adams Papers*, VII, 375–6.

His Excellency Benjamin Franklin Esqr. Minister Plenepotentiary from the United States of America to the Court of Versailles, at Passy.

Addressed: His Excellency / Benjamin Franklin Esqr. / Minister Plenepotentiary from the / Congress of the United States of / America at the Court of Versailles, / at Passy

To William Lee

Copy:[8] Library of Congress

Sir, Passy March 30th. 1779.

I do not recollect ever to have seen the Letter you mention. When Capt. Le Maire came over last year, and made known here the Wants of Virginia,[9] I found three different Merchants of Ability who offer'd each of them separately to supply the whole. I do not know why their Offers were not accepted, & the Business hitherto remains undone.[1] I have heard that Cannon & some Stores, have been obtained of the Government by your Brother but know not the Particulars. I shall be glad to see you on the Subject and to be better informed. I shall dine to day in the City, and will do myself the honor of calling on you, between 5 & 6 à Clock. But if it should be inconvenient to you to be then at home, I will expect you, if you please, at Passy the Morning following— I have the honor to be with great Respect Sir, &c— B FRANKLIN

Honble. W. Lee Esq.

8. In the hand of WTF.

9. Jacques Le Maire de Gimel had delivered William Lee's orders from Virginia; he also brought a letter from Patrick Henry to BF: XXVI, 34–6; XXVII, 361.

1. BF explained this in greater detail to Patrick Henry on Feb. 26: XXVIII, 611–12. The three merchants were Chaumont, Montieu, and a Mr. Bayard: BF to Arthur Lee, July 9 (Library of Congress). The last was probably François-Louis Bayard, who later claimed to have sent five munitions ships to America at BF's instigation; four of them were captured, leading to Bayard's bankruptcy: *DBF; Jefferson Papers,* VI, 399.

From Marie-Nicole Grossart de Virly Gérard[2]

ALS: American Philosophical Society

a versailles ce 30 mars 1779

Je me suis adressée a vous, Monsieur, pour vous prier de faire rachetter une boëte que j'avois envoyée a M. Gerard, vous avez eu la bonté de me promettre de faire faire les démarches necessaires pour cet objet. Comme il y a déjà un peu de tems que je vous ai importunée, permettez moi de vous en demander des nouvelles, je sçais Combien les affaires interressantes dont vous etes chargé doivent éloigner de votre memoire la promesse que je reclame ici. Je prends le parti de vous la rappeller pour faire raison a la bonne volonté et a l'obligeance que vous m'avez marquées.

J'ai l'honneur d'etre, Monsieur, avec la plus haute Consideration, votre tres humble, et tres obeissante, servante

DEVIRLY GERARD

Mr. Franklin

Endorsed: Mad Gerard, 30 Mar 79—concerning a Snuff Box

From David Hartley

ALS: American Philosophical Society; transcript: Library of Congress

Dear Sir London March 30 1779

Yours of March 21st received. I have in my own private thoughts been very much displeased with the delays wch we have met with in the affair of the Exchange of prisoners. I had before the receipt of yours, made some strong remonstrances upon the Subject, and yesterday I went again to the Admiralty with my Complaints. Mr Stephens the Secretary did assure me, upon his honour, that the delays have been unavoidable; that the transport was beat back twice, or I think three times,

2. The wife of Conrad-Alexandre Gérard, the current French minister in Philadelphia: XXVII, 630n. She first had sought American help five months earlier in recovering the box, taken to Guernsey by a British privateer: XXVII, 630–1; XXVIII, 4, 55.

between the Downs & Plymouth; that so far from any wish of delay that they had appointed a Lieutenant to command the Cartel ship, and not a trading owner, who might be tempted to make a job of delay. He gave such full assurances of the intentions of government, that I really hope that they mean to proceed with the quickest dispatch. You may be assured that I will do every thing in my power to press them on.— Every incident, both great and small, concurs in my opinion to make peace most desireable. I know full well that our wishes are in perfect unison, And I assure you that my thoughts & labours are constantly employed upon that subject. If any favorable moment shd happen, even of any chance of *talking* about peace, I am constantly upon the watch. The principles alone upon wch I shall act (if ever I shd have the opportunity of putting my good wishes in to action) are Confidence, certainty, National safety and honour.—Your affecte DH

To Dr Franklin—

P.S. The following note just this moment recd. from the Admiralty—

"Mr. Stephens presents his compts. to Mr. Hartley & acquaints him that the Milford Cartel Vessel sailed the 25th. instant from Plymouth, with American prisoners for France."

Notation: D. H. London March 30. 1779.—

From Marat

ALS: American Philosophical Society

Ce mardy matin 30 Mars 79

MM. les Comissaires seront libres de tenir Seance jeudy, vendredy et Samedy prochains. Monsieur Franklin voudra bien me fixer celui de ces trois jours qui lui conviendra le mieux. Moins il differera lhonneur de Sa visite, plus j'en serai flatté.

LE REPRESENTANT DE L'AUTEUR.

To Stephen Sayre

Copy: Library of Congress

Sir Passy March 31 1779

I have just received your Favour of the 10th inst from Copenhagen. The Account you give of the Disposition of the Swedish Court is very agreeable. I saw in the News Papers that a Deputy of the Congress was at Stockholm; did you obtain the Audiences you mention by assuming that Character?[3] The Informations you did not chuse to venture by the Post from Copenhagen may be safely sent from Amsterdam.

I am not, as you have heard the sole Representative of America in Europe. The Commission of Mr. A. Lee, M. Wm. Lee, & Mr. Izard, to different Courts still subsist. I am only sole with Regard to France. Nor have I Power to give any Employ worth your Accepting.

Much has been said by the English about Divisions in America. No Division of any Consequence has arisen there. Petty Disputes between particular Persons about private Interests, there are always in every Country: But with Regard to the Great Point of Independence, there is no Difference of Sentiment in the Congress; and as the Congress are the annual Choice of the People, it is easy to judge of their Sentiments by those of their Representatives.

The taking of Savannah makes a Noise in England & helps to keep up their Spirits; But I apprehend before the Summer is over, they will find the Possession of that Capital of Georgia of as Little Consequence as their former Possessions of Boston & Philadelphia; and that the Distempers of that unwholesome Part of the Country will very much weaken, if not ruin that Army.

The principal Difficulty at Present in America consists in the Depreciation of their Currency, owing to the over-quantities issued, and the diminished Demand for it in Commerce. But as the Congress has taken Measures for sinking it expeditiously, and the several Governments are taxing vigor-

3. The March 26 issue of the *Gaz. de Leyde* carried an item from Stockholm dated 17 days earlier, which reported the departure for Copenhagen of Sayre, "l'un de ceux qui sont chargés des affaires de *l'Amérique-Unie* en *Europe.*"

ously for that Purpose, there is a Prospect of its recovering a proper Value.[4] In the mean Time, tho' an Evil to particulars, there is some Advantage to the Publick in the Depreciation, as large nominal Values are more easily paid in Taxes, & the debt by that Means more easily extinguished.

I have the Honor to be, Sir &c

Stephen Sayre Esq;

From John Adams

ALS: American Philosophical Society

Sir [Brest] Harbour[5] March 31. 1779

When I arrived at [this place] I found nothing done. Mr Costentin, it is said waited for orders.— And the officers of the Port, expected orders.— But Since my Arrival, as Mr Schweighauser wrote to Mr Costentin to take my Advice, he readily engaged in the Business, and the officers of the Port have afforded Us every facility, consistent with the Kings Service.

Mr Costentin and Captain Landais, I find are both very attentive to Articles of Expence; and do their Utmost to save. The Captain, in this View, has determined neither to sheath his ship in Copper, nor to lay her down to clean, but has applied for proper Instruments to hog her, as their Phrase is, and this operation is now finished so that her Bottom is at present very well cleaned. The Main Top Mast and rigging, is also preparing, the Water will be got on board as soon as possible, and I hope We shall be ready to go from this Port in six or Eight Days.

But there are still a Thousand Difficulties, on board the ship, and every Body is discontented, except the Captain who is as cool a Man as ever I saw.

I have had Petitions to me, from all the Crew, and personal applications from most of the officers. Little Misunderstand-

4. BF's optimism was misplaced; the states failed to pay Congress' huge requisitions: Ferguson, *Power of the Purse,* pp. 33–5.

5. The manuscript is torn where the seal has been removed, and when possible we have conjectured in brackets the missing words.

ings have arisen on Account of the Purser,[6] who is thought to keep the officers to too strict Allowance. But upon the whole I fancy, that Peace may be made and tolerable Content [*word or words missing*] allowing to the officers and Men a small Gratification in Money.

I have the Honour to inclose a List of the petit officers on Board, who are judged by Mr Schweighauser and Mr Costentin to be excluded, by your Excellencys order, from the Benefit of Cloathing which is granted to the Commission and Warrant officers.[7] This is such a Grievance, or at least is considered so, that I cannot avoid interceeding, most earnestly with your Excellency in their Behalf, and intreating that your orders may be given, on this Head, as soon as possible.

Another Thing, I cannot avoid requesting, because, I think the service will be much promoted by it, and without it, I know not what may be the Consequence. It is that Mr Schweighauser, may be ordered to Allow, a small sum of Money to officers and Men, at least to such as the Captain who I am sure is a prudent & frugal Man shall point out.

The Captains Parcimony in other Things will render this less difficult, and the Badness of the Pay, and the little Prospect of Prizes, considering the weak state of the ship in Men, render it an Act of Humanity, of Justice and indeed of Necessity. Many have families at home, and a little sum of Money well laid out here, in Articles of Cloathing, would be a vast Encouragement.

The Punctuality with which [*word or words missing*] as well as the Agent at Nantes and Brest, insist [*word or words missing*] explicit orders for every Thing, make it necessary, that I should request of your Excellency an order to Captain Landais, to give me a Passage in the ship, and to the Agent to furnish me with sea stores. They have all been very complaisant but I see they want, orders.

The Number of Men on Board the ship are not half enough

6. Nathan Blodget; see his letter of March 3.

7. The enclosure is missing. JA discussed the clothing allowance in his letter of March 24. For clothing on order for the *Alliance* see also our annotation of BF's letter to Schweighauser of March 11.

to fight her. If the Prisoners should arrive from England I hope that Captain Landais will be permitted to recruit out of them. I like Captain Jones very well, but I cannot but hope that he will not have all those Men. Landais is very averse, to taking french or English sailors, for my own Part I wish he had an hundred of each, and We would find a Way to suppress Conspiracies.— But He is afraid of Complaints of Partiality to his Countrymen, and of the Treachery, of Britons.

I have the Honour to be sir, your most obedient humble servant
JOHN ADAMS

His Excellency Dr Franklin

Addressed: A Son Excellence / Monsieur, Monsieur Franklin / Ministre Plenipotentiaire des / Etats Unis De L'Amerique / a Passy / Pres Paris—

Notation: John Adams Mar. 31. 79

From Benjamin Bannerman[8]

ALS: American Philosophical Society

Most Honourable Sir.—

City of Roann March 31th. 1779—

I having the agreable happiness of being in your compeny several years ago in America although you may have forgoat me. I also knowed Governer Franklin in the jerseys. I having been a resedenter in that country, 16 years, being Obliged to Advertize to leve the countray for alittle time to go to britain to satle a Smal Estate belonging to a brother. I took a passige in a Vessel going to London and was taken, and brought in to havre de [grace][9] the judge of the Admiralaty detened all my clothing [*word or words missing*] velluable and has also destroyed

8. A man by that name is listed in "Virginia Militia in the Revolution," which covers 1777: *Virginia Historical Magazine,* VI (1889), 400. A Benjamin Bannerman also signed a petition of American loyalists in the autumn of 1778: *W&MQ,* 2nd ser., I (1921), 70.

9. The manuscript is torn where the seal has been removed, and when possible we have conjectured in brackets the missing words.

lost, or mislead bonds [and obligations] to the Amount of Eight hundred pounds Sterling— I have petitioned the Lords of State On this Occesion but having permition granted me to go to England about my intended besiness before any Answre coud be given induces me to give your honnour the truble of this letter, On my way, Praying you to favour me with your Intrest on the Occesion. I am desird to take my passige to america by the way of Nantz and shall dou my selfe the honour of seeing you at paris in my way I have derected my petition to Monseignear De Sartine Ministre and Secretaire d Etat—deted the 17th of March. Your aditional favour in giving the inclosed letter a passige derected To His Excellency Patrick Henry Governer of Virgina will be ever acknowledged. Honourable Sir I am with due regard and Esteem your most Obedt. humble Servant— BENJAMIN BANNERMAN

derect at Capt Robert Beadnall Parish of Shadwell No. 25 Dean Street London

Addressed: To / The Honourable Docter Franklin / Menester for the United States / of America In Paris

Notation: Benjamin Bannerman City of Roann 31. mars 1779.

From Lafayette

ALS: American Philosophical Society

Dear Sir [*c.* March 31, 1779][1]

I went yesterday to pay My Respects to your Excellency, and waïted as long as it was in My power— I wanted telling you that I hope the Expedition will be fix'd upon but the scale yet lessened—[2] So that we Can't do so much as was expected, but however some advantage May be got by this little incursion—Mr de Maurepas thinks it highly Necessary to Converse with Captain, and Mr de Sartine is averse to the pushing on of the preparations Before I have settled the Matter with

1. On April 1 Lafayette wrote Vergennes that the previous day he had left this letter for BF (who was not at home): Idzerda, *Lafayette Papers,* II, 251.

2. The expedition is discussed in BF's letter of March 22 to Lafayette.

the Captain— I therefore am directed By all the Ministry to send for him that I Might thereby get intelligences and lay down the plan— they will afterwards take a last determination, and know if the operation will be undertaken—whatever will be sent I'll have the Command of.[3]

In Compliance with the king's and the Ministry's desire I Engag'd Mr de Chaumont to send for Captain jones and I do expect him with a great impatience—[4] I presum'd to take upon Myself telling to him that you had no objection to his Coming and that even you did wish for it— I din't enter into Any explication with Mr de Chaumont as the stricter secrecy is Reccommended to you and to Me under our words of honor which for my part I took the liberty to engage.

I write to the Ministry this morning for engaging them to Buy some frigattes— I find Myself oblig'd to go to St. Germain for three days, I will saturday to Versaïlles, and Come that Night to Paris. If you have any Commands to lay upon me I shall very heartily obey them. Be so Kind, My dear Sir, as to Give the inclos'd to Mr Blodget of the Alliance.

I wish our expedition little as it is Might take place as it will plague our Good friends, and perhaps Get some Monney for america—with too such points of wiew I'd go Round the world.

With all possible Respect and affection I have the honor to be Dear Sir Yours LAFAYETTE

Notation: Lafayatte 1779

3. Approval for Jones's undertaking was forthcoming (although later rescinded); see Sartine's letter to BF of April 27.

4. Chaumont had long been an intermediary between Jones and the naval ministry and had helped arrange the purchase of the *Duc de Duras* (later *Bonhomme Richard*): XXVIII, 6, 159–60n; Jean Boudriot, *John Paul Jones and the Bonhomme Richard: a Reconstruction of the Ship and an Account of the Battle with H.M.S. Serapis* (trans. David H. Roberts, Annapolis, 1987), pp. 16–17. Lafayette immediately suggested to Vergennes that Chaumont be invited to help plan the expedition; in the process Jones was forced to abandon his own plans to raid the English coast: Idzerda, *Lafayette Papers,* II, 251–3. Chaumont soon was involved in assembling crews and munitions and eventually served as paymaster for Jones's squadron on behalf of the French government: *ibid.*, p. 264n; Morison, *Jones,* p. 192.

From Marat

ALS: American Philosophical Society

Sir Wednesday 29th [*i.e.* 31][5] of March 79.

The honour of your company is desired for thursday or friday next, at ten o clock in the morning, at the hotel of M le Marquis de lAubespine Rue de Bourgogne. F S. G. where MM of the Committee will meet.

The new experiments on the Electrical fluid have been postponed till you are present.

I am with respect, Sir Your most obedient humble Servant

THE REPRESENTATIVE

To Sartine

Copy: Library of Congress

Passy April 1st. 1779

Commodore Gillon has shown me a Project for reducing the English Force in Georgia, by the Help of some Ships from hence.[6] I am not sufficiently a Judge of Military Operations to speak positively of it. I can only say that in my Opinion the Advantage arising from its Success would be very great to the Common Cause; and that the extensive Confidence which appears by his Papers to be placed in Mr. Gillon by the Government of Carolina to whom he is well known, prejudice me much in favour of his Judgement and Abilities in planning such an Undertaking. I therefore beg leave to recommend it to your Excellencys Consideration; and am with the greatest Respect, Your Excellency's, most obedient and most humble Servt. (signed) B. FRANKLIN.

His Ex. M. De Sartine.

5. He must have meant the 31st; he and BF had exchanged letters on the 29th, above.

6. For his plan see our annotation of Sartine's letter of March 22.

From ——— Brault and ——— Demezandré[7]

ALS:[8] American Philosophical Society

Monseigneur A Saint Malo 1er. Avril 1779.

Travaillant depuis plusieurs années dans le commerce, jeunes & pleins d'Ambition, cherchant partout la liberté, nous resolûmes de passer dans les Etats unis pour y etablir une maison. Par le secours d'Amis & de Protecteurs que nous avons a Paris, nous armâmes deux navires considerables. L'un de nous eût alors l'honneur de se presenter devant vous & la satisfaction de recevoir vos avis sur son voyage; enfin, d'obtenir des Lettres de recommandation de Mr. Dean.

Nous partîmes, mais nous ne fumes pas entierrement heureux, un des navires fut pris par les Anglais a l'entrée de la baie de Chezapeack; nous arrivâmes a Charles-Town, in *SouthCarolina,* sur l'autre; mais le haut prix des Indigos & des Tabacs en ce port ne nous a pas permis de realiser ici, il y a eû de la perte. Nous etions repassés pour entreprendre une nouvelle affaire qui put nous dedommager, mais nous avons trouvé les interessés degoûtés & ne voulant pas armer dans le moment present.

Comme les Denrées de l'Amerique sont a valleur égale, beaucoup plus volumineuses que celles qu'on y porte de france nous ne pûmes rapporter que très petite partie de celles qui nous appartenaient en propre, & nous laissâmes le reste a Charles-Town. A la persuasion de MM Parker, Gervais, Thimothy & autres de nos amis,[9] nous en plaçâmes une forte part sur le Trésor de la Caroline-meridionnalle. Mrs. Le Couteulx

7. The latter may well be the same person as the Mézandré whose complaints in 1786 launched a French navy department inquiry into American competition in the St. Domingue trade: Jean Tarrade, *Le commerce colonial de la France à la fin de l'Ancien Régime* . . . (2 vols., Paris, 1972), II, 650–1.

8. In Brault's hand.

9. "Thimothy" is BF's friend Peter Timothy (V, 341n). Jean Lewis Gervais (1741–95) looked after Henry Laurens' property while he was in Congress: *Laurens Papers,* IV, 331–2n. Parker could be the S.C. politician John Parker (*Biographical Directory of the American Congress, 1774–1961* [Washington, 1961], p. 1425) or one of two brothers, the merchants William and George Parker (*Laurens Papers,* III, 31n).

de Paris[1] ont actuellemt. entre les mains deux contracts de vingt mille sept cens pounds, dont ils ne trouveront probablement la négociation qu'avec difficulté.

Cependant le placement de ces fonds, l'espérance de réüssir a etablir notre maison, exigeraient que nous repassassions au plustôt dans le continent, n'importe en quel endroit. Nous ne saurions le faire avec trop de sureté et c'est pour cela, Monseigneur, que nous nous addressons a vous pour vous demander passage sur la frégate L'Alliance, avec quelques effets necessaires a notre etablissement. Car il nous est impossible de faire un armement ni par nous qui n'avons pas eligé nos fonds, ni par nos amis qui ont été degoûtés par les pertes que le Commerce vient d'eprouver depuis quelque tems. M Lelandais qui est le Capne. de la fregate l'Alliance, est notre compatriotte, et il nous a promis son agrément si vous vouliez nous accorder notre demande.

Nous espèrons, Monseigneur, qu'animé du plus grand Zèle pour le bien de votre patrie et porté, par Carractère a la bienfaisance, vous ne refuserez pas deux jeunes gens qui vont y porter de l'industrie & des secours.

Nous ne vous ferons point fatiguer par la sollicitation des grands dont nous pourions eprouver la protection en ce moment. C'est a votre Philosophie a votre empressement a repandre les bienfaits que nous en appellons.

Nous sommes connus particullierement de Mr. Le marquis de la Royerie[2] qui sert encore les Etats unis et de tout saint Malo; si vous voulez des informations Monseigneur, nous emploierons nos amis auprès de vous.

Nous sommes avec le plus profond respect Monseigneur De votre Excellence Les très humbles et très obeïssants serviteurs

DEMEZANDRÉ
BRAULT

Notation: Demezandré & Brault St Malo 1 ap. 79

1. A Parisian banking house with a branch in Cadiz: XXVII, 260n.
2. The marquis de La Rouërie, a fellow Breton: XXV, 383n.

From Jan Ingenhousz

Letterbook abstract: Gemeente-Archief, Statserf, Breda

April 1. 1779

a *Franklin,* que le volume des Trans. philos. contains two papers of mine.[3] That another paper is read upon a new theory of gunpowder which I have imagined.[4] That I desire that his nephew should send me what money he has in hand for that I think trade is too precarious in the present circumstances of time.[5]

From Jonathan Williams, Jr.

ALS: American Philosophical Society

Dear & hond Sir Nantes April 1. 1779.

I have recvd a Letter for Mr Moylan relative to the Bills payable to Mr Dennie, & therefore request you to make no opposition to the Payment of them.—

It is said that a Cartel with the american Prisoners on board is arrived in the River— I am not sure of it, but have no reason to doubt it.—[6]

The american Gentlemen are almost all of them near their Departure— I hope your Order for the Settlement of my accot is on the Road.—

3. Ingenhousz the previous year (XXVI, 439) had acquainted BF with the invention that was the subject of the first paper, entitled "A ready Way of lighting a Candle, by a very moderate Electrical Spark," *Phil. Trans.,* LXVIII (1778), 1022–6, read July 9, 1778. The second paper was "Electrical Experiments, to explain how far the Phenomena of the Electrophorus may be accounted for by Dr. Franklin's Theory of positive and negative Electricity . . . ," *ibid.,* pp. 1027–48, read June 4, 1778.

4. "Account of a new Kind of inflammable Air or Gass, which can be made in a Moment without Apparatus . . . together with a new Theory of Gunpowder," *ibid.,* LXIX (1779), pp. 376–418. Ingenhousz presented the paper to the Royal Society on March 25, 1779.

5. For the background of Ingenhousz's financial dealings with JW, who was handling the investments of both Jan Ingenhousz and his brother, see XXV, 85, and XXVIII, 112. See also JW's letter of April 13, below.

6. On April 2 Schweighauser reported to JA the arrival of the cartel ship *Milford: Adams Papers,* VIII, 21.

I hope the News from Paris to day about the Success of the French in the West Indies & of the americans in Georgia is true.

I am ever most dutifully & affectionately yours &c &

J Williams J

Dr Franklin

Notation: Jon. Williams ap 1. 79.

From Amos Windship

LS: American Philosophical Society

May it please your Excellency, Brest April 1st. 1779.

By the particular direction of Peter Landais Esqr I have sent the Account of my Expences to & from Paris,[7] (as per Receipts) to the Agent at Nantes, together with Capt Landais Orders, at the same time I drew an Order on Mr John D Sweighauser in favor of Mr E I Solomon,[8] who was kind enough to advance the Money for me as Capt Landais was not in Cash at that time,—Nor was it in my Power to do otherways as I brought but three Guineas with me from America, & spent those for my own Amusements when at Paris;—But fearing the Agent might object to answering the Order, Capt Landais judg'd it proper to inform you, setting forth & mentioning particular Charges in the Account.— If the Account should be thought large I can only say that I endeavour'd to be as prudent & frugal as possible, one Reason perhaps of its amounting to so much is the disadvantage I was under in not being acquainted with the language of the Country,—& another the necessity I was under of taking a Carriage by myself when on my Return, from Nantes,—[9] I trust your Excelly

7. Windship arrived back at Brest on Feb. 28 from his trip to Passy; see Landais' letter of March 3.

8. Possibly M. Salomon, the gentleman's tailor of Lorient who in June would present Jones with a large bill for ten uniforms he had made for officers of the *Bonhomme Richard* (Morison, *Jones,* p. 194).

9. We surmise that BF used Windship to carry his Feb. 16, [*i.e.,* 17] letter (XXVIII, 557–8) to Schweighauser at Nantes about fitting the *Alliance* for sea. The journey must have taken under a week, as Windship left Passy for Brest on or soon after the 22nd: XXVIII, 512.

from the present representation will give directions to the Agent to Answer the Order I have drawn in favor of Mr Solomon, & am, with the greatest respect, Yr Excellcys most Obedt. & most Hble Serv AMOS WINDSHIP

His Excellcy Benja. Franklin Esqr

Addressed: His Excellcy. Benja. Franklin Esqr / Minister Plenipotentiary / for the United States / of America, / Paris

Notation: Amos Windship Brest 1er. avril 1779.

From D'Acosta frères

ALS: American Philosophical Society

Monsieur, Paris 3 [*i.e.*, 2] avril 1779./.[1]

Nous prenons la liberté de vous remettre ci-joint un mémoire dont nous vous supplions de prendre lécture: Il a pour objet les fournitures que nous devions éxpedier pour l'Etat de Virginie, d'après les demandes qui nous avoient été faites par M. Lée, & qu'il n'a plus voulu recevoir lors qu'elles ont été prêtes.[2] Nous désirons, Monsieur, que vous nous mettiez à même de donner aux états de nouvelles preuves de notre Zéle par l'envoy de marchandises de premiere qualité dont ils doivent avoir le plus grand besoin.

Nous sommes avec un profond respect, Monsieur, Vos très-humbles & Très-obeissants Serviteurs D'ACOSTA FRERES

1. Because BF and William Lee exchanged letters on April 2 concerning the contents and enclosure of the present one, we assume that this letter was misdated.

2. The memorandum is dated March 26, and recounts the disagreement with Arthur Lee over the contract he had made with the firm on July 1, 1778, to supply military goods to Virginia. The firm has advanced all expenses and stipulated a five per cent commission. Lee refuses to accept the goods; his demand that they be ready for shipping by the end of September was unreasonable, since once supplied, they also had to be individually inspected by Le Maire. Le Maire and his team had worked unceasingly and had only finished their inspection at the end of October. D'Acosta frères, which is willing to send the goods on their own ship the *Courier de l'Europe,* asks BF to oversee the contract and expedite the shipping of these desperately needed supplies. APS. For background on the contract and BF's view of the situation, see in particular XXVII, 361–3; XXVIII, 611–12.

To William Lee

Copy: Library of Congress

Sir

Passy April 2 1779

Before I apply for the Arms you desire, I wish to be informed whether your Brother did not apply for them at the same Time he apply'd for the Cannon he obtained;[3] or since, in Consequence of the Letter you mention to have sent us in January last; and whether they were refused or promised.

Since I had the Honor of seeing you I have received an Application from the Government of Maryland for a similar quantity of Arms & military Stores, which I am requested to obtain in the same manner,[4] and these, with the Orders of Congress, will make so vast a quantity that I apprehend greater Difficulties in obtaining them. I shou'd be glad therefore if a Part cou'd be obtained elsewhere, that the quantity now to be apply'd for might be diminished. On this Occasion, permit me to mention that the d'Acosta's have presented a Memorial to me[5] setting forth that they had provided Arms &c—to a great Amount, in Consequence of a Contract made with you, thro' your Brother; and that for no other Reason but because they were not furnished at the Time agreed there having been a Delay of a Month, which they say was not their Fault, but inevitable, he had refused to take them. Upon this they desire that I wou'd procure Justice to be done them; or that I wou'd approve of their sending the Goods and endeavour to have the Contract comply'd with on the Part of Virginia. I declined having anything to do with the Affair; But I wish you to consider whether it wou'd not be prudent to accomodate this little difference with those People, and take the Advantage of sending those Arms, which have been prov'd good, and I suppose still lie at Nantes ready to be shipt immediately, rather than wait the success of a doubtful Application.

I have the Honor to be Sir &c

Honble. Wm. Lee Esq.

3. See XXVII, 362.
4. See Joshua Johnson's letter of March 27.
5. Described in the preceding letter.

From David Hartley

ALS: American Philosophical Society; transcript: Library of Congress

My Dear friend London April 2 1779

I writ you word in my last that the first hundred of the American prisoners were sailed, therefore I hope that business is in a fair way of getting forward—[6] Peace you know is always my object. If any advice of mine may be influential I assure you it *is* not, nor ever *will be* wanting. I am just at this moment more anxious for the depending events than I can express. If the State of things in Europe shd plunge us all in to a general war, I know not when the end wd come. The misery & destruction wd be universal, and America itself might think the assistance of France dearly bought, if they are to have no settled peace, till a war originally beginning in America, & from American concerns, but afterwards becoming a general European war, shd come to its termination. I think that it is the object of all parties to stop the farther madness of war: But where shall we find sense enough to do it? I think it might be practicable nearly upon the grounds wch I have stated in some of my former letters to you. If any negotiation cd be opened by the intervention of any person or persons, in whom the respective parties cd have Confidence, that wd afford the best, and I shd hope, some probable foundation.[7] Good faith & a national Confidence must lay that foundation. As to myself I can only say, that if that office shd ever be offered to me, consistently with those principles of Justice, and sound policy, (as I think them) wch have been and allways will be the rule of

6. See the postscript of his March 30 letter. Only ninety-seven of the prisoners actually sailed; two had already died and one was "dangerously ill." Charles Herbert, *A Relic of the Revolution* (Boston, 1847), p. 227.

7. Hartley had frequently expressed a desire for peace between England and America. The grounds upon which he thought it might be achieved, however, had shifted over the spring and summer of 1778. In May his proposals had included independence for America, although within a federal alliance: XXVI, 465–6. By August he had eliminated American independence from his propositions, concentrating instead upon ending armed hostilities, freeing prisoners, opening trade, and negotiating a truce for five years: XXVII, 243, 502–3. The "person or persons" who might open a negotiation was, of course, Hartley himself. See XXVIII, 417–18.

my conduct, I shall be ready to devote the utmost of my labours & attention, towards procuring for all parties a just, safe, honorable & permanent peace. Your affecte DH

To Dr Franklin

Addressed: To Dr Franklin

Endorsed: M Hartley

Notation: April 2. 1779.

From William Lee

ALS: American Philosophical Society; copy: University of Virginia Library

Sir. Paris Apl. 2. 1779.

I have recd. your favor of this days date in which you mention a complaint from the House of Penet Da Costa Freres & Co. that the Arms prepar'd in consequence of an agreemt. with me thro' my Br. were refus'd because they were not furnish'd at the time agreed.—

This complaint on the face of it gives its own answr. since they confess that they did not comply with their agreemt.—Why they have thus offended Justice & good Faith they must answer.

That house sign'd an agreemt. the first of July 1778 to send over for the State of Virga. good fusils & a variety of other Articles in the following words— "Et pour plus prompte expedition les Sieurs Penet Da Costa Freres & Ce. s'engagent de les expedier, au plus tard, a la fin de Septembre au déffaut de quoi, ce que n'aura pas èté executé en sera regardé comme non avenu, et les susdits conditions de nul effet."

Not an Article was ship'd agreeable to this engagemt. Some months after they *said* the Fusils were ready for shiping.[8] The Governor of Virginia havg. expressly directed them to be insur'd & that from the delay which they had made, having then

8. The firm's explanation was given in their memorandum of March 26, discussed in our annotation of their April 2 letter.

become impracticable from the general change in Circumstances, it was proposed to them to enter into a new engagement to send the goods on their own risk & be paid in proportion if they got safe. Their former breach of Agreemt. made it necessary to add a penalty on non compliance without which being express'd, it seems according to the Laws of this Country none can be recover'd.

This agreemt. they refus'd to enter into & therefore no farther notice was taken of them.

I have had too much experience on other occasions of the conduct of this house to waste a moments time in making any farther propositions relative to them, because I am sure it wou'd be only time lost, but perhaps Mr. Johnson who is on the spot may be more fortunate & may for the State of Maryland get those arms which they say they have provided for the State of Virga.

As this Company had engaged to ship these Articles my Brother did not enumerate them in what he applyed for to this Governmt.—Therefore I must request that you will apply to the Governmt. here for those of which I gave you a list two days ago & that you will as soon as possible let me know the issue of your application, that if they are obtain'd, I may loose no time in endeavoring to procure freight for them.

A Letter for me sent to Mr. Grands will be duely forwarded.

I have the Honor to be with the Highest Consideration Sir, Your most Obedt. and Most Humble Servt. W: LEE

His Excellency Benja. Franklin Esq. Passy—

Notation: Wm Lee 2d Ap. 79

From Antonio Francesco Salucci et fils

ALS: American Philosophical Society

My lord Leghorn the 2th April 1779

By This Post, We have been honoured, with Your Excellency favours, dated under the 18th: Last. The containing of the Same has Confirmed Us, in the good hopes We have conceived, about our Expedition to America, which Sailed out of Cadiz on The 2th: March, with a Convoy for 200. Leigues of a French Fleet comanded by Sir Espinosa[9] Together with 4. American, and 4. French Ships. If The said convoy, might reach as far as America, we had room, to be more Tranquil.

In The mean while, we Give to Your Excellency our most Sincere thanks, for The happy wishes, that Your goodness advances to Us for the good Success, of this undertaking; and We humbly beg Your Excellency in case of receiving any anticipate advice of the Arrival Theither of this tuscan Ship, to order one of your Secretarys to acquaint us with it. We beg also respectfully of you, to permit us, of Sending to America, Some Letters to our Captain, under the Pacquet of your Excellency, and for Such an Objet, we Took the Liberty to Send one, to Your Secretary by the Last Post, and we advance another in this which is for us equally Important.—

We are with all respect and Submission My lord Your most humble, obedt: and respectble servants

ANTONY FRANCIS SALUCCI & SON

Notation: Ant. Frs. Salucci & Sons Leghorn 2. Ap. 79.

To John Adams

LS:[1] Massachusetts Historical Society; copy: Library of Congress

Sir, Passy April 3d. 1779.

I received the Letter you did me the honour to write to me of the 24th past. I am glad you have been at Brest, as your Presence there has contributed to expedite the Operations of Capt. Landais in Refitting his Ship. I think with you, that

9. Actually Capt. de Coriolis d'Espinouse of the French ship of the line *Caton,* 74. He was the senior captain of a squadron consisting of his ship, the *Destin,* 74, *Magicienne,* 26, and *Atalante,* 26, which arrived at Cadiz from Toulon on Feb. 13, 1779. It sailed from there on March 3, arriving five days later at La Coruña, and finally reached Brest on May 15. Its progress can be followed in the Correspondance Politique: Espagne (AAE).

1. In WTF's hand.

more has been made of the Conspiracy than was necessary; but that it would have been well if some of the most guilty could have received a proper punishment. As that was impracticable under our present Naval Code, I hope you will on your Return obtain an Amendment of it. I approve of cloathing the Midshipmen and petty Officers, agreable to their Request to you, and hope you have order'd it, without waiting to hear from me; and I now desire that whatever else you may judge for the good of the Service, our Funds and Circumstances consider'd, you would in my Behalf give Directions for; as the great Distance makes it inconvenient to send to me on every occasion; and I can confide in your Prudence, that you will allow no Expence that is unnecessary.

My Gout continued to disable me from walking longer than formerly; but on Tuesday the 23d past, I thought myself able to go through the Ceremony and accordingly went to Court, had my Audience of the King in the new Character, presented my Letter of Credence, and was received very graciously.[2] After which I went the Rounds with the other Foreign Ministers, in visiting all the Royal Family. The Fatigue however was a little too much for my Feet, and disabled me for near another Week. Upon the whole I can assure you that I do not think the good Will of this Court to the good Cause of America, is at all diminish'd by the late little Reverses in the Fortune of War; and I hope Spain, who has now 49. Ships of the Line, and 31. Frigates ready for Service, will soon, by declaring, turn the Scale.[3]

Remember me affectionately to Master Johnny, and believe

2. The event is recorded in the March 30 issue of the *Gaz. de Leyde.*

3. Figures undoubtedly provided BF by the French government. Spanish Foreign Minister Floridablanca had promised Vergennes that by the end of May she would have fifty-four or fifty-five ships of the line ready: Dull, *French Navy,* p. 138n. At the moment a scathing critique of the Spanish Navy was en route to Vergennes from Montmorin, the French ambassador: Patterson, *The Other Armada,* pp. 62–4. For the importance of the Spanish Navy to the combined war effort against Britain see our annotation of BF's letter of May 26 to the committee for foreign affairs.

me with great Esteem, Sir, Your most obedient & most humble Servant B FRANKLIN

Honble Jn. Adams Esqre—

Endorsed: Dr Franklin. Ap. 3d. 1779 Ans. Ap. 13. 1779

From Arthur Lee

ALS: Historical Society of Pennsylvania

Sir/ Paris, April 3d. 1779

A Gentlemen calld on me this moment, who wishes for a Passport to gain him admission into the State of Virginia or any other of the United States. Upon my referring him to you, as the only person in this Country who coud give such a Passport, he informs me that he has already waited on you, & that you referrd him to me.

I beg the favor of you to write me, what you wish I shoud do, as it seems to me that it woud be very improper in me to give a Passport here, where you are Minister.

I have the honor to be with the greatest respect Sir yr. most Obedt. Servt ARTHUR LEE

The Gentleman says his name is Hunter.[4]

Notation: Arthur Lee April 3. 1779

To Arthur Lee

ALS: American Philosophical Society; AL (draft):[5] Historical Society of Pennsylvania

Sir Passy, April 3. 1779

As I had no Knowledge of the Gentleman, & he said he had lived in Virginia, I referr'd him to you, imagining you might

4. Perhaps George Hunter, an American previously recommended by two Irish merchants: XXVI, 528n.

5. Written on the verso of Lee's letter of the same day. There are minor differences in phraseology between this and the ALS. The draft, for example, begins "As I knew nothing of the Gentleman . . .". "Character" in the ALS is in the draft, "him or his Connections".

know something of his Character, and whether it would be proper to give him the Pass he desires. If upon conversing with him you apprehend it may be safely done, I would do it on your Recommendation: But as the Use of it is to be in America and not here, I imagine it would be as well for you to give it as me.— I have the honour to be with great Respect, Sir, Your most obedient & most humble Servant

B FRANKLIN

Honble Arthur Lee Esqr

Notation: April 3d. 1779

From Lawrence Boyd

ALS: American Philosophical Society

Brest Road April 3rd. 1779 On Board the Sloop Kingston

Most Worthy Sir/

I hope you will pardon the Freedom I take in addressing myself an entire Stranger to you, but I havg: had the Pleasure of seeing you in London & very well acquainted with your Universal Character & ever Distinguished Mark of Lenity & Compassionate Disposition towards the distressed & this being only on the Behalf of 3 Distress'd Captains & 2 others on Board the Patience Brigg here, whom since I havg: acquainted them of the Cartell for the American's being settled, have applied to me for a Passage to England which I am ready to give them, as havg: large Families & entirely expended what Money they had with being confin'd for near these 12 Months. Therefore most certainly will find it a great Hardship in travelling to St: Maloes, whither I can assure you she is station'd from Plymouth, her Name is the *Milford,*[6] Captn: Levitt, Mr: Nox Lieutenant on Behalf of Governmt: both of whom I am very well acquainted with & with whom I parted in the Downs which I acquainted the Prisoners with at Plymouth. I hope Sir you will take their Case into Consideration & favor me with an Order directed to Mr: Riou[7] to whom I am

6. Which had just arrived at Nantes; see JW's letter of April 1.

7. Pierre Rïou, interpreter at Brest, was in charge of the prisoners on the *Patience:* XXVIII, 210.

ready to give any Discharge you think proper; I have already applied to Adams[8] who informed me you were the only Person that had that Power in France. Therefore I made bold to address these few Lines to you; I shall esteem it a particular Favor of an Ansr: as soon as possible as I am in Expectation of sailing every Day as the Nobleman whom I had the Honor of conveying from England is expected here hourly therefore I hope Sir you will pardon the Haste of Sir Your most Obt: & Hble Servt:

LAWCE: BOYD

1779

Addressed: The Honourable Benjn: Franklin—/ Minister Plenipotentary—of the / United States of America—/ at Passy / Paris

From Dumas

ALS: American Philosophical Society; AL (draft): Algemeen Rijksarchief

Monsieur, 3[–13]e. Avril 1779

Les Etats d'Hollande se sont séparés, pour se rassembler dans 15 jours ou 3 semaines. Il ne se passa rien mercredi, qu'une espece de protestation des quatre Nobles dévoués au St——:[9] dernier soupir, qui ne fait que confirmer la défaite; car 1°. il n'étoit plus temps de protester, il falloit le faire au moment que la résolution passa; & 2°. le partage rend la démarche nulle; on ne peut protester à demi voix.

13e.

L'article ci-dessus ne valant pas la peine d'être envoyé seul,[1] j'ai attendu de pouvoir vous marquer quelque chose de plus. Je sais depuis samedi, de très bonne part, que Sir J. Y. a présenté un Mémoire ici, dans lequel sa Cour déclare à la rep. que malgré les Convois elle fera saisir les Navires chargés de bois

8. In an undated letter listed in *Adams Papers,* VIII, 396. Boyd's application to JA provides the same information given in the present letter.

9. For the four noblemen see Dumas' letter of March 28.

1. We have not located the enclosed article.

de construction.[2] Comme cette menace vaut une déclaration de guerre, je ne doute pas qu'elle ne soit concertée avec certains personnages ici, pour que ceux-ci aient un prétexte de ne pas accorder de convoi.

J'ai vu ici Mr. De N——. Je vous réitere, Monsieur, que j'ai lieu de croire qu'il réussira dans ce que vous savez, pourvu que l'on ne s'impatiente pas & qu'on ne le presse pas. Ce qui est certain, c'est qu'il opere avec le secret requis, & de maniere à ne point commettre indiscretement & prostituer, comme on a fait, le crédit de l'Amérique. Une des causes qui pourront retarder encore quelque temps l'affaire, c'est l'Emprunt considérable que fait actuellement l'Impe. Reine.[3]

Je suis, Monsieur, avec mon respectueux attachement connu, Votre très-humble & très obéissant serviteur, D

P.S. S'il est vrai, comme le dit le Courier du Bas-Rhin, que la France veut faire stipuler au congrès de Tesschen, par un article séparé des Traités, que les Puissances Allemandes reconnoissent l'indépendance de l'Am—— unie, & que ces Puissances n'ont pas montré d'eloignement à cela;[4] Mr. Lee pourroit avoir bientôt de la besogne dans son département: mais je crois toujours, qu'il ne faut hazarder une démarche de ce côté-là, que de concert avec le Ministere de France. Autrement on

2. Yorke's April 9 memorial to the States General criticized the French edicts which exempted Amsterdam and Haarlem from French import duties as an attempt to sow discord. He warned that the French intrigues were designed to foment a war between Britain and the Netherlands. Although George III wished to cultivate harmony between their countries he could not permit the transport of naval stores, particularly timber to France, even if escorted by Dutch men-of-war: Sir Francis Piggott and G.W.T. Omond, eds., *Documentary History of the Armed Neutralities, 1780 and 1800* . . . (London, 1919), pp. 110–11. See also Secretary of State Weymouth's instructions of April 6 to Yorke, which discuss the British objections to Dutch convoying: F.J.L. Krämer, ed., *Archives ou correspondance inédite de la maison d'Orange-Nassau* (5th ser.; 3 vols., Leiden, 1910–15), II, 8–10. Yorke's threats failed to intimidate the Dutch: Daniel A. Miller, *Sir Joseph Yorke and Anglo-Dutch Relations, 1774–1780* (The Hague and Paris, 1970), pp. 76–7.

3. Maria Theresa, widow of a former Holy Roman Emperor, queen of Hungary, and archduchess of Austria.

4. A false rumor.

risque de perdre beaucoup de peine & d'argent pour un éclat vain & nuisible.

J'ai tiré le 10 de ce mois, à l'ordre de Mrs. J. De Neufville & Fils, une Lettre de change sur vous, Monsieur, de £2700 tournois, montant de 112½ Louis d'or, que vous m'allouez selon votre Lettre du 12 Mars dernier & selon nos anciennes conventions de 6 en 6 mois; Ceci étant pour les premiers 6 mois de cette année 1779.

Passy à Son Exc. Mr. Franklin

Addressed: à Son Excellence / Monsieur Franklin, Esqr. / Ministre Plenipe. des Etats-Unis / de l'Amerique / *à Passy.*/.

Notation: Dumas April 3d. 1779

From William Vernon, Sr.

ALS: American Philosophical Society

Sir Boston 3d. April 1779

Permit me Sir. to duplicate my Letter of the 7th. Decr. last,[5] by the Continental Frigate, Alliance Capt. Landais, who Sail'd from hence the 14th Jany. being appointed by the Honable Congress, to carry over the Marquis de la Fayette, who I hope you have long since had the Pleasure of seeing?

Inclosed is a second Letter from Govr. Greene.[6] I made him a Visit, not long since, at his Seat at Warwick, where I had the pleasure of seeing, your Sister Mrs Mecom, in perfect health, gay as the Young Ladies, with whom she was incircled.[7] The air, situation diet, and every thing that is agreeable, is to be found at Govr. Greenes Seat? Can you wonder Sir that old Age is renued & Health abounds, I began to feel my self at

5. In that letter the member of the Eastern Navy Board had introduced his son, William Vernon, Jr. (for whom see below, May 12): XXVIII, 204–5. The present letter follows on the same sheet of paper the duplicate of the earlier one.

6. Possibly another copy of Greene's Dec. 10 letter: XXVIII, 216–18.

7. See her letter of June 23, below.

Twenty five, until disappointed upon mounting my Horse, perceived the want of a horse block.

The good Family wish to Eat hasty Pudding with you at Warwick?

I am with perfect esteem Your Excellency, Most devoted Hble Servt.
WM VERNON

His Excellency Benjamin Franklin Esqr.

Notation: Vernon Wm. 7 Xbre. 1778.

From the Duc de la Rochefoucauld's Secretary

AL: American Philosophical Society

ce 4 Avril [1779][8]

Monsieur Franklin est supplie de vouloir bien faire dire au secretaire de Mr. Le Duc de La Rochefoucauld ladresse de M. le Chevalier de Varaigne Officier d'Artillerie;[9] il à une Lettre pour luy et ne sçai ou le trouver. Il supplie aussi Monsieur franklin de vouloir bien recevoir lassurance de son respectueux hommage.

Addressed: A Monsieur / Monsieur franklin / Ministre Plénipotentiaire / des Etats-Unis dAmerique / A Passi—

8. The duke was in Rouen; see his letter to BF of March 26.

9. Pierre-Bernard Varaigne (1751–1807) was one of the engineers who had accompanied Du Coudray to America in 1777 (see XXII, 462n; XXIII, 272–4n, 289n). He took part in the battles of Brandywine and Germantown, and was captured at Saratoga. He was at the head of the contingent of artillerymen and junior officers sent back to France by Congress in 1778 after it broke the contract Silas Deane had made with these men. Bodinier. See also Lasseray, *Les Français,* I, 101; *JCC,* IX, 876–7.

From James Longwell *et al.*[1]

ALS:[2] American Philosophical Society

Hond. Sir Calais Prison April 4th. 1779

I Hope you will Excuse my freedom of troubling you with these few lines as I Have Been in this Prison Ever since the first day of January and have aplied to the Comissary here for to get me my Releasment but all in Vain my name is James Longwell an american was born in the Upper part of Merryland Joining Chester & newcastle County and did Belong to the Oliver Cromwell Privateer and fitted out a Phildelphia Captn. Carter Commanr. and was taken by the bever Sloop Captn. Jones in the West Indias and sent to England as a Prisioner[3] but I Being Ill was sent to St. Thomas's Hospital from which I Made my Escape and Hearing that There was a fleet of ships Going to America in the Victualing trade I Entered on board of the Amphitrite with a View of getting Home to my Native Country but unfortunately was Cast on the Calais Shore January the first and Ever since that time been in Prison. Honord. Sir I hope you will as it is in your Power alone to Procure me my Liberty and send me to my Native Country once more. Hond. Sir Likewise there is two more Americans besides my self there names are Jacob Good & Willm. Griffiths. Sir I Hope you will be so kind as to Send a answer as soon as possible and we will be in Duty bound and Ever Pray[4]

James Longwell
Jacob Good.
Willm. Griffiths

Addressed: To / Dr. Franklin / American Agent at / Paris / France

1. The three seamen had apparently already sought BF's help; see his letter to Sartine of March 26.

2. In Longwell's hand; he signed for the other two.

3. The Pa. privateer, Capt. Harmon Courter, had been captured by H.M.S. *Beaver* on April 29, 1777, and taken to Antigua; see XXV, 682n; *Naval Docs.*, VIII, 999, 1029; IX, 102.

4. The seamen wrote again on April 7, noting that they had sent several letters but never received an answer. Longwell had also written once only for himself (undated, APS). On April 5, below, Sartine told BF that he had given orders for their release.

From Louis Tardy[5]

AL: American Philosophical Society

Paris 4 April 1779

Louis Tardy presents his respects to Mr Franklin begs the favour that he will be so obliging as to give him the address, in town, of the purser of the ship of war, the Alliance.[6]

If you have any thing Bulky to send to Nantes I shall deliver it safe thither. I set out for that place in one day or two.

Addressed: A Monsieur / Monsieur Franklin / a Passy

Notation: L. Tardy 4 avril 1779. Paris.

From Jonathan Williams, Jr.

ALS: American Philosophical Society

Dear & hond Sir.— Nantes April 4. 1779

This will be presented you by Mr Wilkinson the ingenious Director, and indeed the projector, of a very fine Foundery on this River.—[7]

I am under particular obligations to this Gentleman for his Civility to me and many americans I have conducted to see his Works, the last was Mr Adams, who was much pleased at the Simplicity & Ingenuity of his Machinery.

I beg leave to reccommend him to you & shall esteem every Civility you may show him an obligation confered on me. The Wife of our respected Friend Dr Priestly is Sister to Mr Wilkinson.[8]

5. He first appeared in XXVIII, 467. As far as we know, this is his only extant letter to BF.

6. Nathan Blodget.

7. William Wilkinson (XXIII, 480n) from 1777 to 1780 managed the state ironworks and cannon-foundry on the island of Indret, near Nantes. Charles Singer *et al.*, eds., *A History of Technology* (5 vols., Oxford, 1955–58), IV, 101–2.

8. For Mary Priestley, "a woman of sound culture and good sense," see the *DNB* under Joseph Priestley.

I am most dutifully & respectfully Your affectionate Kinsman JONA WILLIAMS

Addressed: The Honourable / Doctor Franklin. / Passy

Notation: Jona Williams ap. 4. 1779—

To John Bondfield

Copy: Library of Congress

Sir Passy April 5 1779

I received your favours of the 18 & 27 past and have honoured the Draft you mention.

Capt. Jones has not yet apply'd to me for the Cannon you are providing.[9] If he is willing to give for them what they cost, I believe I shall consent to his having them. I will consider about those you tell me are to be sold at Ferrol: Do you know why they were not received for the King's Use? I am glad to hear of the 60 Prisoners on Parole. There is no News here but what you will see in the Papers. I have the Honor to be &c

M. Bondfield.

To Landais

Copy: Library of Congress

Sir Passy April 5. 1779

I am glad to hear that you are at Length clear of your Mutineers; and that your Iron Work is repaired. I hope you will have a good Passage to Nantz.

The Bearer of this, Mr. Joseph Wharton, is a friend of mine, a Merchant of Philadelphia who is about to return thither. If you can conveniently accomodate him with a Passage in the Alliance, you will oblige me. I do not mean to propose that he should have his passage free. He does not desire it; but will

9. Jones had previously written Bondfield about an offer of cannon that he had received; see our annotation of Bondfield's letter of March 27.

make a proper Compensation.[1] I recommend him to your Civilities & have the honor to be, Sir &c

Capt. Landais

To Schweighauser

Copy: Library of Congress

Sir

Passy April 5 1779

I have before me your favour of March 20 & one of a Post preceding without date.[2]

Your Orders to Capt. Landais to finish his Refitt at Brest were good, if he could obtain Permission & Conveniencies there: But I have understood that it could not be, and he writes me of the 28 past, that he proposes sailing for Nantes in 8 Days.[3] I approve much of the Orders you have given to observe Œconomy in that Business. For tho' Capt. Landais may be very prudent, some of the others have been so extravagant in their Demands & Expences, that in general we cannot be too much on our Guard.

The Papers relating to the Prize at Morlaix were but a few Days since put into my Hands. I have looked them over carefully except some Swedish Letters which I cannot read, and as far as appears to me in those Papers, the Vessel belongs to Swedish & the Cargo to Tuscan Subjects, with which Nations we have no War. I send the Papers by this Post to you & desire you to get a Person who understands Swedish to peruse those Letters, & to communicate the whole to Mr. Adams, if at Nantes, for his Advice. If no foundation appears for detaining her, the sooner she is discharged the better, as the Damages (which you are requested to settle in the most equitable Manner) will be the Less.[4]

1. Wharton proceeded to Brest, but arrived after Landais had sailed: Wharton to WTF, April 25, 1779 (APS). He did not reach Philadelphia until about the beginning of August: RB to BF, Aug. 6, 1779 (APS).

2. Both are missing.

3. Landais, however, was unable to sail until April 11; see his letter of April 19.

4. We presume the papers are those Gratien sent BF relating to the Swedish prize *Victoria;* see BF to Gratien of March 27, above.

The Gun Stocks which Mr. Williams contracted for when he had the Management of the Magazine of Arms, ought undoubtedly to be received, & not left upon his Hands. But I doubt whether it is worth while to send them to America, as the freight will be considerable for the Value. Perhaps it will be better to dispose of them where they are.[5]

I hope the Alliance will not be long in finishing her Refit at Nantes. In that Case, it would be best to detain the Morris[6] that she may go under Convoy. I wish to know what her lading will be; I suppose it is on Account of the Congress.

I observe you have drawn on me for ten thousand Livres, which draft I shall accept.

Madame Gerard is desirous of knowing whether the little Picture, of which we formerly wrote to you is likely to be recovered from Guernesey.[7] Please to inform me. I have the Honor to be Sir &c

Mr. Schweighauser

From "Philantropos" ALS: American Philosophical Society

Sir St. Omer 5th. April 1779

Reflecting upon the great advantages, that England, since the Commencement of hostilities between her and France, has obtained over the French by Sea: and least it should be compelled by it's Losses to withdraw its protection from America; which, considering the present great armaments of England, and which would then be totally exerted against America, would, I think, greatly Distress Her; to prevent which, I have taken the Liberty of troubling you with the following Consideration, though far from having an Idea, that I am capable of suggesting anything to a person of your Sagacity, which must

5. JW had asked the commissioners to instruct Schweighauser to provide the necessary receipt so he could terminate his ill-fated venture of repairing and shipping muskets for the American army: XXVIII, 414, 497–9.

6. Capt. Benjamin Gunnison's brigantine, which had been placed under Schweighauser's control: XXVIII, 380–1.

7. See her letter of March 30.

not have occurred to yourself: yet, to the Real Lover of Liberty and Mankind; the probality of anothers having the same Idea, is not a sufficient answer to his Conscience for his Silence in matters of such moment: This is in truth my sole motive for troubling you with this Letter.

It is generally supposed, that Spain intends joining France this Summer; which if it be true, I think, that it ought not to declare War; but give every appearance of a contrary Intention; 'till it was capable of executing immediately after, with France, the following plan; to wit, of convoying with it's entire Fleet, 50,000 French Troops to Ireland; which, I think, might easily be executed; by marching another Corps of 50,000 Men to the Coasts of Brittany, & strengthening the Fleet at Brest as much as possible; And by collecting in the ports of Britanny a sufficient Number of transports to land them in England: which wou'd so alarm Her, as to keep her fleet totally employed in watching the French fleet at Brest. The French Troops, destined for Ireland, might be landed in the Ports between Wexford and Cork both Inclusive; except 5,000 Men, which, I think, ought to proceed with two or three Men of War, and as many frigates, with arms for 20,000 men, to Londonderry. This invasion to be successfull should not have Conquest for it's object: but the freeing Ireland from it's Dependance on England: for in the first Case, they would be opposed, by almost the whole Kingdom; but in the latter, wou'd, I believe, be joined by nine tenths of the People; who have, in general, suffered very much, since the commencement of the American War. The regular Troops in Ireland after the next debarquation will probably not exceed 5,000 or 6,000 Men,[8] about 2000 of which are Cavalry: it is true, that there are ten or twelve thousand Men raised in Companies independent of the Crown; but from the well known principles of most of their officers; and the general Spirit of such sort of

8. According to the army estimates of December, 1778, the number was actually 10,000: Cobbett, *Parliamentary History,* xx (1778–80), 73. The Spanish and French foreign ministers similarly underestimated the troop numbers at this time as they contemplated landing a force in Ireland. Patterson, *The Other Armada,* pp. 72, 109.

Men; instead of opposition, the most important Services ought to be expected from them.[9] I need not point out to you, the most certain successfull Issue of the present War to the Allies from the completion of the above plan: nor can Ireland hesitate what mode of Government to adopt: having so many incomparable Models in America: what an amazing Strength must result in a few years from an intimate Union, and offensive and defensive League between her and America! I ought to have mentioned before, tho' unnecessary, to you, that proper manifestoes ought, immediately on the Landing of the Troops, be published; assuring the People in the most solemn and unequivocal manner of the object of the Invasion and no one is more capable, than you, of drawing them up, after the Irish Debarquation was executed; if the Spaniards instead of returning with the French Transports, would proceed with them to Cadiz and from thence to America with fifteen Sail of the Line, and 10,000 Men to assist General Washington to cut off General Clinton; I think, the most Glorious consequences might be expected from such a manœuvre.

But if it is not the Intention of Spain to join France; I think the most proper Step that France could take, would be to declare all her Ports in every part of the World free Ports, during the Continuance of hostilities; and one year after by which means every Sailor of France might be employed to distress the English Trade, for I can by no means advise France to venture a general engagement at Sea; as from the Superiority of British Seamen over the French the most fatal consequences ought to be expected, without a very great Superiority. In Truth, if France altered Her mode of Taxation, she would have little to dread from the English naval Superiority, considerably encrease her Revenue and add much to the general Ease of her People.

9. Since the Irish government lacked sufficient funds to organize a militia in response to the invasion threat after France entered the war, local elites formed corps known as the Volunteers, who numbered about 10,000 by April. The steady growth of these companies, and the Irish government's lack of control over them made the English government uneasy. Maurice R. O'Connell, *Irish Politics and Social Conflict in the Age of the American Revolution* (Philadelphia, 1965), pp. 71–7, 84–5.

I am Sir with the greatest Respect your Obedient Humble Sert. PHILANTROPOS

Addressed: A Monsieur / Monsieur Franklin Ministre / Plenipotentiaire de Provinces Unies / de L'Amerique Septentrionale / A Paris

Endorsed: Project Attack on Ireland—

From Mary Richardson

LS: American Philosophical Society

Honble Sir Plymo. Apl 5. 1779.

I beg leave to write these few lines to let You know a little of my misfortunes Since I left my Native Country I am the Widow and Daughter of Mary Richardson[1] the occasian of my leaving my Native Country was upon the hearing of the famous Doctor Taylor at London by Advertizement in the Paper[2] my Mother being totally blind she was willing to try for her Sight on that account we came over to England more to my sorrow before we came to London we lost all that we had except a few Changes of raiment that we had in the Cabbin with us by the occation of Shipwreck as soon as we arrived I made application for my Mother but the answer was there was no Cure for her we being left in this Unhappy Situation I with my blind Mother traveled to the West Country in hopes of finding relief of some of her friends as she was born there but to my great Surprize the saying was go to your Rebellious Country I hope Your Honor will take it into Consideration what my Situation must be and I only in the 16 Year of my Age Hearing of Your Honors Goodness that You have bestowed upon those that was in Need of it made me take the Liberty of making my Application to You as being the unfortunate Daughter of the late Anthony Richardson Merchant

1. We presume she means she is the daughter of the widow Mary Richardson.

2. John Taylor (1724–87), oculist to George III, had studied under his father, John (d. 1772), who had been oculist to George II and treated various members of European royal courts. *DNB.*

who was Drowned or Murdered at New York which I could never hear of I am very Loth to trouble your Honor with so long an aspistle but am sensible that your goodness is sufficient to assist me to my Native Country or where you think most proper So that I can once more get out of England And I hope that the Lord will pour Down blessings upon you and your family I hope Your Honors Goodness will be pleased to answer this Letter and direct in the following Manner

To
Mr. Joseph Coad
the Red Cow
Cockside
Plymouth

and I still remain your Honors most Obedient and most humble Servant MARY RICHARDSON

Addressed: To / Doctor Franklin / Ambassador for the 13 United / Sates of America / Paris / in / France / Single Sheet / post paid[3]

Notation: Mary Richardson Plymo. 5 avril 1779.

From Sartine

Copy: Library of Congress

à Versailles le 5. Avril 1779.

J'ai reçu, Monsieur, la lettre que vous m'avez fait l'honneur de m'ecrire le 26. du mois dernier relativement à 3. Sujets des Etats Unis qui étoient sur les Navires échoués à Calais, et qui desireroient servir contre les Anglois. J'ai en consequence donné des Ordres au Commissaire des Classes[4] d'accorder la liberté à ces trois Prisonniers s'ils vouloient servir sur les vaisseaux du Roi, ou sur les Batimens Americains.

3. Written on the address sheet and crossed out: "Return'd to Mary Richardson at Mr. Coads Cockside to pay 4 d. to London——". Written in red ink over the address is, "Pd 4."

4. An official charged with the conscription of sailors; there were fifty of them in France: Didier Neuville, ed., *Etat sommaire des archives de la marine antérieures à la Révolution* (Paris, 1898), p. 446.

J'ai l'honneur d'être avec la Consideration la plus distinguée, Monsieur, Votre très humble et tres obeissant Serviteur.

(signe) DE SARTINE.

M. Franklin Ministre Plenipotentiaire des E. U. &c.

From Landais

ALS: American Philosophical Society

Please Your Excellency Brest April 6th 1779

I received Your favour of the 27th ult. It is true I would Chuse rather all Americains for the Ship's crew than part of it french for that mixture has ever since the begining of the war brought trouble and discontent on board the Ships have had it beside they Should be of litle use having no officers that tock french, However I would prefer to have Some of them to Complet the Ship crew with, than English men; But I believe difficult to obtain french Seamen Since they refuse for this Ship the Americains they have aboard their Ships upon pretence they were taken in english vessels.

I landed according to the Honnble John Adam Consent and Mr shweighauser orders all the Mutiners the 26th ult. I have had the Caulkers and Smiths at work the last ever since the 19th Past, the Iron was So bretle that it is a wonder the Ship came here with her masts Standing.

I received the agreeable news (the 3d) from Mr shweighauser of the arival of a Cartel Vessel at Nantes with ningty Seven Americains aboard,[5] But his orders in the Same letter to take ninety three prisonners out of the guard Ship here to Carry with me to exchange for those Sent at Nantes are venturing Some, in his letter to Mr Cottentin he write him to advise me to put them all in Irons, accordingly I have ordered them to be made immediatly, but all those precautions Might not be Sufficient to prevent the danger of having the Ship taken from us by those prisonners and the mutiners remaning aboard un-

5. The cartel ship arrived about April 1; see JW's letter of that date. Landais eventually enlisted twenty of the exchanged prisoners: Pierre Landais, *Memorial to Justify Peter Landai's Conduct during the Late War* (Boston, 1784), p. 18.

known for to comply with those orders the Securist way, I will do my utmost to get ready to Sail in two days time for to have the benefit of the Company of a french frigate Bound to the Same Harbour if I possibly Can: but I am to observe your Excellency that it was reported to me the Ship Company had resolved not to waigh the anchor unless money be geven to them in which case I Should be yet prevented of getting under Sail tell the agent would order what to do.

Three men have desarted the Ship lately one of which name James mason(?) ran away yesterday morning from the Boat being watering ashore and went to enlist in Dillon Regiment Embark'd unboard french man of war,[6] I was ackwainted with the fact about four in the afternoon by two of my men whom had been in a house where he was confined and had Spoke to him and to the officer belonging the Same Regiment to which they asked for to have the Same man delivered to the guard they had brought with them in which they were denied, as Soon I knew what passed I went for to claim the deserter I Saw him going with the officer in a Boat I followed him onboard a transport Ship Call'd (they told me) the interressant, I told the officer (whose name is Weense[?]) the man he had was belong to my Ship Since Boston and ask'd him to deliver me the man he told me he would not, I aplyed to Mr de la Porte Intendent that Gentlemen told me he could do nothing in that Case, I told him that the deserter was as I thought an American, was maried and had Children in America as I had heard from Some of my Ship Company, but he pruve to be Irishman (that, is nothing to the Case) Mr. De la Porte told me to Seek Mr De La Prevalay that Commander of the Harbour told me he had nothing to do with it, to go to Comte D'orvilliers this Commander here of the Navy told me he could not do any thing but to aply to the Colonel Dillon him

6. Dillon, one of the regiments of the Irish Brigade, was awaiting passage to Martinique aboard the West Indies convoy: Dull, *French Navy,* p. 377. At the beginning of April its 860 men were preparing to embark: Archives de la Marine, B[3]DCLXIV: 224–33. It was commanded by Col. Arthur Dillon (1750–94), for whom see Richard Hayes, ed., *Biographical Dictionary of Irishmen in France* (Dublin, 1949), pp. 60–2.

Self who told me as the deserter he was born an Irisman right to have him and would not part with him. Seeking he is determined to keep the man against all right. I believe my Self obliged to akwaint Your Excellency of the matter that you may do any thing in this case you Well thing proper for to prevent the Same for the futur.

I am with the Greateast Respect Your Excellency, Most Obeidient most humble Servant— P LANDAIS.

To his Excellency Bn Franklin Minister Plenipotentary of the united States of America

Addressed: To / His Excellency Bn Franklin Minister—/ Plenipotentiary of the united States of America / At Passy / *Paris*

Notations in different hands: P Landais April 6. 79. / P. Landais 6th avril 1779. De Brest.

From John Wanklyn ALS: American Philosophical Society

Most excellent and honnourd sire Pariss aprill 6th *1779*

These presents humbley make known to you the distressing Case of your pettitioner who is a dissenting minister (a native of america) who left that country in a very early period of life when his parents went to England with the Rev. Mr Whitefield.[7] I have for four years past been imploy.d in that important work dureing which time I have suffered the sharpest persecution any man could in a professed christian land but that which is the cause of my adressing your excellance this day was my publishing a pamflet reflecting on the Conduct of the English ministry respecting america—and a letter against a clergyman—whom I heard deny the divinity of christ in the pulpit—for which I was brought before a Justice of the peace—in whose power it was not to hurt me—this together with my often defending the cause of my native land in the pulpit Caused the officers of the parrish malliciously to get me

7. For the English evangelical preacher George Whitefield see II, 241n, where the dates of his several trips between America and England are given.

impressd into the English service—who cunningly sent for me at midnight to pray with a person said to be sick at which place a gang was ready to take me on bord a tender where I lay three days and nights denied the use of pen ink and paper—but severall of the impress.d men resolveing to attempt an escape—I escaped with them in which scermish the lieutennant was killd— I fled to Holland—where I was oblidged to sell my watch and ring to pay my passage—and by the aseistance of the humane—I have with much fategue arived at pariss—and am now destitute of the least necessary or farthing in my pocket— my intent is to return to america if it be your excellencies pleasure to afford me a little aid and direction—Resolveing if I can be usefull there in no other character—to serve my country in the field— But hope—if once I was the other side the atlantic to fill up my ministeriall character in peace and comfort. I hope therefore—it may be consistant with your excellencies pleasure to Consider my miserable case—being in a strange land—destitute of money or ability to speak the languadge I am dear sir at the feet of your Mercy hopeing to have Cause to adore the providence of god in influenceing a father of my country to help a child in great need who is sincearly your Excellencies Most Humble servant[8]

J. WANKLYN

N.B If requested am ready and willing to swear alegeance to the Congress

Pleas to Present this to His Excellence

Notation: John Wanklin Ap 6. 79—

From David Wilkin

ALS: American Philosophical Society

Dear Sir Rochel Prison Aprul 6th 1779

I should bee for Ever obleaged to you if your oner woold Clear me of imprisonment & Drect me to Philadelphia as i

8. BF noted in his Cash Book (Account XVI; XXVI, 3) under April 9, that he "Advanc'd to a Methodist preacher escap'd from England 48 *l.t.*" We presume Wanklyn is the man and the date of either the letter or the account entry is off by a day.

have wife & fameley there & at this time i was Going Pashinger on board of the Ship when takin by the barren moumrancy of Rochel bound for nueyork to Get to my famley as they was no orther way for me to Get there from ingland I acted on board as mate for my Pasige i have often times been in the Capesity of master in Philadelphia but at this time Glad to Git home in aney Stachon in hopes your oner will bee Good in Louking in this to Releave me of Imprizonment & Drect me in the way for Philadelphia to my wife & famley in i Should for iver Give you Praise my abestence from there was ocashned by Mr Stocker & warten & Co[9] in Ship of theres the first of the Disturbance She was made an Inglish Propertey Stocker Died & the Ship Sould & i was then taken Pashenger for amireca Bound for nueyork in hopes to Get to Philadelphia as that is my home for twenty years Past there is one Sailer Philadelphia Boarn Pashenger in Prison woold be Glad of the Same Releaf thomas Campbel the Ship taken in fanny Capt Long from London So Long abstent Gives Greet uneasnes & I had no other way to Get home than Going for nueyork & then to Desert over Land to Philadelphia Sir & my famley Should for Ever Regoice at your Percuiring me a Voige there as it has Cost me much trobel Steding to Get there & now Brought to Prison is warce than I Expected. I am a well wisher to my Contrey & thinks Very hard of my Confinement if your oner woold be Good nof to ancer this I Should be for I am as Ever obliaged to you I am Very well youesed as a Prisner at Prisent but not Satisfied abestent from my famley in Philadelphia

Sir Your most Hum Serv DAVID WILKIN

Addressed: To / Mr Dr Franklin Adgent / for Amirica / in Parris

9. Possiby Anthony Stocker and Thomas Wharton, Jr., partners in a Philadelphia merchant firm: XIX, 152–3n. Wharton referred in December, 1777, to his "late Partner, Mr. Stocker": *PMHB,* v (1881), 428.

From Richard Bache

ALS: American Philosophical Society

Dear & Hond. Sir   Philada: April 7th: 1779—

I remain without a single line from you since the arrival of Monsr. Gerard,[1] and esteem myself very unfortunate in so doing, however I continue paying my attentions to you by every opportunity I hear of—this goes via St. Eustatia, and serves to hand to you a circular Letter from Mr. Shee and myself, having formed a Connection with that Gentleman to do business in the Commission way, not only for France, but other Nations in Europe, with whom we wish to form a connection, in a commercial Line—[2] Finding it difficult to obtain here the names of the principal houses in the different ports of France, and elsewhere, I beg leave to trouble you with a number of our circular Letters, to address & forward to such houses as from your general knowledge, in Europe, you think would be likely to do business this way— You will discover that some of the Letters sent you, are particularly calculated for France; the others, for Spain, Holland, or elswhere,—I must beg of you to send me a list of the names of those houses the Letters are sent to—[3] I have wrote to you again and again concerning your different inquiries, I trust some of my Letters have reached you— I hope you have received one of the setts of the bills remitted you for Interest of your Money in the loan Office, the Marquis de la Fayette, carried one sett, one sett, I

1. In the summer of 1778; see XXVI, 202–3, XXVII, 90n.

2. RB had introduced his newly formed firm of Bache and Shee in his letter of Feb. 16: XXVIII, 552.

3. RB eventually received the list, but it took another year and more prompting. He repeated his request, and sent additional circular letters, on Aug. 6 and Sept. 18. On March 29, 1780, he acknowledged receipt of a list from WTF (APS). What is apparently the retained copy of that list is at the APS. Written by WTF with additions by BF, it is marked "Houses Bache & Shees Circular Letters have been sent to," and lists twenty-seven merchants and firms in France, Holland, Germany, and Spain. Bache and Shee continued in business for several years; on Nov. 1, 1783, they asked WTF to serve as their intermediary with traders in Saxony and expressed their gratitude for his grandfather's help (APS).

know was taken, the other I am in doubt about—[4] The Family is well and join me in love & duty— We are expecting an increase of it in a few Months—[5] My love to Ben & Temple—I remain Dear Sir Your affectionate Son RICH: BACHE

Dr: Franklin

Addressed: Dr: Franklin

From Anna Maria Shipley

ALS: American Philosophical Society

Dear Sir Wimbledon Park April 7 1779

I cannot resist the inclination I have to assure you how interest'd we alwaies must feel about a friend whom we have so much loved & esteem'd & whom we now so much admire—It gave us great uneasiness to hear you had the Gout but we hope it will secure you a long long series of health hereafter.

The Genel: Verdiery who breakfast'd with us this Morng. told me he could deliver a letter to you in a few days—[6] it was a temptation I could not resist & I had the less scruple in writing as we please ourselves in thinking you will not be sorry to hear of a family you have so often made happy by yr friendship—had my Sister Georgiana been here I should not have been alow'd this indulgence— I am sorry to say she is confine'd in Town with an Inflamation in her Eyes my Mother is with her, & well so is my Father who is here with us Lord Spencer is so good to lend us Wimbledon for the holidays he

4. For the bills carried by Lafayette see XXVII, 601. According to an Aug. 6, 1779, letter from RB, the second and third sets were carried on the brig *Saratoga* and the snow *Proteus,* both of which were captured (APS).

5. Richard and Sarah Bache's fifth child, Louis, was born on Oct. 7 (I, lxiv).

6. Possibly Charles Verdière d'Hem (*c.* 1729–94), lieutenant general, a prisoner on parole who was exchanged the following November. Lewis, *Walpole Correspondence,* VII, 190.

is in Northamptonshire or I am sure would desire me to express his esteem & regard for you.[7] AMS

Addressed: Benjn Franklin Esqre

Endorsed: Anna Maria Shipley

Notation: M Digges / D

From Mathieu Tillet[8]

ALS: University of Pennsylvania Library

Monsieur et Illustre Confrere A Paris le 7 avril 1779.

M Amelot[9] qui est cette année President de l'Academie des sçiences, vient de m'ecrire qu'il entendroit avec plaisir lundy prochain chez luy après diné les memoires qui sont destinés pour l'assemblée publique du 14 de ce mois. Ayant appris que vous vous proposiez de lire un de ces memoires il m'a chargé de vous inviter à diner chez luy ce meme Jour lundy,[1] où nous aurons le plaisir de vous entendre, en attendant celuy que nous partagerons avec le public: Je suis charmé d'avoir trouvé cette occasion de vous renouveller les sentimens d'estime et d'attachement avec lesquels J'ay l'honneur d'etre Monsieur et Illustre Confrere Votre trés humble et trés obeissant serviteur

TILLET

Notation: Tillet 7. avril 1779

7. John, first Earl Spencer (XIX, 275n), who had a country seat at Althorp, Northamptonshire, and an estate at Wimbledon: *DNB,* under his son, George John Spencer.

8. An agriculturalist from Bordeaux (1714–91) who held the title of *directeur* of the Academy in 1779: *Index biographique des membres et correspondants de l'Académie des sciences . . .* (Paris, 1954), p. 491.

9. Antoine-Jean Amelot de Chaillou, who wrote BF on April 8; see below.

1. It was Le Roy who actually read BF's "Des Suppositions et des conjectures sur la cause des Aurores Boréales": XXVIII, 191. Monday was April 12.

From Samuel Wharton[2]

AL: American Philosophical Society

Hotel de Rome Wednesday afternoon [on or after April 7, 1779][3]

Mr Wharton presents his Respects to his Exellency Mr. Franklin, & sends Him the News paper, and a correct List of all the regular Forces in Ireland. The letter He has just received from a Friend; Who has the best Opportunity of *officialy,* acquiring a State of the Army. Mr. Wharton did not receive A News paper by the last post.

Addressed: A' Son Excellence / Monsieur / Monsieur Franklin / &c &c &c / Passy

From Jonathan Williams, Jr.

ALS: American Philosophical Society; copy: Yale University Library

Dear & hond Sir. Nantes April 7. 1779

You some time since advised me not to meddle in the Affairs of Prisoners, and I have endeavoured to follow your Advice because in fact not being the agent it does not belong to me.—

I cannot however as a private Man help feeling for Distresses I see, and as a private Man I am always willing to

2. BF's old friend, who arrived from England sometime before March 17. On that date WTF wrote JA that Wharton and his son had come and were planning to return to America in a few weeks (Mass. Hist. Soc.). On April 9 Samuel Wharton signed an oath of allegiance as did his son Joseph and a business associate, Joseph Dobson; all are at the APS. For the younger Wharton (not to be confused with his uncle of the same name) see his letter, below, May 31; for his dealings with Dobson see "Selections from the Letter-Books of Thomas Wharton, of Philadelphia, 1773–1783," *PMHB,* XXXIII (1909), 320, 437, 442; XXXIV (1910), 41, 44, 45.

3. The first Wednesday after the date of what we believe to have been the enclosure, a one-page memorandum in an unknown hand labeled "Army in Ireland, April 2d. 1779." It lists 11,030 troops by regiment (with an additional 1,816 still to be recruited). APS. Ireland continued to be a subject of interest to BF, who eventually selected Wharton's fellow stock speculator Edward Bancroft for an intelligence-gathering mission to the island; see the instructions to him, below, May 31.

contribute my Share, but it is impossible to bear all without at once ruining myself.

The Flagg[4] is arrived with 97 americans of which twelve are officers.— The agent has informed them that those who will enter on board the alliance will receive a Guinea Bounty & 20 Sols per day for Board, & that if they do not like these Terms they must shift for themselves. This for Seamen is no doubt proper, except the Board, for I never could board a Sailor under 40. Sols per day in this Place, and the Board encreased to what is realy necessary ought to answer till Capt Landais Capt Jones or somebody else employs them. But Officers certainly deserve some Distinction, especialy those who came forward so early in the War, as to have suffered two Years hard Imprisonment.—When I fitted out the Dean[5] I offered every Man who came from Prison a Passage in her according to his Station, which they willingly accepted, & voluntarily, in Turn offered to assist all in their Power to the Defence & Welfare of the Ship;—I in this Manner procured for that Ship a number of resolute experienced men, who were worth at least double the Number of common Sailors, and the difference between their messing with the under officers & their messing with foremost Men does not form an Object equal to the Difference in their use in Case of action.— This is what I wish to be done as to the twelve officers in Question, and indeed any others also may arrive in similar Circumstances.— They have not a Sol in their Pockets, they eat their Dinners now on Credit, and their Board is at 4 Livres per day.— I therefore in their Behalf request you to order the agent to give them that daily allowance, something to buy Sea Cloathes, and to put them on board the alliance as soon as she arrives on the Terms mentioned. If the Subsistence of Prisoners cannot be allowed as a public Expense, & a Subscription is opened to raise a Fund for the Purpose, I will subscribe 20 Louis and add on future oc-

4. So called because she carried a flag of truce; her name was the *Milford.* See Peter Kemp, ed., *The Oxford Companion to Ships & the Sea* (London, New York, and Melbourne, 1976), p. 142, and our annotation of JW's letter of April 1.

5. The *Deane,* which JW had fitted out in the fall of 1777: XXV, *passim.*

casions as Necessity may require, and my Circumstances permitt. I hope Sir I shall not offend you by taking these Peoples part,—I am actuated by motives of humanity only, for were the Case my own I should think it hard to be turned ashore in a Strange Country without help, or to be obliged to live on half a Sailors Board wages and be turned among People where I might catch the Itch & be covered with Vermin. I have desired these People to write their own Case, in a Memorial which I enclose.— I also enclose a Letter from Capt Johnsons Mate Henry Lawrence with a List of Men who have engaged in the British Service & a List of those who remain in Prison; and another Letter from John Chester master Carpenter to the Same Vessell, to which I will make such answers per return of the Flag as you may think proper.—[6] I request an answer to this Letter as soon as possible and I also again request that you will not be offended at my taking up this Matter (which I indeed endeavoured to avoid) but that you will attribute it to the Proper Motive & believe me to be with the greatest Respect Your dutifull & affectionate Kinsman JONA WILLIAMS J

Addressed: The Hon. Doctor Franklin

Notation: Jona Williams. ap 7. 79.

To John Adams

LS:[7] Massachusetts Historical Society; copy: Library of Congress

Sir, Passy, April 8. 1779.

I did myself the honor of writing to you a few Days since.[8] Last Night I received yours of the 31st past. I am glad to hear the Ship is so far in order. As to the Discontents you find among the Officers and People, it is impossible for me at this Distance to judge of them, or of the means of removing them: I must therefore, as in my last, refer to your Judgment what-

6. The enclosed letters from Lawrence and Chester of the captured brig *Lexington* are missing. Lawrence, Chester, and the ship's captain Henry Johnson, appear on the ship's muster roll: Clark, *Wickes,* p. 377.

7. In WTF's hand.

8. On April 3.

ever you may think for the good of the Service, considering our Circumstances and Funds, and I desire you would give Orders accordingly. If the Officers are dissatisfied with the Purser[9] who is now here, I fancy, but do not speak from Knowledge, that he is not sollicitous about continuing in his Place; and would have no objection to being permitted to stay as long as he pleases in Paris.

I can not at all interfere with regard to the Disposition of the Exchanged Prisoners, by ordering them to go on board one Ship or another. They are Freemen as soon as they land in France, and may inlist with which Captain they please.

I shall by this Post give the Orders you desire to Mr Schweighauser and Capt. Landais, relating to your Passage & Sea Stores; tho' I did not think them necessary.

I have the honour to be, Sir, Your most obedt and most humble Servant B FRANKLIN

Honble. John Adams Esqre.

Endorsed: Dr. Franklin Ap. 8. ansd 13 1779.

To Brault and Demezandré

Copy: Library of Congress

Gentlemen Passy April 8 1779

I received the Letter you did me the Honor to write to me of the 1st. inst. I am sorry for the Disappointments you have met with in your Commerce with America, and hope you will have better Success hereafter. In answer to your Request of a Passage for your selves and Goods in the Alliance, I can only say that no Goods can be taken upon Freight in our Ships of War, the little Room that is left after the Provisions and Water for such a Number of Men are stowed, being all wanted for the Arms, Ammunition & Clothing necessary for our Troops.— As to your Passage, if the Captain can accommodate you and you can agree with him about it, I shall make no Objection to it; tho' in general the taking of Passengers in our

9. Nathan Blodget. JA had recommended the purser and used him to carry a March 24 letter to WTF: *Adams Papers,* VIII, 16.

Ships has been found very inconvenient:[1] But I can give no Orders about it, not knowing whether it is practicable to receive you, of which the Capt. himself is the best judge. I have the honor to be &c

Messieurs de Mezandré et Brault at Malo.

To the Gentlemen at Nantes[2]

LS[3] and copy: Library of Congress

Gentlemen, Passy, April 8th. 1779

Great Objections having been made by the honble. Mr Arthur Lee to the Accounts of Mr Jonathan Williams late Agent for the Commissioners at Nantes, which are therefore yet unsettled, and as not being conversant in mercantile Business, I cannot well judge of them, and therefore, as well as for other Reasons, I did not and cannot undertake to examine them myself, and they may be better examined at Nantes where the Business was transacted than either here or in America. I beg the Favour of you, Gentlemen, that you would for the Sake of Justice and of the Public Good, take that Trouble upon you; and make Report to me thereupon. Which I do hereby agree shall be conclusive and final (subject only to the Revision of Congress) in case Mr Williams shall previously sign an Engagement to abide thereby. If it should not suit you all to attend to this Business, I shall be content with the Judgment of as many of you as can and will attend it, the Number not being less than three. If an equal Number undertake it, and should be divided in their Opinions, I request them to join in chusing an Umpire, that the Matter may be concluded. I did

1. The two men wrote again on May 27 to thank BF. They had shown his letter to Landais, but had been informed by the captain of a change in the destination of the *Alliance.* APS.

2. BF wrote this letter in response to JW's request, on March 23, that he write a second time to the Gentlemen, empowering any group of at least three of them to arbitrate JW's accounts. The first half of this letter duplicates BF's previous one to the Gentlemen, above, March 13. The new ending begins with the phrase "If it should not suit you".

3. In the hand of WTF.

desire Mr Lee, if he had any further Objections to furnish you with them; But he has in a Letter to me declined it.[4]

I have the Honour to be, with great Respect, Gentlemen, Your most obedient humble Servant B FRANKLIN

P.S.[5] Hoping you will comply with my Request, I have ordered Mr Williams to lay his Accounts fully before you.—

To Messrs. Joseph Wharton, Mathiew Ridley, Joshua Johnson, Mathew Mease, John Ross, Jona Nesbitt, ——— Cummings, Joseph Gridley & J.D. Schweighauser, Merchants now at Nantes.—[6]

Notations in different hands: His Excellency Benjamin Franklin to Messieurs J. Wharton M. Ridley J. Johnson M. Mease J. Ross J Nesbit J Cuming J. Gridley & J D Schweighauser Passy April 8. 1779 / a letter from Benjn. Franklin.

To Joshua Johnson

Copy: Library of Congress

Sir Passy April 8 1779

Mr. Wm. Lee has lately been here from Frankfort: he had desired me to make such an Application in Behalf of the State of Virginia, as you request in Behalf of Maryland. Mrs. D'Acosta & Co had complained to me that they had provided what Mr. Lee wanted, in Pursuance of a Contract made with Mr. A. Lee, who had refused to take the Goods off his Hands. I proposed to Mr. Wm. Lee to accommodate this Little Difference, and take those Goods now lying ready at Nantes to be shipt, rather than wait the Event of an uncertain application to

4. See Lee's letter of March 16.

5. In BF's hand.

6. The list of addressees kept changing, according to the merchants' mobility and their willingness to serve on such a committee. The names of W. and D. Blake, Fendall, Lloyd, and Ogilvie had been dropped since BF's letter of March 13; letters of refusal from W. Blake and Fendall are above, March 20 and 21. Although Matthew Mease was not included in the list of addressees for BF's March 13 letter, he was a part of the original group: XXVIII, 57n. Merchants newly included on the list are James Cuming (XXVIII, 206), Joseph Gridley (see his letter of March 17, above), and Jonathan Nesbitt (XXVI, 12–13n).

Government. He absolutely refuses and says you may take them for Maryland;[7] if you please. Pray, let me know, as soon as may be whether, it will not suit you to agree for them with those Gentlemen.

I have the honor to be &c

Joshua Johnson

To Landais

LS:[8] Massachusetts Historical Society; copy: Library of Congress

Sir Passy April 8 1779

Understanding that you expect an explicit Order from me, this is to require you to receive on Board your Ship the Alliance, the Honourable John Adams Esq. with his Son and Servant, and give them a Passage therein to America.

I have the Honour to be Sir your most obedient humble Servant B FRANKLIN

Honbl. Capt. Landais

To Schweighauser

Copy: Library of Congress

Sir Passy, Apr. 8 1779

I have before me your favour of the 3d. inst.[9] I am glad to hear of the Arrival of the Prisoners, & doubt not of your finishing the Exchange as soon as possible. You will, no doubt, answer the Letter of the Commrs.[1] in acquainting them as they desired with the Particulars of the Treatment the English Prisoners have received here. I will endeavour to send you by next Post, what Accounts we have received of the Numbers of Prisoners in the different Ports. If any such Request as you

7. The exchanges of letters are above, under March 30 and April 2.

8. In Gellée's hand. Written at JA's request (as BF told him in his letter, above, of the same day), it now is with his papers.

9. Missing.

1. The Commissioners for Sick and Wounded Seamen. We have not located their letter.

mention, relative to Refreshments, shou'd be made by the Capt. of the Cartelship, you will consult with Mr. Adams if present and follow his Advice, if not, use your own Judgment. I shall not object to what you may think reasonable.

Please to furnish Mr. Adams with what Seastores he may require for himself & son: and charge them in your Acct: and I desire that in supplying the Officers & People of the Alliance, & the Prisoners arrived with Cloaths, Money, or Necessaries of any kind, you would follow his Advice, taking the same in Writing. I have the Honor to be &c

Mr. Schweighauser

To Jonathan Williams, Jr.

Copy: Library of Congress

Dear Jonathan Passy April 8 1779

Too much Business, too much Interruption by friendly Visits, & a little Remaining Indisposition, have occasioned the Delay in answering your late Letters.

You desire a Line "relative to the Complexion of Affairs." If you mean our Affair at this Court, they wear as good a Complexion as ever they did.

I know not what to advise concerning Mr. Monthieu's Proposition. Follow your own Judgement. If you doubt, set down all the Reasons, pro & con, in opposite Columns on a Sheet of Paper, and when you have considered them two or three Days, perform an Operation similar to that in some questions of Algebra; observe what Reasons or Motives in each Column are equal in weight, one to one, one to two, two to three or the like; and when you have struck out from both Sides all the Equalities, you will see in which Column, remains the Ballance. It is for want of having all the Motives for & against an important Action present in or before the Mind at the same Time, that People hesitate and change their Determinations backwards & forwards Day after Day, as different Sets of Reasons are recollected or forgot; and if they conclude & act upon the last set, it is perhaps not because those were the best, but because they happened to be present in the Mind, & the better absent.— This kind of *Moral Algebra* I have often practiced in important & dubious Concerns; and tho' it cannot be mathematically exact, I have found it extreamly useful.—[2] By the Way, if you do not learn it, I apprehend you will never be married.

There is in one Acct. of the Copper, an Article, *des Mines de St: bell 63400*. I suppose it was the Word *mines* & not *Rosette,* that was translated *Ore.*

Let me know if you can, what Answer the Gentleman receives from London, on his Enquiries concerning a supposed Letter.[3]

I send you herewith the Paper you desire respecting the Settlement of your Accts. I send also an attested Copy of Mr. Lee's Reasons for not passing them. In answer to my Letter requesting him to furnish the Gentlemen who are to examine them, with such further Objections as he may have against them, he writes me that "I must excuse him now that it is no longer his indispensable Duty, from concerning himself with a Business which is in much abler Hands: If *Congress,* he adds, should call upon me for farther Reasons than those that I have already given, it will then be my Duty to act and I will obey."[4] I cannot conceive his Reason for not giving his farther Reasons, (if he has any) on the present Occasion, when they would be so proper: But he refuses, & I cannot compel him.

I shall file the Letters & Papers you sent me with your Accounts. I have received back those you inclosed in yours of March 27 relating to Mr. Monthieu's Contract.— I have received also Mess. Horneca & Fizeaux's Invoice, and will return it by next Post with the Order you desire.

I have no Objection to your mentioning the Fact relative to the Censure of Mr. Monthieu's Accts. I am ever your affectionate Uncle B FRANKLIN

Jonath. Williams

2. BF had first recommended the use of "Moral or Prudential Algebra" to Joseph Priestley in 1772: XIX, 299–300.

3. The letter BF was rumored to have written Charles James Fox; see JW's second letter of March 23.

4. Above, March 16. "Congress" is not underlined in Lee's retained copy.

From Antoine-Jean Amelot de Chaillou[5]

ALS: American Philosophical Society

Vlles. le 8 avril 1779

J'apprens à l'instant, Monsieur, que vous vous proposèz de lire un mémoire à la Seance publique de l'academie des sciences qui se tiendra le 14 de ce mois[6]. J'ai l'honneur de vous prévenir que ceux de MM. de l'academie des sciences qui ont des mémoires pour la même séance doivent se réunir chèz moi à Paris le Lundi 12, me faire l'honneur d'y diner, et y faire lecture de leurs mèmoires en présence de MM. les officiers de l'academie.[7] Je serai très flatè que vous veuilliez bien me faire le même honneur, et que cette occasion me procure celle de vous recevoir chèz moi.

J'ai l'honneur d'être avec un sincere attachement, Monsieur, Votre très humble et très obeissant serviteur AMELOT

M. francklin

Endorsed: M Amelot

From Jonathan Williams, Jr.

Copy: Yale University Library

Nantes April 8. 1779.

When I transmitted my last account to the Commissioners I made a memorandum at the Foot showing that when all the demands were paid the Balance would be in my favour. I now enclose the account as it now stands only £2979.19.9. and the

5. Amelot, *secrétaire au département de la maison du Roi,* was president of the Académie des sciences in 1779. *DBF; Index biographique des membres et correspondants de l'Académie des sciences . . .* (Paris, 1954).

6. The meeting at which Le Roy delivered BF's paper on the aurora borealis: XXVIII, 191.

7. Those other guests were Charles Messier and Edme-Sébastien Jeaurat, astronomers, Nicolas-Christian de Thy de Milly, a chemist, Claude-Melchior Cornette, a physician, Raphaël-Bienvenue Sabatier, a surgeon, Jean-François-Clément Morand and Antoine Portal, anatomists. Académie des sciences, *Comptes-rendus,* XCVIII, fol. 88.

Deans anchors,[8] yet unpaid for which Mr. Gourlade this day demands of me amount to £6350..13.—

Being under a Cruel accusation & my accounts under order to be examined, I ought not to pay any thing 'till they are settled & I can obtain a Receipt in full & this I am ready to do at Sight. But M Gourlades demand must be answered and if you desire it I will pay the Balance in my hands toward it, or if you will accept my draft for the Balance which will be due to me after paying M Gourlades demand, I will settle it that way. In Short I will act as you direct which I am Sure will be just & right. I beg your answer for my Government & am with greatest respect

P.S. I also enclose a Copy of Mr. Gourlades account of the anchors: if you will please to look the Deans account you will find that they have not yet been paid for.

Hon: Doctor Franklin, Passy

From Jacques Barbeu-Dubourg[9]

ALS: American Philosophical Society

Paris, 9 avril 1779

Vous vous rappellez surement, Mon cher Maitre, les belles experiences de Physique et de Chymie que vous avez vu faire a M Brongniard, sa dexterité à operer, sa netteté a exposer, sa sagesse a expliquer ce qui peut l'etre et a rejetter les vaines hypotheses auxquelles on a attaché tant d'importance[1]. Si vous en avez eté aussi satisfait que vous me le parutes dans le tems, il se presente une occasion de lui rendre service en concourant a lui procurer une place, où il apportera certainement plus de

8. JW had outfitted the frigate *Deane* for the American navy in the fall of 1777.

9. BF's translator and old friend: XV, 112–13.

1. Antoine-Louis Brongniart (XXVI, 253n) had published, in 1778, his *Tableau analytique des combinaisons et des décompositions de différentes substances:* Larousse. Its publication was announced by the *Jour. de Paris* on March 2, 1779.

zele que qui que ce soit, et où il peut a ce moyen se faire honneur, et se rendre cher au Public. C'est la place de Demonstrateur de Chymie au jardin du Roy vacante par la mort de M Rouelle qui fut enterré hier, qui etoit un excellent Chymiste et un tres mediocre Orateur.[2] Cette place depend presque entierement de M de Buffon,[3] qui connoit deja le merite de M Brongniard, et a qui il a deja eté particulierement recommandé mais vous jugez bien que M Brongniard a des Concurrens, dont quelques uns fort alertes a solliciter seront peutetre d'autant moins zelés a remplir la place qu'ils auroient ainsi obtenue. Voila ce qui lui fait desirer d'etre etayé d'un suffrage tel que le votre, qui certainement seroit du plus grand poids sur l'esprit de M de Buffon, qui ecoutera tout le monde, mais qui sait balancer les autorités. Je vous prie en consequence de vouloir lui marquer ce que vous pensez d'un Candidat que vous avez vu la main a l'ouvrage, et que je dois vous ajouter qui est d'ailleurs un parfaitement honnete homme, et un de mes bons et solides amis, a qui j'ai voué depuis longtems un attachement fidele et constant. J'aurois eté moi même avec lui, si des affaires instantes ne me retenoient icy, mais j'espere aller apres demain vous reïterer ma recommandation,[4] et vous entretenir a loisir de quantité d'autres objets que j'ai laissé accumuler depuis un mois; etant sans cesse obligé de remettre le voyage de Passy d'un jour a l'autre. Mais je m'en vais la semaine prochaine changer de domicile et me rapprocher de vous d'un bon tiers du chemin.

J'ai l'honneur d'etre avec un tendre et inviolable attachement Monsieur et cher Ami Votre tres humble et tres obeissant serviteur

DUBOURG

Notation: Dubourg 9 Ap. 79

2. Hilaire-Marin Rouelle (1718–79) had succeeded his brother, the more famous Guillaume-François (1703–70) in the position of *démonstrateur:* Larousse.

3. The great naturalist was *intendant* of the Jardin des Plantes: *DBF.*

4. Dubourg was successful in his efforts. According to the *Jour. de Paris* for May 27, p. 590, the *Cours de Chymie du Jardin du Roi* was to be inaugurated that afternoon, with Brongniart as the successor to M. Rouelle.

From Thomas Digges ALS: Historical Society of Pennsylvania

Dr. Sir Londo. Apr 9. 1779

Our friend Mr. B——n having given me an oppertunity to convey a letter by a safer conveyance than that of the common post, I make free to inclose it to you in order to be forwarded to Mr W——n should he be out of P——s.[5]

I have but a few minutes before Mr. B—— closes his packet to appologise for the freedom I take & to offer my services here.[6] I am not many hours in London, & shall remain here 'till calld to a western port on the arrival of two Spanish vessels expected there which I guess will be in six or seven weeks. My purpose with these vessels is the same as what has employd me for now nearly two years—the getting out useful articles—The very great wants of which would be much alleviated was an import directly from this Country allowd by mine, for there are hundreds who would adventure largely, & this too without a prospect of *immideate* payment. Not a word of Amn news, & by what I can gather, it is likely the embarkation of troops & Recrts destind for N York (in all about 4,500) have been lately countermanded.[7]

The next W Inda. Fleet will sail abot. the 10 May. 80 to 100 ships.[8] I cordeally wish You every prosperity & am Yours.

T. D——

A Monsieur Monsieur Jacques Vincent Droüillard[9] Bureau des Postes Londres

5. Digges's abbreviations stand for Edward Bridgen (who also carried Christopher Baldwin's letter of March 5, above), Samuel Wharton, and Paris.

6. The Maryland-born merchant had first offered his services to BF the previous September: XXVII, 420–1.

7. Lord George Germain's Jan. 23 orders for stepping up the military campaign in New York and Rhode Island required sending an additional 6,600 men from Britain and Germany to reinforce Gen. Clinton's troops. However, of the 3,000 recruits expected from Britain, only 1,300 were raised. The plan was further disrupted when the transports ordered to sail from the Thames to the Firth of Forth to collect three regiments left five weeks late and did not return with the troops until the beginning of April. Mackesy, *War for America*, pp. 255, 259–60.

8. A merchant fleet.

9. A name he used as a cover for receiving mail.

Addressed: a Monsieur / Monsieur B. Franklin

Notations: Digges London 9 april 79 / April 9 1779.

From Ingenhousz

ALS: American Philosophical Society

Dear Sir London april 9. 1779

Since my last of last weak I saw your old femal friend in town. She came to sea me at my lodgings. She is very wel and in good spirits and desires me to send you her best wishes and to acquaint you that she recieved your kind lettre of Jan. last and will answer it in a short time.[1] I will endeavour to bring you the copper for to roast a chicken in by a bold of iron, which you bought at cheffield when we were there togeather, or, if I can find an earlier oportunity, I will send it to you. Mr Henley has no pretension upon you, his bill being payd within the month of your departure.

As I may possibly go from here earlyer than I expected, the money transaction of my brother might better be omitted till I see you.[2] I expect a lettre from the low countries which will determine my departure from hence. I part with reluctance from a country I like and from friends I esteme, But my duty calls me.

Dr Priestley publishes now a new volum upon air and other articles. It will contain a lettre of mine upon a method of producing at pleasure any quantity of imflammable air without trouble or apparatus.[3] He gave me hesterday a hint which I wish government would adopt viz. to send as soon as possible

1. BF had written to Margaret Stevenson on Jan. 25: XXVIII, 421–3. In that letter he made the inquiries about the copper pot and Henley's bill that Ingenhousz mentions below. Mrs. Stevenson began her reply to BF on March 16 (under which date the letter is published), but did not complete it until April 11.

2. See Ingenhousz's letter of April 1.

3. For Priestley's new work see his letter of March 11, where he promised to send BF a copy. Ingenhousz's contribution to the volume was in the form of a letter to Priestley dated March 1, 1779, and was entitled "A Letter . . . on the Effect of a new Species of inflammable Air, or Vapour." It appears on pp. 474–9, and is an early version of the paper he read at the Royal Society on March 25; see his letter of April 1.

a ship to discovre the North pole. As last sommer was in our hemisphere, or at least in the Northern parts, very hot, and the present winter very mild, it is probable, that the seas will be free from ice.

I am respectfully your most obedient humble servant

J. INGEN HOUSZ

Addressed: A Monsieur / Monsieur francklin / a Passy

Notation: Ingenhousz April 9. 1779.

From Benjamin Vaughan

ALS: American Philosophical Society

After two and one-half years of false starts, editorial anguish, and printer's delays, Benjamin Vaughan was finally sending Franklin the first set of sheets for *Political, Miscellaneous and Philosophical Pieces.*[4] The editor's work was far from finished. He had not yet collected all the pieces he was hoping to include, and he continued to make editorial changes until the book was finished, at the end of the summer. The volume was not released to the public until December 7, 1779; we will discuss the work as a whole under that date.

My dearest sir, London, April 9h:, 1779.

By this conveyance you will receive a printed pacquet of your papers; & inclosed you will receive what is finished in addition. The last proof sheet comes down to p. 320.— I believe in the whole, there will be from 450 to 500 pages; exclusive of index, table of contents, and two or three pages of *explanatory* preface.[5]

4. He had begun the project in the fall of 1776: XXII, 614. In the summer of 1778, the publisher had recommended a hiatus before recommencing work: XXVII, 203. On Feb. 2, 1779, Vaughan wrote to WTF that printing had begun again, and was proceeding "tolerably fast." APS.

5. Vaughan underestimated the edition's length. After he had introduced several new pieces into the body of the work, one of which inspired copious editorial commentary, and he had added six additional items in an appendix, the whole book ran to 550 pages.

Among BF's papers at the APS is a sketchy table of contents in Vaughan's hand, which must have predated this letter since the order of items differs

I have taken sundry liberties with you; but *I* only shall be the sufferer, for I shall in the fullest possible manner get *your* judgment out of the scrape. Italics are put in many places, to serve instead of marking the subject (as in some authors is done) on the *side of the page;* and to prevent an *English* reader running away with a blunder for want of attending to a *particular word* which would have saved his blunder.— The pointing is altered very frequently, your original pointing not being always to be got at; to make the whole uniform. The whole secret of these alterations lies in throwing the sentences into *masses* & members to assist the eye more suddenly in catching & reviewing the sense; and in making abrupt pauses in particular places for the sake of forcing the readers attention to some particular point, either on account of its importance, or as being otherwise equivocal.— Paragraphs and spaces are used with the same sort of license; especially in the Canada pamphlet & the House of Commons examination. With what is done to these two pieces I think you will hardly be displeased: on the former I bestowed much trouble. The writings of very few authors besides yourself, will bear distinguishing into heads. But I think by making the piece more luminous as to the parts, I have only done you infinitely more credit.—[6] However you may be sure of this; that no sort of mercy will be shewn by the editor to *himself.*— The two or three first sheets have been blundered about; not having enough at-

slightly and it does not list several of the pieces which actually appeared in the edition. Entitled "Present intended order of publication," it lists all five sections of the work, giving abbreviated titles for each piece and approximate dates, where known. Vaughan also marked places where he was considering a change in the order.

The one piece that was added to the first 320 pages, not listed in this preliminary table of contents, was BF's "Remarks on a Plan for the Future Management of Indian Affairs."

6. *The Interest of Great Britain Considered, with Regard to her Colonies, and the Acquisitions of Canada and Guadaloupe* . . . (London, 1760) and *The Examination of Doctor Benjamin Franklin, before an August Assembly relating to the Repeal of the Stamp Act &c.* ([Philadelphia, 1766]) are above, IX, 47–100, and XIII, 124–62. Vaughan divided the former into an introduction and seven subdivisions, for which he composed subheadings. In *The Examination* . . . , he introduced extra leading to separate groups of questions by subject.

tended to the subject, or the printer. Mr Jackson in particular is very ill-used, and will have a public & private apology made to him.—[7] However with your permission, I wish that the alterations I have minuted down may be attended to with you, *if not improper;* and that it be expressed in the French translation, that what is altered, is at the desire of the *English editor.*

I am infinitely concerned to tell you that Mr Galloway informed me that "the *rebels* had got at your papers & many of his own; & destroyed them; but that he would *write* me an account, as I should probably feel it more satisfactory, for your information, as to the particulars."[8] I have yet received no letter however: But shall soon urge him again; and wish you would contrive by yourself or Mr Temple Franklin to give me an excuse for pressing him; though at all events it is very easy for me to do the business without you.

About a month ago I took up your paper, on the *vis inertia* to comment upon it.[9] I am impertinent enough to think that I have done a good deal of substantial business, not only respecting that particular subject, but various other subjects of motion. I have been in my time, much teazed & fretted, at seeing so little of the *rationale* on these topics given by others; and little more done than a mere *contention* about laws as they were called or facts, or else a mathematical enumeration & supposed *illustration* of facts. I have written a paragraph on the *theory* or rationale of each of the following subjects without a mathematical figure (one case excepted,) and in a language

7. The blunders in the first several sheets were chiefly errors of spacing, and Richard Jackson's letter to BF, published on pp. 12–23, had more than its share. Vaughan corrected them in the *Errata.*

8. In February, Vaughan had hoped that Galloway would be a source of more MS material for the edition (Vaughan to WTF, Feb. 2, 1779, APS). For the destruction of BF's papers at Galloway's Bucks County house in 1778, see I, xxi. BF had learned the news from his son-in-law and daughter: XXVII, 90, 605. See also BF's answer to Vaughan, below, May 5.

9. BF had sent the paper *circa* July, 1778: XXVII, 202. Gellée had made the copy, which BF corrected. That copy, which was subsequently marked for the printer by Vaughan, is now among Vaughan's papers at the APS.

my sister understands:[1] so that if it is not true, any man's *common sense* will tell him where & why it is false. In short there are nothing but principles; and cases are stated and explained, only for the sake of the principles. I speak proudly *here,* for I speak confidentially, and frankly; but *there* I am very humble. But However, confidentially as I feel myself respecting you, I do not care to trust the paper out of my hands for a fortnight to come, being willing to add & correct. Perhaps the Spanish embassador, if his court has any firmness, will be the bearer.[2] In the mean time I shall get Dr. Pristley & Dr. Price to give their judgments probably.

Comments on the paper.
1. *Confirmation* that the vis inertiæ is a phantom.
2. Rule *substituted,* by which the cases intended to be solved by the vis inertiæ, are better solved.
3. Celerity & force to be *distinguished,* both in theory & effect. Use however of the new conception of *communicated celerity.*
4. Cases shewn in which a small force though continued, *cannot* give more than a certain degree of force to a *given* body; only for want of *celerity.*

General Remarks on other subjects of motion.
5. Manner of projectiles operating 1°: upon unelastic bodies, 2°. upon elastic bodies, 3°. upon elastic bodies that are *lying upon a plane,* according to their accidental projection.
6. Cause of elasticity 1° in compressed bodies, 2°; in springs, 3°. in vibrating bodies 4°. in stretched bodies.
7°. *How* certain bodies *become* endued with their elasticity; as steel. The phænomenon of the Prince Rupert drop explained.
8°. Is not light *elastic* & therefore material, and an emission.

1. Vaughan enumerated the "following subjects" on a single sheet of paper which at some later time became separated from this letter. We are convinced that it belongs at the end of this paragraph (which ends a page in the MS), and have placed it below. The reference to Vaughan's sister may have been to Sarah (1761–1818), his favorite. She and the other three sisters are mentioned in John H. Sheppard, *Reminiscences of the Vaughan Family . . .* (Boston, 1865), p. 26.

2. The marqués de Almodóvar: XXVI, 675.

9°. Of the *direction* of the rebound in elastic bodies.
10°. Whence the versatility arises, with which a given force *practically* resolves itself into other forces.
11°. Of the question, of resistance altering according to the time consumed.
12°. Case of the bullet & candle against a standing board.
13°. Process of a bullet flattening at any obstacle.
14° Curved motion 1°. where the center of motion is *without* the body. 2°. where it is *within,* as in spinning. 3°. where the *parts* are curved within, yet move indifferently as a *whole.*
15°. Of the lever; whence a corollary to be drawn.
16°. Action & reaction to be explained *without* vis inertiæ. 1°. in continued forces. 2°. in single unincreasable projected forces. 3°. In drawing & pushing floating bodies. (which opposed.) 4°. In magnetical & other like forces.
17°. Data given & mistakes cleared relative to the dispute with foreigners, about the *quantity* of celerity used, in communicating given forces. Decided in favor of English & French philosophers. NB All *common sense* language here.
18°. What is force?—The phænomena of force enumerated under *brief* numbered heads.
19. What is *not* force?—the vis inertiæ.—Conclusion; with apology & address to my beloved Dr. Franklin.

The articles that will most amuse you here, are the 1, 2, latter part of the 5, 6, *7,* 11, 14, *17,* & 18.

I have not yet committed a great deal of my electrical conceits, in a regular form, on paper; but I shall soon do it. Ld: Mahon writes me that he is printing a book on the subject.[3]

I have no politics to write you. The country people within these twelve months have sometimes looked as if they were *going* to open their eyes, but France has done us yet so little actual mischief as they think, that they felt that they might go to sleep again. The town too has a good deal lost its hold of the subject: Mr Keppel flattened, Lord Sandwich flattened,

3. Charles, third Earl Stanhope, *Principles of Electricity, containing divers new theorems and experiments, together with an analysis of the superior advantages of high-pointed conductors, etc.* (London, 1779).

budget subjects flattened, every thing flattened.[4] Poor Miss Wray will agitate us for a few days,[5] till Sr. Hugh Palliser's trial comes on; which is fixed for Monday, and Mr Keppel at last summoned. If the court *chooses,* I think *we* can bear the acquittal of this man; they mistake here in thinking it necessary that Palliser should remain under the stigma of the *old* evidence, for they will determine according to the face & with the temper of the *new* evidence.[6] Should Spain really come up to the point, and the vigor of a campaign succeed the winter's calm, we may rouse again; but hardly, for some months. Our prize goods make business & wealth for the moment, and greatly aid the *revenue,* though all other articles of the latter appear falling off. The *tradesmen* seem content to be quiet, with the hope of not losing old debts, and receiving their interest.

4. The acquittal of Admiral Keppel on Feb. 11 had inspired popular as well as parliamentary attacks upon the North administration: XXVIII, 509n. But interest in the Keppel-Palliser affair was waning, and lack of organization on the part of the parliamentary opposition allowed the ministry to beat off their challenge. While the independent members of Parliament might criticize the Earl of Sandwich, First Lord of the Admiralty, they were not prepared to engage in personal attacks on him: Frank O'Gorman, *The Rise of Party in England: the Rockingham Whigs 1760–82* (London, 1975), pp. 385–6. Lord North was able to push his new budget through in spite of protests against the unfavorable terms of the loan he had negotiated and the increase in military spending; see the debates of Feb. 24 and March 1, 1779, in Cobbett, *Parliamentary History,* XX (1779), 155–74. Noting the new taxes that would result, Horace Walpole lamented the ". . . indifference and dissipation of the whole country": Lewis, *Walpole Correspondence,* XXIV, 448.

5. Martha Ray (Reay or Wray), Sandwich's mistress, was murdered as she was leaving Covent Garden Theater on the evening of April 7 by James Hackman, a young clergyman who had sought to marry her. See the *Public Advertiser,* April 9, 1779, and Lewis, *Walpole Correspondence,* XXXIII, 98–101. A pamphlet entitled *The Case and Memoir of the Rev. Mr. James Hackman, and of his Acquaintance with the late Miss Martha Ray* (London, 1779) went through ten editions that year.

6. Sir Hugh Palliser, Keppel's accuser, submitted himself to trial in order to clear his name and was acquitted on May 5, after a tedious proceeding which began on April 12; he had already submitted his resignation: O'Gorman, *The Rise of Party . . . ,* p. 385. Keppel, called as the first witness, made it clear at the outset that he had no interest in testifying against Palliser; see *The General Advertiser and Morning Intelligencer,* April 13, 1779. Throughout its coverage of the trial, this newspaper commented on the government's blatant partiality to Palliser and the shallowness of his defence.

Merchants are clearing off fast; especially with the help of the summer's remittances. I cannot fully explain the *manufacturers;* but I suppose you will pick up useful hands among your privateering & other *prisoners,* who have been accustomed to some thing more beneficial to man than robbery & murder. But lands & loans and luxury of private people, flag very much: It has been the fashion this winter *not to dress,* because they could not buy new clothes till the old were paid for; volunteer & pleasuring expences also are knocked up very much; and Ld. Grosvesnor in my hearing said very seriously, that he should break up his horse-racing, for no money was to be won, and he would not run for £20's. He will keep a few horses that he liked only.— His horse-establishment he said was £6000 a year, and two years ago £9000.[7]

I understand from Adml. Darby's relations, that he is expected to preside at the court-martial; and that the intended commands in the fleet are for Messr. Hardy, Harland, Darby & Digby; but they would not speak too peremptorily.[8]

I wrote to one of the Villesboisnets several articles of news, which I thought he would communicate.[9] In the West India news, our house made some mistakes of little consequence: owing to promotions &c.— Govr. Franklin's letter I hear no

7. Richard Grosvenor (1731–1802) was the largest breeder of bloodstock in England. *DNB.*

8. George Darby (d. 1790) did preside at Palliser's court-martial. His promotion to vice-admiral of the Channel fleet on March 19, 1779, appeared to be part of Sandwich's scheme of juggling political appointments to secure Palliser's acquittal. Sir Charles Hardy (1716?–1780), who had never held an independent command and had not been to sea for twenty years, was made first in command because no active officer would replace Keppel. Sir Robert Harland (1715?–1784) had been second in command under Keppel; he resigned his position on May 10, 1779, with the explanation that his ideas on naval discipline were at variance with those of the other commanding officers. The promotion of Robert Digby (1732–1814) to the rank of rear admiral in March, allowing him to testify at Palliser's court-martial, appeared to be another element in Sandwich's juggling act. Digby had been stationed in Palliser's division and had acted as a witness for the prosecution in Keppel's court-martial. In the summer he became second in command of the Channel fleet under Hardy. For all four men see the *DNB.*

9. The family were important commercial figures in Nantes: XXVIII, 294n.

more about;[1] Govr. Tryon who has written very impertinently here about your country's situation, is to be succeeded by Gen. Robertson as *civil governor.*[2]

I am very glad to hear of your recovery from the gout.— A person who attends my sisters, as music-master, says that during SEVEN YEARS he has taken out his gout, as he calls it I believe with yellow basilicn: [basilicon], lightly spread on tow, and a poultice above. He found the poultice very necessary for some reason I have forgot, and extended the application rather beyond the parts affected; and, when cured, for a day or two wore a little tow on his foot, just *touched* with the basilicn. He writes on a Monday, that he is confined with a severe fit of the gout, but has no doubt but that he shall be able to attend on Thursday: this he has done twice in three months; and kept his word. He says his fits are not only shorter, but he thinks rather less frequent; and is otherwise well. I am as ever, my dearest sir, most ardently, devotedly & gratefully, your BV.

P.S. I wish for a private address to Mr T F,[3] to whom I beg my best compts.

P.S. I write in haste, on very short notice.

Addressed: A Monsr. / Monsr. Franklin, / a Passy, / pres de Paris.

Notations in different hands: Vaughn April 9. 1779 Benjamin Vaughn London / London

1. Possibly a reference to one of the confidential reports on American affairs that WF had written to Lord George Germain on Nov. 12 and Dec. 20, 1778. WF argued that the rebel cause was quickly losing popular support, and that Washington's army and American economic strategy were weak. He described the cruelties that the loyalists were suffering and suggested retaliation. See K. G. Davis, ed., *Documents of the American Revolution 1770–1783* (Colonial Office Series, 21 vols., Shannon and Dublin, 1972–81), XV, 248–53, 293–6.

2. See William Tryon's letters to Germain of Dec. 24, 1778, and Feb. 5, 1779, expressing confidence in a British victory as well as suggesting harsher treatment of prisoners and more monetary rewards for loyalists and troops to induce a more aggressive prosecution of the war: Edmund B. O'Callaghan, ed., *Documents Relative to the Colonial History of the State of New-0 ork* (15 vols., Albany, 1853–87), VIII, 755–6. James Robertson (1720?–1788) succeeded Tryon as civil governor of New York in May, 1779. *DNB.*

3. WTF.

From Robert Gover

ALS: American Philosophical Society

St Vallory Sur Somne[4] Aprill 10: 1779

Robert Gover Aged 25 years Belonging to Baltermore in Maryland Saild from that port September 10: 1775 mate of a ship Bound to London at his Arrivel went out mate of a ship to Senegall returnd Back to London October 1: 1777 Saild from London Febuary 20 for Newyork Intending to git home at his Arrivel at Newyork was not allowd a pass by the mayor of that Town and to git away othor ways was very Difficult so was obliged to Return back in the Ship Saild from Newyork October 18: 1778 was Cast away on the Coast of france January 1: 1779 and is now a prisoner has Applyd to the Comesary of this Place to git Liberty to Enter in the Congress Service has had no Answer from the menester Makes free to Acquant Mr. Franklen of the Same hopes he will be so Obligen to git me Liberty to Enter in the Congress servicce or in a merchant Ship bound to America—[5]

from your &c ROBERT GOVER

Addressed: To / Honorable Doctr. / franklin ambassador / of the America Congress / to the Court of france / to Passy *near Paris*[6]

4. Saint-Valery-sur-Somme, northwest of Abbeville.
5. Gover repeated his appeal in a brief letter dated May 1. APS.
6. The following subtraction series appears on the address sheet:

$$\begin{array}{r} 73300 \\ 5500 \\ \hline 67800 \\ 10\ldots \\ \hline 57800 \end{array}$$

From David Hartley

Transcript: Library of Congress

Ap 10. 1779

I have had some conferences respecting terms of peace wch. I have pressed in the strongest manner whether with effect or no will appear after the holidays.[7] The grounds upon wch. I argued it were confidence & certainty and upon those grounds a friend of yours wd gladly offer his Services, but that friend of yours will never lend himself to transmitt or to negotiate any Specious or fallacious offer to serve as a pretext upon the refusal for the continuation of the War. Peace Peace is the object with the friend. You know so thoroughly my principles relative to America that I can add nothing farther upon that head as to my own Country I wish to reserve its honour as a nation from the importation [imputation] of the crimes of its Ministers. Like the pious Sons of the post diluvian patriarch (the then founder of a new World as this Country is now) I wd Wish to turn my back upon things that are past and to throw a veil over the errors of inabriated Authority.

Let me now refer you to yours feb 22/79 wch. was in answer to mine of Jan 23/79— Thy proposition in mine of 23 Jan/79 was not for you to quit any thing solid to put yourself into a state of receiving what *may* vanish in the discussion. Tho' neither you or I are much Conversant at New market but you may have heard of a customary phrase there, Upon offering a bett *I say Done first.* My Application of this phrase is that *Done*

7. The conferences were with Lord North. The two men had conferred on several occasions over the frustrating delays in the prisoner exchange, most recently in February. George H. Guttridge, *David Hartley, M.P., an Advocate of Conciliation, 1774–1783* (University of Cal. *Pubs.* in History, XIV, no. 3; Berkeley and London, 1926), p. 278. In a letter of March 31 Hartley had tried to persuade North that France was using America to settle a few points of her own against Britain, that "Rest & peace" were America's objectives, and that the continuation of the war was "harassing" to her (Library of Congress). Building on that premise Hartley undertook, in a series of meetings with the English minister during April and May, to find grounds for reconciliation with America and to press for the appointment of one or more Englishmen to open negotiations with BF. See, in particular, his letters of April 22 and May 25, and Digges's of May 12 and 18.

first gives the certainty against vanishing in the Discussion. Take for instance a proposition wch. has been publicly stated in the 4th. letter from an MP to his Constituents and suppose the *Done first* applied to it wch. was not the case in the treaty of last Year, such a *Done first* wd. give every certainty that one nation can give to another. The proposition alluded to is *to withdraw the British fleets & Armies from America & to make an offer of peace to America upon the Condition that the eventual treaty of alliance be relinquished on the part of france.*[8] If we say *Done first* Surely these wd. be terms of certainty and Advantage to America *for if, America is to become substantially independent of Great Britain* No American cd. think it a disadvantage that they shd. become at the same time *independent of France & of all the World.* So much for the *Done first— But the truth is you say you can have no kind of faith* &c in the British Ministry. I abhor the mixture of cunning & fierce as much as you can do. But I think a National *Done first* wd. likewise be an Answer to this objection. It wd doubtless be a strong additional pledge of security.—that the negotiators shd be persons who from principle wd not transmitt any deception [*and*] the negotiation thro' such hands might be mutually carried on upon liberal principles of confidence & good faith. In the conference wch. I have alluded to this point was discussed upon that occasion I Learnt the name of the person who made application to you last year relative to the choice of Commrs. who might have been received in America with confidence. I did not *positively* know the *name* before tho I was not far from guessing.[9] I cd. say a great deal upon the word Magnanimity (vide yours of Jan 25 1779 *a magnanimous & heroic action that is Admired at present by the wise and good through all Europe* &c.) All that I will say is this Motives make Magnanimity.

Treaty of Alliance Act: 2d The essential & direct end of the

8. The statement Hartley presents is from the fourth of his *Letters on the American War* (London, 1778), p. 87. See also XXVIII, 417n.

9. Possibly Sir Philip Gibbes or Paul Wentworth; see XXV, 419–23, 435–9. A number of individuals, however, had sounded out BF in January, 1778, on the prospects for a negotiated settlement, although, to the best of our knowledge, none of them was discussing names of possible commissioners to be sent to America.

present defensive alliance is to maintain effectually the liberty Sovereignty & Independence absolute & unlimited (either formally or tacitly assured Act: 8) of the said united states as well in Matters of Government as of Commerce.[1] Now I put my test of If beyond this essential & direct end and upon grounds totally unconnected with that alliance not upon Motives of Magnanimity *for the relief of an innocent people* but upon distinct & unconnected motives of private European resentments, America shd. be dragged into the consequences of a general European War, She may apply to France the apostrophe of the poet speaking in the Person of Helen to Paris

Non hoc pollicitors tucc[2]

We are both of us engaged in the same cause the restoration of peace but neither you nor I can controul the bent of Nations if the fury of national pride & passions be deaf to the voice of peace. Your Situation puts you more into the Sphere of influential action than mine does. Our hearts are in union for peace. And what so poor a Man as Hamlet is can do to express his love & frending to you God willing shall not lack.[3]

From Richard Bennett Lloyd[4]

ALS: American Philosophical Society

Dear Sir, London 10th. April 1779—

Your obliging favour of the 18th of March came safe to hand, for which I beg you will accept my best thanks. I must apologize to you for the liberty I am about to take but as I have much reason to be assured of your Friendship and as there is no Gentleman who's advice I would so soon follow as

1. For Articles 2 and 8 of the Treaty of Alliance see XXV, 586–7, 589.

2. Correctly written, "non hoc pollicitus tuae." Horace, *Odes,* I, 15, 32. Nereus is prophesying to Paris: "running away like a deer fleeing a wolf is not what you promised your mistress."

3. *Hamlet,* I, 5, 184–6.

4. Lloyd's letter was enclosed with one of the same date to WTF. There he asked for a bust of BF made of Sèvres china, "set on a blue Stone with a gold border—", to be sent care of Pierre Dessin at Calais. APS.

your's—permit me therefore, to ask your opinion on the following scheme—. Mr. William Eden (the late Commissioner, and who I have known for some years) hearing that my stay in this Country would be but short, and supposing that I intended to return to America he has offered to procure a passport should I think of going by the way of New York—.[5]

My answer was, that should such indulgence be granted Government must not expect advantage by it, for on my arrival in Maryland I must take the oath directed by Congress and act agreeably to the laws of that State, or run the hazard of forfeiting my Estate—. I think he replied that perhaps Government would not suppose the allowing a few individuals to return to their Estates that it could effect the point in question—.

I have since received a letter from Mr. Eden saying, that he being sensible that so long a separation from my property must be a pressing Inconvenience to me, he would very readily recommend to the Commander in Chief at New York[6] to permit me and my Family to pass thro the Lines to the Southward: and he had every reason to persuade himself that his Recommendation wd. be sufficient for the Purpose—.

I find the impossibility of leaving my Family in Europe and the taking my little Children the great length of journey to Nantes or Bourdeaux— My *Finances* being exceedingly low (it has been with difficulty I have been able to borrow a few hundreds for the Necessary expences of my Family) this, with the risk of falling into the hands of a Jersey or Grenesey Privateer and my Wife & Children barbarously treated, I confess alarms me much—.

But as this is a Step which requires more foresight than I am able to give it, may I ask for your Friendly advice?—I shall now leave off, beging many pardons for taking up so much of your time— A letter directed for me and put under cover and directed for Messrs. Gale Dawes & Stephenson Little Tower Street London[7] I think will get safe to my hands—.

5. Eden was head of British intelligence (XXV, 435). New York City had been under British control since September, 1776.

6. Sir Henry Clinton.

7. Merchants, listed in *Kent's Directory* (London, 1779), p. 68.

Mrs. Lloyd unites with me in best respects, and I am with the greatest esteem your very obedient humble Servant—

RICHARD BTT. LLOYD

The Honourable Benjamin Franklin Esquire &c: &c: &c:—

Notation: Richard B. Lloyd Londres 10 avril 1779.

From Oliver Pollock

ALS: American Philosophical Society

Sir New Orleans 10th. Apl. 1779

Annexed is Copy of what I had the honor to write you the 29th. April 1778 since which have not been favoured with a line from you.[8] The purport of this letter is to acquaint you that I have this day drawn on Messrs. Saml. & J. H. Delap Sundry Bills of Exchange Viz for p.4000 in favour of Monsr. Jacque Toutant Beaugaud p.1000 in favour of Michael Poupart p.3500 in favour of Cadet Jardin & 2397 in favour of Monsr. F Detmaters the whole amounting to 10897 Dollars all at 90 Days sight being for Sundries Receiv'd from those Gentlemen for the use of the United states to excute the orders I received from Congress and in Consequence I hope in Sight of this you will see them all duly honored—[9] But as in all Probability you may not yet have Received The necessary advices from Congress Respecting those Bills I make no doubt you soon will after this comes [*to*] hand having advised the Honbl. the Congress this day to that purpose but for fear their advice should be retarded by misfortunes or accidents at Sea I have herewith inclosed Paragraphs taken from the Secret and Commercial Committees Letter to me dated 12th. June 24 Octobr. & 21 Novr. 1778[1] as also Copy of a Draft of Exchange drawn

8. For the two letters of that day from Congress' commercial agent at New Orleans see XXVI, 377–8.

9. Pollock is calculating in Spanish pesos or milled dollars.

1. The "inclosed Paragraphs" (now missing) are actually from three 1777 letters from Congress to Pollock: Smith, *Letters,* VII, 185–9; VIII, 171–2, 297–8. We have not found a letter of April 10 from him to Congress advising them on the bills. The committee of commerce, however, wrote BF on July 21 asking him to intercede with the Delaps to see that the bills were honored. At that point Congress owed Pollock $70,000: *ibid.,* XIII, 271–2.

by Capt. Jas. Willing in my favour on Congress to all of which I beg leave to defer you for your better Government and please now to observe that exclusive of paying Congress orders by forwarding Goods to a very large amount for which they have not had it as yet in their Power to supply me with sufficient Funds on Acct. of the Enemies Force at Sea and the Embargo which they think necessary to Continue on their Provisions I cannot negotiate Bills upon them in America nor have I ever had an oppty. of hearing from them on that Subject tho I have been Supporting a Detatchmt. of Troops under the Command of Col. Clark who took possession of the Illinois Country last June as also the ship Morris which I fitted out in a Warlike manner to distress the Enemys Trade in this River to the Islands[2] then heavy advances have obliged me to draw those Bills in full Confidence you will See them duly honored for the Credit of the States which will much oblige your Most Obedient & very Huml. Servt.[3] OLVR. POLLOCK

Copy

From Jesse Taylor

ALS: American Philosophical Society

Sir Belfast 10th. April 1779

Your Excellencies favour of the 18' ult. Came Safe to hand, the Contents were as soon as practicable, Communicated to the princeable Conserned in this town & Neighbourhood— I am by them Instructted to Enforme you, that unless their had been really a Considerable number Resolved on the Expedittion mentioned in my Last of the 21st. Nov., the application

2. For Pollock's financial support of George Rogers Clark and his refitting of the captured British sloop *Rebecca* (renamed the *Morris*) see James Alton James, *Oliver Pollock: the Life and Times of an Unknown Patriot* (New York and London, 1937), *passim.*

3. BF declined to act on Pollock's behalf. He wrote Congress on Oct. 21, 1779, that his resources had been so exhausted by unexpected drafts and expenses that he would have been unable to pay the bills if they had been presented to him. Library of Congress. Pollock's drafts on the Delaps eventually were returned protested, further complicating his accounts with Congress: James, *Oliver Pollock,* p. 352.

had not Been made for the Securitty that was Requested— In their name, I am Desired to Return thanks to your Excelly for your Early Attention to their memorial and to Assure your Excelly, that nothing should prevent their Immediate Compliance with your Commands in sending you the required Discriptive List, But their sence of Danger (which must to your Excelly appear Great) should such a paper be Intercepted, as fall unto Improper hands;—[4] your Excelly Enformation, that the Knight has not Been with you is somewhat alarming to the Conserned, as they have learned he passed through your neighbourhood, in his route to Lausanne, but prehaps he reserves, that honour till his return by same way, this we are Given to understand, will be some time in the presant month, when your Excelly. will prehaps in your Conversattion with that Gentelman Discover sufficent grounds for proceeding to procure and forward, the Securitty so anxiously solicited—[5]

Did not the Concerned hope from their Going in a Body to Desire Concequence; and from the Countenance your Excelly. has been requestted to show this Intended Expedittion, to precure them some degree of Respectabillity, in the place the wish to proceed to—they Could Readily find a safe passage, to that Country whereing they are Desirous to Settel, without troubling your Excelly. for such papers as has been Requested of you—this the frequent Smuglling Expedettions from abought Dublin, to that Country that Comes to the knowledge of the Concerned would readly furnish—But as we do not Deem this mode of Conveyance, Altogether reputtable, they have haitherto Avoided it their wish being to appear on thir arivial what the really are, People who come to settel & Bring propertty with them,—not men who comes for temporary advantage and then Desart that Country, and its Intrist, by which they have been Inriched, should any doubt Remain with you, of our Cincearetty—on Recept hear of—its hoped by the Concerned that your Excelly. will be pleased to ad-

4. The list was hand-delivered; see below. For a discussion of the dangers of emigration see R.J. Dickson, *Ulster Emigration to Colonial America 1718–1775* (London, 1966).

5. The "Knight" was Sir Edward Newenham. See BF to Newenham, May 27, and the reply, June 25.

vise—Inclosing a pasport from that State, to which your Excelly. is Deputted, for one of the Concerned—who will Imeaditly sett of from this to wait on your Excelly., with Such particular Enformattion as your Letter Requires—but if more fortunately for us your Excelly. Doubts, of the memorial Transmitted to you in Nov. Last, bet removed and on Recipt of this, your Excelly. should be pleased to forward the nessacery securitty—I am to Informe your Excelly. that it is the wish of the Concerned, such securitty as you think needfull—should be made out for the Brigt. Elizabeth Willm. Stewart mastar, Burthen abought 150 Tons mounting 14 Carrage Guns &c fifteen Seamen & abought fortty passengers who Goes under the Denomination of seamen & marines, with some weomen & Children—this vessel is solely the property of the writer, & perhaps Stewart may not go Capt, suppose your Excelly would say Stewart, or any other that maybe the Capt. of said vessell—from your Excelly. adressing me as Capt. you seem to recognize a man, who once had the honour of your aquantince when part proprietor, & mastar of a ship who has Carryed from this Country, some hundreds of passengers who he hopes Did approve themselves Good Citizens in America—[6] and Since I was setteled in this place have sent over some thousands—and am now Ressolved on the principals of the memorial transmitted; to Embarque my Person, Wife & Seven Children & part of my fortune In the above mentioned vessel—with many other Gentelmen of Condesetion here—and by our Influance when setteled on the other side, many hundreds of our Countrymen will follow—and they only waight the account of our safe arrivial, & to know we have Established some settelment for them, when they will Instantly sett out (with the Remainder of our property) from a kindom in which they Labour under Insult & opprission,

6. We have found no trace of a previous acquaintance between Taylor and BF. His name appears frequently in the *Belfast News Letter* of the mid-1770's as the owner of vessels sailing from Ulster to various American ports. William Stewart was master of one of those ships which sailed in 1774, carrying Taylor and his family. See Dickson, *Ulster Emigration to Colonial America,* pp. 121, 258, 266–8, 276, 277.

from which they see no other refuge, then what has been Sought from your Excelly— This goes by the Same Conveyance as the former—and in and through the Same Channel your Excelly. will be pleased to send your answer—& as we Presume your Excelly. well knows the handwrite, have not annexed the name for Reasons your Excelly may well know—But Remains with all Respectt your Excellencies most obedt. Humble Sert—[7] J.T.

Addressed: To / his Excelly. Benjamin Franklin / at / Paris / *Cover*

Notations in different hands: J T. Belfast 10. Avril 1779 / Received and Forwarded the 26th. of April 1779.— by your Most Obt Servants Bast. Molewater & Sons of Rotterdam

From Jonathan Williams, Jr.

ALS: Historical Society of Pennsylvania

Dear & hond Sir.— Nantes April 10. 1779.

My Cousin Jona Williams tertius[8] will have the honour of delivering you this.— He lately arrived from America & will therefore be able to give you many pieces of Information which perhaps may have not found their way through a public Channel.— His views in coming to France were principaly to reestablish his Health, having succeeded in this he wishes to see Paris & then return.—[9]

I beg leave to introduce him to your notice & Friendship,

7. The messenger was John Hay, Jr., who met with BF on July 1 and presumably delivered the list of would-be emigrants. That list, now at the APS, contains thirty-four names, including Hay's and those of Jesse Taylor, his wife, and his seven children. Hay left Passy on July 2 with passport in hand: Hay to BF, July 1 and 6. APS.

8. A son of John Williams, the "inspector," he had studied in JA's law office for two years following his graduation from Harvard in 1772: L. Kinvin Wroth and Hiller B. Zobel, eds., *Legal Papers of John Adams* (3 vols., Cambridge, Mass., 1965), I, cxiii.

9. BF received the young man for dinner every Sunday, according to Hezekiah Ford: Butterfield, *John Adams Diary*, II, 364.

we have but one Name between us & from our Infancy we have divided each others affections.—[1]

I am ever Your most dutifully & affecty JONA WILLIAMS J

From James Hutton

ALS: American Philosophical Society

Dear Sir April. 11. 1779

I send the Servant who occasionally does my little messages, for that Protection for the *Good Intent* Capt. *Francis Mugford,* to go to and from Labradore, to the Moravian mission Settlements for the conversion of the Heathen, so kindly promised last Friday.[2] The Person who was to have brought it yesterday never came. I hope it has not miscarried. Many thanks to you for the Readiness with which you oblige your old Friend & Servant JAS. HUTTON

Addressed: To / Doctor Franklin / or His Grandson / Passy.

Notation: M. Hutton April 11. 1779.

To All Captains and Commanders of Vessels of War[3]

Two copies:[4] Library of Congress

Gentlemen, [April 11, 1779]

The Religious Society commonly called the Moravian Brethren having established a Mission on the Coast of Labra-

1. JW also wrote to WTF on April 10, requesting him to show his namesake the sights of Paris. Judging by the appreciative letter the young Williams sent WTF on June 3, the eve of his departure for America, WTF's tour was completely satisfactory. Once back home, the young man's health failed again, and he did not survive much longer than a year. JW reported his death to WTF on Aug. 8, 1780. All three letters are at the APS.

2. The passport, issued on April 11, is below.

3. BF apparently promised this passport to James Hutton on April 9 ("last Friday"), but drafted it in response to Hutton's reminder of April 11, above. He had supplied Hutton with a similar passport the previous spring (XXVI, 667–8), and on May 17, 1780, issued another pass whose wording was virtually identical to this one. The vessel named in the 1780 passport was the brig *Amity,* Capt. James Fraser. APS.

4. The one from which we print is in the hand of WTF.

dor, for the Conversion of the Savages there to the Christian Religion, which has already had very good Effects, in turning them from their ancient Practices of surprizing plundering and murdering such White People Americans and Europeans, as for the Purposes of Trade or Fishery, happened to come on that Coast, and persuading them to lead a Life of honest Industry and to treat Strangers with Humanity and Kindness. And it being necessary for the Support of this useful Mission, that a small Vessel should go thither every Year to furnish Supplies & Necessaries for the Missionaries and their Converts, which Vessel for the present Year is a Sloop of about seventy Tons called the Good Intent, whereof is Master Capt. Francis Mugford. This is to request you, that if the said Vessel should happen to fall into your Hands, you would not consider her as an Enemy, but as employed, in the Service of Mankind in general; that you would not suffer her to be plundered or hindred in her Voyage but on the contrary afford her any Assistance she may stand in need of: Wherein I am confident your Conduct will be approved by the Congress & your Owners.

Given at Passy this 11th Day of April 1779.—

(signed) B. FRANKLIN
Minister Plenipotentiary from the United States, at the Court of France.

To all Captains & Commanders of Vessels of War Privateers & Letters of Marque belonging to the United States of America—

From John Quincy Adams[5]

ALS: Dartmouth College Library

Sir Nantes april 12th 1779

I am obliged to you, for the Mention you have been so good as to make of me in several of your letters to my Pappa, whom I have accompanied to Brest & back to Nantes.[6]

5. This is BF's first letter from the eleven-year-old.
6. They returned to Nantes on April 11: Butterfield, *John Adams Diary*, II, 358n.

I hope you have recovered a perfect state of Health & that you will enjoy it a long time.

I beg of you to remember me respectfully to Mr Franklin & affectionately to Mr Benjamin.

I have wrote several times to my Freinds at Passy[7] but recd no answers. I suspect my Letters have miscarried. I beg you would deliver those inclosed as directed I am with great Veneration sir yours. John Q Adams

From Claude-Mammès de Pahin Champlain de La Blancherie[8]

AL: American Philosophical Society

Le 12 avril. 1779.

M. de la Blancherie présente ses respects à Monsieur frankelin a l'honneur de prier son Excellence de vouloir bien lui accorder enfin l'honneur de sa présence mercredi prochain après la séance de l'Académie. Il attend cette faveur comme les Israélistes attendoient la manne du ciel.

M. frankelin.

7. His former schoolmates BFB and Silas Deane's son Jesse (for whom see XXV, 646).

The young Adams wrote to WTF on April 22 from the *Alliance,* anchored off St. Nazaire, to say that he and his father had arrived at Paimboeuf at 12:00 the night before. He hopes soon to sail for America. APS.

8. The enterprising La Blancherie (for whom see XXVI, 379) inserted a notice about the meeting in the April 14 issue of the *Jour. de Paris:* the *Agent Général de Correspondance pour les Sciences et les Arts,* it reports, will receive scholars and artists in the new location on the rue de Tournon. La Blancherie may have needed BF's presence all the more since he had recently been under attack in the columns of that journal: March 1, pp. 239–40; March 5, p. 255; and March 7, p. 263.

From John Mace: Promissory Note[9]

Two DS:[1] American Philosophical Society

Passy, April 12 1779

I promise to pay to the honbl. the President of Congress or his Order the sum of three hundred & sixty four Livres, twelve sols, for Value recd. of Mr. Coffin at Dunkirk, & of B. Franklin esq; at Passy.

I have signed three Notes of this Tenor & Date to Serve as one.[2]

JOHN MACE

364.12

From Marat

ALS: American Philosophical Society

Sir April 12th 79.

The report of the Commitee's for to morrow has been declined by M. le Roy, & is delay'd till Saturday next.

I again beg earnestly you would be So good as to be present then to give your opinion, which will be requested by M. le Comte de Maillebois.

Was it not now so material a point to the Author, that a candid judgement should be pass'd upon his work, he would trust to time alone. But he is certain that many a Accademical gentleman do not look with pleasure upon his discoveries, & will do their utmost to préjudice the whole Body. Let the cabal

9. Mace appears on the Alphabetical List of Escaped Prisoners where he is recorded as receiving at Dunkirk and Passy 454 *l.t.* 12 *s.* An itemized receipt, dated April 5, reveals his expenses: board for fifty-six days, a pair of shoes, two waistcoats, washing, a nurse and an apothecary's bill, and wine and sundries. Adding on 48 *l.t.* travel money from Dunkirk to Paris, his total is 244 *l.t.* 12 *s.,* which he acknowledges having received from Coffyn. He lists himself as a doctor from North Portsmouth, Virginia. APS.

1. The second of the two is dated April 14.

2. To be sent to America by three conveyances; see BF to Fizeaux, Grand & Cie., June 7.

On May 10, William Willis signed a similar note, drafted by WTF, promising to repay twenty *louis d'ors* (eleven received from Coffyn and nine from BF). His note states that the sum is given to assist him in returning to America. APS. He also appears on the Alphabetical List of Escaped Prisoners.

be ever So warm, it certainly will be Silenced by the Sanction of Such a Man as Doctor Franklin: and how far judgement passed by himself & the Royal Academy can influence public opinion is well known.

If I appèare troublesome, Sir; my consciousness of your benevolence, & my respect for your candour and understanding are my apology THE REPRESENTATIVE.

From John Adams: Two Letters

(I) and (II) ALS: American Philosophical Society

I.

Sir Nants April 13. 1779

I had Yesterday the Honour of yours of the third of this Month.

C. Landais had So much diffidence in Some of his Crew, that he could not think of carrying home any of the most culpable of the Conspirators, especially as he was so weak handed.

The naval Code of the united States, has great occasion for Amendments in many Particulars, without which there will be little Discipline subordination, or obedience.[3]

I am happy that you approve of cloathing the petty officers and thank you for the Confidence you have put in me in desiring that I would give Directions in your Behalf for what I may judge for the good of the Service, Funds and Circumstances considered. A Trust however, that will involve me in difficulties, because I fear the Demands of officers and Men will be greater than I could wish.

Obedience, on Board is So imperfect, that I do not expect the ship can possibly be got to sea, without some Money to the officers and Men.

3. As a member of Congress' naval committee JA had written the "Rules for the Regulation of the Navy of the United Colonies." Its disciplinary articles were less strict than those of the British Navy: *Adams Papers,* III, 147–56.

I expect the Ship here every day, and I hope in 15 days to be at sea, if you have any Letters should be glad to carry them.

Am much pleased with your Reception at Court in the new Character and I do not doubt that your opinion of the good Will of this Court to the united States is just. This Benevolence is the Result of so much Wisdom and is founded in such Solid Principles that, I have the utmost Confidence in its Perseverance to the End.

Spain, too, must Sooner or later see her true Interest, and declare in favour of the same generous Cause. I wish, and hope with you that it will be soon.— If it is not, there is great Reason to fear a very unnecessary and profuse Effusion of human Blood: for the English derive such Spirits from their Captures at sea and other little successes, and War is everlastingly So popular among them, when there is the least Appearance of success however deceitful that, they will go on, at whatever Expence and Hazard.

Master Johnny, whom you have honoured with an affectionate Remembrance, and who Acts at present in the quadruple Capacity of Interpreter, secretary, Companion & Domestick to his Pappa desires me to present you his dutiful Respects.

My Regards if you please to Mr Franklin & Mr Gellée, and the young Fry.

I have the Honour to be with great Respect, your most obedient servant JOHN ADAMS.

His Excellency, M. Franklin, Ministre Plenipotentiary of the U. states

Notation: Jonh Adams Nantes 13 avril 1779.

II.

Sir Nantes April 13. 1779

This Morning I had the Honour of yours of the 8th, and thank you for the order inclosed to Captain Landais, and for those you mention to M. Schweighausser.

The true Springs of the Discontent on board appear to me to be, the Depreciation of Paper Pay, and the Extraction of the Captain. The Purser, may have increased them a little by too much of the Appearance of being a favourite of the Captain, for ought I knew, but without any fault that I knew of.

In short I never knew Discontents openly avowed and Misunderstandings among People confessed without something more solid to say in Excuse for them.

I fancy the Purser, may go home in the Alliance if he choses, and do his Duty without any Injury to the service.—But it should be I think as he chooses, or shall choose.

In Consequence of your repeated Letters to me, I have ventured to Advise Mr Schweighauser, to promiss the officers and Men as much Money as with their Cloaths will make two Months Pay. Without this Indulgence I am convinced the ship would never get to sea, with her present Equipage.

I am perfectly of your opinion that the Americans arrived from England should be at Liberty, and they have been left so accordingly and some have engaged with Captain Jones and some with Captain Landais, so many with the latter as will be a fine Addition to his strength, altho still far short of his Compliment.

I have the Honour to be, sir, your most obedient

John Adams

His Excellency, Dr Franklin

Notation: Adams John. 13 April 1779.

From Stephen Sayre

ALS: American Philosophical Society

Sir. Copenhagen 13th April 1779—

I am favour'd with your Excellencys Letter of 31 March, sent me by Messrs Hopes: for having been taken ill, I had advised them accordingly. I have been many days confined to my Rooms with the *blind Piles;* have suffer'd intolerably, but am now better— My Journey to & from Stockholm, travelling night & day, without rest, probably brought on the complaint—

As I am a correspondent of Messrs Hopes, I venture to state, as nearly as I can recollect, what pass'd, at a certain place.

Your Excy. may easily suppose that after the matters which pass'd at Berlin were become public, I was consider'd, & universally denominated, a Deputy of Congress, and tho I have on some Occasions been under the necessity of denying it, I was not believed—such an Idea predominates so forceably, that no circumstances can remove the Impression, except among my most confidential freinds. Therefore the question was never ask'd me. The who was here at the Review last Summer took particular notice of me, having been pointed out to him as such. Being acquainted with some of his attendants, they told me, they knew it would please him to see me at S——. I was also inform'd that not long since that C—— had made some earnest applications to Spain, for the Island of Porto Rico.[4] Baron N——[5] came on purpose from England to point out the mode of obtaining it &c &c &c &c. I had an Opportunity of an Audience with the K—— very soon after my arrival. I should have remark'd, that he had previously seen his whole C—— introduce themselves to my acquaintance (Ladies & Gentlemen) & saw it with most apparent pleasure. This was at an Assembly where the C—— always attend. I was order'd to wear a pinck colour'd Ribbon in my Hat, at the Masquerade—to answer a signal &c— I was consequently conducted into his s Box, where I had a conference of about half an hour, alone—

His first address was preface'd with assurances of a most friendly disposition, not only to me personally, whose Character he said he well knew, but towards America in General—he was sensible how naturally both Countries might benefit by commerce &c &c. wish'd to bring forward such an Intercourse—desired me, in case I return'd soon there, to present his best Respects to the Congress who he loved & admired. He added, that in the present moment he saw himself critically situated as to England: for that he must inevitably make Re-

4. The story of Sayre's reception in Stockholm ("S——") appears to be an invention; see our annotation of his March 10 letter. Nor do we have any evidence of the Swedish Court's ("C——") interest in Puerto Rico.

5. Baron Gustaf Adam von Nolcken, the Swedish envoy in Britain: *Repertorium der diplomatischen Vertreter,* III, 409.

prisals if his Ships wire not instantly restored, tho' at the same time he had urgent reasons for continuing at peace with all his Neibours.

After several other matters were touch'd upon, I mentioned my Information as to what had been attempted to gain Porto Rico: and suggested the possibility of its being obtain'd on a different principle. That if his would make known such Inclination while the face of public Affairs was making rapid changes, particularly as to West India Possessions, either this, or some other Island, might probably, be thrown in the Scale of . He relish'd the Idea exceedingly—wish'd to know how I thought Congress could, agreeable to thier own Interests, aid such possession instead of making such Island their own. My reply was, that Congress wanted not possession, but the Trade of the Islands—that they would never extend dominion from the Continent— Trade was their only Object— Beside an Island protected by a neutral power—supply'd by neutral Ships—*open, mutually & forever, as to navigation & Rules of Commerce, to both nations:* would during war, be of infinite more advantage to America than if under their immediate Government. That I apprehended the Courts of Paris & Madrid, as well as Congress would studiously endeavour at obliging him, for many political Reasons: knowing the value of his friendship & Influence with Russia & this Kingdom &c &c— In short this Interview induced him to appoint an hour for me to attend his first Minister, next morning; of which he himself gave the Minister notice, to receive me only. After several long Conferences, the following points were settled as clearly desirable. 1t That it would be highly advantagious that the State should upon almost any Terms, gain possession of an Island of any dimensions. 2dlly. That great commercial benefits must soon be derived thro' such Islands, as a Magazine of Commerce, for America, & a door by which their Herring Fishery, & many articles of Export must find a Market. And 3dly. That S——, would by such acquisition only stand on a footing with Denmark, & have a superiority as to many Articles of Export.

It was also agree'd, that if an Island could be obtain'd under any Terms, short of an open Rupture, it should be attempted.

I pointed out some steps to be pursued in the first Stages of the Business, leaving subsequent Matters to time & occasion— Having fix'd all things, as I apprehended, for a train of actual execution, it some how or other came into question whether the Treasurer, who is a man of business, should not be consulted. I made no great difficulty, as I knew little of his Character—he was accordingly call'd on—had a long detail—approved every thing—went farther than the prime Minister, for he proposed sending two Ships of the Line immediately, with a proper person &c. to Congress to try how far they would press the business. &c &c &c—

Extraordinary as it may seem: I never was call'd upon after this meeting or recd. the least intimation to wait longer there. But I understand this Minister has too little principle to do his Master's Business *without being paid for it*—

I also understand, that the   has given him a very severe Rebuke for suffering me to leave S—— under such kind of impressions— The first Minister, must have been bias'd for the moment, but he was candid at first, & is so now— If thereafter any thing is done at this C—— let care be taken to avoid this man— His name begins with L.—[6] I am sorry your Exy. did not give me your opinion as to Dominica which I mentioned— I could have convey'd it to the Minister from hence—Now I am going for Norway—shall probably embark from thence for St Croix or St Thomas, with liberty to stop at St Eustatia— I might from St Eustatia go up to Dominica & secure an Estate I own there. I request again Letters to the Governor for that reason, as I may expect more justice when well supported. If those Letters can be sent immediately to the care of Frederic De Coninck Esqr of this City,[7] they will reach me before I can sail— I have some offers of Business in the West Indies: yet I think I am hardly used to be under the necessity of accepting them: because I know I merit more attention. I did not hesitate a moment to accept any thing offer'd

6. The great Swedish finance minister Jean Westermann, count Liliecrantz or Liljenkrantz (*c.* 1730–1815): Larousse.

7. A wealthy merchant to whose care Sayre had previously asked that letters be directed: XXVIII, 378n.

from America— I shut the door as to England against myself in full confidence of being supported— Pray do me the favour to mention me, once more to Congress— I hope to be with them in some few months— I know your name will do me most essential Service, & strengthen my freinds there—

It is evident from the above rough, undigested account of things that all the civilities I recd at S—— were because I was supposed employ'd by Congress. I trust I have not abused the Character—nor have I assumed it—had the question been put to me, I assure you, I would have acknowledged myself a private man, as I am, let consequences have been what they might.

I am, & ever shall be, with great respect your Excellency's most obedient Humble Servant STEPHEN SAYRE

Notation: Steven Sayre April 13. 79.—

From Jonathan Williams, Jr.

ALS: American Philosophical Society; copy: Yale University Library

Dear & hond Sir. Nantes April 13. 1779.—

I recvd your Favour of the 8th Instant per this days post.— I am surely the most unlucky of all accused Persons for all my Endeavours to bring on a Trial are unsuccessfull. Of the Gentlemen named there remains here only three Mr Johnson Mr Gridley & Mr Schweighauser the two last are so ill as to make their attendance impossible, and Mr S, I have reason to believe, would not attend if he was well.—[8] So I am just where I was.—

I thank you for your advice as to the algebraic Calculation & I will follow it. I have used it already in one or two Instances with some Success, but in the matrimonial Way I a little differ from your Opinion, & instead of my never being

8. JW was continually having difficulties with Schweighauser, as he told John Paul Jones the following week, but had a reason for wanting to maintain cordial relations: he was courting Schweighauser's daughter. JW to Jones, April 22 and 29, Yale University Library.

married if I don't "use it" I am afraid I never shall be married if I do, for the negative Column seems in this Instance the weightiest. Before a Man is married he must *fall* in love and this seems to be as involuntary an act as *falling* into a Well—which requires something more than algebra to get out of.—I begin however to see more reasons on the favourable side than I used to, and I believe the next time I *fall* I shall endeavour rather to make myself content in, than (as I have hitherto done) scramble out.—

Excuse my Badinage & believe me ever with great Respect your dutifull & affectionate Kinsman JONA WILLIAMS J

Inclose a Letter to Dr Ingenhouse which please to read & then forward.—[9]

The Honble. Doctor Franklin

From Daniel Duchemin ALS: American Philosophical Society

Tres respectable Docteur de Londre le 14 avril 1779

Je ne puis menpecher de vous troubler pour vous assurer de mes plus tendre respect et vous donner avis quaprees avoir Etez fait prisonnier deux jour avant lentrée des anglois Dans Philadelphia et detenu depuis ce tems la jé sependant par le moyen d'un amis passé en Engleterre ou je suis presentement mais les perte que jé faite depuis mon Emprisonnement mon mis or Detat de paser En france sans votre secour. Je suis premier Lieutenant dans un corps Comandé par Le Collonnel Armand marquis de la roirie je demeuroit a Philadelphia dans chesnuts Estreet et ay lhonneur detre parfaitement Connu de

9. BF apparently had shown JW the part of Ingenhousz's April 1 letter (of which only an extract survives; see above) that concerned the latter's financial affairs, in which JW was a partner. The answer that JW here encloses, dated April 13, indicates that Ingenhousz had asked that his money, which had been invested in American trade, be remitted to him to be employed in Ireland. JW explained to Ingenhousz the impossibility of commanding the money at the present moment. JW's letter (a copy of which is in the Yale University Library) was forwarded to Ingenhousz along with BF's of May 4[–5], below.

Mr. Tomas moris presentement en franse quy assurement s'il savoit mon Etat present me renderoit des service.[1] Jé lhonneur Detre Connu aussy du marquis de la fayette du General Convoy du Collonel duplessy de monsieur de la Balme du General Déroche fermoy & &.[2] Je vous prie de Grace de ne pas oublié un pauvre miserable quy absent de sa famille depuis plus d'un ans et il ne sessera de prier pour la Conservation de votre respectables personnes par votre tres humbles et trees obeissant serviteur DANIEL DUCHEMIN

premier lieutenant aux Etats unis de lamerique

Mon adresse est: To Mr. Duchemin at Mr. Leroy Green Grosser oposítte St. Geems church Jermyn Street London[3]

Addressed: A Monsieur / Monsieur Le Docteur franclin / agant des Etast unis de lamerique / a Paris

Notation: Daniel Duchemin de Londres 24 avril 1779.

From James Hutton: Two Letters

(I) and (II) ALS: American Philosophical Society

I.

Dear Sir April 14. 1779

I thank you very much indeed for that kind Paper of Protection & Safeguard & Recommendation for our Vessel, which

1. Duchemin was unaware that Thomas Morris had died in 1778: XXV, 568.

2. Augustin Mottin de La Balme (b. 1736), author of a work on horsemanship, sailed for the United States on Feb. 15, 1777, and became inspector of cavalry with the rank of colonel. He resigned in October of that year because the command of cavalry was given to Pulaski. Along with a small contingent of French Canadians, he was massacred by Indians at the Miami in 1780. Bodinier, *Dictionnaire.* Mathieu-Alexis de La Rochefermoy is identified in XXVI, 574n.

3. The writer apparently made his way out of England somewhat later, because in a letter of July 23, from Amiens, he alludes to a visit he paid BF in Passy and to BF's offer of hospitality on his way back. He is now with his family, his shoulder still in bad shape from a wound suffered in America,

you offerd me at once, and which was so kindly and handsomely drawn.[4] I have sent it to England to my Brethren, who know your Good Will, and who will be comforted by it, and will hope for the same thing, in kind, from Mr de Sartine. I sent him a Copy of it that He might know how to form one. Mr Bertin[5] has undertaken to help it forward. It is a matter else little in itself, but in the multitude of affairs unless some kind word be put in, in a happy moment, a Trifle as it may seem, is as hard to get at, as a thing of more Importance. I suppose if you see Mr de Sartine you will say that kind word for the thing, & the sooner it is done the much more kind it will be to me who want much to go on. I feel not at all well, the Noise of this Town, the close Air, the Diet, & many thoughts, the immense fatigue of visiting pressing friends, scatterd over this immense Town at all Ends, Lower my weak Spirits, which are forced beyond their Pitch, in one continued strain, so that if I stay much longer, I shall be seriously ill, I feel it. The Captain, Mate and two Sailors I am trying to get released that we may be able to sail in the proper Season, I am promised 4 French Prisoners in their stead when they are released, but I wished much to have the thing done quietly that the two Sailors may not be immediately pressd at their Arrival, but keep private till the Vessel goes. I want them to go as Passengers to Dover to avoid that, & that they may be preserved for us. You understand the Reasons of this, as you know the execrable Press. If it had been convenient & proper, I think your Protection, in case we could get no other from Mr de Sartine, by only adding, to the Address to your Captains & Commanders perhaps the words *dear Allies* this is only a Thought in Case of need.

---

and has decided to remain in France. He would appreciate reimbursement for the expenses he incurred as first lieutenant and for the two years' pay due him. His address is care of M. Boullet, Amiens. APS.

4. The passport for a Moravian vessel, April 11.

5. Henri-Léonard-Jean-Baptiste Bertin, the former Minister of State who was now manufacturing cannon for the Americans: XXVIII, 92n.

I am sorry that my Deafness hinders me from begging a Ticket for to day at the Academy of Sciences.[6]

I Love to be obliged by you. I shall let Dolly B. know how well & how kind you are. She is a good Creature.[7]

I am Dear Sir your most obliged & obedient humble Servant JAMES HUTTON

I desired Mr Henri Grand[8] to thank you on Sunday night. I see the Paper is bad, but it was my last Sheet.

Addressed: To / Doctor Franklin / Passy

Notation: Hutton 14 Ap. 79

II.

Dear old Friend April 14. 1779 late at night

I gave Mr Du Pont a Lr. for you today.[9] This Evening I recd one from a Brother in London who writes thus. April 9

"Upon the Reciept of your Lr. that afternoon of the 4th Instant, I went immediately to Mr Bell (commissioner for Sick, wounded & Prisoners)[1] & communicated to him what you wrote on the Subject of Capt Mugford & the other three Prisoners, he begged a Copy of that part of your Lr. which relates to this Business & then told me that they had recieved advice that Capt Mugfords Mate and two Sailors were set at Liberty & that thereupon they had set at Liberty a Captain & Mate that were Prisoners at Tenterden in Kent and two Sailors Prisoners at Deal, and that last Tuesday April. 6 or Wednesday April 7. Passports were dispatched to those French Prisoners. This was News of great Joy to me."

So that on our side the Exchange of our 4 Prisoners is done. It remains only that Capt Mugford, the Mate & our two Sail-

6. Where BF's paper on the aurora borealis was to be read; see Matthieu Tillet to BF, April 7.

7. Dorothea Blunt, who sent her letter of March 18, above, via Hutton.

8. Ferdinand's son: XXV, 196n.

9. Pierre-Samuel du Pont de Nemours, a political economist (XV, 118n), and old friend of Hutton (XXV, 413n).

1. John Bell: Elias and Finch, *Letters of Digges,* p. 50n.

ors be actually set at Liberty, which it seems was not yet the Case April 7. when I think Capt. Mugford's last Letter to me was dated which I sent to England for his wife, & our Brethrens Information. They are at Bourbourg, Dunkirk & Bergues under the Care of the Commissary of Marine at Dunkirk. I have wrote to Mr Bertin to desire him to get M de Sartine to send orders for their actual Release. The only thing I want now is such a kind Salvegarde from the French as you was so good as to give me. I wish you could get that Executed soon that I might be gone from hence. I was glad to let you know how things stand at present with regard to our Labradore affair; & to the matters I wrote to you about this morning, & am Dear Sir Yr most obliged HUTTON

Addressed: To / Doctor Franklin / Passy.

Notation: Hutton 14 Ap. 79

From César-François Cassini de Thury[2]

ALS: American Philosophical Society

a Lacademie des Sciences [on or after April 14, 1779][3]

Monsieur

M Le Roy vient de presenter a Lacademie un ouvrage qui minteresse dautant plus que je le regarde comme Le Votre, nÿ auroit til point de lindiscretion a Vous demander un exemplaire en attendant que jay L'honneur de Vous presenter un ouvräge qui est actuellement sous presse.

2. The eminent French astronomer, geodesist, and cartographer (1714–84) who was responsible for producing the first modern map of France: *DBF;* Charles Coulston Gillispie, ed., *Dictionary of Scientific Biography* (16 vols., New York, 1970–80). This was, as far as we know, his only letter to BF.

3. Le Roy delivered BF's paper on the aurora borealis to a public meeting of the Académie des sciences on April 14; it met with an enthusiastic reception. The editor of Bachaumont, *Mémoires secrets,* noted the singularity of seeing a minister of a new republic preoccupied by weighty concerns finding the leisure to "s'amuser à la physique." The paper was written in

Je suis avec respect Monsieur Votre très humble et très obeissant serviteur
CASSINI DE THURY
Dir. de lobservat, Royal

Addressed: A Monsieur / Monsieur francklin / de lacademie des sciences &c / *A Passy*

Notation: Cassini.

From James Hutton

ALS: American Philosophical Society

My dear old Friend April 15 1779

I took courage & went this morning to Versailles to Mr de Sartine who immediately did all I desired. I now therefore can go on my Journey with chearfulness, & thankfulness to you for your kindness to my people & to me. I am sure your giving me that Protection had the wished for Effect here. How many obligations have I & my People in America to you!

It is a hardship for my Heart that Circumstances have not allowed me to visit you. I am glad I saw you that Evening at Mr Grant's.[4]

I was proud of the general approbation I heard at different places given to your Paper read yesterday. You will remember Mr Spangenberg desired you should be consulted on the Aurora Borealis by Mr Crantz several years ago. I think 1769.[5]

I hope this Paper will be printed.

French "parfaitement bien," assisted, it is true, by BF's consultation with Le Roy on its style. *Mémoires secrets,* XIV, 23. A M. Raup de Batistin composed an impromptu quatrain:

> Son cœur dictant les loix du nouveau monde,
> Affranchit son pays qu'il eût pu gouverner:
> En nous communiquant sa science profonde,
> Du feu de son génie il vient nous enflammer.

François Métra, *Correspondance secrete, politique & littéraire . . .* (17 vols., London, 1787), VII, 395.

4. Ferdinand Grand: XXV, 413n.

5. Augustus Gottlieb Spangenberg had been the leader of the Moravian community at Bethlehem from 1735 until his return to Germany in 1762:

I go from Paris to Lyons April 22. In order to have a good place in the Diligence, I book it to day.

I shall always remember your Civilities & kindness to Dear Sir yr much obliged & obedient HUTTON

My Comps. to your kind Landlord & his Family & yours. I go into the Country on Saturday & Sunday next to the Valley of Montmorency.

Addressed: To / Dr Franklin / Passy.

Notation: Hutton 15. April 79

Bill for Benjamin Franklin Bache's Schooling[6]

AD: American Philosophical Society

a Passy Le quinze avril 1779.

Monsieur franklin doit pour la Pension de Mr. son petit fils Les deux quartiers et plusrs. jours de Pension ce qui

fait au total	270	
Six mois de Mtre. de Dessein	108	
6 mois de danse	72	
6 paires de Souliers	27	
Les Semaines	31	12
Lait pour les dejeuner	29	15
6 mois de Perruquier	12	
Les Etrennes des Sous Mtres et domestiques	24	
une Culotte de peau grise et façon	7	

VI, 362n. Among BF's papers at the APS is an undated manuscript entitled "Mr Crantz's Reflections on the Aurora Borealis"; it elaborates on David Crantz, *The History of Greenland* . . . (2 vols., London, 1767), I, 47–50. See also XX, 288n.

6. The final account from his former schoolmaster Le Coeur, where BFB had been since the spring of 1777: XXV, 91n; XXVI, 331–2. The child was now setting off to continue his education in Geneva; see his letter printed under April 20.

une Culotte de Soye noire du 14 fevrier 1779.........	16	20
deux paires de bas de cotton de	5	20
Total........	603 *l.t.*	7 *s.*

J'ai reçu de Monsieur franklin Le montant du présent Mémoire dont je quitte Mondit Sieur pour solde de compte[7]

LE COEUR

Endorsed by Franklin: Pd. by an Order on Grand / Schoolmaster Le Coeur's Receipt. Benny

From John Conner

ALS: American Philosophical Society

Hond: Sir, Dinan Castle 16th April 1779

Being on board of the Virginia Packett bound to Bordeaux in France I had the misfortune to be taken by the Fortune Sloop of War belonging to the English and when I got to England I had my Liberty given me because I was taken on board of an American Merchantman, but being totally at a Loss how to subsist having no money in my Pockett was under the necessity to enter on board of an English Privateer called the Gipsey from Bristol and about two months ago were taken by the French[8] and ever since I have been confined in this place—and am left without any Prospect of returning home to America where I left my Wife and three Children without your Honour will please to intercede for me to be sent hither—

Therefore I now take the Liberty to request the favour that you will procure my Releasement and a Permission to return to Norfolk in Virginia by any Ship going from this Country and you will thereby do a very great act of Charity to me and my Family and will deservedly have the Prayers of them and

7. The payment is recorded in BF's Cash Book (Account XVI; XXVI, 3).

8. The *Gypsey,* Capt. George Hunter, was taken by the French privateer *Amérique* in February, 1779, and sent into St. Malo: J. W. Damer Powell, *Bristol Privateers and Ships of War . . .* (Bristol, 1930), p. 263.

of him who craves leave to subscribe himself Hond Sir Your most obedt. and distressed humble Servt. JOHN CONNER

Addressed: To / His Excellency Doctor Franklyn / Ambassador from the American / Congress residing at / Paris

Notation: John Conner Dinan Castle April, 16, 79

From Dumas

ALS: American Philosophical Society

Monsieur, La Haie 16e. Avril *1779*.

Voici le Memoire, dont je vous ai parlé dans ma derniere du 13e.[9] Je n'ai rien à ajouter, sinon que nous somes ici présentement dans un calme profond, qui ne laisse pas d'être intéressant pour un Observateur attentif. Il n'y a pas plus à s'y fier, qu'à ceux qui regnent quelquefois sur le perfide élément.

Je suis avec bien du respect, Monsieur, Votre très-humble & très-obéissant serviteur D

Passy à Son Exc. Mr. Franklin.

Addressed: à Son Excellence / Monsieur Franklin, Esqr., Ministre Plénipe. / des Etats-Unis de l'Amérique / à *Passy*./.

Notation: Dumas April 18. 79

From J. Pierel[1]

ALS: American Philosophical Society

Monsieur Roscoff le 16 avril 1779.

Jai Lhonneur de vous informer de l'arrivée d'une Prise angloise le 9 du courant sur notre rade de L'isle de bas [Batz] nommée Le Jeune Dominique du port d'environ 30 Thonnaux chargée de Saumons Sallés en futailles faite au Cap de Clare par Le Corsaire particulier Le Prince Noir armé au Port de Celem province de Newhampshire en amerique Capitaine Le

9. The enclosed memoir, a French translation of Yorke's April 9 memorial, is at the National Archives; see our annotation of Dumas' letter of April 3[–13].

1. Or Pieret.

Sieur Nathaniel West.[2] Laquelle prise a été conduite ici par Le Sieur James Barnett[3] ôfficier sur Ledit Corsaire qui s'est adressé à moi & nous allons proceder incessament à la vente de cette Prise & de son chargemt.

Mr Lee qui ma fait Lhonneur de passer 1 jour chez moi est à même de vous rendre compte de la Situation avantageuse de notre Port & de la Commodité de Son entree pour toutes éspeces de Navires ainsi que pour le ménagement des frais. En conséquence je continuerois à rendre à tous les Capitaines americains qui pourroient y venir Tous les Services qui dépendront de moi.

Je Suis charmé que cette ôccasion me Procure l'avantage de vous assurer que je Suis avec un trés profond réspect Monsieur Votre trés humble et trés obeissant Serviteur J: PIEREL

A Monsieur Franklin Ministre Plenipotentiaire des états unis de l'amérique à Paris.

Notation: J. Pierel. Roscoff Le 16e avril 1779.

From the Marquis d'Amezaga[4]

AL: American Philosophical Society

Samedy 17. avril 1779

Mr. D'amezaga, fait ses plus tendres Compliment à Monsieur de franklin, et luy fait demander sil se trouvera demain chès

2. For the *Black Prince,* 18, see Allen, *Mass. Privateers,* p. 84, and the April 30 issue of the *Courier de l'Europe* (v [1779], 280). West achieved considerable post-war prominence in Salem as both captain and shipowner: James D. Phillips, *Salem and the Indies: the Story of the Great Commercial Era of the City* (Boston, 1947), *passim.*

3. Probably the James Barnett, Jr., who had written from southern France the preceding November: XXVIII, 69–70, 246, 322.

4. Born in 1710 to a Spanish family established in Nancy, Ignace d'Urtado, Marquis d'Amezaga, after a career in the military, became first gentleman at the court of Stanislas (the former King of Poland), Duke of Lorraine. In 1754 he married Marie-Anne de Vougny, widow of Jean-Jacques Amelot de Chaillou and mother of Antoine-Jean. *DBF,* II, 604, 614, 642. The stepson had invited BF for dinner on April 12th (see his letter of the 8th), but the present letter refers to the 19th. Several of Amezaga's letters to BF concern joint dinner parties with Amelot.

luy à l'heure du dinner. Mr. D'Amezaga Compte Toujours, que Monsieur de frankin fera Lhonneur Lundy, à Mr Amelot de venir dinner chés luy à Paris où Mr. D'amezaga se rendera.

Addressed: A Monsieur / Monsieur de franklin / a Pacy / a Pacy

From Barbeu-Dubourg ALS: American Philosophical Society

Monsieur et cher Ami Paris 17e. avril [1779]

Je vous recommande avec instance La lettre cy jointe qu'une tendre Mere desire faire passer surement a son digne fils à Philadelphie. Elle est des Amies de Madlc. Basseporte,[5] je crois que cela suffit pour vous faire juger de tout l'interet que j'y dois prendre, et qu'independamment de ma mince recommandation cela suffiroit pour vous y interesser vous meme. Melle. Basseporte a trouvé des jambes pour venir elle meme m'echauffer a ce sujet, s'il en eut eté besoin, recevez ses complimens et mon hommage DUBOURG

From John Bondfield ALS: American Philosophical Society

Sir Bordeaux 17 April 1779

My Motives for inclosing you the Anext detail of conections wherein I have and am embarked springs from the apprehendtion I am under of falling a Sacrefice with many others in the Crush of the times relying on timely returns engaged my extending my concerns further than the Capital we have in Europe will answer. I find myself in a Situation the most disagreable posible owing to the general discredit given by the failure of many Houses and perticularly them in Conection with the

5. BF had met Madeleine-Françoise Basseporte during his first visit to France in 1767; see XV, 115. A painter of birds and flowers who lived at the Jardin du Roi and had given lessons to the daughters of Louis XV, she was, at the time of writing, approaching her seventy-eighth birthday and had only one more year to live. *DBF.* The "Mère tendre" may be Mme. Marie-Charlotte Leullier L'Enfant. On April 15, 1778, Mlle. Basseporte had supported Mme. L'Enfant's request to have a letter forwarded to her son: XXVI, 144.

United States. I have supported without any Assistance all the Checks which the Miscarriage of our adventures have met with and should at this day be entirely disengaged had not the Outfits of our Three Ships at Brest. The Governor Livingston the Hunter and the Mary fearen exceeded the Sums we had allotted for that Service, these Vessels have involved me in a debt of near eighty Thousand Livres which the want of Funds on this Side makes me dread the too pressing instances of them to whom I stand indebted to the hurt of my Credit.[6]

I look up to you for a Credit if to be done without prejudice to your Ministry requesting from your Banker liberty to draw as my Occations may require to a certain extent in so doing you will render me most essential service.

You may and will undoubtedly consider under what pretentions I take the liberty to apply to you. I have no personal pretentions I can have none, but having embarked at the first Opening of the American Confederacy, having advanct as you know in Canada all our Capital at a Crisis for the Support of the American Army. I speak not for myself alone but for Price & Haywood who stand equally interested with me in all our European transactions, having brought with us ten Thousand pounds Sterling which we have and are employing in promoting the Trade of the New Alliances as our force admits haveing establisht ourselves respectably at this City and by our Operations drawn the attention of the French Merchants to Notice our Conduct, independant of the private gratings as a Stab to our Credit would [*torn: word or words missing*]ence would be a hurt to America should we be forced to defer our payments being the only House that have set down from America in this City under their own Support and in the space of twelve months given so active a Spur to the Union.

From these United Circumstances we may probably be thought worthy of your Protection as this application is not

6. The enclosure was a list of nineteen ships and the sums of his cash investment in them. The three ships he names had cost him 252,000 *l.t.;* the other sixteen totalled 164,800 *l.t.* APS. He and his business partners James Price (XXII, 360–1n) and William Haywood (XXVI, 278n) had chartered the ships to Arthur Lee to carry supplies to Virginia: XXVIII, 73n.

with a view to obtain other than a tempory Aid by a Credit until the reentry of sufficient Capital to go without we flatter ourselves to meet in you a protector who will take us by the hand until we are able to go alone which I hope may be before we have any occation to make use of the Credit for which I now apply this being an Act of precaution to stand me in need in case of want and in this I only understand should you engage Mr Grand to be only an Operation on banque not any real advances guarding always to timely remit as drafts become due.

This application will not I flatter myself influence you to my prejudice Trade and Gouverment bind each other and occationally aid to each others support, the distress's occation'd by the Capture of the West Indies Ships belonging to this Port has so checkt the Course of Credit that I cannot make any dependance where twelve Months past I should not have found the least difficulty and being as you may suppose strangers at our Arrival in France it cannot be expected to find that Current Credit which a long Series of application & known Abilities can only procure. I have personally no Cause to complain having met on many Occations striking instances of liberallity from the French Merchants and but for the Calamities the late loss's have created should not doubt their continuance. Circumstances alters Cases and it is our duty to provide against the Storm Committing this my application to your Mature Consideration I remain with due Respect Sir your very hhb Servant JOHN BONDFIELD

To His Excellency Benj Franklin

Addressed: To / His Excellency Benj Franklin / Plenipotentiary from the United States / of America / at / Paris

Notation: John Bonfield Bordeaux 17 avril 1779.

From John Emery[7]

ALS: American Philosophical Society

Sir Bilbao 17 Aprl. 1779

I yesterday recd. the Inclosed Letter from Capt. Sargent Ingersoll of the Saucy Jack, Cutter belonging to Mr. Nat Tracy of Newberry Port & myself—[8] by the Capt. Declaration his Vessell Was taken too Nigh the Shore to be a legal prize & Genl. Oriley[9] gives the Capt hopes of recovering her again, tho from the *Spirited* manner in which the court of Spain have made demands of this sort I confess I have no great hopes myself, yet would not Neglect aney Opportunity of saving my own & partners Intrest should it be convenient to your Honor to mention the affair to the count de Arranda.[1] Perhaps she may be recovred. I expect to Embark onboard Cap. St Barbe[2] for Newberry Port Next week & shall leave this affair in the hands of Messr. Gardoquis who will also write you on the Subject,[3] aney assistance you may think proper to afford them will be ever gratefully acknowledged by Sir Your Most Obt. Hl. Servt.

Jno Emery

7. A Newburyport merchant now residing in Bilbao, where he was associated with the merchant firm of Gardoqui & Sons: xxv, 499n. This is BF's last extant letter from him.

8. In the enclosed letter, dated April 6 (APS), Ingersoll explained that after being pursued by three vessels he anchored a quarter of a mile off the coast. He abandoned ship except for three men, who had orders, if the pursuers proved British, to cut the ship's cable, enabling it to drift ashore. When they failed to do so, they and the ship were captured. Nathaniel Tracy (1751–96) sent 24 privateers and 110 merchant ships to sea during the Revolution (*DAB*).

9. Gen. Alexander O'Reilly (xxvi, 467n).

1. Pedro Pablo Abarca de Bolea, conde de Aranda, the Spanish ambassador at the French court (xxii, 468n).

2. Wyatt St. Barbe was a Newburyport ship captain associated with Tracy: Charles H. Lincoln, comp., *Naval Records of the American Revolution 1775–1788* (Washington, D.C., 1906), p. 466.

3. On April 17, Joseph Gardoqui & Sons wrote BF, enclosing the present letter and asking his help for Emery. They promised to forward any intelligence they received from Ingersoll and reported they expected ships from America to arrive any day. APS.

The prize mentiond was the Fly Cap Penny beloning to Pool[4] which arrived safe & Sold.

Honble. Benjamin Franklin Esqr.

Notation: Emery Jn. April 17. 1779.

From Kéralio

ALS: University of Pennsylvania Library

Monsieur. a l'Ecole Rle. mre. 17e. avril, 1779.

M. L'abbé de la Roche m'a fait espérer que vous vouliés bien me faire L'honneur de venir diner chés moi jeudi 22e.[5] Si vous rendés justice aux Sentiments de vénération et d'attachement que je vous ai voués, vous Savés combien j'en suis flatté. Je vous recevrai comme vous desirés L'être, c'est-a-dire que vous aurés peu de monde. J'espere toutefois que M. votre petit fils sera de la partie et d'ailleurs tous ceux qu'il vous plaira.

Il est un convive que j'attends et que vous ne serés pas faché de voir, c'est Made la Comtesse de Forbach. Je saurai lundi au Soir, si nous aurons le bonheur de La posséder.

Je suis avec Respect Monsieur votre très humble et très obéissant Servr. LE CHR. DE KERALIO

Notation: Le Cher. de Keralio 17. Avril 1779.—

From William MacCreery

ALS: American Philosophical Society

Bordeaux 17th. April 1779

I received the Honor of your Excellencys letter of 18th. Ultimo: am sorry for your indisposition, & sincerely wish a speedy return, & long continuance of Good Health.

In regard to the Duties paid on the exportation of Salt from

4. *I.e.,* the port of Poole on the south coast of England. The prize was a brig bound for Ireland that Ingersoll had captured and sent to Emery.

5. Martin Lefebvre de la Roche was a friend and permanent guest of Mme. Helvétius: XXVII, 590n.

the Ports of France *in general,* & on Shipping it to the *French Colonies* from *this Port,* your Excellencys information was pretty right: but this being a conquored Province, Salt can not be exported to a forreign Market without paying a Duty of *40 l.t. 17.10* on the Pipe of Salt, which costs in Saint Martins only *12 l.t. 0.0.* There are other charges on it, which under the present regulations brings the Price to between four & five Times the first cost, which is, in fact, a meer prohibition. I have myself Ship'd Salt from Nantes, where the Duties are very triffling; & were they no heavier at this Port, I shoud be ashamed to complain.[6]

In place of loading Salt, which wou'd have been proffitable to the Commerce of this Country, as well as to our own, I have been obliged to take in an Hundred Tons of useless Sand, which neither benefits one nor the other, but on the contrary, is a dead loss to the owners of the Buckskin.

I expect the Buckskin will Sail about the 10th. of next Month, and as I purpose going home to Baltimore in her, shall freely take charge of any Letters or dispatches that your Excellency may chuse to send by her.[7]

I have the Honor to be, with the greatest Respect, Your Excellencys most obedient and most humble Servant

WILL MACCREERY

His Excellency B. Franklin Esqr. at Passy

Notation: Will. MacCreery. Bordeaux 17e. avril 1779.

6. In general, the regions of France longest a part of the monarchy paid the highest *gabelle,* or salt tax. Bordeaux and the surrounding province of Guienne and Gascony, conquered from England in the 15th century, paid a lower rate, while St. Martin's on the Ile de Ré paid virtually none. *Hammond's Historical Atlas* (Maplewood, N.J., 1960), p. 25, shows the rates in different parts of the country; for a detailed discussion of the *gabelle* see Larousse, as well as Marcel Marion, *Dictionnaire des Institutions de la France aux XVIIe et XVIIIe siècles* (Paris, 1923, reissued 1969), pp. 247–50.

7. In an April 28 letter to JA, MacCreery gave more details about his proposed return voyage: *Adams Papers,* VIII, 49–50. His plans seem to have miscarried, however; as late as May 28, 1781, he was still at Bordeaux, hoping to return to America in a few months (to WTF: APS).

To Sartine

Copy: Library of Congress

Sir Passy, April 18 1779

By Letters I am daily receiving, I find there are in various Prisons of France a number of American Sailors, who having been forced into the english Service and since taken, remain confined with those of that Nation; but are very desirous of serving their own Country, in any of our Ships of War; and to that end, request I would obtain their Discharge from their present Confinement. To prevent giving your Excellency the frequent Trouble of particular Applications & Orders upon every Occasion, I beg leave to submit it to your Consideration, whether it would not be well to give a general Order to those who have the Care of the Prisons, to examine in each of them those who pretend to be Americans & who desire to enter our Service; and that such as are found to answer that Description be sent immediately to l'Orient & shipt with Capt. Jones, or in the Alliance.

I am, with sincere Respect your Excellency's m. o. & m. h. S.

B Franklin

M. de Sartine.

From Dumas

ALS: American Philosophical Society; AL (draft): Algemeen Rijksarchief

Monsieur La Haie 19e. Avril 1779

Depuis deux mois environ, je suis extrêmement embarrassé de ma conduite ici à l'egard de Mr. l'Ambr. de F——. Accoutumé, ainsi que Mr. l'Abbé Des Noyers son prédécesseur,[8] à me voir leur communiquer sans réserve toute ma correspondance, mes démarches & mes opérations, il m'a paru piqué que je ne lui aie rien dit de ce qui s'est passé entre Mrs. St——r, De N——e, & moi, & que je ne lui montre plus de vos Lettres. Effectivement il n'a pas vu vos 4 dernieres du 11 & 19

8. La Vauguyon's predecessor, Desnoyers, is identified in XXII, 406n.

fevr., 12 & 18 Mars; & sur ce qu'il m'a témoigné ses desirs à cet egard, je lui ai dit respectueusement, que je ne pouvois les montrer à personne sans votre ordre exprès. Il est dans une grande colere contre Mr. St——r, & vouloit absolument que je lui disse où il étoit, ajoutant qu'il y alloit du service du Roi; que la parole que j'avois donnée de ne rien révéler de lui, ne devoit pas tenir contre la raison d'Etat; qu'il ne vouloit pas lui faire du mal, mais qu'il étoit nécessaire qu'il lui parlât; que Mr. St——r étoit un mauvais sujet, à qui il avoit défendu au nom du Roi de se mêler de telles affaires; que Mr. Le R—— de Ch——, & la personne de confiance d'un des Ministres, avoient grand tort de l'employer à cela, & qu'il s'en plaindroit & en écriroit à ce Ministre.[9]

Je l'ai appaisé du mieux que j'ai pu sans faire de bassesse, & sans manquer à mon devoir, c'est-à-dire, en gardant fidelement les secrets qui m'ont été confiés. Mais comme ma liaison & correspondance nécessaire avec Mr. De N——e, & peut-être aussi avec Mr Str., peut m'exposer tous les jours à d'autres difficultés pareilles auprès d'un Seigneur dont le caractere respectable m'en impose à juste titre, & que d'ailleurs j'honore aussi personnellement, j'ai grand besoin d'être rassuré & éclairé. Permettez donc, Monsieur, que je vous demande vos ordres, & les intentions des Ministres du Roi, pour régler ma conduite en conséquence, & que je vous supplie de me les faire parvenir le plutôt possible.

Je sais depuis hier, de bonne part, que l'Espagne s'est enfin déclarée. Cela fera un bon effet ici, & par- tout.[1]

Je suis avec touts les sentimens du respectueux attachement que vous me connoissez pour vous, Monsieur, Votre très-humble & très-obéissant serviteur D

Passy à Son Exc. Mr. Franklin

9. Chaumont's patron was Sartine. Stürler had undertaken a mission in the Netherlands for which Chaumont and Sartine's secretary Baudouin (xxv, 348n) had provided him letters: xxviii, 353–4n.

1. On April 12 Spain and France had signed the Convention of Aranjuez, by which Spain agreed to enter the war. Dumas could have known this only from rumor; not only was the agreement secret but news from Spain

Addressed: à Son Excellence / Monsieur Franklin, Esqr. / Ministre Plenipe. des Etats- / unis de l'Amérique / à Passy./.

Notation: Dumas 19 April 79

From Landais

ALS: American Philosophical Society; copy: University of Virginia Library

Please Your Excellency Sir Nantes april 19th 1779

I left the Harbour of Brest the 11th in Compagny of the French frigate called the Egrette[2] bound to this River but the wind being Contrary we could Sail no farther than the conquet[3] where we staied till the 15th, that the wind came SE, then we get under Sail but I Soon found out we could out Sail all the french frigate or Sloops of war and lasting Sight of them in the night time I made the best of my way towards this River where I came to an anchor the 18th having 93 English prisonners aboard according to Mr Shweighauser order, we are to deliver them to the English Cartel Ship and peeck up what number of Americans we can get out of the number that came in the Said Cartel Ship for to recrut the Ship as well as we can for to get to America when I Shall have Mr shweighauser order to that purpose.

I am with the Greateast Respect Your Excellency Most Obeidient Most humble Servant P: LANDAIS

His Excellency Bn Franklin Minister Plenipotentary of the united States of America

Addressed: To / His Excellency Bn Francklin Minister / Plenipotentary of the united States of America / at Passy Nigh Paris—

required weeks to reach the Netherlands. The convention is printed in Doniol, *Histoire,* III, 803–10; its impact is discussed below in BF's letter to the committee for foreign affairs, May 26.

2. The *Aigrette,* 26; see Dull, *French Navy,* p. 356.

3. Le Conquet, on the coast west of Brest.

Notations in different hands: Landais Apr 19. 1779 / P. Landais Nantes avril 19. 1779.

From John Steward *et al.*

ALS:[4] American Philosophical Society

Honoured Sir St. Mallows Prison Aprill the 19th 1779

We Make Bold to trouble you with these few Lines to Let your Honour know our Situation at present in hopes that your Honour will Be so good as to Relive from our Confinement and Grant us permission to go on Board of Some american Ship Sir we saild out of Nantucket October the 10 Day 1777 Bound to the Brozells a whaling and had the Misfurtune to Be taken By an English ship and Caried to porthmouth and Lay about Six weeks in porthmouth then they Sent us Down word from London that if we would Consent to go a whaling out of England that they would Relive us and the most of us having No friends Nor aquaintances In England we Consented to go And as we was outward Bound we was taken By a french privateteer and Brought to Haverdegrass where we Remain'd four Months then a Capt. of a privateer hearing that we was Americans Came and asked us to go along with him for one Cruse which was to Be But two Months And we told him that we would If that He would Grant us Liberty to go on Borad of a merican vessell after the two Months was Expired So he Caried us to the Comesary of that place and Both the Comesary and the Capt. Declared that we Should have our Liberty to go As Soon as the two Months was up or Before If so be that we met with any united vessell So Pleas your Honour Sir upon these proposals we went on Board and Served our two Months out and at the End of the sd. two months we Came into St. Mallows and hearing of an american Frigate at Brest and another at Lorian we Demanded our Liberty to go on Board of those Ships But the Comesary of this place and the Capt. told us that we should not go on Board of any american Ship an If we would not go in the sd. privateer that we should

4. Steward signed for all the petitioners.

go to prison and sir we Concluded to go to prison In order to Send these Lines to your Honour In Hopes that you try to grant us permision to go on Board of these sd. ships there Is Capt Jones that we hear Is very short of people Like wise the Relience Frigate at Breast and sir we would Not want Greater pleasure at present than to get on Board of one of these ships and If your Honour will Be so good as to hear to these few Lines that we have pen'd and grant us an Answer If not too Much trouble And In so Doing you will most kindly oblide Your Most Humble Servants that would willingly Serve [for our?] Country; Sir your Most affectionate Subject [*torn: word missing*]

John Steward of Capcod
Willim. Barnett of Nantuckett
Robert Wright of Nantuckett
Richard Noldforth of Boston
your Humble servants

Addressed: for / The / Honourable Dr. Frankling / Ambasandor for the 13 united / States of America at / Paris in France

Notation: Petition of several men St. Mallow's Prison April. 19. 79

To Horneca, Fizeaux & Cie.

L (draft):[5] University of Pennsylvania Library

[April 20, 1779]

Where as it is represented to me, and appears by authentic Documents, that[6] the articles of Merchandise mentioned in the annexed Invoice[7] were delivered by Mr—Jona. Williams Junr. at Nantes to Mr. J. D. Schweighauser supposing them to belong to the Public of the United States, and whereas the said

5. In JW's hand. JW sent this draft to BF on March 27, with a partial dateline to be filled in. BF made one addition to the text, noted below; the actual date and BF's initials were added by another hand.

6. BF interlined everything following "Where as", up until this point.

7. The merchandise belonged to Simeon Deane: XXVIII, 221, 580. BF's copy of the two-page invoice, in Gellée's hand, is at the University of Pa. Library.

goods (except case No. 3) have been Since exported to America or otherways employed for the Public Use by the said J. D. Schweighauser, I do hereby request Messrs. Horneca fizeaux & Co. merchants at Amsterdam to replace the said Invoice of goods in quantity & quality (except Case No. 3. Since redeliverd to the sd. Williams the amount of which is deducted from the Invoice annexed) and to transport the Same to Nantes at the risque and Expence of the United States and I engage to reimburse the said Horneca fizeaux & Co. the amount of the said goods with Insurance Freight & all Expences on producing me the proper Invoices, Bills of Lading & accot. of Charges on their arrival & delivery at Nantes.— BF.

Done at Passy this 20 April—1779

Notation by William Temple Franklin: Order upon Messrs Horneca Fizeau & Co. to replace certain Goods sent to America on Acct of Congress, by mistake. according to Invoice. sent to Mr Williams April 20. 1779.

To Jonathan Williams, Jr.

Copy: Library of Congress

Dear Nephew Passy April 20 1779

Inclosed is the Invoice you sent me & the Order you desired. I have kept Copies.[8]

I wish it was in my Power to relieve all the Wants and even to gratify the Wishes of Prisoners, who have suffered in the Cause of their Country. But there are Limits to every thing, and the frequent Intercepting of our Supplies from the Congress by the british Cruizers, has very much narrow'd the Limits in this Case. As to those remaining in Prison, who write for ten guineas a Piece to be sent them, to enable them to escape; the Request, if it were reasonable is not Practicable: the Number would make the sum enormous; and the Proposition is Less necessary now, as the Exchange is begun, and is by Agreement to continue.

One of the Petitions you sent to me, which seems to be from some of the Private men, desires Leave to draw on me for Wages: But it is very improper for me to meddle with the

8. See the preceding letter.

Affair of Wages, as I have neither Authority nor the Means of competent Information: It is impossible for me to know here who were in the Continental Service, or on what Terms, or who were Officers & who Privates; and I have already experienced a good Deal of Imposition among those who have called at Paris in their Way from the Prisons in England to the Sea-Ports of France. The other from the Officers, desires a subsistance till Provision can be made for them to go home, which is reasonable if they are disposed to take the first Opportunity; and as the Alliance is probably at Nantz before this can reach you, I hope they are received on Board her, on the Terms you mention, of having their Passage free, and acting in the Service on Occasion; I make no Doubt, from the Character of Capt. Landais that he will treat them with all due Civility. With Regard to the quantum of their Subsistance as well as that of the common Sailors, while they wait at Nantes, if the ship should not be arrived, I write by this Post to Mr. Adams, whom I have confided in with Regard to other Matters of the same kind, requesting that he would do in it what shall appear to him to be reasonable; and as they will probably go in the Ship with him, there is no Doubt of his being willing to oblige them as far as present Circumstances which he well knows, will admit. I desire You therefore to talk with Mr Adams on the Subject, by his undertaking to give the necessary Directions; you will be free of the Application, & the Gentlemen will, I hope, be satisfied.

I must for a few days, defer answering your Letters of the 8th inst. relating to your Accounts. I am your Affectionate Uncle.

J. Williams

To Woestyn frères[9]

Copy: Library of Congress

Gentlemen

Passy April 20 1779

I am very sensible of the Honor you propose to do me in the naming of your Vessel; to which I have but this Objection,

9. In answer to their requests of March 20 and April 16; see above, under March 20.

that I cannot merit it by taking a Part in the Enterprize. I have communicated your Scheme to some of my Friends; But they are already engaged in such Undertakings as far as they chuse to be. I shall however try some others, and I most heartily wish you all the Success imaginable.

I have the Honor to be &c

Messrs. Voestyn (Dunkirk)

From Benjamin Franklin Bache[1]

ALS: Benjamin F. Bailar, Houston, Texas (1990)

Mon cher bon papa [on or after April 20, 1779]

Je prens la liberté de vous écrire pour vous informer de ma santé aussi bien que de mon voyage ou nous avons essuyé quelques malheurs nous arrivames à Genéve lundi et j'ai été en pension le jour suivant ou je ferai mon possible pour bien travailler et pour vous satisfaire j'espère que je receverai la réponse le plutôt qu'il vous sera possible je suis bien faché de ne pas pouvoir vous ecrire davantage, car si je le pouvois, je le ferois. Je me porte assez bien j'espère que vous vous portez de même Mr Cramer vous fait ses compliments. [2]

Votre tres humble et tres obeissant fils

B. Franklin Bache

1. This is BFB's first letter back to his grandfather after the boy's arrival in Geneva. It is written on the verso of one from Gabriel-Louis Galissard de Marignac dated April 20, below. BF's letter of April 21 to John Quincy Adams, below, explains his reasons for sending the nine-year-old Benny to study abroad. The Cash Book (Account XVI; XXVI, 3) indicates that he gave BFB a going-away present of 12 *l.t.*

2. Philibert Cramer of Geneva, a diplomat and brother of the publisher of Voltaire, accompanied the child on his way. BFB was enrolled at the Academy, founded by Calvin in 1559, his studies to be supervised by Marignac, a regent at the school. Cramer died the following August, and BFB stayed with his widow and their son Gabriel, his schoolmate and life-long friend. See Lopez and Herbert, *The Private Franklin,* pp. 221–2, 227–8, 230; Lucien Cramer, *Une famille genevoise: les Cramer . . .* (Geneva, 1952), *passim.* See also the bill for BFB's schooling, printed under April 20, below.

From Becker & Saltzmann

ALS: American Philosophical Society

Monsieur! Berlin cè 20me. d'Avrile 1779.

Pandant la Guerre en Allemagne, qui heuresement vient d'estre finie,[3] nous avons fait Speculation pour livrer des Uniformes a une partie de l'Armée de notre Souverain, de laquelle nous restent environ quatre mille Uniformes, ne pouvant plus les emploÿer, l'Idé nous est venue, d'envoÿer une Uniforme Complette a Votre Exellençe pour Vous offrir le tout ensemble pour l'Armée en Amerique, en esperant d'autant plus de reuissir, que nous avons deja expedier d'icÿ, il ÿ a deuxs Ans deux mille pieçes de Draps en diverses Coulleurs, principalement en brun et bleu.[4]

Sur la Notte cÿ incluse Votre Exellençe trouvera le dernier prix de jaque Article livré icÿ dans un Vaisseaux pour estre transporté a Hambourg.[5] Nous souhaitons ardemment que Votre Excellençe voudra daigner de faire quelque Reflection la dessus, et nous donner des Ordres en Consequençe, et en meme temp de nous pardonner notre hardiesse, de nous Addresser directement a Votre Excellence.

Nous sommes avec la plus parfaite Veneration de Votre Excellence. Les tres hles. et tres obeissts. Serviteurs

Becker & Saltzmann
Marchands.

Notation: Becker Baltzman 20 avril 1779.—[6]

3. The war between Austria and Prussia; the peace agreement at Teschen was not actually signed, however, until May 13.

4. The Prussian army like the American was predominantly clad in blue uniforms: Christopher Duffy, *The Military Experience in the Age of Reason* (New York and London, 1987), p. 309. A packet containing a complete uniform was forwarded from Strasbourg by the merchant firm of Franck frères (for which see *Almanach des Marchands,* p. 460.) On May 11 they informed BF the packet had been placed on a diligence (public stagecoach) and asked him to reimburse the driver £12 (12 *l.t.?*). APS.

5. The two enclosed lists included prices for cloth, uniforms, shoes, boots, and fusils.

6. On July 3 and July 23 they reiterated their offer and asked BF if he had received the packet (APS). The former letter gives more details about the

From David Hartley

ALS: American Philosophical Society; transcript: Library of Congress

My Dear Sir London April 20 1779

I hope you have heard of your prisoners (viz the first cargo) before this time.[7] I am impatient to receive your answer to some of my late letters to you. You know the Object wch constantly possesses my mind. I wish to bring some material points to issue, upon terms of *certainty* and *Confidence.* Parliament will probably sit for some time yet, and while parliament continues sitting I consider the measures of the year as not yet out of our reach.[8] I shall probably have occasion to write to you again soon. I like to be sure of the ground that I stand upon before any measure of consequence is taken but not to lose opportunities. Opportunity shd be seized by the forelock. You will hear from me again soon—Your affecte DH.

Addressed: To Dr Franklin

Notation: D.H. April 20. 1779.

From Gabriel-Louis Galissard de Marignac[9]

ALS: Benjamin F. Bailar, Houston, Texas (1990)

Monsieur Genève ce 20e. avril 1779

Monsieur Cramer m'avoit écrit de préparer une place dans ma pension à Monsieur vôtre petit fils, je l'ai fait avec plaisir à

packet. It was initially shipped via the widow Ohlenschlager at Frankfurt and contained a coat, some pants and shirts, and a campaign hat. There are two slightly different versions of the July 23 letter; one enclosed a copy of one of the price lists, while the other included copies of the firm's April 20 and July 3 letters. BF eventually received the packet and, although he did not place an order, advised the firm to deal directly with the American states; see his letters of Aug. 1 and Sept. 10 (Library of Congress).

7. For the arrival of the cartel see JW's letter of April 1.

8. Parliament sat until July 3, when it was prorogued until Aug. 5; it was then further suspended until Nov. 25: Cobbett, *Parliamentary History,* XX (1778–80), 1018–20.

9. See BFB's letter of the same date, above.

Philibert Cramer

sa recommandation & a cause de vous; ils arrivèrent hier dix neuf avril en parfaite santé; Je sens bien, Monsieur, que cest à ses bontés que je dois l'honneur de vôtre confiance; mais il est de mon devoir de vous assurer moi même de tous les efforts, que je ferai pour la mériter: les papiers publics m'avoient appris à vous estimer; les sentimens de respect, de tendresse & de reconnoissance, que je tacherai d'entretenir dans Monsieur Franklin pour vous, soutenus par les preuves journaliéres, que je pourrai lui donner de vôtre mérite, ajouteront encore, si cela se peut, à ma façon de penser à vôtre égard: Daignés, Monsieur, m'honorer d'une reponse, Veuillès me donner vos directions sur l'èducation de nôtre jeune homme, & mon empressement à les suivre vous prouvera ma consideration & le profond respect avec lequel j'ai l'honneur d'être Monsieur Votre très humble & très obéissant Serviteur

G L De Marignac

Addressed: A Monsieur / Monsieur Franklin Ministre / Plénipotentiaire des provinces unies / d'Amérique auprès de sa majesté très / chrétienne, adressé à Monsieur Grand / Banquier ruë Monmartre / A Paris

From Sartine

LS: Massachusetts Historical Society; copy:[1] National Archives

Versailles Le 20 Avril 1779.

La Difficulté, Monsieur, de recevoir des Nouvelles de l'Amérique Septemtrionale, et de donner de celles d'Europe au Congrès me fait desirer que vous suspendiez le départ pour l'Amerique Septemtrionale, de la frégate des Etats-unis, l'Alliance; parceque le Roi a ordonné qu'il fût préparé une de ses frégates pour porter en Amérique le nouveau Ministre Plénipotentiaire que sa Majesté y envoye pour remplacer M. Gerard, dont la santé a été très dérangée l'année derniere;[2] et

1. In WTF's hand. BF enclosed this copy and a translation (also at the National Archives) with his of June 2, below, to the marine committee.

2. The new minister was Anne-César, chevalier de La Luzerne (1741–91), whose mission is detailed in William Emmett O'Donnell, *The Chevalier*

afin de remplir une partie des vues que vous pouviez avoir en expédiant l'Alliance pour le Continent des Etats-unis, Le Roi accordera avec plaisir à M. Adams son Passage pour Lui et Sa Suite sur la dite frégate.[3] Sa Majesté desire que cette Proposition puisse convenir avec les arrangemens du Congrès; et dans ce cas, Je vous serai très obligé de vouloir bien donner vos ordres en consequence au Capitaine de la frégate l'Alliance, afin qu'il se rende tout de Suite à l'Orient, où il attendra les ordres ultérieurs que vous lui adresserez.

J'ai l'honneur d'être avec une très parfaite consideration, Monsieur, Votre très humble et très obeissant serviteur

DE SARTINE

M Franklin Ministre Plenipotentiaire des Etats-Unis.—

Notation in Adams' hand: M. De Sartine.

Notation: April 20. 1779.

---

de La Luzerne, French Minister to the United States, 1779–1784 (Louvain, 1938). For the decline of Gérard's health and contrasting views of his accomplishments see Meng, *Despatches of Gérard,* p. 118, and William C. Stinchcombe, *The American Revolution and the French Alliance* (Syracuse, 1969), pp. 42–3.

3. An invitation which had serious consequences for JA's relationship with BF, who enclosed this letter with his to JA of April 24, below. Through Lafayette, BF had asked Sartine for a letter that might serve as an excuse for having to cancel JA's return passage to America on the *Alliance;* see our annotation of BF's March 22 letter to Lafayette and also Idzerda, *Lafayette Papers,* II, 255. This attempt to mollify JA backfired, however, largely because Sartine did not explain that the *Alliance* was being retained in order to sail with Jones's squadron. JA eventually came to the conclusion that BF had arranged the switch to the more lightly armed French frigate *Sensible* in hopes that he would be captured and hence unable to reveal to Congress "some dangerous Truths": James H. Hutson, *John Adams and the Diplomacy of the American Revolution* (Lexington, Ky., 1980), pp. 49–50. See also our annotation of JA's May 14 letter. The *Sensible* sailed for America on June 17.

From Jonathan Williams, Jr.

als: American Philosophical Society; copy: Yale University Library

Dear & hond. Sir.— Nantes April 20. 1779.

The two Boxes for Mr Watson came to hand a few days since and I shall embrace the first opportunity to Ship them.[4] I would do it by the Alliance if I could, but Capt Landais does not think himself justifiable in taking any Goods, Types however (being of public Utility,) may perhaps be an exception.—[5]

I am Dear & hond Sir Most dutifully & respectfully yours— Jona Williams J

The Hon. Doctor Franklin

Notation: Jona Williams Nantes 20 avril 1779.

Bill for Benjamin Franklin Bache's Schooling

ds: American Philosophical Society

[April 20–September 5, 1779]

Doit Monsieur Franklin à Gabriel Marignac pour la Pension de son Petit fils depuis le 20e. Avril jusqu'au 5. 7bre . . . £192.19

4. These were the two boxes of *petit romain* type which bf had ordered from Fournier *le jeune* in September, 1778, and which were ready in February, 1779: xxviii, 505. Watson had entrusted his request for type, along with an advance payment of 1,364 *l.t.* 13 *s.,* to Capt. Robert Niles, who deposited the sum with bf's banker Ferdinand Grand in August, 1778: xxvi, 547n; xxvii, 227–8; Cash Book (Account XVI, xxvi, 3), entry of March 29, 1779. Fournier's bill for these two boxes amounted to only about one third of Watson's account. With the remaining 840 *l.t.,* bf intended to supply Watson with a font of brevier (Cash Book, *ibid.*). This was to be cast at his own foundry in Passy, which was in its infancy; the first recorded payments for salaries and supplies were on April 3 (Cash Book). Watson's font of brevier was completed in 1780, packed in three cases, and placed on the *Alliance* along with these two cases of Fournier's type. Watson died before the *Alliance* sailed for America, and bf directed that the type be delivered to Gov. Trumbull: bf to the commander of the *Alliance,* July 11, 1780 (Library of Congress).

5. bf agreed that type was an item for the public good and, in a letter now missing, gave orders that it be shipped on the *Alliance.* jw conveyed this information to both Watson and Niles in letters of, respectively, April 30 and May 8 (Yale University Library).

Papier, Encre & Plumes	2.5
Ecritoires	.12
Catéchisme	.10
1 Service d'argent pour l'entrée acheté suivant l'ordre de Monsieur Cramer[6]	19.10
8 Paires Bas	13.10
12 Bonnets de nuit	4
Thêmes Mercier	1.10
Blanchissage	3
Epitomé	3.13.6
Apparat	3
Port de lettre double	19.6
Selectae	1.6
Phédre & Distiques	19.6
2 mois de dessein, et fournitures	7.15
Grammaire Grecque	1.10
Histoire Poëtique	.15
donné à Mr. Pinon pour Etoffe d'habit	7.16
Entrée en 5ème	1.10
Cahiers	.6
Grammaire de Perésche	.18
Raccomodage de Bas	1
Payé à Mr. frederich pour toile de Chemises	50.16.6
fournitures et façon des Chemises	7.5
Raccomodage et blanchissage de bas de soye	.10
Ruban de queuë	.6
Blanchissage	2.5
Prix des bonnes nottes	10
Raccommodage de bas	.7
Couteau	.6
Pour raccomoder l'Atlas	.6

6. In an account in WTF's hand dated Dec. 27, 1776–Sept. 6, 1780, and headed "Sums paid by B. Franklin for B.F. Bache," BF noted that he had advanced Cramer 480 *l.t.,* presumably to give to the school. An undated April entry in the same account records a payment by Grand of 644 *l.t.* 2 *s.* for BFB's schooling at Geneva. APS. See also the letter from Gabriel-Louis Galissard de Marignac, above.

Cayers	.10
1 paire Boucles de Côté	. 7.6
Un mois de dessein	3.17.6
Payé au Cordonnier	15.9
A Mr. Pinon pour 1 au [avne]⅓ Serge pour Culottes	4.13.4
Pour ses Dimanches du 20e. Juillet au 5e. 7bre	2
argent Court.	£357.16.1

Ces £357.16.1 Court. font argent de france à 14.*l.t.* 10*s*.6.24 £591. 4.3

PR. ACQUIT MARIGNAC

Endorsed: M. Marignac for Ben's Schooling

From Le Roy

AL: University of Pennsylvania Library

[after April 20, 1779][7]

M. Le Roy prie son illustre ami Monsieur Franklin de vouloir bien s'intéresser auprès de M. De Sartinc pour qu'il accorde à M. Wibert,[8] Lieutenant-Colonel au Service des Etats unis, son passage sur le vaisseau qui portera M. Le Chr. De La Luzerne en amèrique. Monsieur Franklin se rappellera sans doute que M. Adams pendant son sejour ici a donné en plusieurs Occasions les tèmoignages les plus avantageux à M. Wibert[9] et que cet officier ayant eté pris les armes à la main dans le fort Wash-

7. The date on which Sartine informed BF that La Luzerne would sail for America; see the naval minister's letter of that date.

8. The engineer Antoine-Félix Wuybert is identified in XXVIII, 428n. On April 20 BF had loaned him money to return to his regiment and endorsed the receipt, "Wuyberts Notes for 15 Louis." APS. BF, in a letter now missing, instructed Landais to give the engineer passage; see Landais' letter of May 8. As it turned out, La Luzerne and JA sailed on June 17 on the *Sensible;* Wuybert changed plans and joined John Paul Jones on the *Bonhomme Richard* as lt. col. of marines. Morison, *Jones,* p. 204.

9. In fact, JA's recorded opinion of Wuybert, set down while they were both in Nantes on May 7th or 8th, was not particularly favorable: "W. is silent; has something little in his Face and Air: and makes no great Discov-

ington a eté depuis ce tems là Jusqu'au commencement de cette annèe prisonnier des Anglois qui l'ont traité avec toute la dureté possible comme ètant francois et pris au service des Amèricains. Enfin Monsieur Franklin se rappellera que c'est lui même qui a conseillé à M. Wibert de repasser en amèrique pour se faire payer de ses appointemens dont il n'a pas touché un sol depuis plus de trois ans ou depuis le tems qu'il a eté pris par les Anglois &c.

Notation: Le Roy.

To John Adams

LS:[1] Massachusetts Historical Society; copy: Library of Congress

Sir, Passy April 21. 1779

I have received your two Favours of the 13th. Inst. I am much obliged to you for undertaking the Trouble of contenting the Officers and People of the Alliance. I must now beg leave to make a little Addition to that Trouble, by requesting your Attention to the Situation of the Officers and Sailors, late Prisoners in England, which Mr. Williams will acquaint you with; and that you would likewise Order for them such Necessarys and Comforts as we can Afford. I wish we were able to do all they want and desire, but the Scantiness of our Funds & the Multitude of Demands prevent it.

The English Papers talk much of their Apprehensions about Spain: I hope they have some Foundation.[2]

With great Esteem, I have the honour to be Sir Your most obedient & most humble Servant B FRANKLIN

Honble John Adams Esqre

ery of Skill or Science" (Butterfield, *John Adams Diary,* II, 364). By May 22, however, after the Frenchman had complimented him on his French, JA changed his mind and conceded that the engineer "has a good deal in him of Knowledge" (*ibid.*, 377–8).

1. In WTF's hand.

2. On April 1, the *General Advertiser, and Morning Intelligencer* reported war with Spain inevitable; two days later the *Public Advertiser* carried a similar

To John Quincy Adams[3]

Copy: Library of Congress

Dear Master Johnny Passy, April 21 1779

I am glad you have seen Brest and the fleet there. It must give you an Idea of the Naval force of this Kingdom, which you will long retain with Pleasure.

I caused the Letters you inclosed to me to be carefully delivered, but have not received Answers to be sent you.

Benjamin whom you so kindly remember would have been glad to hear of your Welfare; but he is gone to Geneva. As he is destined to live in a Protestant Country, & a Republic, I thought it best, to finish his Education, where the proper Principles prevail.[4]

I heartily wish you a good Voyage & happy sight of your Mama; being really your Affectionate friend BF.

young M. Adams

From Alexander Gillon

ALS: American Philosophical Society

Sir Hotel d'Orleans rue St. Anne 21st. April 1779

As I propose setting off to morrow morning, I shall esteem it a particular favour if your Excellency will be pleas'd to send me per. the Bearer, the Pass I requested of you (when I had the pleasure of seeing you last) for Capt. Joyner[5] & Self, with Servants & Baggage to Holland thro Flanders, & as we propose returning by the Sea Coast, so as to Visit Havre de Grace & perhaps St Maloes, will thank you for extending it to there, & to return here if you think it necessary.— America in Gen-

---

item. Other issues of the two papers discussed Spanish military preparations (*e.g.,* the former on March 30, and the latter on April 7).

3. In answer to his letter of April 12.

4. BF reiterated to other correspondents his intention to make BFB a Presbyterian and a republican. See his letters of April 22 to Jane Mecom and June 3 to Sally Bache, below, and to Samuel Cooper, Dec. 9, 1780 (APS).

5. John Joyner, one of the prospective captains for the vessels, who accompanied Gillon to Europe: XXVIII, 168n. Their visit to the Netherlands apparently was in search of alternate funding for the loan Gillon was seeking; see our annotation of his letter of May 25.

eral, as well as So. Carolina will be much indebted to your Excellency, if you'll be pleas'd to Second my application to His Excellency Mr. de Sartine, for either Selling me the three Frigates wanted, lending me the Money on that States Security to Build them, or if that does not Suit, then for this Government to Join in the Security for the Sum Wanted to those that will lend it me,[6] this latter request can so readily be complied with, that I dare hardly entertain the most distant Idea of its being refus'd. To your personal intercession then do I confide & am with much truth

Your Excellencys Most Obedt hble Servt— A. GILLON

To His Exclly Benja. Franklin Esqre.

Notation: A. Gillon 21. Ap. 79.

To Alexander Gillon

Copy: Library of Congress

Sir Passy April 21st. 1779

Inclosed is the Passport you desire,[7] with which I heartily wish you a good Journey and all the success you hope for. You may depend on my doing what I can for you, but do not depend on my succeeding. I have understood since I saw you, that these Applications of particular States are not agreeable. It is said, that if they are comply'd with, they will encrease, and there is no knowing where they will end: And that all Aids should regularly be apply'd for by the Congress, who can best judge what are necessary and in what proportions, and who alone, by our Constitution, can stipulate with this Court concerning the Terms.[8]

I have the Honor to be with great Esteem &c

Honble. Commodore Gillon

6. A request apparently first made by Gillon a month earlier; see BF's letter to Sartine of March 20 and the reply of March 22. On May 4 Sartine wrote BF rejecting Gillon's proposals.

7. See the preceding letter.

8. BF's interpretation of the as-yet-unratified Articles of Confederation was radical for the time; Article Six merely specified that "No State, without the consent of the United States, in Congress assembled, shall send any

To Schweighauser

Copy: Library of Congress

Sir Passy, April 21 1779

I duly received yours of the 8th inst.[9] I approve of the Assistance you have afforded the American Prisoners. You will consult with M. Adams and take his Directions for what may be farther necessary.[1] I have accepted your late Bills for Livs, and am with great esteem &c—

M Schweighauser

From the Abbé François Rozier[2]

ALS: American Philosophical Society

monsieur Paris 21 avril 1779.

Permettés moi de vous prier de me communiquer votre memoire sur L'aurore Boréale, Pour L'imprimer dans Le journal de physique. J'ose vous faire cette demande au nom de Tous Les physiciens. Vous savés combien tout ce qui sort de votre Plume est interressant Pour eux. Le mercure de France en donnera un extrait, mais un extrait n'est Bon que pour ceux qui ne s'occupent pas Bien sérieusement. Le journal de physique au contraire qui ne parle ni de comedie, ni des Bouquets

---

embassy to, or receive any embassy from, or enter into any conference, agreement, alliance, or treaty with any king, prince or state . . .": *JCC,* IX, 911.

9. Missing.

1. The prisoners had recently arrived on the cartel ship *Milford,* and on April 22 JA oversaw at St. Nazaire (downriver from Nantes) the transfer to that ship of the British prisoners brought from Brest by the *Alliance: Adams Papers,* VIII, 39n.

2. The celebrated agronomist and author (1734–93) who in 1771 created the first specialized scientific periodical, *Observations sur la physique, sur l'histoire naturelle et sur les arts . . . ,* later known as the *Journal de Physique.* A member of the Académie des sciences, Rozier also compiled a four-volume *Tables des matières* of the Academy's papers which appeared in 1775–76. For the abbé see *Nouvelle biographie* and Quérard, *France littéraire;* for the *Jour. de Physique* see Douglas McKie, "The '*Observations*' of the Abbé François Rozier," *Annals of Science,* XIII (June, 1957), 73–89.

à cloris et est fait pour Les Travailleurs et en Travailleurs vous demandent Leur instruction.

Je suis avec Respect Monsieur Votre tres humble et très obeissant serviteur L'ABBÉ ROZIER

M. franclin

Notation: L'abbe Rozier Paris 21e aout 1779

From Sartine

Copy: Library of Congress

à Versailles le 21. Avril 1779.

J'ai l'honneur de vous informer, que Mr. Deshayes Commissaire des Classes à Cherbourg represente qu'il arrive journellement d'Angleterre des Sujets des Etats Unis qui se trouvent sans ressources et qu'il seroit a désirer que vous voulussiez bien nommer un Agent dans ce Port pour pourvoir dans ces Occasions à leurs Besoins.[3] Ce Commissaire s'est jusqu'a present chargé de cet objet de depense, dont il tient un Compte Séparé. Je vous prie, Monsieur, de me faire connoitre vos intentions à cet Egard et si vous jugez à propos que M. Deshayes continue de prendre les soins nécessaires aux Prisoniers Americains et de tenir un Compte des Dépenses qu'ils auront occasionnés.

J'ai l'honneur d'être avec la Consideration la plus distinguée, Monsieur, Votre tres humble et très obeissant Serviteur

(signé) DE SARTINE

M. Franklin.

To Samuel Cooper

ALS (draft) and copy:[4] Library of Congress

My dear Friend Passy, April 22. 1779.

I received your valuable Letter by the Marquis de la Fayette; and another by Mr. Bradford.[5] I can now only write a few

3. Escaped American prisoners at Cherbourg in 1777 had been aided by a local merchant firm, Dulongprey, Coney & fils: XXIV, 270–1.

4. The draft is badly torn on the edge of each page, and we have supplied missing words from the copy.

5. For Cooper's letters see XXVIII, 338–40.

Words in Answer to the latter, the former not being at Hand.— The Depreciation of our Money must, as you observe, greatly affect Salary Men, Widows & Orphans. Methinks this Evil deserves the Attention of the several Legislatures and ought if possible to be remedied by some equitable Law, particularly adapted to their Circumstances. I took all the Pains I could in Congress to prevent the Depreciation by proposing first that the Bills should bear Interest; this was rejected, and they were struck as you see them. Secondly, after the first Emission, I proposed that we should stop, strike no more, but borrow on Interest those we had issued. This was not then approved of and more Bills were issued.— When from the two great Quantity they began to depreciate, we agreed to borrow on Interest, and I propos'd that in order to fix the Value of the Principal, the Interest should be promis'd in hard Dollars.[6] This was objected to as impracticable: but I still continue of Opinion, that by sending out Cargoes to purchase it we might have brought in Money sufficient for that Purpose, as we brought in Powder, &c; and that tho' this Operation might have been attended with some Disadvantage, the Loss would have been a less Mischief than that attending the Discredit of the Bills, which threatens to take out of our Hands the great Instrument of our Defence. The Congress did at last come into the Proposal of paying the Interest in real Money: But when the whole Mass of the Currency was *under Way* in Depreciation, the Momentum of its Descent was too great to be stopt by a Power that might at first have been sufficient to prevent the Beginning of the Motion. The *only Remedy* now seems to be a Diminution of the Quantity by a vigorous Taxation, of great *nominal* Sums, which the People are more able to pay in Proportion to the Quantity & diminished Value; and the *only Consolation* under the Evil is that the Publick Debt is proportionably diminish'd; with the Deprecia-

6. In 1775 BF served on a committee to supervise the printing of $2,000,000 in bills of credit. We have found, however, as we noted previously, no evidence to corroborate his claim that he presented proposals in Congress to prevent depreciation of the currency. See XXII, 54n. In 1764, however, when he was a member of the Pa. Assembly, he had proposed a scheme for interest-bearing notes instead of bills of credit. See XI, 7–18.

tion;—and this by a Kind of imperceptible Tax, every one having paid a Part of it in the Fall of Value that took Place between his Receiving and Paying such Sums as pass'd thro' his Hands. For it should always be remembered that the original Intention was to sink the Bills by Taxes, which as effectually extinguish the Debt as an actual Redemption.— This Effect of Paper Currency is not understood on this Side of the Water.— And indeed the whole is a Mistery even to the Politicians; how we have been able to continue a War four years without Money; & how we could pay with Paper that had no previously fix'd fund appropriated specifically to redeem it.— This Currency as we manage it is a wonderful Machine. It performs its Office when we issue it; it pays & clothes Troops, & provides Victuals & Ammunition; and when we are oblig'd to issue a Quantity excessive, it pays itself off by depreciation.

Our Affairs in general stand in a fair Light thro'out Europe. Our Cause is universally approved. Our Constitutions of Government have been translated & printed in most Languages, and are so much admired for the Spirit of Liberty that reigns in them, that it is generally agreed we shall have a vast Accession of People of Property after the War, from every Part of this Continent, as well as from the British Islands.[7] We have only to persevere to be great & happy. With the sincerest Esteem, I am ever, Dear Friend Yours most affectionately

BF

P.S. My Respects to Messrs. Bowdoin, Winthrop, Quincy, &c.[8]

Dr. Cooper

7. BF was instrumental in having the various state constitutions translated into French by La Rochefoucauld: XXIII, 214, 375–6, 521, 523, 598–9, 606–7; XXIV, 138; XXV, 93–4, 168.

8. James Bowdoin, John Winthrop, and Josiah Quincy, Sr., others of BF's Massachusetts friends.

To Jane Mecom

LS:[9] American Philosophical Society

Dear Sister, Passy April 22d. 1779.

I received your kind Letter of Jan. 4.[1] which gave me the Satisfaction of knowing that you were well, and comfortably situated among your Friends. You mention other Letters you have written, but they are not come to hand. Dont however be discouraged from writing as often as you can; for I am uneasy when long without hearing from you; and the Chance is greater that one Letter out of many should arrive, than one out of a few. I have written to Mr. Williams to assist you from time to time, as you may have occasion: and I confide in his readiness to do every thing necessary for you, as I know he Esteems you, and I have always reimbursed him.[2] If you do not hear from me so often as formerly, impute it to the too much Business upon my Hands and the Miscarriage of Letters, or any thing rather than a diminution of Affection. I have seen nothing of Mr. Casey,[3] whom you mention as the Bearer of your Letter. I suppose he did not come to Paris.

As to myself, I continue to enjoy, Thanks to God, a greater Share of Health and Strength than falls to the Lot of many at my Age. I have indeed sometimes moderate Fits of the Gout; but I think it is not settled among the Pysicians whether that is a Disease or a Remedy. I live about two Miles out of the City, in a great Garden, that has pleasant Walks in which I can take Exercise in a good Air, the Situation being high and dry. The Village has many good Houses & good Families, with whom I live in Friendship, and pass a Leisure Hour, when I have one, with pleasure. The French in general are an amiable People, and I have the good Fortune to enjoy as much of the Esteem and Affection of all Ranks, as I have any Pretensions to. Temple continues with me; but I have last Week sent

9. In WTF's hand.

1. XXVIII, 344–5.

2. BF had a long-standing account with Jonathan Williams, Sr., for the benefit of Jane Mecom and her children (X, 355, 384). Apparently BF had recently written to Williams about a business scheme for Mecom's benefit. See his reply to BF, July 29, 1779, APS.

3. Wanton Casey, identified in XXVIII, 345n.

Benny to Geneva, where there are as good Schools as here, & where he will be educated a Republican and a Protestant, which could not be so conveniently done at the Schools in France.[4] My Love to all that love you, and believe me ever, my Dear Sister, Your affectionate Brother B FRANKLIN

Mrs: Meacom

Addressed: To, / Mrs Meacom / at Govr Greens, Warwick / Rhode Island.

To Josiah Quincy, Sr.[5]

LS:[6] Princeton University Library; AL (draft) and copy: Library of Congress

Dear Sir Passy April 22d. 1779

I received your very kind Letter by Mr Bradford,[7] who appears a very sensible and amiable young Gentleman, to whom I should with pleasure render any Service here, upon your much respected Recommendation; but I understand he returns immediately.

It is with great Sincerity I join you in acknowledging and admiring the Dispensations of Providence in our Favour. America has only to be thankful and to persevere. God will finish his Work, and establish their Freedom: And the Lovers of Liberty will flock, from all Parts of Europe with their Fortunes to participate with us of that Freedom, as soon as the Peace is restored.

I am exceedingly pleased with your Account of the French Politeness & Civility, as it appeared among the Officers and People of their Fleet. They have certainly advanc'd in those Respects many Degrees beyond the English. I find them here a most amiable Nation to live with. The Spaniards are by common Opinion supposed to be cruel, the English proud, the

4. See our annotation of BFB's letter printed under April 20, above.

5. Massachusetts patriot leader and BF's old friend: VI, 3n.

6. In WTF's hand.

7. Samuel Bradford carried Quincy's letter of Dec. 30, 1778 (XXVIII, 301–5).

Scotch insolent, the Dutch Avaricious, &c. but I think the French have no national Vice ascribed to them. They have some Frivolities but they are harmless. To dress their Heads so that a Hat cannot be put on them, & then wear their Hats under their Arms; and to fill their Noses with Tobacco, may be called Follies perhaps, but they are not Vices. They are only the Effects of the Tyranny of Custom. In short there is nothing wanting in the Character of a Frenchman, that belongs to that of an agreable and worthy Man. There are only some Trifles *surplus* or which might be spared.

Will you permit me, while I do them this Justice, to hint a little Censure on our own Country People, which I do in good Will, wishing the Cause removed. You know the Necessity we are under of Supplies from Europe and the Difficulty we have at present in making Returns. The Interest Bills would do a good deal towards purchasing Arms, Ammunition, Clothing, Sailcloth and other Necessaries for Defence. Upon Enquiry of those who present those Bills to me for Acceptance, what the Money is to be laid out in; I find that most of it is for Superfluities, and more than half of it for Tea! How unhappily in this Instance the Folly of our People, and the Avidity of our Merchants, concur to weaken & impoverish our Country! I formerly computed that we consumed before the War, in that single Article the Value of £500,000 Sterling annually.[8] Much of this was saved by stopping the Use of it. I honoured the virtuous Resolution of our Women in foregoing that little Gratification, and I lament that such Virtue should be of so short Duration! Five hundred Thousand Pounds sterling annually laid out in defending ourselves or annoying our Enemies, would have great Effects. With what Face can we ask Aids and Subsidies from our Friends, while we are wasting our own Wealth in such Prodigality?

With great & sincere Esteem, I have the honour to be, Sir, Your most obedient & most humble Servant. B FRANKLIN

Honble. Jos. Quincy Esqre

8. BF may be referring to his 1773 comment to Thomas Cushing that the smuggling of tea and other Indian goods into the colonies deprived Britain of £500,000 sterling per year (XX, 9). As we have noted, however, BF con-

From David Hartley: Two Letters

(I) ALS: Archives du Ministère des affaires étrangères;[9] transcript: Library of Congress; (II) ALS: American Philosophical Society; transcript: Library of Congress

I.

My dear friend London April 22. 1779.

The bearer of this, & of some other papers (Mr. D)[1] is a very sensible & worthy gentleman, with whom I have had the pleasure of contracting an acquaintance, since the commencement of the American troubles, originally upon the business of the American prisoners. It has been a satisfaction to me at all times to have found him a friend to the restoration of Peace between the two countries. It has likewise been an additional satisfaction & confirmation to me in my own thoughts upon that subject, to find that his sentiments, I think upon most, or all of the subjects upon which we have conversed, have coincided with mine. We both seem possessed of the opinion, that some plan of opening a negotiation, upon preliminaries, which each side might find to be a sufficient security to itself, might be practicable: And then, your sentiment, which you gave me in a letter some years ago, might

---

sistently overestimated the effects of American nonconsumption of "superfluities" (XIII, 143; XX, 10n; and XXI, 235–6n). Contrast his criticisms of American behavior expressed here with his prewar prediction (XVI, 117–18). For an understanding of BF's evolving economic ideas see Drew R. McCoy, "Benjamin Franklin's Vision of a Republican Political Economy for America," *W&MQ,* 3d ser., XXXV (1978), 605–28.

9. Presumably BF turned over Hartley's letter to Vergennes, making it clear to the French government that America was unwilling to enter into negotiations with Britain without the knowledge of France. A French translation of the letter was sent to Montmorin: Waldo G. Leland, *Guide to Materials for American History in the Libraries and Archives of Paris* (2 vols., Washington, D.C., 1932–43), II, 479.

1. Thomas Digges. The wording of this sentence is somewhat puzzling since it implies that Hartley is introducing Digges to BF. Digges, however, had written BF in December, 1778, (XXVIII, 251) that he was much in the company of their mutual friend "D—— H——".

have it's free scope & effect; viz, *A little time given for cooling might have excellent effects.*[2]

The sentiments which I have opened to you in my late letters for some months past, & which I have reduced, in an enclosed paper, into a more specific shape, seem to me, upon very repeated reflection, to promise the fairest ground of good expectation.[3] These propositions originate from myself as a mediator; I have communications with both sides, but certainly no authority to make proposals from either; & perhaps neither side, if I were to put the propositions separately to each, (being myself unauthorized,) might give me positive consent. Each side separately might say No from what is called political prudence; & yet, each side might secretly wish that the offer cou'd be made, with *Done first* from the other party. I think the proposition of a truce for 5 or 7 years, leaving all things in the present dispute *in statu quo,* must be advantageous to all parties, if it were only in consideration that a general satisfactory peace to all parties *may* come among the *excellent effects of time given for cooling.* We can but fight it out at

2. BF had suggested in October, 1775, the wisdom of time for cooling on both sides: XXII, 216.

3. The enclosure, "Observations by Mr. Hartley," sets out the grounds for negotiation that Hartley had discussed with Lord North. According to Hartley, North consented to the M.P.'s effort to open talks with BF, and the present "confidential communication" is the result of conferences between North and Hartley. BF's English friend drafted five points to serve as the basis for negotiations: (1) that his majesty appoint five commissioners (any three of whom could act) to "treat, consult, and agree upon" the final settlement upon "safe, honorable, and permanent terms, subject to ratification by Parliament"; (2) that, as a first preliminary, any one of the commissioners have the power to agree to a suspension of land and sea hostilities for a term of five or seven years; (3) that, as a second preliminary, any one of the commissioners be empowered to agree to suspend the operation of any acts of Parliament dealing with America for five or seven years; (4) that, as a third preliminary, "America should be released, freed, and unengaged from any treaties with foreign powers which may tend to defeat the present negotiation"; (5) that a general treaty be undertaken as soon as possible after agreement to the above preliminaries. Wharton, *Diplomatic Correspondence,* III, 130–1. A French translation of the enclosure is at the AAE.

last: War never comes too late: Wisdom may step in between. These matters have stolen upon us, & have arisen to great & formidable consequences, from small & unsuspected beginnings; but henceforward, we shou'd know by experience what to expect. If the rage of war cou'd but be abated, for a sufficient length of time for reason & reflection to operate, I think it wou'd never revive. I cannot pretend to forecast the result of any negotiation, but I think War wou'd not revive; which is all that I want for my argument. Peace is a *Bonum in se;* Whereas the most favourable events of war are but relatively lesser Evils. Certainly they are Evils: *Mala in se;* not *Bona in se.*

I hope that a cessation of hostilities wou'd produce a renewal of reflection: But even to take the argument at the worst advantage, the two parties are at a cooling distance of 3000 miles asunder. If the flames of war cou'd be but once extinguish'd, does not the Atlantick Ocean contain cold water enought to prevent their bursting out again? I am very strongly of opinion that the two nations, of Great Britain & North America, wou'd accord to the proposition of a truce, *for cooling.* I cannot say whether a British Ministry wou'd accord to it, because they won't tell me: nor can I say whether an American Plenipotentiary wou'd accord to it, because probably you will not tell me. I put myself into your hands however, when I tell you frankly I am of opinion that both of you wou'd accord to it, if there cou'd be a *Done first* on either side, to bind the bargain fast. You have the odds of me in this matter, because you know one half of the question; & I cannot give you any proof on the other side, but only my own presumptive judgement upon observation, & upon a course of reasoning in my own thoughts.

—But for France—My judgement wou'd be that if the proposition of the proposed preliminaries, shd. be agreeable to America, France wou'd do very unhandsomely to defeat it by their refusal. I likewise think it the interest of France; because their interest leads them to go to a certain point, & no further. There is a disparity in the operation of the terms of the alliance on the part of France & on the part of America. The more vigorously France interposes, the better for America in proportion to their exertions they create, less or more, a diversion of the British force; This reasoning goes strait forward for America: But it is not so with France. There is a certain point, to France, beyond which their work wou'd fail & recoil upon themselves; If they were to drive the British ministry totally to abandon the American war, it wou'd become totally a french war. The events of a twelvemonth past seem to bear testimony to this course of reasoning. The disadvantage upon the bargain, to America, is, That the efficacy of the French alliance to them, presupposes their continuance in the war. The demur to France, is, That the liberation of their new ally recoils with double weight of the war upon themselves, without any ulterior points of advantage in view, as dependent upon that alliance. I think the interest of all parties coincides with the proposition of Preliminaries. The proposed preliminaries appear to me to be just & equitable to all parties; but the great object with me, is to come to some preliminaries; I cou'd almost add, whatever those preliminaries might be; provided a suspension of arms for an adequate term of years were one. I think it wou'd be ten thousand to one against any future renewal of the war. It is not necessary to enter at large into the reasons which induce me to think, that the British ministry as well as an American Plenipotentiary wou'd consent to the terms of the proposed preliminaries; for indeed I do not know that I am founded in that opinion with respect to either; but still I believe it of both. But what can a private person do in such a case, wishing to be a mediator for peace, having access to both parties, but equally uncertain of the reception of his mediation on either side? I must hesitate to take any public step, as by a proposition in Parliament, or by any other means to drive the parties to an explanation upon any specific proposals; & yet I am very unwilling to let the session pass without some proposition, upon which the parties may meet, if they shou'd be so inclined, as I suspect them to be. I have been endeavouring to feel pulses for some months, but all is dumb shew. I cannot say indeed that I meet with any thing discouraging, to my apprehension either as to the equitableness or practicability of the proposition for preliminaries. If I cou'd but simply receive sufficient encouragement that I shou'd not run any hazard of obstructing any other practical propositions, by obtruding mine, I shou'd be very much satisfied to come forward, in that case, with mine, to furnish a beginning at least which might lead to Peace.

There is nothing that I wish so much as to have an opportunity of seeing & conversing with you, having many things to say to you; but if that cannot yet happen I have only to say, that whatever comunication you may think proper to make to me which may lead to peace, you may be assured that I shall be most strennuous in applying it to that end. In all cases of difficulty in human life there must be confidence somewhere, to enable us to extricate nations from the evils attendant upon national disputes, as they arise out of national passions, interests, jealousies & points of honour. I am not sure whether the extreme caution & diffidence of persons in political life be not the cause, almost as frequently, of the unnecessary protraction of the miseries of war, as of the final production of any superior good to any state. Peace *now* is better than Peace a twelvemonth hence, at least by all the lives that may be lost in the mean while, & by all the accumulated miseries that may intervene by that delay. When I speak of the necessity of confidence, I wou'd not have you to think that I trust to all professions, promiscuously, with confidence: my thoughts are free respecting all parties; & for myself, if I thought it necessary for the end of attaining any additional confidence in your esteem, to enable me to co-operate the more effectually towards the restoration of peace, there is nothing that I wou'd wish you to be assured of but this, That no fallacious offers of insincerity, nor any pretexts for covering secret designs, or for obtaining unfair advantages, shall ever pass thro my hands. Believe me truly to be, not only a lover of my country, but a sincere friend to Peace & to the rights of Mankind; and ever most affectionately yours D. HARTLEY

II.

My Dear friend London April 22 1779

Having heard nothing yet from I have nothing material to add by this days Mail. I send you for your perusal a Copy of an intended bill by a friend of mine some years ago.

You may recollect that I shewed you a written copy of it last year at Passy.[4] Your affate DH

Addressed: To Dr Franklin

Endorsed: Mr Hartley

Notation: April 22. 1779.

From Joshua Johnson

ALS: American Philosophical Society

Honble. Sir. Nantes 22 April 1779

I was duly favoured with your much esteemed of the 8 Instant & in conformity to your recommendation have had two interviews with Mr. D. Acosta on the subject of those Goods he prepared under a Contract with Mr. A. Lee for the State of Virginia & find that he has Shipped all but the Musketts to America on his own Account which makes it utterly Impossible to do any thing with him, indeed from Inquiry I dont think him competant to the undertaking & I again must trouble you with my Solicitations to obtain this Loan if possible for the State of Maryland. I need not point out to you that Money is more advantagious to the State than for Goverment to furnish the Goods wanted, with Cash I can obtain every thing from the first hand and leave a great saving.—You will be pleased to let me know your Intentions & Success in this Negotiation and believe me to remain always most sincerely.— Sir. Your most Obedt. Hble. Servt.

JOSHUA JOHNSON

His Excellency Benjamin Franklin Esqr. Passy.

Addressed: His Excellency / Benjamin Franklin Esqr / American Plenipotentiary / at the Court of / [*in a different hand*] A Passy / Pres Paris / De C. de Versailles

Notation: Joshua Johnson Apr 22 1779

4. The blank in the first sentence was presumably meant for North's name. The "intended bill" is doubtless one of Hartley's own. He had described a plan for conciliation in a letter of Nov. 14, 1775, modified some details, and presented it to the House of Commons on Dec. 7: XXII, 254–60. He could have shown it to BF during his short visit to Passy in April, 1778; see XXVI, 334–5.

From Chrétien-Guillaume de Lamoignon de Malesherbes[5]

LS: American Philosophical Society

A Paris ce 22 avril 1779.

Oserois-Je vous prier, Monsieur, de me faire l'honneur de venir diner chés moi Mardi prochain[6] ainsi que M. votre petit fils. Le Chevalier de la Luzerne qui comme vous le pensés bien, desire beaucoup de multiplier les occasions de vous voir, s'y trouvera. Le Mardi est ordinairement votre Jour de Versailles, mais vous n'aurés pas cet obstacle Mardi prochain puisqu'on est à Marly:[7] si cependant ce Jour ne vous convenoit pas, Je vous prierois de me mander lequel vous conviendroit le mieux de Mercredi, Jeudi ou autres Jours de la semaine prochaine. Vous connoissés, Monsieur, tout l'attachement avec lequel J'ai l'honneur d'être, Votre trés humble et trés obéissant serviteur./.

MALESHERBES

M. francklin.

To Sartine

LS:[8] Archives de la Marine; copy: Library of Congress

Monsieur

Passi ce 23 avril 1779

Je Recois dans ce moment La Lettre que vostre Excellence m'a fait L'honneur de m'ecrire Le vingt de ce mois, et Je m'empresse a faire tout Cequi peut estre agreable a Sa Majesté; en

5. BF had known this great jurist and government minister for some ten years: XVI, 207n; XIX, 372n, XXV, 686n. Since his resignation three years earlier as secretary of state for the king's household he had avoided Versailles and busied himself with various scholarly projects: John M. S. Allison, *Lamoignon de Malesherbes: Defender and Reformer of the French Monarchy, 1721–1794* (New Haven, 1938), pp. 109–10. He was the uncle of the chevalier de la Luzerne; see Charles Carroll's letter of June 2.

6. April 27. JA recorded in his diary that he and BF had dined twice, within a few weeks, at Malesherbes' house, and had dinner with him once at BF's: Butterfield, *John Adams Diary,* II, 387.

7. *I.e.,* the king's weekly reception for foreign ambassadors had been cancelled because he was at his nearby chateau of Marly (often used for hunting parties).

8. In Chaumont's hand. The copy, in English and in WTF's hand, bears a note, "This letter was translated & sent in French."

ecrivant au Capitaine Landais, Commandant La fregatte L'alliance arrivee a Nantes avec quatrevingt treize prisonniers de Se Rendre Le plutost possible a L'orient.[9] Le Dit Cape. trouvera a Nantes quelques Matelots americains echangés, mais pas assez pour estre Bien armé, et Je Suplie vostre Excellence de Donner Ses ordres a L'orient pour quon Luy donne quelques Matelots pour Completer son armement.

Je suis avec Respect Monsieur vostre tres humble et tres obeissant Serv B FRANKLIN

S. Ex. M. de Sartine Secretaire d'etat et Ministre de la Marine

From Gourlade and Moylan

ALS:[1] American Philosophical Society

Honord Sir L'Orient 23 Avril 1779

The Schooner Betsey Cap: Barrett arrived here yesterday from James River Virginia, after a passage of twenty six days. He brings no public papers, but says both Main Armys were, when he saild, in winter Quarters, and that the British one in Georgia had made no material progress in it's advances in that province, that Generals Moutry & Lincoln[2] were marching with a reinforcement for the southern Army, that wou'd be sufficient, at least to recover that province, likewise that the British Sloop of war Swift had got a shore on the Coast of Virginia in chasing the Rattle-snake, who shar'd the same fate, and that the formers Crew was prisoners in Philadelphia.[3] We remain with due respect Hond. Sir Your most obt hle sts

GOURLADE & MOYLAN

The Honble. B. Franklin Esqr.

9. See BF's April 24 orders to Landais.

1. In Moylan's hand.

2. Brig. Gen. William Moultrie and Maj. Gen. Benjamin Lincoln. For Moultrie see the *DAB* and for Lincoln our annotation of Bondfield's letter of March 6.

3. Captain Tathwell of the *Swift* set his vessel on fire before he and his ninety-one-man crew were captured. The *Rattlesnake* was also entirely destroyed in the fray. *Pennsylvania Packet,* Dec. 12, 1778.

Addressed: The Honorable / Benja: Franklin Esqr. / at / Passy

Notation: Gourlade et Moylan L'orient 23 avril 1779.

From Gratien

ALS: American Philosophical Society

Monsieur Morlaix 23 Avril 1779

J'ay Lhonneur De Vous adresser Cy Joint Une Expedition de requete a nous presentée (Concernant le navire suedois la Victoria Detenu En ce port, suivant Detail que Vous avez par Ma Lettre du 19 Mars.).[4] Je Vous prie De prendre Connoissance de L'ordonnance provisoire que J'ay Eté obligé de rendre.

Monsieur De grandbourg secretaire General de La marine recoit ce Jour la même Expedition, Vous pourrez Vous entendre avec luy sur le Tout.

Le consignataire, *Du Papillon* prise faitte par *La marquise De La fayette* Corsaire armé a Bordeaux Sous commission et Pavillon Du congrèz, presse pour obtenir Une Decision, Les morues faisant partie Du chargement, Deperissent chaque Jour Et Seront bientôt sans Valeur.

Je Suis avec Respect Monsieur Votre Très humble Et Très obeissant Serviteur GRATIEN

Lieut Genl De L'amirauté

From Kéralio

ALS: American Philosophical Society

Monsieur. Le 23e. avril, 1779.

Si j'ai bien entendu, bien compris, vous m'avés fait L'honneur de me prier à déjeuner ou à diner pour après demain Dimanche, mais notre Bonne et Respectable amie[5] doit arriver

4. See BF's response of March 27 to Gratien's March 19 letter. For the *Victoria* see BF to Landais, March 2, and to Schweighauser, April 5. On April 20 her captain, Charles Gustave Berg, asked that additional crew be put on board to avert the risk of her being driven ashore; the next day the Morlaix Admiralty promised to investigate and to inform the American representatives: a copy of the memoir and response are at the APS.

5. The comtesse de Forbach, duchesse de Deux-Ponts.

demain au Soir, ou apres demain matin et dans les Deux suppositions il ne me sera pas possible de La quitter: Si au contraire votre obligeante invitation est pour Une date plus reculée, tout pourra S'arranger et je suis persuadé que notre excellente comtesse sera avec plaisir, de la partie. Veuillés donc me donner vos ordres et recevés mes excuses d'avoir aussi mal retenu ce que Vous m'avés fait L'honneur de me dire. Celui que vous m'avés fait hier m'a un peu tourné la tête et je ne suis pas le seul; vous en jugerés par la Lettre qu'un des jeunes gens qui a diné hier avec vous vient de m'adresser,[6] a Son age on ne connoit pas encore Le poids de La chaine.

Le courier de Bretagne arrivé ce soir nc m'a rien apporté ou presque rien. Vous savés que M. d'orvilliers est à paris:[7] il est parti de Brest Le 16 et sa Venue dans ce pays-ci me paroit Une suite des Dépêches reçues d'Espagne Le 10e.,[8] parce que selon

6. The letter must be one of the 23rd to him from a young man called Bellescizes, who declared he had spent the night thinking about BF, the Americans, and current and future revolutions. He enclosed a little poem inspired by his enthusiasm for the doctor:

A ton maintien Respectable et sévère
A tes traits vigoureux où tout est caractère;
illustre et fier Américain;
Chacun dira, sans te connoitre,
Cet homme assurément doit étre
un Philosophe, ami du genrc humain:
Moi Jaurois dit c'est un Republicain.

He added that for one who serves the king such expressions were certainly not prudent, but he trusted Kéralio not to divulge them. On the 25th he wrote Kéralio again, this time in English, forgiving him for having shown his letter to BF and revealing his wish to go to America. APS.

7. D'Orvilliers arrived from Brest on the 21st to report to Versailles on the French fleet's progress. Because of various delays he did not expect to sail until the end of May in support of the planned invasion of England: Patterson, *The Other Armada,* pp. 59–60. For further discussion of the planned invasion see our annotation of Sartine's letter of April 27.

8. The news received from Spain concerned the timing of Spain's entry into the war (and participation in the invasion) should Britain reject her ultimata for ending hostilities with the French and Americans; see Patterson, *The Other Armada,* pp. 50–2. Meanwhile major developments had occurred in the Spanish negotiations with France; see our annotation of the Sartine letter cited above.

moi, c'est d'après ces dépêches que l'on va dresser L'état de guerre (status belli) et Le plan de Campagne. Ou je suis bien trompé, ou L'Espagne a pris une détermination fixe. Toutefois un aussi mince particulier que moi ne peut former que des Conjectures.

Permettés que je Vous renouvelle mes remerciments et les assurances bien sinceres de la Tendre Vénération avec Laquelle je Suis Monsieur Votre très humble et tres obéissant Serviteur LE CHR. DE KERALIO

Notation: Keralio 23 Ap. 79.

To John Adams

LS:[9] Massachusetts Historical Society; copy: Library of Congress

Sir, Passy, April 24. 1779

By the enclosed Letter from M. De Sartine expressing his Majestys Desire that the Alliance should be retained here a little longer, you will see that I am under a kind of Necessity of disappointing you in your Intentions of making your Passage immediately in that Vessel;[1] which would be more unpleasing to me but for these Considerations, that possibly it may be safer for you to go in a Ship where the Crew not being so mixed can be better depended on, where you will not be incommoded by the Misunderstandings subsisting between the Officers and their Captain, and where you will have the Society of the French Ambassador, M. le Chevalier de la Luzerne, who appears to me a most amiable Man and of very sensible and pleasing Conversation. I hope this will in some Measure compensate for the Inconvenience of shifting your Stores from one Ship to the other. And as I shall order the Alliance to l'Orient where the King's Frigate is, that carries the Ambassador, the removal of your Things from one Ship to the other will be more easy. You can even go thither in the Alliance if you chuse it.— The Ships in the American Trade

9. In WTF's hand.

1. Our annotation of the enclosed letter, Sartine's of April 20, above, discusses the consequences of BF's disappointing JA.

which were at Nantes when I offered them the Convoy, of the Alliance, having declined that Offer, and sailed, as I understand, under another & perhaps safer Convoy,[2] makes her immediate Departure for America less necessary; and perhaps she may now make a Cruize in these Seas, for which I understand she will have time; which will be probably more advantageous & therefore more Satisfactory to her People than a direct Return. I hope she may procure us some more Prisoners to exchange the rest of our Countrymen, and at the same time reimburse us the Charges of her Refitting, which you know we stand much in need of.—

M. Dumas writes me from the Hague of the 19th "Je sçais depuis hier, *de bonne part* que l'Espagne s'est enfin declarée. Cela fera un bon Effet ici, & partout." I hope his Intelligence is good; but nothing of it has yet transpired here.

Inclosed I send you a Cover which I have just received from Martinique, directed to me but containing only a Letter for you. The Cover being unskilfully sealed, over the Seal of your Letter, was so attached to it that I had like to have broken open the one in opening the other. I send you also another Letter which came from Spain.[3]

I am obliged by your offer of taking Charge of my Dispatches for America. I shall send them down to you by M. De la Luzerne, who is to set off in a few Days.

With great Esteem, I have the honour to be, Sir, Your most obedient & most humble Servant B FRANKLIN

Honble. John Adams Esqr.

Endorsed: Dr Franklin. Ap. 24. ans. Ap. 29. 1779

2. A convoy for Martinique whose protection had been offered to the American merchant ships at Nantes: XXVIII, 507. BF originally intended for the *Alliance* to escort these ships directly to America (see his letter to Landais of March 2), but her refit at Brest took too long. By the time she reached the mouth of the Loire the American ships had already joined the French convoy; according to an April 25 letter from Joseph Wharton, Jr., to WTF (APS), thirteen of them were at Brest. See also BF's letter to Landais, which immediately follows, and his May 3 letter to Arthur Lee.

3. Missing. *Adams Papers,* VIII, 43n, speculates that the letter from Martinique was written by William Bingham and the one from Spain by the merchant Robert Montgomery (XXVI, 242n).

To Landais

Copies: Library of Congress, American Philosophical Society, Harvard University Library[4]

Sir, Passy April 24. 1779.

I received your Favour of the 6th Inst from Brest, and the 19th from Nantes. I am glad to learn that you are safely arrived with the Prisoners. You will receive some of the exchanged Americans whom Mr Schweighauser has engaged for you: and I have applied to the Minister of the Marine for as many good French Seamen as will make up your Complement, which will accordingly be given to you.[5]

I am now to inform you, that the Ships from Nantes which I at first proposed you should take under your Convoy being mostly sailed; and the King having offered Mr Adams a Passage in one of his Ships which carries his Ambassador to America, there does not seem at present a Necessity for your immediate Return and therefore I purpose that the Alliance should make a Cruise before her Departure, which I imagine will be a Satisfaction both to you and your People as it may give to you an Opportunity of acquiring Honour and to them of Profit: I hope too that both you and they will have the Satisfaction of delivering the rest of our Countrymen from their present Confinement in England by taking a Number of Prisoners to exchange for them: In which Case you may as you desire have your whole Crew composed of Americans only; I am sure your Success in this Respect will make you exceedingly welcome to that Country and the Congress on your happy Return.

With these and other Views my Orders now are that you procced first to L'Orient,[6] where you will receive your Complement of Men and such other Things as may be necessary for your Cruize, and where you will meet the farther Orders I am preparing to send you.

4. The latter two copies are certified by Ludwell Lee.

5. Above, April 23.

6. BF neglects to mention that he had offered JA a passage to Lorient aboard the *Alliance.* JA told BF on April 29, below, that his baggage was already on board and that he would accompany her to that port.

As the Man you lost was Rogue enough to desert, I think we are better without him. And as they will give us a Number of good ones instead of him it is hardly worth while to make a Complaint about him at present.

My best Wishes for your Success, Honour and Happiness will constantly attend you, being with much Esteem, Sir, Your most obedt &ca

Honble P. Landais Esqr

From John Bondfield

ALS: American Philosophical Society

Sir Bordeaux 24 April 1779

Since my last of the 17th Ins I am honord by your favor of the 5th. The Contract for Cannon made with Spain being compleated the Caron Company depended on a renewal and the pieces at Ferrol were lodged there in consiquence Spain alterd her Contract and the Cannon remaind on account of the former Contractors.[7]

The Prisoners carried into the ports of Spain taken by American privateers would form a considerable Body could a plan be pursued to get them to France and would soon in the course of Exchange releive all the American prisoners in England, No arrivals from the United States I expect a vessel dayly from Alexandria she was ready for Sea in February the situation of our Trade is very trying. A French Fleet from Martinico was met on this Coast by two English Men of War who it is said attackt the Convoy its apprehended a shocking Account will be receivd. I have the honor to be with due respect Sr. your most obed H Serv JOHN BONDFIELD

His Excelly B. Franklin

Addressed: His Excellency B. Franklin / Plenepontenciary. des Etats Unies, / a / Paris

Notation: Bondfield John Bordeaux 24 avril 1779.

7. For the cannon see our annotation of Bondfield's letter of March 27.

From C. L. Brust

ALS: American Philosophical Society

Monseigneur Bordeaux Le 24 Avril 1779.

Il s'est elevé divers procés entre les assurés et les assureurs des batiments & Cargaisons partis de L'Amerique Septentrionale pour la françe, et pris par les Anglois ou peris, et je Suis du Nombre de ceux qui Sont en Souffrance par le refus des assureurs de payer les pertes.

Un des grands obstacles a faire finir ces discussions est dans L'Incertitude du rapport de L'Argent de LAmerique a Celui de françe et un tarif qui de Yorktown a eté envoyé ici lannée derniere a eté rejetté par les assureurs faute d'etre revetu d'un Certifficat Authentique, Cest pour Cela que j'ose Supplier Votre Excellence de Certiffier veritable la Copie de ce Tarif cy joint[8] Syl est juste, ou dans le Cas Contraire Oserois je esperer que Votre Excellence daignat men faire parvenir un a laide du quel je puisse parvenir a faire determiner les pertes a payer par les assureurs.

Jai l'honneur d'etre avec le plus profond Respect Monseigneur de Votre Excellence Le Trés humble et Trés Obeïssant Serviteur C. L. Brust

Notation: C. L. Brust Bordeaux 24. Avril 1779.

From Peter Hasenclever[9]

ALS: American Philosophical Society

Sir. Berlin the 24th April 1779

In December 1775 I had the Honour to write to you for Philadelphia and to Send you a Letter from Baron Waitz von

8. The enclosure, dated Yorktown [York, Pa.], Aug. 10, 1778, is signed by Terrasson & Poey. Divided into seven columns, it gives the respective exchange rates of the *livre* or pound (based on a rate of 5 *l.t.* 5 *s.* to a dollar or piaster) in France, South Carolina, New York, Pennsylvania, Virginia, and Georgia.

9. This wealthy manufacturer is identified in XIV, 31–2n. He may have been personally acquainted with BF through WF, who appointed the 1768 commission of inquiry that commended Hasenclever's iron-making enterprise in New Jersey. Since 1773 Hasenclever had been engaged in trade and linen manufacturing in the Prussian province of Silesia: N.J. Hist. Soc. *Proc.*, LIX (1941), 245–7, 250.

Essen, who then was Minister of State here, who told me that he had been acquianted with you at Cassel, this Experienced and worthy Gentleman died Since, and I am in doubt if ever my Letter came to your hands.[1]

I take now the Liberty to Send you the inclosed Letters for Messrs Hasenclever, & R. H. Lee at Philadelphia and Mr Ax Gillon from Charlestown whom I judge at present at Paris, which I beg you will get to be forwarded to their Destiny and Excuse my Liberty.[2]

Yesterday I dined with the American Colonel Baron d'Arend at the Minister of Finances His Excellcy Baron de Goerne; the Colonel was Recommanded to me by my Cousin Mr F. G. Hasenclever now Establishd at Philadelphia, who has been for Some time at Breslau and endeavoured to open a branch of Commerce betwixt their Country and America, from which Place he came directed by the Ministre His Excellcy von Hoym, to the Baron de Goerne[3]; after I had Conversed for an Hour with Colonel d Arend, I observed that he was not experienced in Commercial affairs, and that his proposals could no be accepted, as to form a Company by actions, and to Send Some Ships Loaden with Linnens and Woolens to America, by merchants who live in an inward Country, ignorant of Such undertakings and of Sea affairs, and not knowing to whome the goods with security could be Consigned and in

1. We have no record of a 1775 letter from Jacob Sigismund Waitz, freiherr von Eschen (1698–1776), for whom see *Biographisches Wörterbuch zur Deutschen Geschichte* (3 vols., Munich, 1973). We suspect he was the author of a book on electricity recommended to BF: VIII, 330–1n. His son-in-law is mentioned in Raspe's March 26 letter to BF, above.

2. The letter to Lee is reproduced in *Lee Family Papers,* reel 6, frames 62–4.

3. Henry Leonard Philip, baron d'Arendt, colonel of the German battalion, was on leave from his command: XXVIII, 298n. He wrote on May 16, below, to describe his commercial proposals.

Friedrich Christoph von Goerne, head of the Prussian Overseas Trading Corporation (XXV, 115) had sent greetings through Stephen Sayre a year and half earlier. Although eventually convicted of embezzlement, von Goerne was presently in Frederick's good graces: W.O. Henderson, *Studies in the Economic Policy of Frederick the Great* (London, 1963), p. 158. Karl Georg Heinrich von Hoym (1739–1807) was the directing minister of Silesia: *ADB.*

what manner if they undertook Such an affaire they Should be paid for besides the Danger of the Sea, and Privateering was Such an objection by the Breslau merchants, that they entierly declined this business.[4]

However I have the Honnour to assure you Sir, that it is neighter for want of means nor Inclination, that as yet no trade has been opened direct betwixt This Country and North America, and His Majesty the King has Recommanded his Subjects to trade Directly to America, as Soon as Circumstances will permit it. I have been Called Severall times for this purpose to this Metropolis, and on which account I am here at present, and have almost formd a Plan with the Minister of Finances, in what manner an mutual advantageous trade might be carried on betwixt this Country and the North American Colonies, and there is no doubt or this bussiness will come to perfection, and be of great Importance, Since this Country is So happily Situated, that it provides all the adjacent provinces, with Rice, Tobacco, Caffe, Sugar, and other American and West India Products.

Three year ago I met here a Maryland Gentleman, and Two years ago, when Mr Alderman Lee and Mr Sayre was here I was Send for, but Mr. Lee was departed before I arrived, and Mr Sayre was not accredited for Public business, These Two Gentlemen[5] as well as Colonel d'Arend, were entierly unacquianted with the Nature of Commercial affairs of this Country, as also with the trade of North America, Mr. Sayre made some proposals but they were of Such a Nature, that they could not be executed and Gentlemen become Suspected when they are ignorant of the affairs which they propose.[6]

At present no affairs can be undertaken from this Country To America on account of the war, and difficulty of the Trans-

4. In spite of Frederick's encouragement, the linen manufacturers of Silesia showed no interest in American trade: Horst Dippel, "Prussia's English Policy after the Seven Years' War," *Central European History,* IV (1971), 208.

5. In a footnote at this point Hasenclever wrote, "the Gent. from Maryland & Colonel Arend."

6. For Sayre's proposals see John R. Alden, *Stephen Sayre, American Revolutionary Adventurer* (Baton Rouge and London, 1983), p. 102.

port. But as Soon as peace is reestablishd, we Shall do Some great affairs, we have those Sorts of Linnen and woollen goods which are mostly Consumed in America, and at very reasonable prices, that no Nation can provide them Cheaper, and we can take in Return 7/ to 8000 hheads of Tobacco and about 10 to 12000 Barrills of Rice, and much more of each Sort when affairs are once in their Regular Course.

His Excellency Baron de Göerne Ministre privé d'Etat & de Finance de S. M. Le Roy de Prusse, has desired me to present his Respects to you, as he has a particular Esteem for you Sir, & wishes to be personally acquianted with you; if you find me able to be of any Service to you in this Country, please to Command me and your Commands Shall be Exactly Executed, & you will then direct your letter for me to His Excelly Mr Le Baron de Goerne; it is probable that I may pay you this Sommer a Visit at Paris.

I have the Honour to be with great Respect. Sir Your most Obed humble servant PETER HASENCLEVER

P.S. We Expect His M. the King angainst the 15 May God be thank that Peace and Tranquillity is restablishd[7] I wish it was So with America.

Colonel d'Arend is departed for frankfurt, and has desird me to pay his respects to you.

To Benjamin Franklin Esqr.

Notation: Peter Hasendever Berlin 24. avril 1779

7. An agreement between Austria and Prussia was signed on May 13: see our annotation of Dumas' letter of March 24–5. Frederick returned to Berlin on May 29: *Politische Correspondenz Friedrich's des Grossen* (47 vols., Berlin, 1879–1939), XLIII, 95.

From John Ross: Extract[8]

Reprinted from "Memoir of John Ross, Merchant, of Philadelphia," *Pennsylvania Magazine of History and Biography,* XXIII (1899), 78.

Paris 24th April 1779.

That unless your Excellency affords him speedy relief, agreeable to the express order of that Honble Body (Congress)[9] he must plainly tell your Excellency, that his ruin is immediate and unavoidable, as he has bills running upon him, which he has accepted in perfect confidence and reliance, that the said order of Congress, would be faithfully complied with, and that he should be enabled punctually to discharge them when they become due. (Signed) J Ross.

From H. Sykes

ALS: American Philosophical Society

Sir, Paris April the 24th. 1779—

I should have sent your Spectacles Sooner, but in Complyance with your favor of the 20th: inst:,[1] have cut a Second Pair, in Which I have been Unfortunate, for I broke and Spoilt three Glasses, the Bearer will Deliver them, the Price is 18 *l.t.* a Pair, Which you may Pay him if you think Proper,[2] I hope Sir, they

8. Ross, the agent of Willing & Morris at Nantes, had also purchased goods on behalf of the congressional committee of commerce. As a result of these latter purchases, he appears to have accumulated a debt of perhaps £20,000 sterling: "Memoir of John Ross," *PMHB,* XXIII (1899), 78–9. For the past several months his attempts to obtain funds from the commissioners had been rebuffed because of his reluctance to produce his accounts: XXVIII, 18–19, 290, 321–2.

9. *JCC,* XI, 738–40.

1. Not found.

2. BF drafted a receipt on the verso of Sykes's letter: "Received April 26. 1779 of B Franklin Thirty-six Livres in full of the within mentioned Charge; I say receiv'd for Mr Sykes per me." He noted in his Cash Book (Account XVI; XXVI, 3) that on June 5 he paid Sykes 36 *l.t.* for spectacles. These may have been bifocals, which BF invented and is said to have worn since he was in his thirties. They helped him to understand French, he claimed, by bringing the speaker's features into focus. To George Whately, May 23, 1785 (APS); Charles E. Letocha, "The Invention and Early Manufacture of Bifocals," *History of Ophthalmology,* XXXV, no. 3 (Nov.–Dec., 1990), pp. 226–35.

will Please you, should anything be wanting, you will favor me with your Commands—

As you did not leave your hankerchief here, I hope Sir, you have found it, if not, Please to Recollect where you Call'd, and it is possible you may have left it Elsewhere, Believe me to be with Great Esteem Sir Your most obedient humble Servant

H SYKES

Addressed: A Monsieur / Monsieur Franklin / Député des Etats Unies de / L'Amerique, / á Passy

Notation: h Sykes Paris 24 avril 1779.

To Landais

Copy: University of Virginia Library

Sir

Passy April 25. 1779

The Bearer Mr. Hezekiah Ford who has for some time been in the service of the United States, & always a zealous friend to the cause of Liberty, being about to return to America, if you can conveniently receive him in your Ship as a Passenger when you return thither you will oblige Sir Your most Obedient & most Humble Servant

(Signd) B FRANKLIN

To the Honble. P. Landais Esqr.

I Certify that the above Letter is a true copy from the original signed B. Franklin. L'Orient 23d April 1780.

JOSEPH BROWN JUNR of South Carolina

Notations in different hands:[3] April 25. 1779 Doctr Franklin recommends Mr. Hezh. Ford to Capt P Landais for a Passage to America after he had countermanded her going thither[4] / B. Franklin's Recommends Hezka. Ford to Cap: Lanndois for a passage to America after having countermanded his going thither (25 Apl. 1778.) (1779)

3. The first of which is by Arthur Lee, who on April 23 gave his secretary money for his expenses to America: *Lee Family Papers,* reel 6, frame 57.

4. Ford, however, did find passage on another ship, arriving in Virginia in August to answer charges before the Va. Council: *Jefferson Papers,* III, 65; Butterfield, *John Adams Diary,* II, 364–5n.

From Jonathan Williams, Jr.

ALS: American Philosophical Society

Dear & hond Sir.— Nantes April 25. 1779.—

This will be presented you by Mrs Richards who with her Children, is coming hither to meet & continue with her Husband.— Mr. Richards has been here some time past, & has been employed by Mr Johnson & myself in our 'Counting Houses, as his Intention is to continue in the american Business in this Place, or perhaps to settle with his Family in america, we look upon him as one of us; I therefore request you to consider his Family in the same View, & if any Obstacle should arise on acct of their being English, to facilitate their Departure from Paris so as they may come hither without any Interruption.— Mrs Richards does me the Favour to bring with her my young Friend, who tho' the Fruit of an improper Connection is as dear to me as the tenderest of Natures Ties can make him, and the best proof I can give of a sincere Repentance I take to be a strict attention to the Dictates of Honour, which I am sure my Heart will never allow me in this Instance to swerve from, even were Duty out of the Question. Should he be a moment in your Presence, & should you condescend to grant him your Blessing it would make me happy.[5]

I write thus freely about my Errors because you have already pardoned them, & because I am sure you believe I will do all in my Power to repair them.

I am ever your dutifull & affectionate kinsman

JONA WILLIAMS J

Addressed: a monsieur / Monsieur Franklin / Ministre Plenipotentiaire / des Etats unis / en son Hotel a / Passy prés Paris

Notation: Williams Jona. April 25. 1779.

5. JW had first written BF about his illegitimate son on June 7, 1777: XXIV, 137–8. The boy, named Josiah after JW's late blind brother, was born in late 1775 or early 1776 (JW to WTF, April 4, 1782, APS.) BF seems to have given him a warm reception; see JW's letter of May 26.

To John Bondfield

Copy: Library of Congress

Sir, Passy April 26. 1779.

I am very sensible of your Merit with the United States and wish it was in my Power to serve you under the Difficulties you represent to me in yours of the 17th. Inst. But I have no Money at Command which is not appropriated to answer Contracts we have made here or Drafts of the Congress daily arriving, and I dare not presume to hazard a Possibility of Disappointment, as considering my Situation the publick Consequences of my being render'd unable to pay those Demands might be fatal to the Credit of the States. I hope therefore that either by the Arrival of your Funds or by some other means, your present straits may be relieved and the Inconveniences you apprehend prevented; being with much Esteem, Sir Your most obedt. &ca—

Mr. Bondfield.

To ——— Deshayes

Two copies: Library of Congress

Sir, Passy April 27. 1779.

I understand from his Excellency M. De Sartine that you have taken Care of such poor Americans as arrived at Cherbourg from England, and been at some Expence in relieving them.[6] Please to accept my Thanks, and send me your Account that I may reimburse you. And as you have been so good as to Offer a Continuance of these kind Offices of Humanity I hereby assure you that the same will very much oblige me and that your accounts shall be readily and punctually discharged.

I have the honor to be, Sir, &ca.

M. Deshayes.

6. Above, April 21.

From Sartine

Copy: Library of Congress

Marly ce 27. Avril 1779.

J'ai reçu, Monsieur, La lettre que vous m'avez fait l'honneur de m'écrire le 23. de ce mois.

J'ai rendu Compte à Sa Majesté des ordres que vous avez bien voulu donner au Sr. Landais Capitaine de la Fregatte Americaine l'alliance, de conduire au Port de l'Orient le Batiment qu'il commande. Sa Majesté desire que cette fregatte soit reunie au Vaisseau le Bonhomme Richard et aux autres Batiments qui doivent être employés sous les ordres de M. Jones qui sera le commandant en Chef de cet armement. Sa Majeste desire aussi qu'il puisse être fait usage de ces Batimens pour transporter un detachement de ses troupes destinées pour une Expedition particuliere;[7] et qu'en consequence vous donniez des Ordres à Mr. Jones de recevoir ces troupes a bord de ses Vaisseaux et de les mettre a terre sur les points où l'officier qui en aura le Commandement decidera qu'elles soyent debarquées. Vous voudrez bien alors ordonner pareillement à M. Jones de ne pas perdre les troupes de vue pendant l'Expedition; de proteger leur Operation; d'y concourir en tout ce qui pourra dependre de lui de tenir toujours les Batiments à portée d'assurer la Retraite des troupes, en cas qu'elles fus-

7. The expedition was a smaller-scale version of the one against the ports of the Irish Sea envisaged by Lafayette; see BF's letter of March 22 and Lafayette's of March 31. In the interim Spain and France had signed the April 12 Convention of Aranjuez regulating Spain's entry into the war (for which see our annotation of BF's May 26 letter to the committee for foreign affairs). The second article of that agreement specified that should Spain enter the war the two countries would undertake an invasion of the British Isles in accordance with the French operational plans then being prepared: Doniol, *Histoire,* III, 805. These plans specified a joint invasion of the Isle of Wight, preparatory to an attack on the great British naval base at Portsmouth; see Dull, *French Navy,* pp. 136–43 and, for the current state of preparations, our annotation of Kéralio's April 23 letter. As the plans also discussed diversionary raids, Lafayette's scheme accorded with French strategic thinking; for further details about Lafayette's plan see both the following document and BF's instructions of April 28 to Jones. As we shall see, the French government soon developed second thoughts about the diversionary attack.

sent repoussées; et à tout evenement de les embarquer sur les Batiments qu'il commande quand l'expedition sera terminée.[8]

Je vous serai très obligé de vouloir bien me faire part des ordres que vous avez donnés pour faciliter un projet dont vous avez connoissance.

J'ai l'honneur d'être avec une très parfaite Consideration, Monsieur, Votre très humble et tres obeissant serviteur

(signé) DE SARTINE.

Mr. Franklin Minisistre Plenipotentiaire des Etats Unis de l'Amerique Septentrionale.

To John Paul Jones

LS:[9] National Archives; copies: Library of Congress, Archives de la Marine

Dear Sir, Passy April 27. 1779.

I have at the Request of M. De Sartine postponed the Sending the Alliance to America, and have order'd her to proceed immediately from Nantes to L'Orient, where she is to be furnished with her Complement of Men, join your little Squadron and act under your Command.[1]

The Marquis de la Fayette will be with you soon. It has been observ'd that joint Expeditions of Land and Sea Forces often miscarry thro' Jealousies and Misunderstandings between the Officers of the different Corps. This must happen where there are little Minds actuated more by personal Views of Profit or Honor to themselves, than by the warm and sincere Desire of Good to their Country. Knowing you both as I do, and your just manner of thinking on these Occasions, I am confident nothing of the Kind can happen between you, & that it is unnecessary for me to recommend to either of you

8. See the following letter, which BF wrote after receiving the present one.

9. In WTF's hand, as is the copy at the Archives de la Marine, which BF sent with his letter of May 1, below, to Sartine.

1. See Sartine to BF, April 20, and BF to JA, April 24.

that Condescension, mutual Goodwill and Harmony, which contribute so much to Success in such Undertakings. I look upon this Expedition as an Introduction only to greater Trusts and more extensive Commands, and as a kind of Trial of both your Abilities, and of your Fitness in Temper and Disposition for acting in Concert with others. I flatter myself therefore that nothing will happen that may give Impressions to the Disadvantage of either of you, when greater Affairs shall come under Consideration. As this is understood to be an American Expedition, under the Congress Commission & Colours, the Marquis who is a Major General in that Service, has of Course the Step in Point of Rank; and he must have the Command of the Land Forces, which are committed by the King to his Care: But the Command of the Ships will be entirely in you; in which I am persuaded that what ever Authority his Rank might in Strictness give him, he will not have the least desire to interfere with you.[2] There is Honour enough to be got for both of you, if the Expedition is conducted with a prudent Unanimity. The Circumstance is indeed a little Unusual; for there is not only a Junction of Land & Sea Forces, but there is also a Junction of French men & Americans which increases the Difficulty of maintaining a good Understanding; a cool prudent Conduct in the Chiefs is therefore the more necessary, and I trust neither of you will in that Respect be deficient. With my best Wishes for your Success, Health & Honour I remain, dear Sir, Your affectionate Friend and most obedient Servant B FRANKLIN

Honble: J. P. Jones Esqre.

Endorsed: From Doctr. Franklin inclosing Instructions for a Secret Expedition April 27th. 1779. No. 11.

2. See our annotation of the immediately preceding letter. For Lafayette's role in the expedition see Louis Gottschalk, *Lafayette and the Close of the American Revolution* (Chicago, 1942), pp. 9–16. Lafayette also wrote Jones on the 27th to discuss the expedition (Idzerda, *Lafayette Papers,* II, 258–60), while on the same day Sartine sent his own orders to Jones (Bradford, *Jones Papers,* reel 3, no. 579, summarized in Idzerda, *Lafayette Papers,* II, 256n).

To Sartine

Copy: Library of Congress

Sir Passy April 27 1779

I am much obliged to M. deshayes, Commissaire des Classes a Cherbourg, for the Care your Excellency informs me he has taken of the poor Americans that have escaped from England and arrived at that Port. I shall desire him to send me his Account of the Expence he has already been at in relieving them, that I may discharge it; and I shall request him to continue his kind Care towards such as may hereafter come to Cherburg in the same Circumstances.[3] I am with great Respect &c.

M. de Sartine

From Kéralio

ALS: American Philosophical Society

Monsieur a L'Ecole Rle. mre. 27e. avril, 1779.

Je me mets à vos pieds pour vous remercier de L'honneur que vous m'avés fait Hier et je n'ai point d'expressions pour vous dire combien j'en suis flatté.

Une heure plus tard vous eussiés trouvé notre bonne et respectable amie qui vous embrasse, qui vous fait mille amitiés. Elle aura L'honneur d'aller diner chés vous Vendredi prochain, et L'Excellent Mac-mahon aussi.[4]

J'Espere avec vous que La nouvelle de votre ami de La Haye est bonne: il me semble que la déclaration de L'Espagne ne peut pas tarder, ou La paix se fera.[5] Avés vous lu Le mémoire du chevalier Yorke, aux états-généraux?[6]

Notre jeune homme s'occupe toujours beaucoup de vous et des américains. Voila une seconde Lettre qu'il m'a écrite.[7] Il y

3. BF wrote Deshayes on the same day, above.
4. For Dr. John MacMahon see XXV, 4n.
5. Dumas discussed the subject in his letter of April 19.
6. Yorke's warning on April 9 was against escorting ships with naval supplies; see Dumas' letters of April 3–13 and April 16.
7. Doubtless the letter of the 25th from Bellescizes that we discuss in our annotation of Kéralio's April 23 letter.

a quinze mois au plus qu'il apprend L'anglois; vous voyés qu'il n'a pas perdu son temps.

Recevés toujours avec Bonté L'hommage de la Tendre Vénération avec laquelle je suis Monsieur votre très humble et très obéissant Serviteur. LE CHR. DE KERALIO

Notation: Le Chr. De Queralio Paris 27e. avril 1779.

Franklin's Instructions to John Paul Jones

Copies:[8] National Archives (two), Archives de la Marine, Library of Congress

[April 28, 1779]

Instructions to the Honble: J. P. Jones Esquire, Commander of the American Squadron in the Service of the United States, now in the Port of L'Orient.

1. His Majesty having been pleased to grant some Troops for a particular Expedition,[9] proposed to annoy our common Enemy, in which the Sea Force under your Command might have an Opportunity of distinguishing itself: You are to receive on board your Ships of War, and the other Vessels destined for that purpose, the Troops that shall present themselves to you, afford them such Accommodation as may be most proper for preserving their Health, and convey them to such Port or Place as their Commander shall desire to land them at.

2. When the Troops are landed, you are to aid by all means in your Power their Operations, as they will be instructed in like manner to aid and support those you may make with your Ships, that so by this Concurrence and Union of your different Forces all that such a compounded Strength is capable of may be effected.

8. We print from the copy in WTF's hand at the National Archives. The copy at the Archives de la Marine, also in his hand, was enclosed with BF's May 1 letter to Sartine.

9. See our annotation of BF's April 27 covering letter to Jones. Lafayette expected to embark 650 men: Idzerda, *Lafayette Papers,* II, 258.

3. You are during the Expedition never to depart from the Troops so as not to be able to protect them or to secure their Retreat in Case of a Repulse; and in all Events you are to endeavour their compleat Reimbarkation, on board the Ships and Transports under your Command, when the Expedition shall be ended.

4. You are to bring to France all the English Seamen you may happen to take Prisoners, in order to compleat the good Work you have already made such Progress in, of delivering by an Exchange the rest of our Countrymen now languishing in the Goals of Great Britain.

5. As many of your Officers and People have lately escaped from English Prisons either in Europe or America, You are to be particularly attentive to their Conduct towards the Prisoners which the fortune of War may throw into your Hands, lest Resentment of the more than barbarous Usage by the English in many Places towards the Americans should occasion a Retaliation, and an Imitation of what ought rather to be detested and avoided, for the sake of Humanity and for the Honour of our Country.

6. In the same View altho' the English have wantonly burnt many defenceless Towns in America, you are not to follow this Example, unless where a Reasonable Ransom is refused, in which Case, your own generous Feelings as well as this Instruction, will induce you to give timely Notice of your Intention that Sick and ancient Persons, Women & Children may be first removed.[1]

Given at Passy, this 28th Day of April, 1779.

signed B. FRANKLIN.

M. P. from the U. S. at the Court of France

Notation: April 28 1779 Instructions to Capt. J P. Jones from Doctr. Franklin inclosed in the Doctor's Letter of Octr. 17th: 1779[2]

1. A subject of continuing interest to BF; see his and Lafayette's list of British atrocities, printed below at the end of May. For the ransoming of English towns see also BF to Lafayette, March 22.

2. BF's letter to James Lovell. National Archives.

To Landais

Copies:[3] Archives de la Marine, Library of Congress, Harvard University Library

Sir, Passy April 28th. 1779.

Being arrived at L'Orient agreable to the Orders I sent you when at Nantes, you are to join Capt. Jones, put yourself and ship under his Command as your senior Officer, proceed with him on the Cruize he is about to make, and obey his Orders untill your Return to France.[4] I heartily wish you Success, both with Regard to Profit and Honour, being with great Esteem. Sir Your most obedient & most humble Servant

(signed) B. Franklin

Copy of a Letter to the honble Capt. Landais

To Vergennes

ls:[5] Archives du Ministère des affaires étrangères; copy: Library of Congress

Sir Passy April 28 1779

Enclosed I send your Excellency a Letter I have just received from Mr. Wm. Bingham, Agent of the Congress at Martinique, complaining of the Proceedings of the Judge of the Admiralty there, relating to an English Privateer brought thither by some American Seamen, who have not only been deprived of their Prize, but are thrown into Prison.[6]

The King of England having given Encouragment to all Seamen in the Service of the United States, or in the Service of their Merchants, to seize the Vessels they were employed in, and bring them to England, promising to divide the Value of such Vessels and Cargoes among the Seamen who should ef-

3. The copy at the Archives de la Marine is in wtf's hand and was enclosed with bf's May 1 letters to Sartine. The one at Harvard is in Arthur Lee's hand and is certified by his nephew Ludwell to be a true copy.

4. bf's instructions to Jones immediately precede the present letter.

5. Both the ls and the copy are in Gellée's hand.

6. The story of the privateer *Dolphin* is told in xxviii, 501–3.

fect such Seizures;[7] which Encouragement produced many mischievous Effects, and occasioned the Loss of many Vessels belonging to the Subjects of the States, and bound for France; the Congress after remonstrating in vain against so irregular a Practice as that of enticing Servants to betray their Trust, found it necessary to make Reprisals in the same Way; and accordingly passed an Act promising the same Rewards to those Seamen who should seize and bring in any English Ship they might be on Board of.[8] This Privateer was taken in Consequence. And as I look upon that Act of Congress to be in the Nature of a *general Commisssion,* I apprehend that the Capture was duly made, and that the Captors have a just Title to the Prize. I therefore request your Excellency's Protection in Behalf of those poor American Seamen and that an Order may be sent to discharge them from their Imprisonment, and deliver to them the Value of the Prize in Question.

With great Respect I am your Excellency's most obedient and most humble Servant B FRANKLIN

His Excy. Ct. de Vergennes

Notation: M de Rayneval

7. For examples of the practice see *Naval Docs.,* VIII, 840; IX, 403.
8. *JCC,* IX, 802. See also *JCC,* V, 692.

From Dominique d'O—— de St. Hubert: Receipt[9]

D:[1] American Philosophical Society

[April 28, 1779]

BILLET DE SOUSCRIPTION.

*J'ai reçu de M*onsieur frankelin ministre plenipotentiaire des etats unis de l'amerique la somme de 24 lt *pour payement de* premiere souscription *du* dictionnaire topographique, historique, &c de la france &c *dont ce* monsieur *recevra l*es *Volumes* reliés *sans frais.*

A tarascon—28—avril *1779.*

De st. hubert *Avocat, & Membre de plusieurs Académies.*

From Samuel W. Stockton

ALS: American Philosophical Society

Sir. The Hague April 28th. 1779.

From your kind permission, I have at different times taken the liberty of writing to you.

9. This is the earliest of a series of "receipts," which were really requests for BF to subscribe to a work that never was completed. St. Hubert had written histories of individual French provinces and was now compiling a more ambitious study of the entire country. In an undated letter that may have been written during the spring of 1779, the author requested an interview and told BF that he would certainly be mentioned in the "ouvrage historique." Writing on July 28 and alluding to an earlier letter, St. Hubert identified himself as an *avocat au parlement* whose historical dictionary of France was authorized by the government and would run to twenty-four volumes, the first six of which were due to appear in October, 1779, and the rest to be completed by January, 1780. He would sell the work by advance subscription, and he asked BF to pay the first installment of 24 *l.t.;* he enclosed a handwritten receipt identical in wording to this one. On June 14, 1781, writing for what we believe was the final time, St. Hubert reexplains his project, announces that the first four volumes will appear at the end of July, 1781, asks BF for money, and encloses a new *billet de souscription.* All of these letters are at the APS. For St. Hubert see Quérard, *France littéraire.*

1. The *billet,* a blank form, is printed in italic, and St. Hubert has filled in by hand the pertinent information.

It begins to be generally beleived here, that if Sp——n has not yet declared herself in favor of Ama., that it will not be long before that happy event will take place— Mr. De Neufville of Amsterdam, whose character & sentiments I understand you are sufficiently acquainted with, writes to me in a letter of the 27th. instant thus "It seems however, there is great likelihood that Spain should have given in a declaration, for a certain House, we learned, have sold £60,000 sterling in the Stocks,[2] and this not being an indifferent one, but in the English sentiments, it was followed to day that they were in genl. 3 or 4 per Ct. cheaper than yesterday". Upon the probability of some important event for our country happening soon, I wish to lay in a claim to your attention when any dispatches may be thought necessary to be forwarded for Congress, of which I hope soon to be informed: in the mean time, whereever I may be, I shall strive to promote the interest of my country.

An opportunity for St. Eustatia offering, by which Mr. Dumas writes to Congress, I have taken the liberty of mentioning your health and good spirits in a letter to my friend Dr. Witherspoon of N. Jersey.[3]

I have the honor to be with the most perfect respect Sir your obliged & most obedient Servant. SAML. W. STOCKTON.

His Excellency B. Franklin Esquire.

Addressed: To / His Excellency / Benjamin Franklin Esquire / Minister Plenipotenitary at / The Court of Versailles &c &c &c / Passy.

To Dumas

Copy: Library of Congress

Dear Sir Passy April 29 1779

I received duly yours of the 19 inst. You have my free Consent to communicate the Letters you mention (and any others

2. *I.e.,* British government bonds, which were traded in Amsterdam.

3. Stockton was a member of the Princeton class of 1770, which graduated two years after Dr. John Witherspoon assumed the university's presidency: James McLachlan *et al.*, eds., *Princetonians: a Biographical Dictionary* (3 vols. to date, Princeton, 1976–), I, xix, 622.

that I have written) to M. L. Ambr. de F. He is a wise Man & our Friend,[4] and his Opinion & Advice, when he may think fit to give it, cannot but be useful in our Affairs. As to that M. Str. I saw him twice with Mr. de Ne. when I was ill with the Gout; but I had no particular Conversation with him & know nothing more of him. Pray who is he or what is he? what is his Connection with Mr. de Ne.? and what was the Affair that Mr. Le R—— de Ch—— employed him in? for I know nothing of it: and I am quite at a Loss to guess upon what Subject it is that you desire to have my Orders & the Intentions of the King's Ministers in order to regulate your Conduct.

I wish your Intelligence relating to Spain may be well founded.

They write to me from L'Orient that a Vessel is arrived there from Virginia, which she left the 28th of March; that the northern Armies were still in their Winter quarters, & nothing material had happened between them for some Time. That the British Army in Georgia had made no Progress & that Troops were marching against them from Carolina. That a British Sloop of War, the Swift, had run ashore in Virginia in chasing the Rattle Snake, and her Crew were all taken & sent Prisoners to Philadelphia.[5]

I hear also from Martinique, that some American Sailors who were in an English Privateer, had secured the Rest of the Crew, and carried her into that Island.[6] These are not very important News, but they are the best we have.

With great esteem I am &c

M. Dumas.

To Gourlade and Moylan

Copy: Library of Congress

Gentlemen — Passy April 29 1779

I received the Letter you did me the honor to write me & thank you for the Intelligence it contain'd.[7] There is a Rumour

4. An admiration that Silas Deane shared: *Deane Papers*, III, 12–13.
5. BF learned all this from Gourlade & Moylan's letter of April 23, above.
6. BF described the incident in his April 28 letter to Vergennes.
7. Above, April 23.

here from England of a Battle in Georgia, in which both Armies are said to have suffered extreamly:[8] but I know not whether it has any Foundation. I hear from Martinique that an English Privateer cruizing in those seas had been surprized by some American Seamen who were on Board & who carried her into that Island. I am with great Esteem &c

Mess. Gourlade et Moylan.

To Rozier[9]

Copy: Library of Congress

Sir

Passy April 29 1779

As you do my little Piece on the Aurora Borealis the Honor to suppose it may be agreeable to your philosophical Readers, I have requested M. Le Roi who read it at the Academy & has it in his Hands, to furnish you with a Correct Copy of it, which he has promised to do.[1] With great Esteem I am &c

M. L'Abbé Rozier.

To Sartine

Two copies: Library of Congress

Sir

Passy Apr. 29 1779

I have received a Letter from Mr. Wm. Bingham, Agent for the Congress at Martinique, covering the inclosed for your Excellency, and giving an Account of an unhappy Mistake, in which a Vessel belonging to some Subjects of the U. S. was sunk by one of the Batteries of Guadeloupe, & 17 of the People drowned.[2] I request your Excellency would take the

8. Reports of severe American losses at Briar Creek (on the outskirts of Savannah) in March, 1779, were issued by both Gen. Augustine Prevost and his younger brother Lt. Col. Mark Prevost: Charles C. Jones, Jr., *The History of Georgia* (2 vols., Boston, 1883), II, 349–50. The London *Public Advertiser* for April 21 printed an extract from the former's report.

9. In answer to his of April 21.

1. Le Roy's final manuscript has not survived, but one of his drafts is now at the Library of Congress. Rozier published the paper in the June issue of the *Jour. de Physique*. See above, XXVIII, 190–2.

2. XXVIII, 347–50. The enclosure was a letter to Sartine from the governor and intendant of Guadeloupe about the loss of the *Fair Play*. For further

Matter into Consideration, and if you think it a Case suitable for the Exercise of his Majesty's royal Compassion & Bounty towards the Sufferers, that you would have the goodness to recommend it accordingly. With great Respect I have the Honor to be &c.

M. de sartine.

From John Adams

ALS: American Philosophical Society

Sir Nantes Ap. 29. 1779

I had, Yesterday, the Honour of yours of the 24th. inclosing a Letter from his Excellency M. de Sartine, expressing his Majestys Desire that the Alliance Should be retained here a little longer.

As my Baggage was on board, and every Appearance promised that We should be under Sail in three or four days for America, in a fine ship and the best Month in the Year, this Intelligence, I confess, is a Dissappointment to me. The Alliance has now a very good Crew, and the little Misunderstandings between the officers and their Captain Seem to have Subsided.

The public service, however must not be obstructed for the private Convenience of an Individual, and the Honour of a Passage with the new Ambassador, should be a Compensation to me for the Loss of the prospect of So Speedy a Return home. I cannot but hope, however that the Frigate will go to Some Eastern Port, for I had rather remain here some time longer, or even take my Lott with the Alliance in her Cruise, than go to Chesapeak or even Delaware.

I shall go round to L'orient in the Alliance, and if the Frigate which is to carry the Chevalier de la Luzerne, Sails soon, shall accept with Gratitude to his Majesty, of his obliging offer of a Passage; but I hope that his Excellency, M. De Sartine, will

details see the letters from the Mass. delegates, May 12, and Tristram Dalton, May 13, below.

give the necessary orders, for this Purpose to the Frigate, otherwise, I may be under an Embarrassment still.

I Sincerely join with you in your Wishes that the Alliance may make Prisoners enough to redeem our brave and honest Countrymen who have So long Suffered in English Prisons, and make Prizes enough to reimburse the Charges of refitting.

I wish M. Dumas's Information may be well founded, and indeed it Seems to be favoured by a general Expectation from all Quarters.

A Vessel is arrived at Morlaix And another at L'orient from Virginia—the latter brings nothing that I can learn, tho some favourable Bruits have been propagated, concerning Affairs in Georgia, as from her. As the former has brought Some Virginia & Philadelphia Newspapers, I hope she may have brought, public Dispatches at least some good News. If any of either comes to your Hand proper to be communicated I should be obliged to you, for a share of it.

In a Newspaper of the 1st March, it is said that Mr Deane has asked Leave of Absence,[3] and this is all the material News, that I recollect in it excepting, indeed, G. Maxwells Letter giving an Account of the Affair of Elisabeth Town, by which it appears that the English were repulsed, and lost the Cattle and Horses they had taken, and if they had not fled with uncommon Dexterity, they would have been burgoinisès, a technical Term which I hope the Accademie will admit into the Language by lawful Authority.[4]

I have the Honour, to be with great Respect, sir, your most obedient, humble sert John Adams

His Excellency Dr Franklin

Notation: Jonh Adams Nantes 29 avril 1779.

3. In a piece by Thomas Paine printed in the March 2 *Pennsylvania Packet* and quoted in *Adams Papers,* VIII, 51n. Deane requested on March 15 that the president of Congress inform him whether he would need to testify further before Congress or whether he might return to Europe: *Deane Papers,* III, 403–4.

4. The "Affair" was an abortive February, 1779, British raid against the American position at Elizabeth, N.J.: Freeman, *Washington,* V, 147. Gen.

From Dumas

ALS: American Philosophical Society; AL (draft): Algemeen Rijksarchief

Monsieur, La Haie 29e. Avril *1779*.

Les Etats de la Province d'Hollande sont rassemblés ici depuis ce matin. Mais ce n'est qu'une Assemblée ordinaire; & notre Ami m'a dit plaisamment *Nous ne sommes venus que pour la Foire* (car dans quelques jours d'ici ce sera foire à Lahaie). Il prévoit aussi, que la Résolution des Etats-Genx. ne sera pas telle qu'elle pût engager la France à revenir de son dernier Edit de Navigation.

Une des premieres Maisons d'Amst——, dont la partialité pour l'Angleterre est connue, vient de vendre pour 60,000 £. St. de fonds Angl. Cela met tout en mouvement à Amst——, fait revivre plus que jamais l'idée d'une Déclaration de l'Espagne, & a fait baisser les fonds Anglois à Amst—— de 3 à 4 per cent. Il court un bruit sourd ici, que Mr. D'Estaing a battu Byron:[5] Un particulier ici offre de parier 100 Ducats que cela est vrai. Il pleut des brochures ici contre le dernier Mémoire de Sir J. Y.

Je suis avec tout le respectueux attachement qui vous est connu, Monsieur, Votre très-humble & très obéissant serviteur D

On distribue une suite de feuilles sous le manteau, intitulées *Lettres Hollandoises;* il y en a déjà 5.[6] Cela très violent contre le Stadh——. Elles viennent de Bruxelles. L'auteur travaille un

---

William Maxwell commanded the American defense; the commercial committee of Congress received a letter from him on March 1: *Pennsylvania Evening Post,* March 1, 1779; Smith, *Letters,* XII, 126.

5. In fact the campaign in the Caribbean was still stalemated; d'Estaing lay at Martinique awaiting the arrival of La Motte-Picquet with the troop and warship reinforcements which would permit him to take the offensive against Admiral Byron: Dull, *French Navy,* pp. 159–60.

6. Presumably ——— Dérival de Gomicourt, *Lettres hollandoises, ou Correspondance politique, sur l'état present de l'Europe* . . . (8 vols., Amsterdam, 1779–81).

peu trop vite: car il lui échappe parfois des faussetés: n'importe, on se les arrache des mains & n'en a pas qui veut.

Passy à Son Exc. Mr. Franklin

Addressed: à Son Excellence / Monsieur Franklin, Esqr. / Ministre Plénipotentiaire / des Et. Unis de l'Amérique / *Passy:*

Notation: Dumas la haie April 29. 1779

From Joshua Johnson

ALS: American Philosophical Society

Honbl. Sir Nantes 29 April 1779

Inclosed I forward you Som American Papers which I have rec'ed this Day by a Vessell from Virginia, you will be pleased to give Mr. Jennings the perusial of them when you are done with them.

I have the Honour to be Sir. Your most obed. Hble Servt

JOSHUA JOHNSON

His Excellency Benjn. Franklin Esqr.

Notation: Joshua Johnson 29 April 79

From James Lovell[7]

ALS: University of Pennsylvania Library; copy:[8] Harvard University Library

Sir Philada. April 29th.[–September 17] 1779

As the Books & Papers of the Comtee. of foreign affairs remain on the Table of Congress to be used in the public Deliberations which still continue upon a fruitful Subject begun last September you do not at this Time receive any official Letter from that Committee. But I will not omit the good opportunity by Mr. Smith, Son of the Commissioner of the Loan

7. An active member of the committee for foreign affairs: XXIV, 86n.
8. A retained copy, in Lovell's hand, without the Sept. 17 postscript.

Office here, to assure you individually of my Regards.[9] I hope you have long before now received yr. Credentials as minister Plenipotentiary from the United States. There was a dissagreable Lentor, in the public Proceedings at first, and in the sending forward yr. Testimonials afterwards. From this Source it is, I suppose, that confidential Communications have not been made to you by the french Court, so as to furnish matter for yr. Dispatches to Congress; while such have been made to us in another Channel. Sir, it behoves you much to let yr. Constituents hear often from you, lest it shd. be fully credited among us that there is but one Man in the Universe that can be pleasing to the Court of France as a Minister from hence. The Recall of Mr. Deane has given Birth to very singular Writings and Measures. You have escaped all considerable Injuries, tho you have been comprehended in some Propositions not altogether honorary, as you will shortly see by the Journals which are to be printed weekly.[1] I ought, however, now, to give you the Satisfaction of knowing that the Question about yr. Recall was only a Kind of necessary Consequence flowing from the Adoption of a Fact on which to found a Principle that might destroy the Commissions of Messrs. Lees & Izard particularly Mr. A Lee's.

In my Opinion the improper triplicate appointment for the

9. Samuel Smith, son of Thomas Smith (XXVIII, 442n) was captain of the brig *Kensington,* 14: Charles H. Lincoln, comp., *Naval Records of the American Revolution 1775–1788* (Washington, D. C., 1906), p. 364. Lovell had entrusted him with a number of packets, listed below in the postscript, and a letter of recommendation to an unidentified recipient in France. Smith was captured, and all the packets were lost; the captain presented himself to BF on Sept. 2, and by the following February he had regained control of the *Kensington* and was ready to sail back to America. Smith, *Letters,* XII, 407n; Samuel Smith to BF, Sept. 2 (APS); D'Acosta frères & Cie. to BF, Feb. 8, 1780 (Hist. Soc. of Pa.).

1. Congress voted to begin printing its journals weekly on March 31, 1779 (*JCC,* XIII, 395). Three charges were directed at BF: withholding information from Arthur Lee; concurring in Deane's "disorder and dissipation," out of partiality to JW and Chaumont; being "haughty and self sufficient, and not guided by principles of virtue or honor." *Ibid.,* 367. On April 22 Congress voted not to recall BF: *ibid.,* 500; H. James Henderson, *Party Politics in the Continental Congress* (New York, 1974), pp. 201–5.

Court of France produced, in very natural Consequence, "Suspicions & Animosities."[2] But these Evils ought not to be made Reasons for depriving the public of the Services of Men whose great Abilities Integrity & Industry may be exerted in distinct Trusts without the like future Inconveniences.

Disappointed Views have generated an Implacability against the falsely supposed Cause of that Dissappointment. Nothing short of the Ruin of the Reputation of Arthur Lee will glut the malice of a party formed against him by that Spirit of assassinating Innuendo which so eminently governs his Arch Enemy.

I expect to be able in a few days to communicate to you the Decission of Congress in Regard to the other Gentlemen, and some particular Instructions for your own Government. I refer you to the Gazettes for a general State of military Proceedings, and to common Fame for the ill Condition of our Currency.

I am Sir Your most humb. Servt. JAMES LOVELL

Honble. Doctr Franklin

Copy (private)

P.S. Sepr. 17

I have only this day heard of the Capture of Mr. Smith, and I do not find by my Memoranda that I have sent any Copy of what he carried, which I find to be thus minuted at the time of his sailing. Apr 30th.[3]

4plic: 7 } Hopkinson
3plic: 8 }

my own To J Adams 28th.
To A. Lee 28
To Doctr. Franklin 29
To Jona. Williams 29

2. A phrase from the March 24, 1779, report of the foreign affairs committee to Congress that preceded the charges against the individual ministers. For the entire text see *JCC,* XIII, 363–8.

3. Days later, Lovell told Arthur Lee that he had retained a copy of only one letter, this one to BF: Smith, *Letters,* XIII, 534–5.

Mr. Jays To Doctr. Franklin
To Marqs Fayette
—— Pamphlets and Gazettes to the Doctor

From Dumas

ALS: American Philosophical Society; copy: Algemeen Rijksarchief

Monsieur, Lahaie 30e. Avril *1779*

J'eus l'honneur de vous écrire hier par Rotterdam. Je viens de chez notre Ami, à qui j'ai demandé s'il étoit vrai qu'il avoit dit à g—— F——, que la Ville d'Amsterdam desiroit qu'on n'exécutât pas trop à la rigueur le dernier Edit françois de Navigation? Il m'a assuré qu'il ne l'avoit pas dit; qu'au contraire sa ville comptoit sur l'exécution stricte de cet Edit, puisqu'autrement le parti adverse croiroit que le tout n'est pas sérieux, & s'opiniâtreroit plus que jamais.

Il m'a dit aussi, que le Pensionaire de Rotterdam étoit venu le voir,[4] & l'avoit prié à mains jointes, & d'un ton de désespoir, d'interposer ses bons offices & ceux de sa ville auprès de la Cour de France, pour faire lever l'interdit fulminé contre eux; mais qu'il lui avoit répondu ne pouvoir rien là-dedans, ni lui ni sa ville; qu'il falloit s'adresser à celui qui les avoit plantés dans la bourbe, pour les en retirer.[5] Pauvre consolation pour la Magistrature de Rotterdam, qui, d'un côté, craint une émeute (Car il y a beaucoup de fermentation), &, de l'autre, sent fort bien que la France ne leur fera aucune grace pour l'amour d'un Pce [Prince], qui vient de se declarer si hautement contre elle.

Enfin il m'a répété, que non seulement la Magistrature, mais aussi le gros des Négociants, sont très contents du tour qu'ont pris les choses, & très-résolus de tenir fermes. Ainsi, si l'on disoit ou écrivoit le contraire, croyez que c'est des gens dont les uns trompent, & les autres se laissent tromper. Je réponds

4. Probably Herman van Nederburgh or Nederburg for whom see *NNWB,* v, 357, and F. J. L. Krämer, ed., *Archives, ou correspondance inédite de la maison d'Orange-Nassau* (5th ser.; 3 vols., Leiden, 1910–15), I, 424n.

5. The remainder of the paragraph was written in the margin and marked for insertion at this point in the text.

de la vérité de ce que dessus. Je suis, Monsieur, avec un grand respect, Votre très-humble & très Obéissant serviteur D

P.S. Notre Ami déplore avec moi, toutes les fois que nous nous voyons, l'extrême disette de nouvelles Américaines authentiques. Depuis longtemps on n'en a d'autre ici que par le canal des ennemis, qui ne cessent de prôner sans contradiction leur succès, & de peindre les Am—— comme un peuple désuni & discordant, dont l'union ne subsistera pas, & qui va rentrer en détail sous leur obéissance. Ces répétitions éternelles, sans faire impression sur nous, nous désolent & fatiguent vis-à-vis des ames foibles, que nous devons continuellement rassurer. Nous sommes come Job au milieu de ses parens inquiets & inquiétants.

Passy à Son Exc. Mr. Franklin.

Addressed: à Son Excellence / Monsieur Franklin, Ministre / Plénipotentiaire des Etats-Unis / de l'Amérique / à *Passy*./.

Notation: Dumas la haie April 30. 79

From Benjamin Vaughan

ALS: American Philosophical Society

My dearest sir, London, April 30h:, 1779.

I sent you a pacquet with a number of sheets of your printed papers; which I suppose you have received, though as yet I have not had it signified to me.[6] I send you more sheets which now lie by me; and have still another or two finished, which I believe are with the printer. I send you also all that I have written out of my remarks on *motion* &c &c: it contains a *part* of my annotations only, on Mr Baxter, for I mean him another sentence or two; and it does not go down to the place where I give an apology to you.[7] In the printed collection, I mean to give *two notes* on your paper; one explanatory of the occasion of writing on your part and of Mr Baxter's applica-

6. He sent the packet with his letter of April 9.
7. Vaughan had sent an outline of these remarks on April 9.

tion of his system on the other part; the second note merely affirms that your position, that "equal celerity is the measuring the *same* spaces by moving bodies in equal times", is perhaps not entirely accurate, and that cases where bodies do not move *fast* enough to apply their force to encrease the speed of previously moving bodies (see your 2nd: par:) prove that celerity and force are distinct things.— I do not know whether I express myself clearly here, but I shall study to do it in the note, which I must send to press instantly almost.[8]

I have no news to send you. The public papers will tell you the debates of Friday sufficiently I suppose; I shall therefore say nothing of them.— I believe that Ld. Sandwich will be out of the Admiralty;—out of ministry or favor, are different things. The Marlborough people have done this, we suppose; for had not the cabinet promise been given them, they would have voted against him: But it was thought better to be the work of the *king,* than of opposition.[9] This seems the persuasion of well informed people: But we shall see the event.— We seem in other respects growing more and more quiet. Strong have been the expectations of some, for peace and Spanish neutrality: Of course you have been talked of in the business.— I think all that oppostion have done, has been to convince many in the majority and in the city, and a number also in the country, that the present ministry are a careless, divided, and insufficient set of people; not immediately plun-

8. The footnote appears on p. 483 of Vaughan's edition. For Andrew Baxter see XXVII, 202n.

9. Sandwich's removal from the Admiralty had been moved in the House of Lords on April 23 by the Earl of Bristol, but the motion failed to carry; see *The Public Advertiser,* April 24 and 26, 1779. George Spencer, 4th Duke of Marlborough (XII, 96n), was hostile to Sandwich after the Keppel-Palliser affair but he and his followers were dissuaded by William Eden from voting for Sandwich's dismissal. The following September, Marlborough's younger brother, Lord Charles Spencer (1740–1820), became Treasurer of the King's Chamber: Namier and Brooke, *House of Commons,* III, 459. As late as April 16, Lord North was still making suggestions to George III for reshuffling the cabinet (Fortescue, *Correspondence of George Third,* IV, 325), which may have fueled speculation that Sandwich would be appointed to a different office; see XXVIII, 484n.

dering themselves, but getting *themselves regular* emoluments and honors, and suffering all sort of plunder under them.— There is much want of harmony in the fleet at Portsmouth; but if this man Ld. Sandwich goes out, we shall possibly have Mr Keppel again in command.— I think Genl. B. made a very poor imbecil figure last night; without powers, and a tattered motley cause into the bargain, or rather a very bad one, only that ministry were bad on their side too.—[1] Your friends are all well, and I think every body daily more respects you. Even Ld. North says, that you are the only man at Paris whose hands are pure from stock-jobbing.[2] I need not tell you that my respect never can ebb and go back, but increases, as I would tell you if I could find words stronger than I have already used.

BV.

The bearer is a relation of the Duc de Chartres, and was made known to me one evening in the Shipley family.[3]

Notations in different hands: B. Vaughn Apr. 30. 79 / London

From Chaumont

AL: American Philosophical Society

[*c.* April, 1779][4]

Chaumont a L'honneur de prevenir Monsieur le Docteur franklin que le Courier de Bretagne part aujourdhuy a Deux heures et que si M. franklin a des ordres a faire passer a

1. During the House of Commons inquiry into the conduct of the American war, Burgoyne enumerated the hardships he had suffered and attributed them to "a determined Resolution in Administration to ruin his Military Reputation and Fortune . . .": *The Public Advertiser,* April 30, 1779.

2. Apparently North once thought otherwise. In January, 1778, he believed all the American Commissioners to be stock-jobbing, but Hartley claimed to have convinced him of BF's honesty: XXV, 417n, 691.

3. The bearer was Labussiere. See his letter of May 11 and Georgiana Shipley's of May 1.

4. Probably written between April 20, when Sartine wrote BF of La Luzerne's appointment (although he did not immediately reveal the new minister's name) and April 28, or shortly thereafter, when Chaumont must have left Passy for Lorient (see Chaumont's letter of May 2).

Nantes a M. Landais Commandant La fregatte L'alliance il est Bien important que sa Lettre soit avant deux heures a la grande poste et quelle y soit postée fidelement.

M. le Chever. de La Luzerne demeure au Marais Rue des Blancs Manteaus.

Memorandum on a Proposed Dutch Loan[5]

D: Archives du Ministère des affaires étrangères

[April, 1779]

M. de Neuville d'amsterdam Continue a Donner de Bonnes Esperances Sur L'emprunt de M. franklin, qu'il n'a fait que pressentir parceque L'emprunt de Langleterre, La prise de Ste. Lucie, Celle de Pondichery[6] et quelque tentatives Reelles ou Supposées de M. Neker pour trouver de L'argeant en hollande, luy ont parus trop importants pour operer en mesme tems pour Compte des americains. Les pertes immenses du Commerce de france ne Laisseroient aucun Espoir de Ressource dans Les Banquiers de Paris, qui gardent tous Leurs moyens pour Secourir et encore très faiblement Les Negotiants des Ports. Les Bezoings de M. franklin ne Sont pas urgents et il faut Esperer que M de Neufville aura procuré des fonds avant que Ceux de M. franklin Soyent epuisés.

avril 1779

5. This statement by Jean de Neufville of his continued optimism for the chances of negotiating a loan in Holland is in the hand of Chaumont, who sometimes acted as an intermediary between BF and Vergennes and who presumably furnished the memorandum to the foreign ministry. We believe it provides information intended by de Neufville for BF. The American minister himself discussed French finances in his May 26 letter to the committee for foreign affairs. For his skepticism about the success of de Neufville's efforts see his March 12 letter to Dumas.

6. The March 23 issue of the *Gaz. de Leyde* (no. 24, supp.) carried news of the capitulation five months earlier of Pondicherry, the chief French trading post in India. The Caribbean island of St. Lucia was captured by the British in December, 1778: XXVIII, 347–50.

To Sartine

Copies: Archives de la Marine, Library of Congress[7]

De Passy le 1er May 1779

Conformement à la demande de Votre Excellence je vous envoye cy joint les lettres et les instructions que j'ai adressées aux Captn Jones et Landais.[8]

Je suis très respectueusement De Votre Excellence Le très humble et très obeissant Serviteur B FRANKLIN

Lettre de M. Benjamin franklin

From John Paul Jones

LS: American Philosophical Society; AL (draft):[9] Library of Congress; copies: United States Naval Academy Museum, National Archives

Honored and dear Sir. L'Orient May 1st. 1779.

The letter which I had the honor to receive from your Excellency to day together with your liberal and noble minded instructions would make a Coward brave.—[1] You have called up every sentiment of public virtue in my breast and it shall be my pride and ambition in the strict Pursuit of your instructions *to deserve success.*

If I have any abilities they shall be exerted to the utmost and I am under no fear of disorders under my command— Since I shall treat persons who behave well and do their Duty with all possible civility—and such as misbeheave, must take the consequence agreeable to the rules and regulations, which Congress have instituted for the government of our Marine.— Between the principals in command[2] since they love and esteem one another no disunion need be apprehended—and each will I am convinced do his utmost to promote a general good

7. In English.

8. Sartine's request is that of April 27. The communications to Landais are dated April 24 and 28, and to Jones the 27th and 28th of the same month. All are above.

9. Lacking the postscript.

1. BF's letter is that of April 27, and his instructions were dated the following day. Both were brought by Chaumont: Chaumont to BF, May 2.

2. Jones and Lafayette.

understanding.— Be assured that very few prospects could Afford one so true a satisfaction as that of rendering some acceptable service to the common cause and at the same time Releiving from captivity, by furnishing the means of exchange for, our unfortunate fellow subjects who are Prisoners of war in the hands of our Enemies.

It only remains that I Return your Excellency my most hearty and sincere thanks for the many past instances which I have experienced of your delicate friendship, favor and affection Especially in this last instance of your particular confidence.

I am and shall be to the end of my life with the most affectionate esteem and Respect, Honored and dear Sir Your most obliged Friend & Most obedient very humble Servant

JNO P JONES

N.B. I take the liberty to inclose the Memoire of a young gentleman who has waited here a long time of his own accord to Embark with me[3] as I have a Particular regard for his character if you think fit to Send his paper to Court I Should be glad to have him with me— I Can find no person so proper to Disciplin the Voluntier Soldiers that I have inlisted.

His Excellency Doctor Franklin. &c. &c. &c.

Notation: P. Jones L'Orient 1. may 1779.

From Landais

ALS: American Philosophical Society

Please Your Excellency Nantes May 1st 1779

I Received Your Favour of the 24 ult. and went directly down the River to the Ship to aquaint the Honnble John Adam

3. BF forwarded a memorial to Sartine on the 8th and Sartine's reply of the 18th identifies the author as an officer in the Walsh regiment (of the Irish Brigade) named Stack. This was Edward Stack (1750–1833), who became an officer of marines aboard the *Bonhomme Richard:* Richard Hayes, *Biographical Dictionary of Irishmen in France* (Dublin, 1949), pp. 290–1. He had been recommended to Jones by a captain in his regiment: Bradford, *Jones Papers,* reel 3, no. 516.

with the order you geve me.[4] The wind is So high that no loaded buts can go aboard, I'll do my utmost to fullfil your order as Soon as possible— I have recruted already fourty three fore mast men among the american Prisonners besides the Captains that are willings to enter as volontiers. I which I Should find your futur orders at my arrival at Port L'Orient, and know wheither I am to have the Ship Careen or to go directly on a Cruse for to loose no time in putting them in execution.

I am with the Greateast Respect Your Excellency Most Obeidient Most humble Servant. P. LANDAIS

To his Excellency Bn Franklin Minister Plenipotentary of the united States of America

Addressed: To / His Excellency Bn Francklin / Minister Plenipotentary of the united States / Of America at Passy / Paris

Notation: P. Landais. May 1st 79.

From Georgiana Shipley — ALS: American Philosophical Society

Bolton Street May 1st 1779

As another opportunity offers of conveying a letter to my dear Doctor Franklin, I cannot resist the strong inclination I feel of once more writing to you, especially as I flatter myself that you still retain your former friendship & partiality for this family, & consequently that you will be always glad to hear from any part of it.

Since you left England I am grown a very *great* politician, after this open declaration you will perhaps expect some account of our public affairs, but prudence requires me to be silent on the subject.

I fancy it will not now be long before we visit Twyford, no

4. JA must have told Landais he would accompany the *Alliance* to Lorient (where he would meet the French frigate that would take him to America); see JA's letter of April 29. BF's instructions to Landais had mentioned only that JA would not need passage to America on the *Alliance*.

alterations have been made there since your departure, your Summer-house remains in the same state; I wish there was any probability of your occupying it again, but I dare not allow myself to think that such an happiness is reserved for us.

I know of no late publications worth recommending to you; Johnson's lives of the English Poets is a new work & admired by those whom, I have heard mention it, although it is in parts tainted with his own odious political principles.[5]

Monsieur de la Bussiere will have the pleasure of delivering this letter into your hands, he came to England strongly recommended to us, & we are much pleased with the little we have seen of him, he appears a modest pretty sort of young Man, & very ambitious of being personally known to you; indeed the terms in which he spoke of you, prejudiced us greatly in his favor.[6]

The American Squirrel is still living, & much caress'd; poor fellow! he is grown quite old & has lost his eye-sight, but nevertheless preserves his spirits & wonted activity.[7] Numberless are the prints & medals we have seen of you, but none that I quite approve, should you have a good picture painted at Paris, a miniature copied from it, would make me the happiest of beings, & next to that, a lock of your own dear grey hair would give me the greatest pleasure; my father has had a wax model taken of him, it is not yet finished, but if it should prove like, I will manage to send you one, in the mean time I enclose a shade,[8] which I think you will be pleased with, he never mentions your name without tenderness & admiration; & often laments, that one part of his share in the public misfortunes is to have lost the enjoyment of the most valuable friendship he ever made. Doctor Priestley & Doctor Price two sincere friends & admirers of yours, dined here yesterday when your health was drank with pleasure by the whole com-

5. Samuel Johnson, *The Works of the English Poets. With Prefaces, Biographical and Critical* (68 vols., London, 1779–81). BF had inveighed against this "Court Pensioner" to Bishop Shipley in 1775: XXII, 97.

6. Labussiere wrote BF on May 11, below, about delivering this letter.

7. DF had sent Beebee in 1773 to replace Mungo, his ill-fated predecessor: XIX, 43–4, 59, 300–2; XX, 449; XXI, 397.

8. Silhouette.

pany. Anna Maria is impatient to hear whether you have received a few lines, she sent by Gen. Verdiere.

If I have encroached too much upon your time, pray forgive me; for while I am writing to you the respect & deference due to so great a character is almost lost in the love & affection I feel for an old friend, whose indulgence I have often experienced, & whose esteem it will ever be my pride & happiness to deserve. My Mother & Sisters are well, & unite in good wishes. I am Your gratefull & affecate GEORGIANA SHIPLEY

The ode I send is much admired. The subject has animated the Poet.

From Jonathan Williams, Jr.

ALS: American Philosophical Society; copy: Yale University Library

Dear & hond Sir Nantes May 1. 1779.—

In the Newspapers which Mr. Johnson sent you last post you will see an Extract from one of my Letters to Mr Dean in which the word *Connection* is mentioned and represented as a proof that I had some commercial Concerns with Mr Dean. I send you enclosed a Copy of the whole of the Letter & you will see that the Paragraph has no such relation, & cannot, but by evident malice be so construed.— Mr Dean supposed he had some Enemies here & desired me if I heard anything to his Prejudice to let him know who his Enemies were. I told him naturaly that "my Connection with him being known" People generaly avoided speaking of him before me and so I should have written to any other Friend in a similar occasion. There are some silly People also who dont like you, & these People are ashamed to say anything against you in my Presence, because they know my *Connexion* with you. Does this imply that you & I are trading on the Public money? The Connexion I had with Mr Dean was the same I had with you & with Mr Lee at that Time, and as to commercial Connexions with Mr Dean, I am happy to be able to lay my hand on my heart & declare upon my Honour, that *I have never been, directly or indirectly conserned with him in any trading scheme what-*

ever to the value of a single Livre. As to my desiring an approbation of my Drafts, it was common Sense, for without it, how could I expect any man to buy a Bill of me? And I therefore wrote to the same Purpose to the Commissioners the 14th & 21 of the same month. These very Drafts are accordingly approved by you & Mr Adams.— If I had any private underhand Concerns with Mr Dean, I should have been a Fool as well as a Knave to write the same thing to the Commissioners.— The Part of the Letter which speaks of my Friend C was on acct of the Difference which happened between Mr Carmichael & Mr Dean, and which I tried to accomodate as you will see.—

I am without your answer about Mr Gourlades Demand.— I have written to Mr Cummings & Mr Nesbit requesting them to return to examine my acct free of Expence to them, but am as yet without an answer which surprizes me.[9] I therefore by this Post send them a Copy of my Letter.—

I am ever with the greatest Respect Your dutifull & affectionate Kinsman JONA WILLIAMS J

The Hon. Doctor Franklin.

Notation: Jona Williams May 1. 79

From Chaumont

ALS: American Philosophical Society

Monsieur. L'orient ce 2 may 1779.

J'ay L'honneur de Remettre a Vostre Excellence, La Reponse du Cape. Jones a La Lettre dont vous m'avez Chargé.[1] Je Compte qu'il poura apareiller Le quinze pour executer Les ordres de Vostre Excellence. Permettez moy de vous prier de faire Remettre Sans Retard La Depesche incluse a M. Le Mar-

9. JW had written jointly to James Cuming and Jonathan Nesbitt, both merchants in Lorient, on April 15. They accepted his proposal in a letter written on April 30; JW received it on May 2, and acknowledged it on the same day. Copies of both of JW's letters are in the Yale University Library.

1. Chaumont brought to Lorient BF's April 27 orders to Jones and the April 28 detailed instructions; Jones's response is that of May 1. For Chaumont's assistance in the joint Jones-Lafayette expedition see our annotation of Lafayette's March 31 letter to BF.

quis de la fayette,[2] par quelqu'un qui ne Scache pas d'ou elle vient.

Agreez L'asseurance du tendre et Respectueux attachement avec lequel J'ay L'honneur d'estre Monsieur Vostre tres humble et tres obeissant Serviteur LERAY DE CHAUMONT

Permettez moy de vous prier d'envoyer par M. vostre fils la Lettre a M. de Sartine et qu'il aye la Bonté de S'informer Sil n'est pas a Paris avant de la porter a Marly.[3]

M. le Docteur franklin.

From John Paul Jones

ALS: American Philosophical Society; copies: United States Naval Academy Museum, National Archives

Honored and dear Sir, L'Orient May 2d. 1779

The within paper I have this moment recd.— It comes from some unfortunate Men who were made Prisoners when the Gallant Montgomery fell in his attack on Quebec.—[4] I am so much indisposed to day that I am obliged to write to you in Bed— I have however Sent to ask if the Commandant if he can consistently release these poor Men who have by our Savage Enemies been thus Enslaved—he Sends me word that as the Garrison of Senegal Surrendered conditionally that the Troops in it Should be sent to England—and that as he now

2. Jones's May 1 answer to Lafayette's letter of April 27 (Idzerda, *Lafayette Papers,* II, 258–60, 264–5). Jones's letter reported that Chaumont was attempting to resolve the American's problems with cannon; if he was successful the *Bonhomme Richard* would soon be ready.

3. Chaumont is asking WTF to deliver a letter of May 1 from Jones to Sartine acknowledging receipt (via Chaumont) of Sartine's April 27 orders to transport Lafayette's troops: Bradford, *Jones Papers,* reel 3, nos. 579, 591.

4. The enclosure, now at the APS, is reproduced in Bradford, *Jones Papers,* reel 3, no. 594. When the French had captured the British garrison at Senegal in late January they repatriated their prisoners back to England. Among them, said the enclosed paper, were sixteen Americans first captured by the British at Quebec, who now wished to serve with Jones. BF relayed the request to Sartine: below, May 8.

has Orders to forward them to St. Malo for that purpose it is not in his power to give them up to me without Orders for that purpose from Court.

I need add nothing more than that I am ever with a heartfelt Affection Dear Sir your truely Obligd Friend & Servt.

JNO P JONES

His Excellency Doctor Franklin.

Addressed: His Excellency / Doctor Franklin / American Ambassador at the / Court of France / en son Hótel / a Passy. / (Pres Paris)

Notation: P. Jones L'orient 2 may 1779.

From Arthur Lee

LS:[5] American Philosophical Society; ALS (draft): National Archives; copy: Harvard University Library

Sir/ Paris May 2d. 1779

By letters this day from Nantes, I am informd that the Alliance Frigate is mann'd, & ready to sail. Adverse winds still detain the American fleet at Brest with its Convoy.[6] As that Convoy is destind for the french Islands it will of course leave those Vessels which are intended for the United States before they reach the Coast. Yet there it is that not only from the Enemy's Cruisers, but from the multitude of their Privateers lately fitted out, they will run the greatest risque. Not only the public at large is highly interested in the safe arrival of this fleet, but the State of Virginia depends upon it for supplies essentially necessary for her defence & preservation. The difficulty with which these have been obtaind; & the impossibility of replacing them if lost, makes it of the last importance to use every possible means for their protection.[7]

5. In the hand of Ludwell Lee.

6. For the convoy see BF's response of May 3 to Lee.

7. Lee had intervened in the procurement of arms and war supplies for Virginia, even going so far as to extend his own credit to help cover their

For these reasons I presume to submit to your consideration, whether the Alliance can render a more useful & acceptable service to our Country, than by immediately joining the fleet at Brest, & conveying it quite to our ports.

I have the honor to be, with the greatest respect Sir Your most Obedt Hble Servt.
ARTHUR LEE

The Honble. B. Franklin Esqr

Endorsed: Arthur Lee May 2d. 1779;

To Benjamin Franklin Bache

ALS: Yale University Library

Dear Benny
Passy, May 3. 1779

I received your Letter,[8] and it gave me great Pleasure to hear of your safe Arrival at Geneva, & of your being plac'd in your Pension. You now have a fine Opportunity of learning those things that will be reputable and useful to you when you come to be a Man; and you will make your Father and Mother very happy to hear that you mind your Studies and improve daily, which I hope I shall be able to assure them of.— You ought to be very respectful to Mr Cramer, who was so kind as to take the Trouble & Care of carrying You to Geneva; and as a good Boy I am persuaded you will be very dutiful to M. de Marignac, and attentive to his Instructions.— Your Friends Cochran & Deane[9] dined with us last Sunday & are well. Your Cousin joins his Love with that of

YOUR AFFECTIONATE GRANDFATHER

---

purchase; see XXVII, 361–3, for a summary, and *Jefferson Papers,* III, 90–3. In March, 1779, he went to Nantes to oversee the shipping of the supplies: Louis W. Potts, *Arthur Lee: a Virtuous Revolutionary* (Baton Rouge and London, 1981), p. 222.

8. BFB's first letter from Geneva, printed under April 20, above.

9. BFB's friends and schoolmates at Passy were Charles B. Cochran (XXVII, 262n; XXVIII, 326) and Jesse Deane (XXV, 646).

To Arthur Lee[1]

Copies: Library of Congress, Harvard University Library

Sir Passy may 3 1779.

I did write to the Gentlemen at Nantes concern'd in fitting out the Vessels for America, offering them the Alliance as a Convoy and order'd her to Nantes accordingly.[2] They did not chuse to accept that offer Knowing, as I Supose, her Weakness, but Sail'd for Brest, to go with the french Convoy[3] without waiting her arrival and would probably have been gone long before she could have been fitted for Sea, if contrary Winds had not prevented. I wish your Information were true, that she is mann'd and fit for such Service. It must be from some Person who is unacquainted with the facts, perhaps Mr. ford. I must suppose the Merchants are Satisfied with the Convoy they have put their ships under, as I do not learn that they, have applied for one more suitable. I would readily have sollicited such an Application if I had understood it to be necessary, being equally desirous with you of their arriving safe, and sensible of the Importance of it. But I have not received a line from any of them to any such purpose; and Capitain Landais has assured me, that my supposition of his having Men sufficient to fight his Ship on occasion in going home tho' not enough to man Prizes on a Cruize, was a great Mistake in my informer. He then wanted 150 men,[4] & I have not Since heard of his having recruited more than 40 with the exchanged Americans from England. Mr. ford may probably be accommodated in the same frigate that will take Mr. Adams. I have the honour to be with great respect Sir Y. m. o. h. S.

1. In answer to Lee's of the previous day.

2. XXVIII, 589–90.

3. A convoy to the West Indies which had been joined by American merchantmen; see BF's April 24 letters to JA and Landais. It sailed from Brest on May 1, picked up additional ships at La Rochelle, and reached Martinique on June 27: Auphan, "Communications," p. 345; Dull, *French Navy,* p. 160.

4. On his arrival at Brest Landais claimed to be short at least one hundred crewmen: XXVIII, 488. His letter of March 17, above, echoed his complaint of insufficient seamen to man his ship.

P.S. I am glad to hear from you, that supplies necessary for Virginia are shipt.

Honble. Arthur Lee Esq.

To Vergennes

LS:[5] Archives du Ministère des affaires étrangères; copy: Library of Congress

Sir, Passy May 3d. 1779:

When I last had the honor of waiting upon your Excellency, I mentioned certain Applications from the States of Virginia and Maryland, for Arms, Ammunition and Clothing, which I am desired by their Agents here to sollicit.[6] I should sooner have presented your Excellency a Note of the Particulars, which I now enclose, but that Treaties have been attempted with private Persons to furnish the Articles wanted. Those Treaties not succeeding, I am obliged at length to request your Excellency would take the Trouble of considering the Application, and favour it, if you shall think it reasonable. The respective States propose and promise to pay for what is supply'd to each of them, as soon as the War is over; But as their Letters are dated near a year since,[7] and possibly a part of their Wants may have been supply'd by the Congress, and as the Agents have desired *me* to engage for the Payment I should imagine that if his Majesty should think fit to grant such Aids, they would be best granted to the Congress, who will take care to supply particular States, & be accountable for the whole. In which Case it would be well to double the Quantity of Clothing and small Arms, as the Congress have order'd great Quantities, which we are not able to purchase for want of Money. And could any Part of these Supplies be ready to go with the new Minister, I submit it to your Excel-

5. In WTF's hand.

6. William Lee and Joshua Johnson.

7. Virginia's list of supplies dated from March, 1778, Maryland's from a month later: XXVI, 34–5, 227–8.

lency's Consideration whether it would not be well to put them under his Care; and if all could not be ready, to let him bear the Promise of the rest; as this might be a means of making his Arrival the more welcome; and more generally pleasing, and facilitate his Negociations.[8]

I am with great Respect, Your Excellencys most obedient and most humble Servant. B FRANKLIN

His Exy. M. Le Comte De Vergennes.

Notations: M de Rayneval / M. francklin / rep le 6 may.

The following Articles are wanted for the State of Maryland. viz.

10,000 Stand of Arms compleat, including Cartridge Boxes, &ca.
10. Brass Field Pieces, of 4 & 6 lb Ball with their Carriages and Harness
8 Howits of 9 Inches
50. Pieces of Flannel for Cartridges
5,000. Suits of Soldiers Clothes, ready made
10,000. Pair of Stockings
10,000 Hats
10,000. Blankets
1,000 Tents
20 Tons of Lead
Cloth and Trimmings for the clothing of 350 Officers.

Wanted for the State of Virginia
16. Iron Cannon of 36 lb Ball
20. Do of.......... 24 lb.
8 Brass Do....of 24 lb.
50. Rounds of Grape Shot } For each of
50 Ditto of chain & doubled headed Do } the Cannon
Carriages Rammers, Ladles, and all the necessary Apparatus for the above Cannon
6. Brass Howitzers 5 Inch
4 Do ....5½.

8. The chevalier de La Luzerne was awaiting the departure for America of the frigate *Sensible;* see our annotation of Sartine's April 20 letter.

100. Shells for each Howitzer, with Fuzees, Match-stuff, Carriages, and every thing compleat
20,000 Stands of Fusils and Bayonets compleat
30 Tons of best Cannon Powder
20 Tons Do for Fusils.
Saddles, Carbines, Boots, spurs, &ca. for 100 Light Horse.

These Things the respective Governments engage to pay for. B FRANKLIN

From Madame Brillon

AL: American Philosophical Society

ce 3 may [1779][9] a passy

Je vous remércie bien mon bon papa de l'intérést que vous prenés a ma santé, elle est moins mauvaise mais mon áme est bien malade; c'est cétte áme honneste et trop sensible qui me mine et me tuë: il m'est absolument nécéssaire d'avoir avéc vous une convérsation longue et détaillés; je veux que vous connoissiés a fond mon coeur et ceux qui l'ont bléssé d'une maniére cruélle— il est peut estre important pour vous de sçavoir une chose qui peut un jour vous regardér; voulés vous, pouvés vous me recevoir aprés demain mércredi a dix heures du matin, et faire férmér votre porte une heure, afin que mon áme s'épenche dans la vôtre pour en recevoir des consolations et des conseils: répondés moi un mot sur le champ, il ne faut pas qu'on sache que vous m'écrivés et que j'irai chés vous: adieu vous éstes mon pére, c'est a ce titre que j'ai besoin plus que jamais de la cértitude de votre amitié:

Addressed: A Monsieur / Monsieur Franklin / [*In another hand*] A Passy

9. Mme. Brillon's next two letters, of May 8 and 11 (the latter of which provides the year as well as the month and day), throw light on this one: what she wants to warn BF against is that her husband's mistress, the now unemployed Mlle. Jupin, plans—at Chaumont's suggestion—to manage the Franklin household. For the early stages of this crisis see XXVIII, 8n, 215n, 599n.

From James Conner

ALS: American Philosophical Society

Sir Saumur Castle[1] may 3th 1779

I make bold to truble you with a few Lines to aquant you that I am an Amarican born at Garmaintown Seven miles from Pheladelphea and have at this time a Wife and famley thir so I hope you will asist me in giting me in to my Contreys Servous as I never had an Opertunity in giting thir before now. I shiped my self on board the London Packit Capt Cook[2] to Jamaca and Bristow Just before the Ports was Shut up so I Left hir at Bristow in hopes of giting home and Shiped my Self in Brig Capt Haman bound to Pheladelphea but She altered hir Voiage and toke a Cargo in for the Granadeas wich disipointed me in giting home. And I never had an Oppertunity in giting home Since as we went from the grenadeas to Saltatudes and toke in a Cargo of Salt for Barbadoes and was thir pressed on board an Englash Man of War but Stayed not Long thir be fore I got in to the Marchant Servous.

Sir I would have aplyd my Self to you Sowner but I wrote to Capt Paul Jones and wated with impatious for an answer this Six Weeks Sir if you would be pleaseed to Honour me with answer I Shall take it as the Greatest favours. Sir thir is a Natave of Gannea wen he found I was aplyeing my Self to go into my Contreys Servous begded I would mention him in my Letter that he would be glad to go into the Amarican Servous.

So Sir I remain your Most Obdent Humble Sirvant

James Conner

Addressed: To / Dockter Franklane / in / Paires. / France

Notation: James Conner Saumur Castle May 3d. 1779

From Nicholas Davis

ALS: American Philosophical Society

Sir Amsterdam May 3d 1779

When I had the pleasure of seeing you in Paris Jany. was two years I was in hopes that I was in the high road to

1. Thirty miles southeast of Angers.
2. The ship that carried Thomas Paine to Pennsylvania: XXI, 516.

preferment[3] and honour: As you have no doubt Sir long before now had the particulars of the Ship La Seins being taken by an Eng. Man of War in a few hours after leaving Martinico I imagine it would be unnecessary my adding any thing on that disagreeable subject—[4] I only would beg leave to observe that I used every endeavour on my part and suffer'd myself to be imprison'd sooner than I would (notwithstanding all the threats of the Atty. Genl. at Dominica) answer to Interrog. nor would I have done it at last if I had not been inform'd that the man whom we took on board at Martinico to Pilot us into Boston suffer'd Mr. Binghams order (to the secret Committe at Boston) for the Pilotage of the Ship to be taken upon him, wch. would have Condemn'd her without any thing else.— I got away from Dominica to Martinio. from whence I went to Phila. abot. 3 mos before the British Army got there and my Affairs were under consideration of Congress just at that time.[5]

Money growing short I was oblig'd to leave Phila. and went to my relation Mr. George Mead (who was then at Kennet Square) in order to get some and upon my return to Phila. the British Army were in possession of it—[6] I was frequently solicited by the British to accept of a Majority in their newly rais'd levies which I allways spurn'd at— I took the first Opportunity of a Ship for London where I knew I had some friends that would assist me which I stood much in need of— My father Mr. Anthy Davis[7] was a sugar baker and Distiller in

3. He first wrote "glory". For this American who had obtained money from the commissioners under false pretenses see XXIII, 193. On May 9, below, BF warned Coffyn, Dumas, and Fizeaux, Grand & Cie. against advancing the man any money.

4. For the capture of the *Seine* see XXIII, 560–1. Davis' conduct upon being captured was, according to William Bingham, "perfidious and treacherous": XXIII, 616.

5. *JCC*, VIII, 534. Although the outcome of the Congressional investigation is unknown, letters written by two delegates seem to indicate he was not punished. Smith, *Letters*, VII, 237, 317.

6. Meade (1741–1808) was a prominent Philadelphia merchant: *DAB*. Kennett Square was then a tiny village about thirty miles southwest of Philadelphia. Thomas F. Gordon, *A Gazetteer of the State of Pennsylvania* (Philadelphia, 1832), p. 221.

7. See *Sibley's Harvard Graduates*, IX, 529–30.

Boston which he quitted with his family in 1755 and went to Jama. he afterwards came to Engd. took orders in the Church and return'd to Jamaica where he enjoyd for 10 years an exceeding good living.

Had the La Sein got into Boston I flatter myself I should have shared in the glory and honour which my Countrymen have acquired as well as have avoided many distresses— I should be very glad could I get to France and go out as Capt. of Marines on board some stout Frigate (a Privateer I mean) either french or American by which means if successful I might have it in my power to pay what I am indebted to the Congress which I meant to have paid out of the Proffits arising upon the goods I had on board the La Sein—[8] My present very unhappy and truly distress'd situation will I trust plead my apology for this trespass and flatter myself that I shall find some relief in it's reception— It would afford me infinite pleasure and satisfaction could I be of any service to my Country and wou'd be happy in persuing any plan for that purpose which you might be pleas'd to adopt— The unavoidable expence which attends my stay here compels me to request you'll condescend to honour me with a line by return of Post which will greatly contribute to relieve my present anxiety of mind as well as add to the favours I've allready reced. at your hands.— I am with due defference and respect.—Sir Your most Devoted and Obedt. hble Servant NICHOLAS DAVIS

Notation: Richard Davis Amstordam 3 May 1779

From Dumas

ALS: American Philosophical Society; AL (draft): Algemeen Rijksarchief

Monsieur, La Haie 3e. May *1779.*

Sur les dernieres Requêtes des Marchands de differentes villes Hollandoises, communiquées aux Provinces, les Etats-

8. The commissioners had loaned Davis 720 *l.t.,* and Bingham had given him more: XXIII, 193n, 561; XXIV, 407.

Genx., ayant résumé l'affaire délibérée, avoient pris Lundi 26 Avril, sans que rien en eût transpiré, la Résolution d'équiper 32 Vx. [Vaisseaux] de guerre & frégattes de toutes grandeurs, montés ensemble de 1200 Canons, & près de 8000 h. d'Equipage, pour cette année 1779, pour servir de protection au Commerce de la Rep. avec la France & l'Angle., de maniere qu'il devra y avoir, au moins, tous les mois un Convoi.[9] Notre Ami lui-même ne savoit rien de cette Résolution, jusqu'à Samedi 1er. May dans la matinée, qu'il en eut copie, de laquelle il eut soin de faire envoyer tout de suite copie au Corps des Marchands d'Amst. par leur Procureur ici, avec avis de s'adresser à l'Amirauté pour la prompte exécution de cette Résolution. Je fus Samedi au soir avec Mr. De Neufville chez ce Procureur, qui nous lut la Résolution, laquelle nous surprit bien agréablement. Je me rendis hier matin chez G—— F——, qui eut de la peine à croire la chose, jusqu'à ce que je l'eusse assuré que notre Ami venoit de me la confirmer, & qu'on m'avoit promis de lui faire avoir une Copie de la Résolution. J'en aurai une aussi, dont je vous promets, Monsieur, un Extrait fidele. J'appelle cela une Résolution escamotée: car le secret avec lequel elle est prise, fait voir qu'on a voulu sauver un éclat; & je pense que, pour cette raison, elle ne sera point communiquée aux Ministres étrangers.

Cette nouvelle est importante. Je vous la communique par voie de Rotterdam, parce que je gagne ainsi un jour au moins. Il ne me reste que l'instant de finir par vous assurer, Monsieur, du constant & respectueux attachement avec lequel je suis, votre très humble & très-obéissant serviteur, DUMAS

Le temps viendra où je pourrai faire bon usage de tout ce qui vient d'arriver pour les futures connexions des 2 rep. Mais il faudra laisser meurir encore le projet, que la Commission de

9. The resolution did not specify, however, that ships carrying naval stores would be permitted to join the convoys, and La Vauguyon feared it was a trick on Bleiswijk's part: Fauchille, *Diplomatie française,* pp. 134–6. A French translation of the resolution is given in *ibid.,* p. 134. Dumas sent his own translation (APS).

Chargé d'affaires que vous me faites espérer, facilitera beaucoup.[1]

Passy à Son Excellence M. Franklin, Min. Pl. des Etats unis de l'Am.

Addressed: à Son Excellence / Monsieur Franklin, Esqr. / Ministre Plenipe. des Etats- / unis de l'Amérique / à *Passy./.*

Notation: Dumas la haie May. 3. 1779

From Sartine

Copy: Library of Congress

Marly le 3 may 1779.

J'ai reçu, Monsieur, la Lettre que vous m'avez fait l'honneur de m'écrire le 19 du mois dernier par la quelle vous me marquez que plusieurs Americains qui, après avoir été pressés en Angleterre, ont été pris sur des Vaisseaux de cette nation et conduits dans les Prisons de France desireroient entrer au Service des Etats unis. J'ai deja accordé au Capitaine John la facilité d'engager plusieurs de ces Prisonniers, et je suis informé qu'il en a été remis une assez grande quantité à sa Disposition.[2] Je dois vous observer, Monsieur, que le Roi en Accordant ainsi la liberté aux Sujets des Etats Unis se prive des moyens de la rendre par une échange à ses propres Sujets. Au reste J'ai donné ordre de m'informer du nombre des Americains qui sont encore detenus en France, et lorsque j'aurai pris les Ordres du Roi sur l'objet de votre demande, J'aurai l'honneur de vous faire connoitre les Intentions de Sa Majesté.

J'ai celui d'être avec la Consideration la plus distinguée, Monsieur, Votre très humble et très obeissant Serviteur.

(signé) DE SARTINE

M. Franklin.

1. Dumas had asked on Jan. 25 to be accorded this title, and on Feb. 11, BF agreed to present the proposal at the first opportunity: XXVIII, 427, 507.

2. Sartine's authorization for John Paul Jones to recruit among prisoners taken by the French is reproduced in Bradford, *Jones Papers,* reel 3, no. 510. On May 7 the authorities at Lorient reported work on the *Bonhomme Richard* almost complete: Archives de la Marine, B³DCLXV, f. 47. Jones pro-

From Thomas Viny[3]

ALS: American Philosophical Society

[before May 4, 1779][4]

The condescending respect with which Your Excellency hath in repeated Instances regarded me and mine is matter of gratful contemplation. Permit us to look with sincerest Veneration to the Man distinguish'd amongst a glorious Band of *firm* Characters: who sustain'd by divine Providence, have thus farr, form'd and Fostered the Rising world of Freedom.

May Almighty goodness confirm His pleasure and Reward the magnanimity and persevereing virtue of the People of America by the full Establishment of peace security and FREEDOM—Through out the Continent. That the whole Earth may fear the Lord. The Sword be beaten into plough-share and the speer into pruning hook & the Nations learn war no more.[5]

I cannot think of settling on this-side Jordan but would gladly enter with Çaleb and Joshua into the promised Land.[6] *Forget* most Excellent Sr. where I am and let me be still own'd as Your friend and the friend of Virtuous men. With this Ambition I subscribe Great Sr. Your most devoted T VINY

Notation: Viny

claimed himself satisfied with the number of crewmen he had collected. In an April 30 letter to Chaumont, he said that he had mustered 339 officers, seamen, and volunteer soldiers: Bradford, *Jones Papers,* reel 3, no. 583.

3. For this carriage-maker from Kent who was an old friend of BF and the Stevensons see XVII, 26–7.

4. The date of BF's reply.

5. Micah 4:3.

6. Numbers 14:6–30. Viny and BF had discussed the possibility of the Englishman and his family emigrating to America: XVII, 26–7, 71–2; XXI, 159, 487–9.

From [Jean-François-Paul] Grand[7]

ALS: American Philosophical Society

Monsieur Paris ce 4 may 1779.

Mr. Le Colonel Hope,[8] a ècrit & est venu on ne peut pas plus obligeament lui même, pour vous demander les dèpêches que vous lui aviez annoncé pour la hollande. Il ne seroit pas possible de rencontrer une occasion plus sure ni plus d'emprèssement à vous servir. C'est ce qui fait Monsieur que je vous envoye un èxprès, parce que Mr. Hope part après souper & qu'il faut que les dèpêches soient chez luy Ce Soir avant 9 ou dix heures.

Je suis avec tout le Rèspect possible Monsieur Votre très humble & très obeissant serviteur GRAND

Addressed: A Monsieur / Monsieur Le Docteur / Franklin / *a Passy*

Notation: Grand Paris 4 may 1779.

To Dumas

Copy: Library of Congress

Dear Sir Passy may 4. 1779.

I take this opportunity by Col. Hope of sending you some Papers[9], which you may occasionally make use of to Show the upright Conduct of the Congress, in the Affair of Captures &c. if they have not been already—publish'd— I send also a Copy of my general letter relating to Cap. Cook,[1] which you

7. The eldest of Ferdinand and Marie Sylvestre Grand's sons (d. 1829), he later became a banker himself: Lüthy, *Banque protestante,* II, 341, 451, 614n, 618, 699. Several letters to BF or WTF in his hand are signed "Grand l'ainé."

8. Because of the trip to Holland and the tie to the Grand family we suspect this man was a member, or at least a relative, of the Amsterdam banking family of Hope & Cie., for whom see IX, 367n; XIII, 386; XXVI, 659n; XXVII, 57–8, 129–30; XXVIII, 342–4.

9. See the preceding letter. BF apparently received Grand's letter and then wrote this one. Dumas acknowledged receipt of the enclosed papers in his letter of May 11–14, below.

1. BF's passport for the explorer, under March 10.

may show to any american Cruiser that may happen to put into any port near you.

Inclos'd is what News we have here.

I have received yours of the 29th. past.

I am, with great Esteem Dear Sir Your most obedient & most humble Ser.

M. Dumas.

To David Hartley

Copy and transcript: Library of Congress; copy:[2] Archives du Ministère des affaires étrangères

Dear Sir Passy may 4. 1779.

I received your several favours, viz: One of April the 10 one of the 20th. and two of the 22d. all on the same Day but by different Conveyances.

I need not repeat, what we have each of us so often repeated, the Wish for Peace. I will begin by frankly assuring you that tho' I think a direct, immediate Peace, the best Mode of present Accommodation for Britain as well as for America, yet if that *is not* at this time practicable, and a Truce *is* practicable I should not be against a Truce; but this is merely on Motives of *General Humanity*, to obviate the Evils Men devilishly inflict on Men in time of War, and to lessen as much as possible the Similiarity of Earth and Hell. For with regard to particular advantages respecting the States I am connected with I am persuaded it is theirs to continue the War, till England shall be reduc'd to that perfect Impotence of Mischief, which alone can prevail with her to Let other Nations enjoy *Peace Liberty and safety*. I think, however that *a Short* Truce, which must therefore be an *armed*, Truce, and put all Parties to

2. In WTF's hand. His copy lacks the opening paragraph of the letter and the postscript. It is in two parts, one containing most of the letter, and the other the middle section, beginning with "I will now give you my Thoughts . . ." and including BF's numbered responses to Hartley's five propositions. A French translation of the middle section (in Rayneval's hand) is at the AAE and was sent to Montmorin on May 17.

an almost equal Expence with a continu'd War, is by no means desirable.

But this Proposition of a Truce if made at all should be made to france at the same time it is made to America. They have each of them too much Honour as well as too much Sense to listen separately to any Propositions which tend to separate them from each other.

I will now give you my Thoughts on your Ideas of Negociation, in the order you have plac'd them. If you will number them in your Copy, you will readily See to which my observations refer, and I may therefore be more concise.[3]

To the 1st. I do not see the Necessity, or Use of five Commissions. A Number of Talkers lengthen Discussions, and often embarrass instead of aiding a Settlement. Their different Particular Views, private Interests and jealousies of each other, and fear of misrepresentation from each other are likewise so many rubs in the way of each other:[4] and it sometimes happens that a Number cannot agree to what each privately thinks reasonable and would have agreed to or perhaps proposed if alone. But this as the Parties please.

To the 2d. the Term of 21 Years, would be better for all sides. The Suspension of Hostilities should express'd to be between all the Parties at War. And that the British Troops and ships of war now in any of the united states be withdrawn.

To the 3d. This seems needless and is a Thing that may be done or omitted as you please. America has no Concern about those Acts of Parliament.

To the 4th. The reason of proposing this is not understood nor the Use of it, nor what Inducement there can be for us to agree to it. When you come to treat with both your Enemies, you may negociate away as much of those Engagements as you can; but Powers who have made a firm solid League evidently useful to both, can never be prevail'd with to dissolve it, for the vague Expectation of another *in nubibus:* nor even, on the Certainty that another will be propos'd without Know-

3. For the propositions see Hartley's first letter of April 22.

4. The words between "jealousies" and "are likewise" have been supplied from WTF's copy.

ing what are to be its articles. America has no desire of being free from her engagements to France. The chief is that of continuing the War in conjunction with her, and not making a separate Peace: and this is an Obligation not in the Power of america to dissolve being an obligation of *Gratitude and Justice* towards a Nation which is engaged in a War on her Account, and for her protection, and Would be forever binding, whether Such an Article existed or not in the Treaty. And tho' it did not exist an honest American would cut off his right hand rather than Sign an Agreement with England contrary to the spirit of it.

To the 5th. As Soon as you please.

If you had mentioned France in your proposed suspension of Arms, I Should immediately have shown it to the Minister, and have endeavoured to support that Idea. As it Stands I am in doubt whether I Shall communicate your paper or not, tho' by your writing it so fair it seems as if you intended it. If I do, I shall acquaint you with the Result.

The Bill of which you Send me a Copy was an excellent one at the time and might have had great and good Effects, if instead of telling us haughtily that our humble Petition should receive no Answer, the Ministry had received and enacted that Bill into a Law.[5] It might have erected a Wall of Brass round England, if such a Measure had been adopted when fryar Bacon's brazen Head cried out TIME IS! But the Wisdom of it was not seen, 'till after the fatal Cry of TIMES PAST![6]

The first Cargo of Prisoners is arrived and exchanged; I have not heard that the Milford is Sailed.[7] There have been abundance of high Winds lately, which perhaps have pre-

5. Hartley's proposed bill from 1775; see our annotation to his letter of April 22.

6. As early as 1766 BF had used the tale of the brazen head, a curious invention of Friar Roger Bacon that had the capacity to reveal the secret of defending England, to warn the British that they might wake up to find the time was past for achieving a union between the two countries that would be satisfactory to the Americans: XIII, 269.

7. On May 31 the Office for Sick and Hurt Seamen wrote Secretary of the Admiralty Philip Stephens that they expected daily to hear of the return from France of the *Milford*. Upon its return, one hundred more prisoners would be sent from Forton to Morlaix. National Maritime Museum.

vented. Accept my Thanks for your unwearied Pains in that Affair. Let me know if you can, whether it is intended to send another hundred immediately? In that Case I would assemble from the different Prisons those who are to be returned for them that the Cartel ships may find them ready, & not be obliged to wait for them. We have still a greater Number in Spain.

I am ever my dear friend, Your most affectionately, BF.

P.S. I suppose the Money put into your hands for the Prisoners is expended. Please to let me Know. And also inform me whither two Small Bills I gave you were ever paid.[8]

To Ingenhousz

LS:[9] American Philosophical Society

Dear Friend, Passy May 4.[–5] 1779—

I received your kind Letter of last Month, and I forwarded that Part of it, which related to Mr: Williams. Inclosed you have his Answer.[1]

I shall be glad to see those Papers of yours which you tell me will be in the Transactions, or indeed any thing of your Writing. By the way, mentioning the Transactions puts me in mind that I have received none of the Volumes published since my Departure from England in March 1775. I do not suppose that Politicks have so far taken the Lead of Philosophy in the Society as to judge me unworthy of having them, and therefore request you would be so good as to take the Trouble of sending them to me, by the Stage to Dover, directed to the Care of M. Le Veux, Negociant à Calais. I believe the Carriage should be paid to Dover, which you will charge to my Account. That you may see I have not totally neglected Philosophy, though I have little time for it at present, I send you inclosed some of *my Thoughts,* occasion'd by seeing here one *of the late Northern Lights.*[2] The Paper translated into French

8. Hartley answered on May 11, below.

9. In the hand of WTF.

1. See our annotation of JW's April 13 letter, above.

2. For BF's paper on the aurora borealis see XXVIII, 190–200, and Ingenhousz's letter of May 25, below.

was read in the *Academy of Sciences* and well received, and perhaps will be printed in their Memoirs; I cannot therefore properly propose your giving it to be read at the Royal Society; but after amusing yourself and your excellent Friend with it, I would wish you to deliver it to Mr. Benjamin Vaughan or to Dr Priestly for him: And if you think such a Thing might not be judged improper under present Circumstances, I may perhaps show the Continuance of my ancient Respect for that Society by offering it soon a Paper on a more useful Subject.

With great and sincere Esteem, I am, my dear Friend, Yours most Affectionately B FRANKLIN

P.S.[3] May 5. Since writing the above, I have receiv'd yours of the 9th April, which I shall answer in my next.—

Dr: Ingenhause.

To Richard Bennett Lloyd

Copy: Library of Congress

Dear Sir Passy may 4. 1779.

I received the letter you did me the Honour to write me of the 10th. past. As you Seem to have some Reliance on my Advice in the Affair you mention, I ought to give it candidly & Sincerely. And it must therefore be, not to accept of the offer made you. If you carry your family to America, it is, I suppose, with the intention of Spending the Remainder of your Days in your own Country. This cannot be done happily, without maintaining the general Good Opinion of your Country men.

Your Entring by that Door, will unavoidably Subject you to Suspicions: Those Suspicions will occasion Slights; & perhaps some Ill-Treatment, which will render your situation uncomfortable. I think therefore you had better conclude to Stay where you are till a Peace, tho' under some present Inconveniencies. The Circumstances of such a family will always justify this, wherever you Shall arrive in America. Please to make my

3. In BF's hand.

affectionate Respects accetable to your amiable Lady; and believe me with Sincere Esteem, Dear Sir Y. m. o. m. h. St.

Mr. Lloyd.

To Rudolph Erich Raspe

Copy: Library of Congress

Sir Passy May 4. 1779.

I received the letter you did me the honour to write by Messrs. Waitz & d'Eshen.[4] I happen'd not to be at home when they call'd on me; and they were abroad when I went to wait on them in Paris So that I have not yet had the pleasure of Seeing them;—but Shall be glad of an Opportunity of rendring them any Civilities in my Power on your Recommendation.— I repeat my Thanks to you for your Translation of born & Ferber's tracts, which contain a great deal of observation that may be useful to America.—[5] I hope you are easy & happy in England; being with much Esteem. Sir Your most obedient & most humble servant.

M. Raspe

To Thomas Viny

ALS (draft) and two copies: Library of Congress

Dear Sir, Passy, May 4. 1779—

I received with great Pleasure your kind Letter,[6] as I learnt by it that my hospitable Friend still exists, and that his Friendship for me is not abated.—

We have had a hard Struggle, but the Almighty has favour'd

4. March 26, above.

5. Baron Inigo Born (Ignaz von Born), *Travels through the Bannat of Temeswar, Transylvania, and Hungary, in the Year 1770. Described in a series of letters to Prof. Ferber, on the Mines and Mountains . . . To which is added, John James Ferber's Mineralogical History of Bohemia. Translated . . . with some explanatory notes, and a preface . . . by R.E. Raspe* (London, 1777), which Raspe had sent BF in 1777: XXIV, 435.

6. Printed before May 4, above.

the just Cause, and I join most heartily with you in your Prayers that he may perfect his Work, and establish Freedom in the New World, as an Asylum for those of the Old who deserve it.— I find that many worthy[7] and wealthy Families of this Continent are determined to remove thither and partake of it, as soon as Peace shall make the Passage safer; for which Peace I also join your Prayers most cordially. As I think the War a detestable One: and grieve much at the Mischief & Misery it occasions to many; my only Consolation being that I did all in my Power to prevent it.—

When all the Bustle is over, if my short Remainder of Life will permit my Return thither, what a Pleasure it will be to me, to see my old Friend and his Children settled there. I hope he will find Vines & Fig trees there,[8] for all of them, under which we may sit & converse enjoying Peace & Plenty, a good Government, good Laws & Liberty, without which Men lose half their Value. I am, with much Esteem, my dear Friend Yours most affectionately BF

Mr Tho' Viny Tenterden, Kent.

To Patience Wright

ALS (draft) and copy: Library of Congress

Dear Madam, Passy, May 4. 1779

I received your Favour of the 14th of March past, and if you should continue in your Resolution of returning to America thro' France, I shall certainly render you any of the little Services in my Power: but there are so many Difficulties at present in getting Passages from hence, particularly Safe ones for Women, that methinks I should advise your Stay till more settled Times, & till a more frequent Intercourse is established.—

As to the Exercise of your Art here, I am in doubt whether it would answer your Expectations. Here are two or three who profess it, and make a Show of their Works on the Boulevards;

7. He had first written "brave".

8. A continuation of the Biblical verses that Viny quoted in his letter: "But they shall sit every man under his vine and under his fig tree; and none shall make them afraid." Micah 4:4.

but it is not the Taste for Persons of Fashion to sit to these Artists for their Portraits. And both House-Rent & Living at Paris is very expensive.

I thought that Friendship required I should acquaint you with these Circumstances. After which you will use your Discretion.— I am, Dear Madam, Your most obedient and most humble Servant BF—

P.S.[9] My Grandson, whom you may remember when a little saucy Boy at School, being my Amanuensis in writing the within Letter, has been diverting me with his Remarks. He conceives that your Figures cannot be pack'd up, without Damage from any thing you could fill the Boxes with to keep them Steady. He supposes therefore that you must put them into Post Chaises two & two which will make a long Train upon the Road & be a very expensive Conveyance;[1] but as they will eat nothing at the Inns, you may the better afford it. When they come to Dover, he is sure they are so like Life & Nature, that the Master of the Pacquet will not receive them on board without Passes, which you will do well therefore to take out from the Secretary's Office before you leave London, where they will cost you only the modest Price of Two Guineas and Six pence each, which you will pay without Grumbling, because you are sure the Money will never be employ'd against your Country.[2] It will require, he says, five or six of the long-wicker French Stage Coaches to carry them as Passengers from Calais to Paris, and at least two large Ships,[3] with good Accommodations, to convey them to America, where all the World will wonder at your Clemency to Lord N.[4] that having it in your Power to hang or send him to the

9. Written on the address sheet.

1. The remainder of the sentence is added in the margin.

2. BF made a number of stylistic revisions to the ending of this sentence. He first wrote "never be employ'd against the Americans"; he next substituted "your countrymen" for "Americans", but then cancelled the phrase and interlined "in any public Service of Old England". He crossed that out in turn.

3. He first wrote "but one large Ship may serve to transport".

4. North. Wright made wax effigies of famous figures in Britain with the intention of displaying their true images to the American people: Charles

Lighters, you had generously repriev'd him for Transportation.

Mrs Wright

Notations in Franklin's hand: Postscript to Mrs Wright / Miscellaneous Papers[5]

From John Bondfield

ALS: American Philosophical Society

Sir Bordeaux 4 May 1779

I had the honor to pay my respects to you the 17 & 23 Ulto. I have the pleasure to advise you of the arrival of One of the Ships I expected from Virginia she arrived at Rochforte, the 2d April having had a passage of only Twenty Nine days. The Captain writes me that he shall retain my Letters to deliver them to me himself. I expect the Ship here every Tide we may posibly receive some interesting Inteligence by her on his Passage he met many British Cruizers and had an obstinate contest with a privateer of Sixteen Guns[6] I am happy at this arrival as she releives me from the Anxiety into which my engagements had involved me. Messrs. Andrew & James Caldwell have met with a Loss in a N[*torn*] Brig coming to my address with 132 hhds Tobacco taken and sent to Liverpool.[7] The Seas are cover'd with British Cruizers we have various reports of the Spanish Armaments by last post we are advised of an embargo haveing taken place in order to enrole all the Seamen to man the ships of War order'd to Sea.

Coleman Sellers, *Patience Wright: American Artist and Spy in George III's London* (Middletown, 1976), p. 51.

5. Beneath these notations is a sketch of one of BF's magic squares. For a discussion of the squares see IV, 392–7.

6. The *General Mercer,* loaded with tobacco and outfitted in Alexandria, Va., was commanded by Isaiah Robinson. She defended herself against the privateer *Rosebud,* Capt. Duncan: John A. McManemin, *Captains of the Continental Navy* (Ho-Ho-Kus, N.J., 1981), p. 383. See Robinson's letter of May 11.

7. Both Caldwells, born in Ireland, were partners in a Philadelphia firm dealing in cloth and tea. Andrew is identified in XXVI, 151n.

Mr La Mott Piquet by last advises remaind at Brest, Operations dependant on so many Actors meet with great delays.[8] The Buck Skin Captain Johns for Baltimore will sail from hence in 12 or 15 days.

We have advise of a Vessel belonging to Marseilles being arrived at Isl D'Aix from Virginia but no inteligence of what was do in America is yet at hand. I have the Honor to be with due Respect Sir Your most Obedient Humble Servant

JOHN BONDFIELD

His Excellency Benj Franklin

Addressed: His Excellency / Benj Franklin Esq. / Plenipotentiary from Congress / at / Paris

Notation: John Bondfield. Bordeaux 4e. may 1779.

From Thomas Digges

ALS: Historical Society of Pennsylvania

Sir Hotel de Yorke 4th May/79[9]

I am very sorry to be troublsome to You, but I find great difficulty in procuring my pass, & am not likely to get one without You will indulge me so far as to write a line to the Lieutenant de Police to grant me one. I have taken Dr. Bancrofts advice about it and He advises me to send the inclosd out to You either for alteration or to get a note to the Lieutenant de Police.[1] I am fearful If I do not get it some time in the

8. Toussaint-Guillaume, comte Picquet de la Motte (La Motte-Picquet [XXV, 470n]), commanded the escort for the French-American convoy which had just sailed for the West Indies; see BF to Lee, May 3.

9. In Paris. The previous day Digges had sworn an oath of allegiance to the United States of America before BF at Passy. APS.

1. The enclosure is missing. In a note dated "Tuesday Noon" (May 4 was a Tuesday), Bancroft wrote that he could easily have procured what Digges needed (presumably passage to London) if BF had given him a pass for London; the one to Calais was useless. A line from BF directly to the Lieutenant de Police (Jean-Charles-Pierre Lenoir: XXVII, 578n) would save having to obtain another passport. He would meet Digges at the residence of Edmund Jenings. APS.

forenoon tomorrow I shall be prevented setting out in time to meet the next sailing Packet at Calais.

I shall wait on You early in the morning, as You last appointed, provided I receive from You in ansr. to this no intimation that You will not be ready by that time to dispatch me. You know my object, and may assure Yourself I shall have the highest satisfaction in attending patiently to those or any other of Your Commands.

I am with the Highest esteem Your very obligd & Obt. Servt

THO DIGGES

The Honbe. Dr. B. Franklin Passy

Notation: May 4 1779

From Le Roy

ALS: American Philosophical Society

Mardy au soir [May 4 or 11, 1779][2]

On aime à se parer de votre nom Mon Illustre confrère et on croit qu'il ne peut qu'être accompagné de la fortune et des succes. En conséquence Un Négociant de Dunkerque qui fait construire au Havre une frégate qu'il veut armer en course dèsireroit lui donner votre nom et qu'elle s'appellat *Le Franklin.*[3] Mais il n'a point voulu la baptiser de votre nom sans savoir si cela vous conviendroit ayez donc la bonté de me mander mon Illustre confrere si vous y consentez afin que je lui fasse part de cette bonne Nouvelle si toutes fois vous ne voyez rien qui s'y oppose. Je puis vous dire d'ailleurs qu'elle sera commandée par un très brave capitaine. Le Negociant en question s'appelle M. Woïstin et c'est un des plus considèrables et des plus riches de ce pays là. La fregatte sera de 24 piéces de canon il y a des siécles que je n'ai eu l'honneur de vous voir mon Illustre Docteur et je m'ennuie si fort qu'un de

2. The Abbé Rozier had requested BF's paper on the aurora borealis on April 21, and BF answered him on April 29 that Le Roy had a correct copy and would send it. Based on what he says in the postscript to the present letter, Le Roy must have sent it on a Wednesday, April 28, or May 5, which dates the present letter either May 4 or 11.

3. See the request from Woestyn frères on March 20.

ces jours vous me verrez arriver pour vous demander du Thé le matin ou le soir. Adieu Mon Illustre Docteur vous savez combien je vous suis passionnement attaché pour la Vie.

LE ROY

P.S. J'ai envoyé votre memoire ou l'extrait, au moins faut il le dire, a l'abbé Rozier il y aura demain huit jours.

Addressed: a Monsieur / Monsieur Franklin / Ministre Plenipotentiaire des / Etats unis de L'Amerique / Septentrionale / à Passy.

Notation: Le Roy.

From Sartine

Copy: Library of Congress

à Marly le 4. May 1779

J'ai reçu, Monsieur, la lettre que vous m'avez fait l'honneur de M'écrire le 1er. du mois passé. Je me suis fait rendre un Compte detaillé du projet que M. Gillon m'a communiqué;[4] il en resulte que si le Succès étoit tel qu'il est annoncé, il procureroit éffectivement de grands Avantages; mais pour en tenter l'Execution, il faudroit envoyer sur les lieux au moins trois Vaisseaux de ligne, trois fregates avec deux cutters ou alleges, et cela est d'autant moins practicable, que le Roi a expressement defendu de detacher aucun des Bâtimens qui composent son Armée Navale,[5] Je suis très faché de me trouver par cette raison dans l'impossibilité d'accorder à M. Gillon les demandes qu'il fait et de ne pouvoir lui offrir, que de bons Offices: Je souhaite beaucoup qu'il se presente des Occasions ou ils ne puissent lui être utiles.

4. Gillon had proposed a French attack on Georgia; see Sartine's letter of March 22 and Gillon's of April 21.

5. Almost all French ships of the line were committed to either the West Indies or the pending invasion of England; for their distribution see Dull, *French Navy,* pp. 362–3. In the autumn of 1779, d'Estaing, returning from the West Indies, violated orders by attacking Georgia: *ibid.,* p. 161. For a full account see Alexander A. Lawrence, *Storm over Savannah: the Story of Count d'Estaing and the Siege of the Town in 1779* (Athens, Ga., 1951).

J'ai l'honneur d'être avec une parfaite Consideration, Monsieur, Votre très humble et très obeissant Serviteur;/.

(signé) DE SARTINE.

M Franklin

To Benjamin Vaughan

AL (draft): Library of Congress

Passy, May 5. 1779

I received my very dear Friend's Letter of the 9th April, with the Pacquet accompanying it. I leave the whole Management of that Edition[6] in your Hands with great Confidence, as I am sure my Pieces will be improv'd by your Attention to the Matters you mention.— I have sent a little Paper to Dr Ingenhauss, which I have desired him to give to you, or to Dr Priestly for you.[7]

Mr Galloway's Information about my Papers has not been well founded. My Daughter writes me, that after that Gentleman's Departure, they were brought back to my House at Philadelphia:[8] that the Chest had been indeed broke open, & some of the Papers from the Top were found scattered about the Floor, but these being gathered up, it was thought that very little had been lost. I shall like however to see the Account he has promis'd you.—

I am glad you have taken up the Consideration of the *Vis Inertiae:* The whole Doctrine of Motion & Rest & Communication of Motion, will I hope, now be cleared of the Obscurities & Difficulties & Contradictions with which it has long been embarrass'd. I thank you much for the Information your Letter contains. M. Villeboisnet never communicated to me the News you mention. What was that Letter of Gov. Franklin?— I thank you also for the Receipt against the Gout; but as I am not sure that it is not itself really a Remedy instead of

6. He here deleted "you are doing me the Honour wch to make."

7. His paper on the aurora borealis; see his letter to Ingenhousz, May 4[–5], 1779.

8. XXVII, 605.

being a Disease, I let it take its Course.— Believe me ever, my dear Friend, Yours most affectionately

Mr Benjamin Vaughan, Wanstead near London.

From ——— Baudouin

AL: American Philosophical Society

Ce 5 may 1779.

Baudouin assure monsieur franklin de toutte sa veneration et de son Respect, il prie s. Excellence de vouloir bien faire donner au porteur un recû de la lettre cy jointe.[9]

Addressed: pour / Monsieur franklin

From William Gordon[1]

ALS: American Philosophical Society

My dear Sir Jamaica Plain May 5. 1779

This may probably convey to you a painful article of intelligence, viz, the death of that great man Dr Winthrop,[2] who expired on the 3d instant, & is to be buried on the saturday. The College, the State & the Public have sustained a great loss in his death; but the Orderings of Heaven are all right; & it is appointed unto man to die, no less than to be born. Do we perform the parts allotted us upon the stage of the world, so as to meet with the approbation of our Creator; it sufficeth. Indeed we all perform so illy at certain times, that we need that his pardon should be extended to us, through the Lord Jesus Christ. No material occurrence besides hath happened within the circle of your acquaintance in this neighbourhood, that I at present recollect. The prints will announce to you the capture of a number of vessels going to Georgia with provisions &c, which have been brought into Boston.[3] What makes

9. Possibly Sartine's letter of May 4.

1. For the clergyman's most recent letter to BF see XXVIII, 467–8.

2. The scientist and mathematician John Winthrop: IV, 261n; XXIII, 407–8.

3. The capture of a fleet of schooners and privateers under convoy of the *Jason,* 20, is discussed in the letter from Jean de Neufville & fils, printed

the event the more remarkable is, that most or all the troops at Providence & other ports round Rhode Island would have disbanded by the latter end of the week, had it not been for that provision. Flour is excessive scarce. Through neglect somewhere, no sufficient magazine of that kind hath been collected either in this or the neighbouring State: None being to be had, the brigades, having been without several days, mutinied; Genl [Glover[4]] was with difficulty prevented going off last friday morning. Genl Gates now stationed at Providence sent down immediately, & large quantities of flour designed for the British forces at Georgia [were] travelling by, ever since Lords day morning, so that all things are right again.[5] Mr [Deane] has made a mighty bustle since the beginning of Decr; but a letter from Philadelphia says that he is now down & that the Lee's are more exalted than ever. Your friend Common Sense[6] has detected & exposed him, & I believe he & his party in & out of Congress will be found to be no better patriots than hobley who sold punch in small quantities *pro bono publico.* I must apply afresh for your assistance in forwarding the enclosed, which if they get safe will be of real advantage to Mr Parker,[7] as there are two bills of exchange for a hundred sterling each payable in London. Duplicates & Triplicates shall send immediately from Boston to Holland.

---

after June 28. JW described the event in a letter to WTF of June 29 (APS); see also Gardner W. Allen, *A Naval History of the American Revolution* (2 vols., Boston and New York, 1913), II, 372–4.

4. Possibly Gen. John Glover, who commanded the Continental troops in Rhode Island between March 29 and April 3, 1779. George A. Billias, *General John Glover and his Marblehead Mariners* (New York, 1960), p. 231n. A tear in the MS has obliterated several words, and we have supplied in brackets the most plausible readings.

5. Gates had been transferred from Boston to Providence, where he established his headquarters on April 5. When the troops mutinied in late April, Gates requested supplies from Gen. William Heath in Boston, who complied immediately. Paul David Nelson, *General Horatio Gates: a Biography* (Baton Rouge, 1976), pp. 210–11.

6. Thomas Paine. See his letter of March 4, above.

7. Joseph Parker was trying to resolve his claim against the Mass. government for having seized some of his property in September, 1775. See XXIV, 311n; XXVI, 517; and XXVIII, 467–8n.

Have not heard from You or Mr Adams in answer to what I have wrote once & again: but my letters may not have been recd. Pray my regards to Mr Adams. His family is well. Expect to see them on the friday. With much esteem I continue your sincere friend & very humble servant WILLIAM GORDON

Addressed: His Excellency Dr Benjamin Franklin / Paris

Notation: Gordon May 79

From Ralph Izard and Arthur Lee

ALS:[8] Historical Society of Pennsylvania

Sir Paris 6th. May 1779.—

We have been informed that the destination of the Alliance Frigate has been altered, & that she is not to sail immediately for America. We can not help expressing our great uneasiness at this measure, as we are of opinion that there is no service, in which she can be so usefully employed, as that of convoying the Vessels bound thither. Many of our Countrymen have suffered great distress by having been long detained in France. Some of them have experienced the miseries of imprisonment, to which there is the greatest reason to fear they will return, as very few of the Vessels that sail without Convoy escape from falling into the hands of the enemy.

The persons, & property of so many of our Countrymen, the valuable merchandize, and the essential supplies that Fleet carries, both for the United States, & for that of Virginia, are of such infinite consequence to our Country, that we can not help most earnestly wishing them the protection of the Alliance Frigate. M: la Motte Picquet's Squadron[9] will be a protection to them as long as they can avail themselves of it. But as he is bound to the West Indies, he can be of no service to them on the coast of North America, where there is very great dan-

8. In Izard's hand.

9. La Motte-Picquet, commanded the *Annibal,* 74, *Diadème,* 74, *Artésien,* 64, *Réfléchi,* 64, *Amphion,* 50, and some smaller vessels escorting the Brest convoy for the West Indies; see BF's letter to Lee of May 3 and Dull, *French Navy,* pp. 125, 146, 159–60, 363.

ger, not only from the Ships of War of the enemy, but also from a number of Privateers, fitted out at New York, & Rhode Island. We have another reason for wishing that the Alliance may be ordered immediately to America. Congress have been long without hearing from their Servants in Europe. The Dispatches which we have written to our Constituents, in expectation of their going in safety by the Alliance, and under her Convoy, contain matter of importance for them to be acquainted with, in which their Honour, Interest, & Safety are deeply concerned.

We have the honour to be Sir Your most obedient humble Servants

RA: IZARD.
ARTHUR LEE

Honble B: Franklin Esqr.

From Arthur Lee

LS:[1] American Philosophical Society; ALS (draft):[2] National Archives; copy:[3] Harvard University Library

Sir/ Paris May 6th. 1779

I had not the honor of receiving your letter till today, tho it is dated the 3d. It came by the Penny post.

It was by Mr Adams's information, when on board, that I understood the Alliance "had now a good Crew," & I cannot express my concern on hearing from you that it is otherwise. The persons & property of so many of our Countrymen; the

1. In Ludwell Lee's hand.

2. Lee added an N.B.: "Mr. A Lee having wasted some time without receiving an answer to the above Letter, on the 15th. May I waited on Dr. Franklin to know whether or not he had received it, his answer was that he had, but as the Ships were then sail'd he did not think it necessary to make any answer."

3. In Alexander Gillon's hand. He added a notation observing that the *Alliance* would have had time to join the convoy, which did not sail from Brest until May 10, eight days after Lee had written about it (above, May 2). In fact, the convoy had already sailed by the time Lee wrote; see our annotation of BF's response of the 3rd. Gillon's notation observes that if the ship was manned sufficiently to go on a cruise, she was fit to serve as a convoy.

valuable Merchandize; & the essential stores for the United States & that of Virginia which are on board the fleet at Brest, are of such infinite importance to our Country, that I cannot help trembling for their fate, since I have lately learnt that M. le Motte Piquet will protect them no farther than in his course to the West Indies, & that our Coast swarms with Privateers fitted out from New York, Rhode Island, & Augustine.

The supplies for the State of Virginia were those, which, as I have often had the honor of mentioning to you, were obtaind some time ago from the Crown, consisting of Brass Canon, Mortars, Bombs & Ball.[4] The articles which my Brother sollicited your assistance in procuring, are a second order, & as necessary for the defence of the State as the first; which first only I have fulfilled except in those articles which the house of Penet engaged for, but did not send.[5]

The Gentlemen going to & shipping goods for America, I know lamented that their repeated requests thro the Commissioners to the Ministry for a Convoy *quite to America,* were unsuccessful. They had waited several weeks, & at a great expence, in expectation of it; when the Commissioners sent them a Copy of M. de Sartines final answer to their reiterated applications dated Feby. 6th. & containing these words— "Si ceux qui sont actuellement à Nantes, ayants destination pour les Etats Unis, descendent promptement la Riviére ils seront escortés jusqu'au dela des Caps & plus loin encore, c'est à dire, pendant tout le tems qu'ils voudront suivre la route du Convoi des Batimens françois destinés pour les Isles de l'Amerique."[6]

It was a great mortification to them, that the Alliance was not mannd nor any certainty when she woud be so; which obliged them to put themselves under the french West India Convoy as the best & only one that then offerd.

4. For the supplies for Virginia see our annotation of his letter of May 2.

5. In September, 1779, William Lee wrote Jefferson that "several thousand stand of Arms and some other Articles" had still not been delivered by Penet, D'Acosta frères & Cie.: *Jefferson Papers,* III, 91.

6. The letter was actually from Vergennes, discussing Sartine's response: XXVIII, 476–7. See also Sartine's letter of Feb. 11: XXVIII, 507.

I presume therefore, that it was not their being satisfyd with a Convoy half the way, that prevented them from applying to you, since your late appointment, to obtain for them a more sufficient one; but their knowing *that* application had already been made often, by you & the other Commissioners, without success. It is also probable that their being under sailing orders in Brest road, deprived them of knowing the State of the Alliance at Nantes; but it is most sure, that they woud have been extremely happy to have seen her return to Brest as their Convoy. They had every reason to expect this woud be the Case, if she got men at Nantes, because you had directed them to be informd, that you had given orders for her to Convoy them, which it was understood her want of men only prevented. I cannot therefore doubt but that the wishes of all the American Gentlemen that the Alliance shoud Convoy them, coincide with mine, tho circumstances have prevented them from being expressed.

It was from a persuasion of this, & from an anxiety for their safety as well as for that of the important supplies that go with them, that I venturd to submit to you my opinion of the utility of ordering the Alliance immediately to Brest, which I still most earnestly wish may, if possible, be done.

Most of these Gentlemen have already experienced the miseries of being made prisoners; to which there is too much reason to apprehend they will return, if they are left upon our Coast without Convoy.

It is a long time too since Congress have heard from their Servants in Europe. Mr. Izard & myself have written to our Constituents, in expectation of our dispatches going in safety by the Alliance or under her Convoy, upon matters in which the public honor, interest, & safety are deeply concernd.

I am sorry to have troubled you with so long a Letter, but out of the fulness of the heart, the tongue speaketh; and I am filld with the most anxious concern for the fate of the fleet, if it is to be left unprotected in any part of the voyage.

I have the honor to be with the greatest Respect Sir Your most Obedient Humble Servant ARTHUR LEE

Honble. B. Franklin Esqr.

From Vergennes

L (draft):[7] Archives du Ministère des affaires étrangères; copy: Library of Congress

a Versailles le 6. May 1779.

J'ai reçu, M, la lettre que vous m'avez fait l'honneur de m'écrire Le 3. de ce mois concernant les effets et munitions de guerre demandès par les Etats de Virginie et de Maryland. Vous n'ignorez sans doute pas, que la premiére de ces provinces a obtenu des arsenaux du Roi, par le canal de M. Lée, des canons et autres effets d'artillerie pour une somme considèrable, et que le tout doit etre actuellement en chemin pour l'Amérique;[8] vous jugerez d'après cela, M. qu'en faisant une nouvelle fourniture pour la Virginie, vous vous exposeriez a faire un double emploi. Quant au Maryland personne ne s'est addressé à nous de sa part; nous ignorons les envoys qui peuvent lui avoir été faits, et il paroit que vous ètes dans la même ignorance; cependant il conviendroit que vous fussiez instruit, avant de faire de nouveaux achats:[9] j'attendrai donc, M, que vous ayez bien voulu me donner des eclaircissemens sur cet objet avant de mettre votre demande sous les yeux de Mté.

Au surplus, M, quand même elle seroit agréée dès-à-présent, il seroit impossible de charger les effets donc il est question sur le vaisseau qui conduira en Amerique M. le Chr. de la Luzerne, parce que le depart de ce Ministre est très-prochain, et qu'il y auroit de grands inconvénients soit à le retarder, soit a embarasser la marche de son vaisseau par des marchandises. Si cependant vous aviez des effets prêts à être embarqués, je ne doute pas que M. de la Luzerne ne concoure à satisfaire vos desirs autant que cela sera en son pouvoir et je

7. In Gérard de Rayneval's hand.

8. The arms were being shipped aboard the *Governor Livingston, Mary Fearon,* and *Chasseur;* see Bondfield's letter of April 17. The former two eventually reached Virginia safely, but the *Chasseur* was captured and brought into New York; Bondfield to BF, Sept. 23, 1779 (APS).

9. Deleted from the draft at this point is the phrase "auxquels le Roi ne sera pas éloigné de se prêter". At the end of the sentence, "Mté" was expanded in the copy to "Sa Majesté."

pense que vous ferez bien de vous entendre là-dessus avec luy./.

M franklin

From Jonathan Williams, Jr.

ALS: American Philosophical Society; copy: Yale University Library

Dear & hond Sir. Nantes May 6. 1779.

I have not yet finished my algebraic Calculation[1] relative to my proposed Voyage, because two Circumstances are wanting. *News from America, & the arrival of Mr de Montieu.* The first of these will I believe turn the Balance one way or the other.— If I should hear that my accots. have not been passed by the Committee, and that the malignant Spirit of Party has prevailed to affect my Character as an honest man, I must abandon every prospect of advantage to the support of my injured Reputation, and (if you think as I do) I must take the most direct Method to return to America, & confound my Enemies.— If I should hear the Contrary, my determination will principaly turn on Points of advantage, unless I find I can be of some further Service to my Country, which will always overpower every other Consideration.— I find the American Commissions have not paid the quarter part of the Expences I am obliged as an established Merchant to be at—and I don't see a prospect of their encreasing while the english Cruisers swarm & our Ships coming hither are without Protection. Public employment is not often obtained without sollicitation, and I have not yet, nor can I ever sollicit any. Mr A[2] has during his Residence here been making enquiry about the Situation of the administration of american affairs—& the best footing to put them on in future,—he has asked me many Questions on the Subject and left me many Openings to ask his Interest,

1. See BF's letter of April 8.

2. Adams. For JA's account of his stay in Nantes see Butterfield, *John Adams Diary,* II, 356–66.

but I never have given even an indirect appearance of a desire or, expectation ever to be again in public Employ, although I have often heard he has spoken of me in the highest Manner; and I once heard that after praising me for my Probity Commercial knowledge & french Language, he said I was the only person here who ought to be the agent or Consul.— This I have never appear'd to know, & it would be imprudence as well as foolish Vanity to tell it to any one else, I therefore mention it (entre nous) & the Satisfaction of my own Mind is all the advantage I expect from it.

From all this you will see I am in a State of indecision but I believe it will rather be on the side of staying at least over the Summer than going directly, for I do not expect to be so hardly treated by my Country as to require my immediate Presence and I have seen so much instability in Mr Montieu's Plans that I place no Dependance 'till I see them fixed.—

If you have any Reason for asking me the Question about my proposed Voyage, besides the kind Concern you have always taken in my affairs I shall be glad to know it—

I am ever with the greatest Respect your Dutifull & affectionate Kinsman J WILLIAMS J

Please to answer my Letter about Mr Gourlades demand for the Deanes anchors.— I have not yet executed Mr Greens Order because I have had no Opportunity—[3] I will embrace the first.

The Hon. Doctor Franklin

Notations in different hands: Williams Jona. May 6. 1779. / Jona Williams

3. BF had forwarded to JW the request made by William Greene, governor of Rhode Island, for various goods: XXVIII, 216–17, 522–3.

From John Beckwith[4] ALS: American Philosophical Society

hotel trois Evechées Rue des filles St. Thomas

Sir [on or before May 7, 1779][5]

I write this letter in case I shd. not be fortunate enough to find you at home, the importance of the subject will be a sufficient excuse for the liberty I am about to take desirous ever since the comencement of hostilities in America, to be of service to that cause I have never taken my eyes off their proceedings, & I now find that one substantial check given to the English troops in that Country wd. be in a great measure decisive, flush'd with success the Brittish troops rush on to certain victory, the temperance the prudence of Genl. Washington has hitherto prevented any fatal consequences arising from their victories, perhaps he is the only man in Europe, or America, who cou'd have conducted matters as well.

He certainly wants assistance he cannot alone suffice, his troops want training to that want their misfortunes is principaly to be ascribed, for hitherto there has not apeared any lack of valour or good will but want of discipline in the troops, & perhaps want of vigilance & experience in the comanders, where Mr. Washington has commanded in Person things have never gone very ill sometimes well, but he cannot be every where, permitt me then once again to offer my services, do not be aprehensive I entreat, that a long experience in my profession, perhaps some talents cou'd lead me in any degree to slight virtuous men who strugle for the choicest of all blessings. What I wish, & what indeed I think my self equal too is to be placed ad Latus of the modern Fabius,[6] perhaps it might be in my power, to assist him in his operation, perhaps in case

4. The British major general is identified in x, 329n.

5. On this day Beckwith told Arthur Lee that he recently had communicated to BF his desire to serve in America but was unsure whether BF's promise to inform Congress was "a genteel put off" or the only action he actually had the power to take. Lee replied that he was certain BF's power of appointment was not a general one and confirmed that it was Congress who gave orders to American generals through Gen. Washington: Richard Henry Lee, *Life of Arthur Lee, L.L.D.* (2 vols., Boston, 1829), I, 412.

6. As Washington had become known after his victories at Trenton and Princeton in January, 1777: Freeman, *Washington,* IV, 362–3n.

of necesty he might find me a proper person to employ at a distance perhaps too I might be the means of introducing somewhat more order & discipline, wch. would have every good effect.

You say Sir that you have no authority to treat with a man of my rank, notwithstanding, that it has been observed from early times that Republicks are seldom gratefull, I cannot allow myself to think that the present members of congress can so soon forgett what they owe to their founder as to neglect your recomendation I will then take my chance if you think me a person who may be truely usefull as I flatter myself.

Favour me with a time & I will wait upon.

I have the honour to be with the highest respect Sr. your most humble & obedt. Servt. BECKWITH

To Sartine

Copy: Library of Congress

Sir Passy May 8. 1779.

I have received the honour of your Excelly's: Letter of the 3d. Instant. I am very Sensible of the King's Goodness, in granting Liberty to the Americans who have been taken Prisoners in the English Service as by that means his Majesty Lessons the Number of the Prisoners that may be exchanged for his own Subjects; and I think we ought whenever we can Show our Gratitude by procuring liberty for such of his Subjects as may be in the same Circumstances. We had in America, by the last Accounts many more Prisoners of the Enemy than they had of our People: and I will write to the Congress to advise the obtaining by an Exchange the Discharge of Such French Prisoners as may be confined in New York, tho' I have no doubt of its being done whenever the Cartel shall take place there.

Capt. Jones informs me, that among the English Prisoners brought from Senegal, there are 16 Americans, who having been taken by the English in the unfortunate attack of Quebeck Jan. 1. 1777. had been sent as Slaves to Africa; and that they have petition'd to obtain their Discharge in order to serve under him, and have an Opportunity of taking satisfaction for the cruel tratment they have received: He has apply'd to the Commandant for them, but has received for Answer, that the Garrison having Surrendred conditionally that the Troops in it should be sent to England, it is not in his Power to give them up without Orders from Court.[7] Your Excellency can best judge if this Matter is practicable, either by our replacing them with as many English, or by any other means.

Capt. Jones also writes to me that the Officer mention'd in the enclos'd Memorial[8] has been very Useful in disciplining his Marines, and that he wishes if possible to have him upon the Cruise agreable to his Petition, which is therefore submitted to your Excellency's Consideration.

I am, with great Respect,

M. De Sartine

From John Bondfield — ALS: American Philosophical Society

Sir — Bordeaux 8 May 1779.

I am honor'd with your favor of the 26th Inst. and am truely sensible of your friendly Goodwill which you so obligingly Express in answer to my representation which forecast made me judge incumbent, from dread of events. I am happy to advise you that the Arrival of the General Mercer loaden with Tobacco to my address will effectualy prevent any checks to my too extended Conections.

Captain Robinson Master of the General Mercer arrived here the 5th Instant he has Number of Letters for private persons not a single one for you, as he saild from Virginia and only lately had the Command of this Ship given him his coming this way I apprehend was not known he left Patomack River 25 March, the relation published by Mr. provost was not represented in America in the colours he has painted an advanct party [*torn:* it] was said had been repulsed but of little Consiquence on the other hand there had been many Scirmishes in which the Enemy always suffer'd considerably.[9]

7. Jones raised the issue in his letter of May 2.
8. From Edward Stack; see our annotation of Jones's May 1 letter.
9. See BF's letter of April 29 to Gourlade and Moylan.

This Vessel I shall dispatch with all posible deligence. I hope in the course of three Weeks to have her to Sea. Monsr La Motte piquet lays at Isl D'Aix with the Outward bound Ships for the United States, he has under his Command five Ships of the Line five frigates and a number of Armd Merchant Men of which our three Ships compose a part.

The Number of small Arm'd Vessels fitted out at New York great obstruct our Navigation they run into the Bays and intercept all Ships inwards or outwards. New York and Rhode Island are so situated we never can carry on any Trade til they are reduced. It is imposible to describe the wants of the provinces all European Goods are selling at 20 for 1. Bills I have receivd on you were bought at 10 for 1. It is incredible the Capital required to send a Vessel from America to Europe. Could the plan I laid before you last July be put in practice it would give a quick Sensation to the Value of Continental Money.[1]

I have the honor to be with due Respect Sir your very hlb Servant JOHN BONDFIELD

His Excellency Benj Franklin Esq

Addressed: His Excellency B. Franklin / Plenepoteny from the United States / a / Paris

Notation: John Bondfield. Bordeaux 8e. may 1779.

From Madame Brillon AL: American Philosophical Society

ce samedi 8 may [1779][2] a passy

Mon áme est plus calme mon chér papa, depuis qu'elle s'est déchargée dans la vôtre; depuis qu'elle ne craint plus que mlle j++ ne se retire chéz vous, et n'y fasse votre tourment et celui de votre chér fils: plus je refléchie a sa démarche à ce sujét et a la proposition que vous a fait mr de C++, moins je conçois qu'un homme de son age, qui est peu venu chéz moi;

1. His plan for sinking the paper money: XXVII, 261–2.

2. Dated by two other letters from her in this month, May 3, above, and May 11, below.

ait imaginé de vous offrir de méttre votre confiance, votre amitié, dans une pérsonne dont il ne peut connoistre n'y les talents, n'y le caractére; je le plaindrois sincérement si dans ses affaires pérsonnélles, il ne méttoit plus de refléctions et de soins:[3]

Dans la malheureuse histoire que je vous ai conté l'autre jour; dans les léttres que je vous ai montrés; vous avéz vû l'âme de votre fille a découvert; une éxtrésme sensibillité, de la franchise, une trop grande facillité, nulle méfiance pour se garantir du mal, parcequ'elle ne le soupçonne pas, n'étant pas capable d'en faire; un besoin d'aimér et de l'estre, qui l'a fait se livrér trop promptement a ceux qui affichoient la bonté et la vértu; voila mon ami la cause de toutes mes peines. Aimeraisje moins? Non sans doutte, non; mais j'aimerai moins viste; la raison, la réfléction viendront a l'aide d'un coeur trop tendre et trop foible: plus je m'éxamine et plus je vois, que l'envie d'estre utille a quelqu'un que je croyois malheureux et peu riche; m'a conduit dans un piége affreux: mlle j + + préconisant sans césse la vértu, qu'elle n'a jamais pratiqué; la dellicatésse qu'elle ne sent pas; la franchise, qu'elle ne connoist point; a sçuë aprés s'estre brouillée dans sa famille; s'estre fait chassér de deux maisons; m'abusér au point de tournér toutes ses avantures téllement a son avantage, que je la plaignois, l'aimois, et n'ai jamais voulu écouttér les avis multipliés que j'ai reçus de me méfiér de son caractére; que lorsque j'ai pensés payér de ma vie, l'ingratitude, la fausseté avéc lesquelles elle m'a abusé: mon mari sera encore lomgtems peut estre subjugué par elle; mais j'ose éspérér, que mon attention a lui plaire, la tendrésse de ses enfants, le mépris que tous nos anciens et bons amis ont conçus pour cette fille, et qu'ils ne dissimuleront pas; lui ouvriront un jour les yeux; en attendant, je me livre entiérement a l'addrésse qu'élle vá méttre a taschér de me donnér tous les ridiculs possibles; il étoit important a mon repos; que mon pére, mon bien bon ami fut instruit; quand au public qui m'a toujours jugés avéc indulgence; je

3. All we know about Mlle. Jupin is that by August she was living in St. Germain-en-Laye at the house of a M. de Rochefort (Jupin to BF, Aug. 22 [1779]). APS.

continuerai de lui laissér voir en moi, une conduitte simple, honneste, sans prétention, un grand attachement pour mon mari, mes enfants, mes amis, et surtout pour la vértu; je ne dirai point de mal de mlle j++; malheureusement pour elle son caractére lui en fait assés:

Adieu vous, que je réspécte, que j'aime, mon bon mon aimable papa; gardés mon secrét dans votre áme, gardés y aussi mon coeur que j'y dépose pour le guérir de ses bléssures et de sa foibléssse:

Je vous attends ce soir pour le thé, jamais jamais je n'eus plus de besoin d'éstre quelques heures avéc vous:

From Landais

LS: American Philosophical Society

Please your Excellency aboard the alliance May 8th. 1779

Since I received your orders to Sail for Port L'Orient, I have been Waiting in this River for a boat Loaded with provisions, and fear wind; but now having all aboard and the Wind S E. I am getting under Sail and Expect to be to-morrow at Port-Louis. I have at présent theerten passengers beside the honble. John Adams, his Son and Servant. Please to Write me yours orders about them.[4] I Received a Letter from monsieur De Ray De Chaumont by which he mention that I am to have for Six month vitals aboard, as there is Some goods aboard I Suppose belong to Some of the officers, as I Learned yesterday, I Want to Know What I am to do if I have not room Enough for to put the Said Vitals.

I Received your two Letters Concerning Mr. Herckiah Ford, and M: Wuibert, I have give them the Cabin as I thought your Letters required it.[5]

I am With Respect Your Excellency Most obedient most humble Servant

P: LANDAIS

4. BF had offered JA and his party passage aboard the *Alliance* to Lorient, but had failed to inform Landais; see Landais' letter of May 1.

5. The letter concerning Ford is above, April 25. We know that the military engineer Antoine-Félix Wuybert hoped for passage on the *Sensible* to return to the American army: Le Roy to BF, after April 20. For JA's description of his fellow passengers see Butterfield, *John Adams Diary,* II, 364.

His Excellency B. franklin Minister-Plenipotentiary of the united States of america./.

Notation: P. Landais May 8. 79

From Joseph Priestley

ALS: American Philosophical Society

Dear Sir London 8 May 1779.

The person who will deliver this letter is a priest of the Roman Catholic persuasion, and one of my antagonists in metaphysical matters, but a man of a very liberal disposition, and with whom I have spent many an agreeable hour.[6] He is so obliging as to undertake to deliver to you my *Treatise on Education,* and my *Correspondence with Dr Price.*[7] I shall very soon, by means of Mr Magellan, send you a copy of my new *philosophical work,*[8] which, if you should have leisure to look into it, I flatter myself, will give you some pleasure.

I have just seen, but have had no opportunity to read, a pamphlet in favour of the doctrine of Necessity printed, I think, in 1729, and dedicated to TRUTH. Is this the tract you

6. The bearer was undoubtedly Roger Joseph Boscovich (1711–87), distinguished mathematician, astronomer, and natural philosopher, who had been trained as a Jesuit in Rome, traveled widely as a diplomat, and settled in Paris in 1773, at which time he was appointed Director of Naval Optics of the French Navy and made a French citizen. Priestley and Boscovich had discussed their work during Priestley's visit to Paris in 1774. In 1778, the two men debated metaphysics in an exchange of letters, sparked by the publication of Priestley's *Disquisitions Relating to Matter and Spirit* in 1777.

Boscovich had many friends among the high society of Paris, including leading statesmen and scientists known to BF. His papers, in Yugoslavian archives, are said to contain claims that the Jesuit met BF in London in 1760, and at the home of Vergennes towards the end of the Revolution. No correspondence between the two men is extant. See Robert E. Schofield, *A Scientific Autobiography of Joseph Priestley (1733–1804)* (Cambridge, Mass., and London, 1966), pp. 166–71, 349–50; Lancelot Law Whyte, ed., *Roger Joseph Boscovich* (London, 1961), pp. 64–6, 91–4, 100–1.

7. *Miscellaneous Observations relating to Education* . . . (Bath, 1778), and *A Free Discussion of the Doctrines of Materialism and Philosophical Necessity, in a Correspondence between Dr. Price and Dr. Priestley* . . . (London, 1778). BF lent the former to Count Montfort; see XXVIII, 178.

8. See Priestley's letter of March 11.

told me you wrote, and could not procure me a copy of? I cannot help being desirous of knowing this circumstance.[9]

All your friends are well. You need not doubt that we often talk of you, but we fear there is no prospect of peace, or consequently of our seeing you in England.

In all events, I am, Dear Sir, yours most sincerely,

J PRIESTLEY

Notation: Priestley 8. May 1779.

To Francis Coffyn

Copy: Library of Congress

Sir [May 9, 1779][1]

If one Nicolas Davis should come to Dunkirk, and Demand Assistances as an American in distress, I desire you not to give him anything, he having already defrauded us of great sums. I have the honour to be &

Mr. Coffin

To Dumas

LS:[2] Yale University Library; copy: Library of Congress

Dear Sir, Passy, May 9th. 1779.

I received yours[3] with a Copy of the Resolution of the 26th past which gave me a great deal of Pleasure. If one Nicholas Davis, who lodges in the Warmoes Straat Amsterdam, at the

9. Priestley had probably seen Anthony Collins, *A Dissertation on Liberty and Necessity. . . . And an epistle dedicatory to truth . . .* (London, 1729). Benjamin Vaughan asked BF about the same pamphlet in a letter of July 30 (APS). BF did not answer Priestley, but his letter to Vaughan, dated Nov. 9 (Library of Congress), mentioned Priestley's query and set the record straight.

The essay that BF had written, entitled *A Dissertation on Liberty and Necessity, Pleasure and Pain,* was published in 1725 and dedicated to "J.R." (James Ralph). BF claimed to have regretted its publication almost immediately, and destroyed most of the edition: I, 57–71.

1. In BF's letterbook the present letter immediately follows two letters dated May 9 and precedes one dated May 10.

2. In WTF's hand.

3. Of May 3.

House of Jan Hendrik Consé, should apply to you for Assistance as an American, I desire you to take no Notice of him for he has already cheated us of considerable Sums.

I am ever, Yours affectionately B FRANKLIN

M. Dumas.

Addressed: A Monsieur / Monsieur Dumas / le Hage / Holland

Endorsed: Passy 9e. May 1779 S.E. Mr. Franklin

To Fizeaux, Grand & Cie.[4]

Copy: Library of Congress

Gentlemen Passy May 9. 1779.

I received your obliging Letter of the 3d. Instant,[5] with two Pamphlets, for which I thank you, and shall be glad of any others of the Kind that are esteemed to be well written.

I have received lately two Letters from one Nicolas Davis,[6] who is now in Amsterdam at the House of Jan. Hendrik Conse in de Warmoes-straat, and asks me for Money. I am afraid that if he can find out that you are our friends, he will apply to you likewise; therefore I write to put you on your guard & to request that you would not advance him a farthing. He came to us at Paris in January 1777, and pretending to be an American who had served the India Company some years as an Officer in their Troops, but thought it his Duty rather to serve his Country in this War, he prevail'd on us to furnish him with some Money to bear his Expences thither, We advanced him about 30 Louis & sent him to Havre to take his Passage in a french Ship the seine then bound for Martinique & then to the Continent. At Havre, just going off he shew'd an open Letter of Recommendation we had given him for America, and on the Credit of it took up as much more money, from our friend,

4. On March 12 and on April 20 BF had written this firm under its former name of Horneca, Fizeaux & Cie. After the death of Jean-Jacques Horneca, Georges Grand, hitherto a silent partner, had added his name to the firm. Eventually it became simply Grand & Cie.: Lüthy, *Banque protestante,* II, 335.

5. Missing.

6. One of which is above, May 3; the other is missing.

giving him a Draft upon us for the same, which we thought ourselves obliged to pay. At Martinique he by the same Means got a Credit with our Agent there, & took up the Value of 120 Louis more being afterwards taken in the Ship by the English before the Commencement of hostilities just on going out of Martinique, the Captain claim'd his Vessel as being french & bound to another french Island but this Man inform'd that she was really bound to Boston on which she was condemned at Antigua. Since which he has been with the English at Philadelphia, and I Suspect has abus'd the Recommendation we gave him in other Instances that have not yet come to our Knowledge. It is amazing that after all this he should have the Effrontery to apply again to me for Money. I would rather punish him, if I Knew how. But I suppose it will answer no End to prosecute him in Holland. I wish however, that you Could by Some means learn whether he has still any letter of recommendation from me, and if he shows it get it from him, for I am afraid he may make farther Use of it in defrauding. It Would be well to caution your Magistrates to have an Eye on him.

With great Esteem I have the honour to be Gentlemen

Mrs. Fizeaux Grand & Com.

To John Paul Jones

LS:[7] National Archives; copies: National Archives, Library of Congress

Dear Sir, Passy May 9. 1779.

I received your Favour of the 1st Instant, I have made the Application you desire in behalf of the Officer who wishes to have leave to go with you, and for the Americans who are come from Senegal, and I hope for a favourable Answer.[8]

7. In WTF's hand. WTF had also sent a letter to Jones the previous day conveying the same information as the present letter. National Archives.

8. The request from the Americans captured at Senegal actually had been forwarded by Jones on May 2. BF called Sartine's attention to it when he wrote him on the 8th; with the same letter he enclosed Edward Stack's request to serve with Jones.

I need not tell you that I wish you a good Voyage, and all the Success that I am sure you will deserve; being with great Truth, Your affectionate Friend and most obedt humble Sert.

B FRANKLIN

Honble. Capt. Jones

Addressed: A Monsieur / Monsieur Le Cape. Jones / Commandant la Fregatte / Le Bon homme Richard, / au Service des Etats-Unis / à L'Orient.

Notations in different hands: Letter from Doctor Franklin May 9th. 1779. / No.4 Letter from his Excellency B. Franklin to Capt Jones May 9th 1779—

To John Adams

LS:[9] Massachusetts Historical Society; copy: Library of Congress

Sir, Passy, May 10th. 1779

I received the honour of yours of the 29th past from Nantes. I hope you are before this time safely arrived at L'Orient. M. De la Luzerne is making diligent Preparation for his Departure, and you will soon see him. He and the Secretary of the Embassy[1] are both very agreable and sensible Men, in whose Conversation you will have a great deal of Pleasure in your Passage. What Port the Ship will be ordered to I have not yet learnt, I suppose that it may be partly left to the Captain's Discretion, as the Winds may happen to serve. It must certainly be most agreable to you to be landed in Boston; as that will give you an earlier Sight of your Family; but as you propose going immediately to Congress, being landed at Philadelphia will have some little Advantage, as it saves half your Journey. I shall take care to procure the Order to the Captain from M. De Sartine, which you desire; tho' I should suppose

9. In WTF's hand.

1. François Barbé de Marbois (1745–1837), whose lengthy career was capped by his service as minister of the treasury under Napoleon: *DBF;* Eugene P. Chase, ed., *Our Revolutionary Forefathers: the Letters of François, Marquis de Barbé-Marbois during His Residence in the United States as Secretary of the French Legation, 1779–1785* (New York, 1929), pp. 3–14.

showing the Original Letter of that Minister, which you have, would be sufficient. No publick Dispatches are arrived here since you left us. I see by the Virginia Papers that the 6th of February, being the Anniversary of the signing of the Treaty, was observed with great Festivity by the Congress &c at Philadelphia.[2] From Holland I have just received the Resolution of the States General, of the 26th past, to Convoy their Trade, notwithstanding Sir Joseph York's Memorial, and to fit out directly 32 Ships of War for that purpose; which is good News and may have consequences.[3]

I have the honour to be, with great Regard, Sir, Your most obedient & most humble Servant. B FRANKLIN

Honble: Jn. Adams Esquire.

Endorsed: Dr Franklin May 10. ansd 17th. 1779

To Chaumont

LS:[4] Franklin D. Roosevelt Library; copy: Library of Congress

Dear Sir, Passy May 10. 1779.

I received the Letter you did me the honour to write to me the 1st. inst.[5] That inclosed for the Marquis de la Fayette was sent to him directly. The other for M. de Sartine, was carry'd to Marly by my Son; but he being at Paris, it was brought back and delivered to him there the next Morning. His Answer has been ever since expected, to be return'd by your Express, but not arriving, we suppose he has sent it by some other Opportunity. All Paris now talks of the Marquis de la Fayette's going to America with Troops, &c. From Holland I have certain Advice, that the States General have come to a Resolution to give

2. The festivities included a public entertainment featuring thirteen toasts "drank, under a discharge of cannon": Smith, *Letters,* XII, 25–6n.

3. Dumas described it in his letter of May 3, above; for Yorke's memorial see our annotation of Dumas' letter of April 3–13.

4. In WTF's hand.

5. In his letter, actually May 2, Chaumont had asked BF to forward letters from Jones to Lafayette and Sartine.

Convoys to their Merchant Ships, notwithstanding the last Memorial of Sir Joseph York: and to fit out immediately 32. Sail of Men of War for that purpose. This Resolution was taken the 26th past.[6] With the greatest Esteem and Affection, I am ever, Dear Sir, Your most obedient & most humble Servant.

B FRANKLIN

M. De Chaumont.

From Peter Allaire[7]

ALS: Library of Congress

Sir/

London 10 May 1779

An Offer has been made me, which I think worthy Your Attention, as it may be of Infinite service to the fleets & Armies of America.

A person has Applyed to me to furnish any Quantity (not less then 20 lb weight) of Doctr: James's fever Powders, so well known all over Europe, for fifteen Shill, Ster. an Oz. Each Oz Contains 12 Packages, and the price that James & Newbury sells that at is 2/6 each paper, & to Goverment at 30/per Oz, I am Offered them at one half.[8]

The person before the Death of the late Doct James, was Imployed by the Doctr: for many Years to make them, but since his Death, his Son[9] & Newbury, have Discharged him

6. See Dumas' May 3 letter.

7. For the N.Y. merchant who had sent political and military intelligence to BF on at least two occasions see XXIV, 470; XXVI, 518.

8. Dr. Robert James, who died in 1776, had invented a popular but controversial medicine for fever and inflammation: XI, 202n. Francis Newbery (1743–1818), who had inherited a publishing house and patent medicine business established by his father, held the patent for James's fever powders. *DNB.* The person who offered to furnish the powders was Samuel Swinton, owner of the *Courier de l'Europe,* wine merchant, entrepreneur, and double agent. Claude-Anne Lopez, "The Man Who Frightened Franklin," *PMHB,* CVI (1982), 518–19; Eugène Hatin, *Histoire politique et littéraire de la presse en France* (8 vols., Paris 1859–61), III, 404–6.

9. Pinkstan James (1766–1830), who practiced medicine in London: *DNB* under his son, George Payne Rainsford James.

& having a pattent the Secret is of very little service to him in this Kingdome.

Inclosed I send You Two Oz for Your Inspection & Examination.

If You approve of them & the proposall I shall be happy to think I have been of some little Service to my Country.

I can at all times send them to Calais. I shall Esteem it as a favour, Your Answer to the Above proposal & am With Respect—Your Very humb Servt P. ALLAIRE

N 61 Titchfield Street

a few lines without any Signature will be Sufficient

Benj: Franklin Esqr.

From Chaumont

ALS: American Philosophical Society

L'orient ce 10 may 1779.

Vostre Excellence, Monsieur Le Docteur, peut envoyer quand il luy plaira Sa Benediction au Cape Jones, Je crois qu'il sera en rade le quinze pour partir au plus tard Le vingt, ce que je vous prie de dire a ceux qui s'interessent a son sort. J'attends L'alliance &ca tous Les Jours.[1] Le Cape. Landais m'a ecrit qu'il attendoit unne Barque de Nantes Retenue en riviere par les vents Contraires. Il m'a demandé que Je luy tins prest icy plusieurs objets qu'il trouvera en arrivant. Recevez L'asseurance de mon tendre et Respectueux attachement

LERAY DE CHAUMONT

Addressed: A S. Ex Monsieur / Monsieur Le Docteur franklin / Ministre plenipotentiaire des etats / unis d'amerique a la Cour de / france / (A Paris)

Notation: Chaumont May 10. 1779

1. The *Alliance* sailed from the mouth of the Loire for Lorient on the 10th; see Landais' letter of May 12.

From Dumas

ALS: American Philosophical Society; AL (draft): Algemeen Rijksarchief

Monsieur, La Haie 10e. May 1779

En reponse à la vôtre du 29, je commence par ce que vous me demandez concernant Mr. St——. Il est d'une des meilleures familles de Berne, & peut, en son temps, entrer dans la régence de sa patrie. Il est protégé par le Ministre de la Marine, & employé par le même en Hollande à des affaires particulieres, par Commission signée du Roi, que j'ai vue, ainsi que plusieurs Lettres du Ministre & de Mrs. le R—— de Ch—— & Baudoin. Je suis convaincu de tout cela par mes yeux, & par les aveux qui ont échappé dans un moment de vivacité au G—— F——. Je me suis apperçu dans diverses de ces Lettres, & par les discours de Mr. St——, que le Ch—— G——d étoit fort suspect au Ministre, à Mr. le R—— de Ch——, & à Mr. Baud——, qu'ils desiroient d'être débarrassés de lui, de le voir éloigné des affaires, & du secret de l'Amérique, & de voir Mr. De N—— ou un autre lui succéder. Cela me rappelloit naturellement, & fortifioit certains avertissemens que de braves gens m'avoient donnés 3 mois auparavant sur son crédit vacillant, son malheur en Suisse, son intimité avec Rich l'Espion de Sir J. Y, la partialité que son fils ne pouvoit s'empêcher de montrer dans les conversations (malgré les signes qu'on lui faisoit de se modérer devant moi) en faveur des Anglois, le Gendre commandant un corps contre les Am——, le crédit de l'Am—— indiscretement exposé dans l'affaire de l'emprunt, &c. & voyant que notre ami avoit autant de confiance en N——, qu'il en avoit peu en l'autre, j'ai pris le parti, bien malgré moi, mais en conscience, par devoir, & parce que j'en étois requis, de vous écrire, Monsieur, comme j'ai fait depuis le 25 Janv. dernier.[2] Souffrez, après cela que je vous supplie d'avoir une conversation là-dessus avec Mr. Baudoin: il peut vous mettre parfaitement au fait de ce qui concerne Mr.

2. XXVIII, 426–7; in it he warned of the mishandling of the commissioners' Dutch loan by their agent, Horneca, Fizeaux & Cie.

St——, des ennemis qu'il s'est fait ici, pour s'être mêlé de cette affaire, & du sens dans lequel j'ai demandé vos ordres & les intentions des Ministres du Roi; & je sens maintenant, que vous ne pouvez ni comprendre ma demande, ni y répondre, avant d'avoir eu cet entretien avec lui.

Mr. De N—— n'avoit aucune connexion avec Mr St.; c'est moi qui, sur la priere de Mr. St——, l'ai adressé & fait connoître à Mr. De N——. Selon ses instructions il devoit choisir entre deux Maisons d'Amst——: celle de N—— en étoit une: il me consulta; je lui dis de ne pas hésiter pour Mr. De N——.

Je ne saurois montrer à G—— F—— vos Lettres en original depuis le 11 fevr. Le Chev. Gd. sauroit d'abord quelle part j'ai eue là-dedans et seroit mon ennemi mortel. Je ne puis pas non plus lui montrer votre derniere Lettre du 29, sans exposer le Ministre, Mr. le R—— de Ch—— & Mr. Baud—— avec moi. J'aime mieux lui laisser ignorer que j'en aie reçu une. Je lui donne avec plaisir des Extraits; mais il y auroit de la tyrannie à prétendre voir mes originaux; je ne pourrois à la fin plus rien vous écrire que sous la dictée, & selon les vues d'autrui, peut-être d'un Commis privé, tout dévoué au Chev. Je crois avec vous, Monsieur, qu'on est notre Ami; mais on peut subordonner l'amitié à des vues particulieres, souvent, sans le savoir, à celles d'autrui. Du reste, on est à présent tout accoutumé à ne voir que ce que je juge à propos; & nous sommes bien ensemble; car je puis être souvent utile.

Pour revenir à Mr. St——, vraisemblablement il sera bientôt fort loin d'ici pour affaires du Roi, que Mr. B——n sait. Aussi n'ai-je pas besoin de sa présence, pour veiller avec notre Ami & Mr. De N——, aux Intérêts de l'Am——.

Je sens de plus en plus, Monsieur, le besoin, à plusieurs égards, d'aller vous entretenir pendant une quinzaine de jours. Le supplément que vous m'avez alloué dernierement, me met en état de faire ce voyage, & de raccommoder un peu ma santé par la satisfaction de vous voir enfin. J'espere que ce sera dans 4 à 6 semaines.

Je suis sûr que Mr. De N—— réussira mieux qu'un autre à ce qu'il vous a promis, dès que les circonstances lui rendront la chose possible. Il seroit à souhaitter qu'on eût pris avec son prédécesseur[3] la même méthode qu'avec lui, de ne s'engager à rien que lorsqu'il eût souscrit & garanti toute la somme. Le crédit Américain n'auroit pas été hazardé comme il l'a été.

Vous aurez vu, Monsieur, par ma traduction (faite fort à la hâte) de la résolution des Etats-Genx. du 26 Avril, qu'elle est encore un peu captieuse. Quoiqu'il en soit, la france a publié son nouveau tarif, dont Mr. l'Ambr. m'a donné copie, & que j'ai envoyé aux Gazettiers.[4] Elle a bien fait. Toute la Hollande, excepté Amst. & Harlem, paiera 15 p% de leurs importations en Fce. Je me suis apperçu après coup, d'avoir omis, dans la liste des 32 Vaisseaux qu'on a résolu d'équiper ici, 2 Frégattes de 40 c. & 250 h. chacune.[5] Je suis avec un grand respect, Monsieur, Votre très-humble & très-obéissant serviteur D

Passy à s. Exc. Mr. Franklin

Addressed: à Son Excellence / Monsieur Franklin, Esqr. / Ministre Plénipotentiaire des / Etats-Unis de l'Amérique / à *Passy./.*[6]

Notation: Dumas May 10. 79

3. Horneca, Fizeaux & Cie., whose efforts had failed.

4. A new French tariff of 15 percent on goods imported into France from the Netherlands (except for naval stores) had gone into effect on May 1; the tariff was in addition to regular duties: Edler, *Dutch Republic,* pp. 124–5; Fauchille, *Diplomatie française,* pp. 136–7; *Gaz. de Leyde,* May 11.

5. Each frigate would carry 40 "canons" and 250 "hommes." Dumas included with the present letter a copy of the April 26 resolution of the States General (which he had first mentioned on May 3) and a list of the other ships to be outfitted: six ships of the line of 60 cannon apiece, eight ships of the line of 50 cannon, eight frigates of 36 cannon, seven frigates of 20 cannon, and one snow.

6. On the address sheet is an unrelated list of payments largely duplicating the entry of May 15 in BF's Cash Book (Account XVI, XXVI, 3): 24 *l.t.* to Hemery (a typefounder, for whom see XXVII, 341), 12 *l.t.* to Beauville, 6 *l.t.* to "Girl" and 3 *l.t.* to "Boy." There are numerous similar entries in this account (with varying sums); that of June 12 indicates the four were "In the Foundry."

From Madame Brillon

AL: American Philosophical Society

ce 11 may 1779

Vous avéz bien raison mon bon papa, nous ne devons faire consistér le véritable bonheur que dans la paix de l'áme; il n'est pas en notre pouvoir de changér le caractére des gents avéc lesquels nous vivons n'y d'empeschér le cours des contrarietés qui nous entourent; c'est un sage qui parle et qui tasche de consollér sa fille trop sensible en lui enseignant le vérité: oh mon pére, j'implore votre amitié votre saine philosophie, mon coeur vous entends, vous est soumis; donnés moi de la force, qu'elle me tienne lieu d'une indifférence que votre enfant ne peut jamais sentir: mais mon ami, convenéz que pour celui qui sçait aimér l'ingratitude est un mal affreux; qu'il est dur pour une fémme qui donneroit sa vie sans hésittér, pour assurér le bonheur de son mari; de se voir enlevér le fruit de ses soins, de ses désirs, par l'intrigue, la fausseté—le tems aménera tout a bien mon papa l'a dit, je le crois; mais mon papa a dit aussi, le tems est l'étoffe dont la vie est faitte;[7] ma vie mon ami est faitte d'une étoffe fine et légére que le chagrin déchire cruéllement. Si j'avois quélques reproches a me faire, je n'éxisterois plus depuis bien longtems! Mon áme est pure, simple, franche, j'ose l'attéstér a mon pére, j'ose lui dire qu'elle est digne de lui; j'ose encore l'assurér que ma conduitte qu'il a trouvée sage, ne se dementira pas, que j'attendrai la justice avéc patience, que je suivrai les conseils de mon réspéctable ami, avéc tenuë et confiance— adieu vous que j'aime tant mon bon papa, ne m'appellés jamais que ma fille, hiér vous m'appelliés madame et mon coeur se sérroit je m'éxaminois pour voir si j'avois quelques torts envérs vous, ou si j'avois quélques déffauts que vous ne vouliés pas me dire— pardon mon ami, ce n'est pas un reproche que je vous fais, c'est une foiblésse dont je m'accuse je suis née beaucoup trop sensible pour mon bonheur et pour celui de mes amis; guerissés moi ou plaignés moi, si vous le pouvés faittes l'un et l'autre: C'est demain mércredi, vous viendrés au thé n'est ce pas, croyés mon papa que la jouissance que j'epprouve a vous recevoir est partagée par

7. An echo of Poor Richard 1746, "Dost thou love Life? then do not squander Time; for that's the Stuff Life is made of." III, 64.

mon mari, mes enfants, mes amis, je n'en puis douttér, et je vous l'assure.

Addressed: A Monsieur / Monsieur Franklin / [*In another hand*] A Passy

To Madame Brillon

AL and AL (draft): American Philosophical Society

10 May [*i.e.* May 11 or after, 1779][8]

Vous m'avez dit, ma chere fille, que vôtre Coeur est *trop sensible.* Je vois bien, dans vos Lettres, que cela *est trop vraie.* D'etre fort sensible de nos propres fautes; c'est bon; parceque cela nous mêne de les eviter en futur: Mais d'etre fort sensible & affligé des Fautes d'autres Gens,—ce n'est pas bon. C'est à eux d'être sensible là, & d'être affligées de ce qu'ils avoient malfait:—Pour nous, nous devons rester en Tranquilité, qui est la juste Partage de l'Innocence & la Vertu. Mais vous dites "*que l'Ingratitude est un Mal affreux.*" C'est vrai,—aux Ingrats—mais non pas à leurs Bienfaiteurs. Vous avez conferé des Bienfaits sur ceux qui vous en avez crus dignes. Vous avez donc fait vôtre Devoir, parceque c'est de nôtre Devoir d'etre bienfaisantes; & vous devez être satisfaite de cela, & heureuse dans la Reflection. S'ils sont des Ingrats, c'est leur Crime & non pas la votre; & c'est à eux d'être malheureux quand ils reflechissent sur la Turpitude de leur Conduit envers vous.—S'ils vous font des Injures, reflechissez que quoique ils peuvent être auparavant vos égaux, ils se sont placés par cette moyen au-dessous de vous;— Si vous vous vengez en les punissant exactement, vous les restituez leur Etat d'egalité qu'ils avoient

8. This letter answers point by point Mme. Brillon's of May 11. We presume that she dated her letter correctly since she speaks of a "demain mércredi," and May 11, 1779, was indeed a Tuesday. BF's letter has to have been written after it; he may have drafted his reply and spent some time producing the fair copy before dispatching it to her. Her response (June 4, below) has an immediacy to it that indicates she had just received it. For a linguistic and psychological analysis of this document see Dorothy Medlin, "Benjamin Franklin and the French Language: a Letter to Madame Brillon," *French-American Review,* I (1977), 232–9.

perdue: Mais si vous les pardonnies, sans leur donner aucune Punition, vous les fixez dans cette basse Etat ou ils sont tombées, & d'ou ils ne pouvent jamais sortir, sans une vraie Repentance & pleine Reparation. Suivez donc, ma trés chere & toujours aimable Fille, la bonne Resolution que vous avez prise si sagement, de continuer à remplir tous vos Devoirs, comme bonne mere, bonne Femme, bonne Amie, bonne Prochaine, bonne Chretienne, &c., (sans oublier d'être bonne Fille à votre Papa) & à negliger & oublier s'il est possible les Injures qu'on peut vous faire à present; Et soyez assurée, qu'avec le Tems, la Rectitude de vôtre Conduite gagnera sur les Esprits même des Gens les plus mauvaises; & encore plus sur ceux des Personnes qui sont au fond d'un bon Naturel, & qui ont aussi du bon Sens, quoique pour le present peutêtre un peu egarées par l'Artifice des autres. Alors, tous vous demanderont avec Compunction le Retour de vôtre Amitié, & ils deviendront pour l'avenir des vos plus zélés Amis.

Je suis sensible que J'ai ecrit ici beaucoup de trés mauvais François; cela peut vous dégouter, vous qui ecrivez cette Langue charmante avec tant de pureté & d'elegance. Mais si vous pouvez enfin dechiffrer mes Expressions obscures, gauches & impropres, vous aurez peutêtre au moins cette espece de Plaisir qu'on a en expliquant les Enigmes, ou en découvrant des Secrets.

From ——— de Labussiere[9]

AL: American Philosophical Society

au Palais Royalle le 11 mai 79

Mr De Labussiere emprêssé de s'aquitér des devoirs que lui impose la reconnoisance des bontéz quil vient de recevoir a

9. His identity is a puzzle. Both Digges (May 12, below) and Vaughan (May 31, below) refer to him in terms that suggest he may have been Louis-Joseph-Jean-Baptiste de Boissière, comte de Chambors (1756–1820). Later a maréchal de camp in the French army, he was a gentleman of honor to Charles Philippe, comte d'Artois. *DBF,* under Chambors. In August, 1755, his father had been killed in a hunting accident by the Dauphin who,

Londre de Miss chipley, est au déséspoir que des devoirs le Contrarie sur le desir quil a d'avoir l'honneur de remetre lui mesme a Monsieur Franklin ses Comiscions. Le bonheur eut étté double pour Mr. De Labussiere de joindre les témoignages d'amitié dont il est chargé a seux de réspect et d'estime quil a voué a Monsieur Franklin.[1]

From Dumas

ALS: American Philosophical Society; AL (draft): Algemeen Rijksarchief

Monsieur Lahaie 11–14e. May *1779.*

Aujourdhui 11e. le Corps des Marchands d'Amst—— présente une Adresse à l'Amirauté, pour presser les Convois en conséquence de la Résolution du 26 Avril, sur la foi de laquelle ils ont déjà fait leurs speculations & pris leurs mesures, notamment pour des bois de construction. Nous verrons comment l'Amirauté se comportera.[2]

14e.

L'Amirauté, n'ayant pas répondu d'une maniere satisfaisante à l'addresse susdite des Marchds. d'Amst——,[3] ceux-ci préparent une adresse à L.h.p., pour se plaindre plus fort que jamais. D'un autre côté, la fermentation & le murmure augmentant à Rotterdam, d'où les Marchds. menacent de se retirer pour aller s'établir à Amst——, les Députés de Rott—— — ont fait une proposition à l'Assemblée provinciale ici, pour

in remorse, did all he could to aid the widow and her son born the following January: Cröy, *Journal*, I, 321n. In May the King changed the status of his lands in Chambors to a "comté," though he was always called marquis de Chambors: *Dict. de la noblesse*, under Boissière-Chambors.

1. In another letter, undated, Labussiere, who is just leaving for the country, writes that he has received "nouvélles léttres" from Miss Shipley. Unable to deliver them in person, he sends them care of a trustworthy man. Has BF received the first letters he sent? APS.

2. La Vauguyon had suggested this move to the merchants: Fauchille, *Diplomatie française*, pp. 137–8.

3. The Admiralty replied that it did not consider the States General's resolution of April 26 equivalent to orders to begin convoying: *ibid.*, p. 138.

que l'on prenne enfin, de concert avec les autres provinces, ou, à leur défaut, par la Hollande seule, une Résolution telle qu'il la faut pour mettre fin à tous ces désagrémens, & prévenir la ruine totale de la Ville de Rotterdam. Cette proposition a été faite commissoriale.

C'est en suivant toujours l'impulsion de ma conscience, de mon zele pour l'Amere., & de mon attachement personnel pour vous Monsieur, que je crois vous devoir l'Extrait suivant d'une Lettre que de fort braves gens m'écrivent d'Amst—— en date du 11e.

"Il y a quelque temps que nous reçumes 3 remises tirées de philadelphie, par Holker fils, ordre de Robt. Morris, une sur Buffault,[4] & 2 sur M. le Ray de Chaumont. Elles furent toutes acceptées: mais à l'échéance, les 2 dernieres sont retournées avec protest, faute de paiement. Nous les avons renvoyées à St. Eustache. Ce désastre fera beaucoup de mal au crédit des Amns., dont le papier diminuoit de jour en jour, ensorte qu'on donnoit 5 à 6 Dollars de papier, contre un d'argent, suivant les derniers avis."[5]

Je suis avec respect, Monsieur, Votre très humble & très obéissant serviteur D

P.S. J'ai bien reçu, Monsieur, par Mr. le Col. Hope, votre Lettre & paquet du 4e May; & la Gazette ci-jointe vous fera voir que j'ai déjà commencé à faire usage du contenu. J'ai fait lire au Grand-Pensionaire la Résolution du Congrès touchant le Navire Portugais; il a admiré l'esprit d'équité & d'humanité qui l'ont dicté. Cette Piece, & la Lettre au sujet du Cap. Cook, paroîtront incessamment.[6]

Dans ce moment, Monsieur, je recois la vôtre du 9e. May. Je

4. Probably Jean-Baptiste Buffault, an *agent de change:* Lüthy, *Banque protestante,* II, 528. Jean Holker ("Holker fils") was the French consul in Philadelphia.

5. The dollar was depreciating rapidly in the United States itself; in January, 1779, it took $8.00 in currency to purchase a dollar in specie, in April, 1779, $16.00: Ferguson, *Power of the Purse,* p. 32.

6. The congressional resolution promised reimbursement to the owners of a snow captured by an American privateer: XXVII, 554; *JCC,* XI, 487–9. It and the letter asking safe passage for Cook (above, March 10) appeared in the May 18 *Gaz. de Leyde.*

serai sur mes gardes avec Nicolas Davis; & j'avertirai Mr. De N—— de l'être aussi.

Passy à Son Exc. Mr. F——n

Addressed: à Son Excellence / Monsieur Franklin, Esqr. / Ministre Plénipre. des Etats- / Unis de l'Amérique, à la / Cour de France, / à *Passy.*/.

Notation: Dumas May. 14. 79

From David Hartley

Copy:[7] American Philosophical Society; transcript: Library of Congress

My Dear Friend Golden Square May 11 1779

Yours of May 4th. recd this moment. I cannot see the Commissioners of Sick & Hurt before tonights Mail, but I can equally give you an answr relating to the Prisoners because it was not longer ago than last night that one of the Commissioners calld upon me, in part to hear what was become of the Cartel Ship and anxious to proceed with the Exchange therefore without doubt you may proceed accordingly. The Commissioner, Mr Bell, who is a very well disposd person to forward the Exchange, suggested to me, to renew the application for the Exchange at Morlaix as much more expeditious.[8] Your answer shall be immediately conveyd to the board of Sick & Hurt. If Morlaix should be chosen, I suppose a new passport would be necessary— Querry will a new passport be necessary if the second Exche. should be still at the same port as the first? I must conclude, not having this day a moment to spare. You will hear from me soon— On Nesbit fifteen Guineas, but never paid— On Vaughan twenty Guineas, wch I

7. Possibly in the hand of Thomas Digges. Digges had just arrived in London, probably carrying BF's May 4 letter. The two men were frequently in each other's company in May and June working on both the prisoner exchange and the tentative peace negotiations that Hartley hoped to effect.

8. Hartley had already asked BF to inquire about using Morlaix for future prisoner exchanges: XXVIII, 245–6, 321.

consider not as publick prisoners money, but private upon Your own Acct: therefore remains in my hand—[9] All the other prisoners money has been expended a long while ago. I am Yrs &c. &c D.H—

Compliments from another quarter[1]

Notation: D.H. May 10. 1779.

From Joshua Johnson

ALS: American Philosophical Society

Honbl. Sir. Nantes 11 May 1779

I did myself the honour of Incloseing you some American News Papers the 29 Ultimo which I hope you got safe. Inclosed you have the only one I have received since.

Some time ago[2] you was so obligeing as to write me that you had procured an exemtion of the Duties on my Furniture. I would rather pay ten times the sum than to be troublesome, but the ungenteel behaviour of the Farmers urgeing the Payment will I hope apoligize for my informing you that unless the Director General will send an Order for their acquital that you are under no obligations to him on my Account. I have a small Vessell Just Arrived from Baltimore who departed the 6 April. I have nothing new by her, nor has she brought any News Papers or I would have sent them to you.

In hopes of hearing from you shortly I remain with the greatest esteem Sir. Your most obedt. Servt JOSHUA JOHNSON

His Excellency Benjn. Franklin Esqr.

Addressed: His Excellency / Benjamin Franklin Esqr / Plenipotentiary at the / Court of / Versailles

Notation: Johnson Joshua 11. May 1779.

9. Probably an answer to BF's May 4 query about "two Small Bills." For an earlier inquiry about bills on the bankers Nesbit and Vaughan see XXVI, 526, 539–40.

1. Almost certainly Digges.

2. March 17, above.

From Edward Newenham[3]

ALS: American Philosophical Society

Sir Geneva 11th May 1779

I have the honour to inform your Excellency, that I have this day, received a Letter from my worthy Friends Messrs: Folsh and Hornbostel of Marsailles, enclosing a Copy of his Excellencys the Count de Vergenne's Letter to the Marquiss de Pilles Governor of that City, granting me and my Sons permission, at your recommendation, to remain there;[4] having been constantly travelling ever since, I could not receive that favour Sooner, or I should have acknowledged the particular honour—

I remained at Marsailles, as long as I possibly could without creating a Diffidence or Distrust in Government; having assured the Gentlemen there, that I would not desire to Stay longer, than the Time, I might possibly receive a Letter of Leave; when that Time elapsed, I left that City with much regret; for I would not on any account be even looked upon with a Jealous Eye or Suspected of acting an unworthy part in a Kingdom, where I and my Sons had received accumulated favours—

Permit me to take this earliest opportunity to return Your Excellency my most Sincere thanks for the honour you did me, & to assure you, that you should not have received any discredit from mine or my Sons Conducts, and that your worthy Countrymen shall always receive a reciprocal friendship from me; The warm parts I took in favour of the Liberties of the united states of North America, are well Known in Ireland and England; The Journals of our Parliament record parts of them, by the Motions I made; and many of your Excellency's

3. The opposition member of the Irish Parliament had written from Marseilles in January seeking BF's assistance in obtaining license to stay in that city for the benefit of his sons' health: XXVIII, pp. 330–1.

4. A year earlier J.C. Hornbostel, a merchant in partnership with his father-in-law, the Swedish consul Fölich, had identified himself to BF in a letter applying for a consulship in Marseilles: XXVI, 212. The marquis de Pilles is listed in the *Etat militaire* for 1779, p. 36.

Countrymen have felt my Love for them; Your Friendship will, if Possible, add to my former marks of regard to such of your Brave, Worthy and Virtuous Countrymen, as the fortune of War may render my Country a place of their Temporary Residence— Accident, only, prevented my being in that Land of Freedom last December; having agreed with Captain Smith of Chesnut street in Philadelphia, master of the Ship Resolution, for my passage with my Eldest Son; being determined (if I live) to settle part of my Family in the Jerseys or Pensylvania—[5]

After a Tour through Italy with my Sons, whose health is re-established, I am now on my Journey to Ireland through Germany, and mean to take my Passage from Ostend or Calais, May I Entreat your Excellency will grant me, My Sons and one Servant a Protection against any American Ships of War that may meet the pacquet Boat in which we sail, and to add to that honour, by obtaining me & my Sons the like favour from his Majesty, in Case of meeting any of his Ships or Vessels of War in our passage from Calais or Ostend to England, & from England to Ireland.

I flatter myself that your Excellency will excuse the trouble & Freedom of this Letter, and you may rely upon my not disgracing your favour; I hope to be honoured with an Answer, directed to Sir Edward Newenham, Poste Restante, Ostend, where, I hope to be in about 14 Days—[6]

I have the Honour to be, Sir, with Every *sincere* mark of Respect & Regard Your Excellencys Most obliged & most obedient Humble Sert. EDWARD NEWENHAM

Notation: Eduard Newenham Geneva 11. may. 1779.

5. A year and a half later, Newenham again told BF that he intended to settle in America; he said that he had shipped his belongings in 1777, but was prevented from sailing to New York when the Irish revenue commissioners detained the ship (Nov. 6, 1780, APS).

6. BF suggested that Edward Bancroft meet with Newenham at Ostend; see our annotation of BF's letter to Bancroft, May 31.

From Isaiah Robinson ALS: American Philosophical Society

Honble. Sir Bordeaux 11th May 1779

I arrived here a few days ago from Virga. in a Ship, built there, belonging to Philadelphia, having had leave of absence from the Marine Committee for that purpose. I should have done myself the Honor to have wrote You earlier, aprizing You of the well being of your Family, & Friends in America, had not the Chevalier de Crenis, who came passenger with me, and who is intrusted with Letters for You, proposed setting out for Paris, on our first arrival. He has been detained by Indisposition, but I hope will be enabled to prosecute his Journey in a Day, or two, Your letters by Him will afford You much later, & I doubt not much more Authentick Intelligence, than I can pretend to give You; to these therefore I beg leave to refer You on that Subject.[7]

I trust Your Excellency will not deem me impertinent, or troublesome in Solliciting your information, & advice in an affair, that concerns myself. At the time my late worthy Friend Capt. Lambert Wicks had the Honor of bringing You to France,[8] He, & I entered into an Agreement to share equally whatever prize Money either of Us might be entitled to from any Captures made on our different Cruizes, we had indeed no written Instruments executed between us to that purpose, but there are in Philada. several, who were witnesses of the Contract, the Depositions of some of whom with the proper Certificates I have bought with me; it is supposed in America, that from the number of Capt. Wick's Prizes, his Quota must have amounted to a considerable Sum I have not learnt that any remittence has been Made, nor am I aprized of the proper Channel, thro which to atain to any certain knowledge of what may be done in the Business, since my Arrival here, I have been informed by a Gentleman, a Friend of Mine that a

7. For Martial-Jean-Antoine Crozat de Crénis (1739–1785) see XXIII, 550. Crénis himself writes from Bordeaux, *c.* May 11, that he has arrived by the *General Mercer* carrying letters for BF from the Baches (XXVIII, 386, 390–2). Since illness prevents his immediate departure for Paris, he will, for security's sake, address the letters care of Turgot. APS.

8. For Wickes see XXII, 482n; XXIII, liv, 26–7.

very Valuable part of the prize Goods, were a short time since remaining unsold at Pt. Lorient, I therefore take the Liberty to Sollicit your Excellency's advice, & assistance in the Matter, not at all doubting, from your wonted goodness, & Candour, tho I have not the Honor of being personally known to You, Your affording it me.

As the Ship, General Mercer, in which I am will sail in a few Weeks for Philadelphia, is a remarkable fast Sailer, well armed, mounting Eighteen six pounders, & will be mann'd proportionably, it may be a good opportunity to send to Congress, or Your Friends, whatever you may have Occasion to dispatch in such Case You may depend on my utmost Care, & punctuality Should Your Excellency do me the Honor to write me, Youll please Order such Letters to be put under Cover to, or directed to the Care of John Bonfield to whom my Ship, and Cargoe are Adressd.

I have the Honor to be with most perfect Respect Your Excellency's most Obedt. Servt. ISAIAH ROBINSON

The Honble. Benjn. Franklin Esqr. Paris

Addressed: His Excellency / Benjn. Franklin Esqr / Plenipotentiary / to the United States of America / at the Court / of Versailles / a Passy Pres Paris / de Vlles.

Notation: Isaiah Robinson Bordeaux 11e may 1779.

From Sutton de Clonard

ALS: American Philosophical Society

Sir Ruë Colbert 11 May 1779./.

Mr. Stephen Merchant of Boston, is come from Dunkirk to Sollicite your Excellency for an American Commission to Enable him to Command the Cutter of 16 guns which I mention'd to you—[9] I request you may gratify him therein. This

9. Perhaps mentioned by Sutton de Clonard in person, as his most recent extant letter (above, March 15) did not discuss the cutter (the *Black Prince,* formerly the Irish smuggler *Friendship*): Clark, *Ben Franklin's Privateers,* pp. 5, 23, 29. Marchant's prior attempts to procure an American commission had been unsuccessful; see BF's March 14 letter to him.

Vessel will have a very good Crew, American & Irish; As She Sails extremely well, She must do considerable Execution—

Thomas Wilkinson, formerly Pilot for the Irish Channel, on board the Drake, is not yet order'd to Nantes for being Sent on the Cartel Ship, as you was kind enough to promise—[1] He was lately order'd to remove from St. Pol de Leon, to a town call'd Fougere, where he now is. You'll much oblige me in ordering his Speedy Exchange—

I am, Sir, Your Excellency's most obedient, and most humble Servant De Clonard

Addressed: To His Excellence B. Franklin Esqr / Minr. Plenipy. of the United States / of America / at Passy

Notation: De Clonarg Paris 11e. may 1779.

From Thomas Digges

ALS: Historical Society of Pennsylvania

Dr. Sir London 12. May 1779

My journey hither was a favourable one & I am in hopes will turn out to good account; I have not yet however been able to deliver *all* Your letters—those for the environs of London are yet in my possession, as I preferred keeping them a day or two to make a personal delivery of them, to the risqueing them by penny post. I this day deliverd Miss Shipleys— His Lordship was not at home to join in the general satisfaction & joy expressd by the whole Female part of the Family on hearing from Yourself that you were well & happy— I got a share of consequence by being Your messenger, and was rogue enough to wish (when I saw a hasty kiss given to B F at the foot of Your Letter) to have the beatitude transferrd to me— It is a shame for You to be so great a monopoliser of Hearts.

I understood from the Family that a french Gentn. (I beleive the Ecuyer to the Count D Artois) sets out in the morning for Paris, & I am to send this to the Bishops for forwardance by Him.[2]

1. BF's promise, possibly oral, apparently had been made in response to Sutton de Clonard's March 15 appeal.

2. Labussiere. See his letter of May 11.

Our matter goes on seemingly very well; in a meeting between Mr. H and a certain great man, the later seemd to catch with avidity at Mr Hs. application for an audience, & this night at nine oClock is the hour appointed for a parley:[3] I fear it will not be in my power to forward you the result of that parley by this conveyance; as I am under injunctions from Your Ruby-lipd Correspondant to send my letter this evening; I will however keep it to the last, and at any rate risque sending another letter to the Bishops in the morning. I write You from our friend Mr Hs where I am waiting his return from Westminster Hall & for his Roast beef.

Every thing seems working well for our Country & its cause; I hope no civil discord or nasty cabals will cast a cloud over the promisd fair & serene Western Sky. Arbuthnots Squadron is not yet saild from Torbay but will go with the first fair wind;[4] If a few Ships of War and nearly four thousand Recruits (wch. is the force going with him) can do America any further injury, I am confidant She has my friend Govr Johnstone solely to thank for it; for He stands alone as to opinion that every exertion against America is now necessary for the Safety of this Country.[5]

Ministry seem to speak out dispondingly of their affairs in Ama & particularly for the Southern army. The exposition of the correspondence between them & their Commanders in America has servd to open the Eyes of the people a little, and the Examination into the affairs of the Howes by the evidence wch. have already been given at the bar of the House of Com-

3. See our annotation of Hartley's letter of April 10 for his discussions with Lord North. His letter of May 25, below, reports the results of a private conference with the British minister.

4. Adm. Marriot Arbuthnot (1711?–1794: *DNB*) commanded a convoy destined for New York carrying reinforcements for Clinton. Contrary winds had detained the convoy in Portsmouth; on May 11, the Cabinet created a further delay by ordering Arbuthnot to remain at Torbay until ten of the Channel fleet could escort him. Mackesy, *War for America,* pp. 260–1.

5. See, for example, the speech of Gov. George Johnstone, formerly of the Carlisle Commission, in the House of Commons on April 19: France was now allied with British subjects to bring about the destruction of Britain, and decisive action was needed to compel American submission. Cobbett, *Parliamentary History,* XX (1778–80), 390.

mons, is likely to damn them compleatly;[6] It now appears that instead of vagabonds & poltroons the Americans are a vigilent, well disciplind, and a respectable Enemy. In the House of Lords yesterday, Ld Rockingham gave a very melancholly picture of the state of things in Ireland.[7] It would seem to me that the period is not very distant when that oppressd people will seek relief to their distress from Congress's & assosiations of their own. In the debate on this matter the disunion among both parties, Whigs, & Tories, was a good picture of the distraction of the times. Lord Rockingham makes a motion for the state of Ireland to be laid before the House— Lord Weymouth opposes it with the previous question— The Duke of Chandos & Lord Townsend support Lord Rockingham— The Duke of Grafton & Lord Shelburne oppose Him; & it all ends with giving the Marquis his Motion He cutting off part of His preamble.[8]

The leaders of the Bedford party have veerd about very much of late, & are from all appearances going over to opposition.[9] The quarrels among the Ministry has been the prob-

6. For the exchanges of letters between the ministry and British commanders in America see *The Parliamentary Register . . .*, XI (1778–79), 253–483. The hearings in the House of Commons on the conduct of Sir William Howe and his brother Adm. Richard Howe took place on May 6, 11, 13, and 18. Sir William sought to refute the accusations against them by calling five officers to testify that the colonists were overwhelmingly hostile to Britain and the loyalists uncooperative militarily. For an account of the hearings see *ibid.,* XIII, 1–73, 91–120, and Gruber, *Howe Brothers,* pp. 342–50.

7. The former minister's speech was reported in *The Public Advertiser,* May 12, 1779. He warned of "Ten Thousand People in Arms. . . . Manufacturers and Workmen Starving in the Streets, subsisting on Charity. . . . well-grounded Apprehensions that France, if not America, may offer the distressed inhabitants that Relief which they have implored in vain from England."

8. For Thomas Thynne, third Viscount Weymouth, Thomas Townshend, third Viscount Sydney, and Augustus Henry Fitzroy, third Duke of Grafton, see the *DNB.* For James Brydges, third Duke of Chandos, see Namier and Brooke, *House of Commons,* II, 127. The debates on Ireland are reported in Cobbett, *Parliamentary History,* XX (1778–80), 635–57.

9. The faction formerly led by John Russell, fourth duke of Bedford (d. 1771), had been taken over by his brother-in-law, Granville Leveson-

able cause of this. Lord N and Lord G. G are at cat & dog if not at open rupture.[1] Lord N——'s language is, that Lord G G is such a blundering ass & so great a fool, that it is impossible to act with Him; The other says that North is so treacherous as *never* to support his friends when in need and always leaves them in the Dark.— When rogues quarrel, it is to be hoped honest men will get at their right.—

There has been some accots from N York to Ministry by way of Corke that have not been good enough to give to the publick in a Gazette, consequently they were bad. The talk is that the accots from Byron in the West Indies are but indifferent,—[2] These, together with the reports wch reignd very currently about ten days ago that overtures for Peace were negotiating, having ceasd, has causd the Stocks to fall two & a half per. Ct. lately & the City gentry are rather in the dumps. Hopeing to have an oppertunity given me to write in the morning by the same conveyance with this I shall not add further at present than that I am with very great esteem Dr. Sir Your very obligd and Obedient Servant THO DIGGES

Notation: May 12. 79

From Landais

ALS: American Philosophical Society

Please Your Excellency L'Orient May 12th 1779.

I Sailed from the River of Nantes the 10th. Instt. Came at anchor at Groay Island[3] the 12th and into the harbour of

Gower, second Earl Gower (*DNB*). Gower and Weymouth would, in fact, resign in the autumn in an effort to bring down North and take over the government: Frank O'Gorman, *The Rise of Party in England: the Rockingham Whigs 1760–82* (London, 1975), p. 395.

1. Lord George Germain, secretary of state for the American colonies. *DNB.*

2. The admiral had taken up a position in the Leeward Islands to keep an eye on the French in Martinique. Mackesy, *War for America,* p. 272.

3. The Ile de Groix, near the entrance to the harbor.

L'Orient today,[4] where Monsieur Ray De Chaumond[5] Delivered me the Letter Your Excellency honnoured me with the 28th Ult. Containing Your Order to put my Self and Ship under Capt Jones Command accordinly I went Directly to Seek him and ask'd his orders. I think you Kindly for your wishes.

I am with the Greateast Respect. Your Excellency Most Obedient & Most humble Servant. P: LANDAIS

Excellency Bn. Franklin Minister Plenipotentiary of the united States of America

Endorsed: Capt. Landais May 12. 1779 Complies with the Orders

Notation: 8/

4. The short voyage did not impress JA with Landais' ability. He wrote in his diary of Landais' inactivity and indecision, his jealousy, and his "Silence, Reserve, and . . . forbidding Air": Butterfield, *John Adams Diary,* II, 368–9. Landais blamed the *Alliance*'s master for the ship's poor handling which almost ran her aground: Pierre Landais, *Memorial to Justify Peter Landai's Conduct during the Late War* (Boston, 1784), p. 14.

5. In Lorient, Chaumont corroborated JA's account of the difficulties aboard the *Alliance:* below, May 14.

From the Massachusetts Delegates to Congress[6]

Three LS and copy:[7] American Philosophical Society

Sir Philadelphia May 12th: 1779

The Papers enclosed will inform You of the unfortunate Loss of the American Brigantine Fair Play, with 18 of her Crew, on the 5th: Jany last, by the discharge of the Cannon of a two Gun Battery, near Port Louis in Guadaloupe—[8]

The Governor of the Island thinking it reasonable that the Owners should recieve a Compensation for their Loss, recommended it to the Minister of the Marine of France, in a Letter whereof a translated Copy is enclosed but the Captain of the Brigantine having neglected to take duplicates of the Letter, rendered it necessary for the Owners, of whom Tristram Dalton Esqr. of Newbury port in Massachusetts Bay was one, to take additional Steps, for the recovering of their Interest.

We think it adviseable for Mr. Dalton to obtain a Compensation in the Way proposed by the Governor of Guadaloupe rather than by making a Claim thro' Congress, on the Principle of Right: as the latter may require time, and produce an Altercation neither agreable to the Court of France nor Congress—and as we have no Reason to suppose that there was any Design in the Commandant of the Fort, to insult the Flag of the United States or injure the property or Persons of its Citizens—

6. Or at any rate those presently in attendance. Three other delegates, Francis Dana, Timothy Edwards, and John Hancock did not attend during 1779: Smith, *Letters,* XII, xviii. Three signers of the present letter will be familiar, but Holten has hitherto appeared on our pages only in passing (see XXII, 244). He is Samuel Holten (1738–1816), a physician and early patriot leader: *DAB.* This letter, as well as the papers it mentions, was enclosed with Tristram Dalton's of the following day, below, in support of his claim for compensation in the case of the *Fair Play.* See that letter for further details.

7. The three LS are marked "1st Copy," "3d Copy," and "4th Copy." We print from the last of these, which BF endorsed. The copy is in Dalton's hand and bears BF's notation, "Letter of 4 Members of Congress."

8. On Jan. 5, 1778, William Bingham had written the American commissioners about the incident: XXVIII, 350.

Having stated the Facts we submit to your Determination the Measures proper to be pursued & remain Sir with the greatest Respect your most obt. & very hum Sert

S ADAMS
E GERRY
JAMES LOVELL
S. HOLTEN

Honble. Benj Franklin Esqr. Minister plenipotentiary of the united States at Paris

Addressed: Honble: Benjamin Franklin Esq / Minister Plenipotentiary of / the United States of America / at Paris

Endorsed: Tristram Dalton Esq Papers relating to the Loss of the Fairplay Brigantine—

From Georgiana Shipley ALS: American Philosophical Society

May the 12th 1779

You my dear Sir by your most flattering attention have anticipated my very wishes, this moment I have received from Mr Digges your kind letter & valuable present; it would be difficult to express the real pleasure they have both given me, we all are made happy from your account of your own health, my father desires me to say, that a life so precious cannot be too attentively preserved, long very long may it remain a continued blessing to Mankind.[9]

You ask me "whether I may venture to own my correspondence with an *Out-law.*" Yes I will own it, nay glory in the having some little claim to the friendship & affection of the most respectable of Men.

My father sympathizes with you, in your feelings for the public calamities, the period of which I fear is yet far distant, but you have both this consolation, & a great one it is to

9. BF's "kind letter" is missing. The gift was one of the small Sèvres medallions that BF sent to his friends as souvenirs. Sellers, *Franklin in Portraiture,* p. 135. Digges described, in his letter of May 12, her receipt of the gift. See also her letter of June 6.

minds like yours, that you have done every thing which judgement & integrity could suggest to avert the misfortunes that over-whelm us.

This is the third letter I have written to you lately, reckoning the one Mr Vaughan sent for me, besides which Anna-Maria writ a few lines by Gen Verdiere,[1] it is unreasonable to intrude so often upon your goodness I therefore hasten to conclude, pray continue to believe me Your gratefull & affectionate GEORGIANA SHIPLEY

Will you forgive me, but a lock of Hair from a head I value so much, is all I have now to desire.[2]

Addressed: A Monsr Monsieur Franklin / Passy / pres de / Paris

Endorsed: Miss Ga Shipley

From William Vernon, Jr.[3]

ALS: American Philosophical Society

Sir Bordeaux 12th of May 1779

In February 1778 I embarked with the honble. John Adams Esqr. on board the American Frigate the Boston for France, for the purpose of acquiring a competent knowledge of the Language, manners, customs, manufactures, exports & imports of this Kingdom.[4] I arrived here in April following; and having found, after three Months experience, that the frequent & inevitable company of those who spoke my native Tongue prevented one of the principal & most essential motives of my voyage being answered, I retired into the Country,[5] where I

1. Her two recent letters are dated March 17 and May 1, her sister Anna-Maria's, April 7. All are above.

2. BF finally obliged her in this request early the following year; she thanked him on Feb. 3, 1780. APS.

3. The son of William Vernon, Sr. (for whom see above, April 3): XXV, 641–2n; XXVIII, 204n.

4. JA was sufficiently impressed with the young man to offer him a position as his secretary, an offer which he refused: *Adams Papers,* VII, 35, 80–1.

5. To Montauban in Guienne: Butterfield, *John Adams Diary,* II, 271n.

remained 'till the end of February last. It being, Sir, the intention of my Father that I should enter into a Counting-House for twelve or eighteen months, & I myself being sensible that it is the only means of gaining a knowledge of the Commerce of France, I have made the strictest enquiry for the House of the greatest reputation & most extensive correspondence here; from which it appears that that of Messrs. Feyers freres is upon the most solid foundation & the best adapted in every respect to the ends which I seek. But the improbability of an admittance into it without proper letters of recommendation deters me from attempting it, and (join'd to an ardent desire that I have to execute as soon as possible the views with which I left my native Country & to answer as far as in me lays the expectations of a Parent) induces me to take the Liberty of addressing you upon this subject & of desiring (through the medium of a letter with which I was honored to you by the Honble. John Handcock Esq) that you would take the trouble of writing a few lines to those Gentlemen in my behalf, & of engaging Mr. Le Grand the American Banker, who is a particular Correspondent of theirs, to give them a line in my favour.

I flatter myself, Sir, that you will not hesitate to comply with my request, when you reflect that you will render essential service to one whom a continued remorse disquietes for the loss of that time which ought to be employed in acquiring some knowledge that may make him a fit member for Society, & may qualify him for rendering some service to his Country which will ever be his chief ambition. I beg, Sir, that you will excuse this freedom & accept of the assurance of the most sincere respect & the sentiments of esteem with which I have the honor to be Sir your most obet. & most hlb servant

WILLIAM VERNON JUNR.

Addressed: A son Excellence / Benjamin Franklin Ecuyer / Plénipotentiaire des Etats Unis / de l'Amerique / à Paris

Notation: William Vernon junr. Bordeaux 12. May 1779.

From John Browne

ALS: American Philosophical Society

Sir L'Orient May the 13th. 1779—

I was first Lieutenant, of the Ship Boston, under Captn. Mc.Neil, the first Cruize she made, But when Captn. Tucker got her, I left her,[6] I then got the command of the Continential Brigg Dispatch, to come to France, but had the misfortune to be taken, and Carried to Scotland, and with much Difficulty, got from thence to France, I was at your house in Passey, where I received money, to carry me home,[7] I went to Nantes, where I remained Some time, waiting for a Passage. Captn. Jones, hearing I was there, applyed to me to go his Lieutenant, on which I repaired to L'Orient, to Superintend the fitting Out of the Poor Richard,[8] When Captn. Jones was going to Paris, I told him my Lieutenants Commission, was in Boston, and told him to apply to you for another, but when he returned, he told me you, did not know me, Now Sir I tell you who I am, which Mr Jonathan Williams, can testifie,[9] therefore I Beg you will let me know, if this is a Continential Ship or not, and if she is, and Shou'd be your pleasure I may Sail in her, please

6. Hector McNeill suspended Browne for negligence on Oct. 9, 1777; McNeill himself was relieved of duty in November of that year and replaced by Samuel Tucker. XXVI, 216–17n; Gardner W. Allen, "Captain Hector McNeill, Continental Navy," Mass. Hist. Soc. *Proc.*, LV (1921), 124. For Browne's command of the *Dispatch* see Claghorn, *Naval Officers*, p. 39.

7. Browne received 480 *l.t.* on Nov. 28, 1778: Alphabetical List of Escaped Prisoners.

8. In his capacity as acting commander while Jones was ill, Browne had twelve men on the *Bonhomme Richard* imprisoned for mutinous behavior: Bradford, *Jones Papers,* reel 3, nos. 642, 644.

9. By enlisting Browne as first lieutenant, Jones was trying to replace Peter Amiel (XXVI, 221n), whom he mistakenly believed had disobeyed his orders in April (Bradford, *Jones Papers,* reel 3, no. 598; JW to Jones, April 22 and 29, May 6, Yale University Library). Browne wrote to JW on May 10 to ask for a lieutenant's commission; JW answered five days later (after the present letter to BF had already been sent) that Peter Amiel's appointment superceded any other and that BF, who did not meddle in ships' affairs, ought not to be bothered (JW to Browne, May 15, 1779, Yale University Library). Neither man sailed on the *Bonhomme Richard;* Amiel requested a leave of absence to tend to private business matters, and Browne was appointed pilot on the *Sensible.* Bradford, *Jones Papers,* reel 3, nos. 650, 652, 655, 643.

to Send me a Commission, or your Orders, what I am to do, Also Sir, I was the first Man in all America that Opposed the British Tyranny in the Affair of the Linnen Manufactory—[1]

Sir I remain, your most Humble & Obeidient Servant

JOHN BROWNE

P.S. Sir I was appointed to the rank of first Lieutenant the 15th. Day of June 1776 and received my Commission in October, same year.

An ansr Directed to me at Mr. Solomans S Mercht. L'Orient will Oblige as before

Addressed: To / Doctor Benjamin Franklin / Commissioner for the / United States of America / at Passey near, Paris

Notation: Jonh Browne L'Orient 13 may 1779.

1. The Linen Manufactory House on Tremont St. in Boston was erected in 1753 with public funds, but was active in cloth production only through 1758. Thereafter, the building was leased to two Boston weavers, one of whom was John Browne. In October, 1768, Browne defended the Manufactory against the forcible attempts of Col. Dalrymple's regiment to occupy the building, and also filed legal action for trespass against the sheriff. Gary B. Nash, *The Urban Crucible: the Northern Seaports and the Origins of the American Revolution* (Cambridge, Mass., 1986), p. 119; Samuel G. Drake, *The History and Antiquities of Boston* . . . (Boston, 1856), pp. 751–2; Oliver M. Dickerson, comp., *Boston Under Military Rule* . . . (New York, 1970), pp. 2, 8–10, 37–8.

JA told the story of "Brown of the Manufactory" to the chevalier de La Luzerne, when the *Sensible* set sail and JA realized that Browne was pilot on board. Butterfield, *John Adams Diary,* II, 382.

From Tristram Dalton[2]

Three ALS:[3] American Philosophical Society

Sir Philadelphia May 13th. 1779

I take the Liberty of enclosing to You sundry Papers, relative to the Loss of the Brigne. Fair Play—which Vessel was sunk, last Jany, by Shot, fired from a small Battery, on the Island of Gaudaloupe—[4]

The Depositions of Andrew Giddings & S Mc Clintock, the two principal Officers on Board said Brig, contain the particular Circumstances of this unhappy Misfortune—[5]

The Letter from the Governor of Gaudaloupe, to the Minister of the Marine Department in France, shows his Opinion, that Indemnification ought to be made to the Sufferers, & recommends the same accordingly—[6]

2. Tristram Dalton (1738–1817), one of the owners of the brig *Fair Play,* was a wealthy Newburyport merchant and member of the Mass. House of Representatives. He later was elected one of that state's first U.S. senators: *Sibley's Harvard Graduates,* XIII, 569–78. He entrusted this letter and its enclosures to JA, his Harvard classmate, to forward to BF: *Adams Papers,* VIII, 59–60.

3. We print from the one BF endorsed.

4. All of these enclosures, in varying numbers of copies, are at the APS.

5. The depositions of Capt. Andrew Giddings and Second Lt. Samuel McClintock, Jr., were given before a Newburyport justice of the peace on April 8. According to their testimony, Giddings had gone ashore and been given permission by the commandant of the fort at Port Louis to continue his cruise. As they sailed past a small battery a mile and a half from the fort, it opened fire. Two shots hulled the ship, which sank within six minutes. The justice's attestation was certified (in multiple copies) with the Mass. state seal on April 20. One set of the certified depositions of both men and three additional copies of Giddings' testimony are extant.

6. Dalton enclosed an English translation of a letter dated Jan. 15, 1779, from the island's governor, comte Helle d'Arbaud de Jacques, and its intendant, de Peynier, to Sartine. Two other identical translations are among BF's papers. The French officials support Giddings' appeal, but caution that the commandant of the battery should not be reproached for the accident because orders were in effect for the security of the coasts. On one of the copies is BF's notation, "Translation of Letter from the Govr. of Guadeloupe." The actual letter from the governor, which included a petition by Giddings for redress of grievances, had been sent to BF by Bingham (see the letter from the Mass. delegates, May 12); after he had his secretary Gellée prepare a copy to keep, BF forwarded it to Sartine.

Capt Giddings not having taken proper Care to procure authenticated Copies of the Governor's said Letter, render'd it Necessary, in the Opinion of the concerned, for me to repair to this City, for further Advice—

The enclosed Letter, which the Honl Delegates from the State of Massachusetts, have favor'd me with, shows their Advice as to the Mode of my Proceedings—[7] And the Letter to Monseigr Sartine, which the Minister of France in America has honored me with, evinces his Opinion, in Corroboration of that of the Governor of Guadaloupe, to be, that Indemnification be made us—recommending the same—[8]

The Appraisement of the Value of the Vessel by Gentlemen of Character, under Oath, and who are not interested, must leave the Owners free from Suspicion that they ask any thing more than Justice—indeed, the Sum mentioned therein of 26666 & ⅔ spanish milled Dollars, would have been no Inducement for them to have sold the Brig, when they took into Consideration the Probability of a most successful Cruize, which she was then entring upon—[9]

Having, Sir, thus referred to the several Papers enclosed, I presume to ask the Favor of your kind Assistance to put this Affair in such a Line, at the Court of France, as that the Owners may receive full Indemnification for their Loss—[1] giving Orders for any Intelligence, you may think proper, to be forwarded to me at Newburyport in the State of Massachusetts—

I cannot omit beseeching your Attention also to the Case of the Families of the Eighteen Men, who, by this Accident, unhappily perished—and to the remaining part of the Crew,

7. Their letter of May 12, above.

8. French minister Gérard's letter to Sartine, dated May 11, asks that the owners of the ship be compensated, not because they have a strict right, but out of the "bienfaisance de sa Majesté." The LS and two copies are preserved.

9. The certified appraisal (in quadruplicate) is dated April 12 and signed by four Newburyport merchants. One copy is endorsed by BF: "Papers relating to the Loss of the Privateer at Guadeloupe Tristram Dalton Esqr." Further details about the ship's ownership and worth are given in Allen, *Mass. Privateers,* p. 125.

1. BF had already written. See his letter to Sartine of April 29, above, and the naval minister's reply of May 26, below.

who lost all they had on Board—Any Allowances made on this Acct we wish might be distinguished from the Indemnification to the Owners—and that the whole, which may be granted, be paid into the Hands of Jonathan Williams Esq—or to his Assigns, if He is not in France—subject to my further Directions—

Asking your Excuse for this Interruption to your public, and infinitely more important Concerns, I beg Leave to acknowledge myself to be, with the greatest Respect and Esteem, Sir Your most obedt hble Servt TRISTRAM DALTON

Honle Benjn Franklin Esqre—

Endorsed: Mr Dalton's Letter relating to the Loss of the Brigt. Fairplay, Valuation Families of Persons drowned, &c,

From Jean-Hyacinthe de Magellan[2]

ALS: American Philosophical Society

London 13 May—79

My Dear Dr. and most Respected Friend

You'll allow me these epithets, for the sake of my hearty wishes whatever relates you or to yours. This Vol. lately published, is sent by the author, whose heart you Know well to be as a friendly one, as he is an upright and worthy man.[3] He told me, that he had nothing particular to add: and only to assure you of the Continuation of his and of every other Common friend, good wishes for your wellfare and of all mankind at Large for such is in reality the large Scop, or aim of your actions.

Dor. le Begue du Presle,[4] will Receive, I hope, in a few weeks, some sheets I'll send, to Compleat a set of *Miller's bo-*

2. For the scientist and instrument maker who also transmitted British scientific intelligence to the French government see XIX, 127n; XX, 29n.

3. Joseph Priestley. See his letter of May 8.

4. Achille-Guillaume Lebègue de Presle, physician and friend of BF, is identified in XXIV, 162n. He was the member of the Académie to whom Magellan always sent his reports and remarks.

tanical Collection,[5] a work which you must know, has been Carried into execution, by our worthy friend Dr. Fothergill,[6] who desired I should send it to you, in order to be safely forwarded, if possible, as a present from him to the Philos. Society at Philadelphia. He had no time to write to you at present, or perhaps, nothing moreover to say in the present critical circumstances of the times: only whished to present you with his friendly wishes & Respt.

N.B. The principal part of the above botanical work is already in the hands of our friend Dor. le Begue du Presle: and I have already told him of its destination as soon as it should be compleated.

I ever am from the botom of my heart my dear Dor. & Friend your most obedt. hble. obliged MAGELLAN

Notation: Megellan 13 May 1779

5. John Miller, *An Illustration of the Sexual System . . . of Linnaeus* (London, 1777). Miller (Johann Sebastius Müller), an engraver born in Nuremberg, moved to England in 1744. In 1770, he undertook to make a series of detailed engravings of plants according to the classification system of Linnaeus, which was gradually gaining approval. The plates were issued as Miller finished them; the English naturalist John Ellis enthusiastically recommended the first ones to Linnaeus. The completed work appeared in 1777, in three folio volumes containing more than two hundred plates, half of them colored. The preface included letters of praise by Linnaeus himself. Miller published an octavo edition, intended as a field guide, in 1779. *DNB; Dictionary of Scientific Biography* (16 vols., New York, 1970–80), under Linnaeus.

6. We have found no indication that Fothergill (IV, 126–7n) sponsored this work; however, he was one of Miller's great admirers and had employed him, along with several other artists, to make drawings of the plants in his garden. Betsy C. Corner and Christopher C. Booth, eds., *Chain of Friendship: Selected Letters of Dr. John Fothergill of London, 1735–1780* (Cambridge, Mass., 1971), pp. 323, 397, 398n; R. Hingston Fox, *Dr. John Fothergill and His Friends* (London, 1919), p. 199n.

From John Adams

ALS: American Philosophical Society

Sir L'orient May 14 1779

The Day before Yesterday, We arrived here, in two Days from Nantes, all well:[7]

There is a Frigate now turning into this Port, which is said to be Le Sensible, & if this is true, I hope, it will not be a long Time before We get to sea.

The Chevalier de La Luzerne I hope is sensible of the Value of every Moment in the last half of the Month of May towards a Voyage to America.— If We wait untill the Middle of June, We May very well chance to have a Passage of Eleven or Twelve Weeks.[8]

In my last Letter I mentioned my Hope that the Chevalier would go to the Northward. It is true that I am much interested in this, but I hope my own share in this Buisiness, did not entirely suggest that Wish.— The greatest Concourse of British Men of War is undoubtedly at present between the West India Islands and those Parts of America which lie between Rhode Island and Georgia. Captain Jones in a Vessell from Baltimore, whom I saw at his arrival in[9] at st Nazare which was last sunday night in a Passage of Thirty days told me there were three British Frigates cruising in the Mouth of Cheasapeak Bay. As We have had no Arrival from Philadelphia so long there is great Reason to believe that there is more than one Vessell of War of the Line or Frigates cruising in Delaware Bay.— Therefore I think the Chance of getting safe into Port, is ten Times greater at Boston than Philadelphia, and I presume the Chevalier, wishes to avoid a Captivity as

7. During the voyage JA managed to convince himself that a conspiracy of BF, Jones, and Chaumont had been responsible for the cancellation of his passage to America aboard the *Alliance*. He spoke "very freely" to Chaumont about his suspicions: Butterfield, *John Adams Diary,* II, 369–70. See also our annotation of Sartine's letter of April 20.

8. The *Sensible* sailed on June 17 and JA disembarked on Aug. 2, in Nantasket Roads, near his home at Braintree: Butterfield, *John Adams Diary,* II, 381; Butterfield, *Adams Correspondence,* III, 217n.

9. JA began to write "in Nantes"; he lined through the second word when half-written, but neglected to delete "in".

well as myself, altho in such an unfortunate Case he would probably be treated with more Politeness than I should.

The Transportation of his Baggage by Land, as well as that of Mr Gerard is a Thing that deserves Attention to be sure—But it had better go by Land, to Boston than by sea to New York. As to Mr Gerards I presume, he will bring nothing to Europe with him but what is absolutely necessary, as every Thing he has will fetch in America twice as much as would replace it in Europe—and in this Way Insurance & Risque will be avoided.

Mr Chaumont gave Us the Pleasure of his Company this Morning at Breakfast. His son made Us a Visit before. Both are very well.

I should be obliged to you, if you would present my Compliments to his Lady and Family, and now I have begun with the Ladies, if you think it worthwhile you will oblige me much by making my Compliments acceptable to Madame Bertin,[1] Madame Brillon and Madame Helvetius, Ladies for whose Characters I have a very great Respect. I have the Honour to be with great Respect sir your humble servant JOHN ADAMS

His Excellency B. Franklin Esqr

Notation: Jonh Adams L'Orient may 14 1779.

From Chaumont

ALS: American Philosophical Society

L'orient ce 14 may 1779.

Si vostre Excellence etoit icy, Monsieur Le Docteur, elle verroit avec plaisir Le pavillon americain flotter sur des Vaisseaux franco-americains. J'espere que toutte Cette flotte Legere appareillera du vingt trois au vingt Cinq. Vous devriez venir luy donner vostre Benediction patriarchale, elle en auroit Bezoing, Car les officiers de L'alliance sont prest a devorer leurs Capitaines et Ceux du Bonhomme Richard ne sont pas en trop

1. The niece by marriage of a former controller general; JA had attended a party at Passy where she played the part of the Muse of History and he came to regard her highly: XXVI, 422–3n.

Bonne intelligence.[2] Je veux Relire L'histoire ancienne pour voir si les peuples qui ont amenés de grandes Revolutions sur le globe, sagitoient entre eux ayant mesme un ennemy a Combattre, et si Cela a été J'en Conclueray que vostre amerique sera le principe d'unne grande Revolution, Car vostre agitation est forte. Et en verité, Je n'ay encore vu de vostre païs, que vostre Excellence parfaittement Sage et Excellente. Aussi avez vous Entraisné Nostre veneration, et Je Crois que sans vous nous n'aurions pas tant aimé vos gens du Nouveau Monde, ils me font assez travailler icy a les accorder et a leur procurer leur immense necessaire.

Si vous n'estes pas en Campagne Je vous suplie d'envoyer aussitost que vous le pourez Ma Lettre a M. de la fayette et Celle a M. de Sartines.[3]

J'embrasse vostre Excellence avec Respect et de tout mon Cœur. LERAY DE CHAUMONT

M. Adams est toujours Charmant

M. Le Docteur franklin.

Notation: Chaumont May 14. 79

From Thomas Digges[4]

ALS: Historical Society of Pennsylvania

Dr. Sir Londo 14. May

The reason why you could not find out W. Peters by your letters was that they were directed to Nottingham instead of Liverpoole.—I have done the needful towards Your request & make no doubt of soon hearing frm him for *He is in want.*[5]

2. As far as we know, this is BF's first warning about dissensions among the *Bonhomme Richard*'s officers. The port official at Lorient was unimpressed with the quality of Jones's crew: Morison, *Jones,* p. 193. For the problems aboard the *Alliance* see also Jones's comments in his own letter of this date.

3. BF had already written Chaumont that he had forwarded the two letters: May 10, above.

4. Identified by the handwriting, in spite of his use of an alias.

5. Richard Peters had repeatedly asked BF to help him locate his father William, who had been living in Nottingham, and send him money; see XXVIII, 33.

I gave You a few lines by private conveyance the 12th. Int since which nothing conclusive has been done on the matter I then wrote upon.[6] The beginning of the Business & the stage it is now in promises well, but I am too apt perhaps to doubt of real sincerity. It has been opend by one to three or four others & will from them go to another one to night or tomorrow. In such situation you may easily guess how little I have to say & where the doubt hangs. I am in tolerable spirits about it & hope soon to say more to You.

I Am very truly Your Respectful & Ob Sert

ARTHUR HAMILTON

Notation: May 14 1779

From John Paul Jones

ALS: American Philosophical Society

Honored and dear Sir, L'Orient May 14th. 1779.

I have this day received your esteemed letter of the 9th—The Alliance arrived here the 12th. and the *Sensible* is this day arrived at Port Louis (at the entrance of this Harbour)—There is also this day arrived here a Cutter of 18 Guns from Cherbourg—this last I hope will be added to the Armament—the Pallas with the rest of the small Vessels from Nantes have not yet appeared—and the Cutter called the Leveller from Brest is still absent.[7]

In this situation it is impossible for me to say exactly when this little Armament will be ready to Sail—but I hope to have the Bon homme Richard transported from the Port into the Road on Sunday or Monday next with her Provision and Principal Stores on Board.— I am exceedingly Sorry that I cannot with certainty point out the day When the Marquis ought to

6. Hartley's peace conversations with Lord North that Digges mentioned in his letter of May 12.

7. In addition to the *Bonhomme Richard* and *Alliance,* Jones's squadron eventually contained three warships lent by the French navy, the frigate *Pallas,* the corvette *Vengeance,* and the cutter *Cerf:* Morison, *Jones,* pp. 190–1. The *Leveller* was a captured 14-gun English cutter which Jones unsuccessfully requested Chaumont to add to his squadron: Bradford, *Jones Papers,* reel 3, no. 583.

take leave of Paris—but it will in My Opinion be Unadvisable before the 20th. or 22d. as the arrival of the absent Vessels must depend on the Situation of the Wind.—

I should be unworthy of your generous confidence should neglect to ask your Advice in any difficult situation. The Gentlemen who command Pallas and the other Vessels as they are under the American Flag will naturally expect American Commissions— I have reserved the four blank commissions for this purpose which you entrusted to my disposal—but I will not bestow them in France without your approbation.— If you approve of it I can conclud these Commissions thus

"To continue in force until revoked by Congress, by His Excellency the American Ambassador at the Court of France, or by the commander in chief of an American Squadron."—

Instead of the customary conclusion, thus—

"To continue in force until revoked by this or a future Congress."—

By the former of these conclusions the Commissions can be revoked should it be found expedient when the business for which they are given is compleated.—[8] I am sorry to inform you that the Frigate le Monsieur[9] that was expected to be under my Orders is Sailed— We Shall however I hope be able to proceed without her.—

Since the Arrival of the Alliance I have taken some pains to inform myself with respect to the Misunderstanding on board that Ship.— The Captain appears to me as a Sensible well informed Man—and there seems to be more than enough of Cabal and prejudice among the Officers— I have hitherto taken no part between them—and I am afraid that "they have too contemptible an Opinion of one anothers Understanding"

8. American commissions were given to the commanding officers of the three French warships, *capitaine de brulôt* Denis-Nicolas Cottineau de Kologuen, *lieutenant de vaisseau* Philippe-Nicolas Ricot, and *enseigne de vaisseau* Joseph Varage: Morison, *Jones,* pp. 191, 198.

9. One of two privateers which sailed in company with Jones's squadron in August, but departed a few days afterwards: *ibid.,* pp. 198–9. Lafayette had planned to embark three hundred troops aboard her: Idzerda, *Lafayette Papers,* II, 258.

to be reconciled thro my mediation— It is therefore, as well as to prevent disorders in any other of the Vessels, that I wish for a sufficient number of Officers properly Authorized to hold Courts Martial.— I hope we shall have but little occasion to hold shuch Courts—but without the means of holding them I do not see how it will be possible to keep little Minds in proper Awe.— The first Lieut. of the Alliance I am told is about to leave that Ship—[1] And he will be inexcusable if he does so without leave—Yet I think the Service will Sustain but little loss thro his leaving it.— It is my duty further to ask your Opinion on the propriety of my giving my own Commissions to Lieutenants in the Navy and to Officers of the Volunteer Soldiers that I have inlisted.— If you Approve of it I can make these Commissions revocable at any time.— I submit the thoughts in this letter with profound deference to your Superior Understanding— I know that I have expressed myself but ill—but I have neither time to Copy nor Correct.— I am ever with heart felt affection your Excellencies very Obliged Friend & Servant JNO P JONES

N.B. I recd. a letter this day from the Marquis by his Aid de Camp which I have not time to Ansr.[2] therefore You will greatly Oblige me by communicating to him Such part of this letter as concerns him &c.—

His Excellency Dr. Franklin.

Notation: Capt. Jones May. 14. 1779

William Temple Franklin to Francis Coffyn

Copy: Library of Congress

Sir May 14.—79.

I am Directed by my Grand father to transmit you the enclosed Commission for a Privateer, together with the instructions to the Commander and the bond to be signed by the

1. Stephen Hills, who wrote on June 8 to explain why he left the ship.
2. The aide was Col. Gimat; see Lafayette to BF, May 19.

Owners you are desired carefully to attend to the filling up of the Blanks both in the Commission and Bond.[3]

In the Commission opposite to this (*) mark, after the words "*belonging to*" the owners are to be inserted as also opposite to this (‡) mark after "*The said*" in the Bond their names are to come in nearly at the Top after that of the Capts. you will easily perceive how the other Blanks are to be filled up by what goes before & what after.

I Likewise enclose a Copy of the oath of allegiance to the united states which it is necessary the Captain should take in your Presence before you deliver him the Commission.

I have the honour to be &c. W. T. F.

M. Coffyn.

To Schweighauser

Incomplete copy: Library of Congress

Sir Passy May 15 1779.

I have before me your favour of the 27th. past, & the 1st. & 6th. of May.[4] In these Letters there are several Things upon which you ask my direction, such as the Demand of the Mate and Seamen of the Brigt. Morris, the Propriety of Sending away the Same Brig without Convoy or detaining her till the next, and the Affair of the Swedish Captain's not having produced any Act of Property, which you think excludes his Pretention to Damages.[5] In every thing that relates to Maritime Customs and Usages, and to Commerce, you can certainly, from the Knowledge you have obtained by experience, judge much better than me, who am totally unacquainted with such

3. According to Coffyn's acknowledgement to BF of June 16, below, the enclosed commission and instructions were for the *Black Prince* and her commander, Stephen Marchant. Sutton de Clonard had introduced the captain in his letter of May 11. According to William Bell Clark, Marchant's instructions directed him to bring in as many prisoners as possible for exchange: Clark, *Ben Franklin's Privateers,* p. 22. His commission is reproduced in *ibid.,* facing p. 52; see also p. 22n.

4. All three letters are missing.

5. See BF's April 5 letter to Schweighauser for the *Morris* and the Swedish prize *Victoria.* The latter's captain was Charles Gustave Berg; see our annotation of Gratien's April 23 letter.

Matters; and as you act by Powers from the Committee of Congress convey'd to you thro' their late Agents for Commercial Purposes, it Seems to me that you are fully impower'd to judge and determine in these Cases, without being at the Trouble, and Losing the time, consequent of consulting me at such a distance which must often be attended with great Inconveniencies. With regard to the Swedish Ship in particular, you have in your Possession all the Papers relating to the Transaction from wich any Knowledge of the facts can be obtained; and I must leave it to you to [learn ?] from them how far the Captain is entitled or not to Damages:[6]

I shall pay the Bills you advise me of,[7] amounting to 65100..10..0. Tho' not as approving your Accounts, because I have not yet had time to consider them, I can only Say at present, that the charge of Commissions at 5 per Cent on the Delivery of the tobacco's Seems to me very extraordinary, of which I Shall Say more in my next.[8]

I have the honour to be Sir

Mr Schwieghauser

From Landais

ALS: American Philosophical Society

Please Your Excellency L'Orient May 15th 1779.

Since I tooke the Command of the frigate Alliance My officers have join together against me,[9] Even before I left Boston,

6. The letter is in a copybook, from which the remainder of the page has been torn. The letter resumes at the top of the following page.

7. The remainder of the sentence is in another hand.

8. The next extant letter from BF to Schweighauser is that of June 21. In the interim BF complained to JA about what he regarded as exorbitant commissions charged by Schweighauser: below, June 5. The commissioners had made a similar complaint: XXVII, 395, 454. The tobacco in question had arrived on the brigantine *Baltimore: Adams Papers,* VIII, 73n.

9. According to JA's diary, Landais told him, "The Officers deceive you! They never do their Duty but when you are on deck. They never obey me, but when you are on deck. The Officers were in a Plott vs. me at Boston, and the Navy Board promised to remove them all from the ship and yet afterwards let them all come on Board." Butterfield, *John Adams Diary,* II, 368–9.

I was promissed that I Should have another Set, but being ready to Sail the Hounble Navy board thought they woold behave better when at Sea, but to the Contrary it has been gradualy worse and worse to a peack that I am Compel to acquaint you with it that your Excellcy May take proper method for to remedy it, Moreover if there is no other one I'll rather Chuse to leave the Command than to have officers wich are against me: the first lieuft Hill[1] has Said he had heard all the bad Caracter of me and has propagated it amongs all, of which I told him three days ago, amongs other things he threatened me to leave the Ship I told him he might, but he want My Consent by writing what I cannot do without your order.

I am with the Greatest Respect Your Excellency Most Obedient and Most humble Servant P: LANDAIS

His Excellency Bn Franklin Minister Plenipotentiary of the united States of America

Endorsed: Capt. Landais May 15. 1779 complaining of his Officers.—

From Maximilien-Henri, Marquis de Saint-Simon[2]

ALS: American Philosophical Society

Monsieur A utrecht Ce 15 may 1779.

Mr Le comte de Sarsfield m'a fait Esperer que vous voudriez bien vous occuper un moment des nottes que nous vous avons Laissées, et dont vous connoissez toute l'importance pour mon ouvrage: je ne les rappelle à vôtre Souvenir que pour vous temoigner ma reconnoissance, et La confiance avec Laquelle j'attens un temoignage si precieux de vôtre amitié.

1. Stephen Hills and his fellow officers had sent their own complaints to BF on March 2, above.

2. The French writer and translator (*c.* 1720–1799) was a distant relative of the duc de Saint-Simon (1675–1755), author of the *Mémoires,* and a cousin once-removed of the comte de Saint-Simon (1760–1825), the economist. The marquis had retired from military duty in the 1740's and established himself in Utrecht. Larousse. This is his only surviving letter to BF.

Je me sens D'autant plus d'ardeur pour Suivre mon plan, que j'y Suis encouragé par Ceux mêmes qui prennent Le plus de part aux affaires, et je vois avec plaisir que Le denouement ne peut pas manquer detre heureux, si L'union et L'harmonie subsiste toujours dans Le congréz, et si l'intrigue ne reussit point a diviser des hommes que l'argent n'a pû Corrompre.

Je vois toutte La campagne qui s'ouvre en vos diverses contrées, tourner en projets illusoires qui ne peuvent etre adoptées que par des ministres ineptes et soutenus par Les majorats des deux chambres rendus à leurs caprices. Le feu ne s'etendra point avec vivacité dans L'europe, et vous acquererez une consistance d'autant plus solide, qu'elle ne dependra plus de quelques operations locales, ou de quelques evenemens inatendus, et vous direz comme hidalla dans le poëme de Temora

but let us move in our strength, slow as a gathered cloud. then shall the mighty tremble; the spear shall fall from the hand of the valiant..—[3]

et prevost après burgoyn et d'autres encore accompliront cette prophetie amere.

Si vous avez La complaisance de remettre à Mr grand ce que vous aurez à me faire passer, il Le fera parvenir à son frere qui me le fera tenir dabord.

Je voudrois avoir quelqu'occasion de vous donner des temoignages de L'estime sincere et du veritable attachement avec lequel j'ay L'honneur d'etre Monsieur Votre tres humble et tres obeissant Serviteur LE MARQS. DE ST. SIMON

Notation: Marquis de St. Simon Utrecht le 15 may 1779.

3. Hidalla tries to calm the rivalries among the allied chiefs, vying for the privilege to battle Fingal's forces. From "Temora," *Book I: An ancient epic poem, in eight books: together with several other poems, composed by Ossian, the son of Fingal. Translated from the Galic Language by James Macpherson.* (London, T. Becket and P. A. De Hondt, 1763), p. 8. Although fragments of Macpherson's counterfeit Ossianic poems had appeared in French translation in several literary journals soon after the original publication of *Fingal* (1762) and *Temora* (1763), Saint-Simon was the first to make one of these epics known in its entirety when he published his French translation of *Temora: Temora, poème épique en VIII chants, composé en langue erse ou gallique par Ossian . . .* (Amsterdam, 1774). On Saint-Simon's translation and the importance of

From Samuel Wharton

ALS: American Philosophical Society

Dear Sir Paris 15 May 1779

I have sent a parcel of Papers about Vandalia, which it may be proper, That you should have a Copy of.[4] I am with the sincerest Respect & Esteem Dear Sir Your's most affectionately

SAML. WHARTON

His Excellency Benjamin Franklin Esqr. &c &c &c—

Notation: Wharton Paris 15 may 1779.

From Jonathan Williams, Jr.

ALS: American Philosophical Society

Dear & hond Sir. Nantes May 15. 1779.

On looking over some Papers I found a Congress Commission & Warrant, which remaind after filling up those for the Dean. As it is probable you may want them for Capt Jones, and as they ought to be at your Disposal only, I herewith transmit them and request you in the next Letter you write me to do me the favour to mention the reception of them.

A Dutch Vessell is arrived here, the Capt Reports that in the Bay he met 5 Spanish ships of the Line & a Frigate, that the latter brought him too, & finding he was dutch Property told him that had he been english he would have been a lawfull prize, he told him further that the 5 Ships & himself were bound to Brest.— This *may* be true but I have generaly found Sea news erroneus.[5]

Ossianism in 18th century France see Paul van Tieghem, *Ossian en France* (2 vols., Paris, 1917; reprinted, Geneva, 1967), I, 261–7 and *passim.*

4. BF and Wharton were still partners in the proposed colony to be founded on lands purchased from the Indians: XXII, 19–21. Wharton continued to pursue their claims with Congress: George E. Lewis, *The Indiana Company 1763–1778: a Study in Eighteenth Century Frontier Land Speculation and Business Venture* (Glendale, Cal., 1941), p. 249. On July 1 Wharton wrote to WTF requesting "the fair & rough Copy of the Memorial concerning Vandalia." APS.

5. He had first written "uncertain".

Gov. Greens Goods are ready & I shall put them on board the three Friends under Convoy of the Alliance.[6] If it is not improper I shall be glad to know if Capt Jones & the Alliance go together, I ask only to be able to regulate the 3 Friends for Convoy.—

I am with the greatest Respect Dear & hond Sir Your dutifull & Affectionate Kinsman JONA WILLIAMS J

The Hon. Doctor Franklin.

Notation: Williams Jona. May 15. 1779.

From the Baron d'Arendt[7]

ALS: American Philosophical Society

franckfort sur le Mein, ce 16me. de Maÿ, 1779.

Monsieur,

J'ai l'honneur de Vous avertir de mon arrivée icy, et que l'etat de ma sante est beauccoup meilleur qu'il etait avant ce tems,[8] je desespêre pourtant d'être parfaitement retabli. Il y a six semaines que je Vous avois donné des mes nouvelles par une lettre incluse dans celle de Mr. William Lee, mais malheureusement cette lettre a eû le sort des deux autres, et n'est pas parvenüe a Lui, et je me trouve jusqu'a present très incertain de la cause de cette perte. Je suis bien en peine d'avoir manqué de trouver Mr. Lee icy,[9] pour lui communiquer mes observations et ce que j'ai appris a la Cour en quéstion ou j'ai fait

6. See JW's previous letter, May 6. The *Three Friends* was owned by JW; her captain was James Colman, and JW's letterbooks contain a complete list of her cargo dated June 5, 1779 (Yale University Library).

7. Identified in Hasenclever's letter of April 24.

8. Arendt was, at this time, nine months into the year's leave he had been been granted for health reasons. He resigned his command of the German battalion (technically the 8th Maryland regiment) on Jan. 1, 1781: Heitman, *Register of Officers;* Fred Anderson Berg, *Encyclopedia of Continental Army Units . . .* (Harrisburg, 1972), p. 47.

9. A puzzling statement as Lee was in Frankfurt that very day: Ford, *Letters of William Lee,* II, 636.

jusqu'a present mon sejour.[1] C'est dans ce moment, ou la paix vient d'etre conclüe, la juste epoque, a ce qu'il me semble, ou on pourroit entreprendre quelques negociations avec succes. J'ai eû des frequentes conferences avec un Ministre a qui j'etois addressé par une ordre du Roi touchant cette affaire, et il est fort de mon avis. Je ne crois cepandant pas, que cette cour declarera a cette heure l'independence de l'amerique etant empechée par des autres mesures, qu'elle a a garder, ny qu'elle signera ouvertement une traite de commerce par la même raison, ny qu'elle voudroit envojer des vaissaux marchands chès nous, par ce qu'elle n'entretient pas de marine, qui pourroit escorter les autres, neanmoins je Vous assure, que ses dispositions sont trés favorables pour nous, et qu'elle fera tout pour nous, sans faire ces demarches publiques. J'etois informé que cette Cour tient fort au coeur l'etablissement du commerce des ses toiles, qui ont, comme Vous scaures Monsieur, une trés bonne reputation, et qui se vendent a meilleur marche a proportion que presque les autres de l'univers, j'ai fait donc sentir au dit Ministre les grands avantages qu'on retireroit en faisant le commerce avec les americains en cet egard, il convenoit aisement sur ce point mais il souhaitait que cette nation venoit elle même pour faire l'achat des ces marchandises par ce qu'il etoit maintenant impossible par les raisons alleguées de les transporter directement chès elle. Il se faisoit fort de procurer alors la permission aux Vaissaux americains de pouvoir entrer dans les ports de sa couronne et de faire leur negoce, permission, qui a ce qu'il disoit etoit autrefois refusée.[2] Vous sentes bien Monsieur, que ce commerce engagera bientôt la dite cour aux demarches plus determinées et a nous favoriser pour ses propres interets. Le Ministre m'a demandé des nouvelles sur ce point, Je suis convaincu, d'avoir pú pousser ma pointe plus en avant, si j'aurais eté muni d'un pouvoir ou d'une autorite par le Congrés même ou par ses Commissaires en Europe, et

1. That of King Frederick II. The minister he saw may have been von Goerne.

2. On Jan. 2, 1779, William Lee had been told by the Prussian government that American ships needed no special permission to use their ports: Paul Leland Haworth, "Frederick the Great and the American Revolution," *American Hist. Rev.*, IX (1903–4), 472–3.

Vous apprendres aisement Monsieur, que je n'ai rien negligé pour seconder Vos interets. Je me flatte que si on vouloit reïterer les tentatives, qu'on se pourroit alors servir de moi assés utilement, aÿant deja travailé dans cette affaire et franchi le chemin, etant connû du Roi et de la cour, et connoissant moi même le terrain, il me semble même qu'on entreroit plus aisement en affaire avec moi, qu'avec un Etranger, et qu'elle avanceroit alors plus vite. Ce n'est pas mon interet qui me porte a le dire, mais c'est notre interet commun. Je serois autorisé alors par Vous et je me reglerois uniquement sur Vos instructions.

J'attens Votre reponse Monsieur aussitôt qu'il se pourra, et Vous aures la bonte de me dire, si Vous croyes qu'on voudra faire quelque chose et se servir de moi, ou si je dois me rendre a Paris pour entrer dans un plus long detail touchant cette affaire, ou si je dois attendre le retour de Mr. Lee, enfin tout ce que Vous trouver necessaire a me dire. Je suis decidé de retourner en amerique, si je ne t ouve pas que je Vous puisse être utile en Europe, car Vous seres convaincû par tous mes demarches, que c'est l'unique zêle pour la cause commune qui me guide.

J'ai l'honneur d'être très parfaitement, Monsieur Votre très humble et obeissant serviteur, BARON DE ARENDT.

Colonel Americain.

Vous aures la bonte de marquer sur Votre lettre, qu'on la rende dans *l'auberge du Lion d'or,* ches Mr. Fritsch. Faites agréer mes Compliments a Monsieur Chaumont.

Notation: Arendt Baron De: 16. may 1779.

From Georges-Marie Butel-DuMont[3]

ALS: American Philosophical Society

Monsieur, à Paris ce 16. Mai *1779*

J'ai l'honneur de vous envoyer un Billet d'associé et trois autres billets dont vous pouvez disposer pour entrer à L'as-

3. For this historian see XXV, 637n.

semblée publique que la société libre d'Emulation[4] tiendra le Vingt de ce mois dans une salle de l'hôtel de soubise.

Je suis avec une profonde vénération, Monsieur, Votre très humble et très Obéïssant serviteur

DU MONT Secrt. de la société.

Notation: Du Mony Paris ce 16e. may 1779.

From Benjamin Duffield[5]

ALS: American Philosophical Society

Dear Sir/. Bourdeaux May 16. [1779][6]

You will probably be much surprized at receiving a Letter from this Place, and from one who has so much disgraced the Introduction you were so kind as to favour him with. I cannot without deep Confusion, attempt to address you again— I cannot attempt to excuse my past follies and Indiscretions otherwise than by pleading a natural Volatility and a great flow of Animal Spirits. These joined to Youth and Health hurried me into Imprudencies that I have since severely repented of. I have bought Experience dearly. Distress and Necessity have taught me a Lesson that I never, never shall forget: and I am now by my regular Conduct, and prudent behaviour, endeavouring to regain that Reputation that I once enjoyed. The Advice and Assistance of my amiable Friend H: Conyngham[7] have been of the utmost Service to me, and as the first step towards reinstating myself in the good Opinion of my father,

4. BF had been put in touch with the society shortly after his arrival in Paris, and he attended its meetings thereafter; see XXIII, 451n, and subsequent volumes. The society lasted only until 1780.

5. The son of BF's old friend the Philadelphia clock- and watchmaker Edward Duffield (VII, 211n; XXVIII, 392n). Benjamin (1753–99) had gone to Edinburgh in 1774 to complete his medical studies, and BF had provided him with an introduction to Lord Kames: XXI, 268–9, 523–4.

6. The year is supplied from the notation.

7. David Hayfield Conyngham (XXIV, 412–13) was the cousin of the ship captain Gustavus, whose cruises had created diplomatic difficulties for the American commissioners (XXVII, 552). Hayfield had sailed for Europe in

he advised me to return, & most generously furnished me with everything necessary to accomplish that Intention. I was within a few Days of sailing, when I received a small Bill from my father—with a Letter strongly marked with that cool Inflexibility for which you my dear Sir well know he is so remarkable. Indeed he has Reason to be much offended—but his Education being much confined, and his Ideas of Men and Things not the most liberal, he magnifies my offences. However; if he is implacable there is a Door open for my Reception. The Army of my Countrymen shall be my Resource; and as I am happy in an excellent Constitution and possess some degree of firmness of Mind, I hope to bear his Slight and Displeasure with Patience and Resolution. I am already resigned to it, I am so fully convinced of having deserved it.

Mr Conyngham (whose Name I shall never mention but with the most sincere Gratitude) has promised to procure me a Passage in a Letter of Marque to America. I shall officiate in the way of my Profession if called upon—tho if in that Quality I could get on Board a Cargo Privateer it would be much more acceptable to me; and perhaps profitable as my Finances are but slender. My Bill was for £85; Part of this I employed in liquidating some Debts that my Pride and folly led me to contract—the Remainder being 28 Guineas I have with me—and as I am in want of cloaths If I can embark either in one method or the other with a very few Guineas in my Purse I shall be contented.

If you do not think me quite unworthy your Notice—if you have any Compassion for my unhappy situation, may I request the favour of your advice. I look upon your Character as sacred, & as I am shut out from Parents and all that I hold dear, and that once held me high in their affection and Esteem, will you condescend to mark out a Line for my Conduct which I promise most religiously to observe. I have seen my

September, 1775, resided at Paris and Bordeaux, and returned to Philadelphia in 1779: Horace E. Hayden, "The Reminiscences of David Hayfield Conyngham," Wyoming Hist. and Geological Society, *Proc. and Coll.*, VIII (1904), 196–8.

Errors in the strongest Light, and will endeavour to make my future Conduct as bright as my faults were deep before.[8]

I am my dear Sr your most obliged humble servt

B: DUFFIELD

Addressed: Dr: Franklin

Notation: 79

To John Beckwith

Reprinted from William Temple Franklin, *The Private Correspondence of Benjamin Franklin, LL.D. F.R.S. &c* . . . (2nd ed.; 2 vols., London, 1817), I, 36–7.

Sir, Passy, May 17, 1779.

Having assured you verbally that I had no authority to treat or agree with any military person, of any rank whatever to go to America, I understand your expressions, that "*you will take your chance if I think you may be useful,*"[9] to mean that you will go over without making any terms with me, on a supposition, which you also mention, that my recommendation will be regarded by the Congress, and that you shall thereupon be employed in our armies.

Whoever has seen the high character given of you by Prince Ferdinand (under whom you served) to Lord Chatham,[1] which I saw when in London, must think that so able an officer might have been exceedingly useful to our cause, if he had been in America at the beginning of the war. But there is a

8. As far as we know, BF never replied. The young man returned to Philadelphia, acquired a large medical practice, and was an early lecturer on obstetrics: *Summary of the Transactions of the College of Physicians of Philadelphia,* n.s. IV (1874), 449–50.

9. See Beckwith's letter printed under May 7, above.

1. At the end of the Seven Years' War, the Prussian field marshal Prince Ferdinand of Brunswick had recommended Beckwith to the King of Prussia for his services with the British forces in Germany. Beckwith became a Prussian general and was appointed governor of Emden. Richard Henry Lee, *Life of Arthur Lee, LL.D.* . . . (2 vols., Boston, 1829), I, 411; Sir Reginald Savory, *His Britannic Majesty's Army in Germany during the Seven Years War* (Oxford, 1966), p. 224n and *passim.*

great difficulty at this time in introducing one of your rank into our armies, now that they are all arranged and fully officered; and this kind of difficulty has been found so great, and the Congress has been so embarrassed with numbers of officers from other countries, who arrived under strong recommendations, that they have been at above 100,000 livres expence to pay the charges of such officers in coming to America and returning to Europe, rather than hazard the discontent, the placing them to the prejudice of our own officers who had served from the beginning, would have occasioned. Under these circumstances they have not merely left me without authority, but they have in express terms forbid me to agree with or encourage by any means, the going over of officers to America in expectation of employment. As to my recommendation, whatever weight it might have had formerly, it has in several instances been so improperly employed through the too great confidence I had in recommendations from others, that I think it would at present be of no importance if it were necessary; but after that above mentioned of so great a general, and so good a judge of military merit as Prince Ferdinand, a character of you from me would be impertinence.

Upon the whole, I can only say, that if you choose to go over and settle in our land of liberty, I shall be glad to find you there on my return as a fellow citizen, because I believe you will be a very good one, and respected there as such by the people. But I cannot advise or countenance your going thither with the expectation you mention. With great esteem, I have the honour to be, &c. B. FRANKLIN.

To [Dumas][2]

Incomplete copy: Library of Congress

[between May 17 and 19, 1779][3]

in a Week. The Business has required a longer [*remainder of line missing*] is the Only cause of the Bills not being paid according

2. In response to his of May 11, above.

3. This document is in a letterbook from which the top half of the page, containing the beginning of the letter, has been torn. It follows an incomplete letter of May 17 and precedes one of May 19, hence our dating.

to the Acceptance. But whatever the Cause, I do not See why that Should as your friend Supposes *faire beaucoup de mal au credit des Americains.* M Holker is not an American but a Frenchman lately arrived in America. If a frenchman at Amsterdam should draw on another frencheman at Paris who refuses or neglects to pay his Bill, ought that to hurt the Credit of Holland? As to M. De Ch I think he has many friends here who would in his absence readily have paid the bill for his honour if they had known of it before it was protested and sent back.—[4] The Depreciation of the American Paper is solely owing to the excessive Quantities, they have been oblig'd to issue, and not to any doubt of their ability to redeem it. Quantity in every thing tends to Lessen value. Gold and Silver—

To Woestyn frères

Incomplete copy:[5] Library of Congress

Gentlemen Passy May 17. 1779.

Before the Rect. of your last favour of the 11 Inst.[6] I had assured M. Le Roy who wrote me on the same subject that tho' I could not take a Part in your Ship I was very Sensible of the Honour you proposed to do me by giving her my Name, and therefore should make no objection to it. But since you desire my Consent in Writing, I hereby give it; wishing most sincerly to her and her Owners all the success that can be imagined. I have the honour to be, Gentlemen your most obedient

Mrs. Woestyn, Neg. Dunkerque

4. In fact, friends did offer to pay; see Dumas to BF, May 21.

5. The remainder of the page in the letterbook, including the rest of the complimentary close and anything else that might have followed it, is missing.

6. Described in our annotation of their letter of March 20, above.

From John Adams

ALS: American Philosophical Society

Sir L'orient May 17. 1779

Your Favour of the 10th. I received the Day before Yesterday, and am glad to hear that the Chevalier is making diligent Preparation for his Departure, for I wish, most impatiently to see him. Every day, now is a great Loss.

In a Letter I wrote a few days ago I mentioned Some Reasons for prefering Boston to Delaware.[7] I think there can be no doubt that there are at least Several Frigates in Delaware River which there will be no Chance of escaping. However, after submitting my Reasons to consideration I shall be very willing to submit to the Decision. As to my going to Congress.— I have not taken any Resolution nor made any Promises about it: But upon the whole my prevailing Opinion is that I shall not go, unless I should be ordered, very soon.

The Resolution of the States General, to convoy their Trade and fit out 32 ships of War for that Purpose, has an Appearance of Decision, and I hope will have some Tendency to bring the English to Reason. They have given one Symptom of some remaining Justice and Humanity in the late Exchange of Prisoners, which is the only Instance of any Appearance of Candor or sincerity, that I can recollect in their Conduct, since the Repeal of the Stamp Act.

We have an odd Report, here of Six ships of the Line, before St Maloes, which Nobody can account for.[8]— Surely it is impossible that Six ships should insult, this Coast so near to Brest.

Private Letters from England by Yesterdays Mail say that the last Proposals of Spain, have been rejected, with ill humour.—[9]

From America, no News can be obtained.— Of five Vessells

7. Above, May 14.

8. Adm. Arbuthnot's squadron; see our annotation of BF's May 26 letter to the committee for foreign affairs.

9. On May 3 Secretary of State Weymouth informed Spanish Ambassador Almodóvar that the Spanish proposal for a truce between the British and Americans was unsatisfactory: Patterson, *The Other Armada,* pp. 66–7. For further discussion see our annotation of BF's May 26 letter to the committee for foreign affairs.

arrived, within a few Weeks, one at Morlaix, one at L'orient one at Nantes and two at Isle, d'aix, not one has brought any Dispatches, nor all together above 4 or 5 News papers.— These are all from Cheasapeak.

The Frigate Le sensible, has been here several days. The Poor Richard appears to be almost ready for sea, and she has a set of very fine officers, but what Character the ship deserves and her Equipage, which is very much mixed I dont know, But I hope and believe, that the officers will keep them in order.

The Characters you give of the new Ambassador and his secretary, give me much Pleasure.— The Name of the latter I have not yet heard. Shall be happy to form an Acquaintance with both, and in an opportunity to shew them the Town of Boston before they go to Philadelphia. It may be Usefull, to see, so large a Part of America, and they will be very sure of a cordial Reception.

I have the Honour to be, with great Respect, sir Your most obedient servant JOHN ADAMS

His Excellency B. Franklin Esqr

Notation: Jonh Adams L'orient 17 may 1779.

From Marc Le Fort[1]

ALS and copy:[2] American Philosophical Society

Monsieur Marseille le 17: may 1779.

Nous sommes très reconnoissans de la peine que vous avés pris de nous faire part, par votre lettre du 23. juillet de l'année passée,[3] de ce qui etoit venu à votre connoissance concernant le rembours ordonné par le congrès de Williamsbourg de la valeur du senau l'Elegante & la Cargaison & qui a eu son Effet, pour la somme de 5000 pounds; Nous prenons encore la

1. A retired or semi-retired partner in the Marseillais shipping firm of Faure, Douneau & Cie. The firm was half-owner of the snow *Elégante,* captured by the British at the mouth of the Rappahannock: XXVI, 502–4.

2. The copy which Le Fort made as part of his letter to BF of Feb. 23, 1780 (APS).

3. Missing.

liberté de recourir à vos bontés & vous prier de vouloir donner Cours à lincluse pour le sr: Antoine Gautier notre preposé & chargé de nos affaires à Williamsbourg,[4] le recommander aux Magistrats pour l'aider à se faire rendre compte du Capne. Collineau[5] de Bordeaux qui a mal agi dans la gestion du susdit Senau & refuse de vuider ses mains des fonds qu'il a en maniement;

Nous vous prions de plus Voulloir engager le Congrès de Williamsbourg de recevoir en depost du sr: Ante. Gautier la somme de sept mille pounds en payant l'interest annuel de 6% le dit Gautier nous marquant en date du 17. Janvier dernier que le Congrès ne prenoit plus d'argent à interest, nous savons cependant que divers particuliers en ont placé de meme en d'autres Provinces, & nous craignons que ce ne soit Un pretexte dont se sert le sr Gautier pour garder ses fonds en maniement. Si vous pouviés nous procurer les moiens de retirer cette somme par lettres de Change, ou autrement, nous Vous en aurions une veritable obligation. Daignés Monsieur prendre en Consideration cette affaire, & agréer les sentimens de la respectueuse Estime avec laquelle nous sommes Monsieur Vos très humbles & très obts serviteurs

ppre. de Mrs. faure Douneau & Cie: LE FORT

Nous evaluons le pound 17 *l.t.* 5 *s.* argent de france.

Mr. B. Franklin à Passy

Notation: Le Fort 17. May 1779.

From ——— Morel

ALS: American Philosophical Society

Monsieur Versailles ce 17. Maÿ 1779.

Je prens la liberté de présenter a Votre Excelance; Le Tableau des forces actuelle de la france; Tant par Terre, que par Mer; ouvrage que J'ai deja eu L'honneur de présenter aux Princes; et Seigneurs de La premiere distinction ainsÿ qu'a quelque uns des Ministres Etrangers.; M. Le Marquis de La

4. Gautier was the other half-owner of the ship: XXVI, 502–3.
5. Who commanded the *Elégante: ibid.*

Faÿette a qui J'ai eu L'avantage den offrir; ma fait L'honneur de me demander si Jen avoit presenté une pareille à votre Excellance; sur ce que il ma fait l'honneur de me faire dire que c'est ouvrage pouroit peut être vous faire plaisir cest ce qui me détermine à avoir L'honneur de vous presenter ce fruit de mes Mediocres Talens;

Je Serai Trop heureux si mes Travaux peuvent Mériter L'honneur du suffrage de votre Excelance.

Je Suis avec Le plus profond respect de Votre Excelance Le Trés humble et Trés obeissant Serviteur[6]

Morel
fils dun ancien officier au service des Troupes du Roi.

Notation: Morel Versailles 17 may 1779.

From Stephen Sayre

ALS: American Philosophical Society

Sir Amsterdam 17th May. 1779

I this moment arrived in the City, & have only time enough to request your Excellency, if not done already, to send me Letters of recommendation for the Govr. of Martinico, or Dominica, as I mean to sail from hence to St Eustatia, from thence visit those Islands.[7]

I am with all possible Respect your Excellency's most obedient Servant

Stephen Sayre

Addressed: A Son Excellence / Benjn Franklin / Embassadour extra: / de Americque. / a Paris—

Notation: Sayee Stephen 17 May 1779.—

6. On May 22, in a similar letter, Morel added that his father was formerly *l'aide-major* in the regiment of Toul (an artillery regiment). APS.

7. For BF's reaction see his letter to Dumas of June 4.

To All Captains and Commanders of Vessels of War

ALS (draft): American Philosophical Society

Gentlemen, [May 18, 1779]

The Bearer of this, Mr. George F. Norton,[8] a Native of Virginia, and returning thither with his Family, has, during his Residence in England, manifested on all Occasions his Attachment to the Cause of Liberty, and his Compassion towards his Countrymen confin'd in the English Prisons, many of whom he has assisted in their Distresses with a liberal Hand, as they have acknowledged to me with grateful Expressions of their Obligation to him.—[9] I therefore recommend it earnestly to you, that if in his Passage you should happen to meet with him, you would not consider him as an Enemy on Account of his having lived in England; but treat him as a Friend & Countryman with all Civility, not retarding him in his Voyage, but affording him all the Assistance in your Power that his Situation & Circumstances may render necessary. With best Wishes for your Success in your Cruizes, I have the honour to be Gentn Y. m. o. h. S.— BF.

M. P. of the U.S.

To all Captains & Commanders of Vessels of War, Privateers & Letters of Marque belonging to the United States of America,

At Passy, this 18th. Day of May— 1779.—

Notation: Pass for Mr Norton.

8. George Flowerdewe Norton (b. 1751), son of the Virginia tobacco trader John Norton, who became a partner in the firm of John Norton & Sons in 1774. George had been sent to London for schooling at the age of ten, and was joined by his family three years later. Since the summer of 1778 he had been plagued by ill health and failing finances; by the spring of 1779 the family had planned to remove to America. Frances Norton Mason, ed., *John Norton & Sons, Merchants of London and Virginia* . . . (2nd ed.; Newton Abbot, 1968) pp. 367, 417, 422, 515–16.

9. The only evidence in BF's papers of Norton's assistance is an extract of a letter he wrote Matthew Ridley on Sept. 30, 1778, which Ridley forwarded to BF and which was docketed by both WTF and JA. Norton reminds Ridley of the "Friends whom I hope by this time you have seen," who had received from him twenty guineas. APS.

From Thomas Digges

ALS: University of Pennsylvania Library

Dr Sir —18 May—79

Mine of the 12th. & 14th. Inst. have I suppose got safe to hand— The last would give you some idea how matters stood at the parting of our friend with another personage in regard to a certain matter: The opening was auspicious & the parting favourable to our wish— Since that period till yesterday the affair remaind in embrio; *others* I apprehend were consulted upon the occasion of the first parley, and those others recommended it should be laid before a principal or cheif Phisician,[1] which I suppose was done on Sunday last. As I apprehended the business alluded to ought to be pushd forward or settled with as much expedition as possible for fear of any other interposition, I urgd my friend to look to another consultation— He did so very lately, & the answer was "I will speak to you soon I am not yet ready for you." In this situation it now rests—appearances tell me the Phisick is working powerfully— You know what a heavy dose it is.

Genl Howes evidence is yet before the House, & from the vast strength of proofs as to improbability of success in Ama. it would appear that Ministry will give up the idea of subjugation— Howe has 10 or 12 more Officers to call in proof thereof, and their weight of evidence is to be ballancd by about as many Mac's from the Highlands and twenty or thirty American Torey refugees now in England with Joe Galloway at their head.[2] The fleet for N York & Georgia is still at Torbay,

1. George III.

2. Digges had previously written about the Parliamentary hearings on the Howes' conduct: above May 12. Joseph Galloway, BF's former friend, had begun leading a campaign against the brothers shortly after his arrival in London in December, 1778, arguing that most Americans preferred to remain united with Britain, and that the rebels' success was due to the incompetence of the Howes. Since this interpretation of events also shifted blame away from the ministers, North and Germain were suddenly more attentive to the loyalist refugees' claims: Mary Beth Norton, *The British-Americans: the Loyalist Exiles in England 1774–1789* (Boston, 1972), pp. 158–61.

& likely to be there while these western storms prevail—[3] Sr. J. Wright has returnd to London a little down in the mouth.[4]

I am very truly & wth much esteem Yrs. V. J. D——D

Addressed: A Monsieur / Monsieur—B—F—/ Passy

Notation: Digges 18. May 1779.

From Dumas

ALS: American Philosophical Society

Monsieur, Lahaie 18e. May *1779*

Vous verrez, par l'imprimé ci-joint, que je n'ai point tardé de faire usage de ce que vous m'avez envoyé dernierement. Les mêmes pieces sont insérées aussi dans les gazettes Hollandoises.[5]

Voilà dequoi il faut remplir les papiers, & non des altercations entre particuliers, tristes effets de la mésintelligence, de l'ambition peut-être & de l'envie.

J'espere que ma démarche, ci-jointe, auprès du Gd. Pre., aura votre approbation.

Il n'y a rien de nouveau ici. Une personne bien instruite a voulu parier tout ce qu'on auroit voulu, en bonne compagnie, qu'un grand personnage saura bien traîner & éluder les convois pour les munitions navales jusqu'à-ce que la guerre soit finie. Tant pis pour lui: cette mauvaise volonté diminuera d'autant son crédit, & l'amour que lui portoit la nation. Pour nous, il ne nous importe guere qu'on donne ou non ces convois: mais il nous importe d'avoir un fort parti ici contre tout ce qu'il voudroit faire de plus pour la Cour Br., & Dieu merci nous l'avons.

3. Adm. Arbuthnot's squadron, which spent three weeks becalmed there after its brief foray to the French coast: John A. Tilley, *The British Navy and the American Revolution* (Columbia, S.C., 1987), p. 165; JA to BF, May 17.

4. Sir James Wright (XV, 94n) was reluctantly preparing for a return to Georgia and a resumption of his governorship in compliance with a ministerial plan to restore refugees to their former positions in areas that the British had retaken. Norton, *The British-Americans,* pp. 107–8.

5. BF had sent the papers on May 4, and Dumas acknowledged them in his letter of May 11–14.

Je suis avec un très-grand respect Monsieur Votre très-humble & très-obéissant serviteur, D.

Copie d'une Lettre que j'ai écrite au Gd. Pre. d'Hollde.

Monsieur Lah. 7e. May 1779

Mr. l'Avocat Tullinghh d'Oldenbarnevelt m'a adressé un paquet de papiers, duplicats & triplicats, contenants Requête au Congrès-Général des Etats-Unis de l'Amérique, Procure en blanc, & nombre de Pieces justificatives, pour servir à réclamer & constater la proprieté Hollandoise d'un bâtiment & Cargaison de Rotterdam, pris il y a deux ans environ par un Armateur Americain, & condamné comme propriété Angloise par l'Amirauté de Charlestown en Caroline;[6] avec priere de faire parvenir ces papiers à mes Amis en Amérique, & de les intéresser à cette cause, pour que protection lui soit accordée, & justice rendue. Il a ajouté de bouche, que comme il ne paroissoit pas à propos que, dans les conjonctures présentes, la République intervienne dans cette affaire, Vre. Exc. avoit conseillé aux Réclamants, de se servir de mon Ministere pour la fin susdite.

Je me ferai un vrai plaisir, Monsieur, de rendre service aux sujets d'un Etat, sous la protection duquel je goûte depuis longtemps la douceur de vivre, si je puis obtenir quelque assurance de la part de Vre. Exce., que mes offices ne déplairont point au Gouvernement, & qu'il les verra, au contraire, d'un oeil analogue à la bonne intention qui me porte à les rendre.

Je suis avec un très-grand respect, &c.

Je ne m'attendois pas à une réponse par écrit. Le Pre. ne pouvoit me la faire sans trop se commettre. 3 ou 4 jours après j'allai lui en demander une de bouche. Il m'avoua qu'il m'avoit renvoyé cette affaire dans les termes qu'on me l'avoit dit; & que je ferois plaisir de m'en mêler, pour éviter un éclat & des désagrémens à l'Etat.

6. Isaac van Teylingen was the agent for the owners of the Dutch sloop *Chester,* for whose misadventures see XXV, 122, 657–9; XXVII, 482–4; *NNBW,* II, 1426.

J'ai déjà expédié tout cela conséquemment en Amérique.

Passy à Son Exc. Mr. Franklin

Addressed: à Son Excellence / Monsieur Franklin, Esqr. / Ministre Plenipotentiaire / des Etats-unis de l'Amérique / à la Cour de France / à *Passy.*/.

Notation: Dumas May 7. 79

From Sartine

Copy: Library of Congress

Marly le 18. May 1779.

J'ai reçu, Monsieur, la lettre que vous m'avez fait l'honneur de m'écrire le 8. de ce mois relativement à 16. Americains qui se trouvent parmi les prisonniers provenant du Sénegal et qui desireroient entrer au Service des Etats Unis. Une des Conditions expresses de la Capitulation acceptée par M. Le Duc Lauzun portant que tous les prisonniers seroient renvoiés en Angleterre aussitôt leur arrivée en Europe, vous concevez, Monsieur, qu'il n'est pas possible de s'ecarter de ces Dispositions.

A l'égard du S. Edmont Stacht[7] officier au Regiment de Walcht qui demande un Congé et la permission de s'embarquer Sur la fregate le Bonhomme Richard; j'envoye son mémoire à M. Le Prince de Montbarrei[8] avec l'article de votre Lettre qui est relatif à cette demande.

J'ai l'honneur d'être avec la Consideration la plus distinguée Monsieur, votre très humble et très obeissant Serviteur.

signé DE SARTINE.

M. Franklin,

7. Edward Stack; see our annotation of Jones's May 1 letter.
8. Montbarey, the French minister of war.

To Chaumont[9]

LS:[1] Yale University Library; incomplete copy: Library of Congress

Dear Sir, Passy May 19. 1779.

I am sorry and very much ashamed of the Quarrel on Board the Alliance: But I beg you would not form an Opinion of the Americans in general from this Accident. Where a Number of Men of whatever Nation are together with little or nothing to do they are apt to be mutinous and quarrelsome. I hope when they are fully employ'd they will behave with more discretion and more good Nature to each other. At this Distance I cannot judge between them. They are now under the Orders of Commodore Jones, whose Authority exercised with Prudence and Temper, will I hope be sufficient to compose these Dissensions and re-establish good Order and Harmony among those People, and to him I must leave them.

I forwarded immediately your Letter to M. De Sartine and the Marquis de La Fayette. I suppose you have herewith their Answers.

I hear from Holland that a Bill of M. Holker fils, drawn on you and accepted, is gone back protested for Nonpayment.[2] I suppose this Accident happened by your being out of Town. I am sorry I did not know of it in time to prevent its being return'd. I hear it is gone back to America via St Eustatia. As that is a round-about Voyage, a Letter from you by the Ambassador may reach Mr Holker before the Protest arrives, and you may by that means save his Credit. It is for this Reason I mention it.

With the sincerest Esteem, I am Dear Sir, Your most obedt humble Servant. B FRANKLIN

M. De Chaumont.

9. In answer to Chaumont's of May 14.

1. In WTF's hand. The copy, on a torn page of the letterbook, contains only the opening paragraph of the letter.

2. Reported by Dumas on May 11–14. See also BF's reply, printed under May 17.

To John Paul Jones

LS[3] and copy: Library of Congress

Dear Sir, Passy, May 19. 1779.

I received yours of the 14th, & communicated to the Marquis what related to him. I send you enclosed two more Commissions, which I have found since your Departure. It is difficult to revoke Commissions once given, and there might be some Inconvenience in French Officers retaining those Commissions unrevoked after the occasion of giving them is past; I therefore am of Opinion, that the Conclusion might be better thus, "to continue in force during the Expedition or Expeditions intended under the Command of the honourable J. P. Jones Esq." By this means they will continue if you should make more Expeditions, and become void of themselves when the Force is dissolved, and the French Ships are withdrawn from under your Command.

I am sorry for and ashamed of the Divisions on board the Alliance. I hope these Commissions will enable you to compose them. I do not know enough of the Navy Law to judge of the Propriety of your giving Commissions to Lieutenants, and therefore can give no Opinion about it. I send you all the Warrants I have, will they not serve instead of Commissions, 'till such can be obtained?[4] My best Wishes attend you, being ever, Dear Sir, Your faithful Friend and most obedt humble Servant.

B Franklin

Hon. John Pl. Jones. Esqr.

Endorsed: From his Excellency Dr. Franklin Passy May 19th. 1779. recd. L'orient May 23d.

To Landais

Copy: Library of Congress

Sir Passy, may 19. 1779.

I received yours of the 12th. and 15th. Instant. I was glad to hear of your safe Arrival at l'Orient, but what you write me

3. In WTF's hand.

4. These were certificates of appointment for officers of lower rank than commissioned officers. JW had recently sent BF a blank warrant and commission that Jones might use: above, May 15.

about the Officers of your ship afflicts me exceedingly. At this Distance I can do nothing towards remedying the Disorder. I must therefore leave it to Commodore Jones whose Authority with the Aid of Courts martial, if necessary, will I hope be sufft to compose these Dissensions—[5] I have the h. t. b. w. m. Esteem. Sir., Y. m. o. and m. h. S.

Honble. Capt. Landais.

From Dumas

ALS: American Philosophical Society; AL (draft): Algemeen Rijksarchief

Monsieur, Lahaie 19e. May *1779.*

Aujourdhui les Marchds. d'Amst. & de Rottm. présentent des Requêtes à L.H.P. Celle d'Amst., courte & ferme, se plaint de la réponse évasive qu'ils ont reçue de l'Amirauté, qui, sans tenir compte de la Résolution du 26 Avr., prise après celle du 26 Janv., laquelle avoit annullé la resolution du 19 Nov. dernier, qui excluoit les bois de constructn., leur a repondu n'avoir point reçu ordre d'accorder des convois illimités:[6] ajoutant, que ce n'est pas pour être frustrés de la sorte, qu'ils ont consenti à payer double droit d'Entrée & de Gabelle.— Celle de Rottm., aussi énergique que volumineuse, représente à L.H.P. la ruine inévitable de leur ville, si leurs requêtes, tant auprès d'Elles qu'auprès du Stadhr. continuent de rester sans effet.— Vendredi L.h.p. besogneront sur ces deux requêtes.— Le Cte. de Welderen avoit eu ordre de L.h.p. de demander à la Cour d'Angle., en vertu de l'Article XII. du Traité de 1674, une ré-

5. On May 27 and on June 6 Landais asked Jones, apparently without success, to convene either a court of inquiry or a court martial to hear the *Alliance* officers' charges against him and his against them: Bradford, *Jones Papers,* reel 3, nos. 629 and 636.

6. For a detailed discussion of the French pressure which caused the States of Holland on Jan. 26, 1779, to annul their Nov. 19, 1778, vote against convoying ships carrying timber see Fauchille, *Diplomatie française,* pp. 85–114. The April 26 resolution of the States General and the Admiralty's attempt to evade it are discussed in Dumas' letters of May 3 and May 11–14.

vision politique des Jugemens rendus par les Juges du Royaume au sujet des prises faites sur les Hollandois: Ld. Weymouth a répondu, *que les Loix du Royaume ne permettoient pas une telle revision.* Ainsi les Anglois se croient en droit de ne pas observer un art. du Traité parce qu'il ne leur convient plus, un autre, parce que les Loix de leur royaume s'opposent à son exécution.[7]

Je suis avec un grand respect, Monsieur Votre très-humble & très obéissant serviteur D

J'ai pour garant de tout ceci notre Ami. Cette Lettre partira demain par voie de Rotterdam, pour gagner un jour sur la poste d'ici.

Dans ce moment je viens de recevoir la Visite de Mr Nicolas Davis. Il étoit allé se présenter à l'Ambassadeur, qui me l'a envoyé. Je l'ai reçu conformément à ce que vous m'en dites, Monsieur, dans l'honneur de la vôtre du 9e. May.

Passy à S.E. Mr. Franklin

Addressed: à Son Excellence / Monsieur Franklin, Esqr. / Min Plenip. des Et Un. de l'Am. / en France / à *Passy.*/.

Notation: Dumas May 9. 79

From Lafayette

ALS: American Philosophical Society

Dear Sir Paris 19he May 1779

Inclos'd I have the honor to Send you a letter from Mons. de Gimat[8] giving an account of a very dangerous division Be-

7. Welderen is Jan Walraad, graaf van Welderen, the Dutch ambassador in London (XXVII, 129n), who had already protested to Secretary of State Weymouth the British seizure of Dutch ships carrying naval stores; XXVII, 396, gives an example. Such matériel was not listed as contraband in the 1674 Anglo-Dutch commercial treaty; see our annotation of Dumas' letter of March 29–31.

8. Jean-Joseph Gimat de Sourbadère, Lafayette's aide-de-camp: XXV, 495n. His letter to Lafayette (also at the APS) warns of a conspiracy among the *Alliance*'s officers to ruin Landais' character; see Idzerda, *Lafayette Papers,* II, 267n. Gimat must have already met BF, as his fellow aide Maj. Capitaine mentions Gimat's having shown BF a map drawn by Capitaine: to WTF, May 20 (APS).

twen the officers of the Alliance—that I had foreSeen long ago, and I believe Some thing or other Must be done, in this affair.

I also send you the ideas for prints I have Somewhat increas'd, and I Could indeed Make out an immense Book upon so Rich a Matter—[9] but, My dear doctor, tho' I hate the British Nation, I however am oblig'd to Confess that those Ministers and theyr Executors are unhappily of the Same Nature (whatever Corrupted it Might be) as the rest of Mankind— do'nt you feel any Shame in thinking those people are by theyr features Some thing like men? But as they Must be known By the future American posterity, I great deal love our project, and want to be Concern'd in it as much as possible.

I'll do Myself the honor of waïting on you friday Next, and whatever intelligences I may Collect among, and Get out from Ministerial Bosoms on american affairs I will Communicate to you.

With the Sincerest affection and esteem I have the honor to be Dear Sir Your most obedient and Most humble servant

LAFAYETTE

They Say ireland is Rather in Motion; Do You think a corps of two thousand Men with four thousand Spare arms Might not Crowd awround them Many lovers of Liberty, and Many Ennemies to the English tyrannical governement.

Endorsed: Marquis de la Fayette & Col Gimat 19 May 79 relative to the dangerous Animosities on board the Alliance.

9. See BF and Lafayette's list of prints to illustrate British cruelties, printed below at the end of May.

From ——— Bazin: Receipt for China and Earthenware

D: American Philosophical Society

May 20[–21], 1779

1779	Fourni a Monsieur francklin, Par Bazin Md fayancier rue des fossés st Germain L'auxerrois, hôtel de Lizieux a Paris			
20 May	15. Douzaines d'assiettes fayance blanche a 6 *l.t.*	90*l.t.*	"	"
	2. Grands plats ronds	9	"	"
	6. Dits plus petits	12	"	"
	12. Dits d'Entrée	14	8	"
	12. Dits d'Entremets	12	"	"
	4. Grands plats Carré	6	"	"
	4. Dits petits	4	16	"
	2. Grands plats ovals	9	"	"
	2. Dits moyens	6	"	"
	2. Dits	4	"	"
	4. Dits	4	16	"
	4. Dits	4	"	"
	2. Terrines ovals	24	"	"
	2. Saladiers	3	"	"
	6. Coquetiers de porcelaine blanche	7	4	"
	14. Pots a jus Id	24	10	"
	1. Moutardier et Cuilliere doré	8	"	"
	6. Caraffes a lEau de Cristal	4	4	"
	24. Goblets a glaces de Cristal	6	"	"
	24. Assiettes porcelaine bleu	48	"	"
	1. Jatte porcelaine de sèvre a fleurs	12	"	"
	2. Couvercles de theyeres	8	"	"
	2. Seaucieres et plateaux	4	8	"
	1. Theyere blanche	1	10	"
	12. Goblets de Cristal Taillé	7	4	"
	12. Dits unis	1	4	"
	2. Pots a lEau blanc	1	10	"

1. Cuilliere a Moutarde	"	18	"
1. Jatte bleu	1	4	"
Port a passy	15	"	"
	353*l.t.*	16 *s*	"

Jay reçu de Monsieur francklin la somme de trois cent cinquante trois Livres seize sols pour solde du present memoire a paris ce 21 may 1779 BAZIN

Endorsed: Bazin's Acct for Earthen & China Ware 353 Livres.. 16s.

From John Paradise and William Jones[1]

Reprinted from Jared Sparks, ed., *The Works of Benjamin Franklin . . .* (10 vols., Boston, 1836–40), VIII, 366n.

Hotel du Port Mahon, Rue Jacob, May 20th, 1779.

Mr. Paradise and Mr. Jones present their best respects to Dr. Franklin. They are just arrived at Paris; and, as they were desired by their worthy friends, Dr. Price and Dr. Priestley, to deliver to him their publications,[2] they have left the books and

1. John Paradise (1743–95) was an unpublished scholar who hosted convivial gatherings of London artists and literary figures, most notably Dr. Samuel Johnson. He and his close friend William Jones, the celebrated Orientalist (XVIII, 201n), were fellows of the Royal Society and members of the Club of Honest Whigs. In 1769, Paradise had married Lucy Ludwell of Virginia, sister-in-law of William Lee. Fearing the loss of his wife's portion of her family estate after the Sequestration Act, Paradise had made Jones his legal adviser. It was probably Jones who suggested that he seek BF's assistance. *DNB;* Archibald B. Shepperson, *John Paradise and Lucy Ludwell of London and Williamsburg* (Richmond, Va., 1942), pp. 5, 11, 120, 136–8.

2. Priestley had recently arranged to send a number of his pamphlets to BF, including a published correspondence with Richard Price; see his letters of March 11 and May 8. Price had lately reissued two works of 1776–77 as *Two Tracts on Civil Liberty, the War with America, and the Debts and Finances of the Kingdom* . . . (London, 1778). His latest publication was *A Sermon, Delivered to a Congregation of Protestant Dissenters* . . . (London, 1779), which asserted the sovereignty of the people and provoked controversy. See Roland Thomas, *Richard Price, Philosopher and Apostle of Liberty* (Oxford and London, 1924), pp. 86, 91–2.

letters at Passy, where they propose to have the honor of waiting upon the most respectable of patriots and philosophers, on any morning when they hear that he is likely to be at leisure.

From Samuel W. Stockton

ALS: American Philosophical Society

Sir. The Hague May 20th. 1779.

I did myself the honor of writing to you the 28th. ulto.—it rather gives me pain to trouble you so soon after, but the kindness expressed in your's of the 18h. March that I might rely on such friendly offices as might be in your power, gives me my best apology.

I think myself unfortunate, that (from the present scantiness of my finances) I am deprived of paying my personal respects to you at Paris before I depart for Ama.: I am obliged therefore thro' this channel to tell you how much I shall thank you for any dispatches you may expect soon to forward for Congress, and as I know of no immediate conveyance from this country, you will permit me to remain in hopes of your friendly attention: In the mean time, as I am informed Mr. Pringle[3] intends to leave Paris for this Country about the last of this month, may I request you for a few recommendatory letters, by him, to individuals in different parts of Ama. as I know not in what part of the continent I shall arrive? And as I have for this last year been in the public service, I need not say how much I shall be obliged for a few lines in my favor to The Honble The Committee of Congress for foreign affairs, if you think it proper. As a foundation for these letters I beg leave to subjoin the following copies (the original of the first being in your own possession) without troubling you with others.— "Dear friend. London May 16. 1778. The bearer Mr. Stockton, brother of your friend Richard Stockton Esquire of

3. Izard's secretary, John Julius Pringle, who recently had unsuccessfully solicited a mission to England to negotiate an exchange of prisoners: XXVIII, 496, 516n. He soon would return to Charleston: *DAB*.

New Jersey, wishes much to be introduced to you. I have not had the pleasure of Mr. Stockton's acquaintance, but my brother is intimate with him, and assures me that, upon all occasions, from the beginning of the controversy between the United States & this Country, he has shewn himself a zealous & steady assertor and supporter of the rights of America. May I therefore be permitted to recommend Mr. Stockton to your notice & protection. I am with the greatest respect & esteem, dear friend, your's most affecty. His Excellency Benjamin Franklin Esqr. &c &c &c. Saml. Wharton."[4]

You will permit me to add an extract of a letter from Wm. Lee Esqr. to Mr. Cushing of Boston dated March 8th. 1779. "Dear Sir. I am happy to have it in my power to introduce to your acquaintance a worthy countryman Saml Witham Stockton Esqr. This gentleman has been some time with me in the service of his country, to which he has rendered considerable advantages, and which has much more to expect from his abilities & zeal in the cause of liberty. He now returns home & may possibly visit your city, in which case I beg leave to recommend him to your friendship & civilities &c &c."

There is no news of importance here— Your cautionary letter to Mr. Dumas respecting Nicholas Davis[5] has prevented the latter from imposing on several persons in this country.— I was induced to hope for some advantages for Ama. from the conferences at Teschen.—[6]

The Prince of Or——e is again endeavoring to delay the equipment of the convoys, & the timid, lethargic souls of the 7 Provinces, I am afraid, will require a declaration from Spain or an attack upon their convoys by the English, before they will be thoroughly awakened, or before the patriotic party in this country can get the better of the intrigues of the Br: Court.

I am just now informed by a letter from Amsterdam of Mr.

4. Stockton had sent this recommendation to BF on June 3, 1778: XXVI, 582n.

5. Above, May 9.

6. Where an agreement between the Austrians and Prussians had just been reached; see our annotation of Dumas' letter of March 24–5.

S. Sayre's being in that city, having arrd. there a few days ago from Copenhagen by water.[7]

I have requested Mr. Pringle to wait upon you for the above mentioned letters, before he leaves Paris— Your good offices in this instance will greatly add to my obligations & gratitude for your friendliness already experienced.

That you may long continue in health & the discharge of your public duties, and at length once more give Ama. an opportunity of personally testifying her highest & most grateful approbation for your important services in her glorious cause, is the sincere & most ardent wish of Sir Your most obliged & most respectful Servant. SAML. W. STOCKTON.

His Excellency Benjamin Franklin Esqr.

Addressed: To / His Excellency / Benjamin Franklin Esquire / Minister Plenipotentiary at / the Court of Versailles &c &c &c / at Passy / near Paris.

Notation: Stocton S. W. 20 May 1779

From Vergennes

L (draft):[8] Archives du Ministère des affaires étrangères

A Versailles le 20 May 1779.

J'ai l'honneur de vous envoyer, M, un mémoire qui concerne M. de Vatteville, issu d'une des meilleures maisons du canton de Berne;[9] vous verrez que cet officier souhaiteroit d'entrer au

7. Sayre reported his arrival on May 17: to BF, above.

8. In Gérard de Rayneval's hand.

9. Perhaps the Capt. Nicolas Amedé de Vatteville (Watteville) who was a company commander in the Erlach regiment: *Etat de messieurs les officiers qui se trouvent aux services étrangers . . .* (Bern, 1773), p. 6. The memoir, endorsed by BF "Vatteville his Memoire," describes him as about forty years of age and recounts his military experience. After four years as a volunteer in the Dutch corps of artillery he resigned in 1758 to raise a company for Prussia. He was wounded and captured at the Battle of Landeshut (1760); after his exchange he served as an aide-de-camp to Prince Henry of Prussia. At the end of the Seven Years' War he returned to Bern, becoming a Lt. Col. of Artillery. Dissatisfied with his present lack of opportunities he now wishes

Service des Etats-unis: les témoignages avantageux que l'on donne de ses talents militaires, me persuadent que le Congres feroit une très-bonne aquisition, et si des obstacles invincibles ne vous arrêtent point, je vous serois particulierement obligé si vous voulez bien seconder ses desirs./.[1]

M. franklin

From the Loge des Neuf Soeurs

AL:[2] American Philosophical Society

The Nine Sisters had known nothing but tribulations since they had held, on November 28, 1778, a grandiose commemoration of Voltaire—with Franklin's rather rash participation.[3] The American may not have gauged the intensity of anger aroused in the Church by Voltaire's anticlerical pronouncements and the problems confronted by Louis XVI, who was both a Mason and a devout Catholic. The royal displeasure was vented on the Lodge through the masonic channel of the Grand Orient de France, headed by the King's own cousin, the duc de Chartres. First, the Nine Sisters were evicted from their spacious quarters on the rue du Pot-de-Fer and relegated to a small locale in an annex. Then, on December 22, the current *Vénérable,* Joseph-Jérôme de Lalande, was roundly reprimanded for having, among other infractions, admitted two women to the ceremony. More trouble occurred—or was deliberately provoked—on March 9, 1779, when the Lodge, in order to mark the anniversary of its foundation, held what was called a "loge d'adoption," *i.e.,* a special convocation for women, all of them of high birth and related to Masons, to be enrolled in philanthropic endeavors. In the ensuing clamor, the Nine Sisters came close to being abrogated but three of

for employment with General Washington. He is trained in mathematics and fluent in French and German. One of his brothers and three other relatives are in French service. AAE.

1. BF wrote Richard Peters on July 12 (Library of Congress) that Vatteville was going to America with the intention of settling in Pennsylvania. Vatteville was the bearer of that letter, and carried with it the present one.

2. In the hand of Court de Gébelin, who signed for the others.

3. See XXVIII, 286–7.

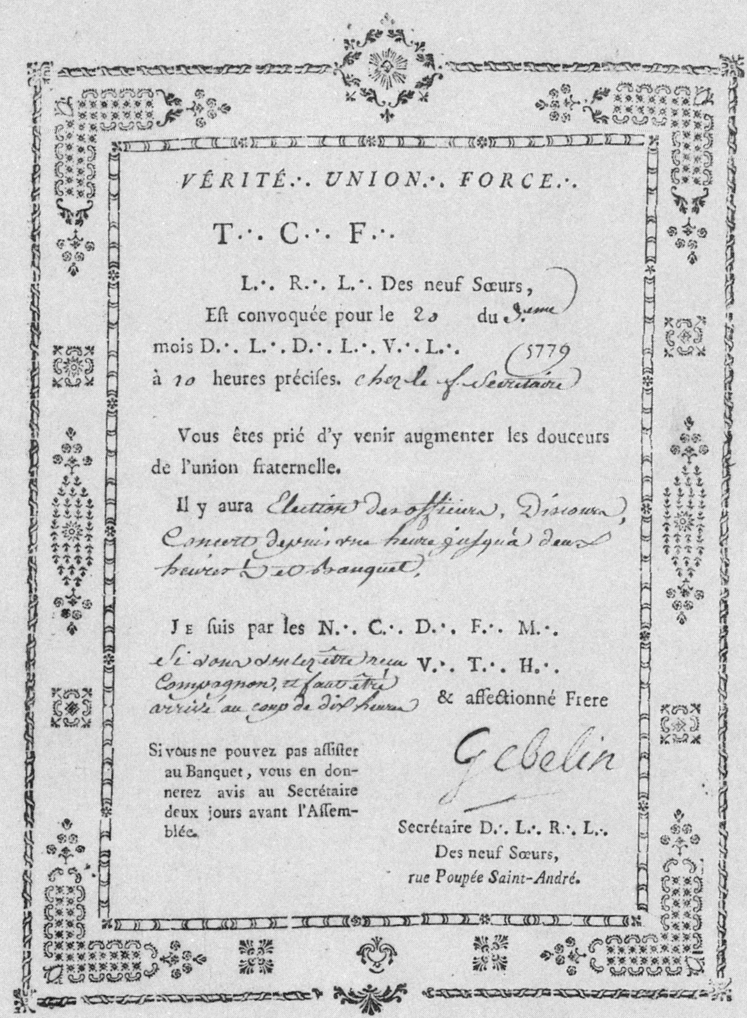

VÉRITÉ∴ UNION∴ FORCE∴

T∴ C∴ F∴

L∴ R∴ L∴ Des neuf Sœurs,
Est convoquée pour le 20 du 3ème
mois D∴ L∴ D∴ L∴ V∴ L∴ 5779
à 10 heures précises. chez le f. Secrétaire

Vous êtes prié d'y venir augmenter les douceurs de l'union fraternelle.

Il y aura Election des officiers, Discours, Concert depuis une heure jusqu'à deux heures et Banquet.

Je suis par les N∴ C∴ D∴ F∴ M∴
V∴ T∴ H∴
& affectionné Frere

Si vous voulez être reçu Compagnon, il faut être arrivé au coup de dix heures

Gebelin

Si vous ne pouvez pas assister au Banquet, vous en donnerez avis au Secrétaire deux jours avant l'Assemblée.

Secrétaire D∴ L∴ R∴ L∴
Des neuf Sœurs,
rue Poupée Saint-André.

Noubliez point de vous munir de vos ornemens.

∴ ∴ ∴

Invitation to a Masonic Ceremony

their defenders reacted so eloquently that the Grand Orient, as mentioned in the document below, finally backed down.[4]

The choice of Franklin as next *Vénérable* is wrapped in the usual masonic mystery, but his election certainly was an important factor in cooling the atmosphere. The author of Bachaumont's *Mémoires secrets,* no friend of Freemasons, commented sarcastically on May 26: "Il est merveilleux de voir M. Franklin, malgré les grandes & nombreuses affaires dont il est chargé, trouver assez de temps pour jouer à la chapelle, & suivre les assemblées de franc-maçons, comme le frere le plus oisif: jeudi dernier [May 20] il a été élu vénérable de la loge des Neuf-Soeurs, & une députation est allée à Passy lui en faire part." The chronicler went on to predict trouble because the publication of La Dixmerie's *Mémoire* had provoked the *garde des sceaux* [minister of justice] to order the prefect of police to stop its distribution and do his utmost to discover its publisher. His gleeful conclusion: ". . . voilà matiere de quoi exercer le zele du nouveau vénérable."[5]

But the "nouveau vénérable," perhaps because of his personal friendship with the head of police, M. Lenoir, steered clear of trouble. "L'inventeur du paratonnerre devait, ici encore, écarter la foudre."[6]

There were a few more aftershocks during the summer and fall of 1779, but Franklin held himself apart from them and they eventually subsided.

[before May 21, 1779][7]

Deputés de la R. L. des IX. Soeurs auprès du F. Dr Franklyn pour l'informer & le prier d'agréer le choix que la R. L. a fait unaniment du F. Franklyn pour son Venerable, dans l'assemblée pour les Elections le 20. de ce mois

F. Comte de Milly premier surveillant de la L.
F. Court de Gebelin second surveillant

4. The chief defender was Nicolas Bricaire de la Dixmerie (1731–91), a man of letters who composed a *Mémoire pour la loge des Neuf Soeurs* (Paris, 1779) on which L. Amiable bases his account of the events: *Une Loge maçonnique d'avant 1789* (Paris, 1897), pp. 95–129. La Dixmerie's *Mémoire* is discussed at length in Bachaumont, *Mémoires secrets,* XIV, 61–2 (May 23, 1779) and XIV, 70–1 (May 30).

5. Bachaumont, *Mémoires secrets,* XIV, 65.

6. Amiable, *Une Loge maçonnique,* p. 137.

7. The date of BF's election as *Vénérable.*

F. DE LA DIXMERIE Orateur auxquels s'est joint
LE F. ABBÉ CORDIER[8]

On a la faveur de l'informer que Le Grand Orient a annullé sa sentence contre la L. des IX. Soeurs.

F. de la Lande se trouve Ex-Venerable par les Reglement du G.O. qui ne permettent pas qu'on soit continué au delà de trois ans.

From Thomas Digges

AL: Historical Society of Pennsylvania

Dr Sir 21 May 79

I was in hopes to have given you some tidings as to the bargain I was about to make for the House but as yet I am little advancd. My Brother[9] this day slightly urgd the necessity of another meeting &a. on the business but it was "*a serious matter deserving contemplation & should be attended to*"—

I have done the needful as to Mr W—— P——s[1] but have not yet got his answer as to what He wants &ca—; I am told he is very poor. Should he want a small supply I have wrote him I will assist him as to negotiating the Bill. It is not unlikely He may draw upon Me for a small sum on yr. accot & I suppose it will not be disagreeable to you for me to repay myself by drawing on you. If you will allow Me to include in such bill the sum I advancd J. Brehon & four others (ie £20—for wch. You have seen a bill & promisd a friend of Yrs. You would pay)[2] it will be a help to Me & lighten in some measure a heavy debt I have for similar services; for I can assure You I am not at present cursd with a great deal of ready Cash.

8. Nicolas-Christiern de Thy, comte de Milly, is identified in XXIII, 128n, Antoine Court de Gébelin in XIX, 342n. Abbé Edouard Cordier de Saint-Firmin (*c.*1730–1816), a particular target of the Lodge's adversaries, was a writer. Larousse.

9. Presumably Hartley, a "brother" in the efforts for peace.

1. William Peters; see Digges's letter of May 14.

2. James Brehon and a number of others escaped from Forton prison in late 1778: XXVIII, 389.

I was favord this Eveng with a sight of the letter which coverd the underwritten note & am desired to give to you with Comps &c &c.

The Commrs for Sick & hurt Seamen &c—present their Comps to Mr ———,[3] and return him thanks for the communication in his note to Mr Bell relative to the Milford transport which saild with the Amn Prisoners; And as by the orders the Commrs at present are under, further numbers will be sent as long as there are any English Prisoners taken by Americans to be returnd in Exchange for them, they would be obligd to Mr ———[4] for any information he may be able to give them, or for procuring such as may be relied upon, as to the number of such Prisoners on the other side the water, as well as for giving such intimations[5] there, as may be the means of having the numr of Prisoners to be returnd for the next hundred that will go from hence, at hand to be embarkd without detaining the vessel unnecessarily— By Mr ——— not mentioning any thing relating to Morlaix, the board concludes he has not recd any ansr upon that point, & should be glad, if He thinks proper, that it might be mentiond again, as it would be a much more convenient port.

The Cartel Vessel is not yet returnd & every party concernd wonders very much at her delay as the winds have been fair

A Packet from Ja——a is arrivd & brings no news that is yet let out consequently none good. She saild the 4 Apr—& might have brought accots from St. Kitts to the 25 March.—[6]

The following illustrious names are summond to give evidence to the Ho. of Commons as to the expedience of the prosecution of the Amn War & to over throw the testimonies

3. Hartley.

4. He first wrote "Mr H".

5. Replaces "informations".

6. On May 26 *The General Advertiser and Morning Intelligencer* did print a letter from Kingston, Jamaica, dated March 31, which had arrived by the *Duke of Cumberland* packet on May 21. It reported the loss of a British privateer, d'Estaing's activities in Martinique, and the British possession of Georgia.

of Lord Cornwallis Genl Grey, Coll Montresor, Capt Hammond &c &c. &c—[7]

Jno Maxwell Esq. Jos Galloway Esq—Andw. Allen Esqr—Jno Patterson Theos. Morris—Enoch Storey—& Jebas Fisher— I think they should have added James Delancy[8]

Addressed: A Monsieur Monsr. Franklin

Notation: Digges 21. May 1779.

From Dumas

ALS: American Philosophical Society; AL (draft): Algemeen Rijksarchief

Monsieur, Lahaie 21e. May *1779*

Je vous ai parlé dans une de mes dernieres, de 2 Lettres de Change Americaines protestées.[9] Voici ce que les mêmes Amis me marquent en date d'hier.

"Par le Courier de Mardi dernier, nous reçumes une Lettre de Mrs. Sellonf. & Perrouteau, nos Correspondants à Paris,[1] avec avis que Mrs. J. Cottin & fils & Jauge[2] avoient offert de

7. The Howes had called a total of five officers to testify in their defence: Lt. Gen. Charles Earl Cornwallis, Maj. Gen. Charles Grey, Sir Andrew Snape Hamond of the frigate *Roebuck,* Capt. John Montresor of the royal engineers, and Sir George Osborn, muster master general in America. Gruber, *Howe Brothers,* pp. 342–3.

8. Galloway and the other refugees were to testify that loyalists constituted a sufficient force in support of the British army: *ibid.*, p. 345. Andrew Allen had been attorney general of Pennsylvania and recorder of Philadelphia. John Patterson, an officer in the British army who had emigrated from Ireland in 1759, had been the deputy of customs in New York when the Revolution broke out (Palmer, *Loyalists*). Enoch Story of Philadelphia, once an acquaintance of BF, had arrived in England in 1778: XIV, 308n. Jabez Maud Fisher of Pennsylvania, who became a merchant in New York, came to England to address the King in 1779 and died the same year. John Maxwell and Theodore Morris were summoned to testify but were never examined (Sabine, *Loyalists*). James De Lancey was a notorious partisan leader. *DAB.*

9. Above, May 11–14.

1. A Parisian banking firm with whom BF had had contact: XXV, 206n.

2. A Bordeaux merchant firm with whom BF eventually had extensive dealings: XXVII, 48n.

payer nos effets sur le R—— de Ch——. Mais comme nous avons profité de la premiere occasion pour renvoyer les dits effets & le protest à notre Remettant, nous ne sommes pas à même de faire usage de leur offre. Nous en sommes bien fachés; car quoique les sommes ne soient pas très-importantes, le crédit des Américains & de leurs amis en France en souffrira beaucoup. En attendant nous communiquerons l'offre de Mrs. Cottin & Jauge à nos amis en Amérique, pour les tranquilliser sur le sort des Lettres de Change qu'ils pourroient avoir remis postérieurement."

Je dois voir notre ami Ami au sortir de l'Assemblée. S'il m'apprend quelque chose de nouveau, je l'ajouterai par Postcrit.

Je suis avec tout le respectueux attachement que vous me connoissez, Monsieur, Votre très-humble & très-obéissant serviteur D

L'Assemblée n'a rien conclu, & s'est ajournée à la huitaine. On vient de Me dire que Mr. Sayre est arrivé à Amsterdam.

Passy à Son Exc. Mr. Franklin Min. Pl. des E.U.

Addressed: à Son Excellence / Monsieur Franklin Esqr. / Min. Plenip. des Etats-Unis / &c. / *Passy.*/.

Notation: Dumas. 21 May 79

From John Bondfield

ALS: American Philosophical Society

Sir Bordeaux 22 may 1779

A Small Sloop arrived here last night from the Eastern shore of Maryland she left Motompkin [Metomkin] a small port without the Cape the 17 April. The Captain informs me all appeard perfectly quiet no movements of any Note he brought no Letters nor any papers.

I received yesterday the inclosed. The writer Joseph Baily and his Companion Phillip Chapman are Prisoners at Bayonne taken on Board an outward bound Whaleman a Prize to our Privateer the Marquise de Lafayette referring to their petition not having any instructions from you on this head I shall not presume to apply for their release unless I am authorised [*torn: several words missing*] do.[3]

Monsieur La Motte piquet has had favorable weather since he left Isle d'Aix the 7th Instant various are the conjectures of his destination my Ideas conducts him to the 14th province.

I shall not be able to get the General Mercer Capn. Robinson to Sea before the 7 or 10th June he will go direct to Philadelphia any articles you may wish to transmit to your family I shall carefully provide & forward. I have the honor to be with due Respect Sir your very hhb Servant

JOHN BONDFIELD

His Excellency B. Franklin Esq

Addressed: His Excellency B. Franklin Esq / Plenipotentary from the United / States / a / Paris

Notation: John. Bondfield. Bordeaux 22 may 1779.

From the Abbé André Morellet[4]

ALS: American Philosophical Society

à auteuil dimanche à 11 heures. [May 23, 1779?][5]

Monsieur

Madame helvetius apprend que mesdelles Alexandre viendront lui demander à diner aujourd'hui à auteuil. Elle est engagée à diner chès Mr. l'abbé Rochon avec sa societé des dimanches et il ne lui sera pas possible par cette raison de

3. Bailey had earlier petitioned BF; see his letter of March 21.

4. The abbé had translated in 1766 a piece published by BF in *The London Chronicle* under the title of "On the Price of Corn, and Management of the Poor"; see XIII, 510. The two men eventually met in 1772 at Shelburne's estate in High Wycombe. For a biographical note on Morellet see XIX, 177n. As BF's relationship with Mme. Helvétius deepened, so too did his friendship with Morellet.

5. We agree with the dating of this document proposed by Dorothy Medlin, Jean-Claude David, and Paul LeClerc, eds., *Lettres d'André Morellet* (1 vol. to date, Oxford, 1991), I, 393n. The Alexander family moved from Auteuil to Saint-Germain-en-Laye during the spring of 1779, but the daughters—Bethia, Mariamne, Christine, and Jane—frequently came back to visit Mme. Helvétius: *ibid.*

recevoir Melles Alexandre. Elle a pensé que comme vous dines chès vous vous voudries bien venir à son secours et recevoir ces demoiselles. Elle ira les rejoindre chés vous après le diner. Je me rendrai demain lundi à l'invitation obligeante qu'elle m'a faite de vôtre part. C'est toujours un grand bonheur pour moi que de vous voir. Je suis avec le plus profond respect Monsieur Votre très humble et très obeissant Serviteur

L'ABBÉ MORELLET

Addressed: a Monsieur / Monsieur Franklin / ministre plenipotentiaire des etats / unis de l'amerique / à Passy.[6]

Notation: L'abbe Morellet D'autueil.

From the Crew of the *Drake*

ALS OR L:[7] American Philosophical Society

Fougere May 24. 1779—

The Humble Petition of the remaining part of the Drake Sloop of War's Crew, Sheweth—

That whereas your Honour truly Sensable of the Miseries attending the said Ships Company at there being taken and during their Imprisonment, did Vouchafe of your Goodness to Order them Cloths and other Necessaries in Order to proceed in a Carteel to England which Order was punctually executed except to such as were sick & wounded then in Brest Hospital.—[8] Hope your Honour will take it into Consideration and Extend your Humanity to those few who are in a Miserable Necessitous Condition not having wherewithal to Cover there Nakedness or keep them from the Inclemency of the weather—and shou'd We be so happy as to Experience this Act of your Clemency shall Jointly be bound ever to Pray for your Health & Preservation—

JAMES PINKERTON
EPHRAIM CREATON

6. Some arithmetic calculations, apparently unrelated, are on the address sheet.

7. The letter and all signatures are in the same hand.

8. For BF's orders about providing the prisoners with clothing see his March 19 letter to Schweighauser.

John Rickets
Richard Cross—
John Wright
William Bailey
William Chirton
Adam Mc. Adam
Andrew Mc. Comb
James Letow—
Thomas Ralph—

P.S. Your Honr. will be pleased to favour us with an answer as soon as Convenient.

N.B. Charles Arthur acting gunner woud be Glad if your Honour wou'd be pleased to order him out on Perole, as the Master at arms has had his Enlargement.

To the Honourable Dr. Franklin—

Addressed: The Honourable—/ Dr. Benjn. Franklin / Commissioner for the Americans / in Passy. / France—

Notation: vu Bon a [*torn*] fougere le 26 may 1779 Macé Chirurgien interprete

From J. Rocquette, T. A. Elsevier & P. Th. Rocquette[9]

ALS or L: American Philosophical Society

Monsieúr! Rotterdam 24 May *1779.*

Nous nous empressons à vous acheminer un paquet que nous avons reçu aujourdhui pour vos Graces par un navire arrivé de St. Eustache, nous L'adressons par precaution a nos Amis Messieurs Vandenyver freres et Co. a Paris,[1] qui vous la fairont tenir, comme on nous recommande ce paquet très particulierement nous vous prions de vouloir bien nous faire L'amitié de nous en accuser la reception pour notre Satisfaction.

9. The firm began corresponding with BF and his fellow commissioners in late 1777: XXV, 170–1.

1. The Parisian relatives of an Amsterdam banking house: XXV, 521.

Permettez nous de nous prevaloir de cette occasion pour vous prier de nous faire le plaisir, de nous marquer ou nous pourrions negocier le plus avantageusement Les Bank notes des Provinces unies de L'Amerique en datte du 8 fevrier de cette annêe pble. au 8 fevr. de L'année 1782. avec L'interet à raison de 6 per Cent, & à quel Cours ce papier est negociable. Nous en avons en portefeuille pour vint mille Dollars.

En attendant de vos nouvelles, & après vous avoir Reiterê en toutte occasion L'offre de nos plus devoues Services, nous avons L'honeur d'etre avec La consideration La plus Respectueuse, Monsieúr: Vos tres humbles & três obeissants Serviteurs J. ROCQÚETTE T: A: ELSEVIER, & FRERES ROCQÚETTE

P.S. Veuillez aussi avoir La bonté de nous dire Si les Interets des Bank notes des Etats de L'Amerique Se payent annuellement & dans ce Cas ou on peut recevoir ces Interets.—

Si vous avez quelques Effets, ou Lettres a faire passer a L'Amerique par voye de nos Isles, Laquelle nous paroit la plus Sure dans Les Circonstances actuelles: nous nous estimerons heureux d'etre Employez a vottre Service LESDITS

Monsieur Benjamin Franklin. Ministre Plenipotentiaire des Etats unis de L'Amerique à Paris

Notation: J. Rocquette/: A Elsevier et freres Rocquette. Amsterdam 24e. may 1779.

To Anna Maria Shipley

ALS (draft): American Philosophical Society

Passy, May 25, 1779

I received by General Verdiere a few Days since the very obliging Letter my dear and amiable Friend did me the honour of writing to me from Wimbledon, dated April 7. He had it seems been detain'd somewhere by Sickness.— The kind Remembrance & unchang'd Affection of old Friends whose good Opinion I always highly valued, is in these times of publick Calamity, one of my greatest Consolations. I often think of the happy Hours, now never to be repeated, that I have formerly passed under your hospitable Roof, with a Family whose Tempers are all so good, and whose Conversation so constantly pleasing. My best Wishes attend you all. Present my Respects to Lord S.[2] if you think they will be acceptable, and believe me ever with sincere Esteem, my dear Friend, Yours very affectionately BF.—

[*torn: word missing*] Anna Maria Shipley.—

From Baudouin

ALS: American Philosophical Society

Monsieur a Paris le 25. May 1779

Je suis bien honteux d'etre obligé de vous faire connoitre toutte l'etendue de mon etourderie je ne me suis appercu de la meprise, que lorsque la sottise a eté faitte, je prie V. Excellence de me pardonner cette faute, je luy jure, que cela n'arrivera plùs. J'espere qu'elle voudra bien me traitter dans cette occasion cy avec son indulgence ordinaire et agréer les hommages de la proffonde veneration et du trés respectueux attachement avec lesquels j'ay l'honneur d'etre monsieur votre tres humble et tres obeissant serviteur BAUDOUIN

Notation: Baudoin. Paris 25e. may 1779.

From Thomas Digges

ALS: Historical Society of Pennsylvania

Dr. Sir 25.th. May. [1779][3]

On the business of the purchase which I have wrote you about by every post *save the last* for four or five back, I have nothing now to say, as nothing new has arose:[4] There has been another item from the person who has it in contemplation, "that the affair was properly attended to, that it requird deliberation, and the answer should be given as soon as possible"—nothing therefore can be further urgd by my friend

2. Lord Spencer; see her April 7 letter.

3. In his letter of May 31, 1779, below, Digges writes that his last letter was the 25th.

4. A disguised reference to the negotiations between Hartley and Lord North.

until an opening is given by the person with whom he has to deal. I have every reason to beleive it was taken so seriously, that a messenger was dispatchd to a quarter where You are very conversant, in order to probe to the bottom what might appear dark, or palliate offensive parts of the proposition. This is not unlikely from the length of time taken to give an answer, and a seeming disinclination not to give one, or to throw any cloud over the matter, for a few days to come, when in all probability the answer may be returnd. If my surmises have any foundation, I make no doubt but you have discoverd or had a hint of what has been attempted.

We have no news here that is good save the arrival of the Wt. India fleet with the loss only of *one* ship wch founderd—this has given us vast spirits & contradicts the reports of the Brest fleet being out to intercept them.[5] The report so current some days ago that DEstaign had been beaten by Byron & lost 14 Ships is now totally discredited; but a similar ridiculous storey even told as coming from N York will be again beleived & swallowd. It is yet asserted as a fact that La Motte Picquets Squadn. is dispersd & many of the Amn Ships lost.[6]

There was nothing material at New York the 10th Feby. nor no appearances of any active exertions on either side. The plan there now, I find, is to procure a revolt in the Jerseys for this purpose there had been sundry Torey Gentn let to go freely into that Country. Jeb Fisher is one of those and after being twice there is at length arrivd in London and is much with the Ministerial People evincing the probability of still succeeding by such a maneuvre— Eden & Gov Johnstone lean to the same opinion, & it has got out from one of them that Govr Franklin is to be the chief Engine for the business—

5. The merchant fleet arrived in Falmouth on May 23, having narrowly escaped an encounter with the French. *Public Advertiser,* May 28, 1779.

6. *The Public Advertiser* had reported the story of a victory by Byron over d'Estaing on May 24. The next day the newspaper accused the government of propagating the false story to keep the public's mind off thinking about Arbuthnot's delay. It also relayed a correspondent's report that Picquet had not been beaten back but was on his way to America. *The General Advertiser, and Morning Intelligencer* of May 25, on the other hand, stood by the story that four of Picquet's squadron were lost off La Rochelle.

He is to go into the Jerseys, insinuate himself into the good graces of some of the leading people & then to be supported by the Army when he sees proper to hoist the Kings Standard.—[7] Wild as all this may appear to you, I am nevertheless of opinion there is one branch of the Admn that will encourage its being put into execution.— The Examination to come on before the House this week of the Torey Refugees—Galloway, Allen, Fisher &c &c—will probably throw some new light on this matter.[8] It does not appear that the Ministry are yet tired of murder & devastation, but I think it high time for them to be warnd against the errors they have frequently been led into by hungry Governors & discontented Toreys driven from their freinds & Country by their wicked & insidious conduct. No accots yet of the sailing of the fleet from Torbay.[9] I am &c &c

ALLEN HAMILTON

I should be glad You will not forget Yr. promise to help me to a drawing from a certain picture I spoke to you & Mr. F——n about.[1]

7. WF was collaborating with Gov. William Tryon of New York on a plan for turning the associated loyalists into an active military force. Edward H. Tebbenhoff, "The Associated Loyalists: an Aspect of Militant Loyalism," *The New-York Hist. Soc. Quarterly,* LXIII (1979), 126–7, 129. In a letter of Feb. 5, WF informed Germain that an association of refugees from New Jersey and New York would make depredations in rebel territory in retaliation for those that the loyalists had suffered. They called themselves "The King's Military Volunteers" and received WF's encouragement and assistance. The following month the former members of the Carlisle Commission privately proposed to Germain the creation of a "civil establishment" that would assist the commanders-in-chief, ease relations with the inhabitants, and make decisions about the restoration of civil government to recaptured territories. WF was suggested as a member of the proposed council. K.G. Davies, ed., *Documents of the American Revolution 1770–1783* (Colonial Office Series, 21 vols., Shannon and Dublin, 1972–81), XVII, 53, 81–2.

8. These American loyalists are identified in our annotation of Digges's letter of May 21, above. Examination of the administration's witnesses in the inquiry into the conduct of the American war did not actually begin until June 8; see Cobbett, *Parliamentary History,* XX (1778–80), 803–6.

9. Adm. Arbuthnot's squadron had in fact set sail for New York the previous day, escorted by the Channel fleet under Adm. Darby: Mackesy, *War for America,* p. 261.

1. WTF. Digges was probably referring to the Duplessis portrait of which BF had promised a miniature to Georgiana Shipley; see her letter of June 6,

From Phillip Faure: Promissory Note[2]

Two DS:[3] American Philosophical Society

Passy May 25. 1779

Received of his Excellency B. Franklin Esqr Two Louis d'ors, to assist me in returning to America which I promise to repay to the honble. President of Congress, or his Order. I have signed three Notes of this Tenor & Date to serve as one.

PHILLIP FAURE
Surgeon of the Frigate Hancock.

Notation in William Temple Franklin's hand: Philip Faure's Notes of hand for 2 Louis

From Alexander Gillon

ALS: American Philosophical Society

Hotel de Modene Tuesday 10 a Clock [May 25, 1779]

Sir

I much regret that I had not the pleasure of meeting your Excellency at Home on my first visit to you since my return

below. Digges's request went unheeded. On May 24, 1780, he asked BF to sit for a full-length portrait, "to oblige a deserving and ingenius Engraver" who would produce good prints from his copy while leaving Digges to enjoy the original. Elias and Finch, *Digges Letters,* pp. 209–11.

2. This promissory note differs slightly in form from the one which BF used earlier in the spring; see that from John Mace, April 12, above. Over the next few months BF will issue, in identical format, several more of these promises by escaped prisoners to repay money lent them at Passy. The dates, amounts, and names are as follows: on July 1, eight louis for Eli Vickery; on Sept. 13, ten louis for Jean de Guio; and on Oct. 24, the same sum for John Pleini. Vickery's, Guio's, and Pleini's notes exist in two copies. All the documents are at the APS. The Alphabetical List of Escaped Prisoners confirms the amounts, and provides the additional information that Guio was a Canadian and Pleini from Charleston, S.C. Guio will reappear in vol. 30, seeking his return passage to America; see BF to Schweighauser, Sept. 13. Library of Congress. Philip Wagner (for whom see our headnote to the favor seekers, March 6, above) also signed one (in three copies, one in French). APS.

3. Numbered "No. 2." and "No. 3."

from Holland.[4] I was as unlucky Yesterday, being detain'd by unforeseen Events, so that I cou'd not wait on you till the Afternoon, missing you then also, I tho't it best to come here in hopes of seeing you this day;—will your Excellency therefore be pleas'd to Admit my waiting on you,[5] at any Hour or place you will please to name to the Bearer, that I may crave your advice, on what I wou'd wish to lay before His Excellency Mr. de Sartine. After dinner, he having favour'd me with that oppty, by Honouring me with an Invitation to dine with him to day, I crave your Excellencys Pardon for troubling you at this Period, but as I learn there are sundry safe opptys for America in a few days, the State of So. Carolina will expect I shou'd write them the particulars of my Conduct, & applications in France, which I can not do till I have His Excellency Monsr. de Sartine's answer to the different requests I have made,[6] you will therefore oblige me, & the State will I am sure thank you, if you will please to aid me in getting any assistance for them, or a reply this day. The Bearer waits you answer & I am with very much Esteem.—

Your Excellencys Most Obedt & most Hble Servt

A. GILLON

Addressed: His Excellency / Benjamin Franklin Esqre. / Minister Plenepotentiary / at the Court of / Versailles

Notation: A. Gillon May 25. 1779

4. Gillon told the S.C. congressional delegates on June 15 that he had found a commercial house in Amsterdam to undertake a loan on his behalf: "Letters from Commodore Alexander Gillon in 1778 and 1779," *S.C. Geneal. and Hist. Mag.*, X (1909), 133.

5. Gillon has here written and then crossed out "this Forenoon".

6. Gillon described for the delegates the result of his discussions with Sartine. The naval minister had earlier refused his request for three frigates (see Sartine to BF, May 4); Gillon now proposed with equal lack of success that the French provide him with a single frigate for which Gillon would give over the money he presently had, the remainder to be repaid within two years: "Letters from Commodore Alexander Gillon," p. 133.

From David Hartley[7]

Transcript: Library of Congress

My Dear friend London May 25 1779

I was in hopes to have had something material to have communicated to you before this but I presume that matters of so much importance & difficulty require long & repeated consideration— In a very long conference of above two hours I enforced every argument for peace upon the terms wch I have explained to you, or nearly upon similar terms, but at all events for a real & sincere negotiation, I received a very serious attention but I cannot make any judgement as to the result.[8] I stated the proposal to extend to the three parties, & it has since occurred to me whether this Court may not have thought it adviseable to sound the Court of Versailles but this is mere conjecture. I attribute to this Conjecture amongst other possible causes the delay of determination. I mention this merely as a conjecture & to suggest to you that if any preliminaries cd be entered into wch might draw on a negotiation in consequence it wd be very immaterial in what place they shd begin or by whose intervention. I am very anxious to lay the foundation of peace. I am inclined to hope that the delay of giving me an answer bespeaks a serious consideration of the Matter. My chief motive for writing to you when I had nothing to write about but mere conjecture, was to suggest that (as I conclude the road allways to be open between the two Courts for any intercourse or proposal wch either side chuses) if any proposition shd be suggested on your side of the water wch might serve for a beginning upon similar grounds with my propositions the delay of an answer thro my hands might not impede that good beginning. I will send you the earliest intelligence that I may have to communicate. In the mean let me assure you that nothing shall be wanting on my part to the utmost of my power towards forwarding a general peace. I am Your affecte DH

7. See Digges's letter of May 31 below, with which the present letter was probably enclosed.

8. He had recently been conferring with Lord North; see our annotation of Hartley's letter of April 10, above.

From Ingenhousz

ALS: American Philosophical Society

Dear friend. London May 25 1779

I reciev'd your lettre of the 4 of May and thank you for the communication of your paper upon the Aurora Borealis, which I find to contain very natural and truly philosophical Suppositions. I had scarce reciev'd it, but it was known by many I had it, tho I did mentioned to no body, except to Dr. Priestley. After having taken a copy of it I sent it to Magellan, who had allready enquired after it, and who would forward it to Mr. Vaughan.[9] It has given a general satisfaction. As it has been allready read at the Royal Academy I think it can for that reason not with propriety be read at the R. S.. But Dr. Priestley and others were very glad to hear you would soon favour the Royal society with a paper upon a more usefull subject. Dr. Priestley desired me to let you know, that he desires much you should direct it to him for to be presented at the Society, and send it soon. For my part I rejoice to see, that you still take delight in Philosophical pursuits and cannot but hope that this taste will groe upon you.

At the next council of the Royal Society the matter of your copies will be taken up, and the copies certainly granted as your property:[1] I will forward them as you direct it, if I doe not find some better oportunity. I will send also your roasting vessel.[2]

As I could not possibly finish my book upon the smallpox, being so often interrupted,[3] I thought, that, if I quit this coun-

9. Ingenhousz's copy, entitled "Suppositions and conjectures forming an hypothesis for the explanation of the Aurora Borealis," is at the Library of Congress. Vaughan later published the piece, varying the title slightly, in his *Political, Miscellaneous and Philosophical Pieces* . . . (London, 1779), pp. 504–9.

1. The next meeting was on June 3. BF's request for volumes of the *Phil. Trans.* that he had not yet received was granted without discussion. From information kindly supplied by Sheila Edwards, Librarian of the Royal Society.

2. See Ingenhousz's letter above, April 9.

3. Ingenhousz had made a similar complaint the previous fall: XXVII, 504. His work with inoculation was well known, but there is no evidence that he ever published a book on the subject.

try before finishing it, it may possibly have the same fate, as had my Latin translation of your book. I therefore have asked leave from my Imperial Masters to spend the summer and part of the winter here. I intend to retire in a country house for the summer season for to work quietely, but near the town. Letters directed to my name at *Dun & Taylor. N. 6 Fleet Street* will be forwarded to me. Two papers of mine upon Electricity are in the press, if they come out before the volume of the transactions reaches you, I will by some or other oportunity forward a copy of them to you.[4]

I draw'd up a paper upon a new method of suspending magnetical needles, which did please much to those of my friends, to whom I communicated my idea.[5] Mr. Nairn[6] was so much strukt with it, that he thought much of securing a patent for him of the invention. A new theory of mine upon the nature and explosive force of gunpowder gave much satisfaction to the R Society. No body thought before me upon the true explication of this awfull ingredient. Dr. Priestley having red my paper, acknowledges, I hit at the true theory, and that his theory is far inferior to mine.[7]

Our respectable friend[8] is very well, now at Bath.

Recieve my thanks for the care of the article to your

4. One of these papers offered a clever way of lighting a candle by generating an electric spark; the other explained the workings of Volta's electrophorus by applying BF's theory of positive and negative electricity. See the annotation of Ingenhousz's letter, above, April 1. They were both published in part II of the *Phil. Trans.* for 1778, but that volume may not have appeared until the fall of 1779: *Gentleman's Mag.*, XLIX (1779), pp. 554–6.

5. "On some new Methods of suspending Magnetical Needles," *ibid.*, pp. 537–46, read June 17, 1779. In order to keep compass needles from quivering and ranging imprecisely, Ingenhousz proposed to suspend the magnetized needles in a liquid; water worked well, but linseed oil had the advantages of not freezing and not causing the needles to rust.

6. For Edward Nairne, F.R.S., one of the foremost instrument makers of the 18th century, see X, 171n.

7. For the paper on gunpowder see Ingenhousz's letter of April 1. Priestley does acknowledge this theory, but in somewhat more circumspect terms than Ingenhousz here describes, in a letter to Giovanni Fabroni, June 20, 1779: Robert E. Schofield, *A Scientific Autobiography of Joseph Priestley (1733–1804)* (Cambridge, Mass., and London, 1966), p. 171.

8. Sir John Pringle.

Nephew whose answer I found with much satisfaction inclosed in yours.

I am very respectfully Dear friend Your Most obedient humble servant J. INGEN HOUSZ

Addressed: Mr Tourton / A Monsieur / Monsieur Le Docteur / francklin / *a Passy*

Notations in different hands: Ingenhouss May 25. 1779. / Le d.. Ingenhou [torn] / Dr Ingenhauss

From Sartine

Copies: Archives de la Marine, American Philosophical Society, Library of Congress (two)

A Versailles le 26. May 1779;[9]

J'ai recu, Monsieur, la lettre que vous m'avez fait l'honneur de m'ecrire au sujet du Brigantin du Sr. Giddins, de Newbury qui a été coulé a fond pour méprise sous une Batterie de la Guadeloupe.[1] Sur le compte que j'ai rendû au Roy de cet accident et de votre demande en faveur de ce Capitaine, Sa Majesté a bien voulû lui accorder une indemnité proportionnée à sa perte, et j'ai chargé les Administrateurs de la Colonie de la régler d'après les connoissances locales qu'ils se procureront.[2] Je joins ici le Duplicata de ma dépêche que je vous prie de vouloir bien faire passer au Sr. afin qu'il la présente lui même aux Administrateurs. Les Etats-Unis trouveront dans cette décision du Roy une nouvelle preuve de la bienveillance de Sa Majesté.

J'ai l'honneur d'etre avec un Sincere attachement, M, votre très humble &c.

A M. franklin Ministre plenipotentiaire des Etats unis de l'Amerique à Passy

9. Published out of our usual sequence because the following letter indicates the present letter had already been received.

1. Above, April 29. For Giddings' testimony in the case see Tristram Dalton's letter of May 13.

2. Sartine eventually decided to compensate the ship's owners in the amount of 15,000 *l.t.:* to BF, June 25, 1780 (APS).

To the Committee for Foreign Affairs

LS:[3] National Archives; AL (draft):[4] Library of Congress; copies: Library of Congress, South Carolina Historical Society; transcript: National Archives

Gentlemen, Passy, May 26th. 1779.

The Marquis de La Fayette, who arrived here the 11th of Feby. brought me yours of Oct. 28. and the new Commission, Credentials and Instructions the Congress have honoured me with.[5] I have not since had an Opportunity of Writing that I could trust; for I see by several Instances that the Orders given to private Captains, to throw their Dispatches into the Sea, when likely to be taken, are sometimes neglected, and sometimes so badly executed that the Letters are recovered by the Enemy; and much Inconvenience has attended their Interception. You mention that you should speedily have Opportunities of forwarding Duplicates and Triplicates of these Papers; None of them have ever come to hand, nor have I received any other Line from you of later Date.

I immediately acquainted the Minister for Foreign Affairs with my Appointment and communicated to him as usual a Copy of my Credential Letter, on which a Day was named for my Reception. A Fit of the Gout prevented my attendance at that time, and for some Weeks after, but as soon as I was able to go through the Ceremony, I went to Versailles and was presented to the King and received in all the Forms.[6] I delivered the Letter of the Congress into his Majesty's own Hands, who in the most gracious manner express'd his Satisfaction. And I have since constantly attended the Levee every Tuesday

3. In WTF's hand. The letter was carried by La Luzerne aboard the French frigate *Sensible,* which brought JA back to America and arrived in Nantasket Roads on Aug. 3 (BF to JA, June 5, below; Butterfield, *John Adams Diary,* II, 400). On Aug. 17, having reached Philadelphia, the letter was referred to a committee of congressional delegates (Laurens, Lovell, and Meriwether Smith): *JCC,* XIV, 972.

4. The draft's numerous emendations and marginal insertions were all incorporated into the LS.

5. XXVII, 633–46, 654–5.

6. Described in his April 3 letter to JA.

with the other Foreign Ministers, and have taken every proper Occasion of repeating the Assurances I am instructed to give, of the grateful Sentiments of Congress, and their determined Resolution to fulfil religiously their Engagements. Much Pain is constantly taken by the Enemy to weaken the Confidence of this Court in their new Allies, by representing our People as weary of the War and of the Government of Congress, which Body too they represent as distracted by Dissensions &ca. but all this has very little Effect; and when on some Occasions it has seem'd to make a little Impression & create some Apprehensions, I have not found it difficult to remove them. And it is my firm Opinion, that notwithstanding the great Losses suffer'd by the Commerce of this Kingdom, since the Commencement of the War, the Disposition of the Court to continue it ('till its Purpose of establishing our Independence is compleated) is not in the least changed, nor their Regard for us diminished.

The End of that Part of the Instructions which relates to American Seamen taken by the French in English Ships, had already been obtained. Capt. Jones having had for some time an Order from Court directed to the Keepers of the Prisoners, requiring them to deliver to him such Americans as should be found in their Hands, that they might be at Liberty to serve under his Command. Most of them have accordingly been delivered to him if not all.[7] The Minister of the Marine having entertained a high Opinion of him, from his Conduct and Bravery in taking the Drake, was desirous of employing him in the Command of a particular Enterprize; and to that end requested Us to spare him, which we did, and sent the Ranger home under the Command of his Lieutenant.[8] Various Accidents have hitherto postponed his Equipment, but he now has the Command of a 50 Gun Ship, with some Frigates all under American Commissions & Colours, fitted out at the Kings

7. See Sartine's letter of May 3 and, for the instruction to BF, XXVII, 635–6.

8. The *Ranger,* commanded by Thomas Simpson, Jones's former lieutenant, had arrived in Portsmouth, N.H., more than seven months earlier: XXVIII, 186n.

Expence, and will sail it is said about the 1st of June.[9] The Marquis de la Fayette was, with some Land Troops, to have gone with him, but I now understand the Marquis is not to go, the Plan being a little changed.—[1] The Alliance being weakly manned at first, and the Captain judging it necessary to be freed from 38 of his Men who had been concerned in a Conspiracy, and unwilling to take French Seamen I thought it best to send him directly home, as his Ship might be of some Protection to the Vessels then about sailing to America, and Mr Adams who was desirous of returning soon, might be accommodated with a Passage in a swift sailing Vessel.[2] I accordingly offerd her as a Convoy to the Trade at Nantes; but the Gentlemen concerned, did not think fit to wait for her getting ready, as a French Convoy offer'd for at least Part of the Voyage and the Minister requesting she might be added to Capt. Jones's little Squadron, and offering to give a Passage to Mr Adams in the Frigate with the new Ambassador, and to compleat the Alliance's Complement of Men,[3] I thought it best to continue her a little longer in Europe, hoping she may in the projected Cruise, by her extraordinary Swiftness, be a means of taking Prisoners enough to redeem the rest of our Countrymen now in the English Goals. With this View, as well as to oblige the Minister, I order'd her to join Capt. Jones at L'Orient, and obey his Orders, where she now is accordingly.[4] There have been great Misunderstandings between the Offi-

9. Jones's squadron did not sail until mid-June; for the use to which it was put see BF's June 3 letter to the marine committee and Jones's letter of June 18.

1. Four days earlier Lafayette had announced to Jones the cancellation of their planned joint operation: Idzerda, *Lafayette Papers,* II, 267. Louis Gottschalk, *Lafayette and the Close of the American Revolution* (Chicago, 1942), p. 15, blames the minister of war for the cancellation. Montbarey had in fact devised plans for a different diversionary attack (against Plymouth) should circumstances permit: Patterson, *The Other Armada,* pp. 70–1. An operation entirely under French control and linked to the progress of the invasion attempt against the Isle of Wight presented obvious advantages over an independent operation with an American naval commander.

2. As he had instructed Landais on Feb. 22: XXVIII, 589.

3. See Sartine's letters of April 20 and 27.

4. His orders to Landais are dated April 28.

cers of that Ship and their Captain, and great Discontents among the latter for want of Clothes and Money. I have been obliged to make great Advances to appease those Discontents, and I now hope the Authority and Prudence of Capt. Jones will be able to remove, or at least prevent the ill Effects of those Misunderstandings. The Conspirators are detained in Prison; and will remain there subject to such Direction as the Congress may think fit to give concerning them. The Courts here would not, because they properly could not, undertake to try them; and we had not Captains enough to make a Court Martial for the purpose. The sending them to America, with Evidence to convict them, will be a great Trouble and Expence, and perhaps their Offence cannot be so clearly made out as to justify a Punishment sufficient to deter by its exemplary Severity: Possibly the best use that can be made of them is to give them in Exchange for as many Americans in the Cartel now operating here.[5] The perfidious Conduct of English and Scotch Sailors in our Service, a good deal discourages the Idea of taking them out of those Prisons in order to employ them.

This Cartel is at length brought about by the indefatigable Endeavours of an old Friend of mine and a long declared one to America, Mr Hartley, Member of Parliament for Hull. The Ship employ'd has already brought us one Cargo from the Prison at Plymouth. The Number was intended for an hundred, but proved 97: and she is returned with as many in Exchange, to bring us a second Number from the Prison at Portsmouth. This is to continue 'till all are exchanged.[6] The Americans are chiefly engaged with Capts. Jones and Landais. This Exchange is the more remarkable, as our People were all committed as for high Treason.

5. In the draft, the paragraph first ends here; the next sentence is added in the space remaining at the end of the line. BF also revised "Their Conduct" to "The perfidious Conduct".

6. The hope proved illusory; the exchanges ended in July because of the lack of American-held prisoners: Catherine M. Prelinger, "Benjamin Franklin and the American Prisoners of War in England during the American Revolution," *W&MQ*, 3rd ser., XXXII (1975), 276.

Agreable to the 7th. Instruction, I have earnestly recommended the Reduction of Halifax & Quebec.[7] The Marquis de la Fayette joined me warmly in the Application for this purpose; and I hope we shall in due time see some good Effects from it.

I have also in various Ways and thro' various Channels laid before the Ministry the distressed State of our Finances in America. There seems a great Willingness in all of them to help us, except in the Controller, M. Necker, who is said to be not well disposed towards us, and is supposed to embarras every Measure proposed to relieve us by Grants of Money.[8] It is certain that under the Resolution, perhaps too hastily declared, of the King's imposing no new Taxes on his Subjects for this Year, the Court has great Difficulties in defraying present Expence, the Vast Exertions to put the Navy in a Condition to equal that of England, having cost immense Sums.[9]

7. The *eighth* article of BF's instructions (an article later rescinded) ordered BF to indicate to the French government the significant advantages that would result from capturing Halifax and Quebec: the ruination of the Newfoundland fisheries and the destruction of the British marine. BF does not mention here that he exceeded these instructions by asking France to send an expeditionary force to the United States: XXVIII, 603–6. He later abstained from further requests for troops because, as he wrote Lafayette on October 1, 1779, he had no orders to seek them: Idzerda, *Lafayette Papers,* II, 320. The proposal for a French expeditionary force languished until revived by a letter from Washington to Lafayette: Jonathan R. Dull, *A Diplomatic History of the American Revolution* (New Haven and London, 1985), pp. 115, 117–8.

8. In February, Necker, responsible for the government's finances, had complained to the influential abbé de Véri, "Je me trouverais à l'aise sans les demandes que la guerre occasionne": Jehan de Witte, ed., *Journal de l'abbé de Véri* (2 vols., Paris, [1928–30]), II, 196. His opposition to the war and its enormous expenses would continue to grow; see Richard B. Morris, *The Peacemakers: the Great Powers and American Independence* (New York, 1965), pp. 91–111.

9. During 1779, the French navy cost some 150,000,000 *l.t.,* compared to a normal peacetime budget of 27,900,000 *l.t.* per year (while the government's annual revenues were approximately 400,000,000 *l.t.*); expenses over the preceding three years had also been heavy: Dull, *French Navy,* pp. 345–50; J.F. Bosher, *French Finances, 1770–1795: from Business to Bureaucracy* (Cambridge, Eng., 1970), p. 90.

There is also a prevailing Opinion that the most effectual Service to us, is to be expected from rendring their Marine superior to that of England.[1] The King has however, to encourage our Loan in Holland, been so good as to engage under his Hand to be Security for our Payment of the Interest of three Millions of Livres; but that Loan has not yet amounted to more than about 80,000 Florins.[2] Dr. Price, whose Assistance was requested by Congress, has declined that Service, as you will see by the Copy of his Letter enclosed.[3] To me it seems that the Measure recommended by the Wisdom of Congress for diminishing the Quantity of Paper, by Taxes of large nominal Sums, must have very Salutary Effects.

As to your Finances here, it is fit that you should know the State of them. When the Commissioners of Congress made the Proposition of paying the Interest at Paris of the Money borrowed in America, they understood the Loan to be of Five Million of Dollars.[4] They obtained from Government Sums more than sufficient for the Interest of such a Sum. That Sum has been increased, and if they could otherwise have provided for it, they have been from time to time drained by a Number of unforseen Expences of which the Congress had no Knowledge, and of others occasioned by their Orders and Drafts; and the Cargoes sent to the Commissioners by the Committees have some of them been treacherously run away with by the Seamen, or taken by the Enemy, or when arrived have been hitherto applied towards the Payment of Debts, the Tobaccos to the Farmers General according to Contract, and the Rice and Indigo to Messrs Hortalez and Co. from whom by the Way, we have not yet been able to procure any Account.[5] I have lately employed an Accountant, the Son of our Banker, to form compleat Books of our Accounts to be sent to Con-

1. In the draft, this sentence is added in the margin. Vergennes recently had instructed Gérard to use this argument with Congress: Meng, *Despatches of Gérard,* p. 611.

2. See our annotation of Vergennes' letter of March 18.

3. His letter of Jan. 18: XXVIII, 393.

4. XXIII, 469–70.

5. BF complained about Beaumarchais in more detail in his March 19 letter to JW; for Beaumarchais' side see XXVIII, 523–31.

gress.[6] They are not yet ready. When they are, I shall send them by the first safe Opportunity. In the mean time I may just mention some Particulars of our Disbursements. Great Quantities of Clothing, Arms, Ammunition and Naval Stores, sent from time to time; Payment of Bills from Mr Bingham 100,000 Livres; Congress Bills in favour of Haywood and Company above 200,000. Advanced to Mr Ross about £20,000 sterling.[7] Paid Congress Drafts in favour of returned Officers 93,080 Livres. To our Prisoners in England and after their Escape to help them home, and to other Americans here in Distress, a great Sum, I cannot at present say how much. Supplies to M. Hodge for fitting out Capt. Cunningham, very considerable.[8] For the Freights of Ships to carry over the Supplies, great Sums. To Mr Wm Lee, and Mr Izard £5500 Sterling.[9] And for fitting the Frigates Rawleigh, Alfred, Boston, Providence, Alliance, Ranger &c I imagine not less than 60 or 70,000 Livres each, taken one with another: And for Maintenance of the English Prisoners I believe when I get in all the Accounts I shall find 100,000 Livres not sufficient, having already paid above 65,000 on that Article. And now the Drafts of the Treasurer of the Loans coming very fast upon me, the Anxiety I have suffer'd, and the Distress of Mind lest I should not be able to pay them has for a long time been very great indeed. To apply again to this Court for Money for a particular Purpose which they had already over and over again provided for and furnished Us, was extreamly awkward. I therefore repeated the *general* Applications which we had made when together, for Aids of Money, and received the general

6. Presumably Jean-François-Paul Grand, identified in our annotation of his May 4 letter to BF.

7. For the payments to Bingham see our annotation of his March 3 letter to the commissioners. William Haywood, formerly a Montreal merchant and now a business associate of Bondfield, had been reimbursed by the commissioners for help given the Continental Army in Canada: XXVI, 278n. Ross's accounts are discussed in his letter of April 24.

8. XXIII, 585n; XXIV, 243; *Deane Papers,* III, 17–19.

9. According to Silas Deane, Lee received 72,000 *l.t.* (about £3,000 sterling) and Izard 60,000 *l.t.* (about £2,500 sterling): *Deane Papers,* V, 252. For payments to the two see XXV, 497n, 626; XXVIII, 380, 401n. See also Lee's account of his conversation with BF, above, March 15.

Answers, that the Expence of Government for the Navy was so great, that at present it was exceedingly difficult to furnish the necessary Supplies. That France, by sending a Fleet to America, obliged the Enemy to divide their Forces, and left them so weak on the Continent as to aid us by lessening our Expence, if it could not by giving us Money, &c. &c;[1] and I was asked if we did not receive Money from Spain? I know indeed of some Money received from thence, and I have heard of more, but know not how much. Mr. A. Lee as Minister for Spain, having taken to himself all the Management of that Affair, and will account to Congress. I only understand that there is none of it left to assist in Paying Congress Bills.[2] I at length obtained, as above mentioned, the King's *Bon* for Payment of the Interest of Three Millions, if I could borrow it in Holland or elsewhere; but tho' two eminent Houses in Amsterdam have undertaken it, and had hopes of Success, they have both lately written to me, that the great Demands of Money for Germany and for England had raised Interest above our Limits, and that the Successes of the English in Georgia and St Lucia, and in destroying the French Trade, with the supposed Divisions in Congress, all much magnified by the British Ministry and the pressing Applications to borrow by several of our States separately, had made the Money'd People doubtful of our Stability, as well as our Ability to repay what might be lent us, and that it was necessary to wait a more favourable Moment for proceeding with our Loan.[3] In this Situation I have been applied to by Mr William Lee, and lately thro' our Banker by Mr Izard, for more Money for their Expences, and I am told there is much Anger against me for declining to furnish them, and that I am charged with *disobeying an Order of Congress,* and with cruelly attempting to distress

1. In the draft, from here through ". . . Congress Bills." was added in the margin.

2. For the results of Arthur Lee's 1777 Spanish mission see XXIII, 498–500, and for his accounts, Wharton, *Diplomatic Correspondence,* III, 15.

3. Jean de Neufville & Cie. continued to hold out hope for the success of the loan; see the memorandum on the proposed Dutch loan that we publish at the end of April.

Gentlemen who are in the Service of their Country. They have indeed produced to me a Resolve of Congress *impowering them to draw* on the Commissioners in France, *for their Expences at Foreign Courts;* and doubtless Congress when that Resolve was made, intended to enable us to pay those Drafts.[4] But as that has not been done, and the Gentlemen (except Mr Lee for a few Weeks)[5] *have not incurred any Expence* AT *Foreign Courts,* and if they had, the 5,500. Guineas, received by them in about 9 Months seem'd an ample Provision for it; and as both of them might command Money from England, I do not conceive that I *disobey'd an Order* of Congress; and that if I did, the Circumstances will excuse it; and I could have no Intention to distress them, because I must know it out of my Power, as their private Fortunes and Credit will enable them at all times to pay their own Expences. In short the dreadful Consequences of Ruin to our Public Credit both in America and Europe, that must attend protesting a single Congress Draft for Interest, after our Funds were out, would have weigh'd with me against the Payment of more Money to those Gentlemen, if the Demand had been otherwise well founded. I am however in the Judgement of Congress, and if I have done amiss must submit dutifully to their Censure. Thanks to God, I have this last Week got over the Difficulty so far as relates to the Bills, which will all be punctually paid; but if the Navy Boards send more Ships here to be fitted, or the Congress continue to draw for the Payment of other Debts, the Ships will be disappointed, and I shall probably be made a Bankrupt; unless Funds are at the same time sent over to discharge such Demands.

With regard to the fitting out of Ships, receiving and disposing of Cargoes and purchasing of Supplies, I beg leave to

4. For BF's refusal to supply more funds to William Lee see the latter's account of their conversation, March 15. We have no record of Izard's latest attempt to obtain more money, but BF had earlier been a strong opponent of such funding: XXVIII, 335–7. The congressional resolution was that of May 7, 1778, which empowered Lee and Izard to draw on the commissioners: *JCC,* XI, 473.

5. During his unsuccessful mission to Vienna; see our annotation of Dumas' letter of March 24–25.

mention, that besides my being wholly unacquainted with such Business, the Distance I am at from the Ports renders my having any thing to do with it extreamly inconvenient. Commercial Agents have indeed been appointed by Mr Wm Lee, but they and the Captains are continually writing for my Opinion or Orders, or Leave to do this and that, by which much time is lost to them, and much of mine taken up, to little Purpose from my Ignorance. I see clearly however that many of the Captains are exorbitant in their Demands, and in some Cases I think those Demands are too easily comply'd with by the Agents, perhaps because their Commissions are in Proportion to the Expence. I wish therefore the Congress would appoint the Consuls they have a Right to appoint by the Treaty, and put into their Hands all that sort of Employment. I have in my Desk I suppose not less than Fifty Applications from different Ports praying the Appointment, and offering to serve *gratis,* for the Honor of it, and the Advantage it gives in Trade:—[6] but I should imagine that if Consuls are appointed they will be of our own People, from America, who if they should make Fortunes abroad, might return with them to their Country. The Commissions demanded by the Agents, seem to me in some Cases very high. For Instance Mr Schweighauser in a late Account charges 5 per Cent, on the simple Delivery of the Tobacco's to the Officer of the Farmers General in the Port, and by that means makes the Commission on the Delivery of the two last Cargoes amount to about £630 sterling. As there was no Sale in the Case, he has in order to calculate the Commission valued the Tobacco at 90 Livres the 100 wt. wheras it was by our Contract with the Farmers to be delivered at about 40 Livres. I got a Friend who was going upon Change to enquire among the Merchants what was the Custom in such Cases of Delivery. I send enclosed the Result he has given me of his Enquiries. In consequence I have refused to pay the Commission of 5 per Cent on this Article; and I know not why it was, as is said, agreed with him at the time of his Appointment, that he should have 5 per Cent on his

6. The same estimate BF had made to Gridley on March 17.

Transactions, if the Custom is only 2 per Cent, as by my Information.[7]

I have mentioned above the Applications of separate States to borrow Money in Europe, on which I beg leave to remark, that when the general Congress are endeavouring to obtain a Loan, these separate Attempts do interfere, and are extreamly inconvenient, especially where some of the Agents are impower'd to offer a higher Interest, and some have Powers in that Respect unlimited. We have likewise lately had Applications from three several States to this Court to be furnished with great Quantities of Arms, Ammunition & Clothing or with Money upon Credit to buy them; and from one State to be supplied with naval Stores and Ships of War.[8] These Agents finding that they had not Interest to obtain such Grants, have severally applied to me, and seem to think it my Duty as Minister for the United States, to support and inforce their particular Demands. I have endeavour'd to do so, but I find the Ministers do not like these separate Applications, and seem to think that they should properly come only thro' Congress, to whom the several States in such Cases ought first to make known their Wants, and then the Congress could instruct their Minister accordingly. This would save the King's Ministers a good deal of Trouble, and the several States the Expence of these particular Agents. Concerning whom I would add a little Remark, that we have in America too readily in various Instances given Faith to the Pretensions of Strangers from Europe, who offer their Services, as Persons who have powerful Friends and great Interest in their own Country, and by that means obtain Contracts, Orders or Commissions to procure what we want; and who when they come here are totally unknown, & have no other Credit but what such Commissions give them; or if known, the Commissions

7. We have not found the enclosure. Schweighauser's supposedly excessive commissions had been the subject of complaint for many months; see XXVII, 395, 454, and also BF's June 5 letter to JA.

8. South Carolina wished ships of war, Maryland and Virginia military supplies.

do not add so much to *their* Credit as they diminish that of their Employers.—

I have received two Letters from a Frenchman settled in one of the Ports of Barbary, offering himself to act as our Minister with the Emperor, with whom he pretended to be intimate, and acquainting me that his Imperial Majesty wonder'd we had never sent to thank him for being the first Power on this Side the Atlantick, that had acknowledged our Independence, and opened his Ports to us; advising that we should send the Emperor a Present.[9] On Enquiry at the Office in whose Department Africa is included, I learnt the Character of this Man to be such, that it was not safe to have any Correspondence with him, and therefore did not answer his Letter. I suppose Congress has received the Memorial we presented to this Court respecting the Barbary States, and requesting the Kings good Offices with them agreable to the Treaty; and also the Answer expressing the Kings Readiness to perform those good Offices whenever the Congress should send us Instructions and make Provisions for the necessary Presents,[1] or if these Papers have not yet got to Hand, they will be found among the Copies carried over by Mr Adams, and therefore I only mention them by way of Remembrance. Whenever a Treaty with the Emperor shall be intended I suppose some of our Naval Stores will be an acceptable Present, and the Expectation of continued Supplies of such Stores, a powerful Motive for entring into and continuing a Friendship.

I should send you Copies of several other Memorials and publick Papers. But as Mr Adams goes in the same Ship, and has the whole of our Transactions during his Time, it is not so necessary by this Vessel.

The Disposition of this Nation in general continues Friendly towards us and our Cause; and I do not see the least Diminution of it, except among the West India Merchants and Planters, whose Losses have render'd them a little Discontented.

9. A notation in the margin identifies him as "D'audibet de Caille" (Etienne d'Audibert Caille), for whom see XXVI, 285n. The sultan of Morocco was Muhammed III, who reigned from 1757 to 1790.

1. XXVII, 313, 468, 481–2, 663.

Conde de Floridablanca

Spain has been long acting as a Mediator, but arming all the time most Vigourously. Her Naval Force is now very great indeed, and as her last Proposition of a long Truce in which America should be included, and treated with as Independent in fact tho' not expressly acknowledged as such, has been lately rejected by England, it is now thought that her open Junction with France in the War is not far distant.[2] The Commissioners here have a Power in general Terms to treat of Peace, Friendship and Commerce with European States, but I apprehend this is scarce explicit enough to authorize me to treat of such a Truce if the Proposition should again come upon the *Tapis*. I therefore wish the Congress to consider of it, and give such Power as may be necessary to whom they may think proper; that if a favourable Opportunity of making an advantageous Treaty should offer, it may not be slipt.

Admiral Arbuthnot who was going to America with a large Convoy and some Troops has been detained by a little Attempt upon Jersey, and contrary Winds since that Affair was over, have detain'd him farther 'till within these few Days.[3]

2. In the draft, the remainder of the paragraph is added in the margin. For the Spanish truce proposal see XXVIII, 358–9. BF was not aware that at the beginning of April Spain had made a final attempt at mediation which would not have guaranteed American independence. Through their ambassador in London they proposed a truce in place in North America. The Convention of Aranjuez, signed on April 12, called for Spain to enter the war if Britain rejected this proposal (as it eventually did): Doniol, *Histoire,* III, 805; JA to BF, May 17. Spain imposed on France a high price for her joining the hostilities: a promise to continue the war until Gibraltar was recaptured from the British, help in obtaining a variety of other territorial objectives, and a commitment to share the risks of an invasion of England (for details of which see Sartine's letter of April 27): Doniol, *Histoire,* III, 805–10. Vergennes was able to convince Louis XVI that France had no choice but to pay whatever price Spain asked; the French Navy had failed to win a decisive victory and henceforth would be badly outnumbered by the British Navy unless it received the help of Spain: Dull, *French Navy,* pp. 126–43, 361–4. Spain's help to the United States, however, would be indirect; she reserved the right to make her own arrangements with the Americans whose independence she had not recognized (and in fact had little interest in assisting). For BF's reflections on Spanish-American relations see Croÿ's account of a dinner with him, March 1.

3. The French threat to the Channel islands did in fact cause Arbuthnot to recall to port the huge convoy of nearly 400 sail while he reconnoitered

Since I began writing this Letter I have received a Packet from the Committee by way of Statia and Holland sent by Mr. Lovell, containing his Letters of Decr 8 Jan 29. and Feb. 8. with one from the President dated Jan 3d. Several Papers are mentioned as sent with them, and by other Opportunities but none are come to hand, except the Resolution to postpone the Attempt upon Canada; and these are the first Dispatches received here since the Date of those sent by the Marquis de la Fayette.[4]

I have also just received a Letter from Mr Bingham, acquainting me that the Ship Deane and the General Gates are just arrived at Martinico and apply to him to be careend refitted and procure a fresh Supply of Provisions; and that tho' he has no Orders, he must draw upon me for the Expence.[5] I think it right to acquaint you thus early that I shall be obliged to protest his Bills. I have just obtained from his Majesty Orders to the Government of Guadaloupe to make reasonable Reparation to Capt. Giddens of Newbury, for the Loss of his Vessel, sunk in mistake by a Battery of that Island.[6]

Great Preparations are now making here with much activity in all the Sea Ports, Taking up Transports, and Building small Vessels proper for Landing of Troops, &c. so that many think an Invasion of England or Ireland is intended. The Intention whatever it is, may change; but the Opinion of such an Intention which seems to prevail in England, may tend to keep their Troops and Ships at Home.

General and Lord Howe, Generals Cornwallis and Grey, Col. Montresor, Captain Hammond and others have formally given it as their Opinion in Parliament, that the Conquest of America is impracticable.

---

the area with his five ships of the line: W.M. James, *The British Navy in Adversity; a Study of the War of American Independence* (London and New York, 1926), pp. 170–1. Their eventual departure for New York was reported to BF by Thomas Digges on May 25, above.

4. XXVIII, 206, 334–5, 438–9, 492; the resolution was enclosed with Jay's of Jan. 3 and is discussed in our annotation of it.

5. The letter is Bingham's to the commissioners of March 3, above.

6. Sartine informed BF on the same day of the orders for reparations to be made to Giddings; see the letter immediately preceding the present one.

This Week, as we hear, John Maxwell Esqre Joseph Galloway Esq. Andrew Allen Esq. John Patterson, Theophilus Morris, Enoch Storey, and Jabez Fisher are to be examined to prove the Contrary. One would think the first Set were likely to be the best Judges.[7]

Be pleased to present my dutiful Respects to the Congress, and assure them of my most faithful Services.

I have the honour to be Your most obedient & most humble Servant

B FRANKLIN

To the honble the Committee for Foreign Affairs.

Notation: Letter from B Franklin Esqr Min. plen. Passy 26 May 1779 Comtee. for. Affrs. Read Aug 17. 1779 Referred to Mr Laurens Mr Lovell Mr Smith.

From John Paul Jones

ALS: American Philosophical Society

Honored and dear Sir, L'Orient May 26th. 1779.

Since I had the honor to receive your kind and polite letter of the 19th. I have waited with impatient expectation of seeing the Marquis here.— The Bon homme Richard the Alliance, the Pallas, the Scerf & the Vengeance are now ready in the Road for the Embarkation of the Troops— I have sent Officers and Men to Brest for the Leveller and I expect the Appearance of that Vessel every hour— This little Armament was not I may say begun before the 12th. of this Month, since then the people concerned in it have been employed Night and Day—and I have flattered myself with hopes of Success and Honor—

Judge then of my disappointment when instead seeing the Marquis I have recd. a letter from him which tells me that "the Kings disposition concerning our plan is entirely changed and

7. For the Parliamentary hearings see Digges's letters of May 12 and 21. The testimony of the officers mentioned in the preceding paragraph was reported in the May 11, 14, 18, and 21 issues of the *Courier de l'Europe,* v (1779), 302–3, 307–10, 319, 323–5.

that instead of meeting me he is now going to take command of the Kings Regt. at Saints."[8]

Extraordinary as this change is it is not my place to enquire into the Reasons of it—and tho the expence of the Armament may perhaps exceed the usual amount yet I am certain that the Alteration cannot be attributed to any want of Activity on my part.— Indeed it is my Opinion that no season could be so fit for our purpose as the present—for supposing the fleet to sail from Brest about the 1st. of June—the Enemies Attention would be fully engaged and I think they would find employment enough without attending to the little Armament at L'Orient.—

I am ready to follow any plan you please to adopt, or if any thing is left to me you may depend on my best endeavours either in Europe or America— In both I think I can see Openings— It would have added greatly indeed to my happiness to have been Joined in command with a Character so amiable as the Marquis and I am very Unwilling to drop the expectation of his coming here.— His letter was but this moment brought to my hands, and to Save the Post I am Obliged to Shorten my letter.—

I have the honor to be with honest Affection and Esteem in all changes— Honored and dear Sir Your very Obliged Friend and Obliged Serv JNO P JONES

His Excellcy Doctor Franklin &c &c &c.

Addressed: His Excellency / Doctor Franklin / American Ambassador at the / Court of France. / en son Hôtel à Passy.— / (pres Paris)

Notation: P. Jones L'Orient 26 may 1779.

8. Lafayette to Jones, May 22: Idzerda, *Lafayette Papers,* II, 267. The cancellation of Jones's and Lafayette's joint expedition is discussed in our annotation of BF's May 26 letter to the committee for foreign affairs.

From Lafayette

AL: American Philosophical Society

Dear Sir [*c.* May 26, 1779][9]

I have just now Receiv'd a letter from the President of Congress which I think Should be in Compagny with Many others—[1] I therefore wish to know before My departure when did the pacquet sail from America, what kind of ship she was, what News or what people she brought with her— that I do'nt only desire as an american citizen who wants to hear from his Country, but moreover I expect Some aids de Camps with dispatches who Might have arriv'd with that ship, and whom I should expect instead of going to Saintes.[2] Farewell; pray answer fully to my scribling.

How was the paper currency?

Addressed [*in another hand*]: A Monsier / Monsier Le docteur Frankin / a pasy

Notation: La Fayette.

From Jonathan Williams, Jr.

ALS: American Philosophical Society

Dear & hond Sir.— Nantes May 26. 1779.—

I am much obliged to you for the kind Notice you were pleased to take of my little Fellow.—[3] I may be partial but I think him the finest Lad I ever saw, and I shall take care to give such an Education & to impress his mind with such prin-

9. When Lafayette's expedition into the Irish Sea was cancelled, he was ordered to report to his regiment, the *dragons du Roi,* stationed at Saintes (near Rochefort). Lafayette wrote Vergennes from the area on June 1; we assume he left Paris about May 27: Idzerda, *Lafayette Papers,* II, 228n, 267, 270–1.

1. The letter announced Congress' decision to abandon a proposed Franco-American attack on Canada; Lafayette told Vergennes on June 1 about receiving it: XXVII, 633–4; Idzerda, *Lafayette Papers,* II, 217, 270.

2. Probably his aides Maj. Neville and Capt. de la Colombe, whom he wished to join him at Saintes. He also expected a Boston merchant and a Pa. regimental commander; see Idzerda, *Lafayette Papers,* II, 269n.

3. His son Josiah; see JW's letter of April 25.

ciples as will, I hope, prevent his being unworthy of the Blessing you were pleased to bestow upon him.— I had a Brother who bore your name, at about 9 years of age he fell thro' the Ice in a large Pond, & was drowned.— Every Feature of my poor Brother & every one of his actions are revived in this charming Boy.

Please to let me know if you advanced any money on my accot & what Sum.—

I am just setting off to L'orient to dispatch the three Friends.[4] I shall be glad if you will drop me a Line about the Anchors, as Mr Gourlade will no doubt ask me for the payment. The Balance of my accot I am ready to pay, but I think it is hard to be obliged to make an advance, which will only perhaps be another disputed article, to an already cruely disputed accot.—

I have at last obtained the Consent of 4 of the Gentlemen to sit on my accot, two of them who have been a long time at L'orient, I intend to bring back with me for that purpose.—[5]

I am ever with the greatest Respect your dutifull & affectionate Kinsman JONA WILLIAMS J

Please to direct to me about the Anchors under Cover to Mr Gourlade at L'orient.

Addressed: a monsieur / Monsieur Franklin / Ministre plenipotentiaire des / Etats Unis / en son Hotel / a Passy / prés / Paris

Notation: Jones Williams Nantes 26 may 1779.

4. The name of his ship.

5. Gridley and Johnson from Nantes, and Cuming and Nesbitt from Lorient. Gridley had recovered from his illness; Schweighauser, however, was still too ill to serve. JW to Cuming and Nesbitt, May 2, 1779, Yale University Library.

To Edward Newenham

Reprinted from William Temple Franklin, ed., *The Private Correspondence of Benjamin Franklin, LL.D, F.R.S., &c* . . . (2nd ed., 2 vols., London, 1817), I, 37–8.

Sir, Passy, May 27, 1779.

I should sooner have sent this Passport, but that I hoped to have had the other from this Court in time to send with it.[6] If you should stay a few days in England, and will let me know how it may be directed to you, I can send it to you per post.

I received some time since a letter from a person at Belfast, informing me that a great number of people in those parts were desirous of going to settle in America, if passports could be obtained for them and their effects, and referring me to you for future information.[7] I shall always be ready to afford every assistance and security in my power to such undertakings, when they are really meant, and are not merely schemes of trade with views of introducing English manufactures into America, under pretence of their being the substance of persons going there to settle.

I admire the spirit with which I see the Irish are at length determined to claim some share of that freedom of commerce, which is the right of all mankind, but which they have been so long deprived of by the abominable selfishness of their fellow subjects. To enjoy all the advantages of the climate, soil and situation in which God and nature have placed us, is as clear a right as that of breathing; and can never be justly taken from men but as a punishment for some atrocious crime.

The English have long seemed to think it a right which

6. BF's draft of a passport, dated May 26, 1779, attested that Newenham "hath on various Occasions manifested himself a firm Friend of Liberty and of America, where he purposes as soon as may be to settle himself, Family and Fortune:—" He requested that Newenham and his family be treated as friends if captured on any part of their journey from Ostend to England, from there to Ireland, and on to America. APS.

On the verso of the passport is an unrelated social note in BF's hand: "J'irai volontiers avec la bonne Famille. Avez vous une Place vacante dans votre Carosse—Non.— Il faut que je viens dans le mien. Je le ferai & je me rendrai chez vous à 5 heures precises."

7. See Jesse Taylor's letter of Nov. 21, 1778: XXVIII, 147–8.

none could have but themselves. Their injustice has already cost them dear, and if persisted in, will be their ruin. I have the honour to be, with great esteem, Sir,

Your most obedient and most humble servant,

B. FRANKLIN.

From Dumas

ALS: American Philosophical Society

Monsieur, Amst. 27e. May *1779*

J'ai profité de l'ajournement de certaine Assemblée, & de l'obligeante invitation de Mrs De N——[8] pour passer cette semaine ici chez eux. Cette petite excursion a été utile: car elle ma donné des lumieres, que je ne pourrai cependant vous communiquer que de bouche: ce qui, j'espere, pourra arriver dans peu de semaines. Je dois me borner ici à vous assurer généralement, que je suis plus que jamais dans la persuasion, que cette maison vraiment Hollandoise, patriotique et amie de l'Am——, est la seule qui doit & devra être toujours la maison Americaine à Amst——; qu'elle vous sera utile dès à présent, & qu'elle pourra vous l'être beaucoup plus encore, à mesure que vous vous entendrez avec elle directement. J'éprouve une cordialité & une franchise, qui est le parfait contraste de la réserve que d'autres ont eue, & de leur subtilité. C'est par le moyen de Mrs. De N—— que je puis, dans ce même jour-ci, rendre un service essentiel au crédit Américain. Mais cette petite particularité est aussi trop délicate pour pouvoir vous être racontée autrement que de bouche.

Hier nous eumes dans la maison la compagnie de 4 Américains Mrs. Sears, Cordes, Alexandre Cofin, et Sayre.[9] Les 2 premiers sont ici depuis certain temps déjà, pour affaires de Commerce. Cofin ne fait que d'arriver avec un navire, parti de Baltimore le 20 Mars, & de la Côte le 6 Avril, chargé princi-

8. Jean de Neufville and his son and partner Leendert de Neufville (*NNBW,* VIII, 1213).

9. David Sears was a Boston merchant: XXVIII, 465n. Joseph Cordis testified on behalf of Sayre's ship design; see Sayre's letter of June 7. Alexander Coffin came from Nantucket and later commanded privateers: Allen, *Mass. Privateers,* pp. 69, 176; Sayre to BF, June 7.

palement de tabac. Ils sont tous 4 de Boston. Quant à Mr. Sayre, ci-devant Banquier à Londres, le même que Ld. Rochefort avoit fait mettre à la Tour,[1] qui vient d'arriver ici d'une tournée en Suede, Norvege & Danemarc, il fait le sujet principal de cette Lettre: & ce que j'ai à vous dire à son sujet, demande une prompte réponse, & doit rester secret de vous à moi. J'ai eu quelque conversation avec lui. Il a l'abord très-prévenant. On voit qu'il a vu le grand monde; & il me paroît fort entendu dans les grandes opérations financieres. Mais il m'a paru en même temps, que Mrs. De N—— seroient bien aises de savoir, s'il jouit de votre confiance & de celle du Congrès. Car de la maniere dont il leur a parlé, il peut leur être envoyé, soit pour espionner les affaires de l'Amérique (sans peut-être s'en douter lui-même) soit pour ôter à cette maison les bonnes graces des Etats-unis & les vôtres. Mais, d'un autre côté, si Mrs. De N—— pouvoient compter sur ce qu'il leur a dit, ils m'ont avoué qu'il pourroit être avantageux d'entrer dans les idées d'un homme entendu comme lui dans les grandes affaires. Je ne doute pas que ces Messieurs ne vous écrivent eux-mêmes au sujet des plans qu'il leur a communiqués. Il m'a paru cependant nécessaire de vous en parler aussi, & d'attendre votre sentiment, Monsieur, le plutôt possible, afin d'en faire part à ces Messieurs. J'entends de toutes parts tant de bien de votre digne ami Mr. Bencroft que je me fais une vraie fête de faire sa connaissance & de lui demander son amitié. Pour cet effet, quand je serai à Paris, je tâcherai de louer une petite chambre dans la même maison, s'il se peut, où il loge, où du moins dans son voisinage: car je me promets de sa liaison divers bon effets pour le service de l'Am——.

Je ne puis m'empêcher, Monsieur, de terminer par une réflexion qui m'occupe de plus en plus. C'est qu'il faut, coute qui coute, que ce Pays ici devienne Créancier de l'Am——, & plutôt pour des sommes fortes que pour de moindres, qui mettroient dans la nécessité d'y revenir trop souvent; que par une telle opération on rétablira et fera respecter ici le crédit

1. On the orders of the Earl of Rochford, one of the secretaries of state, Sayre in 1775 had been imprisoned in the Tower on suspicion of conspiring to abduct King George III: John R. Alden, *Stephen Sayre, American Revolutionary Adventurer* (Baton Rouge and London, 1983), pp. 67–86.

public & particulier de l'Am—— dans la circulation du papier; qu'on ruinera d'autant celui de vos ennemis; que pour de tels objets il ne faudroit pas s'arrêter à l. ou deux pCt. de plus; & que les effets & les suites d'une telle opération dédommageroient amplement du sacrifice.

Je suis avec tout le respectueux dévouement pour vous, & tout le zele que vous me connoissez pour la cause, Monsieur Votre très-humble et très-obéissant serviteur D

P.S. Si ces Mrs. ne vous écrivent pas aujourd'hui sur les ouvertures de Mr. Sayre, ce sera l'un des ordinaires suivants.

Notre ami tient de bonne main, qu'il est question à Tesschen de la paix entre la Fce. & l'Angle.

Je me suis apperçu aux discours d'un Tory, qu'on en veut aux Gazettiers d'avoir inseré la Lettre au sujet du Cap. Cook,[2] & qu'on se plaindra peut-être d'eux. J'ai donné à entendre que les Nouvellistes n'ont fait que copier fidelement un Acte de bienfaisance, dont il seroit aisé de produire l'original. Je n'en ai plus entendu parler.

Passy à S.E. Mr. Franklin M. P. des E.U. en France

Addressed: à Son Excellence / Monsieur Franklin, Esqr. / Min. Plen. des Etats-Unis &c. / à *Passy./.*

Notation: Dumas 27 May 79

To John Paul Jones

Copy: Library of Congress

Dear Sir Passy, May, 28. 1779.

You may remember I once Spoke to you concerning some young American Gentlemen, who had come to France with Views of being employ'd as Mid Shipmen in three Ships of War which Commodore Gellon of S. Carolina was sent to procure in Europe.[3] Tho' That Design is not likely to Succeed,

2. See Dumas' letter of May 11.

3. In a March 5, 1779, letter to the S.C. congressional delegation Gillon gave their names as Spencer, Warters, and Doville: *S.C. Hist. and Geneal. Mag.* x (1909), 80. None of them appears, however, on the roster of the *Bonhomme Richard:* John S. Barnes, ed., *The Logs of the Serapis-Alliance-Ariel*

they continue to have as I understand, the laudable Desire of improving themselves in marine knowledge, and that under your Command. You were So good as to Say that you would receive them if they Should come to you. Some of them will have the Honour of delivering this Letter, and I earnestly recommend them to your kind Notice and Protection. With great and sincere Esteem, I have the honour to be &c—

Capt. Jones

From Louis-Casimir, Baron de Holtzendorff[4]

ALS: American Philosophical Society

Sir Paris May 28th. 1779./.

You have been so Kind as to forward some Letters, from your country, to London, which I had the honour to give you when I arrived; therefore I do myself the pleasure to send you hereby three other ones, I received Lately from carolina I can't tell by which way, hoping you will be so good again as to forward them too.[5]

As for the rest, I'm flattring myself, that Congress, by your interposition, will at length do me the justice I merit from them,[6] & I dare say I wait for their favorable answer with the more impatience, as I would be entirely ruined, if they should not comply with my just claims & their own resolves, in a

Under the Command of John Paul Jones 1779–1780 (New York, 1911), pp. 3–16; Augustus C. Buell, *Paul Jones, Founder of the American Navy: a History* (2 vols., New York, 1906), II, 407–13. John Spencer distinguished himself aboard the *Alliance:* Landais to BF, Oct. 9, 1779 (APS).

4. A former colonel in the American army, who had resigned his commission in early 1778: XXIV, 267n; XXV, 384n, 706.

5. When Holtzendorff returned to Europe he brought letters to BF from Michael Hillegas and Richard Peters, and presented his own memorial: XXV, 706–7; XXVI, 53; XXVIII, 296–7. We have no record of either of the sets of letters he wished forwarded to London.

6. Holtzendorff had written on several occasions to ask BF's help in obtaining reimbursement for his travel expenses: XXVIII, 364–5. Meanwhile he elected to pursue a career in the French army; he was named captain in the regiment of Anhalt on April 29, 1779: Bodinier, *Dictionnaire.*

convenient manner: I had, I believe, the honour to tell you lately, that I applied to the Count de Vergennes and begged his most Christian Majesty's protection by Congress about that Subject; & me thinks, Congress will take that recommandation into their most Serious consideration.— You will, Sir, do me a very singular favour to let me Know their answer whatsoever it may be as soon as you receive any.

I have the honour to remain very respectfully Sir—your most obedient humble Servant BARON DE HOLTZENDORFF

The honble. Dr. Benjamin Franklin./.

Notation: Baron de holkendor. Paris 28 may 1779.

From William Jones

AL: American Philosophical Society

28 May 1779.

Mr. Jones presents his best respects to Dr. Franklin.

Since I had the honour of seeing you last, I amused myself with the enclosed translation of a curious fragment of Polybius; which, as it may possibly afford you also some little amusement, I take the liberty of sending to you.[7]

It will be both an honour and pleasure to Mr. Paradise and myself to be charged with any commissions, letters, or messages, that you may have for England. We leave Paris on Wednesday morning.[8]

My friend will always remember with gratitude the kind-

7. The work was actually a thinly disguised allegory presenting terms of conciliation Jones thought might be acceptable to the British government. In it a private citizen of Athens addresses his old acquaintance Eleutherion, an eminent philosopher zealous for the cause of liberty, who has been sent by the united islands of Chios, Cos, Lesbos, and Rhodes to Caria, an ally in the struggle by the united islands for liberty. Realizing that Athens will never recognize the independence of the islands, Eleutherion's friend sets forth a plan of a treaty acknowledging the natural union between their countries. The new relationship is one of sisters rather than parent and child. It recognizes the rights of all citizens of Athens and proposes a policy of reciprocal representation between the assemblies of Athens and the islands. Printed in Sparks, *Works,* VIII, 543–7.

8. Among the letters may have been answers to communications from Richard Price and Joseph Priestley; see Paradise and Jones to BF, May 20.

ness you have shown him.[9] Accept my hearty thanks for your obliging attention to me, and be assured of my eternal veneration and esteem.

Addressed: To / His Excy. Dr. Franklin, / Minister Plenipotentiary / from the United States of / America— / at Passy.

Notation: Mr. Jones 28th May 1779—

From John Torris[1]

ALS: American Philosophical Society

Sir Dunkerque 28th. May 1779.

I have the Honnor to Inform you, that I am Security for, & have a Procuration from Capt. Stephen Merchant of the Black Prince Cutter, fitted out here; & from all his Crew, to act for them all, as also for the owners & Concerns, & represent the former as their Sole agent in the sale of all the Prises they Shod. make, & to do all Transactions whatsoever relative to the said Privateer, wherein I am myself Deeply Interested— In consequence of these Powers, I Shall have the honnour, Sir, to acquaint you with all the Proceedings of this Vessell, & be very exact in advising you all the Particulars.

As the Commission of Instructions from Congress you gave to Capt. Merchant,[2] do not make any exceptions whatsoever in the Takeing of all British Vessells &ca, & If the Intention of

On Oct. 14 Price thanked BF for the note he had sent via Paradise and Jones. APS.

9. BF had appealed to Thomas Jefferson to help Paradise retain his wife's property in Virginia. *Jefferson Papers,* v, 610.

1. A Dunkirk merchant, who was half-owner (with the Irish smuggler Luke Ryan) of the cutter *Black Prince;* see Sutton de Clonard's letter of May 11, and Clark, *Ben Franklin's Privateers,* pp. 5–6, 23–4. Clark speculates that Ryan and Torris selected Marchant as captain for the *Black Prince* in order to win BF's approval for the privateering venture, but that they planned for Ryan as second-in-command to exercise the real authority: *ibid.,* p. 25. Henri Malo, *Les Derniers Corsaires: Dunkerque (1715–1815)* (Paris, 1925), p. 117, points out that by arming the privateer as American Torris avoided having to pay the *Invalides de la Marine* 6 *d.* per *l.t.* on the value of his prizes.

2. On May 14, above, WTF wrote Francis Coffyn, the American agent at Dunkirk, enclosing a blank commission and bond for Marchant.

Congress & your own, Sir, had been to deffend Takeing at sea the British Packets going from Dover to Calais, & Backward from Calais to Dover, with or withot. the Licence of the Court of France, you wou'd, most Certainly, have mentionned it, Because you are unavoidably Informed of this Intercourse; Capt. Merchant Intends to Cruise on these Packets, & Strives to Take & bring them as Prises back again to Calais or to this Port,[3] & I think it, Sir, my Duty to acquaint you with these Projects, & as your answer might reach before he sails, I beg the favour of your honnouring me with an Answer per the return of the mail, whether these wou'd not Prove wrong Steps, against the Intentions or determinations of yourself & Congress, But if it is, as Mr. Merchant expects, to be deemed Lawfull Prises with the help of your Justice & good offices, I beseech you will be so kind to give me, or Mr. Merchant, your own Private directions how to act. My Character in Business & Titles, answer for my discretion & gratefull use of your generous Informations, But If you do not think Proper to favour me with an Answer, I beseech you will do it forthwith to Mr. Merchant directed to my Care.

I am with great respect Sir Your obedient most Humble Servant J. TORRIS

Addressed: A Monsieur / Monsieur Benj. Franklin / Ecuïer Ministre Plenipotentiaire des Etats Unies de L'amerique / Septentrionalle / A Passy / près Paris

Notation: Torris Dunkerque 28 May 1779.

From John Walsh

ALS: American Philosophical Society

Honoured Sir Fougeres in Britany May the 28th. 1779

With greatest Respect, I take the present Liberty to acquaint you that the prisoners late on board the patience Brig at Brest road, Receiv'd the Honour of your kind and oblidging

3. Clark believes the idea was Ryan's: Clark, *Ben Franklin's Privateers,* p. 27.

answer to our Memorial of the 16 March past,[4] attended with the desired Effect, and in consequence, I did Myself the honour (agreable to your desire) to send you an account of the provisions which were Served us by Mr. Riou, from the 1st. September 1778 until the 1st March 1779 with our most Greatfull acknowledgements for your humane Interference on our Behalf.— Believe me Sir, it is with the greatest Reluctance that I now find meself oblidged to Renew my complaints of the Harsh treatment I undeservedly Receiv'd from Mr. Riou of Brest, that Gentelman not being contented with having wrongfully used every Means in his power to Enrich himself by treating us in the Manner I had the honour to Inform you by my letter of the 2 Ult,[5] he, trew Malicious Motives and contrary to the long Established Custom of Exchangeing Such commanders or officers of Kings Ships, or vessells, who might have Been made prisoners of War, as Soon or Sooner than the crews who formerly Served under Such commanders or officers.—Deprived me of Returning to England with Seventy two of the Drakes late crew, who were the 9th ult sent to Nantez there to embark in a carteel.—[6] The consequence of my being seperateed from many of them as being necessary Witnesses on my Court Martial may be fatal to me, and furnishes me with Motives Sufficient to Justify the present Liberty I take of most humblely Requesting that your Excellency be most gratiously pleased to allow me with four others of my late Crew, whose names are here annexed the Liberty to Return to England as Soon as possible where I shall use my outmost Endeavours to get you as many Americans Returned for us, I have Wrote Mr. Stephens Secy. of the Admiralty for that purpose and am in hopes [*torn:* I?] may not be Refused that favour. Your Secretarys Name not being known to me is the cause of my thus Writeing Directly to your Excellency,

4. He presumably meant Feb. 16 (XXVIII, 554–6); BF replied on March 2, above.

5. Missing. For Rïou and the prisoners on the *Patience* see Lawrence Boyd's letter of April 3.

6. On May 26, above, BF wrote the committee for foreign affairs that the first cargo of prisoners for the *Milford* had left for England.

who I hope will Excuse the Liberty, and Regard with a propitious Eye the very unhappy Situation of him who is with the greatest Respect and Veneration Honoured Sir Your very obedt: and humble Servt &. JOHN WALSH
late Master of the Drake—

I beg leave to Remind your Excellency that there are here and it environs between 70 & 80 prisoner to the american arms—

Peoples Names whom the late commdng. officer of the Drake begs to be allowed to go to England with him a soon as possible for the purpose of giving Testimony at a Court Martial how said Sloop Drake was taken and the Diffence she had made on the 24th April 1778[7]
Mr. Thomas Wilkinson pilot
Wm. Sweeny Quarter Mastr.
John Butcher Do—
James Hays—

To His Excellency the Honorable Docter Bengamin Franklin.—one of the commissioners from the united states of America at Paris

Addressed: To / His Excellency The Honorable Doct. / Bengamin Franklin—one of the / Commissioners from the united states / of America / a Paris

From Samuel Wharton

ALS:[8] Archives du Ministère des affaires étrangères; copy:[9] American Philosophical Society

May 29 1779.

The Memorial of Samuel Wharton of Philadelphia respectfully sheweth.

That Thomas, and Robert Burdy left England about twelve Months ago, and settled at Diepe with Messieurs Richard

7. The date of the *Drake*'s capture: XXVI, 535.
8. BF forwarded this memorial to Vergennes on June 13.
9. In the hand of WTF.

Neave & Son,[1] intending, when an Opportunity offered to go and settle in Pennsylvania, One of the said United States.

That the aforesaid Thomas & Robert Burdy took with Them from London to Brighthelmstone,[2] with an Intention of transporting Them to Diepe, several Trunks containing their wearing Apparel and other Necessaries, and from thence to have shipped Them to Pennsylvania aforesaid; But finding on their Arrival at Brighthelmstone, that it was impracticable to send the same at that Time, from thence to Diepe, They left Them under Care of Captain Burton with Orders to bring Them, when He should sail for Diepe.

That on the 26th of this present Month of May, The said Captain Burton arrived with his small Vessel from Boulogne sur la Mer, having a Pass from the Judge of the Admiralty at the said port, and brought the said Trunks; But notwithstanding the said Pass, The Judge of the Admiralty at Diepe seized, and detains the same, very much to the Prejudice of the said Burdy's and Messrs. Neave & Son.

That your Memorialist is ready to testify, That the said Persons (one of them, To wit, Richard Neave the younger, is a Subject of the United States aforesaid)[3] always prepared, and meant soon to embark, and settle in Pennsylvania,[4] and That the said Trunks, or packages do not contain any Articles, But only wearing Apparel, Linen for Shirts, and some few other Articles, necessary for the personal Use, and Voyage of the said parties to Pennsylvania aforesaid. Your Memorialist therefore, with all Respect, prays, That your Excellency will

1. The Neaves, formerly London-based merchants, had fled to France during the Revolution: XII, 151n.

2. Brighton.

3. Actually it was not until Aug. 9 that the father and son swore an oath of allegiance to the United States. APS.

4. The emigration plans of these Englishmen continued to require BF's assistance. On Aug. 2 he provided for Thomas Burdy a passport from Ostend to England. Public Record Office. Seven months later, the Neaves requested BF to intervene with Wharton on their behalf. They had been in France three years, with assurances from Wharton for passage to America and support until his departure. Having caused their ruin, he was now withdrawing his promises of passage and financial support: to BF, March 5, 1780, APS.

take such Measures in the premises, as your Excellency may Think best for the speedy Restoration of the said Packages (mentioned particularly on the other side) to the said Burdy's & Neave's, And your Memorialist, as in Duty bound, shall ever Pray. SAML. WHARTON

A List of Articles seized, and detained by the Judge of the Admiralty at Diepe, referred to in the within Memorial

Vidzt.

1 Letter directed to Richard Neave Junior at Diepe.
1 Trunk
1 Chest
2 Boxes
A paper Parcel, containing, a few old Magazines, & Pamphlets. & a parcel of loose papers,—Letters, Memorandum Books; & A manuscript Map of Pennsylvania.

N.B. The foregoing Articles were taken out of the Trunks &c and put into a Bag, & carried to the Admiralty Office at Diepe;—Where They now remain.—

To his Excellency Benjamin Franklin Esquire Minister plenipotentiary from the United States of America, at the Court of Versailes

Notation: 1779. Mai 29.

To Thomas Digges

Copy: Library of Congress

Dear Sir Passy, May 30[–31]. 1779

I received your favours of the 14th. 18th. and 21st. Instant. You mention one of the 12th. which is not come to hand.

I never had nor have I now the least Expectation that any Good can come of the Propositions made to certain Persons.[5] Whatever is reasonable and prudent for them to do, Seems to be out of their sphere: for hitherto they have constantly rejected the best Measures and chosen the worst.—

I am obliged much by your Attention to the affair of W.

5. A reference to his friend Hartley's peace proposal to Lord North.

Peters. If he is in want and should draw on you for any Sum within 100 £. I will repay it. I have paid Brehon's Bill.

Mr. Schweighauser has undertaken to write to the Commissioners for Sick and Hurt sea men and give them the Informations they desire relating to the Prisoners here. I have mention'd Morlaix again and have found the Ministers of the Marine not unwilling to permit the Cartel's using that Port. But as I know some others of the Council are strongly against it, I do not expect to obtain any Change. The old Pass will be allow'd good as long as the Exchange continues.

I shall be glad to see the Examinations of those American Worthies you mention.[6] If they have Judgmt. and hope ever to return to their Country, they will join with Cornwallis, Grey, &c in the Opinion of Impracticability— If they Strive to support the contrary Opinion they inevitably fix their Ruin.

I am, with great Esteem. Your &c

Be so good as to procure from Mr. Almon the remembrancers Debates in Parliament since the American Disputes and all Such other Pamphlets as may be of use to an Historian, who proposes to write the late revolution.[7] And Send them to Holland to the House of Horneca, Grand & Co. Amsterdam. I will pay your Draft for the Amount.

May 31st. Since writing the above I have received yours of the 24th. It confirms me more in my Opinion that your friend ought to expect nothing from his Laudable Endeavours with those People. They are expert in little Parliamentary Crafts but have none of that true Wisdom which comprehends the extensive and great Interest of their Country Domestick and Foreign, present and Future.

M Digges.

6. Galloway and the other loyalist refugees summoned to testify on behalf of the administration in the inquiry on the conduct of the American War.

7. John Almon's *The Remembrancer, or Impartial Repository of Public Events . . .* : XXIII, 242n. The historian was William Gordon, who was working on *The History of the Rise, Progress, and Establishment, of the Independence of the United States of America . . .*, not published until 1788: XXIII, 391n.

From Benjamin Franklin Bache[8]

ALS: American Philosophical Society

Dear grand papa the 30 of May 1779

I take the liberte to wright to you for to tell you that I am in good health M Marignac Gives his compliments to you and says that I am a good boy I will do all that can for to be the first of the class M. Cramer is in good health give my compliments to my cossin and to cochran and to Deine A have notings mor for to tell you for the presente.

I am your affectionaite Son B. FRANKLIN. B.

Addressed: A Monsieur / Monsieur Franklin Ministre / Plenipotentiaire des Provinces unies de l'Amerique / auprés de Sa Majesté Trés Chrétienne, recommandée / à Monsieur Grand Banqr. ruë Montmartre / *A Paris.*[9]

From Mary Hewson

ALS: American Philosophical Society

My dear Sir Kensington May 30. 79

I left Cheam yesterday morning, my mother and children all well. My mother received your letter the day before, inclosed in one from young Alexander, informing her that his father was returned, and he should join him in a few days at Calais.[1] I brought your milk pot, & lodged it at Mr Lechmere's and wrote to Mr Alexander desiring him to take charge of it. The Copper vessel my mother gave to Dr Ingenhouez several weeks ago, and she believes he left London soon after, but we are not sure.[2] My mother cannot recollect anything of the But-

8. Who had now been in France and Geneva long enough to have lapsed into a rather gallicized English. His letter may be in response to his grandfather's of May 3.

9. An apparently unrelated numerical calculation appears on the cover sheet. The address is in Marignac's hand.

1. BF's letter to Margaret Stevenson is missing. The "young Alexander" is probably William Alexander's eldest son, William (XXV, 364–5n).

2. BF received neither his milk pot nor this letter until Ingenhousz delivered them by hand in early 1780; see BF to Mary Hewson, Jan. 10, 1780, and Ingenhousz to BF, Nov. 18, 1779 (both at the APS). For the copper vessel see Margaret Stevenson's letter printed under March 16.

tons. The Pearces are well, they have now a son to their two daughters. I hope they will thrive, for I believe indeed he is a very industrious good man, and she does as much as she can. Mrs Wilkes has lately taken a house at Richmond for the accommodation of young ladies, and as there was a detached apartment sufficient for Pearce's family & business she offered it to him rent-free, this will be a help to them. Mr W. is *going* to Algiers.[3] I write in great haste therefore can only add my mother's love & she begs you will not be in a hurry about the account. Mrs Blunt sends her love and thanks for your letter.[4] Adieu! my dear Sir. I wish we could meet! Your affectionate

MARY HEWSON

Addressed: Dr Franklin

Notation: Mary Hewson May 30. 1779—

3. For James and Sally Franklin Pearce, who had received financial assistance from Dorothea Blunt in 1776, and BF and Polly's old friend Elizabeth Wilkes, see XXII, 590n, 595. Elizabeth's husband Israel, elder brother of the notorious politician, John Wilkes, had been disappointed by his lack of financial success and was going to Africa in search of business opportunities. Horace Bleackley, *Life of John Wilkes* (London, New York, and Toronto, 1917), pp. 167, 366.

4. Missing.

To [Edward Bancroft][5]

AL (draft): American Philosophical Society

May 31. 79.

When at Bt.—[6] acquaint the People that have a mind to remove to America, that they may do it with great Safety to themselves & Effects.—[7] It is said there are great Numbers in those Parts. Represent the happy Living of Thousands of Families that have already passed from thence. On Occasion, State the Advantages to those that remain, of a free Trade with A. so large & growing a Country. Vent for their Manufrs. &c.

Learn what are the 10,000 in Arms, spoken of lately in Parliamt.—[8] Of what People compos'd?—Where? and with what Views?—

It may not be amiss to write some little Things now and then for the Newspapers, in which Matters may be discreetly hinted, & Ideas suggested that may have good Effects. The shorter the more likely to be copied in all the Papers.—Some in form of Letters, Some in Articles of News. &c.

Notation in Franklin's hand: Instructions to Dr B

5. These instructions to Bancroft are connected with the French foreign ministry's project to evaluate the possibility of raising a rebellion among Irish Presbyterians as a diversion for the planned Franco-Spanish invasion of England. Lafayette had suggested Bancroft for the mission. (BF's involvement was minimal, although he did propose, unsuccessfully, that Bancroft stop at Ostend en route to meet with a "vehement member of the opposition party in the Irish parliament," undoubtedly Sir Edward Newenham.) Unknown to Lafayette, Vergennes, or BF, Bancroft was a British secret agent. His eventual report to Vergennes discouraged any hope of an Irish rebellion; no one had yet thought of independence and the Irish were too afraid of England and too divided by religion: Idzerda, *Lafayette Papers,* II, 268–9, 287n; Patterson, *The Other Armada,* pp. 72–6.

6. Belfast (?).

7. BF had recently granted a passport to some prospective Irish emigrants; see our annotation of Jesse Taylor's April 10 letter.

8. Probably the Marquis of Rockingham's comment in the House of Lords on May 11 about 10,000 supposed troops in independent corps and companies there: *The Parliamentary Register . . . ,* XIV (1779), 335. See also our annotation of "Philantropos" to BF, April 5.

From Thomas Digges

ALS: Historical Society of Pennsylvania

Dr. Sir Londn. May 31.[–June 1] 1779

I have wrote You from time to time since I had the pleasure of seeing You, about a matter we conversd upon, and my last was by post the 25 Int.; since which time nothing matereal has transpird, nor any circumstance appeard to cast a damp upon the business I wish so ardently to be brought forward; on the contrary we have reason rather to be elated, for altho there has been delays in giving answers that might be expected, these very delays indicate to me a serious consideration of the matter by the partys most concernd.

I have just heard of a Mr. Panchaud returning to Paris and solicited his care of this letter.[9] The Inclosd was written a few days back & intended for a private conveyance, but it came to my hand too late; I dare say my friend has explaind Himself to You in that letter.[1]

I mentiond in a former letter to You the probability of having found Mr. W. Peters's proper direction, which Mr Penn told me was at *Liverpoole* instead of Nottingham as You directed to Him, but I have been disapointed.[2] I took care to mark on my letter that it should be returnd to me if Mr Peters could not be found, and it was this day returnd to me markd "Mr Peters is not to be found in Liverpoole." I acquainted Mr Penn of this, & solicited his further assistance among his Phila. friends to find Mr Peters out, but he is fearful he must be dead, because Mr Peters wrote to Him about four months ago from the same direction in Liverpoole, & mentiond that He was old & very infirm. I intend to try another letter to Mrs. Roberts at whose house he lodgd, & shall do what you request provided he can possibly be found.

I mentiond this oppertunity of writing, to Mr Penn last night & he said he would send me a letter for You or to be

9. Earlier in the year the banker Isaac Panchaud (XXVII, 37n) had brought books from London for BF: Richard B. Lloyd to WTF, Jan. 8, 1779. APS.

1. Hartley's of May 25, above.

2. For Richard Penn's involvement in the Peters affair see XXIII, 275n. The former lieutenant governor of Pennsylvania had last written to BF on Oct. 20, 1778: XXVII, 579–80.

forwarded by You to Phia. I do not recollect wch, but if it comes in time you shall have it enclosd in this.

I have a letter forwarded me by J. Johnson of Nantes; which from its contents must have been brought from Maryland by my Younger Bror. about the first Feby. in a Ship to Bilboa, to which place He was bound for the recovery of his health in a consumptive case.[3] I am fearful from Johnsons not mentioning how it got to his hands & my Bror. not accompanying it with a line from himself that He may have died upon the passage; but if this should not be the case, & he may think proper to travel quietly on to Paris (wch. he probably may do to inform You how matters stand in America) I am to beg a share of Your usual civility & attention to Him. He is a young Man brot up to Phisic, has had an excellent Education, & is very clever; His politics & conduct will I am sure do him Credit with You.

The letter forwarded Me was from my Bror. whom You knew at Paris[4] but contains nothing but what you must be apprisd of, as there have been one or two arrivals from that quarter to France since I saw you.

There has been rather a gloom over the faces in the City and at Loyds[5] since the late dispatch's from Byron and it has not been lessend by the Mediterranean advices, those from N York by way of Corke or by the more domestic movements in Ireland & Scotland.[6] Spain, tho more likely than ever to be upon the back of this Country in a few months, is not now talkd of.

3. Dr. Joseph Digges (1747–80) was a prisoner on parole in Teneriffe. He failed in his effort to escape to the south of France and died on the island in February. Elias and Finch, *Digges Letters,* pp. xlviii, 55n.

4. George Digges (1743–92) had been in Europe from 1775 to 1778: *ibid.,* p. xlvi.

5. Lloyds Coffee House near the Royal Exchange was the center of shipping transactions and marine insurance: XXIII, 63n.

6. A letter from Byron of April 2, received on May 28 via the *British King* which had landed at Cork, reported much French activity around Martinique and a failed attempt to engage d'Estaing's squadron: *The London Gaz.,* May 29, 1779. Privateering on the Mediterranean had become so threatening to trade that inhabitants of Minorca petitioned the British government to send a naval force. The latest express from Gibraltar described a French

The chit chat of the day is the probable inexpediency of prosecuting the war in America, for since the American Enquiry before the Ho. of commons, some parts of the Admn hold this kind of language. If they had been wise they would have made these kind of enquirys before they fought & became disgracd.

It is said that the Bedford party shew visible discontent as to continuing the War in America, & I believe Lord N. is heartily sick of it.[7] Ministry do not seemingly pull well together; fattend with the spoil it is likely they are becoming restive, & I live in hopes they may soon kick up some good. I shall keep this letter open till I go in the City to see Mr Panchaud to inclose you any thing that may be new at Loyds. I am with the highest esteem Dr Sir Yr very obligd & ob Sert.

V. J. D——D

1st. June—please to turn over

A meeting (wch. carrys the appearance of more meaning than any preceeding one) is appointed for tomorrow.[8]

There is much conversation to day about a probable speedy rupture with Spain & it has found its effects on the Stocks.

You may perhaps think me (as a person totally unconnected or concernd the least for Ama) a little impertinent by wishing so ardently for peace or throwing out any probable terms that *may be listend* to but You must allow me intrude upon You a

---

attack on a homeward-bound convoy. *The General Advertiser and Morning Intelligencer,* May 27, 29, 1779. In Parliament on May 5, Lord George Gordon had represented Scotland as ripe for rebellion over religious issues. On May 27 Rockingham had complained that the ministry was ignoring Ireland's distress, and the Duke of Richmond had pointed out that Britain would be in grave danger should the French invade while the ministers were allowing rebellion to foment. Cobbett, *Parliamentary History,* XX (1778–80), 622–3, 651–4.

7. Lord Gower was engaged in negotiations to depose North and bring the Bedford party into office; see Jenkinson to the King, May 29, 1779, in Fortescue, *Correspondence of George Third,* IV, 344–6. North was so dispirited that he welcomed this plan, and on June 15 would beg George III to relieve him of his office: *ibid.,* 355–6.

8. Doubtless he refers to a meeting between Hartley and Lord North. Digges was overoptimistic regarding the outcome; see Hartley to BF, June 11.

few propositions. A hint in the common way of conveyance under a direction You are possessd of may find its effect.[9] As preliminarys only suppose—first. Commissioners to be appointed to treat subject to ratification of Parlt. 2d a Truce for 10 or 12 years (to commence immediately) *uti Possidentis.*[1] Third all acts of Parliament specially regarding America (excepting such articles as relate to Dutys on import & thereby effecting the Revenue) to be suspended during the term of the truce. 4th. a truce for ten or twelve years (to commence immediately) *uti Possidetis* between Gr. Britain & France. 5th. upon these preliminaries a negotiation to be opend as soon as conveniently may be. What say you to this?

I am going to Mr. P——d, and it is not unlikely I may give him a bill on you for the twenty Pound formerly mentiond to you for supplys to J. Brehen, Dr. Sims & three others.[2] On receiving it from You he may transmit me an order to receive a similar sum from a french Ho. he is connected with here, which will be a much better mode than any common negotiation.

Mr. R. P——n[3] has not sent the letters & I begin to be more fearful from what I hear, that Mr. Peters is dead.

Notations in different hands: May 31 1779. / May 31 79 / May 31

From Dumas

ALS: American Philosophical Society

Sir

Amst. 31th: May 1779

Last Friday I had the honour to write to you a Letter of which I had no oportunity to keep a copy for myself.[4] The same will be the case of the present; other wise I would lose te post.

9. In his letter of Dec. 19, 1778 (XXVIII, 248), Digges had informed BF how to direct letters to him.

1. Each retaining all territory and possessions currently under their control. Digges's preliminaries are a variation of those earlier proposed by Hartley; see our annotation of his April 22 letter.

2. "Mr. P——d" is Panchaud. For James Brehon and other American prisoners who had escaped from Forton see Digges's letter of May 21.

3. Richard Penn.

4. He did write on May 27, a Thursday, above.

The vessel Hannah, Capt. Alex. Coffin, gone from Baltimore the 20th. of March, from the Capes the 6th. of April, & arrived here the 24th. had a cargo of tobacco chiefly, consigned partly to Mrs Clifford & Tisset, & partly to my old friends Mrs De la Lande & Fynje, of this City.[5]

The 27th arrived another Ship, the Hannah, Captn. Richd. Inkson from Virginia,[6] consigned to Mr. Hudson Mercht. of this City.

The 29th. arrived here another, the Sloop Poppus Captn. Martin,[7] saild from Maryland the 1st. of May, & from the Capes the 6th. Inst. belonging to the hon. Rob. Morris, & consigned to Horneca Fizeaux & Compe. Capt. Martin has brought news, that when he set sail, there arrived at Baltimore a Carolinian Gentleman, with the report, that the Brittish troops having set out from Savannah to attack the continental troops, were totally defeated, with the loss of 100 to 150 killed on the Spot besides prisoners & wounded, & obliged to retreat to Savannah, leaving in our hands all their bagage. & that an Express was in his way to philadelphia, to bring this news to Congress. I congratulate you of it with all my heart.

I am since 8 days lodged here at Mr. N——'s. I have not seen & will not see, for obvious reasons, the Chev. Gd. nor his Associate. I hope to dine to morrow with Capt. Martin, by the politeness of Mr. N——. I think to return immediately after dinner to the hague where I shall meet again our friend, with whom I have had the honour to dine some days past.

You will be so good as to excuse my venturing to write to you in bad English. I am with very great respect Sir yr. most obedient & faithful servant D

I am a little more acquainted with Mr. Sayre, & do find him a very intelligent & sensible Man; but will Still expect your Sen-

5. Clifford & Teysett were European correspondents of Robert Morris: Ferguson, *Power of the Purse,* pp. 81–2. For Jacob de la Lande and Hendrik Fynje see XXV, 700–1n.

6. A young Pennsylvanian who later commanded the brigantine *Delaware*: Claghorn, *Naval Officers,* p. 163.

7. The Maryland sloop *Porpoise,* commanded by Nicholas Martin: *ibid.*, p. 197.

timents & directions on his account, before growing more intimate with him.

I have received yr. respected favour of the 22d. inst.[8] & make good use of it with some gentlemen of this City.

Passy to his Exc. the hon. Dr. Franklin, Esqr., Plenipy. &c.

Addressed: To His Excellency / B. Franklin Plen. of the United / States, &c. / at *Passy.*/.

Notation: Dumas 31. May 1779.

From Jean de Neufville & fils

ALS:[9] American Philosophical Society

Ever Honourd Sir! Amstdn. the 31st. May 1779.

We intended Severall times to write to yoúr Excellency aboút the Loan for America recomanded to oúr care, for which she was so good, as to allow ús what patience we wanted, Some time ago; and which we are to begg for again: tho' we found circumstances, and by the late news that came in from Virginia,[1] groing better from time to time.

We cannot however conceal from yoúr Excellency that Some days ago Mr. Sayre was introduced to oúr hoúse as, born in America, having been Establishd in England, coming lately from the North and, which was the principall with ús as a Gentleman of trúe American sentiments; this last made him the more welcome, and he professed them openly; bútt what most surprised ús, that in a private Conversation, he asked for, he fell Directly upon talking aboút a Loan for America, and tho' he confessed he had no Commission nor from Congress, nor from yoúr Excellency, yett he spoke aboút the matter With Judgement.[2]

8. Missing.

9. In the father's hand, as are the subsequent letters from the firm in this volume.

1. Presumably the news brought by a ship from the Virginia Capes that the British in Ga. had suffered a defeat: *Gaz. de Leyde,* June 4, 1779.

2. Sayre reported to BF on May 17 his arrival in Amsterdam. He appears to have borrowed money for himself from Dumas' old business associates

Tho' no subscribers could be found as yett for any Súmm of Consequence as matters go, we are in hopes to lay in those before your Excellency What may be done and expected on this purpose.

Mr. Dumas promised ús to write to yoúr Excellency aboút Some late and good tidings that came júst in from Virginia; Some Luck will be very promoting to the American Credit.

We make bold again to desire yoúr Excellency would be So Kind as to favoúr ús with his powerfúll recomendation to Congress and any Private Acquaintance in the Mercantile way for their Connections with Holland, as will reckon it as a favoúr and great part of oúr Duty from principall to be to every one of them with all regard and affection and in particular Ever Honour'd Sir. Yoúr Excellency's Most obedient & devoted Servant JOHN DE NEUFVILLE & SON.

Notation: Neufville John & Son 31 May 1779

From Benjamin Vaughan

ALS: American Philosophical Society

My dearest sir, London, May 31, 1779.

I have no pretensions to trouble the person affording me this conveyance with a large pacquet, otherwise I might send you more sheets. We are indeed just finished; only that I have expectations of procuring your preface to Mr Galway's speech, and in consequence the epitaph;[3] all which can very easily be inserted. Indeed it was through great carelessness that I did not apply to Mr Wharton before his leaving England for these articles.[4]

Your paper on the *Auroras* I can give no greater praise to,

Jacob de la Lande and Hendrik Fynje: John R. Alden, *Stephen Sayre, American Revolutionary Adventurer* (Baton Rouge and London, 1983), p. 115.

3. BF's preface to *The Speech of Joseph Galloway, Esq. . . . In Answer to the Speech of John Dickinson, Esq. . . .* (Philadelphia, 1764), and his famous Epitaph: XI, 267–311; I, 109–11.

4. Samuel Wharton had arrived in Paris sometime before March 17; see our annotation of his letter to BF, printed under April 7.

than by saying it is *your own*. I have myself no doubt of its containing the fundamentals of the true theory. I am ashamed to say that I was so wonderfully struck with it, as off hand to pretend to carry it to considerable minutiae: I shall now omit sending you my comments, for the reasons above; but in the course of a week or so, I am tempted to think you will receive something from me.— As to the paper on the *vis inertiae,* till you started it to me, I had never thought 5 moments on the subject; as indeed that there is scarce a subject in politics or philosophy on which I have speculated, where you did not give the occasion and for the most part the rudiments;—but, as to this paper, I have had so much business put into my hands by others, as not to be able to write it out. What you say about it, makes me blush a little; and I am clear I shall deceive what you state to be your expectations, at least if they are metaphysical ones. The part of it perhaps that will be most practical & important is that which relates to *resistance coupled with time.* You would not however think I knew much on this part of the subject, by giving so clumsy an instance, as that of a ship of war sailing *through seas* &ca to be pushed on by a mosquito, to illustrate my reasonings; particularly when I had so neat an instance as one of your *vast globes* before me, subject neither to attraction friction nor resistance, with the self-same mosquito to push it forwards.[5] The fact is, I took the instance carelessly, when I had gone but a little way on the subject, and it never occurred to me when I wrote it out, of what nature it was. I shall however change it, for what I mention; and put a tennis ball for my *New Market racer,* which last is another very absurd instance.— I say all this upon the supposition that you have received a *fragment* of the paper I had promised on this subject, which fragment I was induced to send, from its lying before me on the table at the time I sent you a second pacquet of printed sheets;—it was, I think, by A Monsr: le Marquis de Bussyere, or some such person, a relation of the Duke de

5. In BF's essay questioning the existence of this property in matter, he had used the illustration of a mosquito producing motion in "two Globes each equal to the Sun and to one another, exactly equipoised in Jove's Ballance": III, 85–6.

Chartres.— I have no news. You will observe nothing from me relative to Irish or Scotch politics yet. I am, as ever, my very dearest sir, your devoted & grateful BENJN. VAUGHAN

Notation: B Vaughan May 31. 79

From Joseph Wharton[6] AL: American Philosophical Society

Hotel de Rome 31 May 1779

Mr. Joseph Wharton present's his best Respects to his Excellency Dr. Franklin and by Desire of his Father returns the American Papers with many Thanks.—

Addressed: A Son Excellence / Monsieur / Monsieur Franklin / &c &c &c / Passy

6. A son of Samuel Wharton: Anna H. Wharton, *Genealogy of the Wharton Family of Philadelphia, 1664 to 1880* (Philadelphia, 1880), p. 15n. He had recently arrived from England with his father; see our annotation of Samuel Wharton to BF, under April 7. He remained in France for more than a year: in August, 1780, he was in Lorient, where he made and attested a copy of an Oct. 15, 1779, letter from BF to John Paul Jones (Library of Congress). Reportedly he was killed during an uprising on Jones's *Ariel* during her passage to America in early 1781: Anna Wharton Morris, ed., "Journal of Samuel Rowland Fisher of Philadelphia, 1779–1781," *PMHB,* XLI (1917), 415. We follow present usage and call him Joseph Wharton, although he sometimes signed himself Joseph Wharton, Jr.; his uncle, Joseph Wharton, Jr., in contrast, generally signed himself Jos Wharton.

Franklin and Lafayette's List of Prints to Illustrate British Cruelties[7]

AD (draft):[8] Library of Congress

[*c.* May, 1779][9]

1. The Burning of Charleston (Date)[1]
   A fine Town by the Waterside, being a Port, but without any Defence.
   A Spire rising among the Houses, belonging to the House of Worship.
   A Belfrey belonging to the Town House all in Flames.—
   The Inhabitants had all left it.
2. The Burning of Falmouth (Date Nov. 1775)[2]
   A fine Town & Port, but without Defence
   Ships firing hot Shot, & throwing Bombs & Carcasses into the Town; English Colours.
   The Houses partly in Flames
   Sailors with Torches setting fire to others.
   The Inhabitants flying out of it carrying off the Sick and Aged

7. On Feb. 2, 1780, BF told Hartley that Congress expected him to make a school book of the accounts taken by congressional order concerning British atrocities; moreover, he was ordered to have thirty-five prints designed in France to illustrate the book: Smyth, *Writings,* VIII, 7. BF also hoped to use the designs on coinage; see his Oct. 2, 1779, letter to Edward Bridgen (Library of Congress). Congress was interested in publicizing British war crimes (*e.g., JCC,* VII, 276–9; VIII, 565), and BF's own outrage at British atrocities had been provoked recently: XXVIII, 256–9, 420. Such atrocities would form the topic of one of his most celebrated satires, the 1782 "Supplement to the Boston *Independent Chronicle*" (Smyth, *Writings,* VIII, 437–42).

8. Of which the first sixteen, the first five words of the seventeenth, and the final two proposals are in BF's hand; the remainder are in Lafayette's. For an illustration of one of the pages see Idzerda, *Lafayette Papers,* II, 266.

9. When Lafayette seems to have made his suggestions; see his letter of May 19. He inquired on July 12 about the progress of the book: Idzerda, *Lafayette Papers,* II, 292.

1. Charlestown, Mass., burned during the Battle of Bunker Hill: XXII, 72n. For BF's reaction to the destruction of this and the other cities subsequently mentioned here see XXII, 125, 196, 200, 242, 393.

2. Actually, on Oct. 18, 1775: Mark Mayo Boatner III, *Encyclopedia of the American Revolution* (New York, 1966), p. 215.

Women with Children in their Arms.
Some kill'd as they go off, and lying on the ground.—

3. The Burning of Norfolk[3]
fine Town & Port, several Churches
Town House
Inhabitants flying as above, & Ships firing

4. The Burning of Bedford[4]
5. The Burning of Esopus[5]
6. The Cannonading of Bristol[6]
7. ——— of Stoningtown[7]
People flying, &c—
(4–7: all defenseless Places.—)

8. The putting Prisoners to death in cold Blood after having surrendred their Arms, & demanded Quarter.— Baylor's Troop[8]

9. Prisoners dying in their Goals, with Hunger Cold & want of Fresh Air.

10. Dunmore's hiring the Negroes to murder their Masters Families[9]
A large House
Blacks arm'd with Guns & Hangers
Master & his Sons on the Ground dead,
Wife & Daughters lifted up in the Arms of the Negroes as they are carrying off.

11. Savages killing and scalping the Frontier Farmers and their Families, Women and Children, English Officers mix'd

3. On Jan. 1, 1776: *ibid.,* pp. 810–11.

4. Bedford, Mass., burned Sept. 5–6, 1778: *ibid.,* p. 66.

5. Esopus (or Kingston), N.Y., burned Oct. 16, 1777: *ibid.,* p. 583.

6. Bristol, R.I., bombarded Oct. 7, 1775: *ibid.,* p. 114.

7. Stonington, Conn., bombarded on Aug. 29, 1775: Richard Buel, Jr., *Dear Liberty: Connecticut's Mobilization for the Revolutionary War* (Middletown, Conn., 1980), p. 47.

8. A hundred soldiers from Col. George Baylor's 3rd Continental Light Dragoons were ambushed while sleeping on Sept. 28, 1778: Boatner, *Encyclopedia,* pp. 64, 1085–6.

9. In November, 1775, Gov. Dunmore of Va. issued a proclamation freeing "indentured servants, negroes, or others" who would fight under British colors: Ivor Noël Hume, *1775: Another Part of the Field* (New York, 1966), pp. 393–6.

with the Savages, & giving them Orders & encouraging them.

12. Governor Tonyn sitting in State, a Table before him, his Soldiers & Savages bringing in Scalps of the Georgia People, & presenting them. Money on the Table with which he pays for them. [1]

13. The Commanding Officer at Niagara, receiving in like Manner the Scalps of the Wioming Families.- -[2]

14. The King of England, giving Audience to his Secretary at War, who presents him a Schedule intitled *Acct. of Scalps.* which he receives very graciously.

15. American Prisoners, put on board Men of War, & whips to make them fight against their Countrymen & Relations

16. Americans put on board Ships in Irons to be carried to the East Indies, & Senegal, where they died with Misery & the unwholesomeness of the Climate.—[3]

17. Burning the Wounded with Straw at the Crooked Billet Small place in pensilvania[4]

18. Prisonners kill'd and Roasted for a great festival where the Canadian indians are eating American flesh, Colonel Buttler an english officer Setting at table

19. British officers who being prisonners on parole are well Receiv'd in the Best American families, and take that opportunity of corrupting Negroes and Engaging them to desert from the house, to Robb, and even to Murder theyr Masters

20. American officers who as they arrive in the British Camp are insulted By an enrag'd Soldiery—theyr Monney,

1. Patrick Tonyn was governor of East Florida, where Indians were not seriously discouraged from taking American scalps: J. Leitch Wright, Jr., *Florida in the American Revolution* (Gainesville, 1975), p. 36.

2. The American settlements of Wyoming Valley, Pa., were destroyed in July, 1778, by an Indian and loyalist raiding party led by Maj. John Butler from Niagara: Boatner, *Encyclopedia,* pp. 1221–8.

3. The American Commissioners had protested this practice to North: XXVI, 593. See also BF to Sartine, May 8, above.

4. Lafayette mentions this incident at Crooked Billet, Pa., in Idzerda, *Lafayette Papers,* I, 98.

theyr Cocades, theyr sword, and all theyr Cloathes are taken a way from them—

21. A durty prison ship where American officers are Confin'd without Being at liberty to take the Air, and so Crowded that they Can live but a few days—British officers Come to laugh at 'em and insult at theyr Miseries.

22. British officers plundering with theyr own hands farm houses, abusing the old people of the house, insulting the young land lady, and frightening the children

23. An honorable Captain Corning last Spring in the house of A Gentleman Call'd Mr West at White Marsh, Rushing in the Room where Miss West and An other Young lady Were sleeping at two o'clock in the Morning—the Captain and soldiers jump to the Beds of the two ladies, and with fix'd Bayonnets Upon theyr Breasts Make Several inquiries, and laugh at theyr dreadfull situation in the Most abusive Manner

24. An other Right honorable Captain Going out on a detachement an killing defenceless people.

25. General Gage's Perfidy to the Inhabts of Boston.[5]

26. Counterfeiting the Paper Money[6]

Notations in Franklin's hand: Ideas for the Prints / List of British Cruelties

From Madame Brillon: Two Letters[7]

(I) and (II) AL: American Philosophical Society

I.

ce mercredi a 3 h. [before June, 1779]

Mon chér papa, monsieur le Comte de Stroganoff vient de nous proposér d'allér voir le sérvice de l'impératrice de Russie

5. Described in XXII, 92.

6. See XXVII, 644.

7. Presumably sent at a two-hour interval on an unspecified Wednesday, these two notes refer to a proposed visit to the Sèvres manufactory where a huge dinner service (seven hundred and forty-four pieces) was being

a la manufacture de séve; s'il vous convient d'y venir avéc nous, nous vous donnerons le thé au retour: un mot de réponse a votre fille; nous partirons a 5 heures précises:

II.

ce mercredi 5 heures [before June, 1779]

La fille du papa ne pouvant se résoudre a passér une journée d'un mércredi sans le voir; lui demande le thé au retour de séve pour elle et pour ses amis.

Addressed: A Monsieur / Monsieur Franklin / A Passy

To [Vergennes]

LS:[8] Archives du Ministère des affaires étrangères

ce 1er Juin. 1779

Le Refus qu'à fait M. Le Directeur General[9] de se prêter aux propositions de M. Franklin, & ses besoins urgents, le determinent pour n'avoir rien a se reprocher, si les Evenements qu'il craint arrivent, de revenir a la charge auprès de l'Administration pour les prevenir, il demande en consequence, & a titre de pret, un Million quoique cette Somme ne remplisse pas ses besoins,[1] il espere que d'icy a ce qu'elle soit employée il pourra reçevoir d'autres Secours d'Amerique, ou par l'Emprunt dont il est chargé, & pour lequel il a fait imprimer des Promesses, au Nom des Treize Etats Unis, rem-

---

readied for shipment to Catherine II. According to Kira Butler, "Sèvres for the Imperial Court," *Apollo,* CI (1975), 454–6, the turquoise service, known as the Cameo, was completed in June, 1779—hence our dating—and shipped in a Dutch vessel to St. Petersburg, where it arrived in October. Some of the pieces can still be seen at the Musée de l'Histoire de la Porcelaine at Sèvres. For a somewhat different version of the transaction that dates the completion of the service in 1788 see William Burton, *A General History of Porcelain* (2 vols., New York, 1921), I, 178–9. Count Stroganoff was a fellow Mason of BF at the Nine Sisters; see XXVIII, 286n.

8. In the hand of Henry Grand.

9. Jacques Necker, *Directeur Général des finances.*

1. The last quarterly installment of a 3,000,000 *l.t.* loan had been paid on Nov. 1, 1778: Account XII (XXV, 3); XXV, 207–8. BF's appeal for a new loan was successful; payments of 250,000 *l.t.* were made on June 10, Sept. 16, Oct. 4, and Dec. 21, 1779: Account XII.

boursables dans dix ans a Paris, ainsi que les Interrets chaque Année.[2]

Il offre de remettre de ces Promesses pour la Même Somme qui lui sera fournie, & si l'Administration ne trouvoit pas a les realiser d'icy a leur echeance, Il s'engage de les retirer des premiers fonds qu'il aura de libres pour cela.

Quoique par cet arrangement, cette Operation paroisse plûtot un placement qu'un Secours M Franklin n'en sentira pas moins le prix du Service qui lui sera rendu par là il peut même dire que l'Interret des deux Nations le necessite aujourdhuy pour ne pas s'exposer a perdre le fruit de leur Union.

B FRANKLIN

Notation: 1er. juin 1779.

To Jonathan Williams, Jr.: Extract[3]

Extract: Library of Congress

Passy June 1. 1779.

I think it will be best for you to pay what Ballance you suppose in your hands towards the Anchors, and draw on me for the Rest. This will answer the present purpose of satisfying M. Gourlade, and Errors if any may be rectified in the final settlement of your accounts.

Part of a Letter to Jonathan Williams

From Barbeu-Dubourg

ALS: American Philosophical Society

ce 1er. juin 1779

J'ai l'honneur de souhaiter le bonsoir a Monsieur franklin et de le prevenir que le diner projetté pour demain chez M Le Pot d'Auteuil ne peut pas avoir lieu, et qu'on lui proposera de

2. BF enclosed a sample blank promissory note with coupons. AAE.

3. In answer, finally, to JW's letter of April 8. The extract is written in BF's letterbook.

le remettre a vendredi. Mais c'est une affaire a traiter jeudi chez M Grand[4] DUBOURG

Addressed: A Monsieur / Monsieur franklin / A Passy

From [Vergennes][5]

L: University of Pennsylvania Library

A Versailles le 1er. Juin 1779./.

Avant qu'il puisse être délivré un passeport du Roi sur le Certificat ci joint de M franklin, il est nécessaire d'expliquer *ou sont nès* ces Messrs Jones et Paradise, de quel Royaume ou Souveraineté ils sont Sujets, et le nombre de domestiques qu'ils ont à leur service et qu'ils doivent emmenner avec eux en Angleterre par le port de Calais.

Notation: Note a Mr. Le Dr. franklin. Versailles 1er. juin 1779.

From John Paradise and William Jones

AL: American Philosophical Society

1 June 1779.

Mr. Paradise and Mr. Jones present their best respects to Dr. Franklin. Being informed that the King's passport was *absolutely* necessary for them to go out of France, they sent to Versailles for that purpose, and have just received the enclosed answer.[6] May they trouble his Excellency to insert in his passport what they seem to want namely, that Mr. Paradise is an American gentleman *born in Greece*[7] (if *où ils sont nès* must be

4. The affair was the French loan BF was trying to raise through his banker Grand and Grand's *notaire*, M. Le Pot. Dubourg to BF, Aug. 10 (APS), and BF to Dubourg, Aug. 13 (Library of Congress).

5. Enclosed in the following document.

6. Above.

7. Paradise was born in Salonica where his father, Peter, was British consul. His mother, née Lodvill, was half Greek. John Paradise actually never had set foot in nor sworn an oath of allegiance to America. Archibald B. Shepperson, *John Paradise and Lucy Ludwell* (Richmond, Va., 1942), pp. 25, 147.

taken literally,) and that Mr. Jones is an Englishman with one valet de chambre. They are ashamed of giving his Excellency this trouble and wish him perfect health and happiness.[8]

Addressed: A Son Excellence / Mr. Benj. Franklin / Ministre Plenipotentiaire / des Etats Unis / de l'Amerique

Notation: Paradise et Jones 1er juin 1779

To Richard Bache

Incomplete copy: Library of Congress; extract: reprinted from William Temple Franklin, *The Private Correspondence of Benjamin Franklin, LL.D. F.R.S. &c.* . . . (2nd ed.; 2 vols., London, 1817), I, 40–2.[9]

Dear Son Passy, June 2. 1779.

I have received yours of june [Jan.] 16.[1] You observe that you Seldom hear from me, I have the Same reason to complain; but I do not complain of you. This ['Tis] the Loss of Ships, and the Sinking of Dispataches when chas'd that cuts our Correspondence to pieces.

8. On June 5 the Englishmen wrote from Calais: they had arrived there the day before and would embark for England in two hours. They thanked BF for his hospitality and expedition in procuring them a pass from Versailles; they were obliged to BF for the passport he had sent, which, although not immediately useful to them on the voyage, would remain a testimony of his friendship. They promised to deliver his two letters and please his friends with an account of his health. APS.

9. Because the incomplete copy and the extract bear the same date, and the order of the subjects discussed in them follows closely that of RB's letter of Oct. 22, 1778 (XXVII, 599–602), we believe they were originally one letter, of which no whole version survives. The incomplete letterbook copy contains the salutation and the first four paragraphs of the text, which ends in midsentence at the bottom of a page. The remainder of the letter and the signature come from the printed extract. We have used suspension points to separate the two parts.

1. Undoubtedly a mistake introduced by BF's French amanuensis; RB's letter was written on Jan. 16 (XXVIII, 386). This is the first of many such obvious errors, a few of which were corrected by a contemporary hand, but the majority of which remain. Where we are confident of the original wording, we indicate it, as here, in square brackets. When the meaning is so garbled as to defy our attempts to unscramble it, we let it stand.

Yours of Oct. 22. gave me a good deal of Satisfaction, in informing me of the Adventures of your family, your return to philada. Welfare &c.

You desire me to set the Price of the printing house Sold to Virginia, but I have received no Account of the Particulars where of it consisted.[2] Did they take the Cases as well as the Types; and what were the Number? There was a large Mahogany Press that cost me 25 Guineas and a Small one that cost 12 Guineas. Did they take those? And did they take all the Letters, flowers, &c &c. except the six Cases of Money Types which you Say the Congress have taken?— If so, you may make out the Account in this Manner.— As the Price of the Types in England was for Some 25 a pounds, Some 156, and some a Shilling, and the flowers, of which there was a great Quantity 5s—and it will be difficult now to come at the Weight of the Several Sorts. I Suppose it may be equitable to estimate the whole Weight at 18d. and the Cases at 3s each,[3] all Sterling and then allow me such and [an] Advance in Sterling also as European Good [Goods] Sold for at the time. I hope indeed they did not take the Presses, for I Should be unwilling to part with Them, as they were made under my own Inspection with Improvements,[4] and also a stone belonging to the press and a Number of Iron Chases or frames for fixing the Pages, and many other things which I know not

2. RB had written several times about the types that he had sold to Virginia: XXV, 552; XXVII, 89, 599–600. Gov. Patrick Henry had requested them in July, 1777, for an edition of the state laws: William Wirt Henry, ed., *Patrick Henry: Life, Correspondence and Speeches* (3 vols., N.Y., [1891], reprint ed., 1969), III, 84.

3. We can make little sense of these figures, but suspect they could benefit from a few decimal points. Type was sold by the pound and priced according to its size and condition. Seven-year-old brevier, for example, was valued at 1*s.* 3*d.* per pound when BF sold his printing office in 1766. For the itemized valuation of that printing office, and an explanation of its terminology, see XIII, 60–3. The type that RB sold to Virginia was probably that which BF had bought at auction in 1773: XX, 232n; XXI, 102, 210.

4. The mahogany presses that BF valued so highly (XIV, 177) "fell into worse hands," as RB subsequently reported. During the British occupation of Philadelphia some officers gave the presses to James Robertson, a Loyalist printer, who took them to New York. RB to BF, Sept. 18, 1779, APS.

whether they have taken or not which may be valued by any Printer.

The Scripts Letters which the Congress have taken cost me double the Price of common Letters of The Same sizes. The long Pica and long primer Bill I remember amounted to forty pound Sterling. What I gave for the larger Sort I leave have forgotten, but Suppose about ten Pounds. You may there fore Settle, that in the Same manner as to the advance &c. and when you are paid, you may Send . . .

I am very easy about the efforts Messrs. L. and ***[5] are using (as you tell me) to injure me on that side of the water. I trust in the justice of the Congress that they will listen to no accusations against me, that I have not first been acquainted with, and had an opportunity of answering. I know those gentlemen have plenty of ill will to me, tho' I have never done to either of them the smallest injury, or given the least just cause of offence. But my too great reputation and the general good-will this people have for me, the respect they show me and even the compliments they make me, all grieve those unhappy gentlemen; unhappy indeed in their tempers, and in the dark uncomfortable passions of jealousy, anger, suspicion, envy, and malice. It is enough for good minds to be affected at other people's misfortunes; but they that are vexed at every body's good luck, can never be happy: I take no other revenge of such enemies, than to let them remain in the miserable situation in which their malignant natures have placed them, by endeavouring to support an estimable character; and thus by continuing the reputation the world has hitherto indulged me with, I shall continue them in their present state of damnation; and I am not disposed to reverse my conduct for the alleviation of their torments.

I am surprised to hear that my grandson, Temple Franklin, being with me, should be an objection against me, and that there is a cabal for removing him.[6] Methinks it is rather some merit that I have rescued a valuable young man from the dan-

5. Arthur Lee and Ralph Izard.
6. XXVII, 600–1, 604.

ger of being a Tory, and fixed him in honest republican Whig principles; as I think from the integrity of his disposition, his industry, his early sagacity, and uncommon abilities for business, he may in time become of great service to his country. It is enough that I have lost my *son,* would they add my *grandson!* An old man of 70, I undertook a winter voyage at the command of the Congress, and for the public service, with no other attendant to take care of me. I am continued here in a foreign country, where, if I am sick, his filial attention comforts me, and, if I die, I have a child to close my eyes and take care of my remains. His dutiful behaviour towards me, and his diligence and fidelity in business, are both pleasing and useful to me. His conduct as my private secretary has been unexceptionable, and I am confident the Congress will never think of separating us.

I have had a great deal of pleasure in Ben too. 'Tis a good honest lad, and will make, I think, a valuable man. He had made as much proficiency in his learning as the boarding school he was at could well afford him, and after some consideration where to find a better for him I at length fixed on sending him to Geneva. I had a good opportunity by a gentleman of that city who had a place for him in his chaise, and has a son of about the same age at the same school. He promised to take care of him, and enclosed I send you the letters I have since received relating to him and from him.[7] He went very cheerfully, and I understand is very happy. I miss his company on Sundays at dinner. But if I live and I can find a little leisure I shall make the journey next spring to see him, and to see at the same time *the old 13 United States* of Switzerland.

Thanks be to God, I continue well and hearty. Undoubtedly I grow older, but I think the last ten years have made no great difference. I have some times the gout, but they say that is not so much a disease as a remedy. God bless you. I am your affectionate father, B. FRANKLIN.

Mr. Bache.

7. Probably the letters dated April 20, above, from BFB and Marignac.

To [William Carmichael][8]

Incomplete copy: Library of Congress

[June 2, 1779][9]

. . . Copies of the Letters, Votes &c relating to that Amiable and excellent young Man.[1] He was mighty well received, at Court, and has a Regiment given him. Ever Since his arrival he has been industrious in moving or projecting Something or other for the Advantage of America.

I am Sorry to hear of Dissensions in Congress, You are now one of that Body, and will, I hope, contribute to heal them;[2] I See, as you Say, that we have Wedderburnes in france as well as in England. They quarrel *at* me, rather than *with* me; for I will not quarrel with them. They write me long abusive Letters which I never answer, but treat the Gentlemen with The same Civility when we meet as if no Such Letters existed. This I think most prudent for public Character but I Suspect my Self of being a little malicious in it, for I imagine they are more vex'd by Such neglect than they would be by a tart Reply. Such malignant natures cannot long agree together even in mischief no revenge is necessary from me, I need only leave them to hiss, bite sting & poison one another.

Permit me to recommend to your Civilities the Cher. De La Luzerne who Goes over to replace Mr. Gerard. He is a Nephew of that Great man Mr. de Malesherbes President of the Cour *des Aides;* is much Esteemed here for his personal qualities and has a hearty Good will to the american cause.[3]

8. In answer to his letter of Oct. 30, 1778: XXVII, 664–6.

9. The letter is in a letterbook from which the date, salutation, and possibly some of the text have been cut. The letters preceding and following it are dated June 2; hence our dating. On this and the next two days BF wrote half a dozen other letters of recommendation for minister designate La Luzerne to various prominent Americans. The others are below.

1. Lafayette had carried Carmichael's letter to BF; in it Carmichael had recommended that BF personally take to the French court the letters and resolutions in praise of the returning hero: XXVII, 664–5.

2. Maryland elected Carmichael to Congress on Nov. 13, 1778: Burnett, *Letters,* III, liii.

3. La Luzerne was not only a nephew of the celebrated jurist Chrétien-Guillaume de Lamoignon de Malesherbes (above, April 22), but also a

All goes as well here as I could wish; except that you are not come over as expected to assist me in the Business. A Dieu, and believe me ever Dear Sir, Yours most affectionately.

To Charles Carroll[4]

Copy: Library of Congress

Dear Sir Passy, June 2. 1779.

This will be delivered to you by the Chevalier de La Luzerne, who Succeds M. Gerard. He is a Gentleman of a most amiable Character here and a Sincere wellwisher to America. As Such I beg leave to recommend him to your Civilities. You must have heard much of M. De Malesherbes Son of The Chancellier *Lamoignon,* and late President of the Cour des Aides, famous for his Eloquent, free, and Strong Remonstrances to the late king; This gentleman is his Nephew.

Correspondence between friends in America and Europe is now miserably cut to pieces by the Captures of Vessels. When one writes and the Letters do not get to hand; or if they get to hand The Answers miscarry, by degrees we may come to forget one another. But I Shall never forget the Pleasure I had in your Compagny on our Journey to Canada. Please to remember me when you write to your other Compagnons de Voyage, and belive me ever with Sincere Esteem and affection. Dear Sir, Your most obedient and most humble Servant BF.

P.S. to Mr. Carrol's Letter.

In looking over a Letter you favour'd me with, dated Aug. 12. 1777.[5] and which gave me great Satisfaction at the time. I find one Passage which I did not then answer. It relates to the

cousin through the maternal line of one of France's greatest military commanders, the *maréchal* de Broglie. One of La Luzerne's brothers became a cardinal, another minister of the navy: William E. O'Donnell, *The Chevalier de la Luzerne: French Minister to the United States, 1779–1784* (Bruges and Louvain, Belgium, 1938), pp. 39–40.

4. BF's fellow commissioner to Canada in the spring of 1776, Carroll of Carrollton subsequently had been elected to Congress, where he served sporadically from 1776 to 1778: XXII, 380n; *DAB.*

5. XXIV, 417–21. BF's answer has not been found.

Sending over Artificers of various kinds. You can have no Conception of the Numbers that apply to me with that View; and who would go over if I could assist them, by obtaining a passage for them without expense. If this Should be thought useful, and Congress could afford the charge and could confide in my judgement of the Persons and knowledge of the Arts wanted among us, I am persuaded I could send you over many People who would be valuable acquisitions to our Country.

Carrol of Carrolton Esqr.

To Chaumont

ALS: Yale University Library

Dear Friend Passy, June 2. 1779

You stay long from us, and every body wishes your Return. The Paving in the Court is finished, and the Passage thro' the Terras nearly so. Your Garden is in great Beauty, with Plenty of Green Peas & Cherries: Will you stay till they are all eaten?

Since my last, I received the following Paragraph in a letter from Holland; it is quoted from a Letter written at Amsterdam to my Correspondent at the Hague;[6]

"Par le Courier de Mardi dernier, nous reçumes une Lettre de Messrs Sellonf. & Perronteau, nos Correspondants à Paris, avec Avis que Messrs. I. Cottin & fils & Jauge avoient offert de payer nos effets sur M. le R. de Ch. Mais comme nous avons profité de la première Occasion pour renvoyer les dits Effets & le Protest à nôtre Remettant, nous ne sommes pas à même de faire usage de leur Offre. Nous en sommes bien fachés; car quoique les sommes ne soient pas trés-importantes, le Credit des Americains & de leurs Amis en France en souffrira beaucoup. En attendant, nous communiquerons l'Offre de Messieurs Cottin & Jauge a nos Amis en Amerique, pour les tranquilliser sur le Sort des Lettres de Change qu'ils pourroient avoir remis posterieurement.—"

I had before written to my Correspondent that I was sure

6. And Dumas quoted it to BF on May 21, above.

many of your Friends here would have paid the Bills in your Behalf if they had known of them.—[7]

My Love to Ray,[8] & believe me ever My Dear Friend, Yours most affectionately B FRANKLIN

To [Horatio Gates][9]

LS:[1] New-York Historical Society

Dear Sir, Passy, June 2. 1779.

I received your obliging Letter by the Chevalier De Ramondis who appears extreamly sensible of the Civilities he received at Boston, and very desirous of being serviceable to the American Cause; his Wound is not yet right, as he tells me there is a part of the Bone still to be cut off.[2] But he is otherwise well and chearful, and has a great Respect for you.

The Pride of England was never so humbled by any thing as by your Capitulation of Saratoga. They have not yet got over it, tho' a little elated this Spring by their Success against the French Commerce. But the growing Apprehensions of having Spain too upon their hands, has lately brought them down to an humble Seriousness that begins to appear even in Ministerial Discourses [*torn:* and the Papers?] of Ministerial Writers. All the happy Effects of that Transaction for America, are not generally known; I may sometime or other acquaint the World with some of them. When shall we meet again in chearful Converse, talk over our Adventures, and finish with a quiet Game of Chess.

The little Dissensions between Particulars in America are much magnified in England, and they once had great Hopes from them. I consider them, with you, as the Effects of appar-

7. To Dumas, printed under May 17.

8. The younger Chaumont's Christian name was Jacques: XXVIII, 239n. He had accompanied his father to Lorient; see JA's letter of May 14.

9. An old acquaintance: XXII, 249n. In April, 1779, Gates moved his headquarters to Providence, R. I. Paul David Nelson, *General Horatio Gates: a Biography* (Baton Rouge, 1976), p. 210.

1. In WTF's hand. The signature, which we assume was BF's, has been cut off.

2. For Gates's letter see XXVIII, 184–5, and for the chevalier de Raimondis and the circumstances of his wound see XXVIII, 490.

ent Security; which do not affect the grand Points of Independence and Adherence to Treaties; and which will vanish at any renew'd Appearance of Danger.

This Court continues heartily our Friend, and the whole Nation are warm in our Favour; excepting only a few West Indians & Merchants in that Trade, whose Losses make them a little uneasy.

With sincere and great Esteem and Affection I am ever, Dear Sir, Your most obedient and most humble Servant

[B FRANKLIN]

Endorsed: Letter from Dr. Franklin, dated passy, 2d: June, 1779:—

To John Jay

LS:[3] Royal Library, Windsor; copy: Library of Congress; transcript: Columbia University Library

Dear Sir, Passy June 2. 1779.

I received a few Days since by way of St Eustatia, the Duplicate of a Letter you did me the honour to write to me of 3d Jany.[4] But the Act of Congress of Decr 23d which you mention is not yet come to hand. Col Diricks whom the Secretary names to you called here in his way to Holland, and brought me a Recommendatory Letter from Govr. Trumbull;[5] but neither himself nor that Letter mentioned anything of his Business in Holland except to see his Friends; so that I yet know nothing of the purport of that Act. The other of Jany 1st. is come to hand. Besides The Reasons given in it for deferring the Expedition to Canada, there is one that would weigh much

3. In WTF's hand.

4. Jay's letter (XXVIII, 334–5) enclosed the two congressional resolutions that BF discusses in the present letter. The first one (*JCC,* XII, 1246–7) ordered Jay to provide BF with an introduction for Lt. Col. Jacob Gerhard Dircks who, with his friend Gosuinus Erkelens, was promoting a loan in the Netherlands; see Dumas' letter of June 24, below. The second one (*JCC,* XIII, 11–14) rescinded the instructions for BF to solicit French help in invading Canada.

5. XXVIII, 223–4.

with me, and that is our Want of a sufficient Quantity of hard Money. The Canadians are afraid of Paper and would never take the Congress Money. To enter a Country which you mean to make a Friend of, with an Army that must have occasion every Day for fresh Provision, Horses, Carriages Labour of every kind; having no acceptable Money to pay those that serve you; and to be obliged therefore, from the Necessity of the Case, to take that Service by Force, is the sure Way to disgust, offend, and by Degrees make Enemies of the whole People, after which all your Operations will be more Difficult, all your Motions discovered, and every endeavour used to have you driven back out of their Country.[6]

I need not recommend the Chevalier de la Luzerne to the President of Congress. His publick Character will recommend him sufficiently to all the Respect and Consideration due to the Minister of so great and good a Prince as the King of France our Ally. I shall only mention that his private Character here is an excellent one, and that he is connected by Relation to some of the greatest and best People of this Country. I hope that his Residence with us will be made agreable to him. I have written largely to the Committee. By our last Advices from Holland, the English Interest diminishes there; and from England they write, that the daily Apprehensions of a War with Spain, begins to have a serious Effect in disposing People generally to wish for Peace. Great Preparations are making here in all the Sea-Ports; and this Summer will probably produce some important Action. With great Respect and Esteem, I have the honour to be, Sir Your most obedient and most humble Servant. B FRANKLIN

Honble. John Jay Esq.

Endorsed: Doct Franklin 2 June 1779 answ. 26 Sep 1779

6. BF had witnessed at first hand the consequences of an American army in Canada with inadequate hard money: XXII, 413–15.

To John Paul Jones[7]

Copy: Library of Congress

Dear sir Passy June 2. 1779.

I know no more than you the Reasons of the Change respecting the Marquis But suppose they are good ones. I have no new Instructions to give. Perhaps you will receive some Instruction of the King's Pleasure.[8] I can only wish you Health and success, being ever, with great and Sincere Esteem Dear sir y. &c.

Capt. Jones.

To James Lovell

LS: Massachusetts Historical Society; AL (draft): Library of Congress; copies: Massachusetts Historical Society, National Archives, Library of Congress

Sir, Passy June 2. 1779.

I received a few Days since, via Eustatia & Holland the Triplicates of your several Favours of Dec 8. Jan. 29. and Feb. 8.[9] The preceding Copies of the same Dates never came to hand. I thank you very much for the News-Papers, tho' the Disputes I see in them gave me Pain. You observe rightly that the want of good Conveyances obstructs much the punctuality of our Correspondence. The Number of long Letters I have written to America have almost discouraged me from writing, except by such an Opportunity as this: You may judge of the Uncertainty of Letters getting to hand, when I tell you that tho' you mention the having sent me Quadruplicates of my Credentials, only those by the Marquis de La Fayette have yet appeared.

I am glad to understand that you are taking Measures to restore the Value of your Money, by taxing largely to reduce the Quantity. I believe no Financier in the World can put you upon a more effectual Method. The English have had a little

7. In response to Jones's May 26 letter.

8. New plans for Jones's squadron were already under discussion; see our annotation of BF's June 3 letter to the marine committee.

9. XXVIII, 206, 438–9, 492.

Flow of Spirits lately, from their Success against the Trade of France, and the News of the imagined Conquest of Georgia: but the growing Apprehension of a War with Spain also, begins to sober 'em; and like People who have been drunk with Drams, they now seem to have both the Head—and Heartake. The late Letters from thence are in a more humble Stile, and some printed Papers by the last Post, known to be Ministerial, appear intended to prepare the Minds of the People for Propositions of Peace.[1] But these Ebbs & Flows are common with them, and the Duration of neither are to be relied on.

As I do not find by any of yours, that a long Letter of mine to you in July last has come to hand, I send you herewith a Copy of it, (tho' now a little Stale,) as it serves to show my continued good Opinion of a Gentleman, who by the Papers you have sent me Seems to be hardly used.[2] I have never meddled with the Dispute between him and Mr. Lee; but the Suspicion of my having a Good Will to him, has drawn upon me a great deal of Ill-Will from his Antagonist. The Congress have wisely enjoyned the Ministers in Europe to agree with one another.[3] I had always resolved to have no quarrel, and have therefore made it a constant Rule to answer no angry, affronting or abusive Letter of which I have received Many and long Ones from Mr Lee & Mr Izard, who I understand, and see indeed by the Papers, have been writing liberally, or rather ill-liberally against me, to prevent, as one of them says here, any Impressions my writing against them might occasion to their Prejudice: But[4] I have never before mentioned them in any of my Letters.

1. Lovell's acknowledgment of this letter on Sept. 16 (University of Pa. Library) referred to "Mauduit's Speculations." We believe BF sent a broadside by the famous pamphleteer Israel Mauduit (for whom see the *DNB*) urging Parliament to declare the colonies independent: *A Hand bill advocating American Independence, inspired by the English Ministry, and written and published at London in March, 1778* (ed., Paul L. Ford, Brooklyn, 1890).

2. BF's July 22 letter (XXVII, 135–42) had defended Silas Deane.

3. XXVII, 655n.

4. In his draft BF here first wrote and then crossed out "it is another Rule of mine which I hope I shall always observe, because it is a just one, to accuse no Man to his Superiors at such a distance without sending".

Our Scheme here for Packet-Boats did not continue.[5] I wish Congress could fall on some Method of sending some little light Vessels once a Month, to keep up a Correspondence more regularly. Even the receiving Letters of a certain Date, tho' otherwise of no Importance, might serve to refute the false News of our Adversaries on both Sides the Water, which have sometimes too long their intended Effect before the Truth arrives. I see that frequently little Pilot Boats of 25 or 30 Tons burthen arrive safe from Virginia, the Expence of such would not be great.

I beg leave to recommend earnestly to your Civilities M le Chevalier De la Luzerne, who goes over to succeed M Gerard as the King's Minister to the Congress. He bears here a most amiable Character, has great Connections, and is a hearty Friend to the American Cause.

With great Esteem, I am Sir, Your most obedient & most humble Servant B FRANKLIN

Honble. James Lovel Esq.

Notations in different hands: June 2d. 1779 Doctr Franklin's to J L recd. Aug. 30 answd Sept. 16 / Deane Lee Izard Pacquet Boats Luzerne.

To Robert Morris

LS:[6] Boston Public Library; AL (draft) and copy: Library of Congress

Dear Sir, Passy June 2d 1779.

The Chevalier de la Luzerne, who goes over to succeed M. Gerard, will I hope have the Pleasure of delivering this into your hand, and of being by that means introduced to your Acquaintance. He has a most amiable Character here, and I am persuaded will make himself very acceptable to our People, as he has the most sincere Good Will to our Cause & Country, and the strongest Disposition to serve us. I therefore

5. See XXIII, 543–5.
6. In WTF's hand.

take the Liberty of recommending him warmly to your Civilities: Permit me at the same time to assure you of the unchangeable Esteem & Affection, with which, I am ever, Dear Sir, Your most obedt. & most humble. Sert. B FRANKLIN

Honble Rt. Morris Esq.

Addressed: The honble Robert Morris Esqr / Member of Congress, / Philadelphia

Endorsed: Passy 2d June 1779 Doctr Franklin by the Chevr Luzerne—

To Jonathan Trumbull

LS:[7] Mrs. C. Phillip Miller, Chicago, Illinois, (1963); incomplete copy: Library of Congress

Sir Passy June 2 1779

I received by Col. Dircks, the Letter your Excellency did me the Honour to write to me of the 12th December last.[8] I also had the great Pleasure of reading your Letter to Mr. Vander Capellen, agreeable to your kind Permission.[9] Col. Dircks went from hence immediately to Holland, and I have not since heard of him. There is a good Disposition in that Country towards us, but the English Interest thro' the Stadtholder is still very prevalent, tho' diminishing. In general thro'out Europe, we have the good Will and good Wishes of both the Princes and the People; the one glad to see the Power and Insolence of Britain diminished, the other to see an Asylum established for Liberty. Continued unanimity & Perseverance, with God's Blessing will effect this, and crown all our Labours with Success. I have the Honour to be with the sincerest Esteem and Respect Sir your most obedient and most humble Servant B FRANKLIN

The Fleets of both Nations are expected to be soon at Sea

7. In Gellée's hand.

8. XXVIII, 223–4.

9. For Gov. Trumbull's relationship with Joan Derk van der Capellen tot den Pol, the pro-American Dutch nobleman (XXVI, 349n), see XXVIII, 224n.

Notation: Passy 2nd June 1779 Doct B Franklin de Coll Dircks—disposition of European Princes & people towards America recd—15th—Augt. vespere

From Bordot[1]

ALS: American Philosophical Society

Sir, Rochelle, wednesday June 2d, 1779.

Two English Privateers, one under the name of the Defiance, from falmouth, and the other call'd the Ladies Resolution, from London, were brought Yesterday into these Roads by the frigate L'hermione;[2] the first mounting 18 four and Second 18 Six pounders; both of them taken the latter end of last week, about fifty leagues off the Channel.— As they made very little resistance, if any at all, there has been no loss of People on either Side.— The Crews, to the Number of 194 in the whole, are Just landed and Sent to Prison, most of them mere Boys.

I have the honor to be with great respect, Sir, Your most obedt. and Most hble. servt. F BORDOT

Mr. B. franklin

Notation: Bordot 2 june 1779. La Rochelle.

From ——— Hardoüin[3]

ALS: American Philosophical Society

Monsieur a Paris ce 2. juin 1779.

Les sieurs Witel et fauche imprimeur a Neuchatel en suisse[4] mon fait scavoir de vous donner avis que Lon delivroit ac-

1. Who several months earlier had sent BF a similar letter; see BF's reply of March 11.

2. A 26-gun frigate recently launched at Rochefort: Dull, *French Navy,* p. 357. The news of her captures was reported in the June 18 issue of the *Courier de l'Europe:* V (1779), 392.

3. A bookseller who in 1777 had brought trouble upon himself for selling a banned book: Bachaumont, *Mémoires secrets,* X, 152.

4. From whom BF had ordered the *Encyclopédie:* XXVII, 594–5.

tuellement chez moy, La premiere Livraison des œves. [œuvres] Complette de M. charle Bonnet 3 volumes in 4°. ou en 6 volumes in 8°. Le prix de l'in 4°. est de 12 *l.t.* chacque volumes et L'in 8°. 3 *l.t.* Mr, si vous estes jaloux dacquerir cette ouvrage qui a le plus grand succes, vous voudrez bien monhorer d'une Reponse et suis avec Respect Votre tres humble et tres obeissant serviteur Monsieur[5] HARDOÜIN

libraire Rue des pretres st. german Lauxerois

Addressed: A Monsieur / Le docteur / Monsieur franklin / a Passy / pres le Bois de Boulogne

Notation: hardouin 2. juin 1779

To Sarah Bache

Reprinted from William Temple Franklin, *The Private Correspondence of Benjamin Franklin, LL.D. F.R.S. &c.* . . . (2nd. ed.; 2 vols., London, 1817), I, 42–5

Dear Sally, Passy, June 3, 1779.

I have before me your letters of Oct. 22, and Jan. 17th:[6] they are the only ones I received from you in the course of eighteen months. If you knew how happy your letters make me, and considered how many miscarry, I think you would write oftener.

I am much obliged to the Miss Cliftons for the kind care they took of my house and furniture.[7] Present my thankful

5. The complete works of Bonnet, the Genevan-born philosopher and naturalist (1720–93) were issued between 1779 and 1783: Quérard, *France littéraire.* BF ordered the three volumes in quarto, for which he paid Hardoüin 37 *l.t.* 4 *s.* on Sept. 5: Cash Book, Account XVI, (XXVI, 3). When Hardoüin offered the second installment of four more volumes, on June 12, 1782 (APS), BF added those to his library. BF's set of *Oeuvres d'histoire naturelle et de philosophie de Charles Bonnet,* eight volumes in all, is now at the Library Company of Philadelphia.

6. XXVII, 602–5; XXVIII, 390–2.

7. Anna Maria Clifton and her sister watched over BF's home during the British occupation of Philadelphia; see XXIII, 425–6n; XXVI, 488; XXVII, 602.

acknowledgments to them, and tell them I wish them all sorts of happiness.

The clay medallion of me you say you gave to Mr. Hopkinson was the first of the kind made in France.[8] A variety of others have been made since of different sizes; some to be set in lids of snuff boxes, and some so small as to be worn in rings; and the numbers sold are incredible. These, with the pictures, busts,[9] and prints, (of which copies upon copies are spread every where) have made your father's face as well known as that of the moon, so that he durst not do any thing that would oblige him to run away, as his phiz would discover him wherever he should venture to show it. It is said by learned etymologists that the name *Doll,* for the images children play with, is derived from the word IDOL; from the number of *dolls* now made of him, he may be truly said, *in that sense,* to be *i-doll-ized* in this country.

I think you did right to stay out of town till the summer was over for the sake of your child's health.[1] I hope you will get out again this summer during the hot months; for I begin to love the dear little creature from your description of her.

I was charmed with the account you give me of your industry, the table-cloths of your own spinning, &c. but the latter part of the paragraph, that you had sent for linen from France because weaving and flax were grown dear; alas, that dissolved the charm; and your sending for long black pins, and lace, and *feathers!* disgusted me as much as if you had put salt into my strawberries. The spinning, I see, is laid aside, and you are to be dressed for the ball! you seem not to know, my dear daughter, that of all the dear things in this world, idleness is the dearest, except mischief.

8. The medallion was one of those made by Jean-Baptiste Nini at Chaumont's faïence factory near Onzain. See XXIV, 23n; XXV, 273n; Sellers, *Franklin in Portraiture,* pp. 344–5.

9. On June 1 WTF wrote to his aunt that he was sending her as a present, "the Bust of my best Friend your venerable Father." He also included directions for unpacking it. APS. The bust, however, never arrived. After a long wait at Lorient it was put aboard the *Marquis de Lafayette,* which was later captured. WTF to Sarah Bache, Sept. 14, 1781, Library of Congress.

1. Elizabeth, or Eliza, Franklin Bache had contracted smallpox (XXVII, 602).

The project you mention of removing *Temple* from me was an unkind one; to deprive an old man sent to serve his country in a foreign one, of the comfort of a child to attend him, to assist him in health and take care of him in sickness, would be cruel, if it was practicable. In this case it could not be done; for as the pretended suspicions of him are groundless, and his behaviour in every respect unexceptionable; I should not part with the child, but with the employment. But I am confident that whatever may be proposed by weak or malicious people, the Congress is too wise and too good to think of treating me in that manner.

Ben, if I should live long enough to want it, is like to be another comfort to me: as I intend him for a Presbyterian as well as a Republican, I have sent him to finish his education at Geneva. He is much grown, in very good health, draws a little, as you will see by the inclosed, learns Latin, writing, arithmetic and dancing, and speaks French better than English. He made a translation of your last letter to him, so that some of your works may now appear in a foreign language. He has not been long from me. I send the accounts I have of him, and I shall put him in mind of writing to you. I cannot propose to you to part with your own dear *Will:* I must one of these days go back to see him; happy to be once more all together! but futurities are uncertain. Teach him however in the mean time to direct his worship more properly, for the deity of *Hercules* is now quite out of fashion.[2]

The present you mention as sent by me, was rather that of a merchant at Bourdeaux, for he would never give me any account of it, and neither Temple nor I know any thing of the particulars.

When I began to read your account of the high prices of goods, "*a pair of gloves seven dollars, a yard of common gause twenty-four dollars, and that it now required a fortune to maintain a family in a very plain way,*" I expected you would conclude with telling me, that every body as well as yourself was grown frugal and industrious; and I could scarce believe my eyes in reading forward, that "*there never was so much dressing and plea-*

2. XXVIII, 391. BF had once referred to young William Bache as an infant Hercules: XXII, 67.

sure going on;" and that you yourself wanted *black pins and feathers from France,* to appear, I suppose, in the mode! This leads me to imagine that perhaps, it is not so much that the goods are grown dear, as that the money is grown cheap, as every thing else will do when excessively plenty; and that people are still as easy nearly in their circumstances as when a pair of gloves might be had for half a crown. The war indeed may in some degree raise the prices of goods, and the high taxes which are necessary to support the war may make our frugality necessary; and as I am always preaching that doctrine, I cannot in conscience or in decency encourage the contrary, by my example, in furnishing my children with foolish modes and luxuries. I therefore send all the articles you desire that are useful and necessary, and omit the rest; for as you say you should "*have great pride in wearing any thing I send, and showing it as your father's taste;*" I must avoid giving you an opportunity of doing that with either lace or feathers. If you wear your cambric ruffles as I do, and take care not to mend the holes, they will come in time to be lace; and feathers, my dear girl, may be had in America from every cock's tail.

If you happen again to see General Washington, assure him of my very great and sincere respect, and tell him that all the old Generals here amuse themselves in studying the accounts of his operations, and approve highly of his conduct.

Present my affectionate regards to all friends that enquire after me, particularly Mr. Duffield and family,[3] and write oftener, my dear child, to Your loving father, B. FRANKLIN.

To the Marine Committee of Congress

LS:[4] National Archives; copy: Library of Congress

Gentlemen Passy June 3 1779

I received the Honour of yours[5] by the Marquis de la Fayette, who arrived safe and well in the Alliance Fregate, which you were pleased to put under my Orders.

3. Edward Duffield; see his son Benjamin's letter, above, May 16.
4. In Gellée's hand. The copy is dated June 2.
5. Dated Oct. 27, 1778: XXVII, 651–2.

There had been a Conspiracy on Board to seize and run away with the Ship to England. Thirty eight of the Crew concerned in the Plot were brought in under Confinement, and the Captain was much embarrass'd with them, and Suspicions of many more. We could not try them here, for Want of Officers sufficient to make a Court Martial. The French Admiralty could not take Cognizance of their Offence. The Captain objected to carrying them back as both troublesome & dangerous. In Fine We got Leave to land and confine them in a French Prison, where they continue till further Orders.

Captain Landais desired much to have his Ship sheathed here with Copper. But having neither Orders, nor Money in my Hands for that Purpose I was obliged to refuse it. There was a great Misunderstanding between him and his Officers: and great Discontent among his Officers themselves, who were in Want of Cloathes and Money: The Ship too, tho' new, wanted great Repair, all her Iron Work being bad. The Agent Mr. Schweighauser required my Orders about every Thing: And I had Letters from him from the Officers, or from the Captain, by almost every Post. My total Unacquaintedness with such Business made it very perplexing to me. I have got thro' it at Last, and I hear the Officers are more contented; But I hope to have no more such Affairs on my Hands.

Being informed by the Officer who came up from the Captain with the Dispatches,[6] that She had not Hands sufficient to man Prizes if she should be sent on a Cruise, that the Captain did not care to supply the Deficiency with Frenchmen, that if She were again at Boston now that her Character for a swift Sailer, and that of the Captain for a good Officer were established, of which the Seamen were before doubtful, there was the greatest Probability that She would be fully manned immediately; And as Mr. Adams wished for an Opportunity of going home, and I heard that some Ships were bound to North America from Nantes, to whom the Convoy of a Fregate quite to the American Coast might be convenient, I determined to

6. Amos Windship, surgeon of the *Alliance;* see Landais' letter of March 3.

send her back directly; and accordingly offered her as a Convoy to the Trade. But as M. de la Mothe Piquet was about to sail from Brest with a Squadron, before our Frigate could be fitted, and as he offered to take Care of all outward bound Ships who should join him at Brest, the Offer I made was not accepted, and all the American Ships went from Nantes to join his Fleet. She was however still to go with Mr. Adams, but receiving the enclosed Letter from Mr. de Sartine Minister of the Marine, who at the same Time offered to man her compleatly if I comply'd with his Request,[7] I thought it right to oblige him, as the Inconvenience would be only a little longer Delay to Mr. Adams in getting home, and by her extreamly swift Sailing, of which they relate Wonders, she might in the proposed Cruize take Prisoners enough to redeem by the now established Cartel the Rest of our unfortunate Countrymen still in the English Prisons. I accordingly acquainted Mr. De Sartine that I would, agreeable to his Desire, order her to l'Orient; where She now is a Part of Capt. Jones's little Squadron, which is ready to sail, if not already sail'd on the intended Expedition.[8]

After all this was thus arranged, Mr A. Lee wrote to me, to urge the sending her with the Merchant Ships, and to carry over some Dispatches of his & Mr Izards, that were of great Importance:[9] But as those Ships were by this Time Sail'd, and the French Frigate with the new Minister and Mr. Adams was to sail in a Week or two and might carry those Dispatches, the Contents of which I was not acquainted with, I did not see the Necessity of retracting the Promise I had made to the Minister, and thereby deranging the Expedition.

7. Above, April 20.

8. See BF's April 23 letter to Sartine and his May 26 letter to the committee for foreign affairs. Now that Jones's squadron was no longer needed for the Irish Sea expedition Sartine suggested to Chaumont on June 2 that it be used in the Gulf (*i.e.,* the Bay of Biscay) for convoying and the fighting of British privateers: Charles H. Lincoln, comp., *A Calendar of John Paul Jones Manuscripts in the Library of Congress* (Washington, D.C., 1903), p. 89. It was soon put to such use; see our annotation of Jones's June 18 letter.

9. See Lee's letter of May 6 as well as Lee and Izard's joint letter of the same day.

As our Ships of War that arrive here, require an amazing Expence to fit them, and the Prizes they bring in, often occasion Law Suits and all the Embarrassement and Sollicitation & Vexation attending Suits in this Country, I must beg the Committee would be so good as to order the several Navy Boards to send no more to be outfitted here, without sending Effects to defray the Expence: and that if our armed Ships should be still ordered to cruise in these Seas, a Consul or Consuls may be appointed in the several Sea Ports, who will thereby be more at Hand to transact maritime Business expeditiously, will understand it better, relieve your Minister at this Court from a great Deal of Trouble, and leave him at Liberty to attend Affairs of more general Importance.

With great Esteem and Respect I have the Honour to be Gentlemen your most obedient and most humble Servant

B FRANKLIN

The Honble. the Marine Committee of Congress.

Notations in different hands: The Honourable Benjamin Franklin esqr. Passey. June 3d 1779 / No 2

From Thomas Conway: Certificate

ADS: American Philosophical Society

[June 3, 1779]

Je certifie que j'ai eu L'honneur De servir en amerique avec Mr De saintuary;[1] que cet officier qui ÿ servoit a ses Depens, etait aimé et consideré par ses superieurs. J'ai vû Mr De santuary montrer Beaucoup De Zêle et D'activité aux Batailles De Brandÿweine et De Germàntown. Je certifie que Mr De santuary a eté fait prisonnier en Novembre 1777 auprés De philadelphie, et que Le Congrés par satisfaction, pour sa conduite a proposé D'echanger Mr De santuary contre un officier anglois qui eut Le rang De Major.[2] Ces faits sont a La Con-

1. The baron St. Ouary: Fitzpatrick, *Writings of Washington,* x, 155.
2. *JCC,* IX, 991.

noissance Des officiers francois qui ont fait La Guerre a L'armée Du General Washington.

fait a paris Le 3. juin 1779 CONWAŸ

Endorsed: M. Conway's Certificate concg. M. de Saintuary

To Dumas[3]

ALS: Haverford College Library

Dear Sir, Passy, June 4. 1779

It is not a pleasant thing to be called upon for one's Sentiments of Persons & Characters; but when Matters of Importance to our Country, our Friends or ourselves, depend on a true Judgment of Men, it is right to ask one another's Opinions & to give them frankly in confidence that no inconvenient Use will be made of them.

Mr. S. has always been a Friend to the Cause of America. He fail'd as a Banker, in consequence of some imprudent Schemes & Operations, which did not succeed. He spent as much as he could of his Wife's Fortune, then came to France. Mr A. Lee took him as a Companion to Berlin; there they differ'd as I understand, and Mr Lee return'd without him. He has since been rambling about the North, proposing magnificent Plans of Commerce to Ministers and Merchants, and taking upon himself the Character of a Minister or Agent of Congress without having any Authority for so doing. Whether he has borrowed Money on the Credit of that Character, to subsist on, which I suspect, or whether he has drawn his Subsistance from England, I know not.[4] He has desired of me to give him Letters of Recommendation to some French Governors in the West Indies. I wish him well, but I do not care to commit myself, not knowing what Use he may make of them, and therefore have neither sent him such Letters, nor answer'd his Letter requesting them.[5] I do not approve his Conduct;[6] I do

3. In response to Dumas' query of May 27.

4. For Sayre's banking career, marriage, and activities in Berlin, Copenhagen, and Stockholm see John R. Alden, *Stephen Sayre, American Revolutionary Adventurer* (Baton Rouge and London, 1983), pp. 49–52, 91–4, 100–14.

5. See Sayre's letter of May 17.

6. From here through "Prudent Man;" is added above the line.

not know him to be dishonest, but I think him rather an artful than a prudent Man; I desire to have no Difference, with him and therefore keep this to yourself.— If you come to Paris, come directly to Passy where I shall have a Bed at your Service, being with great Esteem, Dear Sir, Your most obedient humble Servant B FRANKLIN

The English Fleet has left St. Lucia, much weaken'd by Sickness.—[7]

Mr Dumas,

To William Greene[8]

LS:[9] American Philosophical Society; copy: Library of Congress

Dear Sir, Passy, June 4. 1779

I received your kind Letter of Decr 10. with the Bills of Exchange for two hundred and sixteen Dollars, & with the List of Goods you would have in return. As I live far from any Seaport and am unacquainted with Merchandize, I sent the Bills, with your Order directly to my Nephew at Nantes, who will I doubt not accomplish it to your Satisfaction.[1]

I shall be glad of any Opportunity of being serviceable to your Son-in-law, both for your Sake and his Father's.[2]

Your Letter with the first set of the Bills did not come to hand; which I regret the more, as by that means I have lost Mrs. Greene's Letter which you tell me was inclosd. Present

7. Although BF could not yet have received news of it, Byron's fleet had left St. Lucia May 25 on cruise: W.M. James, *The British Navy in Adversity: a Study of the War of American Independence* (London, 1926), p. 145.

8. Husband of BF's old friend Catharine Ray Greene and governor of Rhode Island since 1778. His letter is in XXVIII, 216–18.

9. In WTF's hand. The four corners of the MS are torn, and we have supplied missing words from the copy.

1. BF had sent the orders on Feb. 13: XXVIII, 522–3. The goods were shipped on the *Three Friends:* JW to Greene, May 26, 1779, Yale University Library.

2. Greene's son-in-law was Samuel Ward, Jr., son of former R.I. governor Samuel Ward (XXVIII, 216n).

my affectionate Respects to her; and my Love with that of my Grandson to honest Ray, of whose Welfare I am very glad to hear and of his Progress in his Learning.[3]

If my Sister continues under your hospitable Roof, let her know that I did not receive hers of the 7th: that you mention;[4] that I have not time now to write to her, but will by the next Opportunity; and that I am well and love her as well as ever.

With great Esteem & Respect, I am, Dear Sir, Your most obedt and most humble Servant B FRANKLIN

P.S. If the Chevalier De la Luzerne should pass thro' your Government, I recommend him warmly to your Civilities. He goes over to supply the Place of M. Gerard, as his most Christian Majestys Minister to the Congress. He is a Gentleman of a most amiable Character here, has great Connections, and is a hearty Friend to America.

His Ex. Wm. Greene Esq.—

To Francis Hopkinson

LS:[5] American Philosophical Society; copy: Library of Congress

Dear Friend, Passy June 4. 1779.

I received your kind Letter of the 22d Octr. last, which gave me great Pleasure as it inform'd me of your Welfare, and of your Appointment to the honourable Office of Treasurer of Loans.[6] I think the Congress judg'd rightly in their Choice. An Exactness in Accounts, and scrupulous Fidelity in Matters of Trust, are Qualities for which your Father was eminent,[7] and which I was persuaded were inherited by his Son when I

3. BF had interested himself in Ray Greene's education since he took the ten-year-old boy to the Academy of Philadelphia in 1775. The youth had met WTF at that time: V, 502n; XXII, 253n, 254n, 273n; XXVIII, 217–18.

4. XXVIII, 217.

5. The MS is torn, and we have supplied the few missing words from the copy.

6. Hopkinson was elected to the post on July 27, 1778: *JCC,* XI, 724. For his Oct. 22 letter see XXVII, 605–7.

7. For Thomas Hopkinson see I, 209n.

took the Liberty of naming you one of the Executors of my Will, a Liberty which I hope you will excuse.[8]

I am sorry for the Losses you have suffer'd by the Goths and Vandals, but hope it will be made up to you by the good Providence of God, and the Good Will of your Country to whom your Pen has occasionally been of Service. I am glad the Enemy have left something of my Gimcrackery that is capable of affording you Pleasure. You are therefore very welcome to the Use of my Electrical and Pneumatic Machines as long as you think proper. I inclose you a little Piece or two of Oxford Wit, which I lately recd hoping they may afford you a few Minutes Amusement.[9] Present my Respects to your good

8. Hopkinson accepted the appointment in his Sept. 5. reply (APS). The will that actually named him to the post is dated July 17, 1788 (Smyth, *Writings,* X, 493–510). BF's earlier wills, dated [June 22, 1750], and April 28, 1757, are above: III, 480–2; VII, 199–205.

9. The enclosure has not survived, but Hopkinson had it published in the Sept. 4 issue of the *Pennsylvania Packet or the General Advertiser* (as he wrote BF on Sept. 5). Characterized as a "piece of Oxford wit," the poem reads

Upon the tressel *pig* was laid
A dreadful squeaking, sure, he made:
Killpig stood by with knife and steel—
"Cans't not lie quiet? Why dost squeal?
Have I not fed thee with my pease?
And now, for such trifles such as these,
Dost thou rebel?— So full of victual—
Can'st not be cut and slash'd a little."
To whom thus *piggy* in reply—
"How canst thou think I'll quiet lie?
Or that for pease my life I'll barter"—
"Then *piggy* you must show your charter,
Prove you're exempted more than others,
Or go to pot like all your brothers."
(Pig struggles)
"Help neighbours, help—this *pig*'s so strong,
I fear I cannot hold him long—
Oh help, I say! See, by my blunder,
He's gone and broke his bands assunder."
Exeunt omnes.
Pig running, Killpig after him, neighbours following,
God knows whither!

Mother and Sisters,[1] and believe me ever, My Dear Friend, Yours most affectionately B FRANKLIN

P.S. Permit me to recommend the new Minister, M. le Chevalier De la Luzerne to your Civilities as a Gentleman of most amiable Character here, and a hearty Friend of the American Cause. If you can in any Respect be serviceable to him, you will much oblige me.

Fras. Hopkinson Esqr—

Notation: Franklin. Donnée par Mademoiselle Elisabeth hopkinson. à Philadelphie.—

To the Massachusetts Council

LS:[2] Massachusetts Archives; copy: Library of Congress

Honble Gentlemen Passy June 4 1779

The Commissioners at this Court received the Letter you did them the Honour of writing to them, recommending the Marquis de la Fayette. I immediately sent it to be perused by the Minister, who desired to have a Copy of it. He was very favourably received by his Majesty, and has had given him a Regiment of Dragoons.[3] He retains the warmest Zeal for the American Cause, and Affection for the People; and has been continually moving something or other with the Ministry for the Advantage of America, ever since his Arrival. The Chevalier de Ramondis too retains the most grateful Sense of the Attention paid him by your Government during his Illness, under the Loss of his Arm: Several other Officers speak highly in Favour of our Country on Account of the Civilities they received there, which has a very good effect here, and evinces the Wisdom of the Conduct you are accustomed to pursue with Regard to Strangers of Merit. I thought it right to acquaint you with these Circumstances, and I do it with more

1. XII, 124–5n.
2. In Gellée's hand.
3. For the letter from the Massachusetts Council and BF's to Vergennes see XXVIII, 351, 536.

Pleasure, as it gives me an Opportunity of assuring you of the great Respect with which I have the Honour to be Gentlemen, Your most obedient and most humble Servant B FRANKLIN

P.S. If the Chevalier de la Luzerne who is going to America to succeed M. Gerard as Minister from this Court, should happen to put into Boston, you will find him every Way deserving of the Civilities he may receive independent of his public Character. He is much esteemed and respected here, has great Connections and is a hearty Friend to the Cause of Liberty and America

The Honble the Council of the Massachusetts Bay

Notation: Letter from Benja Franklin June 4th: 1779

From the Marquise de Boulainvilliers[4]

AL: American Philosophical Society

ce 4 juin [1779][5]

Puisque nous n'allons point a passy il faut aumoins avoir lhonneur et le plaisir de nous rapeller au souvenir de Monsieur francklin; il y a des Siecles qu'il n'a eu le bontés de se Souvenir de nous: sa bonne amie s'en plaint parcequelle luy est: toujours tres attachée.[6] Elle sera saigné demain samedy et gardera quelques jours la Maison: Monsieur francklin deveroit bien nous faire lhonneur de venir diner avec Nous les premiers jours de la semaine prochainne le plus tot sera le Mieux nous le prions seulement de vouloir bien nous Mander le jour pour pouvoir luy donner des personnes de sa Connaissance. Monsieur de boulainvilliers est toujours incomodés il Compte partir incessament pour les eaux de Spa: si Monsieur francklin veut venir prendre du thè un de Ces jours independamment

4. Identified, along with other members of her family, in XXV, 389n.

5. The "demain samedy" indicates that this was written on a Friday. June 4 fell on a Friday in 1779.

6. BF's "bonne amie," the former Mademoiselle de Passy—whose marriage to vicomte Gaspard-Paulin de Clermont-Tonnerre was noted in XXVIII, 284n—was pregnant with her first child, the future Aimé-Marie-Gaspard, comte, then duc de Clermont-Tonnerre (1779–1865): *DBF.*

du diner il nous trouvera car nous ne sortons point; nous le prions de permettre que nous disions Mille choses a Monsieur son petit fils; nous esperons aussi avoir lhonneur de le voir.

From Madame Brillon

AL: American Philosophical Society

ce 4 juin [1779][7]

J'aurois cértainement un grand plaisir mon bon papa á devinér des énigmes que vous auriés faittes, et a taschér de découvrir vos secréts; cependant cet espéce d'exercisse entraisne avéc lui une sorte de fatigue, que je n'éprouve point en lisant vos léttres; la vértu, la sagésse s'y montrent a découvért; j'y trouve des conseils dictés par une áme dont la force se trouve adoucie par la sensibillité; mon bon papa je ferai mes éfforts pour vous ressemblér, mais ma consistance phisique qu'un coup de vent dérange, influë sur ma consistance morale: sensible a l'éxcés, je manque de force; je sçais bien prendre assés sur moi, pour ne pas détruire le bonheur de mes entours, pour y sacrifiér mesme mes gouts mes penchants; mais je souffre mon ami! Souvent seule, mes yeux se couvrent de larmes—Je serai toujours une fémme douce, vértueuse; taschés de me rendre une femme forte, ce miracle vous est peut estre résérvé—Mon ami je ne suis pas injuste, je sçais que l'homme auqu'el le sort m'a lié, est un homme de méritte; je le respécte autant que je le dois et qu'il le méritte; je l'ai peut estre toujours aimé au dela de ce que son coeur peut me rendre; vingt quatre ans de différence dans nos ages; son éducation austére; la miénne peut estre un peu trop soignée du costé des talents agréables, ont resséré son coeur et exhalté le mien—[8] Mon papa les mariages dans ce pays ci, se font au poid de l'or; on m'est d'un costé de la balance la fortune d'un garçon, de l'autre celle de la fille, quand l'egallité s'y rencontre l'affaire se términe au contentement des parents; on n'imagine pas de consulter le gout, l'age,

7. Her reference to "samedi" at the end of her letter persuades us that she was writing on Friday, June 4. See our dating of the preceding letter.

8. JA noticed this discrepancy; he would write much later in his autobiography that "Mr. Brillon was a rough kind of Country Squire. His Lady all softness, sweetness and politeness." Butterfield, *John Adams Diary*, IV, 47.

le rapport de caractéres; on marie une jeune fille dont le coeur renférme le feu de l'age et ses besoins, a un homme qui les a éteints:[9] on éxige que cétte fémme soit honneste—Mon ami cétte histoire est la miénne, et celle de tant d'autres: je ferai mes éfforts pour que ce ne soit pas celle de mes filles, mais hélas, seraisje maitrésse de leur sort? Adieu vous óh mon ami, vous que je revére, que j'aime; je vais lire, relire votre léttre; je me conformerai aux vérités qu'elle renférme, je tascherai de devenir la digne éléve d'un philosophe d'un sage; je tascherai de prouvér au meilleur des papas et des amis, que sa fille ne fait pas seulement consistér l'amitié qu'elle a pour lui, dans le plaisir de le voir et de le lui témoignér; qu'elle ne veut pas se contentér de lui plaire par des agréments qu'il rencontre tous les jours a un plus haut degré dans beaucoup d'autres fémmes; mais par le complément et l'assemblage de toutes les vertus, qui la rendront a juste titre l'amie de son bon papa, fut elle vieille, laide, fut elle homme etc.: enfin, fut elle loin de l'état qui fait que les sens sont pour quelques choses dans l'hommage qu'on rend aux femmes: a demain, c'est demain samedi mon papa, et vous n'estes pas venu mércredi.

From Marat

ALS: American Philosophical Society

Sir Paris the 4th June 79.

The honour of your company at dinner on thurday next (with Mrs le Comte de Maillebois, de Montigni, le Roy & Sage)[1] is desired by the author of the experiments on the igneous fluid.

The honour of Mr ..... your grand-son company is likewise desired. If the time keeps clear; it will be to him an oportunity to see the experiments.[2]

9. She here deleted "par le libertinage".

1. The four members of the commission previously appointed by the Academy to report on Marat's experiments.

2. As his March 25 letter had indicated, sunny weather was needed for the use of the *microscope solaire*.

The dinner on the table at tow o clock at the hotel of M. le Marquis de l Aubespine Rue de Bourgogne F. S. G.

If you have perused the manuscript treatise on the fire, Sir, & will be so good as to deliver it to the bearer with your judgement, it will be esteemed a great favour.[3]

I am with great regard, Sir Your most humble obedient Servant THE REPRESENTATIVE.

Notation: M. Marat 4 June 79.

From François-Pierre de Séqueville[4]

LS:[5] Historical Society of Pennsylvania

Monsieur, Paris, le 4 Juin 1779.

Le Roi ne verra point Mardi prochain[6] huit du mois, Messieurs les Ambassadeurs et Ministres étrangers.

DE SÉQUEVILLE
Secrétaire ordinaire du Roi, à la conduite des Ambassadeurs.

Addressed: A Monsieur / Monsieur francklin / Ministre Plenipot. de La / Republ. des Provinces Unies / de l'Amerique Septentrionale / a Passy / De Sequeville.

Notation: Advertisements & ceremonial Notices.

3. His *Découvertes sur le Feu . . . ,* for which see the headnote to his letter printed under March 13.

4. In 1761 Séqueville (1725–93), a *commis* in the foreign ministry, became the court official dealing with the ministers of foreign states: Jean-Pierre Samoyault, *Les Bureaux du Secrétariat d'Etat des Affaires étrangères sous Louis XV* (Paris, 1971), p. 306.

5. A printed form with only the word "huit" and the date written by hand. There are thirty similar notices from Séqueville among BF's papers at the APS and one at the University of Pa. Library. None of the others is fully dated.

6. The day of the week on which the king received foreign diplomats accredited to the French court.

To John Adams

LS:[7] Massachusetts Historical Society; copy: Library of Congress

Sir, Passy June 5. 1779.

The Chevalier de La Luzerne sat out Yesterday for L'Orient, and will be with you perhaps before this comes to hand.[8] You will find him a very agreable sensible Man, and a hearty Friend to the Cause of America.

As you may land in Boston and are not certain of going directly to Philada: I have put under his Care my Dispatches for Congress, and request yours for those to New England.

Mr Bondfield has drawn on me for 18,000 Livres on Acct of the Canon. I cannot find the Agreement that was made with him for that Article. If you have it and can easily get at it, be so good as to send it to me or a Copy of it.[9]

Mr. Schweighauser in a late Account charges a Commission of Five per Cent. on the simple Delivery of two Cargoes of Tobacco out of the Ship into the hands of the Officer of the Farmers General, all attending Expences separately charged; and to make the Commission rise the higher, he has valued the Tobaccos at 90 Livres, the Price it now sells at in the Ports, and not at 40 Livres, which it was to be delivered at by our Contract; by this means the Commission on those two Cargoes comes to 630 £ sterling. Thinking this an exorbitant Demand, I got a Friend to enquire of the Merchants upon Change what was the Custom in such Cases, and received the following Answer. "I have spoken to more than ten Merchants, who all have told me unanimously, that One per Cent was not only the general Custom, but as high as could be

7. In WTF's hand.

8. He arrived on the 11th: Butterfield, *John Adams Diary,* II, 380.

9. The commissioners had ordered him to purchase and ship fifty-six cannon: XXVII, 275. On May 25 the firm of Louis Sazerac l'aîné & fils at Angoulême sent Bondfield forty cannon, for which they charged 30,914 *l.t.:* Francis James Dallett, "Une Fourniture de canons à la marine américaine par la maison Sazerac d'Angoulême (1779–1782)," *Mémoires de la Société Archéologique et Historique de la Charente* (1965), 115–19. Its bill to Bondfield is at the University of Pa. Library.

claimed being half Commission: For if there had been a Sale in the Case, it would have been two per Cent. which is the general Usage in the Trade and not 5 per Cent." I have wrote to M. Schweighauser that I objected to that Article of his Account, but he seems not dispos'd to give it up.[1] I find myself too little acquainted with Mercantile Business to be a Match for these People, which makes me more and more desire to see Consuls appointed in the Ports, who might take it off my Hands, and I wish, if you are of Opinion it would be right, that you would press it upon Congress. My Grandson desires I would present you his affectionate Respects, and joins with me in heartily wishing you & our young Friend a prosperous Voyage & happy Meeting with your Friends and Family. I shall take care to present your Respects to the good Ladies you mention.[2] All goes well here: Countenances begin to brighten, and the contrary in England (according to our last Advices) from the Aprehension of certain Event,[3] which may God prosper. I am with great Esteem and Respect, Sir, Your most obedt & most humble Servant. B. FRANKLIN

Hon. Jn: Adams Esqr—

Endorsed: Dr Franklin June 5. 1779

1. BF alluded to the matter in his letter to Schweighauser of May 15 and discussed it in his May 26 letter to the committee for foreign affairs. Schweighauser eventually did lower his commission to 2 1/2 percent: *Adams Papers,* VIII, 73n.
2. See JA's letter of May 14.
3. Spain's entry into the war as an ally of France.

From Dumas

ALS: American Philosophical Society; AL (draft):[4] Algemeen Rijksarchief

Monsieur Lahaie 5e. Juin *1779.*

Je dînai Mardi passé chez Mrs. De N—— avec 7 Américains, savoir Mrs. Sayre, Sears, Cordes, West,[5] & les Capitaines Cofin, Inkson & Martin. Votre Santé, Monsieur, n'y fut pas oubliée. L'honnête Cofin m'a fort prié de vous présenter ses respects: il m'a dit que vous le connoissiez de longue date, & que c'étoit lui qui fut le porteur, de votre part, des Lettres qui démasquerent les Traîtres Hutchinson &c. aux Américains.[6]

Hier au soir j'eus le plaisir de prêter un apartement chez moi pour un Entretien secret, à G—— F—— & à notre Ami, à la requisition du premier.

Le Committé nommé par les Etats d'Hollde. au sujet des requêtes d'Amst. & de Rotterd——, a décidé, à la pluralité de 10 contre trois, de s'en tenir aux résolutions prises en faveur des Convois illimités, & de presser les convois en conséquence.

Mardi, à mon départ d'Amst——, le bruit y couroit que Sir J. Y——, dans un Meme. présenté,[7] avoit en quelque maniere

4. Containing only the second, third, and fourth paragraphs. While we have called the entries in Dumas' letterbook at the Algemeen Rijksarchief AL (drafts), in the paragraph immediately preceding the complimentary close of the present letter he refers to his retained versions as copies.

5. Perhaps the William West who wrote Samuel Stockton from the Texel on Aug. 28 (Hist. Soc. of Pa.)

6. For BF's role in the affair of the Hutchinson letters see XIX, 399–413. Cushing wrote BF on March 24, 1773, that he had just received the letters (XX, 123); it seems unlikely that Coffin carried them since his ship arrived in Boston on April 12: *Diary of Mr. Thomas Newell,* Mass. Hist. Soc. *Proceedings,* 1st ser. 15 (1876–77), 337.

7. Of which Dumas encloses a copy, which indicates that the memoir is from Sir Joseph Yorke to the States General and is dated May 25. Yorke therein complains that the Dutch papers, particularly the *Gaz. de Leyde,* are full of indecencies and calumnies against Britain. He cites in particular an article (from the May 18 issue of that journal) about a memoir delivered to the British government by Count Musin-Pushkin, the Russian ambassador. The Russian memoir, which announces the intention of the empress to

déclaré la guerre à Amst—— & à Harlem, en les déclarant Alliées de la France, &c. La même chose me fut confirmée à mon passage à Leide. *Parturiebant montes:* à mon arrivée ici, j'ai trouvé le *ridiculus mus,*[8] la déclaration, ci-jointe, de guerre contre mon pauvre ami, à qui pourtant il n'arrivera rien de sinistre: Notre Ami me l'a assuré. Cela fera pourtant un sujet de déliberation pour les provinces, à qui la piece a été communiquée. Sir J. a engagé une très grande Dame à écrire à Cleves contre le Courier du Bas-rhin. On vient de me dire, que les fonds Anglois ont baissé de 5 pour cent subitement que ceux d'Amst—— ont reçu des Lettres de Fce. & peut-être même d'Angle., portant que les Espagnols se seroient emparés de la Jamaique. Cette nouvelle me paroît mériter confirmation avant que je la croie. *Timeo Danaos,* c'est-à-dire les Agioteurs, *& dona ferentes.*[9] Ce qui est sûr, c'est qu'il manque trois paquebots d'Angle. qui n'arrivent pas, & que l'un d'eux, attaqué par des Dunkerquois, a jetté sa malle à la mer.

J'ai eu l'honneur de vous écrire 2 Lettres d'Amsterdam, sans pouvoir en garder copie. Il en sera de-même de celle-ci, pour ne pas manquer la poste.

Je suis avec un très-respectueux dévouement, Monsieur, Votre très-humble & très-obéissant serviteur D

Presque tout ce que les vaisseaux arrivés d'Amérique à Amst—— ont apporté est propriété de Mr. Rob. Morris.

Le nouvelliste de Leide s'étoit déjà rétracté de lui-même, en donnant dans une feuille postérieure la déclaration exacte de la Russie, qui, dans le fonds revient au même que celle au No.

---

initiate naval patrols, is, according to Yorke, misquoted. (The article in question portrays the Russians as threatening Britain with reprisals if they attempt to stop any ship carrying the Russian flag; for an account of the actual memoir see Isabel de Madariaga, *Britain, Russia, and the Armed Neutrality of 1780: Sir James Harris's Mission to St. Petersburg during the American Revolution* [New Haven, 1962], p. 89.) The British minister forwards a declaration by Musin-Pushkin disavowing the news item and demands a retraction. The June 1 issue of the *Gaz. de Leyde* did print a retraction and a revised statement of the memoir.

8. "The mountains were in labor and a ridiculous mouse was born": Horace, *Ars Poetica,* 139.

9. "I fear the Greeks, especially bringing gifts": *Aeneid,* II, 49.

40, à la différence près de quelques termes: différence qui ne vient que de ce qu'il avoit traduit une traduction.[1] Son vrai crime auprès de Sir J——, c'est d'être notre ami, & bon républicain.

Leide a tourné casaque, & est l'une des 2 villes qui ont voté pour la limitation des convois dans le Committé. Horn est l'autre.

Le Vaisseau venu de Philadelphie, Cap. Robinson, a apporté des Depêches de Mr. Gerard, qui ont été acheminées à Mr. l'Ambr. qui m'a dit les avoir reçues par Mr. Fizeaux; les Capitaines m'avoient dit que Clifford & Teisset les avoient reçues. Peut-être que Clifford les a remises a Fizeaux. Ce qui me paroît une bêtise. A sa place, j'aurois mieux aimé en avoir le mérite directement auprès de Mr. l'Ambr.

Passy à S.E. Mr. Franklin &c.

Addressed: To his Excellency B. Franklin Esqr. / Min. Pl. of the united States &c / *Passy.*/.

Notation: Dumas Juin 5. 79

From Schweighauser — ALS: American Philosophical Society

Nantz 5. June 1779

Since the Letter, I had the honor of adressing your Excellency the 22. ultmo. I am without any of your esteemed favor. The purpose of this will serve to inclose the Account of my disbursements for the Alliance

amounting to	79237. 9.	*l.t.*
& the account of those made for the Brig Morris	12177. 7.10	
together	91414.16.10.	*l.t.*

1. Number 40 is the May 18 issue of the *Gaz. de Leyde.* The paper's editor was Jean-Etienne Luzac (XXIII, 461n). For a recent study of his newspaper and its warm support of the American cause see Jeremy D. Popkin, *News and Politics in the Age of Revolution: Jean Luzac's* Gazette de Leyde (Ithaca and London, 1989), pp. 75–9, 146–57, 188–91.

on account of which I have already drawn at 10 days date	10000.	
ded. 1/3 % loss	33.6.8	
		9966.13.4
remains for ballance		81448. 3.6. *l.t.*

Which I have this day taken the liberty to draw on Your Excellencÿ at 20. days date as per the note at foot[2] which I hope will meet your approbation, by the first safe Conveyance I will send you my Vouchers if requisite, as also a recapitulation or State of the Arsenal, that is of the number of Articles Shipt & of those now remaining.[3]

In Sending You the account of what has been paid for the forementioned Continental frigate & brig Morris at Lorient I will add whatever other accounts appear as also the last from Brest which I have not yet received.

I hope the Morris is actually Safe arriv'd at Lorient

With profound Respect I am Your Excellency's Most obedient & most humble Servant J. DL. SCHWEIGHAUSER

To His Excellency Benjamin Franklin Esqr. Minister Plenipotentiarÿ from the United States of America at the Court of France Passÿ

2. On a separate sheet Schweighauser listed twenty-nine separate drafts on BF totaling 81,857 *l.t.,* 9 *s.,* 6 *d.* minus 1/2 percent loss (409 *l.t.,* 6 *s.*) for a net total of 81,448 *l.t.,* 3 *s.,* 6 *d.*

3. For the arsenal and for the brig *Morris,* mentioned in the following paragraph, see BF's letter to Schweighauser of April 5.

From the Duc de Chaulnes[4]

AL: American Philosophical Society

ce Dimanche 6. Juin [1779][5]

M. De Chaulnes a L'honneur de faire tous ses complimens a Monsieur franklin, il na pas encore pu aller lui même s'informer de sa santé, comme il l'auroit desiré, parcequ'aprés une longue absence, les embarras sont nécéssairement considérables au moment du retour. Il aura cet honneur aussitost qu'il le pourra; en attendant il prie Monsieur franklin de lui faire scavoir, le titre, et les moyens d'acquérir un ecrit sur le transport du bois des Pyrrénnés, que M. Vaughan la prié d'acquerir pour lui, et dont il lui a dit que Monsieur franklin avait la connaissance.[6] M. De Chaulnes lui serait trés obligé, s'il pouvait lui faire ce plaisir, lui Mander des nouvelles presentes de sa santé, et a l'honneur de le saluer.[7]

Addressed: A Monsieur / Monsieur Benjamin franklin / Ambassadeur des Etats unis / de L'Amérique / en son hotel ./. *A Passy.*

Notation: De Chaulnes

4. Marie-Joseph d'Albert d'Ailly, duc de Chaulnes, is identified in XXIII, 408n.

5. The only other year during BF's stay in France that June 6 fell on a Sunday was 1784. According to our practice, we publish the letter at its earliest possible date.

6. Vaughan and the Duke may well have met in Paris in late 1776 under BF's auspices: XXIV, 539n. The work in question is probably *Mémoires sur les travaux qui ont rapport à l'exploitation de la mâture dans les Pyrénnées,* published in Paris in 1776, but with a London imprint to bypass the restrictions of the Paris censors. The work is generally attributed to Julien-David Le Roy (1724–1803), a brother of Jean-Baptiste. He was an architect and a member of both the Académie des inscriptions et belles-lettres and the American Philosophical Society: Quérard, *France littéraire,* VII, 215–16, 219. He wrote on ships and the navigation of rivers, and he will correspond with BF in the mid-1780's.

7. In another letter, addressed to BF as "Ministre plenipotentiaire" and dated only "ce dimanche," the Duke wrote that he was forwarding to BF several packets from Vaughan. APS.

From the Vicomte de Sarsfield[8]

AL: American Philosophical Society

6 juin [1779?]

Le Vicomte de sarsfield a l'honneur dEnvoyer a Monsieur francklin La Lettre cy jointe—. Le derangement de sa santé Là Empechè d'Avoir L'honneur de Le Voir depuis longs temps— Il ira Le Chercher a Passy dans la Semaine prochaine— Il A L'honneur de l'assurer de son sincere attachement.

Il Supplie Monsieur francklin d Avoir la bonté de Luy Envoÿer les Nouvelles Gazettes americaines et de Luy faire dire les Nouvelles quil a recües

From Georgiana Shipley

ALS: American Philosophical Society

Bolton Street June 6th 1779

You absolutely spoil me, my dear Doctor Franklin, by your indulgence, for I now expect, with the utmost impatience, the copy from Du Plessis's picture; altho before I received your last letter I was perfectly happy & content with the small head you had the goodness to send me by Mr Digges:[9] the wax model that has been taken of my father is by no means a good representation, however I will endeavor the next opportunity to procure a cast from it.[1] At present I send you a small draw-

8. Jacques-Hyacinthe de Sarsfield had been introduced to BF by his brother, the comte, in XXIII, 231n. We now believe that the present letter, which had originally been catalogued as *c.* 1779, was the sequel to Sarsfield's note of April 16, 1778, and should have been published in vol. 26. But no internal clues, other than the mention of an illness, argue in favor of any one year over another. We therefore publish it here, without further explanation. Another undated note from the vicomte, written on a "dimanche," sends a present of several cheeses. APS.

9. For Digges's delivery of the gift see Georgiana Shipley's letter of May 12, above. On Feb. 3, 1780, she acknowledged receiving a "copy" of Joseph-Siffrède Duplessis' "Grey Coat" pastel portrait of BF, in the form of a miniature mounted on a snuff box. APS. See our annotation of Digges's May 25 letter and Sellers, *Franklin in Portraiture*, pp. 128–9, 135, 267.

1. She may have attempted the cast and found it unsatisfactory, but she did send BF a watercolor copy of Reynolds' portrait of the Bishop; see her letter of May 26, 1780. APS.

ing that you may be able to judge whether I am improv'd since you left England, & I flatter myself that you will accept & value it for my sake; the subject is, Venus giving the cestus to Juno.[2]

Yesterday we dined with Mr Vaughan at Wanstead & were received with the greatest hospitality by that worthy family, our esteem for them you may believe was not lessen'd by the respect with which they mentioned our long-absent friend: in the evening we were shewn many experiments on electricity, & a few quite new to me, Mr Vaughan has by far the largest machine I ever saw, when in proper order it will give a spark 16 inches distant;[3] apro-pos to electricity I am pleased to find by your conjectures on the Aurora Borealis, that the active part you have of late years taken in public affairs, has not prevented your continuing your philosophical studies.

Tuesday next we leave town & retire to Twyford, without any regret on my part, as many of my friends have already quitted the metropolis, & exclusive of their society, I own I prefer the country, on account of the leisure it affords for reading drawing &ca. Doctor Price has promised to spend the month of July with us, he is a most excellent Man, & his friendship for you endears him to all this family.

The parliament still continues sitting & it is uncertain when it will be prorogued, but no material business is expected to come on, as many of the Members are already gone into the Country, the affairs of Ireland are put off till the next sessions, & I question then whether they will obtain any effectual relief; the feeling you express for the calamities of others encourages me to hope that the conduct of one sett of Men will not make

2. Aphrodite (Venus) lent Hera (Juno) her magic girdle to render her irresistible to Zeus and thereby distract him from the Trojan war: *Iliad,* 14:214–15. In a letter probably written to Georgiana in March, 1781, of which only a fragment is extant, BF lamented that she had not given to Juno, Venus, and Cupid the faces of her sisters Anna-Maria, Emily (Amelia), and Betsy. Library of Congress.

3. The electrical machine was designed by Joseph Priestley and built by Edward Nairne: Robert E. Schofield, ed., *A Scientific Autobiography of Joseph Priestley (1733–1804)* (Cambridge, Mass., and London, 1966), p. 53. See also XX, 433–4n.

you judge too severely of a nation, where you have spent many happy years in tranquility, & where your character continues to be admired & respected by numbers of the inhabitants; besides a general peace is a blessing so much to be wished-for by all parties, that I know the benevolence of your disposition will incline you, to exert every method of promoting it.

The hurry of business occasioned by our approaching departure, obliges me to release you from this scrawl, & only permits me time to assure you once more, of the continued friendship & esteem of this family. I am dear Dr. Franklin yr affecate & obliged G: SHIPLEY

To Fizeaux, Grand & Cie.

Copy: Library of Congress

Gentlemen Passy June 7 1779.

I received the honour of yours of the 31 past[4] and thank you for the News it contained, tho' not yet confirmed.

I know nothing of that Mr. Miller But if he appears to you to be an honest Man, I consent to your supplying him to the value of ten Guineas which I will repay. Please to take three Notes for the sum, that I may send them over by different Conveyances. It is impossible for me to supply every Bodys Wants equal to their Expectations.

I have the honour to be &c.

Mrs. fizeaux Grand & Co

From Rocquette, Elsevier & Rocquette

ALS: American Philosophical Society

Sir! Rotterdam 7 June 1779.

We observe with pleasure by your much esteemed favour of the 31st. of past month, the reception of the pacquet we sent you the forwarding of it, deserved no thanks, we shall allwaÿs

4. Not found.

be happy in finding opportunity to be usefull to you, and renew you to that End our most devoted Services.[5]

According to your permission we enclose you Two bills Issued by the States of America, they are Each of 1000 dollars and dated the 8th. of february 1779. pble. at same day of the year 1782. with the Intrest of 6 per Cent and Number 2348 & 2349. We'll be oblidg'd to you to return us Same, with your Sentiments on the place where this paper is negotiable at the most advantageous footing; & what it's Currencey is, as also if the Intrest is payable annually, or that it is onley payd once at maturity, & if it is payd in Europe, or in America.

We have the honour to be most Respectfullÿ Sir! Your most obedient & very Húmble Servants

J. ROCQÚETTE, T. A:
ELSEVIER, & BROTHERS ROCQÚETTE

The Honble. B: Franklin Esqr: Minister Plenipotentiary of the united States of America, at Passÿ

Addressed: To / the honble: B. Franklin Esqr. / Minister Plenipotentiary of the / of the united States of America / at / Passy near / Paris

Notation: J. Rocquettes: A Elsevier et Brothers Rocquettes, Amsterdam 7e june 1779.

From John Ross

AL: American Philosophical Society

Paris 7th June 1779 Hotel de York

Mr. Ross Respects wait on his Excelly. the Minister plenipoty of the United American States—and send some American papers received today via Holland, by a Vessel arrived from Philada.

Mr: Ross has got several letters from America, but none later then 24 March, and not a single Sylable of News from any of his friends—[6]

5. BF's of the 31st is missing. Theirs, accompanying the packet, is dated May 24, above.

6. Ross was apparently more conscientious in forwarding items than was BF. Among BF's papers at the APS is an April 29 letter addressed to him for

From Stephen Sayre

ALS: American Philosophical Society

Sir Amsterdam 7th June 1779—

I wrote your excellency a few Lines upon my arrival here.[7] I requested the great favr of some Letters that might aid me when I arrived in Dominica: for unless I am encouraged from your Excellency to stay longer in Europe, my resolution is to get into America as soon as Opportunity offers, after I have secured some little property for myself in Dominica. [Ever]y difficulty attends procuring such Letters. I must beg you will state it in your answer, and be kind enough to give me a Letter yourself to the Governor of Martinico, Guadaloupe or Dominica. Perhaps no Person[8] in France, let his Station be ever so favourable, can give me a better than your Excellence— I shall be detain'd here some two or three weeks, & hope for the favour of an Answer &c &c—

I am somewhat at a loss to guess the reason why your Excely is totally silent as to that part of my former Letter respecting a new constructed Ship, so singularly superior. I suppose you can give no credit to so extraordinary a matter. I have a Model now with me, for explanation, so far as regards the better sailing, & better safety of a Ship in a Sea or Lee-shore &c &c. and the Captains who are now present from America, Cordice & Coffin,[9] whom I have consulted on her points of novelty, stand decidedly convinced she has infinite, & hetherto inconceivable advantages over any Ship that ever was built: & they are willing to attest [*torn:* their?] opinion, tho' previous to seeing her they believed no improvement could be made beyond an English Ship. I shall keep out of sight the principle on which I would construct a Ship for fighting untill I have Opportunity to explain myself to Congress. I

forwarding to Ross. Its author, a Mr. Carmichael, offered to sell masts, cables, sails, and rigging for a ship Ross had under construction. This Carmichael is probably the dealer in provisions described in Butterfield, *John Adams Diary,* II, 359–60.

7. He wrote on March 21.

8. He first wrote "man".

9. Joseph Cordis and Alexander Coffin; see Dumas' letter of May 27 and Coffin's of June 28.

am clear in the Opinion, & am confirm'd by daily experiments, that I can contrive a Ship so much superior to any now in use, as to be morally sure of success over every thing on the Seas—nothing can take her but another after the same form— I could render the whole British Navy totally useless with a very few, not larger than Frigates, on my construction—they may also be built of the softest pine, at a very small expence: for half the labour only is necessary.

I have red. Letters by the last post from London, which request my Interest with your Excellence, to know how far, or in what manner, you would now give aid to Ireland. It is thought that in case a War with Spain takes place, a Fleet might with safety be sent on the Coast of Ireland: but that it will be necessary that an American should come over in it with powers as to the Fleet, & have proper Instructions as to his conduct with the people. In short, the aid must be American, to avoid prejudices &c &c— I am requested to take that Commission if thought proper— Would my coming to Passy be of any use?— I am desired to tell your Excellency that a Doctor Moore gives Lord North constant information what is going forward in Paris—he was a Clergeman—I know him to be a dirty fellow.[1]

I am with great Respect Your Excellency's most Humle Servt.

STEPHEN SAYRE

Addressed: A Son Excellence / Benj: Franklin / Ministire Plenipotentiere / de Etats Unie de Amerique / Paris—

Notation: Sayce Stephen 7 June 1779.

From William Bingham

ALS: American Philosophical Society

Dear sir, St Pierre Mque June 8th 1779

I flatter myself that you will excuse the Liberty I take in recommending to your Notice & Protection during his Stay at

1. Probably Dr. John Moore (1729–1802), who published in 1779 *A View of Society and Manners in France, Switzerland, and Germany* (2 vols.) telling of his experiences accompanying the young Duke of Hamilton on a five-year "grand tour" of Europe: *DNB.* Moore, although the son of a clergyman, was not one himself.

Paris the Bearer Richard Harrison Esqr—a Gentleman who was employed in this Place in the public Character of Agent for the States of Virginia & Maryland & who has rendered his Country some essential services by his Exertions in that Line—[2] After discharging the Duties of his Station with honor to himself & Satisfaction to his Constituents, he returned to his native Country, & has now left it with an Intention of entering into a commercial Establishment at Cadiz or some other Port of Europe—You cannot procure more full & candid Information of the Situation of Affairs in America than what the Gentleman can furnish you with—

I shall make no Apology for introducing him to your Acquaintance, as I am sensible that your own Feelings must be gratified by conferring your Favor on Men of Mr Harrison's Merit, so truly deserving of them—

I have the honor to be with unfeigned Respect Your Excellency's most obedient & very humble Servant

WM BINGHAM

Notation: Bingham June 8. 1779.

From Félix António Castrioto[3]

ALS: American Philosophical Society

Sir Lisbon 8 of Jun 1779.

Having wrote to you several times, giving information of what was passed respecting the Comission I was charged with: and not recieving the honnour of any answer, it would perhapes be proper to desist from the atempt to obtain it, and spare me self the trouble of importuning you any more. But it

2. As a member of the committee of secret correspondence BF had corresponded several years before with Richard Harrison, the Baltimore merchant who represented Maryland and Virginia in Martinique: XXII, 447–9. While there he and Bingham were in partnership in various privateering ventures: Robert C. Alberts, *The Golden Voyage: the Life and Times of William Bingham 1752–1804* (Boston, 1969), p. 50.

3. A former editor of the *Gazetas de Lisboa,* who had carried to the Portuguese court a memorial from the American commissioners: XXIV, 289–90n. This is his last extant letter to BF.

is impossible for me to belive that, if my lettres was come to your hands, you could have any reason to refuse me the satisfaction at least of knowing that you had recieved them: and in fact who could expect that a man who was the first foriner that undertook in Public the defence of your Peoples rights, exposing the justice of their cause in three different pamphlets, which, I can without presumption assert, made a deep impression in many peoples minds:[4] a man who offered himself to negotiate in his country the interesses of your Nation, and hazarded his own by the excess of his zeel in acquiting himself of this comission, when he gives acount of the effects of his endeavours, you should juge him not deserving your answer? To think, that the success of my efforts having not answer'd your expectation made me not worthy of your attention, should be inconsistent with the opinion I intertain of your principles, and I can not help to belive that a person who strives to be useful to your People must be estimable to you, independent of the success of his ardour. So persuaded, I am inclinable to supose that my letters, tho' adressed as you ordered, have been misled: and now, Sir, that your public caracter renders unnecessaire any precautions, I take the liberty to felicitate you upon the progresses of the American prosperity, and upon the justice done to your merit by your Governement.

If my suposition, about the letters I wrote to you, is right, you must be otherwise informed that my representations of your pretentions were not at first successeful, and even it was found improper that I should be so eager in promoting them; but I found afterwards our Ministers better disposed to treat this matter, and I was realy achemed of not finding meself authorised with a letter from you to proceede in the negotiation: Circonstances becoming more favourable my zeel could have been more effectual: at least I am sure nobody could with more efficacity manage your interesses, as nobody ever showed more afection for your new Republic, without any

4. For Castrioto's previous letters from Portugal see XXV, 232–3, and XXVI, 136–7, 572; we have found no reply to any of them. For what we know about his pamphlets see XXIV, 553n.

personal interest, or other inducement, then the attachement to the rights of human kind, of which I look upon the Americans as the Defenders. It is however natural I should aspire to see meself estim'd by those which I estime so much: and to wish that the effects of my sentiments should excite alike ones in my favour. You promised me to send to the Congress some of my pamphlets, and to enform them of my offers to serve their Cause; how could the opinion of their justice be so well founded, if it would fail in this particular instance? How could their known gratitude disregard so candide a well wisher? The only mark of theirs and your regard I could desire was to give me an oportunity of imploying meself in their sirvice: I was flatered with the notion of having found that; but, deprived of an answer, my satisfaction soon vanished. The same sentiments, not withstanding, still excite me, and they are sincer, so is the particular estime and respect with which I am Sir Your most humble and affectionate servant

FELIX ANTONY CASTRIOTO.

P.S. If I can at last merit your answer my name is sufficient for adress.

Notation: Castrioto Felix Antoni 8. Juin 1779.—

From Dumas

ALS: American Philosophical Society; AL (draft): Algemeen Rijksarchief

Monsieur La Haie 8e. Juin 1779

Il y a une erreur de précipitation dans ma derniere. Ce n'est pas aux Provinces, c'est à l'Assemblée d'Hollande que l. h. pes. ont envoyé le Meme. de Sir J. Y.[5] Il a eu le sort mérité, c'est-à-dire, de ne pas produire le mauvais effet qu'on en attendoit. Mr. le Gd. Pensione. lui-même a justifié le Gazettier, en produisant la sa feuille 44, où la Déclaration Russe se trouve rec-

5. Sir Joseph Yorke's memorial, a copy of which Dumas had enclosed with his letter of June 5.

tifiée.[6] L'Assemblée a acquiescé à cette justification, & a seulement chargé la ville de Leide, d'exhorter le Gazettier à prendre garde le plus qu'il pourra, de ne pas insérer des choses qui puissent offenser des Puissances étrangeres.

Le papier ci-joint[7] vous donnera, Monsieur, une idée de ce qui se passe à l'Assemblée provinciale ici. Vous voyez que ce n'est plus Amsterdam (who sits down contented with the french Interdict) mais le reste de la Hollande, notamment Rotterdam & Dort, qui se trouvent dans la détresse, & aux prises avec la Cour & son parti.

Je reçois dans ce moment l'honorée vôtre du 4. Soyez sûr, Monsieur, que vous ne serez commis avec personne. Mr. De N—— même ne saura pas que vous m'avez écrit sur cette matiere. Je me contenterai de le précautionner de mon chef, plus décisivement que je n'ai osé le faire d'abord. Ce que vous m'apprenez confirme ce que j'ai tiré successivement de la bouche de Mrs. Stockton & Sears.

I have the most gratefull sense of your very obliging intentions respecting my person when at Paris. I shall be all obedience to your pleasure of disposing of it, after you will have heard from me the reason of my mentioning to have a little room at or in the nighbourhood of your good bosom friend.[8]

Les fonds Anglois sont & restent bas. Notre Ami croit plus que jamais que l'Espagne va se déclarer; G—— F—— aussi.

Je suis avec grand respect, Monsieur Votre très-humble & très obéissant serviteur D

Une ancienne connoissance Tory m'a dit il y a quelque temps: "On vous pardonnne vos connexions Am——; mais non celles avec certain hôtel & certaine ville."

Passy à Son Exc. Mr. Franklin &c.

Addressed: à Son Excellence / Monsieur Franklin, Esqr. / M. P. Des E. U. &c. &c / Passy./.

6. "Feuille" 44 was the June 1 issue of the *Gaz. de Leyde;* see Dumas' June 5 letter.

7. Discussed in our note, below.

8. Bancroft; see Dumas' letter of May 27.

8e. Juin *1779*

Hier Mr. G—— F—— me fit chercher, & me remit un papier écrit de sa main, contenant ce qui suit, pour servir de matiere à un entretien qu'il me pria d'avoir avec notre ami.[9]

Notations: Dumas 8. Juin 1779. / Dumas 8 Juin 1779

From Stephen Hills and Joseph Adams[1]

ALS:[2] University of Pennsylvania Library

Sir Ship of war alliance Loriant June 8th 1779

After Receiving your kinness Every officer on Bord the Ship was Content and was Determined to stay on Bord to fulfill what we wrote to your honnor[3] Butt our hopes of this kind soone vanished for Capt Landis his mettod of Govrning his Ship so Contry to all Nations In the world that it is impossable for humane natur to Live with him I would Inform your honnor of our treetment Butt it would tier your pashants and Rather Impose on your Goodness But Refer to the Honble John adams & John Poul Jones Eqrs for they have heard all the treetment and Capt Jones has tried all that Lays In his power to Reckensile matters which he has ackted The Gentlemans part Butt to no purpose for sir we have put up with Ill Treetment as Long as humane nater Can possible Bare for the

9. Dumas here provides a copy of a letter written by Ambassador La Vauguyon to serve as a basis for a dialogue with the Pensionary of Amsterdam, van Berckel. It warned that the pro-British party in the States of Holland would use delaying tactics and demanded that the States force the stadholder to issue the necessary orders to implement convoying. This is an example of the unremitting pressure applied by the French: Fauchille, *Diplomatie française,* p. 141. Dumas concluded by giving van Berckel's reassurance that the States certainly would give France satisfaction before separating.

1. Hills and Adams were first lieutenant and second mate of the *Alliance:* XXVIII, 478n. Jones warned BF on May 14, above, that Hills was going to leave the ship, and on June 18, below, wrote that the two officers had left.

2. In the hand of Joseph Adams.

3. The March 2 letter from the *Alliance*'s officers, above, promised that they would give every service in their power.

sake of our Cuntry and The Cause in which we are in Gaged But alass wee are obliged to use meanes to Leave the ship sir I suposse you will hear of this By another hand But Blame us not to seeke for That Sweet Thing Cald Liberty from Tyrany which we have so Long Contested for But Good sir we air willing to answer for our Conduct when we arive In amerca we apealle to heaven and Every officer on Bord for our justification Tho we are sorry from our hearts that things of this natur has arived to This pitch tho not one officer on Bord is satisfied with Their Treetment from PL sir we Remain your honnors most obedent most humble servants and yours to serve

STEPHEN HILLS
JOSEPH ADAMS

Addressed: His Excel. / Benja. Frankling Esqr / Plenepotentiary for The / united States of America / Cort of Versails / Parris

Notation: Officers of the Alliance June 8. 1779

From Jeremiah Peirce[4]

ALS: American Philosophical Society

Sir Tenterden Jun 8thd 1779

I Beg Lef to eyequant your honnour with my Setuation at Present I am a french Presnour on Porrole at Tenterden I was first Leutannant of the Six Gun Cutter She was Called the alla Croushua from facomp Commanded by Capt Charles fequet[5] Sir I will Inform your honnour how I Com on Bord of a french Cutter as I am an amarican and a Natef of the State of Rhodisland in and When I am at hom East Greenwich is my Dweling Place the twenty Six of may 1778 I Saelled from Bos-

4. Probably the son of Jeremiah and Margaret Peirce of East Greenwich, R.I., born in 1751, and married to Mary Gorton in 1773. He died in passage from Jamaica to Charleston, S.C., in 1799. James N. Arnold, *Vital Records of Rhode Island . . .* (21 vols., Providence, R.I., 1891–1912) I, part I, p. 90; part 2, pp. 139, 140.

5. Along with this letter came a certificate in French of the same date from Capt. Charles Fiquet stating that Peirce had been his first lieutenant on *La Racrocheuse* of Fécamp, taken Oct. 1, 1778, and that he had been released on his parole in Tenterden in Kent. APS.

ton In the Brigenteene Called the Angelaca of Sixteen Guns Commanded By Capt William Dennes I was a Prise Marster on Bord the Brigg the twenty Six of may we Saelled on a Cruse from Boston and we were only five Days on a Crouse befoure we Were taken by a twenty Eaight Gun freget Called the Andromeda from amarica Bound to England With Generel howe on Bord tha Set fire to the Brigg and Destroyed hir and Everething Belonging Except the men the Second of July we a Rived at Porth Smith the Six we were Sent to forten Prison[6] the twenty first of July & if Im not mistake my Capt and the Capt of the alford fregget and Eaight men more maid there Escape out of forten Prison and all Got Clear[7] the Six of September I and maney others made our Escape By Cuting a hole threw the flower and Diging under Ground there was five of ous that went to Gether we Stered about twenty miles Back in the Contry and then Stered to the East word til we Got about half ways to Dover then we Steared to Southword for the See Side there we traveld Severel Nights Back word and for words on the Be(?) See Side bef we Cold find a bote but at Last we found one Small Roe Bote and we Set of we were forty four hours before we Got to france we were fourteen Days from Prison before we Got to france I only Eat five meles of vittels In that time I met with a misforten to Lose my Shoes Giting out of the Prson when we a rived at france we ware taken up for Spice as thare was a English Cutter Site that moing. But Soon Cleard we a medetly Rote to your honnour and the next morning we Set out to travel we Got to fecomp that Day But It fetegue me So that i was not abel to Go no feuther and my Compney Left me and ther I agreed to Go one months Cruse In the french Cutter and now I am Prisonour agin It is very Bad for a Prisnour to have no money and I have none only what is a Louded to Prisnours tho have no money

6. Peirce is listed in Kaminkow, *Mariners,* as having been committed to Forton on July 7, 1778. He is cited there under "John," and confused with the crewmember of the *Bonhomme Richard* of that name. For other prisoners' accounts of the capture of the *Angelica* see XXVII, 132, and *Adams Papers,* VI, 293–4.

7. Elisha Hinman, captain of the *Alfred,* had bribed the Forton guards and walked out: XXVII, 276n.

I have a Good frind Mr Viney[8] I have a wife In East Greenwich and I have Ben a Long time from hom and as I have no frind In france I omble Beg the favour of your honnours to Get my Exchange I would taket It very kind If your honnour would take the troubel to Rite me a few Line wethe I Can be Exchanged or no for my Suteation at Present makes me very un happey and So No more But I Remain your honbel Servent JEREMIAH PEIRCE

To the honnourabel Doctor Franklen[9]

Addressed: To / His Excellency / Dr Benjn: Franklin / Passy

Notation: Deirce Jeremiah 8d. June 1779—

From John Torris ALS: American Philosophical Society

Sir Dunkerque 8th. June 1779.

I have had the Honnor of Informing your Excellency the 28th. of last month, that Capt. Stephen Merchant of the Black Prince Cutter Privateer, was to sail in a few days, and in consequence of the Tenor of his Commission and Instructions, he had an Intention to Cruise on the Packet from Dover to Calais & from thence to Dover.

I Persuaded him to differ sailing untill you had favor'd me, or him, with an Answer to my Said Letter, the contents of which I Communicated to him; Mr. Merchant granted Same with great relectuancy, but finding your Excellency had not thought Proper to answer yet, He does Interpret your Silence as a Clear approbation to Take these Packets, & will no longer delay Sailing when the wind & weather Permit,[1] & he is fully

8. Thomas Viny (whose undated letter BF answered on May 4) appended the following message underneath Peirce's signature: "I fully Credit the Narrative of honest Jerh. Peirce whose cause and Conduct are worthy Your attention and as I can do it heartily, at his Request, recommend him affectionately to my Hond. & dear friend— The Cordial of May 4th does *us* much Good thanks everlasting from Your unworthy but affece. TV."

9. Peirce had made his way to Passy by March 22, 1780, when BF gave him 4 *louis d'or,* or 96 *l.t.* His receipt is at the APS; the amount is also listed in the Alphabetical List of Escaped Prisoners.

1. He sailed four days later; see Marchant's letter of June 23.

persuaded your Excellency's Justice wou'd not Leave him in any dilemma, & that your silence shows you'll grant him all assistance to make these Prises be Condamned to his Proffits &ca— If Mr. Merchant shou'd Persist & Succeed in his attempt, I shall do myself the honnour to Inform your Excellency of it Immediatly, as well with every Particular whatsoever that might occur relative to this armement made under the Protection of Congress.

I wait for your Excellency's Commands & am with great Respect Sir Your obedient most Hble Servant J. TORRIS

Addressed: A Son Excellence / Son Excellence Monsieur Benjn. / Franklin Ecuier Ministre / Plenipotentiaire des Etats Unis / de L'amerique Septentrionalle a la / Cour de france A Passy / par Paris

Notation: J. Torris Dunkerque 8e. june 1779.

From Vergennes

L (draft):[2] Archives du Ministère des affaires étrangères; copy: Library of Congress

A Versailles le 8. Juin 1779.

J'ai eu l'honneur, M, de vous prévenir, le 13. 7bre. d.,[3] que M. de Sartine enverroit aux administrateurs de la guadeloupe l'ordre de faciliter au Sr. Stewenson les recouvrements qu'il avoit à faire dans cette ile. Vous verrez par la letre du 4. juin que ce Ministre vient de mécrire sur cet objet que le debiteur du Sr. Stewenson a versé dans la caisse du Roi une somme de 9569 *l.t.* argent des iles, et que cette somme sera remboursée à paris por le Trésorier de la marine;[4] il n'est question que de Savoir à qui elle doit être remise; des que vous maurez ré-

2. In the hand of Gérard de Rayneval.

3. Expanded in the copy to "dernier"; Vergennes' earlier letter is printed in XXVII, 396–7.

4. Vergennes enclosed a copy of Sartine's letter (Library of Congress), which identified William Stevenson's debtor as a Sieur Testos.

pondu à cet égard, M. de Sartine donnera les ordres nécessaires pour que le payement n'éprouve aucun retard./.

M. franklin

From Jonathan Williams, Jr.

ALS: American Philosophical Society

Dear & Hond Sir L'orient June 8. 1779

I have recvd your Favour of the 1st Instant & shall do all I can for Mr Dubourg.—

I have sent to Nantes for the amt of what I owe the Commrs & expect next Post to receive it when I shall settle with Mr Gourlade as you propose.

I shall send Mr Bache the Things you order by the Chr de Luzerne—[5]

The 15 Louis to Mr Richards are to your Credit.—[6]

I beg your private perusal of the Enclosed & your excuse for this hasty Scrawl.

I am ever your dutifull & affectionate Kinsman

JONA WILLIAMS J

The Hon. Doctor Franklin.

Addressed: a monsieur / Monsieur Franklin / Ministre plenipotentiaire des / Etats Unis / en son Hotel / a Passy prés Paris.

Notation: Williams Jona. June 8. 1779.

5. These appear to be items which BF had requested for his daughter Sally. JW informed her, on June 13, that he was placing the articles on the *Three Friends,* along with the baggage of La Luzerne (Yale University Library). See also his letter of June 29.

6. For Richards, an employee and friend of JW, see JW's letter of April 25.

From Dumas

ALS: American Philosophical Society; AL (draft): Algemeen Rijksarchief

Monsieur, Lah. 9e. Juin *1779* au soir.

En vous confirmant mes Lettres des 5 & 8 du court., je me hâte de vous rendre compte d'un entretien que je viens d'avoir avec N. A.[7]

Mrs. du College de l'Amte. d'Amst. sont venus ce soir chez Mrs. les Dep. de la Ville d'Amst., leur témoigner l'extrême embarras où ils se trouvent, quant au préavis que l'Amté. d'Hollde. doit donner après demain vendredi sur l'affaire des Convois. *Nous leur avons répondu,* dit N. A., *des choses* TRÈS-SENSIBLES; & notamment ceci, par où ils ont fini: *Si vous voulez continuer de vous laisser conduire par V. D. H.*[8] (le Sece. de l'Amté. de Rott——, l'ame damnée du parti Angl., & un maître f——be[9]) *vous en êtes les maîtres; pour nous, comptez que nous tiendrons ferme, & que nous saurons parler sur le ton qu'il faut.*

Il est arrivé à Amst., par les dernieres Lettres d'Angle. un *Avis secret,* portant qu'en Irlande, si l'on vouloit y entreprendre quelque chose, & si l'Am—— offroit sa protection aux Irlandois, ceux-ci l'accepteroient; & qu'on a écrit en ce sens, de leur part, à Son Exc. Mr. Franklin.—[1] Jugez, Monsieur, si nous sommes envieux, N. A. & moi, de savoir au juste ce qui en est. Nous prévoyons cependant que, si l'avis est fondé, l'importance & la nécessité du secret vous fera garder le silence.

N. A. est dans l'idée que la Déclaration de l'Espe. est faite ou se fera dans 6 ou 7 jours.[2]

Un cinquieme navire, l'Indépendance, Cap. Brown de Vir-

7. "Notre ami," viz., van Berckel.

8. Jacob van der Heim, secretary of the Admiralty of the Meuse (also called the Admiralty of Rotterdam); see Dumas' March 1 letter.

9. "Fourbe," *i.e.,* cheat or swindler.

1. See BF's letter to Bancroft of May 31.

2. Not a bad prediction; on June 16 the marqués de Almodóvar, the Spanish ambassador, delivered to the British government a list of Spanish grievances and on the 18th he left the country: Francis Piggott and G. W. T. Omond, eds., *Documentary History of the Armed Neutralities, 1780 and 1800* . . . (London, 1919), pp. 119–21; Dull, *French Navy,* p. 150.

ginie,[3] est entré le 7e. au Texel, consigné à Mrs. J. De Neufville & fils. Il leur porte nouvelle de deux autres, dont l'un est pris, & l'autre, chassé par 4 Corsaires, a échoué: cependant les appareils de ce navire vendus le paieront.

Les Anglomanes ont commencé à lâcher des feuilles, qui tendent à irriter la populace contre la France. Je suis avec un très grand respect, Monsieur Votre très humble & très obéissant serviteur D

Passy à S. E. Mr. Franklin

Addressed: To His Excellency / B. Franklin Esqr. / Min. Plen. of the United States / &c. / at *Passy.*/.

Notation: Dumas 9. Juin 1779.

From John Jay

Two LS: American Philosophical Society, Historical Society of Pennsylvania

Sir, In Congress Philadelphia June 9. 1779.

I enclose you an act of Congress of the 8th. of this Instant June, directing that Bills should be drawn upon you to the amount of three hundred and sixty thousand Livres Tournois for the purpose of importing Military Stores.[4] I have accordingly drawn four setts, payable to the Honble: Henry Laurens, Francis Lewis, James Searle, & John Fell the Commercial Committee of Congress[5] or the order of either of them vizt.

3. Although sailing from Virginia the ship was Boston-owned and was commanded by Francis Brown from New Haven and Beverly: Sears to BF, below, June 10; Allen, *Mass. Privateers,* p. 187; Claghorn, *Naval Officers,* p. 36.

4. The enclosure is missing, although an extract from the minutes giving the report of the committee on the treasury from June 10 accompanies each LS. For the act of June 8 see *JCC,* XIV, 707–8. BF received with this letter an invoice of supplies desired; see his response of Sept. 30, printed in Wharton, *Diplomatic Correspondence,* III, 354.

5. Lewis had served with BF on the secret committee of Congress: XXII, 204n; XXVI, 552–3n. James Searle (1733–97) of Pennsylvania and John Fell (1721–98) of New Jersey were first elected to Congress in November, 1778. *DAB.* Searle began a private correspondence with BF in September, 1780, when he arrived in France.

one sett, for One hundred and fifty thousand, one, for one hundred thousand, one for seventy thousand, and one for forty thousand Livres tournois. Our Disappointment in not receiving the Supplies which we expected from France has render'd this measure indispensably necessary, and we flatter ourselves that you will be able to make such Representations to the Court of France on this subject, as to induce them chearfully to put it in your power to honor these drafts.

I have further to add that through the assistance of Monsr. Gerard, the Minister Plenipotentiary of France at this Court, there is some prospect that the Military stores of which we stand in need, may be obtain'd from the Royal Magazines in the French West Indies.[6] In that case, the Bills will not be presented for payment.

I have the Honor to be with great Respect & Esteem Sir Your most obedient Servant JOHN Jay President

To The Honble: Benja. Franklin Minister Plenipotentiary for the United States at the Court of France.

Addressed: The Honnble. Benjamin Franklin Esquire / Minister Plenipotentiary for the United States of / America at the Court of France.

From Stephen Sayre

ALS: American Philosophical Society

Sir Amsterdam 9th June 1779—

I have more Letters from some Gentlemen in London pressing the affairs relating to the present State of Ireland mentioned in my last.[7] They assure me that nothing more is required than a small Fleet, under a proper person Commissioned from America. I therefore must beg your Excellency's immediate Reply to the following questions.

Do you think you can, consistently, impower any person, who you supposed might be worthy, to conduct the Enterprize?

6. Gérard made enquiries particularly about powder and lead but they could not be spared: Smith, *Letters,* XIII, 42n.

7. Above, June 7.

Do you think France could furnish a proper fleet for such an undertaking?

Could you furnish the person so entrusted with blank Commissions, to be given to proper leaders of the Revolt, upon landing there? Those Coms. would be of the last importance: because any delay such as must be the case, if any legal arrangements are to be first settled, would perhaps prove fatal: whereas order, subordination, command, &c would directly take place under such Commissions—nor would the consequences be the same under our Commissions in case of failure, as we should protect such persons from capital punishment. My Situation & conduct has been such in former times, that I flatter myself your Excellency will not think me an improper person for this business. If however you differ with me in Idea, as to this point, I shall no longer support the correspondence, because I am unequal to the whole matter, if unequal to the execution; & those Gentlemen run great risques too serious for an ineffectual purpose— They suppose the fleet will be supported by a proper force by land, long before any ships could arrive from England to oppose them—Should such support be inadequate they might depart in due time. There are not more than 2000 effective men now in the Island, while they have near 12000 excellent Militia,[8] nor is it supposed that the Militia of England would move, if only an offer of freedom stood in the question.

If there are any number of American navy officers now in France, they would do great Service, as the language from those in command should be as universally English as possible—

Mr Vander Capel,[9] comes here this day, to sound the City with regard to America. There is a strong party for us, who are not ashamed to avow it. Can your Excellency see the propriety of my Services in any manner, while I remain here? Am I doom'd to receive no countinance from the Country to which I sacrifise all private Consideration? Others are sup-

8. See the letter from "Philantropos" of April 5.

9. Joan Derk van der Capellen tot den Pol; see BF's June 2 letter to Trumbull.

ported, I know not how, after accusations that, if true, ought to hang them. Yesterday arrived another Vessell from Virginia this makes five now lying here—

Let me, with the most sincere respect, request an Answer immediately—

I am most devotedly your Excellency very obedient humble Servant STEPHEN SAYRE

I wish my Letter may come under cover to Monsr de Neufville here— Hope is too much on the side of England[1]

Addressed: Son Excellence / Benj: Franklin / Ministere Plenepotentiere / de Etats Unis de Amerique / Paris

Notation: Stephen Sayre 9. Juin 1779.

From Jean de Neufville & fils

ALS: American Philosophical Society

High Honourable Sir! [before June 10, 1779?][2]

We should have been extreemly happy, if Y: E: had granted us already the papers relating the Loan, to be in the terms we had requésted, in case we could there on succeed to engage oúr Subscribers; for we should have gone already a great way and do no doúbt as we had the honoúr to observe; we should have offerd Y E a Sufficient summ to go on upon before there could be any answer from Congress.

Some of oúr frinds had intented long ago, to try the American búsiness under Ours Coloúrs; we should be again obliged to yoúr Exclly, in case there would be any pasports, or any other formalities wanted, that we might be informed there aboút, as Oúr Zeal for the American intrest will make ús embrace every opportúnity to give these of the strongest proves; as we are in particular with all respectfúll Regard High Honourable Sir Your Excellencys Most obedient devoted servants

JOHN DE NEUFVILLE & SON

1. Dumas said much the same thing about the Amsterdam bankers: XXVII, 129–30.

2. The only clue to a date is the reference to "papers," which may be those discussed by the firm on June 10, below.

From Jonathan Loring Austin

ALS and copy:[3] American Philosophical Society

Sir, Boston 10th June 1779

I cannot omit the present favorable Opportunity by Capt Thompson, who proposes going himself to Paris,[4] to return your Excellency my most sincere Thanks, for the many Civilities you were pleased to honor me with while in France— The important News I had the Honor of carrying to Passy,[5] which operated so favorably for our Country, the Disposition of all Ranks of People, their Attachment to our Cause, added to the Confidence reposed in me by the Commissioners, in employing me so near their Persons, render'd my Stay in France very agreeable. Had not some particular Business calld me to Holland, from whence I expected to get to my native Country in eight or ten Weeks, I should have thought myself happy to have continued for some time in the same Situation—

Soon after my Arrival at Amsterdam, finding I should be obliged to come to this Continent by the way of St Eustatia, what you was pleased to mention to me at Passy immediately occur'd "that I should find this Rout very tedious & disagreeable," my Inclination was to return once more to France, & enter upon the same Employment agreeable to Mr Adams's Invitation, but the Trouble & Expence of getting myself & Baggage back discouraged me; I had Reason however, after embarking to wish these Discouragements had not prevented it, a Detention of 50 days in the Texel, followed with a passage of 45 brought it to the 20th Feby before I landed at St Eustatia, the middle of April I got to Virginia & it was the 29th Ulto. when I arrived in this Town—

The Letters you were pleased to honor me with for your Friends (as I expected to make some Stay at 'Statia) I for-

3. The copy is included with his letter of July 12 (APS).

4. Capt. James Thompson reported on July 22 his arrival at Brest with letters from Boston. APS. As the captain of the *Rising States* he appears frequently in vols. 23 and 24; he now commanded the schooner *Lee:* Claghorn, *Naval Officers,* p. 309.

5. The news of Burgoyne's surrender at Saratoga: XXV, lx, 99, 102–3.

warded to the Continent by a fast sailing Vessel enclosing them to the president of Congress, this Vessel was unfortunately taken or lost as she has not been heard of—[6]

For public News I beg Leave to refer your Excellency to the Papers I have the Honor to forward to Mr. Adams by this Opportunity.[7] The Depreciation of our Currency may possibly make our Enemies exult that its Credit will soon be ruined, but if they consider our Situation & the Difficulties we struggled with when this Contest commenc'd, Difficulties infinitely more formidable than any that have since occur'd, it will damp their Joy— The Spirit which first animated our Countrymen in this glorious Opposition, still exists, & as our Armies are respectable, & we shall never I hope be destitute of a sufficient Force to exclude from this Continent, every cruel hostile Invader;— in this America appears unanimous—

I am so well pleased with the Climate of France, & have so great an Inclination to make myself Master of the Language, that I should be enduced to take another Voyage, provided I could meet with proper Encouragement to under take it— should your Excellency think my small Abilities would be in any Respects serviceable to my Country in some vacant Employment, your Remembrance of me would be thankfully noticed, & any Intimations to Congress gratefully acknowledged—[8] With my kindest regards to Mr Franklin (with whom I should be glad to correspond in French)— I am with all Respect Your Excellency's most Obedient & very humble Servant

Jon Loring Austin

My Father begs leave to present you his best compliments.[9]

His Excellency Dr. Franklin

Notation: J. L. Austin June 10. 79

6. On Sept. 19, 1778, Austin had informed the commissioners of his intended return to America and offered to carry their letters: XXVII, 423. For letters that we know, or suspect, he carried see XXVII, 446–7; *Adams Papers,* VII, 57–9.

7. Austin wrote JA on June 7: *Adams Papers,* VIII, 76–8.

8. BF replied on Oct. 20, that he knew of nothing to propose that was worthy of Austin's acceptance. Library of Congress.

9. For Austin's father, Benjamin, see XXV, 102n.

From Demezandré[1] ALS: American Philosophical Society

Monseigneur. St. malo le 10. Juin 1779.

Les Bontés que ma temoigné votre Excellence Dans le passage que javois demandé Sur la fregatte l'alliance et l'intèrest vif que je prends aux etats unis m'engage à vous donner avis que hiers matin 9. du Courant, il est entré le navire le Sartinne de st. malo Venant de charles Town en *trente jours* étant Sorty de ce port le 9 may. Un officier de ce Bord de mes amis Croit que le gouvernement de la Carolinne n'a chargé le Sartinne D'aucun paquet pour votre Excellence; c'est particulierement dans cette Crainte que je vais à la hâte vous faire part de ce que j'ay appris.

Les anglois ont descendu dans les georgies avec 3000 hommes & Volontaires de new york et quelques thorie. Ils se Sont avancé dans les terres et ont pris Savanas qu'on croit avoir eté Vendue par le Général hauve qui n'a fait aucun mouvement de deffense.[2] Alors le Conseil de Charlestown à rappellé ce général qui a été renvoyé au congrès, lon à remis M. *Rottelege* prisident; il est arrivé de philadelphie un ingenieur françois qui a fait en peu de temps fortifiér charlestown. Les anglois ont été chassés du terrein dont ils s'etoient emparé en georgie, mais Comme s'ils l'avoient fait exprès, ils n'ont quitté Savana que pour se Replier Sur charles town et ils n'étoient qua 20 mille de Cette Ville lorsque le Sartinne est Sorty.[3] Le Capne. et Les officiers de ce nre. [navire] pensent que cette ville est maintenant assiegée, mais ils la Croyent en etat de Resister et ne Croyent pas que les anglois Reussissent. Ce qui les fortifient dans cette pensée c'est que le 7 mais ils avoient le pilotte à leur Bord pour les mettre dehors lorsqu'il lui vient

1. One of two St. Malo merchants who first wrote BF on April 1, above, to request passage to America on the *Alliance.*

2. Maj. Gen. Robert Howe, blamed widely for the poor state of Savannah's defenses, was acquitted by court martial of any misconduct "with highest honor": Mark M. Boatner III, *Encyclopedia of the American Revolution* (New York, 1966), pp. 521–2, 980–2.

3. Gen. Augustine Prevost had arrived with 900 British troops. He retreated, however, when he learned that Gen. Lincoln's 4000-man army was returning from its siege of Augusta: *ibid.*, pp. 1034–5; Ward, *War of the Revolution,* pp. 684–5.

une deffense de le faire Sous peine de mort. Tout le lendemain ils ne virent Sur la rade, ordinairement assez mouvante, pas la moindre pirogue. Le capne. *Roussel* prit le party de faire Sonder la Barre—Et hazarda Sa sortie tout Seul pour ne pas S'exposer à un troisieme Embargo, car il etoit retenu depuis notre sortie C'est a dire depuis 7 à 8 mois. Il a été heureux et Comme le Sartinne marche Superieurement il a Eu une Courte traversée. Les officiers de ce nre. disent que les affaires vont assez Bien depuis que mr. Rottelege Est president et depuis qu'il y a de nouveaux généraux, cependant ils Croyent que charles-town recevroit des secours avec bien de la joye. Tout y est d'une Cherté horrible. Une chemise vaut 50 punds & tout en proportion, il n'arrive plus de secours de france—Le Rhum vaut 60 punds le galon; la farine vaut 100—je dis cent ponds le cent, un dinde 15 punds, le Boeuf, en proportion, le Ris 28 ponds. Cela est a peine Croyable. On croit que le peu de Confiance du papier, dont les contrefactions fourmillent, est Cause de cette extrême Cherté.

Il seroit Bien à desirer que M. de la fayette quon dit être embarqué a lorient avec 1200 hommes tournât ses pas vers cette contrée aujourd'huy la plus pressée.

Pardonnez-moy Monseigneur la précipitation avec laquelle je vous Ecris. Le depart du Courier me presse extraordinairement.

J'ay l'honneur dêtre avec le plus profond Respect Monseigneur Votre tres h. & t. o. sr. DEMEZANDRÉ

Addressed: A Son Excellence / Monseigneur Monseigneur / de franklin ambassadeur des / etats unis de l'amerique à lui / même. / *A Paris*

Notation: DeMazandre St. Malo le 10. juin 1779.

From [Pierre-Ulric] Dubuisson[4]

ALS: American Philosophical Society

Paris 10 juin 1779. hôtel des 3 milords rue traversière *st. h.*

Monsieur,

Lorsque je publiai, il y a six mois, l'abrégé de la révolution de L'Amérique Anglaise, j'eus l'honneur de vous en porter un exemplaire; n'ayant pas eu celui de vous trouver chez vous, je le laissai, avec mon adresse, à quelqu'un de vos gens, & j'ai toujours attendu depuis que vous voudriez bien me faire savoir s'il vous était parvenu.

Quoique cet ouvrage ait eu un succès assez flatteur, & qu'il ait été analysé dans les journaux d'une manière d'autant plus satisfaisante pour moi que je ne connais aucun de leurs rédacteurs, je vous avouerai, Monsieur, que l'incertitude où je suis, Si mon travail a pu vous être agréable, m'a déjà causé plus d'un regret de l'avoir entrepris.

L'air de réprobation que votre silence semble lui imprimer me trouble & m'aflige. Plusieurs personnes m'ayant demandé si vous connaissiez mon ouvrage & ce que vous en pensiez, ma franchise ne m'a point permis de leur déguiser ce que j'avais lieu de présumer.

Aujourd'hui que l'on me sollicite de donner le tableau des événemens qui se sont passés en Amérique pendant l'année dernière, j'ai résolu de ne me livrer à ce travail qu'autant que j'y aurai été encouragé par vous-même, Monsieur, & même aidé dans la serie des faits du théâtre desquels je suis maintenant trop éloigné pour en vouloir assurer aucun sans votre garantie.

4. Pierre-Ulric Dubuisson (1746–94) resided at St. Domingue, where he sometimes used the title *directeur général des postes.* While there he learned of the American situation and, claiming to be an authority on the colonies, wrote a book, *Abrégé de la Révolution de l'Amérique Angloise;* its publication was announced in the *Jour. de Paris* on April 20, 1778. He subsequently wrote a number of plays and operas, accompanied Dumouriez on a campaign, and, after the latter's defection, was guillotined. *DBF* and Quérard, *France littéraire,* where his name is erroneously given as Paul-Ulric. This is the only extant letter from him to BF.

J'attends l'honneur de votre réponse, & je suis avec respect Monsieur, Votre trés-humble & très- obéïssant serviteur

DuBuisson
américain

Notation: Dubuisson 10. Juin 1779.—

From William Lee

ALS: American Philosophical Society; copy: Virginia Historical Society

Sir Frankfort June 10th. 1779.

I had the Honor of writing to you the 30th. of March & 2d. of April last, requesting the favor of you to apply to the French Ministry for certain Canon, Arms & Ammunition for the State of Virginia; since which, I have not heard any thing from you on the Subject; you will therefore I hope excuse me for desiring to know, whether you have made this application, and whether there is a liklyhood of our obtaining the Articles wanted, as at this time a very favorable opportunity has occur'd, for transporting them expeditiously to Virginia.

I have the Honor to be Sir, with the highest Consideration, Your most Obedient & most Humble Servant W: Lee

Addressed: To The Honorable / Benjamin Franklin Esqr / Minister Plenopentiary from the United / States of America to the Court of / Versailles, at Passy near / Paris

From Jean de Neufville & fils

ALS: American Philosophical Society

High Honour'd Sir! Amsterdam the 10 Júne 1779.

The principall motive of the present is to desire Yoúr Excellency's Kind assistance in forwarding the annexed Mercantile Letter by the first conveyance from France, it contains the arrivall of Some Vessells with ús; the Independance came to oúr adress from Virginia, which we may reckon we hope de bonne aúgúre.[5]

5. Sears discusses this ship in the letter immediately following.

It hath not been possible as yett to gett a sufficient quantity of subscribers on the papers Yoúr Excellency was so Kind to entrúst me with; every Nation múst in those things have something allowed for prejudice. Bútt we have under hand consulted what might be the best, and oúr frinds, the most fitted for this bússiness, gott the papers ready dressed for ús, which we hope to lay in short before Y.E: after having them translated; and when we will have those Sign'd we may try the subscription,[6] and, as we hope, we will succeed to satisfaction. We expect however first Mr. Van de Capellen from Overyssell, to consúlt likewise with him again, he comes over very soon, to consúlt with ús what might be done in the American caúse, which we in particúlar will always promote the best in oúr power. & so acknowledging the favoúr yoúr E: honoúrs ús with, We Remain with all devotion, and Regard High Honour'd Sir Yoúr Excellencys most Obedient humble Servants

John de Neufville & Son

Mr. Sayre desired ús we should forward the enclosed.[7]

Addressed: A Son Excellence / Monsieur B: Franklin / Ambassadeur & Ministre Plenipotentiaire / du Congres des treize Etats unis de L'amerique / &a &a &a / a Passi

Notation: Neufville John & Son 10 June 1779.—

From David Sears[8]

ALS: American Philosophical Society

Sir Amsterdam June 10th. 1779

Yesterday came up to Town the Sloop Independance belonging to Mr Isaac Sears & Co of Boston she left Virginia the 16th Apl last and came north about but brings nothing so late as you must be already furnish'd with—[9]

6. For the loan on behalf of Congress that the firm was attempting to raise.

7. Presumably Sayre's June 9 letter to BF.

8. A Boston merchant; see our annotation of Dumas to BF, May 27.

9. The arrival of the *Independence* was also reported in Dumas' letter of June 9. Isaac Sears (1730?–86), prominent in the New York Sons of Liberty

I have settled my affairs in Europe and shall now return to Boston in the above mentioned Vessell (at least I shall take passage in her) because I know her to be a very fast sailing Vessell she has been running all this War—[1] The reason that I so particularly mention this matter to your Excellency is that I wish to be charg'd with something from you to our Country and you now have a tender of my best services what ever may be put under my care shall be strickly attended to and all orders carefully obey'd but if your Excellency should have frequent and better opportunities from France I cannot expect you'l write by this quarter— however if you can repose a Confidence in me and have any thing which you think proper to communicate that will be agreeable in America I should wish the honor of a line from you. I beg your Excellency will excuse this uncommon freedom in me which has arose barely from a desire to carry something new and agreeable—

It has been said here that Mr Adams & the Marquis de la Fayette went out in the Fleet of Monsr la Motte-Piquet but that they were damag'd in a storm and oblig'd to return I hope it is not so—

I have nothing further for your detention only that you'l accept my best wishes for your health and welfare & believe me to be with much esteem Your Excellencies Most Obet Most Humle Sert— DAVID SEARS

To His Excellency Benjn Franklin Esqr Passy near Paris—

P.S. I am at Messrs John de Neufville & Son in this City and I believe Capt Brown in the Independance will actually be ready in 10 or 12 days. D S—

N.B. I have Inclos'd this under cover to my Bankers Messrs Vandenyver Frere & Co of your City (Paris)

---

at the beginning of the war, lived in Boston from 1777 to 1783: *DAB.* He and David Sears were great-grandsons of Capt. Paul Sears (1637/8–1707/8): Samuel P. May, *The Descendants of Richard Sares (Sears) of Yarmouth, Mass. 1638–1888* (Albany, 1890), pp. 41, 113, 167.

1. Sears reached home safely after a narrow escape from an English frigate: *ibid.,* p. 168.

Addressed: To his Excellency / Benjn Franklin Esqr / at Passy / near / Paris—

Notation: Sears, David.

To Morel[2]

Copy: Library of Congress

Sir Passy, May 31. [*i.e.,* after June 10][3] 1779

It was *two* Guineas that I gave the Person who brought me your Charts, tho' you mention to have received but *One.* This makes me think that he is not a Person to be trusted, or else I should send them back to you by him: for Tho' I would not undervalue your Labour; yet not being Rich I cannot afford to give you three four or five Guineas as you say other Gentlemen have done, and I must content myself with the Printed Accounts. Therefore whenever you please to call or send for them. I shall return them to you, wishing you a better Purchaser, I have the honour &

Mr Morel

To Sartine

Copy: Library of Congress

Sir Passy, June 11 1779.

I received and read with great Pleasure the Letter your Excellency did me the honour to write to me the 26 past, acquainting me with his Majesty's Goodness towards the Sieur Giddins, who had the Misfortune to lose his Brigantine by the Mistake of a Battery at Guadeloupe.

I beg you would present and make acceptable to his Majesty

2. See his letter of May 17, above.

3. This letter is clearly in answer to one from Morel dated June 10, 1779, and we therefore conclude that BF's is incorrectly dated in his letterbook. Morel's letter states that about a month ago he sent BF charts of the French army and navy. They represent over two weeks work and, "Tous les Traits des Lignes sont d'or en Conquille." He has twice sent the porter to BF's lodgings to collect payment, but the man brought back only one louis. Other foreign ministers have given three or four for his work, and he hopes BF will treat him as generously. APS.

my most thankful Acknowledgements for this Act of his Beneficence, added to the many which have long Since gain'd him the Hearts of all the Americans. Please to accept my Thanks for the care you have taken of this affair, and believe me to be, with the Sincerest Respect Your Excell.

M. De Sartine.

To Vergennes

LS:[4] Archives du Ministère des affaires étrangères; copy: Library of Congress

Sir, Passy, June 11th. 1779.

The Congress having been extreamly embarrassed and put to great Expences by the Number of Foreign Officers that went to America in Expectation of Employment, and who could not be employed, our Armies being already arranged and more than fully Officer'd, have signified to me their Pleasure that I should give no Encouragement, or Expectation for the future, to any Officer whatever.[5] I cannot therefore make any Contract with M. De Vatteville, nor give him any kind of Assurance that he will find Employ in that Country: But I did acquaint a Friend of his, soon after I had the honour of receiving your Excellency's Letter relating to him, that if he resolved to make the Voyage, I would in respect to your Recommendation, give him Letters of Introduction to my Friends, who would receive him as a Gentleman, and a Stranger of Merit, and endeavour to make his Residence there agreable to him.[6] This being all in my Power on this Occasion, I hope your Excellency will excuse my not accomplishing your Wishes more perfectly, and believe me nevertheless to be, with the sincerest Esteem and Respect, Your Excellency's, most obedient & most humble Servant. B FRANKLIN

His Exy: the Count De Vergennes.—

4. In WTF's hand.

5. Congress' prohibition actually was less comprehensive: *JCC,* VII, 177. Both Lovell and Washington did write BF to discourage any more foreign officers from coming: XXIV, 266–7, 440–3.

6. See Vergennes' letter of May 20 recommending Vatteville.

From Thomas Digges

ALS: Historical Society of Pennsylvania

Dr. Sir London 11 June 1779.

I receivd Your favour of the 30th ulo. & find by it only one of my letters have miscarryd. By mentioning the dates of my letters I did not mean to draw you into answering any of them but meerly to assertain their safety; I well know how much better Your time is employd than by answering letters of little import, never mind me, but when you have any thing to do which you may think proper to require of me to transact. I have never yet found any letters have miscarryd under Your last direction, but this will not do for such Towns as have french Prisoners in the neighbourhood, because there is a rule to open them in order to find out if the letters are not for prisoners; In London it will do well, but as I am going to Bristol for a few weeks having some goods to Ship on Spanish bottoms expected & now there I should be glad to receive any commands of Yours under direction *Mr. William Singleton Church Post Office Bristol.*

I have made every application in my power about W Peters, & shall continue my endeavours to find him out & do what you require; I have wrote to Mrs. Roberts at Liverpoole, the house he lodgd in, to find out from her when he left that place, where gone &ca, but as yet I have no ansr.

I wrote to you by Mr Panchaud who went by the packet of the 1st Int. and as you had mentiond to me You would pay the bill on Brehon when it again appeard, I took the liberty to draw one for 20£ to Mr Panchaud, wch on Rect. He was to remit it to his friend here. As You mention in Yr. last you had paid Brehons Bill this will of course be cancelld & returnd to me.

I shewd DH[7] that part of Yr. letter which relates to the Cartel of Prisoners & the mention of the Port of Morlaix in preference to Nantes &ca. He spoke to Mr Stephens abt it before me, who did not seem at all averse to letting the whole remaining prisoners go in the next voyage, but abt this, Lord Sandwich was to be consulted: They are, both at the Admy &

7. David Hartley, also referred to later in the letter as "our friend."

board of Sick & hurt, very much surprisd that there is as yet no accots whatever from the transport which carried over the first hundred, & say She must be either lost or detaind for want a like number of British Sailors to return for those who were sent. Much surprisd also to hear that there are prisoners in Spain.

The Books You order to be forwarded to Messrs. Horneca Grand & Co. of Amsterdam are now in the packing up, & will be sent in a Ship to sail in about ten days calld the Anna Maria Christiaan Roeloffs Master they will be put in as small a deal box As possible and markd BF directed also on a card to Horneca & Grand, so that you may give the necessary orders to Amsterdam about them. I have got some friends trying to collect annecdotes & matter to help Dr. Gordon in his work. General Washington two years ago wrote to me to forward him some books, & give what assistance I could.[8] I was with Dr Price to day & mentiond such a work to him as well as our valuable Bishop In whose family, thanks to you, I have been more than once very happy they all went into Hampshire on tuesdy & I believe Yours was the last name mentiond in the town House by Miss Georgiana.[9] Wilkes also promisd Me some annecdotes, and Mrs. MaCaulay to use her pen, but the former is so busied in rectifying the errors of Christianity & putting all Religions upon the level of the haram, that I have little hopes from him; and I guess Madam is too much engagd as yet in the joys of new wedded Love and envelopd in the embraces of Her Young highlander to take up her pen.[1]

8. William Gordon was at work on *The History of the Rise, Progress, and Establishment, of the Independence of the United States of America* (London, 1788); see BF to Digges, May 30[–31], above. The Digges and Washington families were friends of long standing: Elias and Finch, *Digges Letters,* p. 428.

9. Georgiana Shipley. The bishop is her father, Jonathan Shipley, Bishop of St. Asaph.

1. John Wilkes, in a debate on granting further relief to Protestant Dissenters, inveighed against bigotry and argued for toleration of all religions and sects: Cobbett, *Parliamentary History,* XX, 309–20. The marriage on Dec. 17, 1778, of the historian Catherine Macaulay (see XXVII, 204n, 474n) to William Graham, a surgeon's mate twenty-six years her junior, subjected her to ridicule and the loss of many friendships. *DNB.*

I gave You from time to time, as often as any new occurrence arose, the progress of the business I have lately been upon, & which I had most seriously at heart, and as I was well convincd it was taken up seriously & properly by the parties most interested in it I gave it *all* my attention & constantly held it in view. I wish I knew all the actors as thoroughly as You know them, but I have attended long enough to their moves to discover they are very expert in little dirty parliamentary craft, but have none of that true wisdom which comprehends the extensive and great Interests of their Country. I am sorry our friend got so little by his laudable endeavours to serve both Countries. There was a decision negative to the first & leading proposition of a ten years truce, because it was in fact giving Independence. This is the sum total & I dare say I need not enter into particulars. The plan of Ministry is to try another years work in Ama. The idle scheme of Govr. F which I mentiond in my last to You, however ridiculous & absurd it may appear, is to be adopted;[2] much expectation is formd from it, from dissentions & cabal in Congress, disunion & distress among the people &ca. &ca. Whatever Negotiations the ministry at present have in view are certainly intended to be offerd thro Sr. H Clinton who will probably be armd with a new Commission & fuller powers.— Something similar to this & very great offers for the Georgians are gone over to Prevost.[3]

There will be some conversation to day in the house on a motion of Sir W. Merediths for ministry to declare what they intend to do; Our friend will hold forth on this occasion, & probably tomorrow will open some new lights.[4]

2. Actually it was his letter of the 25th which reported WF's activities.

3. Eden was urging that Henry Clinton be encouraged to use any means of persuasion, including bribery and threats, to bring over Americans to their side. The commission he proposed to aid Clinton was not formed until the following year. Carl Van Doren, *Secret History of the American Revolution* (New York, 1941), pp. 233–4. Maj. Gen. Augustine Prevost, headquartered in Savannah, had been left in charge of establishing civil government in Georgia. For details of that operation see Paul H. Smith, *Loyalists and Redcoats: a Study in British Revolutionary Policy* (Chapel Hill, 1964), pp. 104–6.

4. Sir William Meredith's "motion for preparing peace with America" was seconded by Hartley; the house did not act on the measure: Cobbett,

The Evidence of the Torey Worthies who are calld in by Lord G.G to overweigh the evidence of Lord Cornwallis Genl Grey &c &c. has not yet extended further than to Genl Robertson, who has been three intire days at the bar giving as dull a narrative as was ever heard in that house. It is thought Galloways will come next, and so on down to the worthy little Jebas.[5] Many are of opinion parliament will rise on thursday & cut short this enquiry, & deprive these Gentn. of an oppertunity to clinch the nail of their ruin in America; for I cannot help thinking if they controvert the evidence of Cornwallis Grey &ca. and aim at establishing an opinion of the practicability of carrying on the war and subjugating america they will innevitably fix their ruin in both Countries. Genl Robinsons evidence was generally much ridiculd & laughd at; It tended to exculpate Lord G.G of any inattention to the necessary supplies of Men Ships &ca. &ca., to the crimination of Genl Howe, and to prove to all the world (except those who are already well informd of the state of facts) that Washington with twelve or fifteen thousand men (never *more*) has baffled every effort of the British and mercenary armies of upwards of 40,000 men commanded by Sr. W Howe and aided by a fleet of 80 to 90 Sail of Men of War; But his Evidence more than all clearly serves to prove that this wise & good ministry have projected and carryd on the war by the advise & recommendation of Fools, and they now bring these very fools to prove it.

An Express armd Vessel is arrivd from N York the 4th. May. The accots. nearest the truth & which are believd at Loyds are as follows. A Detatchd Army of 7 Regts. Under Erskine abot:

Parliamentary History, xx, 836–8; Frank O'Gorman, *The Rise of Party in England: the Rockingham Whigs 1760–82* (London, 1975), p. 389. For Meredith see Namier and Brooke, *House of Commons*, III, 130–3.

5. Maj. Gen. James Robertson (whom later in the paragraph Digges calls "Robinson") was examined at length from June 8–10, and again on the 14th. Of all the loyalists summoned, only Joseph Galloway actually testified before Parliament. For the hearings see *The Parliamentary Register*, XIII, 273–349, 370–97, 422–42, 448–71. The committee was dissolved after Howe did not appear for the examination of evidence ordered on June 29: *ibid.*, 537.

2,500 men was on the point of sailing to the So.ward on some expedition, said in N York to be sent as a Reenforcement to Prevost, but more probably from Mrs. Tryons accot. to be bound to Chesepeak Bay, either to support some discontents on the Eastern Shore or to act on the Virga. side as a divertion in favor of the Georgia Army which if report speaks truth, has receivd two checks from Lincoln & was obligd to retire nearer to their head quarters at Savannah.[6]

Seven Sail of Victualling transports under convoy of the Jason frigate bound from N York to Georgia with supplys for the Army in the South, were taken convoy & all by three American Cruisers on the Coasts of Carolina.[7]

The Revenge Capt Cunningham after taking in all about forty sail of prizes, was himself taken by an English frigate near Bermudas & carried into New York.[8]

No appearances of any active exertions of the British army from New York, but there was a current talk that Govr F with a body of Amn Loyalists & a few troops were going into the Jerseys from which quarter there was strong desertions & every confirmation of the disunion & distress of the People.[9]

Since I wrote to You about my Bror. a Cozn. of mine Dr Stewarts Son of Annapolis has been with me; he saild in the same vessel with my Brother the doctor & was taken & car-

6. Maj. Gen. Sir William Erskine was not involved in this expedition; he returned to London later that summer. Mark M. Boatner III, *Encyclopedia of the American Revolution* (New York, 1966), p. 349. Maj. Gen. Edward Mathew led this army into the Chesapeake to intercept Washington's reinforcements and destroy enemy supplies. Mackesy, *War for America,* pp. 269–70; Richard K. Showman, ed., *The Papers of General Nathanael Greene* (5 vols. to date, Chapel Hill, 1976–), IV, 49–50n.

7. For the capture of the *Jason* convoy see our annotation of William Gordon to BF, May 5, above.

8. Conyngham, aboard the *Revenge,* which recently had been fitted as a privateer, was captured by the British ship *Galatea* on April 27, shortly after reaching his cruising ground out of New York (*DAB*). His severe treatment in Pendennis Castle and Mill Prison will become an object of concern to BF in future volumes.

9. These plans were abandoned because of Clinton's lack of support: Van Doren, *Secret History,* p. 224.

ryd into N York.[1] I have a full detail of the state of things in that quarter of Ama. Their greatest evil is the failure for now two years of the Crop of Wheat. Mr Stewart being a Scotsmans Son got interest to come to Europe gratis, but my Brothers politics being well known & his having been much about the person of Genr Washington for the last two or three years, he could not obtain permission to die at Sea & was left a prisoner in N York very near wore down in a Consumption.

If any thing new transpires to day I will give you a line by common post to night. This is intended for the Spanish bag. I am with great truth & the highest esteem Dr. Sir Yr very obligd & Obt Servt. T.D——

Notation: June 11. 79

From Dumas

ALS: American Philosophical Society; AL (draft): Algemeen Rijksarchief

Monsieur La Haie 11e. Juin *1779*.

En attendant que je puisse vous parler de ce qui se passe aujourd'hui à l'Assemblée, il est bon de vous rendre compte de la maniere dont a fini l'affaire du Gazettier de Leide.[2] Voici l'extrait des deux dernieres lettres qu'il m'a écrites, en date des 7 & 10 du court. C'est moi qui lui avois envoyé copie du Meme. de S. J. Y.,

7e. "Je vous suis obligé de la Conférence avec Mr. V. B., & de la communication de ses informations (savoir du précis de ce que l'Assemblée avoit décidé). Je ne craignois, il est vrai, pas beaucoup; mais il est toujours désagréable d'avoir à se

1. His brother was Joseph; his cousin was David Stewart, third son of Dr. George Stewart, who had emigrated from Scotland in 1721, and held various offices in the colonies before returning in 1775 to claim estates inherited from his brother. David had been register of the Land Office in Annapolis from 1774 until 1777, when he refused to cooperate with the rebels. He had made two previous attempts to sail from New York. Elias and Finch, *Digges Letters,* p. 62n.

2. Jean Luzac; see Dumas' letter of June 5.

defendre, quand on n'est pas d'humeur fléchissante, ni d'un naturel à mâcher les choses. N'ayant eu aucun Message de nos Messieurs jusqu'à cet après-midi, je croyois qu'on s'épargneroit même la peine de nous en parler. Mais aujourd'hui à 5 h. nous avons été mandés à l'hôtel de ville pour demain matin. Il faudra voir sur quel ton on le prendra. Je le présume benin, parce qu'on a tant tardé."

10e. "J'ai été moi-même à l'hôtel de ville. Il n'y avoit que le Président & les 2 Secretaires. L'on a commencé par me dire, *que je me rappellerois, qu'il s'étoit trouvé dans la Gazette un Extrait de Mémoire, rectifié ensuite, que sur des plaintes, faites au sujet de cette premiere insertion, il avoit été pris par les Etats une Résolution, dont le Secretaire me feroit lecture.* Celui-ci a demandé au Président, à voix basse, s'il devoit lire toute la Résolution?—*Non, simplement le dispositif.* On me l'a lu, à peu près dans les mêmes termes que vous me l'aviez marqué. J'ai demandé si Messieurs jugeoient à propos de m'en donner copie, pour que je la communiquasse à mon Oncle,[3] ou si je devoir seulement lui faire mon rapport de bouche?— *Non, de bouche, cela suffit.* J'ai continué, qu'il me paroissoit étrange, que Mr. l'Ambr. se fût plaint de l'insertion d'un Article, publié à Londres même; qu'il étoit bien plus naturel de s'en prendre à la source; que me doutant de l'objet qui m'avoit fait mander, j'avois pris avec moi le Papier Anglois, que j'étois prêt à faire voir à Messieurs.— *Non, cela n'est pas besoin: Mais nous vous recommandons de vous conformer à la Résolution* (v. ma Lettre du 8): *vous montrez trop, dans toutes vos feuilles, de quel parti vous êtes.*— PAS PLUS, MONSIEUR LE BOURGUEMAÎTRE, QUE NE L'EXIGE LE DEVOIR D'ÊTRE VRAI.— L'affaire étant finie, je me suis retiré. Ainsi vous voyez, mon cher Ami, que l'on a cru ne pas même devoir nous faire connoître le Mémoire en question, qui plus digne d'une Poissarde que d'un Politique, répond bien mal à l'idée que je m'étois faite d'ailleurs de l'habileté de celui dont il porte le nom."

J'apprends dans ce moment que l'Assemblée d'Hollde. vient d'être prorogée, & que ces Mrs. partent demain pour leurs

3. Etienne Luzac (1706–87), former editor of the *Gaz. de Leyde: NNBW,* I, 1290.

villes. Je ne pourrai voir notre Ami que ce soir. Il est allé dîner hors de ville. On n'aura rien décidé encore. Mr. l'Ambr. est allé ce matin à Rotterdam au-devant de Made. la Duchesse.

Je suis avec un grand respect, Monsieur Votre très-humble & très obéissant serviteur D

Il est arrivé des Lettres de la Cour de L——, comme quoi elle consentiroit (bien de la grace) à laisser faire à la rep. son commerce avec la Fce., pourvu que la rep. s'engage à ne pas y laisser envoyer des bois de construction. C'est le chat qui tombe toujours sur ses pattes. Cela est visiblement concerté avec ceux d'ici. N'importe laissons-les faire. La Fce. ne manquera pas de bois pour cela;[4] & les Anglomanes n'y gagneront que de se rendre toujours plus odieux, & d'affoiblir leur influence dans l'essentiel. C'est un très-mauvais service que leur rendent leurs bons amis.

Passy à S. Exc. M. Franklin

Addressed: To his Excellency / B. Franklin Esqr., / M. Plen. of the United States, &c. / at *Passy.*/.

Notation: Dumas 11. Juin 1779.

From David Hartley

Transcript: Library of Congress

My Dear friend London June 11 1779

Before you receive this you will probably have received my last, by a private Conveyance.[5] You will find by that letter, that I have not been successfull in the negotiation in which I was so desirous to give assistance. Let me just ask you; if a truce of ten years be not practicable, what wd you think of a truce for one Year as a foundation for treating. My bias leads me so strongly towards pacification that in my own private opinion I shd incline even to a truce for a single year, rather than to

4. By this time large quantities of wood ordered by the French navy were accumulating at Amsterdam and Hamburg, awaiting convoy through the Strait of Dover: Dull, *French Navy,* p. 174.

5. His last letter was May 25.

the continuance uninterrupted of the war. *A little time given for cooling may have good effects.* I will write again soon Your affecte. DH—

From Richard Bennett Lloyd

ALS: American Philosophical Society

Dear Sir, London 11 June 79.

I have just received two letters from Maryland, one from my Uncle Lloyd, the other from my Brother—. I enclose you Copies of them, and earnestly request the favour of you to think if I can take up the money in France as my Friends expect by drawing on them in Maryland—.[6] Shd. you imagine my presence at Paris would make this necessary, I can easily come over—. I beg many pardons for being so very troublesome but you are the only Person who's advice I can put sufficient confidence in with an affair of so much importance to me—Mrs. Lloyd is at this time in the Straw—[7] She joins with me in best respects—

I am, Dear Sir, your obliged & obt. humble Servant

R. B. LLOYD

I write this in a hurry being late at night—

Addressed: A Monsieur / Monsieur Franklin / à Passy

Notation: R. B. Lloyd Londres 11. juin 1779.

6. Lloyd's brother Edward had written from Annapolis on March 5, informing him that enemy privateers made it impractical to send remittances in tobacco; instead, Edward was having Jean Holker, French consul at Philadelphia, send bills of exchange in the amount of £1,000 sterling. University of Pa. Library. The letter from Lloyd's uncle, Col. Richard Lloyd (*Md. Hist. Mag.*, VII [1912], 427), is missing. On July 12, however, BF wrote in answer to the present letter that he had received the copies of both letters. Library of Congress.

7. In childbed.

To Robert Cochran[8]

LS:[9] Princeton University Library; copy: Library of Congress

Sir, Passy June 12. 1779

I received yours of Augt 16. a long time after the Date.[1] I am happy that any little Notice I have been able to take of your Son is agreable to you. He is truely a fine Boy, ingenious, active, industrious, and capable of any Improvement you may think fit to bestow upon him in his Education.— From his good Dispositions of Mind, there is great Reason to hope, that his Parents will have much Satisfaction in him. I am, Sir, Your most obedient humble Servant. B Franklin

Capt. Cochran.

To Christopher Gadsden

Copy: Library of Congress

Sir, Passy, june 12. 1779.

I received the honour of yours by Commodore Gillon, and have done every thing in my Power to forward his Undertaking.[2] But the present Circumstances here have prevented that Success which at another time he might have promised himself.

I am glad to hear that you Continue well and active in your Country's Cause, being, with Sincere Esteem Sir Your most obed. & most hum. ser.

Honble. Christ. Gadsden Esqr.

8. This S.C. shipyard owner and ship captain was the father of Charles Cochran, BFB's best friend: XXIII, 38n; XXVII, 262n.

9. In WTF's hand.

1. Thanking BF for his friendship and kindness to his son: XXVII, 262–3.

2. The Charleston merchant had written on July 15, 1778, to introduce Gillon: XXVII, 98–9.

To Rawlins Lowndes

Copy: Library of Congress

Sir [June 12, 1779][3]

I received by Commodore Gillon the Letter your Excellency directed to The Commissioners at this Court; Dated the 18th of July last.[4] It would have been a great Pleasure to me If I could have been of Service in enabling him to obtain a Loan here for the accomplishing the purposes of his Voyage hither; But the great Sums wanted by the Governement here, and the high Interest given in holland, by Germany and England, had engross'd all the Money that could be found to borrow in Europe so that the Loan was impracticable. He appears to have with a great Zeal for our Cause, much Intelligence in sea affairs and unCommon activity, which makes me regret exceedingly that he could not Succeed in obtaining the frigates, as I am persuaded he would have been very useful in his Station.

I have the honour to be with great Respect Your Excellency's most Obedient & most humble servant BF

His Excelly. Rawlins Lowndes Esqe. Governor of South Carolina.[5]

To Arthur Middleton

Copy: Library of Congress

Sir Passy, June 12. 1779.

I received the honour of yours per Commodore Gillon.[6] It would have been a great Pleasure to me if I could by any Endeavours of mine have enabled him to accomplish the Ends of his Mission; But the Circumstances of the Times made it impracticable. I shall always pay great Respect to your Rec-

3. Dated on the assumption that BF wrote on the same day to the four South Carolinians who had recommended Gillon.

4. XXVII, 118–19.

5. Actually president of South Carolina. He did not run for reelection in 1779, and his successor took the title of governor; see Lowndes's entry in the *DAB*.

6. The S.C. politician had recommended Gillon on July 4, 1778: XXVII, 47.

ommendation, being with Sincere Esteem, Sir Your most obedient & most humble Servant.

Honble. Arthur Middleton Esqe.

To John Rutledge[7]

Copy: Library of Congress

Sir

Passy, June 12. 1779.

I received by Commodore Gillon the Letter you did me the honour of writing to me, dated the 9th. of July last.[8] Since his arrival, he has been extremely industrious in endeavouring to accomplish the Ends of his Mission but various Circumstances have concurred to disappoint him, which I am sorry for, as from his intelligence and Zeal for the Congress, I should have great Expectations of his usefulness in his Station. It gives me much pleasure to understand that the Treaties we have made here are so universally acceptable, and that they have your Approbation. With great & Sincere Esteem I have the honour to be Sir, Your m. o. & m. h. S.

Honble. John Rutledge Esqe.

To Vergennes

LS:[9] Archives du Ministère des affaires étrangères; copy: Library of Congress

Sir,

Passy June 12. 1779

Since the receipt of the Letter your Excellency did me the honour of writing to me of the 6th of May past, I have enquired concerning the Munitions of War supply'd from the King's Arsenals to Mr Lee, and which are gone to Virginia; and I find that they are different from those now desired for

7. Lowndes's predecessor as president of South Carolina: XXVII, 67n.
8. XXVII, 67.
9. In WTF's hand.

that Colony, and were a Part only of the Order received, of which the List I sent to your Excellency is the Remainder.[1]

If upon reconsideration of this Matter, your Excellency should think fit to lay it before his Majesty, and the Request of that State should be granted, Mr Wm: Lee will take Care of shipping the Goods to Virginia, by the first good Opportunity, he being their Agent.—[2]

The Agent for Maryland, M. Johnson, who resides at Nantes, presses me to endeavour obtaining for that State the Supplies of Arms, Ammunition, Clothing, &ca. contained in the Invoice that acompany'd my Letter to your Excellency of the 3d of May.[3] I do not find upon Enquiry that any considerable Quantities of those Articles have been sent thither; And as during a Year past the Exportations from France to America have been much diminished, private Merchants being discouraged by the many Captures, and the Commissioners have not been able to fulfil the Orders of Congress for want of Money, I begin to apprehend there may be a general Scarcity of such Supplies if no means are taken to furnish them. I am sorry to be so frequently troublesome to your Excellency, who have so many more weighty Affairs to employ your Attention, but the apparent Necessity of the Case compels me to request you would take this Application also into Consideration, and enable me to give some Answer to the Agent of that State.[4]

With the greatest Respect, I have the honour to be, Your Excellency's, most obedient, & most humble Servant,

B FRANKLIN

His Exy. M. le Comte De Vergennes.—

From Edward Byrne

ALS: American Philosophical Society

Sir Cherburg June 12th 1779

I Writt you of my misfortins Sir in which it lys in your powr to Send mee hom to wher I blong to Feladealfea Sir, I was

1. BF included the list of goods wanted by Virginia and Maryland in his letter of May 3, above.

2. See William Lee's letter of June 10.

3. Johnson's latest extant letter on the subject is dated April 22, above.

4. As far we know, Vergennes did not answer BF's request.

takn by the Winchilsey frigat wee was bownd to martninq and Kiped one Board of hir Six months and I run away from hir in Jemeaky and Cam to Liverpool and then gat meet of a brigg bownd to Limerick in Irland and from Limerick to London and was Taken by the Privater sloope the 13th of May and Cared into this port of Cherburg Sir pleas your Honer to geet mee my Librty and to Send mee hom to Filedlfea as my Realitions and frinds Lives ther my onkl Cips the Sin of Ship in Wallnot Street[5] and if Not to Send mee to aney pleas or port in aney Ship or Vesel your Honer pleases in amerika Sir I am your Humbl Servant EDWARD BYRNE—

Mr Franklen

Addressed [*in a different hand*]: A Monsieur / Monsieur franklin Ministre / Plenipotentiaire des Etats / unis de L'Amerique / *A Paris*

To Rocquette, Elsevier & Rocquette

Copy: Library of Congress

Gentlemen Passy, June 13. 1779

I received your favour of the 7th. Instant, inclosing two Notes of the United states for 1000 Dollars each for my Inspection, which I return inclos'd. I have not yet seen the resolution mentioned therein but by what I can recollect from the face of the Notes themselves, I judge that the Dollars for which the notes are given were of Paper Money borrowed, and that the interest will be payd and the principal repaid in the same paper which is now in state of great depreciation. If before the time of Payment it should fall still Lower, the possessor of the Notes will be so much a Loser, if on the Contrary

5. He may refer to the Pat Byrne who kept a well-known tavern on the corner of Front and Walnut streets, the sign of the Game Cock. A Patrick Byrne (1734–1808), pew-holder in St. Mary's Church, lived on Front St. in Philadelphia between Walnut and Spruce. *PMHB,* XCVIII (1974), 141; Joseph Willcox, "Historical Sketches of Some of the Pioneer Catholics of Philadelphia and Vicinity," American Catholic Historical Society of Philadelphia *Records,* XV (1904), 413–4.

they should rise in Value (of which from the Measures taken for that purpose, there is great Appearance) the possessor will be in proportion a Gainer the Interest will be payd every year but is payable only at the Loan office in America, from whence the Bills issued, and to that End they must be produced there, that the payment may be indorsed.[6] These Bills have therefore been improperly brought to Europe, being of less value here, as they must return to have their Effect; and being *Sola* Bills, payable to the Bearer, they have not the same security from the Dangers of the sea that Bills of Exchange usually have, for they may not only be lost or destroy'd by Accidents, but if taken the Ennemy will reap the Benefit of them— The Insurance of them back is therefore a proportionate Diminution of their Value. At What Value they are at present current in America, I cannot inform you, that depending on the fluctuating State of the Paper there; nor do I know where they can be so well negociated as in the place where they are payable.[7]

I have the honour to be Gentlemen

Messrs. J. Rocquette T Elsvier and Brothers Rocquette.

To Vergennes: Two Letters

(I) LS:[8] Archives du Ministère des affaires étrangères; copy: Library of Congress; (II) copy: Library of Congress

I.

Sir, Passy June 13. 1779.

I have communicated to Mr Lee the Letter your Excellency did me the honour to write to me of the 8th: Instant, relative to the Money placed in the Kings Treasury for Acct of Mr Stevenson;[9] and also the Copy of the Letter to M. De Sartine

6. The interest was payable in paper money, which was rapidly depreciating; nevertheless, the loan certificates sold well and held their value much better than did currency; see Ferguson, *Power of the Purse,* pp. 39–40.

7. On June 24 the Rotterdam firm acknowledged with thanks the return of the two notes and renewed its offer of whatever services it could render (APS).

8. In WTF's hand.

9. Arthur Lee was a friend of William Stevenson: XXV, 406–7.

which it enclosed: Mr Lee having no particular Orders from Mr Stevenson to receive the said Money, thinks it best that it remain in the hands of the Treasurer of the Marine, (if this may be permitted without Inconveniency) subject to the Drafts of Mr Stevenson, when they shall appear. We are much obliged to your Excellency & to M. De Sartine, for the Care and Trouble you have so kindly taken in this Affair.—

With great Respect I am, Sir, Your Excellency's, most obedient and most humble Servt. B FRANKLIN

His Exy. M. le Comte De Vergennes.

II.

Sir Passy, June 13 1779.

I beg Leave to submit to your Excellency's Consideration the enclos'd Memorial relating to some Goods Seized at Dieppe, belonging to Persons going to America;[1] and if the Facts on Enquiry Shall appear to be as stated in the memorial, and that no fraud was intended, I would request that the Goods may be restored to the Persons on their Paying the Duties.— With the greatest Respect.

I am &c.

M. De Vergennes.

From John Kendrick[2]

ALS: American Philosophical Society

Lisbon June 13. 1779—

Have taken the liberty to inform Your Excellency that I Commanded the Brig Count De. Estaing a privateer of Sixteen Guns from Boston belonging to Messrs. Isaac Sears Paskel Smith & Company[3] that on the 7. of April in Latitude 38:40

1. See Wharton to BF, May 29.

2. The Massachusetts navigator and trader (*c.* 1740–94) who during the Revolution commanded several privateers. *DAB;* he is also mentioned above, XXIV, 443.

3. The *Count D'Estaing* was commissioned Dec. 16, 1778: Allen, *Mass. Privateers,* p. 105. For Isaac Sears see David Sears's letter of June 10. Paschal Nelson Smith was Isaac's son-in-law: John A. Stevens, Jr., *Colonial Records of the New York Chamber of Commerce . . . Sketches Biographical and Historical* (New York, 1867), p. 161.

N—and Longitude 33:30 West. from the Meridion of London I was taken By the Ship Brutus of 28 Guns and her Tender of Ten Guns from London the Brutus was Commanded by Samuel Hill of Boston and the tender by one Ross of Boston, Both In the Brittish Service— I remain'd Prissener on Board till the 22. Instant when Graciosa one of the western Islands Bore SW. from us ten Leagues Capt. Hill Gave me Boat and Order'd me on Shore with thirty more of my Ships Company whare we arrived that Day—we was Very Sevilly treated by the Inhabitants, I remained there fourteen Days, then got to the Island of Tersary,[4] where we was Likewise well treatted By the General of the Islands who made Provision for me and my people & after a Stay of Sixteen Days there the General provided me and all my peopel with a passage to Lisbon on Board a Sweddish vessel, & put on board Provissions and what was Nessary for Our Subsistance all att. the Exspence of the Queen of Pertengill, I arived att. Lisbon the first of June Comeing on Shore I Fortannately found a Gentleman that is a very Sensiar Friend to the Cause of Liberty to Say Arnold Henry Dohrman Esqr.[5] who has not only Furnish'd myself Officers & people with such appearel as they Stood in Need of. & provissions, But with Sufficensy of money to Bare our Exspences to Spain, for which place we set on to day.

I am Your Excellency Mt. Servt. JOHN KENDRICK

P.S. Please to Foward the Inclos'd—

His Excellency Benjamin Franklin Esqr.

Addressed: His Excellency Benja. Franklin Esqr. / The American Ambassador, a / Paris

Notation: Hendrick John—Juin 13 1779—

4. Terceira, another island in the central Azores.
5. This American merchant in Lisbon is identified in XXVI, 211–12n.

From James Lovell

ALS: American Philosophical Society (three), University of Pennsylvania Library;[6] copy: National Archives

Hond. Sir June 13th. 1779 Philada.

By way of Martinique I forward to you Gazettes, Journals and one or two Pamphlets. The Situation of Things in Congress has been such for some time past that the Committee of foreign Affairs has been drawn on to look dayly for some interesting Decisions to communicate to you, which must account for their Silence many Weeks. I am once again left alone, and therefore in a too delicate Circumstance to pretend to give you any detail of Matters agitated but not concluded respecting your Commission. I inclose one late Resolve to which I beg your Attention;[7] and I intreat that you will believe me, to be with much Respect Sir Your most obedient Friend

James Lovell

Honble. Doctr Franklin

Addressed: Honorable / Doctor Franklin

Notations in different hands: James Lovell Phyladelphie 13. juin 1779. / These were left by the Capt. of the Martinico-Man by Mistake

From Dumas

ALS: American Philosophical Society; AL (draft): Algemeen Rijksarchief

Monsieur Lahaie 14e. Juin *1779*

Après le départ de ma Lettre du 11e., voici exactement ce que j'ai appris de notre ami.

6. Three of the documents are marked respectively "Copy," "Triplic:," and "4plicate" (U. of Pa. Library); we print from the one with no marking.

7. The resolution, dated June 5, directs the committee for foreign affairs to request the commissioners in France to "transmit an account of their proceedings in Mr. Beaumarchais' accounts." *JCC,* XIV, 692. Four copies are at the APS. For subsequent Congressional actions see John Jay to BF, below, June 18.

Le préavis de l'Amirauté d'Hollde. a éte en apparence assez bon, savoir, de faire de fortes remontrances à L. H. P., pour les presser de se conformer tout de bon à la resolution de la province d'Hollde., quant à la prompte & efficace prestation des Convois illimités.—[8] Mais Mrs. d'Amst. ont remarqué là-dessus, que c'étoit encore trop vague; qu'il s'agissoit de contenter la France, afin de faire lever promptement l'interdit; qu'il falloit donc limiter le terme d'un mois à L. H. P. pour se décider, au bout duquel, à leur défaut, la Province d'Hollde. prendroit séparément les mesures qu'il falloit pour la protection de son Commerce; qu'en ce cas Mrs. d'Amst. s'offroient, pour secourir les Villes souffrantes, d'interposer leur médiation auprès de Mr. l'Ambassadr. de fce., afin de le porter à obtenir, pendant ce terme, une suspension de l'Edit & du Tarif: mais qu'ils avertissoient en même temps, qu'après avoir ainsi fait tout ce qui dépendoit d'eux pour sauver ces Villes, ils ne pourroient rien de plus, se tiendroient tranquilles, &, pour justifier leur conduite à la postérité, feroient insérer dans les Actes une Annotation, d'avoir fait tout ce qui avoit dépendu d'eux pour prévenir la ruine des dites villes, ruine dont le parti contraire, en ce cas, auroit seul à répondre. Ceux de Dort & de Rotterdam ont été entierement de l'avis d'Amst., & ont reconnu que cette ville venoit de faire pour elles tout ce qu'on pouvoit attendre d'une bonne confédérée. Rotterdam, surtout, a parlé très-fortement, & menacé rondement de fermer sa caisse.— Mais le Corps de la Noblesse s'est opposé violemment à l'addition proposée (Mr. d'Obdam, ci-devant du bon parti, ayant tourné casaque).—[9] Enfin toute l'Assemblée est tombée en confusion; les villes non contentes du préavis ont

8. Fauchille, *Diplomatie française,* pp. 141–2, argues that this change of heart was occasioned by yet another French trade regulation, which restricted the exemption from the 15 percent tariff to naval products only. In any case the admiralty urged the deputies from Holland to solicit the other members of the States General "de la manière la plus vive et la plus pressante, de se conformer à la détermination des Etats [of Holland] d'accorder au commerce une protection illimitée": La Vauguyon to Vergennes, June 15, 1779, quoted in *ibid.*, p. 142.

9. Jacob Jan, graaf van Wassenaer-Obdam (1724–79): *NNBW,* II, 1539.

pris la chose *ad referendum,* & l'Assemblée a été prorogée à mardi prochain en huit.— Ceux de Dort, leur brave Pensionaire[1] étant, pour leur malheur, depuis longtemps fort mal, ont prié celui d'Amst. de leur donner des Memoires instructifs de tout ce qui s'est passé jusqu'ici, & de ce qu'ils avoient à faire; il le leur a promis, & il y travaille.

J'ai observé à notre Ami, que je ne concevois pas comment L. H. P. pouvoient avoir besoin d'être pressées de résoudre ce qu'Elles ont déjà résolu. Il m'a dit, "Votre observation est juste: mais que voulez-vous? ils veulent que ces résolutions ne disent pas ce qu'elles disent, que la lumiere ne soit pas lumiere: Ce sont des puérilités, des subterfuges d'enfants: Mais que répondre à ceux qui vous disent que le noir est blanc, que 2 & 2 ne font pas 4? Toute dispute dès-lors est finie."—Avec tout cela notre Ami est content de la situation des Affaires: il dit que cela ne sauroit finir qu'à l'avantage du bon parti. Effectivement, Amst. joue un beau rôle; il devient de plus en plus brillant: Rotterdam sa rivale-même lui adjuge maintenant la palme de la sagesse, de la modération, de la générosité & du patriotisme.

Le G—— P—— a encore joué un mauvais rôle là-dedans: mais, dit N—— A——, il s'en répentira.

Je pars demain matin pour Amst., je reviendrai ici après demain. Je suis avec un très-grand respect, Monsieur, Votre très-humble & très-obéissant serviteur D

Passy à S. E. Mr. Franklin

Addressed: To his Excellency / B. Franklin, Esqr. / Min. Plen. of the Un. States / &c. / *Passy.*/.

Notation: Dumas 14. Juin 1779.

1. Cornelis de Gijselaar (Gyzelaer or Gyselaar) (1751–99) had been pensionary of Dordrecht (Dort) since 1776: *ibid.*, x, 309–10. JA later praised him highly: Wharton, *Diplomatic Correspondence,* v, 688.

From Thomas Mante

ALS: American Philosophical Society

Sir Au fort L'Eveque[2] 14 June 1779.

This morning the Count de Landreville[3] paid to the concierge of this prison, two Guineas that he received from your humanity,[4] by means of which, I am in a situation to preserve the chamber in which I am lodged, and which I trust will enable me to preserve it, till the justice of the parliament may relieve me from the most tyrannical cruel oppression that ever one man dared to commit on another.[5]

It is necessary to see this place, and the horrid situation from which I am extricated, to conceive a just idea of the impression that Your goodness has made on my mind: accept Sir, as this sole return that I can at present make for your bounty, the most ardent wishes that you may enjoy a perfect state of health, and that thereby you may be enabled to prosecute effectually, the great plan of restoring liberty to Your oppressed country. I have the honour to be with respect Sir, Your most obliged obedt humb servt. DE MANTE[6]

Notation: De Mante du fort l'Eveque 14 juin 1779.

From John Bondfield

ALS: American Philosophical Society

Sir Bordeaux 15 June 1779

By advices yesterday from Bilboa a vessel arrived at that port from Salem which place he left the 8 May. The Frigates

2. For-l'Evêque, the jail in which Mante had been imprisoned: XXVII, 349n.

3. Innocent-Hector de Maillart, comte de Landreville, son of a lieutenant-general, now deceased: *Dictionnaire de la noblesse,* XII, 810–11. On an otherwise unspecified Thursday, he wrote BF from Passy asking for a brief interview—possibly to intercede on Mante's behalf. APS.

4. A June 13 entry in BF's Cash Book (Account XVI, XXVI, 3) reads, "Charity to M. Me an able writer . . . 48 *l.t.*" At the current exchange rate 48 *l.t.* (or 2 *louis*) was worth about two British guineas. BF had aided Mante previously; see XXVII, 348.

5. Mante was complaining of the comte de Boisgelin, for whom see XXVII, 348.

6. He sometimes signed himself as "de Mante": XXIII, 255n.

the Queen of France, the Warren and the Ranger on a Cruize fell in with a small fleet of Transports from New York bound to Georgia, took eight of them loaden with Arms Amunition Artillery & Stores with many Officers on board and sent them into Boston.[7]

The Spanish Fleet from Ferrol lay in the Bay of Currona when the post came away.[8] The Operation of Spain attract the Commercial Attention we flatter ourselves the measures pursueing will cause a fall in the Insurances and admit the reasuming the Trade with the United States that the high rate of the Premiums have for some time Suspended I have the honor to be with due respect Sir your very hhb Servant

JOHN BONDFIELD

His Excellency B. Franklin

Addressed: His Excellency / Benjamin Franklin / Plenipontiaries des Etats Unies / a / Paris

Notation: John Bondfield. Bordeaux 15e. juin 1779.

From Francis Coffyn

ALS: American Philosophical Society

Paris 16th. June 1779.

I duly receiv'd the honnor of Mr. H. I. Franklin's letter dated 14th. ultmo.[9] covering a Commission, instructions, and other papers for the Cutter Black Prince, Stephen Merchant Commander, which I intended to carry to Dunkirk, to deliver the same to said Captain, and to get the bond Executed by Mr. John Torris, owner of said privateer; but first a Sudden indis-

7. See William Gordon's letter of May 5 and one from Jean de Neufville & fils printed after June 28. Joseph Olney commanded the *Queen of France,* John B. Hopkins, the *Warren,* and Thomas Simpson, the *Ranger:* William James Morgan, *Captains to the Northward: the New England Captains in the Continental Navy* (Barre, Mass., 1959), pp. 156–8.

8. The Ferrol fleet was moved to La Coruña because of the convenience of that port to Cape Finisterre, the rendezvous point for the Franco-Spanish fleet: Dull, *French Navy,* p. 149. See Bondfield's letter of June 22 for further details.

9. Coffyn must have misread the "W. T." in WTF's signature for "H. I."; the letter is above.

position, and then some unexpected business having detained me here, I was under the necessity of sending Said papers to my house, with the instructions respecting the filling up of the blanks in the Commission and bond; all which having been duly Executed, the bond, and the oath of allegiance to the united states, the former Sign'd by the Captain and owner, and the latter by the Captain only, have been return'd to me here; I intended to wait on your Excellency to have the honnor of delivering Said papers into your Excellency's hands, but a return of a Sore throat and fever, has kept me confined to my room Since the beginning of this month. To avoid any further delay, I take the liberty to send the Said vouchers inclosed, requesting the favour of your Excellency's answer by the bearer, acknowledging the receipt thereof. I am further to acquaint your Excellency that I receiv'd advise yesterday, that said privateer sail'd from Dunkirk road the 11th. inst.[1]

I have the honnor to Subscribe my Self with due respect. Your Excellency's Most obedt and most devoted Humble Servant FRANS. COFFYN

To His Excellency Dr. Benjn. Franklin at Passy.

Notation: frans. Coffin Paris 16. juin 1779.

To William Lee

Copies: Library of Congress, University of Virginia Library

Sir Passy, June 17. 1779

I made the Application you desired to the Ministry for the State of Virginia[2] and it is still under Consideration. But it being known that the contract made for the Same things with D'Acosta & Co. has been executed by them, and the greatest part already sent over on their own Account, as you refused to take them, I know not how I can well urge a Compliance with your particular request. I have however, lately repeated the Demand for such a supply to be sent to the Congress, who

1. We have not located the enclosure. The *Black Prince* actually sailed on the 12th; see Capt. Marchant's letter of June 23.

2. To Vergennes, June 12.

may furnish Virginia with it if still wanted or dispose of it otherwise where the general Good shall most require it, and I hope I shall succed tho the great Affairs now on the tapis here, may occasion some present Delay. I have the honour to be with much respect, Your most obedient and most humble servant.

Honble. Wam. Lee Esq.

From Alexander J. Alexander[3]

ALS: American Philosophical Society

Dr: Sir St Germain, 17th June 1779

I propose doing myself the Pleasure to call upon you on sunday Morning to communicate some letters that have past between a friend of yours & myself you may probably guess what the Subject is[4] I hope I shall find you at home I beg my Complements to your Son & am most sincerely Dr Sir your Most Obt Humble Servt A: J: ALEXANDER

Addressed: A Monsieur / Monsieur Franklin / A Passi

Notation: A J Alexander st. Germain 17 june. 1779.

3. This is the first extant letter of the handful that BF received from the brother of his good friend William Alexander. Two years earlier William had told BF he was expecting him soon from the West Indies: XXIV, 199–200.

4. The letters probably concerned a legal tangle involving the two brothers. Between 1763 and 1771 they (and a third brother, now deceased) had purchased two large estates in the recently captured Caribbean island of Grenada. William Alexander's financial difficulties soon thereafter forced them to mortgage the estates to the banking firm of Walpole & Ellison. When William Alexander went bankrupt in 1775, Alexander John Alexander fought a delaying action in the courts of Grenada to prevent their joint properties from being seized by Walpole & Ellison. The French capture of the island in July, 1779, threw the dispute into the French courts: Price, *France and the Chesapeake,* II, 696–9.

From Baudouin

ALS: American Philosophical Society

Monsieur A La Porte de Longchamps ce 17 Juin 1779

Mr. de Sartine, que j'ay vú ce matin, m'a chargé d'avoir l'honneur de vous dire, qu'il luy est revenu, qu'un corsaire ameriquain se disposoit a intercepter le paquebot de douvres à calais, que le capitaine de ce corsaire vous avoit ecrit pour vous communiquer son projet, et que n'ayant pas recû de reponse de vous, il prenoit ce Silence pour un consentement, et qu'enfin il se dispose a executter ce projet.[5] Mr. de Sartine prie instamment V. Excellence d'ecrire le plùs promptement et le plùs fortement possible a ce capitaine, qu'il ait a s'abstenir d'attaquer aucun pacquebot de douvres à calais;[6] cette communication peut à la verité etre de quelqu'utilité à nos Enemmis communs; mais à bien des Egards, que Ve: Excellence devinera sans peine elle nous est avantageuse et meme necessaire, et je ne doutte pas que la cour de france ne la conserve aussi longtems, que celle de Londres voudra la laisser subsister.[7]

Je proffitte avec Empressement de cette occasion pour renouveller a Ve. Excellence toutte ma veneration pour elle ainsy que le tres respectueux attachement avec lequel j'ay l'honneur d'etre, Monsieur votre trés humble et très obeissant serviteur

BAUDOUIN

Notation: Baudouine à la porte de Lonchamp ce 17. juin 1779.

From Dumas

ALS: American Philosophical Society

Monsieur, Amst. 1779, 17e. Juin

Je me trouve ici, depuis une couple de jours, chez Mr. De N———. Avant que j'eusse pu le précautionner, par lettre d'a-

5. See Torris' letter of June 8.

6. On May 7–8 the French government had closed the coast to all traffic with England *except* for the Calais-Dover packet boat. The packet boat service was still important to the French because Spanish Ambassador Almodóvar had not yet left England: Dull, *French Navy,* pp. 149–50.

7. The British government stopped the packet boats at the end of June in order to hinder French gathering of intelligence: Fortescue, *Correspondence of George Third,* IV, 379; Patterson, *The Other Armada,* pp. 99–100.

bord, & plus amplement de bouche, sur ce que vous m'avez confié par votre Lettre du 4e. Mr. S——[8] lui avoit remis une Lettre pour vous, qu'il n'a pu refuser poliment de recevoir, & par conséquent de faire parvenir. Aujourd'hui il s'est passé une petite scene de dénouement, que Mr. De N—— m'a requis de vous communiquer. Mr. S—— l'a abordé, pour lui demander s'il avoit réfléchi sur les plans qu'il lui avoit proposé, & s'il avoit résolu quelque chose en conséquence. Mr. De N——, pour couper court, lui a donné à entendre, qu'il étoit en correspondance directe avec vous, Monsieur, sur la matiere qui faisoit l'objet des dits plans, & qu'ainsi il n'avoit pas besoin de l'intervention d'un tiers: sur quoi Mr. S—— l'a quitté & s'est retiré d'un air mécontent. Ceci nous a confirmé dans l'idée que les démarches de Mr. S—— étoient un commencement d'intrigues, dans lesquelles il servoit d'instrument à certaines maisons ici. Je ne vous en aurois pas écrit, Monsieur, si je ne voyois la possibilité, que rebuté par Mr. De N——, il ne fît agir quelqu'une de ces maisons pour vous faire des propositions directement, qui, dans la conjoncture présente, où Mr. De N—— se donne des mouvemens pour réussir sans risquer le crédit de l'Am——, ne pourroient être que des pieges tendants à faire manquer tout.

J'écris ceci au moment de mon départ pour La Haie, où je vais tout préparer pour me mettre en chemin vers la fin de ce mois, afin de pouvoir, s'il est possible, célébrer sous vos yeux, l'heureux anniversaire de l'Indépendance Américaine.[9]

Le bruit se soutient ici, depuis quelques jours, du départ de la Flotte de Brest, pour se joindre à celle d'Espagne, comme aussi, du depart du M. D'Almodovar de Londres.[1]

Je suis avec le plus respectueux dévouement, Monsieur
Votre très-humble & très-obéissant serviteur D

Passy à S. E. M. Franklin &c.

8. Sayre, against whom BF had warned on the 4th.

9. He was unable to leave The Hague before July 6: Dumas to BF of that date (APS).

1. The Brest fleet sailed on June 3 for a rendezvous off the Spanish coast with fleets from Cadiz and Ferrol, preparatory to an intended invasion of the Isle of Wight; see our annotation of Bondfield's letter of June 22. Am-

Addressed: To his Excellency / B. Franklin, Esqr. / Min. Plenip. of the United / States / at Passy./.

Notation: Dumas 17, Juin 1777.

From Jean de Neufville & fils

ALS: American Philosophical Society

High Honourable Sir! Amstdm the 17 June 1779.

The spirit for the American caúse beginns to revive here, and may be I feel the more impulse for this manner of thinking, which hath been always so agreable to me as we enjoi'd many Conversations on trúe liberty with Mr Van der Capellen Mr. Dúmas and severall American Gentlemen, among which, one introdúces himself every where with proposalls, after having claimed with ús some intelligence with Yoúr Excellency and desiring me some days ago to cover a Letter, for which we begg pardon again as Mr. Dúmas told ús he should be of no fúrther notice to ús as that of an American intitled to general politeness.[2]

Having consulted different people here on the manner in which the Loan for Congress might be best proposed, Your Excellency will give me leave to join to this present the following papers as An aúthorisation on yoúr Excellèncy from Generall Congress.

An order or bond from Yoúr Excellency on ús both dressed in the manner as they should appear in publicq & joint to the Obligation we should give to any particular person for proves we were thereto Aútorised.

Fúrther the particúlar conditions on which yoúr Excellency should give ús permistion to open the loan, and by which she will be so kind as to aprove of the prescribed form, the terms are most the same as which were allowed when I had the

bassador Almodóvar's departure from London, in effect a declaration of war, did not occur until June 18; see our annotation of Dumas' June 9 letter.

2. Dumas had written on June 5, above, about meeting with several Americans. The one presenting proposals was Sayre; see the immediately preceding letter, which was enclosed with the present one.

honoúr of attending and paying my respects to yoúr Excellency at Passy; we charged now those in only 2 per Ct. at the end of the loan or the repayment recd besides the 10 per Ct. allowed to ús 2 per Ct. more, this we were adviced to ask for, in the present circúmstances as we will be obliged to allow perhaps greater gratifications to have a sufficient qúantity of subscribers; and we were flatterd and so we hope that before the Aútorisation from Congress should retúrn we may obtain the two Million.[3] Accomplish'd even will we say to anyone that in a Countrary Case we will desist from opening this loan, offering the same to some particular persons bútt Conditionaly, and not attempting to offer it before we saw occasion to fulfill one Million as it is expressed in the third paper, this is the Only Safe way for the honoúr of yoúr Excell: and of Congress; so we may flatter oúr Selfs that she will be convinced intirely of oúr trúe Zeal to serve the American Caúse; May we now begg yoúr Excellency to pay some attention to the forms we proposed,[4] as we were required to have this stiled before ever any body should intent to subscribe, and to give ús her reflexions, in case any thing might occúrr which was not intirely to her liking and Could be alter'd. And which perhaps after we were inform'd there of, could be illucidated by Mr. Dúmas, who intends to pay his complimts. in short to Yr. E: and so we hope to bring it soon to some Conclúsion, at least what can be done safe all honoúr and with the utmost care for the Credit of America will be menaged with a trúe Zeal.

As we have employed some time ago oúr time in the American intrest oút of a spirit for Liberty and Patriotism Mr. Dúmas seeing that we were Concernd in that Trade(?) advised us

3. The firm in fact was to raise 1,500,000 florins rather than the far larger sum of £2,000,000 sterling: XXVIII, 629–30; BF to Dumas, March 12.

4. The firm had asked BF for the title of "Commissioners for Trade and Navigation and Treasurers of General Congress, and every private State of the Thirteen United States of North America, through the Seven United Provinces": XXVIII, 630. On July 28 de Neufville wrote Congress to ask for the title for himself and his son (National Archives); Congress received the request on Nov. 24 and referred it to the committee for foreign affairs, where apparently it died: *JCC*, XV, 1302.

that we should write to Congress, and as there will be some body we used who should do the búsiness and meddle him self with some matters that might offer either in trade or Navigation that we should offer oúr services to Congress, that she might give us a Caracter withoút any [*illegible*] as Commissioners for trade and Navigation and Treasúrers for Generall Congress and every private state of the Thirteen United States of North America, so may we begg Y. E. to write Likewise in oúr favoúr on this head; and Certainly there is no doubt when circúmstances grow more favoúrable in the futúre bútt what we have done and are promoting still for as múch as it lays in Any ones power for the intrest of America may consist in such Connections to ús as were always Cheafly of oúr department and this would perhaps and very likely be highly despúted to ús as soon as a reverse of State matters may change all oúr Tory hoúses in Whighs for the Sake of intrest; This however we are to wish should not be farr off; the generall Caúse will Always prevail with ús on private intrest. Mr Dúmas however doth not mention this in his Annexed Letter; bútt we hope he'll give in short to Y: E the same reasons for it on oúr side, and that Y E. may approve there of, as we will be able at the same time to act the parts of Consúls Agents of what fr. [foreign?] trade might be reqúired, and oúr Mercatile Commission would be oúr Salary.

One thing again remains to observe aboút the loan, we certainlÿ without the subscription or engagement we intend to pursúe will have occasion as we have already a few of private persons who might have money without employ; and should desire to offer it before the loan could Admitt paying intrest, in the manner as we múst propose it for the Sake of delicacy; we are in hopes Y E. will allow ús the facúlty of receiving those summs of money and to pay intrest for, of which be it múch or little we would directly Acquaint Y E with Further oúr intimate intelligence with Mr. Van Berckell Mr Van de Capellen & Mr. Dumas, will we doubt not make every thing easy and the intrest of America promoted in oúr City, even through the Whole Republicq, as much as either in the Way of Politicqs or by Trade or any other Connections it should be possible; May the time of the Conclúsion of the Treatÿ be soon coming, it is now in Mr Dumas hands, and only known to those who were there in from the beginning Concerned, That will fire the Union of the Twenty States in Two Republicqs forever.[5]

We Recomand oúr selfs to the obliging frendship of Y:E: with all acknowledgement and Remain with all devoted regard High Honourable Sir! Yoúr Excellencys most Obedient humble Servant JOHN DE NEÚFVILLE & SON

Notation: Neufville John & Son 17. June 1779.—

From Samuel W. Stockton

ALS: American Philosophical Society

Sir. Amsterdam June 17. 1779.

I am unfortunate in not having had it in my power to give you earlier information of my determination to make use of the opportunity which now offers for America from hence. I was induced to beleive these vessels would not sail so soon as I find since my arrival here, they intend.

The vessel I expect to go in will sail for Philadelphia or Baltimore & is very small about 40 or 50 tons, and therefore I am in hopes we may escape the vigilance of our enemies, tho' I must expect the reverse of every convenient accommodation during the voyage.

I hope Sir you may have sufficient time to favor me with your commands by return of the post as the vessel expects to sail Saturday the 26th. of this month. You may depend on my best care of them, and should you honor with letters to individuals or dispatches for Congress, you may be assured they shall be delivered as soon as possible after my arrival.

I will not detain you with a recital of the political reports of this country, but must again thank you for friendly offers and

5. *I.e.,* a treaty of commerce between the Netherlands and the United States, a project in which Dumas had been involved for the past nine months: XXVII, 352–3.

request your kind attention once more. Your packets addressed to the care of either the house of Mesrs. Jean De Neufville & Fils or of Fitzeau & Grand will be immediately delivered to me.

I must now take my leave of you, wishing you every happiness.[6] My best wishes also attend young Mr. Franklin who will please to accept my compliments. I have the honor to be with the greatest respect and esteem Sir your most obliged and most obedient Servant S. W. STOCKTON

His Excellency Benjamin Franklin Esqre. &c &c &c

Addressed: To / His Excellency / Benjamin Franklin Esquire / Minister Plenipotentiary / at the Court of Versailles / &c &c &c / at Passy / near Paris. / Mr. Grand is requested to send this immediately

Notation: Stocton S. W. June 17 1779.—

From Benjamin Vaughan AL: American Philosophical Society

My very dearest sir, June 17, 1779

In about 3 weeks time I hope to send you every thing complete, relative to a certain collection. There will be an engraving of the head of the party, taken from the larger medallion, of which you sent a miniature-size to Miss G: S.—[7] The motto, given by her father at my request, is "His country's friend, but more of humankind." I wanted something that should answer to "*complectitur orbem*";[8] which this does only in

6. This is the last extant letter from Stockton to BF. He reached Boston in December, 1779, and subsequently became one of the most distinguished residents of Trenton, eventually holding the office of N.J. secretary of state: James McLachlan *et al.*, eds., *Princetonians: a Biographical Dictionary* (5 vols. to date, Princeton, 1976–), I, 623–5.

7. Vaughan used for the frontispiece of his edition a line engraving by an anonymous artist. Years later he said that he had selected this likeness as the best then available. Sellers, *Franklin in Portraiture*, p. 368. BF sent Georgiana Shipley the miniature within a fortnight of her May 1 request, above, to him. See also her letters of May 12 and June 6.

8. "He embraces the world." The verb can also mean "explains," "understands," or "cherishes." The motto ultimately used was *Non Sordidus Auctor*

one sense of "*complectitur*": however it is infinitely the more important sense, and that which will most please you; and I like it too the better, as it will look with *some,* like making friends with England; which kind of incidents I always take in.— The above stands round the *engraving;*—in the *title page* you know comes, "*hominum* rerumque repertor," from Virgil.—[9] We have got the preface to G:'s speech, all but the *epitaph;* which is promised me, as I suppose from Mr Wharton and is much wanted.[1] My negligence in not asking for this in *good* time, as I thought it might be had at *any* time, is inconvenient to us a little.— As to G. himself, I have not yet been able to see him; but I shall probably see him today, as his examination I believe continues to day at the house. He answered almost every single question of Lord G. G:'s, in the affirmative.[2] He said that at the taking up arms, only 5 were for independence; but that the party had *begun* in the chief towns, ever since 1754 for in order to abuse the Howe's for not quelling the revolt, they seem to consent to acknowledge that they *made* it. But it is impossible to go into the particulars of what he said, they were so very multiplied; but it turned out, that in fact your people had "*recruited*" at *least* on as good terms as ours, whether in America or even almost in England; and that your bounty money for "*substitutes,*" as it was called, was less than the Liverpool & Manchester people gave for *their* regiments in many instances.— The Spanish manifesto's[3] being *announced,* as yet has had little effect; for the people seem to feel as if they had *acquitted* themselves of "being afraid of foreign enemies," by their pannic a year ago; which they take for granted has been proved *needless,* by the event and the

---

Naturæ Verique: "No common judge of nature and of truth." Horace, *Odes,* I, 28, 14–15.

9. "Creator of men and things," referring to Jupiter: *Aeneid,* XII, 829.

1. Vaughan had requested them on May 31.

2. On June 16 Lord George Germain began Galloway's interrogation before the House of Commons committee on the American papers: *The Parliamentary Register . . . ,* XIII (1779), 422–42, 448–71. For the motives of Germain and Galloway, see our annotation of Digges to BF, May 18.

3. See Dumas to BF, June 9.

folly of their enemies. The ———[4] seems to think he has made way both at home & abroad; and all, the CONSEQUENCE of his firmness; and as the prospect now is not held so black as it was a year ago, you may guess whether he is likely to be moved by the *present* prospect. I think nothing but mobs & events will move him. They tell me he has even signified, that if the Marlboroughs & Bedfords (at present a split party in several shapes) leave him, he will be the same: and in consequence, Ld. Denbigh & the Duke of Chandois, (notorious court lords) have given Ld Sandwich the first commendations in the house; the meaning & source of which you will easily understand.—[5] He thinks not only the people subdued, opposition subdued, but the navy subdued, and Mr Keppel put by for ever: as to the *Irish,* I believe he hardly thinks much about them. Indeed my own opinion is, that good sense might bring that matter lastingly to rights; but that these people will not impossibly blunder it into an insurrection, if not a rebellion. Prey Burn this scrawl.[6]

P.S. The letter of Govr. F. was stated to contain accounts of the difficulty America found in getting and supporting an army. He is since stated to be a firm-govt man, and to be the man likely enough to have a considerable civil command in our

4. The King.

5. The Marlborough and Bedford factions are described in our annotation of Vaughan to BF, April 30, and Digges to BF, May 12. George III was determined to keep the administration intact, despite North's efforts to have Gower, leader of the Bedford party, replace him as chief minister; see our annotation of Digges's letter of May 31, and Fortescue, *Correspondence of George Third,* IV, 355–6, 369–70. Contributing further to the cause of political stability, the House of Lords voted against the Duke of Richmond's motion to investigate the alleged mismanagement of the Greenwich Hospital for retired seamen, in which the Earl of Sandwich was strongly implicated. James Brydges, 3rd Duke of Chandos, subsequently moved that Sandwich be thanked for his dedication to the Hospital's welfare. A week later, in debate on Richmond's motion to print all evidence and discussion, Basil Feilding, 6th Earl of Denbigh, urged that the enquiry be printed, "for it would place that Noble Lord's Character in a still fairer Light to the whole World." *Public Advertiser,* June 8, 15, 1779.

6. The sentence is barely legible; this reading is our best guess.

expected conquests.[7] But this is mere vulgar town-talk; and I have no authorities.

Notation: Vaughn June 17th: 1779

From Peter Vesey *et al.*[8]

L:[9] American Philosophical Society

Hounnered Sr. Bouling[1] 17th of June 1779

We that Have our Name Hear prescribed Have hade the Misfourten To Be twise taken the first time Taken By the english when we wase Bound from Boston to Cape fransaay & Carried to Jemac'a & then Sent Hom prisoners to england & after making our eskeep we got to London where we had got a voyage for Hallifax in Hopes of geating to our own homes But fourtun Would Have it So that we most fall in with Two french Cutters Wo Carried us in to Bouling Wher we are in Prison. And if you Pleas to Clear us we are willing to go on Board aney American Ship. This is from your most Obedint Humbel Servants.—

Peter Wesey Boren in Boston Wif & 2 Childers
John Cern Boren in Do.—
Hennery Bringwal Boren in Neubory Port.
Peter Williamson Boren in Newyork was Living in Boston
Thomas Bleke Boren in Newyork was Living at the east eand of Long island
Hennery Williams Boren in Newyork

7. For WF's letter see our annotation of Vaughan to BF, April 9. For his efforts to form armed loyalist brigades see Digges's letter of June 11.

8. We know nothing about these three men other than the story they offer here and repeat in two subsequent appeals dated July 8 and Sept. 22 (University of Pa. Library; APS). The latter two letters were penned by Peter Vesey, whose English is heavily influenced by Dutch; we spell his name here the way he later signed it. In both of the later appeals, Vesey wrote on behalf of Henry Bringwall and John Danelson. To the best of our knowledge, none of these letters elicited a response.

9. The letter and all the signatures are in the same unidentified hand.

1. Boulogne.

Honnered Sr. we Desire the favour you Would Send us Two Lines from your hand To Let us No whether you will exept of our Servise or No.

Addressed: To / His Excellency Sir Pitter / Frankling / A / Parris

To Baudouin[2]

Copy: Library of Congress

Sir Passy, June 18. 1779.

I shall write immediately as you desired to the Capitain of the American Privateer forbidding him to meddle with the Pacquets betwen Dover and Calais.[3] I did not attend much to the Capitains Letter, supposing that if they were under the protection of the Governement they would if stopt by him produce that protection, and that he would of course discharge them. Please to assure M. De Sartine of my Respects, and believe me to be with great Esteem, Sir,

Mr. Baudoin

To John Torris and Francis Coffyn

Copy: Library of Congress

Sir Passy, June 18 1779.

I received the Letters you did me the honour of writing to me the 20th. of May and The 8th. Instant.[4] I did not immediately forbid Capt. Merchant's intercepting the Dover Pacquets supposing that if they were protected by this Governement, he would, on their showing him their Passports, discharge them, and if not protected there would be nothing improper in taking them.— But as I now understand that such an Interruption of the Correspondence between the two Nations would be disagreable to the government as being prejudicial

2. In response to his of the previous day.

3. See the following document.

4. BF's copyist apparently mistook "28" for "20"; Torris' letters were dated May 28 and June 8. He also miscopied "Marshal" for "Marchant" and (possibly) "or" for "&" in the inside address line.

to Commerce,[5] I do here by desire you would acquaint Capt. Marshal, that he will not be contenanced in that Entreprise that if he should take any of the Pacquets they will not be condemn'd to him, and that he is strictly for bidden to meddle with them. With much Esteem I have the honour to be, Your most obedient et most humble Servant BF.

Mr: Torris or Mr Coffin.

From Thomas Digges

ALS: Historical Society of Pennsylvania

Dr. Sir June 18. 1779

My letters under the dates of the 11th. & 15th. Inst—[6] will inform You very fully of the final conclusion of the business I was lately upon, and I make no doubt but the rejection has been lamented by another party concernd fully as much as by me & my friends.

The Books You orderd are already Shipd on board the Dutch Ship Anna Maria Captn. Christiaan Roeloffs which will sail for Amsterdam in six or seven days. There is a mark on the box in which they are packd thus W and a card is also naild upon it directed thus (Books) For Messrs. Horneca Grand & Co. Merchs. Amsterdam. I will accompany it with a line or two to them Gentlemen giving information that the books are forwarded to their care by your order, as by so doing it may save a custom house search of the box & the unpacking the Books. I have not yet got the bill of the exact contents of the box or the amount of the Cost &ca., but I shall do it soon and repay myself as you direct— In this way or whatever other You may please to command Me I shall be ever ready and willing to serve You or Yours.

As Your letter of the 30th. May informs me You had paid Brehons Bill, I am in expectation that the other drawn in favr of Mr Panchaud will be soon returnd to me. The want of the usual intercourse as to negotiation of bills inducd me (from

5. See Baudouin's letter of June 17 and BF's response of June 18. The *Black Prince* missed the packet on her June 12–22 cruise: Clark, *Ben Franklin's Privateers*, pp. 33–41.

6. That of June 15 is missing.

Yr. mentioning You would pay the money advancd to Brehon & others) to get Mr. P. to carry the bill to Paris & to remit me the 20 £ to his friend in London, & I unluckily gave him the bill but a very few days before I found from Yr. letter that You had paid it.

We are all in an uproar here about the late maneuvere of Spain, & the word perfidious is now transferd from the Court of Versailles to that of Madrid. The notification was given to the House of Commons last Wedy. with a smiling face from our Primier who was pretty severely handled for treating lightly so momentuous a matter. It was read yesterday to the Commons, & long, tho not very spirited or interesting debates ensued thereon; the house of Lords treated it in a higher stile & there has been much commendation on the speeches of Lord Shelburne and the Duke of Richmond. In both houses many hints were thrown out about the propriety of withdrawing the Army from America in order that the whole force might act directly against the house of Bourbon. It will be a sad effort for this Ministry to abandon intirely the prospect of subduing America, but nevertheless there was a hint from the Treasury bench (from W Ellis) that the withdrawing the army might be adopted as a future measure and that the Independence of America was *no very improbable event.*[7] It apears to me that one of the Ports of N York or R Island will be soon evacuated not unlikely the former as the later being an Island may be longer tenable. I have no doubt this would have been a measure some time ago adopted had not fresh proofs of disunion & discontents in Ama given ministry some hopes of subduing the Country—they are now seeking these proofs to

7. Some newspapers made much of North's "smiling and joyous countenance" as he informed the House on June 16, that the Spanish Ambassador had delivered to Lord Weymouth a manifesto declaring that Spain had joined France in the war. The following day these papers described in glowing terms Shelburne's and Richmond's speeches attacking North's ministry and calling for a withdrawal of troops from America; see *The General Advertiser, and Morning Intelligencer* and *The Public Advertiser* for June 17–18, 1779. Welbore Ellis, treasurer of the Navy (XII, 120n), had in fact voted against the motion for an address to the King to direct all British forces against the Bourbons. Fortescue, *Correspondence of George Third,* IV, 359.

the eternal disgrace of this Country, by the evidence of Torey Refugees who never again can go to Ama. I suppose Galloways evidence will finish this night. Lord S. has been finely baited for not having the fleet out (28 sail of the line & 6 frigates) before yesterday.[8] I understand two of them are put back. It is said here that the Spanish fleet saild twelve of the line & frigates &ca on the 27th May and 20 sail of the line &ca. on the 2d. June. The Brest fleet of 28 sail of the line & several frigates on the 3d. June. This is generally beleivd, & the consequence of such apparent superiority causes much discontent & a general gloom upon the faces of every one. The ministry are yet haughty & carry it with a high hand, & talk of being equal to all this force even if joind by Holland & Portugal.

It appears pretty clear that the 2000 men wch Saild from NY the 5 May, are gone to Chesepeak said to be in support of a party of discontents to the Congress measures on the Eastern Shore of Maryland.[9] There appears to be no line of battle Ship in Ama. & but few frigates, there was but three of the line went with Arbuthnot, and four of Byrons fleet unfit for active service are now on their way home.

Much alarm as to an invasion of Ireland, but the most general receivd opinion as to the Brest fleet is, that it is gone Southward to join the Spaniards.[1]

Mr. Hartley gave notice yesterday he would make a motion to bring in a bill to lead to some terms to be offerd Ama. It was to be debated upon to day, but put off till Monday on accot of Lord N non attendance on acct of his having lost an infant Son. He read to the house some articles for pacification or negotiation six in number, which he mentiond as terms he thought probable America would not totally reject, & of which the Minister had had some confidential information

8. Rockingham criticized Sandwich in the House of Lords on June 14, citing this as an example of his gross neglect of duty. *The Parliamentary Register . . .*, XIV (1778–79), 498–9.

9. See our annotation of Digges's letter of June 11.

1. *The Public Advertiser* reported this on June 17, but also predicted that France and Spain would first attack Ireland.

about & had rejected.[2] This Gentn. is indefaticable in his laudable endeavours to do good, but from the present lethargic disposition of all ranks of men there seems little prospect of success.

I am in hopes the late movements in Spanish affairs here will induce some of my acquaintance's near You to take a journey soon;[3] I am the more anxious for it, as I am certain You Sir will be left more at ease and to your wish, setting aside the public Good. I cordially wish you happiness & Success and am with great truth and Sincerity Your Obligd & Obt. Servant W.P.——

Notation: June 18. 79 Digges.—

From Dumas

ALS: American Philosophical Society

Monsieur, La Haie 18e. Juin *1779*

Mes dernieres étoient du 14e. & 17e. La derniere a été écrite d'Amsterdam à la requisition de Mr. De N——. Il y a joint une des siennes pour vous,[4] dont il m'a lu des morceaux, qui demandent quelque éclaircissement de ma part. Il m'a demandé s'il pouvoit écrire directement au Congrès, pour demander le titre de *Trésorier général en Hollande* des Etats-Unis?[5] J'ai dit que, quant à moi, il le pouvoit, &, sur ce qu'il desiroit que je l'appuyasse, je lui ai fait entendre que je ne le ferois qu'après vous avoir consulté, & sous votre approbation. J'ai compris, par ce qu'il m'a lu, que c'est un titre bien plus étendu,

2. Dudley North (b. 1777) fell ill on June 16 and died two days later: Alan Valentine, *Lord North* (2 vols., Norman, Okla., 1967), II, 109. Hartley's terms of negotiation can be found in *The General Advertiser, and Morning Intelligencer,* June 19, 1779. It was not until Tuesday, June 22, that he made a lengthy speech and motion for reconciliation with America; it was negatived without debate. Cobbett, *Parliamentary History,* XX (1779), 901–15.

3. Probably a reference to Arthur Lee, who wished to return to Madrid; see Louis W. Potts, *Arthur Lee: a Virtuous Revolutionary* (Baton Rouge and London, 1981), p. 226. For Digges's relationship with the Lees see Elias and Finch, *Digges Letters, passim.*

4. Above, June 17.

5. De Neufville also asked it of BF, but Congress buried the request in committee; see de Neufville's letter of June 17.

qu'il ne me l'avoit dit dans la conversation, qu'il sollicitoit. Il vous parle aussi, dans sa Lettre, d'autres personnes de ce pays, qui peuvent avoir des connexions d'estime réciproque avec des personnes respectables en Amérique, comme particuliers, mais qui n'ont pu me produire aucune preuve d'être autorisés par le Congrès à se mêler des affaires de l'Am——. J'ai donc cru devoir être circonspect, & ne pas entrer avec elles dans les mesures à prendre, dont elles se disent chargées. Le reste, je vous le dirai, Monsieur, de bouche. Il suffit, en attendant, que vous soyiez prévenu en termes généraux. J'ajouterai, qu'il ne manque pas de gens qui voudroient faire leur fortune avec l'Amérique, à présent qu'ils y voient de l'apparence: mais ce n'est pas ceux-là dont elle a besoin, ni des *Plan-Makers;* l'essentiel est de trouver de puissants souscripteurs, comme on vous l'a promis. J'arrange à présent mes affaires, pour partir avant la fin de ce mois: car, outre qu'il est grand temps que nous entretenions de bouche sur bien des choses, je serois charmé de pouvoir vous présenter en personne, le 4e. Juillet, tous les sentimens que m'inspire cet heureux anniversaire, avec ceux du respectueux attachement avec lequel je serai toute ma vie, pour vous, Monsieur, Votre très-humble & très-obéissant serviteur D

Je n'ai pu garder Copie de ceci

Passy à S. E. M. Franklin

Addressed: To his Excellency / B. Franklin, Esqr. / Min Plen. of the un. States / *Passy.*/.

Notation: Dumas 18. Juin 1779.

From the Baronne de Frëÿ[6]

ALS: American Philosophical Society

Monsieur A paris le 18 juin 1779

Cest Madame de Fréÿ epouse de Mr le baron de fréÿ premier Capitaine de la légion de pulauswki au Service des etats unis de l'amerique, qui a l'honneur de vous ecrire pour vous prier Monsieur de vouloir bien faire parvenir à Son mari la lettre cy jointe.[7]

Je prends Monsieur la liberté de m'adresser à vous parce que de 6 a 7 lettres que jai ecritte à mon mari depuis Son depart aucune ne parois lui etre parvenue, et que la Seulle lettre que jai recue de lui est Celle qui m'est venue par Monsieur Le Marquis de la fayette[8] quoique Suivant Cette meme lettre il me marque m'en avoir ecrit plusieurs aûtres en se plaignant de mon pretendu Silence.

Permettez moi Encore Monsieur de profiter de Cette occasion pour vous Suplier d'accorder à mon mari l'honneur de votre protéction immédiate Si Comme jai tout lieu de le penser le Congreés est Content de ses services, les bontées dont il me marque que Monsieur le Marquis de la fayette l'honnore est un titre pour autoriser cette liberté.

Des raisons tres fôrtes Monsieur m'empechent d'avoir l'honneur d'aller vous faire moi même ma priere et mes excuses, Monsieur de Malésieu[9] veut bien avoir la bonté de vous presenter mon paquet Si vous aviez quelques choses à me faire dire au Sujet de Mon Mary vous pouvez le dire Monsieur en toutte Confiance a Monsieur de Malesieu.

6. Her use of accent marks seems indiscriminate; her husband used none at all. He is Joseph-Pierre-Charles, baron de Frey, whom BF had recommended to Washington: XXIV, 156–7; *DBF.*

7. Missing.

8. In 1778 Congress had appointed Frey an aide to Lafayette for his projected expedition against Canada: *JCC,* X, 107.

9. Most likely this was one of the distinguished Malézieu family, several of whose members appear in Christine Favre-Lejeune, ed., *Les Secrétaires du roi de la grande chancellerie de France: Dictionnaire biographique et généalogique (1672–1789)* (2 vols., Paris, 1986), II, 918–19.

Je Suis avec respect Monsieur Votre tres humble et tres obeissante Servante PARIEN DE FRËŸ

Notations in different hands: Madame de freÿ rue des deux porte st. severin. vis a vis l'hotel d'orléans / De Frey Paris 18. juin 1779.

From John Jay

LS:[1] American Philosophical Society (two), Historical Society of Pennsylvania, University of Pennsylvania Library, Harvard University Library, His Excellency M. Jacques Delarue Caron de Beaumarchais (1976); copy: Library of Congress

Sir In Congress Philadephia June [18][2] 1779.

I enclose you Acts of Congress of the 5th. and 18th. Instant[3] respecting Bills of Exchange for two Million four hundred thousand Livres Tournois Principal and four hundred thirty two thousand Livres Interest drawn on you in Favor of Monsieur de Beau Marchais, and payable in the several Sums and at the respective Periods specified in the enclosed Schedule.[4]

1. The six LS vary in capitalization, punctuation, and spelling. We print from the one in the Bache Collection at the APS, which bears BF's endorsement.

2. We have supplied the date from the LS at the Hist. Soc. of Pa.

3. The enclosures are at the Hist. Soc. of Pa. and the APS. The act of June 5 includes the full report of the Congressional committee appointed to investigate Beaumarchais' claims and to negotiate a settlement with his agent, Jean-Baptiste-Lazare Théveneau de Francy (for whose mission see XXVIII, 528). The act is printed in *JCC,* XIV, 690–2, and discussed in Smith, *Letters,* XIII, 80–1n. James Lovell included an extract from the report in his letter of June 13, above. In the act of June 18 the committee on the treasury provided for repayment to Beaumarchais through the issuing of bills of exchange on the U.S. minister plenipotentiary in France: printed in Smith, *Letters,* XIV, 746–7.

4. The repayment schedule, referred to in the act of June 18, provided for fifty sets of bills of exchange containing six bills in each set, amounting to 2,400,000 *l.t.* principal. They were payable on June 15, 1782. APS. Also at the APS is a bill of exchange dated June 15, 1779, for 20,000 *l.t.* pursuant to the June 5 act of Congress, signed by John Jay and attested by Charles Thomson. The notation reads "Presented the 24 Decr. 79." A rudimentary

Sensible of Monsieur Beau Marchais's Efforts to serve these United States and of the seasonable Supplies he has from Time to Time furnished Congress are earnestly disposed to make him this Payment.[5] They would gladly have done it in Produce; but the State of our Finances, and the hazardous Navigation render it impracticable. We flatter ourselves that you will be able to discharge the respective Drafts with Punctuality. If Difficulties occur you will have Time to represent them to Congress who will exert all the Means in their Power to prevent any Loss or Disappointment to Monsieur de Beau Marchais.

I have the Honor to be Sir with great Respect and Esteem Your most obedt Servant JOHN JAY
Presidt.

To The Hon'ble Benjamin Franklin Esqr. Minister Plenipotentiary for the United States of America at the Court of France.

Endorsed: Letter J. Jay Esq Dated June 1779 with Papers relative to M. Beaumarchais' Affairs. recd. June 12. 1780

From John Paul Jones

AL (draft): National Archives; copy: United States Naval Academy Museum

On board the Bon homme Richard At Anchor
under the Isle of Groa[6] June the 18th. 1779.
5ôClock P. M.

Honored and dear Sir,

I have this moment Anchored here. M. de Chaumont will communicate to you the Object of my present destenation[7] as

repayment schedule, beginning with 20,000, is written on the bill of exchange.

5. Congress was less in agreement than Jay implies; see Paine's letter of March 4, above.

6. The Ile de Groix, off which was Lorient's roadstead.

7. At some later date Jones began making notations in the margins of his drafts for use in his dispute with Landais. Here Jones inserted "To convoy a fleet from Groix to the Different Ports in the Bay of Biscay send them to Cadiz for Privateers on my return to Groix."

well as inform you where I mean to anchor about Ten days hence to receive your final Orders.—[8] I have had a most disagreeable Task to compose Affairs on board the Alliance—The two principal Officers Lieutenants hill and adams have at last left her *without a Congée*[9] And I believe in consequence that a better Understanding will Subsist between the Officers that remain.— The inclosed letter respecting Mr. Amiel[1] I hope will meet with your Approbation and when I anchor to receive your orders I can take him again on board or not as you direct.

I am with real Sentiments of honest Esteem and Affection Dear Sir Your truely Obliged Friend and very humble Servant

His Excellency Doctor Franklin.

Notation in Jones's hand: His Excellency Doctor Franklin—Passy—Bon homme Richard June 18th. 1779 at Anchor under the Isle of Groa No. 11.

From Jonathan Williams, Jr. Copy: Yale University Library

Dr. & hond Sir. Nantes June 19. 1779

This serves to inform you that I have this day Settled with Mr. Gourlade for the Deans Anchors in the following manner agreeable to your order .... Vizt:

The anchors amount to as per bill................6445.18.—

I have pd. the ballance due from me to the Commrs £2799.19.9

8. On June 19, at Sartine's request, Jones sailed from Lorient with the *Bonhomme Richard, Alliance, Pallas, Vengeance,* and *Cerf* to escort French merchantmen to various ports in the Bay of Biscay. The squadron returned to Lorient on July 1 after a cruise marred by a collision between the *Bonhomme Richard* and *Alliance:* Morison, *Jones,* pp. 193–4; Idzerda, *Lafayette Papers,* II, 268n; Peter Landais, *Memorial to Justify Peter Landai's Conduct during the Late War* (Boston, 1784), pp. 18–20; Jones to BF, July 1 (APS).

9. *I.e.,* without leave. See their letter of June 8. On June 13 Jones chaired a hearing attended by JW and others which unsuccessfully tried to reconcile the conflict between Landais and his officers: Landais, *Memorial,* pp. 16–18.

1. Granting his secretary Lt. Peter Amiel leave of absence; see our annotation to John Browne's letter of May 13. A copy of Jones's letter is at the APS.

I have drawn on you at this date in favr.
M Gourlade 3 days do. 3645.18.3
£6445.18.

This Ballance this Object and my account with the Commissioners.

Doctor Franklin Paris.

From the Duchesse de Deux-Ponts

ALS: American Philosophical Society

Ecolle Militaire[2] dimanche 20 juin 1779

Voici Monsieur Les Ciseaux que je Vous ait promis. Vous Voyez que je Multiplie autant que je le puis Les Moiens de me rapeller a Votre souvenir, pardonnéz Moi charmant homme les petites ruse que Linteret de Mon Coeur Me suggere, ce sont les seule dont je sois Capable; en changeant de chemise, en vous promenant,[3] et en ecrivant, vous Voila forcés de songér a Moi, mais vous y penseréz encor bien plus surment mon cher monsieur francklin Lorsque que vous voudres vous occuppér des gens qui vous Aiment et qui vous revere le plus tendrement. DE FORBACH DOUAIRIERE DU SME. DUC DE DEUXPONTS

Addressed: a monsieur / Monsieur francklin Ministre / des Etats unis a La Cour de / france / *a passis*

Notation: De forbach Paris 20. juin 1779.

To Schweighauser

Copy: Library of Congress

Sir, Passy, June 21—79.

I received yours of the 5th. Inst. acqg. me with your Drafts on me for 91,414 *l.t.* 16. 10. I shall pay them as they appear,—except so much of them as are founded on the Commn. of 5

2. She must have been visiting her friend Kéralio on that day.

3. BF eventually lost the walking stick that she had given him, but she replaced it with one decorated with the Phrygian cap of liberty. Bequeathed by the Doctor to George Washington, it now resides in the Smithsonian Institution: Lopez, *Mon Cher Papa,* pp. 189–90.

per Ct. charged in your Accts. on the Delivery of the tobaccos, which I cannot allow being well informed that one per Ct. in such Cases is the Usage and fully sufficient.[4] I request therefore that you would retain in your hands and not issue so many of your Drafts as amount to that Difference. I have the honour to be &c.

Mr Sweighauser

From Samuel Wharton ALS: American Philosophical Society

Dear Sir Hotel de Rome Monday Morning Jun 21/79

I send you the News Paper. The Spanish Declaration was not made on Tuesday, But I have a Letter, which says, That it was to be deliver'd on Wednesday. They write from London, That the New York Mail brings Advice,—of General Clinton's detaching three thousand Men upon an Expedition (to sail the 8th of May) and That Genrl Washington supposing it to be to Virginia on a desolating Plan, and to make a favorable Diversion for Prevost,—had apprizd the Governor of that State, of it.[5] It seems, The Frigate which convoyed the seven Transports towards Georgia, and which with Them are carried into Salem,—had Twenty six Thousand Pounds sterling worth of Indian Goods on Board.[6] A seasonable and important Supply for the use of the States, and at the Rate, The Indians were accustomed to be supplied by the Traders,—would be equal to above One hundred thousand Pounds worth. Mr. Craig,[7] a faithful American, writes Mr. Ross, The Truth of this Capture may be depended on. If your Excellency had any News yester-

4. See BF to JA, June 5. BF explained his objections at length in a July 25 letter to Schweighauser (Library of Congress).

5. For the British raid on Virginia see our annotation of Digges's June 11 letter. We find no record of Washington's having written Gov. Patrick Henry, but for his reaction see Fitzpatrick, *Writings of Washington,* XV, 90–2, 150–1, and *Jefferson Papers,* II, 265.

6. The convoy captured by the *Warren, Queen of France,* and *Ranger;* see Gordon's May 5 letter.

7. Possibly the Philadelphia merchant John Craig (XXVI, 260n), who had been with Ross in Nantes.

day in your Letter, I should be much obliged to Billy, To favor me with the important Parts of it.

In great Truth, I am, with the utmost Respect, Dear Sir yr. Excellency's most obedient & humble Servant S. WHARTON

Please to turn over

One of my Friends writes me as follows.

"Our Grand Fleet will fall down to St. Helens to morrow, with Orders to put to Sea the first fair Wind; It consists of 29 Ships of the Line, 8 Frigates, five Fire ships, and two Cutters. It will probably be reinforced with three or four More Ships of the Line."[8]

I cannot conceive, That the English have such a Fleet at Portsmouth, except They include Darby's Squadron, which I do not find by the News paper, was returned from convoying Arbuthnot.[9]

His Excellency Benjamin Franklin Esqr. &c &c &c—

Notation: S. Wharton Paris 21. juin 1779.

From ——— Allemand with Franklin's Note for a Reply

LS: American Philosophical Society

Monsieur à Paris le 22 Juin 1779.

J'ai l'honneur de vous adresser la Note que vous m'avés demandée; je me reproche la peine que vous voulés bien prendre pour coopérer à la perfection de mon ouvrage sur les Canaux.[1] C'est un tribut d'estime que je paye à votre Nation,

8. On June 16 the main British fleet of thirty ships of the line sailed from its anchorage at St. Helens, Isle of Wight: Patterson, *The Other Armada,* pp. 107, 168.

9. Vice-Admiral George Darby, the second in command of the British fleet, had taken a detachment of ten ships of the line to escort Adm. Arbuthnot and his convoy clear of the coast; Darby had returned to port on June 10; see our annotation of BF's May 26 letter to the committee for foreign affairs and Patterson, *The Other Armada,* pp. 104–5.

1. The enclosure was a list of eight specific questions (with a generous amount of space left for answers) on the construction, dimensions, and

et dont je me plais à m'acquitter, en la proposant pour exemple à ma patrie.

J'ai l'honneur d'être avec un très-profond respect Monsieur Votre très humble et très obéissant serviteur. ALLEMAND

M. allemand, ancien Conservateur des eaux et forêts de l'Isle de Corse, rue Guénegaud, hôtel d'artois

Endorsed: No Canals have hitherto been constructed in the Countries of the United States, unless that called the *Thorough Fare,* of Duck Creek in Delaware State, should be deemed one.[2] It is said to have been made in one Night by a Number of People concern'd in the Navigation of the Creek, which formerly had such a Turn in it, that after sailing 40 Miles one came round to within a Mile of the same Part of the Creek that had been passed. As the Ground of the Isthmus was flat & soft, and some high Tides nearly cover'd it, Proposals had often been made to the Owner of the Land to permit for a Sum of Money, a Cut to be made there, which he had also refused.

Notation: Allemand 22 Juin 1779.—

From John Bondfield — ALS: American Philosophical Society

Sir — Bordeaux 22 June 1779

The Union of the two Fleets which took effect at Currona the 13 Instant leaves no longer in doubt the resolutions of Spain, it is said the Spanish Fleet saild from Cadiz the 11th

---

operation of any working or projected canals in America. BF had presumably requested Allemand to put his questions in writing. When faced with them, however, he drafted only a general response on the bottom of Allemand's cover letter. Allemand's *Introduction et plan d'un traité général de la navigation intérieure, et particulièrement de celle de la France . . .* was published in 1779. For his subsequent publications on interior navigation, and a brief biography, see the *DBF.*

2. BF's friend Thomas Gilpin had written to him about the prospect of constructing a canal between the Chesapeake and Delaware bays, at Duck Creek: XVI, 216–18.

Inst. Letters of the 9th from Cadiz say they only waited a fair Wind. Letters from Madrid say they are at Sea.[3]

A Vessel of 28 Guns is arrived at Bilboa from America but we are without the Name of the ship or the place she saild from on her passage she took four prizes two with provisions that she sent to America the other two with Salt wch. she destroy'd they have many Prissoners. Captain Jones in his new Ship has convoyd into this port many coasting Vessels he has besides his Ship two Frigates in Concert I expect we shall soon hear of his feats he has on board they tel me Eleven hundred Men which certainly are not intended to be inactive.[4]

The Buckskin saild yesterday for Mary Land. The pilot Boat William, with the General Mercer Cap Robinson will sail on Saturday for Philadelphia they will convey inteligence of the junction of the Fleets. I [coud?] wish before they sail to see some publick Act to transmit of the event. I have the honor to be with due respect Sr your very hhb Servant

JOHN BONDFIELD

His Excellency B. Franklin Passi

Addressed: His Excellency B Franklin / plenipotenre. des Etats Unies / a / Paris—

3. The recently expanded plans for the invasion of England now called for 30,000 troops from St. Malo and Le Havre to capture first the Isle of Wight and then Portsmouth. Before they could sail, however, a Franco-Spanish covering fleet would have to reach the English Channel from its rendezvous point at Cape Finisterre. Twenty-eight French ships of the line had sailed from Brest on June 3 for the rendezvous. Eight Spanish and two French ships of the line from La Coruña joined them off Finisterre at the beginning of July, but the main Spanish contingent of thirty-two of the line lay becalmed at Cadiz from June 4 until June 22. Beset by contrary winds, it took another month to reach the rendezvous; only then could the huge combined fleet sail for the Channel: Dull, *French Navy,* pp. 147–54, 362–3; W.M. James, *The British Navy in Adversity: a Study of the War of American Independence* (London and New York, 1926), pp. 170–7. For a full account of the campaign see Patterson, *The Other Armada.*

4. An abbreviated French translation of the first two paragraphs of the present letter is among BF's intelligence reports (National Archives). For Jones's cruise see our annotation of his June 18 letter.

Notations in different hands: Bourdeaux / J. Bondfield. Bordeaux 22. juin 1779.[5]

From Dumas

ALS: American Philosophical Society

Monsieur, Lahaie 22e. Juin *1779*

La grande nouvelle que nous reçumes hier par la malle d'Angleterre, & qui nous a été confirmée par les Lettres de france aujourd'hui, de la Déclaration & jonction de l'Espagne à la France, & par conséquent à l'Amérique, est trop importante pour ne pas m'empresser de vous en complimenter de tout mon coeur.[6]

Vous aurez compris, Monsieur, par ma derniere de Vendredi dernier,[7] que toujours fidele à mon grand principe, de subordonner tout au service de l'Amérique, j'ai cru devoir vous précautionner contre l'ambition d'un particulier, qui peut être très-utile à l'Amérique en s'évertuant dans sa sphere, qui est la mercantile, mais qui ne seroit ni capable, ni à portée, ni propre à la servir dans le politique, & qui ne penseroit certainement qu'à convertir à son propre avantage les pouvoirs dont on le révêtiroit.

There is another Gentleman, living constantly on his country-seat in a remote province.[8] I know the former has made, or will make mention of him to you. But I don't see by his political and other circumstances that he can be useful at all. His having declared himself a friend to the Americans some years ago, must not distinguish him from many others in this Country, so much as to be entitled to more than to the esteem and friendship of the Americans. He has attacked, without any aparent hope of success, some darling preroga-

5. In addition to these notations there are various numbers and calculations on the address page (such as the division of 25,000,000 by 24), having no apparent connection with this letter.

6. A reference to Almodóvar's June 16 manifesto, which was printed in the June 25 issue of the *Gaz. de Leyde.*

7. June 18.

8. Van der Capellen, who was from the rural province of Overijssel: Schulte Nordholt, *Dutch Republic,* p. 22.

tives of a Great personage in this Country, who, for this reason, looks on him as his personal enemy.[9] Therefore, all what should be proposed by such a channel, would be very unwelcome. We want here water to be poured in the fire, not oil. This young gentleman is too restless & too hot. When things will be brought to maturity, I hope we will have here a wise American, *pietate gravem ac meritis virum quem, doctum regere dictis animos, & pectora mulcere.*[1] Till this time I think I must carry on the business as hitherto with our friend alone, without communicating any thing of it with the Gentleman. I beg this Letter may not be seen by any body.

J'ai eu l'honneur de présenter ce matin Mrs. Pringle & Stockton à Son Exc. Mr. l'Ambr. de Fce.

Je suis avec un très grand respect, Monsieur Votre très-humble & très-obéissant serviteur D

Je ne saurai que ce soir, de notre ami, si je pourrai partir avec la fin de ce mois, comme je me l'étois proposé. Pour peu que je voie de pouvoir être utile, j'attendrai que l'Assemblée d'hollde., qui rentre demain matin, se sépare.

Passy à Son Exc. Mr. Franklin

Addressed: To his Excellency / B. Franklin, Min. Plenip. / of the United States / *Passy.*/.

Notation: Dumas 22. Juin 1779.

From Magellan

ALS: American Philosophical Society

Monsieur & cher confrere Londres 22 June—79

Celle-ci est pour un acte d'amitié & d'humanité, auquel je suis sur que vous prendrez tout parti, & vous employeres pour reussir. C'est en faveur d'un ami,[2] de celui que vous connoissez & voyez à Passy. Son frere Richard Nairne, capitain

9. The stadholder; see *ibid.,* p. 26.

1. A garbled version of Virgil, *Aeneid,* I, 151–3: "If they should see a man respected for his dutifulness and services they will fall silent . . . His words rein in their spirits and soften their positions."

2. Edward Nairne.

du vaisseau Marchand nommé the *generous Friends.*, en venant de Newfound Land, fut pris par la Fregate *Flora*, commandée par le Marquiz de Castellan dans le 30 Mars dernier: & fut amené à Toulon.[3] Ce Monsr. Richard Nairne se trouve actuellement *sur parole* à Aix en Provence, chez Messrs. gregoire. Vous n'avez qu'à dire à la personne que vous savez le nom de ce Monsr., qui est frere de celui du meme Nom, faiseur d'Instrumens de Mathematique, & deja Membre de la Soce. Rle. qui demeure vis à vis la Bourse de Londres, & qui est son antien & bon ami: & je suis persuadé qu'il fera tout ce qui sera en son pouvoir pour obtenir la Liberté de son frere.[4] Monsr. Nairnc Lui meme a eté ce matin avec moi pour cet affaire: mais il n'a pas jugé de bien faire en ecrivant en droiture à la Personne que vous savez. Ainsi je vous recommande cet affaire de coeur. L'humanité et amitié m'engage et je comte sur la votre. Vale & ama tuum MAGELLAN

N.B. Il ne m'a pas été possible de trouver l'ouvrage de Home sur le croup.[5]

Notation: Magellan 22. Juin 1779.

From Samuel Wharton AL: American Philosophical Society

Rue L'Universite Hotel de Rome June 22d. [1779]

Mr. Wharton presents his Compliments to Mr. Franklin & sends the News Paper, containing the Spanish Declaration of War.[6] Mr. W's Friends write Him, That the Merchants & Stock Jobbers keep the Price of Stocks, from an Opinion, That

3. The *Flore*, 26 guns, commanded by de Castellane-Majastre, was part of the Toulon fleet: Amblard-Marie-Raymond-Amédée, vicomte de Noailles, *Marins et soldats français . . . pendant la guerre d'indépendance des Etats-Unis (1778–1783)* (2nd ed., Paris, 1903), p. 376.

4. BF must not have acted on this letter. Richard Nairne, still detained at Aix-en-Provence, wrote to solicit his help on Aug. 19 (APS).

5. Francis Home, *An Inquiry into the Nature, Cause, and Cure of the Croup* (Edinburgh, 1765).

6. Almodóvar's declaration was published in London newspapers on June 19.

Spanish War was a *good Thing* & would produce great Quantitys of Silver & Gold.[7]

From Stephen Marchant: Two Letters

(I) and (II) LS:[8] American Philosophical Society

I.

Sr/ Black prince Cutter Road of Morlax June 23d. 1779

I set Sail on My Cruize June 12th. after taking in my propper Stores for the same, and Steered to the Westward from the Road of Dunkirk at 11 in the Morning fell in with a portuguese brig having English Manufactured Goods on board. I took her and sent her to Calais being the nearest port and at one Next Morning took a prize as I Imagined she being bound from Denmark to Dublin laden with Lumber I took her to Calais road and According to My Instructions Applyed to the Court of Admiralty when the two brigs were discharged they not being deemed Lawfull prizes to the United States so I weighed Anchor and Stood out to Sea Cruized for three or four Days and met no Enemy Spoke to several Neutral Ships when upon the 16th of this Instant June being with in a few Leagues of Beachy[9] on the English Shore at 2 OClock in the Morning Discovered 6 Sail—5 of them Brigs and one Dogger Spoke to the Dogger Chased the 5 Brigs and about 8 in the Morning came to an Engagemt. with them and wd. certainly make a prize of them but it being a Small bay and almost with in Shot of an English Fort on Shore I being in 4½ Fathom Water was Obliged to be Satisfied with running them on Shore, about 10 Oclock I stood out to Sea Saw Several Armed Vessels Convoying a fleet of Coasters, along shore, about

7. Silver and gold were no doubt expected from captured Spanish treasure ships. These shipments, however, had already arrived safely in Spain: Dull, *French Navy,* pp. 127–8n.

8. In the hand of Timothy Kelly, one of the *Black Prince*'s crew: Clark, *Ben Franklin's Privateers,* p. 40. For a map showing this and Marchant's later cruises see *ibid.*, p. 89.

9. Beachy Head, on the coast of Sussex.

Noon I perceived an Armed Vessell in pursuit of me she Coming up Very fast upon me I fought my Stern Chases[1] for half an hour when she came up and poured in upon me a whole broadside which I returned with Interest by giving his for the space of an hour 4 Guns for her one I wd. surely make her a prize only she Sheered off I wd. pursue but seen an English Frigate under my Starboard Bow so I set out to Sea and Stood to the Westward on the 17th Inst. I spoke to a Spanish Ship on my lee Quarter an English Frigate on my Weather Bow the Spaniard Informed me that the Spanish Fleet had Set Sail on the 18th Instant my Course S by E Ile of Wight bearing N.E distant 4 Leagues Poverin point N. distance 4 Leagues sale the English Fleet of Men of War[2] Sailing to the Westward Bearings from me N. NEast distance 4 Leagues the 19th. Inst. Course S:W: b W Wind Westwardly fine Weather at 8 in the Morning 20th June saw an English Frigate on my Weather Quarter I steered S: E and b E untill I got clear then tacked and Steered N: W & b W saw Several Ships in Sight mostly Frigates & Men of War Sailing Westerdly, at 6 in the Evening Close to the Lands end I saw the English Fleet the Lands end bearing N.NW. Wind North Easterly distance from Lands end 6 Leagues. At 8 O Clock in the Evening close to the Lands End took an English brig called the blessing in ballast from Tinby bound sent his to France— At 9 in the Evening took another brig called the Liberty Bound to Milford sent her to France at 11 in the Evening took a Sloop the Sally Laden with Coals from Swansey to Falmouth sent her to France 21st June at 2 in the Morning took a brig the Hampton laden with Coals and Earthen Ware from Liverpool to London sent her to France at 3 in the Morning took a Sloop the Elizabeth from Caermarten in Wales to Falmouth laden with Coals Butter and Oats sent her to France at 12 Oclock took a brig the 3 Sisters in ballast from Bideford to Swansey she being but a poor Vessell and unwilling to Weaken my Crew to much by send-

1. Guns firing astern.

2. Admiral Hardy's fleet of thirty ships of the line which had sailed from the Isle of Wight on June 16; see our annotation of Wharton's letter of June 21. "Poverin point" is Peveril Point on Swanage Bay in Dorsetshire.

ing her to France and having a prospect the same Night of more prizes According to Instructions I ransomed her for 70 Guineas[3] at 2 in the Evening still Coasting at the Lands end took a Brig the Orange tree from London to Cork Laden with Kings Stores sent her to the nighest Port of France Likewise at 4 in the Evening took a brig the good will from London to Waterford laden with Porter Iron and dry Goods sent her to France. At 6 in the Evening Wind Northerly Stood out to Sea and Sailed for the French Coast 22d June Course SSE fair Wind an English Frigate near the French Shore gave us chase I sent away our brig prize that was in Company with me being to Windward of the Frigate he Chased us in Vain for 6 Hours and better untill we got Clear of him—

23d Course W, Wind S: S: East [*torn*] the Morning taked [tacked] and stood for the French Shore with a fair Wind saw one of my Prizes the sloop Elizabeth in Company with the English Frigate who Attempted to Chase me but soon gave it over I being near the French Shore was in great fear of my prizes being taken by the frigate. At 4 in the Evening my Prize the Good Will brig and us came to Anchor in Morlax Road, when to my Grief I found that six of our prizes were retaken by the English[4] together with 21 of my Men, having so many Prisoners and my Crew being weakened by sending them in the Prizes I was Constrained to sett Some of them at Liberty and put them in the ransomed Brig Aforesd. kept 21 Prisoners which I have brought in my Cutter to France this is a brief Account of my Cruize from the 12th untill the 23d Inst June— I remain with all respects to yr Excellency Yr Excellencies Most Obedient humble Servant STEPHEN MARCHANT

Addressed: To / His Excellency Benjamin / Franklin Minister of the United / States of North America at the / court of France, Passy / by / Paris

Notation: Capt. Merchant—June 23. 1779

3. Details of the ransom are given in Clark, *Ben Franklin's Privateers,* p. 38.

4. By the frigate *Quebec: ibid.*, p. 39. The July 13, 1779, issue of the *Courier de l'Europe* (VI, 32) reported they had been retaken by the sloop of war *Cabot.*

II.

On board the black prince cutter Morlax Road June 23: 1779

Sr/

In my other Letter bearing an equal date with this I did Acquaint yr Excellency in a brief Manner the transactions that has happened since the 12th. untill the 23d Inst June, in this I acquaint yr Excellency with the Names of the Prisoners I have taken and their Quality, as likewise the Names of 21 of my Men who have been made prisoners by the English, being in my 6 prizes that were retaken their Names as follows—

Americans taken by the English	English taken by me	
Viz.	William Reed Junr Capt,	Brig Named Blessing
Bryan Rooney Gunners Mate	William Reed Senior Owner	do.
Edwd. Duff Boatswains Mate	John Davis Mate	do.
Richard Molloy	Jerimiah Webb	do.
Michael Doran	William Thomas	do.
John Watson	William Pritchard Capt.	Elizabeth Sloop
John Herrin	John Hughes Mate	do.
John Mc.Fadan	William Power Capt.	Brig Goodwill
Terence Kearney	James Currin Owner	do.
Hugh James	William Hederinton Mate	do.
Luke Aver	John Burness	do.
James Collins	Luke Morrissy	do.
James Markin	Richard Williams	do.
James Longwell	James Kenedy	do.
Maurice Creemon	William	

	Knighton Capt	Brig Hampton
Edwd. Brangan	John Kingwell	do.
John Connelly	George Closen	do.
William Griffiths	William Wogan Mate	Brig Liberty
Jacob Wood	Peter Babb	do.
John Hore	Robert Rossitter Mate	Orange tree brig
Robert Wild	William Bale	Sally Sloop
Charles Provoy		

Yr Excellency sees there is an Equal Number of Prisoners on both sides the Men I sent in the diferent prizes were good Men I am a great Loss for them which will a while retard my Cruize I having a fine prospect before me of Distressing the Subjects of Great Britain and to Maintain the Honour of the United States, yr Excellency may be Assured I never will as long as Congress permits me to have my Commission never to Derogate from that noble Spirit of an American Still means to Act with prudence and Caution will knowing my own force and that of the Enemy whom I hope to Harris greatly, I hope yr Excellency will use yr. Influence and Authority in having an Exchange made of the Prisoners taken by me and my Men taken by the English there being an Equal Number and I being Retarded from pursuing my plan of Opperation untill I get my Men Exchanged makes me so Solicitious with yr Excellency to use yr Endeavours as Soon as possible to have the Cartel made, I remain with all respects yr Excellency's most Obedient humble Servant STEPHEN MARCHANT

Addressed: To / His Excellency / Benjamin Franklin / Minister of the united States / of North America at the Court / of France, Passy / by Paris

Notation: Capt. Merchant June 23. 1779

From Jane Mecom

ALS: American Philosophical Society

Dear Brother

Warwick June 23d—1779

As I would not omit writing you by an opertunity which I expect espeshal care will be taken to Deliver, I have complied with a Request made me by Mr Casey whose son I wrot by last fall, in favour of a Mr Elkanah Wattson, Conl. Wattson's son of Plimoth. I have given him to understand I will Inform you what he says of the young Gentileman (which is that he served an Aprentisship with Mr John Brown of provedence who gives him a very good Charrecter & that His Father is a man of a plentifull Estate) & I tell him if he has merritt He may be able to Recomend Himself.[5]

I have wrot you many Leters (some of which I hope you have recd) Informing you of Every thing concerning me worthy yr atention, I have not yet recd. a line from you since that by Mr Simeon Dean,[6] but bless God I now & then hear of yr helth & Glorious Achievments in the political way, as well as in the favour of the Ladys ("since you have rub'd off the Mechanic Rust and commenced compleat courtier") who Jonathan Williams writes me clame from you the Tribute of an Embrace & it seemes you do not complane of the Tax as a very grat penance.[7]

We have Just heard that the Fleet of Transports from France are arived at Baltimore where I hope my Poor unfourtunate

5. For Silas Casey and his son Wanton, and the letter which the latter carried to BF, see XXVIII, 344–5. Elkanah Watson, Jr. (1758–1842), the future merchant and canal promoter, traveled to Europe carrying dispatches and money for BF at the request of the Brown family, merchants of Providence, R.I. Watson formed a partnership with M. Cossoul in Nantes and may also have had mercantile dealings with JW. See XXVII, 63n; *DAB;* James B. Hedges, *The Browns of Providence Plantations: the Colonial Years* (Providence, 1968), pp. 246–54. Watson's memoirs contain numerous anecdotes about BF's life in Passy. Winslow C. Watson, ed., *Men and Times of the Revolution; or, Memoirs of Elkanah Watson . . .* (New York, 1856).

6. Simeon Deane carried several dispatches when he left France in January, 1778 (XXV, 320), and he may have carried BF's letter of Oct. 5, 1777 (XXV, 28–9).

7. Jane Mecom is quoting a story that had been circulating in London and found its way into the American press. An article dated London, July 7, 1778, in the Nov. 10, 1778, issue of *The Connecticut Courant and the Weekly Intelligencer* (Hartford), for example, reported that

A gentleman just returned from Paris, informs us, that Dr. Franklin has shaken off entirely the mechanical rust, and commenced the compleat courtier. Being lately in the gardens of Versailles, shewing the Queen some electrical experiments, she asked him in a fit of raillery, if he did not dread

son in law Collas is so far saif among them,[8] & as I heard Jonathan Williams was coming with them hope for leters from you by Him, we have Grat News of the Defeat of the Britons at Carolina; which we hope is trew but have had no pointed acount of it yet.

God grant this may put a final Stop to these Ravages, my Grandson whome I am with lives where we have frequent alarmes they have come & taken of the stock about 3 quarters of a mile distant & burnt houses a few miles from us, but hitherto we are preserved.

I have as much helth as can be Expected in comon for won of my years & live in a very Pleasant place tho not Grand as I sopose yrs is it gives me grat delight the Famely is kind & courtious; my Grandson is a man of sound sense, & solid Judgment, & I take much Pleasure in his conversation tho he talks but litle, they have won child which they call Sally.[9] Govr. Greene & famely are well I had wrot you there Eldest Daughter was married to Govr. Wards Son they have now a fine son, Ray is still at Mr Moodys scool a promising youth.[1]

---

the fate of Prometheus, who was so severely served for stealing fire from Heaven? "Yes, please your Majesty, (replied old Franklin, with infinite gallantry) if I did not behold a pair of eyes this moment, which have stolen infinitely more fire from Jove than ever I did, pass unpunished, though they do more mischief in a week, than I have done in all my experiments."

On Oct. 25, BF replied to Mecom that the anecdote was a fabrication, one of many instances of the liberties that English newspapers took with him. Van Doren, *Franklin-Mecom,* p. 198.

8. She was still awaiting the return of her son-in-law Peter Collas a month later: Mecom to RB, July 21, 1779, APS.

9. Sarah, daughter of Elihu and Jane Flagg Greene (Mecom's granddaughter), was born on March 16, 1778. Louise Brownell Clarke, comp., *The Greenes of Rhode Island . . . Compiled from the Mss. of . . . George Sears Greene* (New York, 1903), p. 211.

1. Samuel and Phebe Greene Ward's son was William Greene Ward, born on April 1, 1779. John Ward, *A Memoir of Lieut.-Colonel Samuel Ward,* . . . (New York, 1835), p. 17. For Phebe's brother Ray Greene's schooling see our annotation of BF to William Greene, above, June 4. Samuel Moody was the proprietor of Dummer's (now Governor Dummer) Academy. William Greene Roelker, ed., *Benjamin Franklin and Catharine Ray Greene: Their Correspondence, 1755–1790* (Philadelphia, 1949), p. 85.

I see few persons hear of yr acquaintance which deprives me of much pleasure I used to have in conversing about you but I now & then see somthing in the paper which pleases me in perticular there Placeing you alone in won of the Arches at the Exhibition made on the Aneversary of the French-Trety.[2] Mr Casey calls for the Leter & that puts all Els I designed to write out of my mind only to beg to hear perticularly about Temple & Ben & that I am Ever your affectionat sister

JANE MECOM

the Inclosed coppy[3] comes to my hand which I send least you should not have recved the other

From the Comte de Sarsfield

AL: American Philosophical Society

mercredi 23 Juin [1779][4]

M De sarsfield Envoie Savoir des Nouvelles de Monsieur franklin et le prier de lui faire Lhonneur de diner demain chez lui avec Made la duchesse d'Enville. Elle n'est a paris que pour fort peu de Jours[5] et Monsieur franklin aura peu d'occasions de la voir parce qu'elle y est Sans Sa maison.

Addressed: A Monsieur / Monsieur franklin Ministre / plenipotentiaire des Etats / Reunis d'Amerique / A Passy

2. The exhibition was held in Pluckemin, N.J., but was delayed until Feb. 18, 1779, by Washington's absence from headquarters. In addition to a dinner and a ball, the celebration included an elaborate fireworks display near a "temple" with thirteen illuminated arches. On each arch was depicted a significant event of American history. The eighth honored the "American Philosopher and Ambassador extracting lightening from the clouds." *The New-Jersey Gazette* (Trenton), March 3, 1779.

3. Not found.

4. One of two years (the other is 1784) during BF's stay in France that June 23 fell on a Wednesday. According to our practice we publish it at the earliest possible date.

5. Indeed, Turgot informed a friend on July 3 that the duchess, mother of the duc de la Rochefoucauld, had left: Schelle, *Œuvres de Turgot,* v, 592.

From Sartine

Copy: Library of Congress

Versailles le 23 Juin 1779.

J'ai l'honneur, Monsieur, de vous envoyer le memoire que le Sieur deguis prisonnier en Angleterre vous adressé et qui s'est trouvé souscrit à mon adresse.[6]

J'ai l'honneur d'etre avec la Consideration la plus distinguée votre tres humble et très obeissant Serviteur.

(signé) De Sartine.

M. Franklin.

Invitation to an Independence Day Celebration

d: American Philosophical Society

Franklin's celebrated press at Passy has left surprisingly few traces beyond the now-rare imprints which were its products, and even those are sometimes impossible to date. No one knows precisely when the press was established, or from whence Franklin procured the initial printing equipment. We do know that he had met Jean-François Fournier fils in the summer of 1777, and ordered from him fifty pounds of type. Fournier tried to convince the American that he needed a full font, at least fourteen times that amount. Franklin settled on a modest 261 pounds of *gros romain* or 18-point great primer, roman and italic, which was delivered in October, 1778.[7] Why we have no evidence of any printing activity before mid–1779 remains a mystery. This particular blank invitation form for a dinner celebrating the anniversary of American Independence, printed in Fournier's *gros romain,* is the sole surviving example of the earliest Passy imprint that can be dated with any certainty.[8]

The occasion for which Franklin seems to have inaugurated his press was a special one; it was his own formal introduction to the American community as sole minister plenipotentiary. A year earlier, he and John Adams had hosted a similar dinner in Passy on the fourth of July, to which they invited all the Americans in the vicinity

6. Missing. The prisoner may have been Charles-Antoine Guez, a young surgeon BF had once recommended: XXIII, 580n, 581–2; XXIV, 476.

7. See XXIV, 500–1, and XXVII, 618.

8. Luther S. Livingston, *Franklin and his Press at Passy* (New York, 1914), pp. 78–9.

Dr. FRANKLIN, presents his Compliments to
and desires the honour
of Company at Dinner, on Monday the 5th
of *July*; in order to celebrate the ANNIVERSARY of the
DECLARATION of AMERICAN INDEPENDENCE.

Passy, 1779.

An Answer if you please.

Invitation to an Independence Day Celebration

of Paris, and a few local French "Gentlemen." The animosity which Franklin felt toward certain of those Americans, especially Ralph Izard, had reached such a pitch that he refused to invite them; they would not have attended had Adams not insisted upon issuing invitations in his name alone.[9] A year later, exuberant in his post, Franklin printed his own invitations, setting his name in capital letters, and sent them to those very Americans remaining in Paris who had worked so hard for his recall. Although none of the issued invitations has survived, a partial guest list can be compiled from the replies now among Franklin's papers, the first of which is dated June 24.[1] The celebration itself, delayed by one day since July 4 fell on a Sunday, will be discussed in volume 30.

[before June 24, 1779][2]

Dr. FRANKLIN, presents his Compliments to and desires the honour of Company at Dinner, on Monday the 5th of *July;* in order to celebrate the ANNIVERSARY of the DECLARATION of AMERICAN INDEPENDENCE.

Passy, 1779.

An Answer if you please.

9. See Butterfield, *John Adams Diary,* IV, 143–4. Among the group BF would have omitted JA named only Izard and Dr. Smith (James Smith, for whom see XXVI, 387n, and subsequent volumes), but he implied that there were others. He also listed some of the French *invités:* Messrs. Chaumont, Brillon, Le Veillard, Grand, Beaudoin (presumably Sartine's secretary Baudoin), Gérard de Rayneval, and the abbés Chalut and Arnoux. He went on to note the general disapproval with which the court ministers regarded BF's circle of friends.

1. In chronological order, they are from Edmund Jenings, Ralph and Alice Izard, Arthur Lee, Samuel Petrie, the abbés Chalut and Arnoux, Samuel Wharton (who will bring his son Joseph), Montfort de Prat, Ferdinand Grand, Barbeu-Dubourg, and on July 7, having only just returned to town and found his invitation, Laneuville.

2. The date of the first extant reply.

From Dumas

ALS: American Philosophical Society; AL (draft): Algemeen Rijksarchief

Monsieur, La Haie 24e. Juin *1779* au matin

Je fus mardi au soir chez notre Ami. Nous nous félicitames réciproquement du grand événement qui vient d'avoir lieu. Quant à l'Affaire des Convois, les deux Villes privilégiées (who, as I have said already, have reason to sit down contented) ne peuvent rien de plus, que d'appuyer les villes souffrantes: c'est donc le tour de celles-ci d'agir: nous verrons comment elles se comporteront.— Quant à la déclaration d'Espe., si la Cour d'Angle. demande secours ici, comme il y a apparence qu'elle fera, je sai positivement que les deux Villes ne souffriront jamais qu'on l'accorde, & que, sans daigner entrer dans l'examen du cas, elles se contenteront de dire, que, comme l'Angle. a allégué, que la convenance & la conservation de soi-même la dispensoit d'observer ses Traités, les mêmes raisons existent pour la rep.[3]

J'ai été franc avec notre ami sur le chap.[4] de N——. Il a convenu qu'il étoit remuant & trop ambitieux, ainsi que le Bar—— de C——:[5] & de mon côté j'ai été de son sentiment, que, comme Négociant, Démagogue à la Bourse, Anti-Angl. &c. &c. le premier peut être plus utile que d'autres; qu'il est bon, par conséquent, tout à la fois, de le ménager & de le contenir dans sa sphere.—Quant au B—— de C—— He has no power (being now excluded from any share in the Government of his little Province), & too much rashness, to do good. He is busy with publishing some Letters he has received from Govr. Trumb——, Govr. Livingst——, & Genl. Gates, who,

3. The two privileged cities were Amsterdam and Haarlem, which were exempted from the French trade restrictions. The British government in July did formally request military assistance under the terms of the Anglo-Dutch military alliance of 1678: Daniel A. Miller, *Sir Joseph Yorke and Anglo-Dutch Relations, 1774–1780* (The Hague and Paris, 1970), p. 77. Britain had been avoiding her obligations to follow the provisions of the Anglo-Dutch *commercial* treaty of 1674. For the French view of the situation see Fauchille, *Diplomatie française,* pp. 148–9.

4. "Sur le chapitre," or *re* de Neufville.

5. The Baron de Capellen, *i.e.,* Joan Derk van der Capellen.

he tells us, cannot but have written them by consent of Congress.[6] His friend, Lt. Col. Diriks, of the regt. of Proctor, has brought over a plan for a Loan, framed, they give out, by authority of Congress, by one *Erkelens,* a Dutch Merchant establish'd some years since in America; & he proposes it, I fear, very imprudently, for, besides what he has told me of himself, I have found it the matter of conversation in our public boats.[7]

Je viens de témoigner ma joie, & offrir mes services à Mr. le Comte de Herreria Env. d'Espe.[8] Il a accepté compliment & offres avec politesse & plaisir, me disant, *Je sai que vous en avez rendu de grands.* Il m'a averti qu'on m'espionnoit beaucoup. Je lui ai demandé s'il ne paroîtroit pas bientôt un Traité d'Amitié & de Commerce entre l'Espe. & l'Am——, & si je pouvois lui présenter les Américains qui me seroient adressés de bonne part? Il m'a remis, pour s'expliquer, au temps où il aura reçu ses instructions, qu'il attend.

24e. au soir

La Province d'Hollande vient enfin de prendre une résolution très-vigoureuse & unanime, telle qu'Amsterdam l'avoit avisée, selon ma Lettre du 14e., c'est-à-dire, de donner aux autres Provinces le terme d'un mois, au bout duquel, si elles ne se conforment pas à la Résolution du 30 Mars, la Prov. d'Hollde. déliberera sur les mesures qu'elle aura à prendre séparément pour la protection de son Commerce.[9] Le Gd. Pe. a déjà distribué pour cet effet les Lettres circulaires, conçues dans des termes *aussi forts,* dit notre ami, *que nous eussions pu le faire nous-autres.* Cependant, comme on n'a pas voulu autoriser, dans la Résolution, la Ville d'Amst. à la médiation qu'elle avoit

6. For Jonathan Trumbull's letter see XXVII, 366; for William Livingston's, Carl E. Prince *et al.,* eds., *The Papers of William Livingston* (5 vols., Trenton, 1979–88), II, 488–94.

7. For Dircks (whose former commander was Col. Thomas Proctor) see BF's June 2 letter to Jay; for Erkelens' loan see XXVII, 366n; XXVIII, 334.

8. Alvaro de Nava, vizconde de la Herreria, Spanish minister plenipotentiary in the Netherlands from 1771 to 1780: *Repertorium der diplomatischen Vertreter,* III, 435.

9. In response to this decision by the States of the Province of Holland, France extended the exemption from the trade edicts and new tariff for the entire province for four weeks: Edler, *Dutch Republic,* p. 126.

offerte pour faire suspendre l'Edit & le Tarif, suspension qu'elle garantissoit en ce cas, elle n'a pas laissé de faire insérer dans les Actes l'annotation dont je vous ai parlé, en témoignant d'ailleurs être contente de la Résolution. Ceux de Dort & de Rotterdam, de leur côté, ont aussi fait insérer une annotation pareille. Voilà donc Amsterdam triomphante, justifiée par ses rivales-mêmes, & couverte de gloire. Sir J., au milieu de tout cela, fait triste figure, *d'autant plus triste,* dit notre Ami, *qu'il va se plaignant de nous autres à tout le monde.* C'est un grand personnage qui seul a empêché que la motion, pour obtenir la suspension, n'a pas été adoptée. Il l'a fait pour conserver son crédit, non seulement en Angleterre, mais aussi, & surtout, dans les autres provinces, où il est tout-puissant, & où il voudroit toujours l'être.

Mrs. De N—— viennent de m'écrire qu'il leur est arrivé deux petits Sloops de l'Amérique (en voilà donc 7 à Amst——) Le Diamant Cap. Joseph Cook, & la Diane, Cap. Wm. Klaydon. Les Anglomanes sont furieux de cela: Hier, étant en bourse au milieu de ses Américains, les Anglomanes lui crierent; *Now you may stand upon your toes.* Ces derniers-venus ont apporté les nouvelles suivantes:

Boston 22 Avr. Le Navire du Continent entra vendredi dernier. Il avoit pris un Corsaire Anglois de 14 pieces, par lequel ils eurent connoissance de la prise de 8 Vaisseaux de vivres & fournitures destinés de N. York pour la Géorgie. Le convoi étoit de 10; ainsi 2 seulement échapperent. Les chargemens seuls de ces prises sont estimés £80 m. st.; encore cette perte n'est rien en comparaison du malaise où elle aura laissé les royalistes en Géorgie. Le Jason Cap. Rotterfield [Porterfield], Esqr. de 20 pieces, la Marie de 16, & le Hibernian de 8 pes., en étoient.

Bost. 26 Avr. Jeudi dernier entra la Frégatte du Continent la Reine de France, Cap. Orney [Olney], avec la prise la Marie de 16 pes., trois Brigantins, & le Hibernian, qui entra le dernier des 8 prises faites par le Warren, la Reine de France, & le Ranger.[1]

1. For the cruise which Dumas describes see Gordon's May 5 letter; Dumas' account seems to accord with that quoted by de Neufville, below, after June 28.

Je prévois que je n'arriverai pas assez tôt à Passy pour y célébrer le 4 Juillet: patience; je ne puis me résoudre à laisser ces gens assemblés ici. Je crois devoir vous apporter la fin du roman, & sacrifier plutôt mon plaisir; *for my heart was set upon it.* La raison pourquoi j'avois pensé à me procurer un gîte près de Mr. Bancroft, c'est que j'espérois de pouvoir vous approcher en sa compagnie plus souvent & sans cérémonie, &c. car on m'avoit dit (peut-être à dessein) que je ne pourrois avoir que rarement audience, & toujours en la faisant demander avec apparat. On m'avoit dit aussi, que vous étiez allé demeurer dans l'Hôtel-même de Mr. De Ch——. Mr. Pringle vient de m'assurer le contraire. Disposez donc de moi dans quelque endroit de votre hôtel qu'il vous plaira; j'y attendrai les moments de loisir où vous me ferez appeller, avec ce respectueux dévouement que j'aurai toute ma vie pour vous, Monsieur, Votre très-humble & très-obéissant serviteur, D

Mrs Pringle & Stockton sont partis pour Amst., où ils s'embarqueront dès qu'ils pourront. Je les regrette tous deux. Je m'étois fait une douce habitude de la société du dernier, le trouvant aussi prudent que zélé pour sa patrie.[2] Cette Lettre ne peut partir que demain 25.

Passy à Son Exc. Mr. Franklin

Notation: Dumas 24. Juin *1779.*

From David Hartley: Two Letters

(I) and (II) transcript: Library of Congress

I.

My Dear Friend London June 24 1779

I shall hope soon to have an opportunity of writing to you by a private hand, & shall defer what I have to say till that opportunity. In the mean time let me only tell you that I am still of the same opinion that I have always held that there is

2. See Dumas' June 22 letter. Stockton returned to Boston, Pringle to Charleston: Smith, *Letters,* XIV, 206; *DAB* under Pringle.

not yet any alienation between the nations of GB & NA. I think likewise that what has passed in the way of feeling pulses for negotiation may in the end do good as laying a foundation wch by way of reference may be a line for some approximation towards peace in some more fortunate hour. This is a point wch I will never lose sight of. I hope that our Consultations may some day or other meet with better success. Yrs. &c DH

II.

Dear Sir, Lond June 24 1779

Another Cargo of prisoners for exchange is either sailed or under orders from Portsmouth, viz Forton prison, to Nantes—[3] You writ me word that your Agent at Nantes wd keep up directly a correspondence with The Commissioners of Sick and Hurt on Towerhill London. That is what they desire, for the sake of expedition.[4] I believe they are worried by *reports*. I believe some of the prisoners returned have *reported* that they dont *believe* that there are many more prisoners in the neighbourhood of Nantes. Then the Commrs. write to me, being apprehensive of losing their labour by going to Nantes, or of staying there a long time to collect prisoners from a distance. I have prevailed with them to dispense with these doubts, and to send another cargo to Nantes. If your agent wd keep up a correspondence himself all these little doubts & embarrassments wd be avoided. Let him send returns of numbers now & then and say by such or such a time I cd exchange 100 or 200 or 300, for now that we have made a beginning, I think the Commissioners wd be willing to sweep away greater Numbers then 100 at a time, if they had a specific certainty to depend upon.— So much for this, I am moreover desired to propose to you again Morlaix, if approved by the french Ministry, & I confess I do not see what reason can obstruct such a

3. In fact twelve American prisoners wrote Hartley from Forton Prison on June 26 that the cartel had arrived on the 25th and would be ready to take them on board in five or six days. D.A.F.H.H. Hartley Russell Papers, on deposit in the Berkshire County Record Office.

4. Hartley had previously asked BF to designate an agent at Nantes or Lorient, and BF named Schweighauser: XXVIII, 245, 321.

proposition. I was desired to suggest to you at the same time, whether the french prisoners might be exchanged at the same place, combining the two sets of prisoners; and Morlaix to be the general *entrepôt.* One Agent there might correspond with our Commissioners & dispatch business quickly.— I am commissioned to consult with you likewise about the exchange of prisoners wch you have in Spain. As you know the Circumstances of place & Numbers, Pray give me your thoughts & propositions upon that Subject.— Dont let us quit the exchange at Nantes till we can be fully arranged for Morlaix, wch wd be infinitely more convenient if consented to by the french Ministry. Your affecte DH

To Dr Franklin.

From the Baron de Holtzendorff

ALS: American Philosophical Society

Sir Paris, june 24th. 1779.

I think it incumbent on myself to inform you, that yesterday in the after noon I found young Mr. cocheran quit Sick, possessed by a very strong Feever, which I fear may be the Effect, or consequence, of an accident, called in french, *un Effort,* he proved, so told me Mr. Le coeur, on thursday last week.[5] His father, very much estimed, I believe, by yourself, would be undoubtedly exceedingly obliged to you, if you will sent to the young gentleman a good Surgon, or doctor, where care would prevent the ill consequences of such bad Events for the young people. I ardently take this opportunity for renewing to yourself the very respectful Sentiments with which I have the honour to remain Sir your most obedt. honnbl servant

LE BARON DE HOLTZENDORFF

Notation: Baron D'holkendor Paris june 24e. 1779.

5. The young Cochran recovered from what was probably a hernia; for his adult career see XXVII, 262n. Holtzendorff presumably had met the father, Robert Cochran (above, June 12), and his family while he was in Charleston; see Lasseray, *Les Français,* I, 242.

From Edmund Jenings

ALS: American Philosophical Society

Sir Paris June 24. 1779.

I Have the Honor of receiving your Excellency's obliging Invitation to Dinner, in order to celebrate the Anniversary of the Declaration of American Independancy, which I should accept of with the greatest Pleasure, if I was not setting out on my intended Tour. I shall Keep the Day in my remembrance & Concur with you in wishing perpetual Liberty & Happiness to our Country. I am Sir your Excellencies Most Obedient & devoted Humble Sert. EDM: JENINGS

Notation: Edm. Jenings, june 24 1779. Paris.

From Thompson, Farley & Co.[6]

ALS:[7] American Philosophical Society

Sir! Nantes 24 June 1779

Dr. Busch who came from England the beginning of May took charge of a Small parcell with some letters and papers given him by Mr Thompson at Dover to be delivered us here, where he proposed coming after paying his Respects to you at Passy. Since that time we have been in daily expectation of seeing him but without Success; we therefore are under the necessity of giving you this Trouble to be informed if that Gentleman still remains at Paris and to request you will desire him to deliver the same to Mr. Olivier, Rue Bourg L'abbé unless he is soon coming to this City; We pray Your Excellency will be pleased to excuse this Trouble we could not avoid giving you and that you will Consider us with the greatest Respect Sir Your most Obedient and most devoted humble Servants THOMPSON FARLEY & CO.

His Excellency B Franklin

6. For Henry Farley and the business he had established with two sons of Thomas Thompson of Dover see XXVIII, 187–8. BF had recommended that Farley be permitted to settle in Nantes: XXVIII, 346–7.

7. In Farley's hand.

Addressed: A S. E / S. Excellence M. Franklin / Ambassadeur des Etats unies / de l'amerique / a Passy / Pres de Paris

Notation: Thompson Farley 24 Juin 1779.

From C——

ALS: American Philosophical Society

My Dear Friend. June 25. 1779

Your Letter of the 17 April[8] gave me infinite Pleasure & I am more exceedingly obliged to you for the very kind reception you gave my Son, as well as your warm commendations of him.

I wish this detestable war was at an End, that Friends who love each other might cordially meet & embrace, & I am sure you wish you could put an End to it.

All your Friends here besides the Two particular ones you mention love & esteem you equally, especially those who were once of the Family of *Sugar* Loaf Hall Hampstead. You shall have the London Chronicle soon.

We have not seen good Mrs. Stevenson these 100 Years nor Mrs. Hewson.

My whole Family unite in cordial & affectionate wishes for you, & I am Dear Sir, Your most obedient humble Servant.

C

P.S. Kind regards to Mr Temple.

As no more Packets are to go between Dover & Calais—you had best apply to the Postmastr. of Calais (Monsr. Caffieri)[9] for the Chronicle.

Addressed: A Monsr. / Monsr. B. Franklin / a Passy / pres de Paris.

Notation: No Name.

8. We have no record of BF having written any letters on this date, nor have we been able to match the handwriting of the present letter with any of the extant correspondence between BF and his old friends from London.

9. Known to us only as Caffiéri l'Aîné, this *directeur des postes* at Calais had previously forwarded books to BF: XX, 491–2. At the end of June Britain halted the Dover-Calais packet; see our annotation of Baudouin's letter of June 17.

From Thomas Digges AL: Historical Society of Pennsylvania

25th. June 1779

I am happy to inform You that I have found out Mr. Peters after I had given over hopes of Him & supposing Him dead. He desires of me to place the remittance intended for him in the hands of Messrs. Fuller & Co. Bankers in London to whom I have applyd to accept my bill on You for the one hundred pound you limit Me to go to, but they being unusd to negotiate French Bills desird me to look out among the French Merchts. to get the Bills negotiated & the amount paid to Fuller & Co. for Mr Peters's use. I think of looking after this business before the next packet sails & if it can be done I will draw the Bill on You payable at the House of Monr. Grand & advice You thereof by next packet.[1]

The box of books were sent as you directed and I shall by first oppery. send You the Bill of Parcells wch. amount to £9:19:6 the Charges of Cocket &ca. &ca. two or three shillings more, so that I shall make my draft on You an equal ten pounds: It will be better I include this sum in Peters's Bill & make it one hundd & ten pounds but I shall inform You in the course of Post if this mode is adopted. M. Peters writes me he is old & rather infirm and lives near Nottingham. My two former letters to that quarter miscarryd by being directed to Mrs. Roberts's but I have wrote to him to find them out. I am &ca &ca &ca.

Dr. *Franklin*

1. In another letter, which refers to this one as having been sent by "last post," Digges informed BF that the regular packets had stopped, and that he had been advised to draw from Grand at ten days' sight. He would thus draw in *livres* the equivalent of £110 sterling at the London exchange rate, made payable to Messrs. French and Hobson, since Fuller and Co. lacked the necessary connections in Paris. He asked BF's advice on how to direct bills to Ostend, since the immediate conveyance had now ceased. This second letter bears a date of June 19, but must have been written at the end of the month. The next of Digges' letters, dated July 6, mentions having written BF "a few days ago" about drawing a bill on Grand. Both letters are at the Hist. Soc. of Pa. and are printed in Elias and Finch, *Digges Letters,* pp. 66–9.

From John Green[2]

ALS: American Philosophical Society

Sir Bourdeaux June 25th 1779

I sailed from Philada: 2nd. May last Commander of a new Brigt: named the Nesbitt bound to France laden'd with Tobacs.[3] and on the 1st of June before day light fell in with a British Cruzer of 18 six Pounderes about 23 Leauges to the Westward of Bell Ilse who overpowered us with sail & Took and carryed us into Falmouth, on the 13th Inst: made my Escape and arrived here last night on board a Burning Brigt: my hands that were on board my Vessel was delivered up to the press gang at Falmouth and sent on board the Tender in order to sent on board a Man of Warr—

I had no Dispatches from Congress but was given four Packages from Mr. Holker directed for the Minister of France with orders to commit them to the Deep rather than they should fall into the hands of the enemy. I had several other Letters all of which shared the same fate—

A few days before I left Philada: an express arriv'd to Congress from Capt: Hopkins of the Ship Warren of his taking 7 Sail of Transports under Convoy of a 20 Gun ship & an armed Brigt laden'd with provisions and accoutrements for 250 Horse with dry Goods to the amount of 52 Thousand sterlg. some Officers and several Merchants whom sailed from New York and bound for Georgia, there was in Compy. with Capt: Hopkins the Ship Queen of France & Ranger when the above Fleet was taken—

It was believed the Brittish troups would soon evacuate Georgia the loss of the Troupes would [*be*] greatly felt a Sloop arrived in Philada from the inhabitants of Bermudas beging assistance from Congress that several hundreds of the Inhabi-

2. A Philadelphian formerly associated with Willing and Morris (XXIV, 143–4n), Green had been commissioned captain of the *Queen of France* at Nantes in February, 1778 (XXV, 716). He brought her cargo of clothing and stores into Boston in May: William James Morgan, *Captains to the Northward: the New England Captains in the Continental Navy* (Barre, Mass., 1959), p. 142.

3. The ship was owned by John M. Nesbitt & Co. of Philadelphia: Charles H. Lincoln, comp., *Naval Records of the American Revolution, 1775–1788* (Washington, D.C., 1906), p. 404.

tants had already perished for want of food, that many had not tasted bread for several weeks, it was mentioned in Philada that some assistance would be given as soon as possible—[4]

Several privateers are swarming from south Carolina to New York and has taken many of our Vessells, but I'm in hopes they are all destoyed before this as several Continental Vesselles were ordered to cruize on the coast—A large Brigt. sailed in Compy. with me from Philada: bound to Martinico laden'd with flour lost her Mainmast on the same Day & was oblidg'd to put back—The Coast of France from Ushant down to Bell Ilse are many British privateers, 3 Large Cutters & 2 Guernsey Luggers spoke us—

I hope in a short time the Ship Dean Capt Nicolson[5] will be in France and I believe Mr: Carmichael will come in her, she lay in the Delaware when I came a way.

I am with Respect you Humble Servt. JNO GREEN

Addressed: The Honourbl: Benjamin Franklin Esqr / Plenipotentiary to the United / States of America / at the Court of / a Pasy pres paris

Notation: Jn Green 15. Juin 1779

From Richard Bennett Lloyd

ALS: American Philosophical Society

Dear Sir, London 25th June 79—

I beg pardon for giving you this trouble but as the enclosed Letter is of some consequence to the writer of it, I take the

4. The memorial was referred by Congress to committee on April 19: *JCC,* XIII, 471. It finally authorized Delaware, Maryland, and Virginia to ship 1,000 bushels of corn: Henry C. Wilkinson, "They Built Small Ships of Cedar: Bermuda and American Independence" in Charles W. Toth, ed., *The American Revolution and the West Indies* (Port Washington, N.Y. and London, 1975), pp. 162–4.

5. Samuel Nicholson, commanding the *Deane,* had accompanied Green on the ocean crossing and landed at Portsmouth on May 1, 1778: XXVI, 400. In early 1779, he sailed to Martinique: Bingham to commissioners, March 3. On June 25, in fact, Nicholson, now at Philadelphia, was ordered to cruise off Bermuda: Gardner W. Allen, *A Naval History of the American Revolution* (2 vols., Boston and New York, 1913), II, 398, 401.

liberty of placing it under your care—. Mr. Stephenson is the Gentleman who waited on you at Passy about eighteen months ago— He is a Friend to our Country and a particular Friend of mine—[6] I flatter myself I shall be favoured with a Letter from you by this Day's mail, and I am, with very great respect, your obt. and most humble Servant R. B. LLOYD

Addressed: A Monsieur / Monsieur Franklin / à Passy

Notation: R. B. Lloyd Londres 25 juin 1779.

From Edward Newenham

ALS: American Philosophical Society

Sir Dunkerck 25 June 1779

On my arrival at Ostend this morning, I had the honour of your Excellency's Letter[7] with the two passports, for which I return you my most Sincere and gratefull thanks; I was delayed on my Journey to Ostend much Longer than I expected, or should sooner have acknowledged the receipts of your Letters & favours, which I assure your Excellency *never* shall be disgraced by me—

I did not mention it in my former Letter, least, as I was not personaly Known to you, it might appear like a modern Compliment only done with a View of a return, but now I have the honour to acquaint Your Excellency, that in April last I recieved an answer to a Letter I wrote to Mr: Nat: Parks of Dublin, where-in he informs me, that to oblige Lady Newenham and me, he had obtained the release of Six American Prisoners belonging to the John & Sally of Philadelphia, and that he had given 30 s to Carry them on Board the Ufrow Maria bound to Amsterdam; I have also (in may last) at the Request of Mrs: *Doges* (alias Verges) *now at Rochelle,* wrote to have her husband permitted to go where he pleases, He was Captain of

6. William Stevenson complained in January, 1778, that the American commissioners had reneged on their request that he carry dispatches to Congress: XXV, 406–9. On Feb. 25 he sailed for America on the *Deane:* XXV, 494. The enclosed letter is missing.

7. Dated May 27.

a Transport bound to Martinico in February last and Carried into Corke, & was, when I wrote, a Prisoner in the Town of Bandon In Ireland—it was Mr: *Germain of Lausanne,* who solicited me in her favour—

I think myself so highly honoured by the Confidence you have placed in me, that I wish to prove to *my* Countrymen, that my Steady Conduct in Support of the Liberties of the united states of North America, has been noticed by Your Excellency, therefore, if perfectly agreable, I should be Glad to shew them the favour done, & the Confidence reposed in, me; but not without your permission, which I shall hope to receive by the Time I reach Ireland—

As to those Persons who addressed Your Excellency from Belfast, it is very true, they wrote to me, before I Left Ireland, upon that Subject, but in a Matter of Such importance, I could not hazard my Character by recommending them, without being more fully acquainted with their Characters, Names, & *Designs;* If I find them fit objects, after making a proper enquiry, I shall Certifie it to your Excellency; but if I find the smallest tendency in them, inimical to the Liberties or Manufactures of the united states of America, I shall inform you thereof; If any others should write to you on that Subject, if you honour me with a Letter, I shall give a *faithfull* account of them—[8]

With the sincerest wishes for yours & your familys health and happiness, and with the Greatest respect for so Exalted a Character.

I have the Honour to be Your Excellencys Most obedient & most obliged Humble Servt. EDWARD NEWENHAM

P.S. Please to present my compts: to yr: Grandsons—my address is, Belcamp near Dublin, Ireland—[9]

Notation: Edouard Newenham Dunkerque 25. juin 1779.

8. BF had already offered to help the Belfast emigrants; see his letter to Jesse Taylor, March 18.

9. Newenham wrote from Calais on the 29th requesting a new passport for the journey from England to Ireland after officers at the French port informed him that BF's pass was by then out of date. He would await BF's reply in London, at the Graecian Coffeehouse, Temple. APS. *The Public*

From Joshua Steele[1]

ALS: American Philosophical Society

Howland Street, Tottenham Court London 25th.
June 1779—

Dear Sir,

The political difference between our Nations, can not make me forget or suspend the Affection & Esteem that grew out of an acquaintance with private worth: I therefore take the opportunity of conveying to you, by the favour of Ser. Anduaga secretary of the Spanish Embassy,[2] my friendly & Affectionate Respects: And tho' I must suppose you are much employed in affairs of the greatest moment, yet as I know human Nature requires relaxation, from such heavy Cares, by light Amusements, I send you, by the same opportunity, some printed papers, being forty Copies of an Abstract of the Claims of five Candidates for the *premiums* offered by the Society (of which you are a perpetual Member) for an *invariable Standard for weights or Measures.*[3]

During the public Misfortunes of my Country, which I was in no capacity to prevent, I have endeavoured to divert my thoughts by these & such like philosophical speculations.

I will beg the favour of you to present one parcel of them to the Royal Academy of Sciences, requesting them to make them as public as they can, & I could wish some of them were sent to Geneva & Switzerland; The Rest are at your own Disposal, for America or where you please.

This premium has been continued five years, at first annual,

Advertiser of Aug. 17 printed an extract of an Aug. 2 letter from Ireland reporting that Newenham had lately returned from France with a report that 60,000 men were ready to invade Ireland, and with a manifesto offering the Irish independence and free trade.

1. A London friend who had long been a member of the Royal Society of Arts: xx, 312n.

2. Probably José de Anduaga, later a diplomatic envoy to Sweden, Holland, and England: *Repertorium der diplomatischen Vertreter,* III, 430, 433, 435, 442.

3. The premium was a gold medal, or one hundred guineas, "for discovering to the Society an invariable Standard for Weights or Measures, communicable at all times and to all nations, by means of letters or characters," and had been extended to "persons residing in any country whatever." The deadline was March 16, 1779. Royal Society of Arts, *Premiums Offered by the*

then Biennial, as the first year produced nothing worth notice: And you will see by two Copies, of the Claims made in 1777, wch. I send you, how little our *desideratum* was then understood.

We have made some Trials on the *apparatus* of Candidate E, which have answered exactly, according to what he has advanced; But we are preparing for more accurate ones, in which we shall try what difference, moisture, dryness, Heat, and Cold, will make in the Horsehair: And we hope good Experiments will be made in several other places; & that this will set other Heads at work to improve it, or to find out something better.

I have one more hope, that is, that a Ray of good Sense may enlighten us, so as to bring back peace, & put a Stop to miseries that degrade & disgrace us.

I am, dear Sir, wth. perfect Esteem, Your most Affecte. friend &ca J STEELE.

Addressed: To His Excellcy / Dr Franklin / paris

From John Bondfield

ALS: American Philosophical Society

Sir Bordeaux 26 June 1779

Captain John Green arrived here the 23d Inst. to which port he had been carried by a privateer that took him on his passage from Philadelphia,[4] he destroy'd all his Letters & papers these miscarriages cruelly suspend the execution of the proposed Operations of our friends on the other side whose disapointments as well as Loss's come heavy.

A Courier from Madrid past thro' this City yesterday in the afternoon with dispatches for Versailles by the last advices The French & Spanish Fleets were stil at Couronna. We are without any interesting occurences on this Coast. I have the Honor to be respectfully Sir Your most Obedient Humble Servant JOHN BONDFIELD

Society, Instituted at London, for the Encouragement of Arts, Manufactures, and Commerce (London, 1777), p. 47.

4. See his letter of the 25th, above.

the Captain had Letters for Mons De Vergennes & the Comte D'Arranda wch he destroy'd

Passi His Excellency B Franklin Esq

Addressed: His Excellency Benj Franklin / Esq / Plenipoty. from the United States / at / Paris

Notations in different hands: Jonh. Bondfield. 26. juin 1779. / Bourdeaux

From the Duchesse de Deux-Ponts

ALS: American Philosophical Society

Samedis 26 [June, 1779][5]

Je fait demander a Monsieur francklin des Nouvelles de sa santes, ses ordres pour Lalemagne, et La Lorraine, et sil a recue Les Ciseaux que jai eut Lhoneur de Lui envoyér il y a quelques jour

DE FORBACH DOUAIRIERE DU SME. DUC DE DEUXPONTS

Addressed: a monsieur / Monsieur francklin / Ministre des etats unis / a La Cour de france / a *passis*

From John G. Frazer[6]

ALS: American Philosophical Society

Sir, Bordeaux, 26th. June 1779

You will please to excuse me for taking the liberty of inclosing to you a Letter from one of our unfortunate countrymen, now a prisioner at Aix in Provence,[7] he wou'd be very happy to obtain his liberty and return to his native Country, (Virginia) he is a young Gentleman of very good Family and Fortune in that Country—and is very capable of rendering some service to his country if requested, you will please to observe

5. She had sent the scissors mentioned in this letter on Sunday, June 20, above.

6. A Virginian in France, for whom see XXVIII, 408n.

7. The enclosed letter (now missing) was from Cradock Taylor, who wrote BF on June 29, below.

he has mentioned in what manner he was forced into the service of the English—which you may rely upon to be the Truth— If his liberty can be procured you will serve him in a particular manner, & infinitely oblige me—I have the Honour to be, Sir, with the greatest respect, your most obet. & Mo. Hbl. Servt— JNO. G. FRAZER

Addressed: His Excellency / Benjamin Franklin Esqr. / Plenipotentiary to the / United States of America / at Paris—

Notation: Jno. G. Frazer 21e. juin 1779. Bordeaux.

From Ralph and Alice Izard

AL:[8] American Philosophical Society

Paris 26th. June 1779.—

Mr. & Mrs. Izard present their Compliments to Dr. Franklin, & will have the honour of waiting on him to dinner on Monday the 5th. of July.—

Addressed: A Monsieur / Monsieur Franklin / Ministre Plenipotentiaire / des Etats Unis de l'Amerique / à Passy.—

From Le Couteulx & Cie.[9]

LS: American Philosophical Society

Monsieur Paris 26. Juin 1779.

Nous avons l'honneur de vous remettre avec la presente une lettre de Mrs. P: M: de Murquia et Isidore de la Torre Membres de la Compie. des Assurances de Cadiz.[1]

Quoique nous pensions inutile de joindre nos Sollicitations

8. In the husband's hand.

9. A Paris banking house whose Cadiz branch, Le Couteulx, Le Normand & Cie. (XXVII, 260n), acted as intermediary in the present business.

1. Written in Spanish and dated May 21, the enclosed letter from de Murquia and de la Torre sought BF's help in obtaining an indemnity for the cargo of the brig *Nuestra Señora de la Merced.* She had been captured by an American "fragata" (actually a Massachusetts privateer), while en route from Cadiz to London. APS.

a celles de ces Messieurs pour vous determiner a acquiescer a leur demande, nous venons vous prier de vouloir bien appuier leurs pretentions de votre Recommandation aupres du Congres;[2] et de nous marquer ce que vous jugez convenable de faire en cette occurrence pour accelerer la Justice qu'ils ont droit d'attendre d'un Corps aussi recommandable et respectable a tous egards.

Comme la lettre et les pieces cy jointes vous informront de l'objet en question, nous pensons que le Detail que nous pourrions vous en faire seroit superflu & nous nous bornerons a vous assurer que nous avons l'honneur d'etre avec le plus profond Respect. Monsieur Vos tres humbles et obeissans Serviteurs.

LE COUTEULX & COMP.
rue Montorgueil

Si par hazard vous aviez besoin de la traduction des pieces cy incluses vous pouvez nous les retourner et nous nous ferons un vrai plaisir de la faire de suitte.

Passy les Paris Mr. Le Docteur franklin

From Arthur Lee

AL: American Philosophical Society

Paris June 26th 1779.

Mr A. Lee returns his Compts to Dr. Franklin; & will have the honor of waiting upon him on the 5th. of July.

Mr Lee will be very much obligd to Dr. Franklin, if he will order an authenticated copy to be made for him, of the Letter, from the Commissioners, to Count de Vergennes, on the agreement with Hortalez & Co., dated Passi Sepr. 10th. 1778[3]

2. In October the case, originally heard by the Mass. Board of Admiralty, was referred to the congressional Committee on Appeals: *JCC*, XV, 1159. The opposing party apparently were the owners of the privateer, headed by Samuel Cabot, a Beverly shipowner. The eventual decision restored the brig and part of the cargo to the Spaniards but ruled that the remainder was lawful prize: Henry J. Bourguignon, *The First Federal Court: the Federal Appelate Prize Court of the American Revolution 1775–1787* (Philadelphia, 1977), pp. 278–9.

3. XXVII, 382–3.

with a copy of his Excellency's answer which Mr. Lee does not remember to have seen.[4]

Notation: A Lee. Paris 26. juin 1779.

From Robert Montgomery[5]

ALS: American Philosophical Society

Sir Alicante 26th: June 1779

I find Myself under the Necessety of Troubling your Excellency to Inform you, that Notwithstanding I have Every time that the foraigne Merchants Established here ware Called by the Governour to Declare of what Nation they ware, always declared and Subscribed Myself a Subject of the Thirteen United States of North America yet Yesterday on A proclamation of war being Made here Against England I was Arrested my Property Seized and House filled with Soldiers, I Immediately produced My Certiffcate and Passeport Given Me, by you Mr Lee and Mr Adams when I had the Honour of Attending you at Passy Last August on My way to this Place,[6] but have had No Answer nor Relief in Consequence of them, I Insisted to Know if Spain had Declared war Against the States of America to which Am Answerd in the Negative but without Any Relief or Apearance of it. And as I know myself Guilty of No fault; but the Exect Semillarity between us and the English (Except in Sentiment) I Must Request your Excelly will Immediately write the Count De Ricla Minister of War at this Court,[7] that he may Consider Me, As I am, a Subject of the

4. We have no record of a response by Vergennes.

5. An American merchant who for the last two years had been residing on the Mediterranean coast of Spain: XXVI, 242–3. He had corresponded occasionally with JA; see, for example, *Adams Papers,* VIII, 5–6, and our annotation of BF to JA, April 24. He sent to JA a letter almost identical to the present one, and it is now with BF's papers at the APS. A French translation of the present letter is at the Archivo Historico Nacional Estado, Madrid.

6. See XXVII, 414.

7. A cousin of the current Spanish ambassador to the French court, the conde de Aranda, Ricla had become minister of war in 1772: Anthony H. Hull, *Charles III and the Revival of Spain* (Washington, D.C., 1981), p. 184.

Allies and Order the Embargo to be taken off My house and Business, please Also Indicate to Me who is Charge des Affairs for the States at Madrid, if yet Appointed that I may Appley to him in future Should Any Simoller Injustice be done Me, I Rely Entirely on your freindship and Justice for the Releif I Claim from My Present distressed Situation, and dont dout to have Your Ansr. as it will Otherways be Very Deficult for Me to Extricate Myself and Save the Credit and Perhaps Ruin of Your Excellys. Most Obedt humble Servent

ROBT MONTGOMERY

Benjaman Franklin Esqr,

Addressed: To / His Excellancy Benjamin Franklin Esqr: / Plenipotenciary from the / united States / Passy / Paris

Notation: Montgomery 26. Juin 1779.—

From Samuel Petrie[8] AL: American Philosophical Society

Rue Ste: Anne. Saturday June 26. [1779]

Mr. Petrie presents his Compliments to Dr: Franklin &, if he is able, will have the honour of waiting on him, Monday se'nnight.[9]

Addressed: Son Excellence le Ministre / Plenipotentiare des Etats Unis / de l'Amerique.

When he learned of Montgomery's plight he reprimanded the local governor and ordered him to support and protect the Americans as friends and allies: *Adams Papers,* VIII, 96; Montgomery to BF, July 6, 1779 (APS).

8. For the Scottish merchant see our annotation of BF's March 14 letter to Oliver.

9. *I.e.,* on Monday, July 5, for the Independence Day celebration.

To the Duchesse de Deux-Ponts

AL (draft): University of Pennsylvania Library

[after June 26, 1779][1]

I received my dear Friend's kind Present of the Scissors, which are exactly what I wanted, & besides their Usefulness to me have a great additional Value by the Hand from which they came. It is true that I can now neither walk abroad nor write at home without having something that may remind me of your Goodness towards me; you might have added, that I can neither play at Chess nor drink Tea without the same Sensation: but these had slipt your Memory. There are People who forget the Benefits they receive, Made [Madame] de Forbach only those she bestows.— But the Impression you have made on my Mind as one of the best, wisest & most amiable[2] Women I ever met with, renders every other means to make me think of you unnecessary.—[3] My best Wishes will attend you to Germany, & wherever else you may happen to be, being with the sincerest Esteem & Respect, (will you permit me to add Affection) Your most obliged & obedient humble Servant.

Notation: Franklin rough copy of letter to Mme. de Forbach

From the Abbés Chalut and Arnoux[4]

AL:[5] American Philosophical Society

passy dimanche 27. juin [1779]

Les abbés Chalut et Arnoux assurent de leur respect Monsieur franklin, ils auront l'honneur de se rendre à son invitation pour Celebrer l'heureuse et éternelle independence de l'amerique.

1. In answer to her letter of that date.
2. BF inserted "& most amiable" above the line.
3. Here BF wrote and then deleted, "That Impression will remain as long as the Heart in which it is stamped."
4. Elderly friends of the American cause (XXV, 382), replying to BF's invitation, printed before June 24, above.
5. In Arnoux's hand.

Addressed: A Monsieur / Monsieur franklin Ministre / plenipotentiaire des états / unis d'Amerique / *à Passy*

From William Lee

ALS: American Philosophical Society; copy: Virginia Historical Society

Sir. Frankfort 27th. June 1779

By the Letter you did me the Honor to write to me the 17th. instant, I perceive you are still under a mistake relative to the Contract made with D'Acosta & Co.— There never was to my knowlege any Contract made with that house for the same things that I requested you to apply for to the French Ministry on account of the State of Virginia.

D'Acosta & Co. contracted to send some thousand fusils & other triffleing Articles for the State of Virginia, which they expressly stipulated to ship from France before the end of last September, otherwise the Contract was to be entirely void.

This House fail'd to comply with their Contract, and even without making any Apology, or giving any reason for so doing; which I have since thought a most fortunate circumstance not only for the State of Virginia but indeed for America, having authentic information, that within the course of 12 Months past, many thousand fusils have been sent from Leige to a Clerk of that house, many of them of so base a quality as to cost only Seven Livres the fusil & bayonet.

In my Judgement it is an unpardonable cruelty to put such instruments into the hands of brave Men who are not only fighting for their own Lives, but in defence of the Liberties of their Country.

The most important part of the Supplies that the French Ministry were requested to furnish for the State of Virginia are the Canon, Howitzers, Mortars, Powder Ball & Shells; none of which have ever been contracted for with any one, & if they shou'd be sent to Boston or Charles Town for Congress, they cannot be of any more use to Virga: while the War continues & the Enemy have the Superiority in the American Seas, than if they were in France; & as the principal Military operations this year, will most likely be in the Southern States, there is much reason to apprehend that the want of fusils will be severely felt in that quarter. I therefore hope you will endeavor to get the Supplies requested sent to Virginia as soon as possible, since they may be even now got there before the Campaign is ended.

In doing this you will certainly render an essential Service, to the Common Cause & highly oblige him who has the Honor to be with very great respect Sir Your most Obliged and Obedient Humble Servant W: LEE

Honorable Benjamin Franklin Esqr. &c &c &c

Addressed: The Honorable / Benjamin Franklin Esqr. Minister / Plenipotentiary, to the Court of / Versailles, from the United States / of America. / at Passy / near Paris

Endorsed: Wm Lee Esqr about the Arms

"The Morals of Chess"

Reprinted from *The Columbian Magazine,* I (December, 1786), 159–61; incomplete copy:[6] American Philosophical Society

Franklin and chess have long been associated in the popular mind largely because of this bagatelle, which was the most widely re-

6. In the hand of Barbeu-Dubourg, who acknowledged receiving BF's manuscript on June 28, below. The first half is in English, up to the phrase, "which is to pass the time agreeably." Thereafter, on the last surviving page, Dubourg translated into French, and then crossed out, the enumerated courtesies up through number four. The remainder of the manuscript has been lost. There are slight differences in capitalization, punctuation, and wording, between the copy in Dubourg's hand and the *Columbian Magazine* text. The significant discrepancies are noted below.

There were evidently two versions of "The Morals of Chess" which circulated during Franklin's lifetime. The second text, whose first half more closely resembled Dubourg's English version, appeared mysteriously in [Richard Twiss], *Chess* (London, 1787). That text was reprinted many times in other publications, beginning with *The Gentleman's Magazine.* For a publishing history of the bagatelle see Ralph Hagedorn, *Benjamin Franklin and Chess in Early America* (Philadelphia, 1958) pp. 21–7, 83–4; Richard E. Amacher, *Franklin's Wit & Folly* (New Brunswick, 1953), pp. 158–61.

printed product of his Passy press. Made public for the first time in 1786, it would be reprinted at least a dozen times by the end of the century, and translated into French, German, and Russian.[7]

Franklin played chess with a single-mindedness that threatened to exclude all else. The story has already been told in these volumes of Mme. Brillon's being detained in her tub while he, oblivious, played chess in her bathing room well into the night.[8] Tales of Franklin's chess games became magnified over time. Le Ray de Chaumont's grandson Vincent maintained that the Doctor's tireless passion for late-night games was checked only by his supply of candles, and that once, at the home of a French minister, Franklin refused to receive an important dispatch from Congress until after a match had finished.[9]

"The Morals of Chess" poses certain infuriating problems for the textual editor. No manuscript copy has survived, and although we know that Franklin printed the bagatelle on his Passy press,[1] not a single imprint has surfaced. Because he sent the essay to Barbeu-Dubourg in June, 1779, its composition has commonly been dated *circa* that time. However, we believe that the essay was originally formulated as early as 1732, and that Franklin in the spring of 1779 was once again recalling material from his earlier life for the amusement of his circle at Passy.[2]

Our evidence comes from the commonplace book that Franklin kept from 1730–38. He used it primarily for two purposes: composing pieces which would find their way into the *Pennsylvania Gazette,* and drafting rules, procedures, and papers which he would present to his secret society, the Junto. A sketchy outline of "The Morals of Chess" appears in the commonplace book between a fictitious letter

7. See Hagedorn, *Benjamin Franklin and Chess,* p. 83. The Franklin Collection at Yale University contains forty different independent editions, including translations into Italian, French, and Danish.

8. xxv, 204.

9. Vincent Le Ray de Chaumont, *Souvenirs des Etats-unis* (Paris, 1859), pp. 6–7.

1. He wrote as much to Mme. Brillon on April 8, 1784 (APS).

2. Other examples of BF's reworking earlier material for his French circle are the "Ephemera" (XXVII, 430–5), based on an article he had read fifty years earlier, and two drinking songs he had written as a young tradesman and recalled later in 1779. One of them he wrote out *verbatim,* the other he turned into a lengthy stream of punning French prose: Lopez, *Mon Cher Papa,* pp. 292–6.

for the *Gazette* and a set of private proposals and queries to be asked the Junto, dating from June, 1732.[3] Based on Franklin's mandates that every Junto member "produce Queries on any Point of Morals, Politics or Natural Philosophy" at each meeting, and four times per year address the group on a subject of his own choosing, we suspect that Franklin originally drafted this essay for presentation to his club of leather apron men.[4]

What might have brought the essay to mind in 1779? Franklin was certainly playing chess with his Passy neighbors and friends (Dubourg, Le Veillard, Mme. Brillon and the duchesse de Deux-Ponts, among others) but even more important was his recent sifting through the early papers he had with him, looking for previously unpublished material to add to Benjamin Vaughan's edition of his writings. One of the pieces Franklin sent to London, probably in the spring of 1779, was a list of standing queries for the Junto.[5] This suggests that Franklin either had his commonplace book with him in Passy, or that he had copies of early papers relating to the club. One of those may well have been his "Morals of Chess."

In the absence of the original manuscript or Passy imprint, we publish the text of "Morals" as it appeared in the 1786 *Columbian Magazine* because we believe that the magazine reproduced most closely the essay as it was issued from Franklin's press. One of the magazine's editors, Mathew Carey, had worked for a short time as

3. See I, 259–64, 270, and the headnotes on pp. 254–6. The draft reads as follows:

The Antiquity & universality of it
Has been practis'd by the most famous Men
Usefulness. Wrestling of Bodies strengthen them, this a W of Minds
In the Conduct of Life
Caution & Circumspection
Foresight in looking for Advants & discovering Disadvs
Consideration of Consequences

It teaches the ill Consequences of Rashness, of Inattention to our Affairs, of Neglect of Circumspection—
tis a constant Lesson of Morality—
Nothing shows so much the [*the* MS *breaks off here.*]

4. This hypothesis was proposed, without evidence, in *The Good Companion Chess Problem Club*, v (April, 1918), pp. 170–1.

5. I, 255–9. By May 31 (as he wrote to BF, above) Vaughan had in hand nearly everything for the edition, which included the queries. They were printed in *Political, Miscellaneous and Philosophical Pieces* on pp. 533–6.

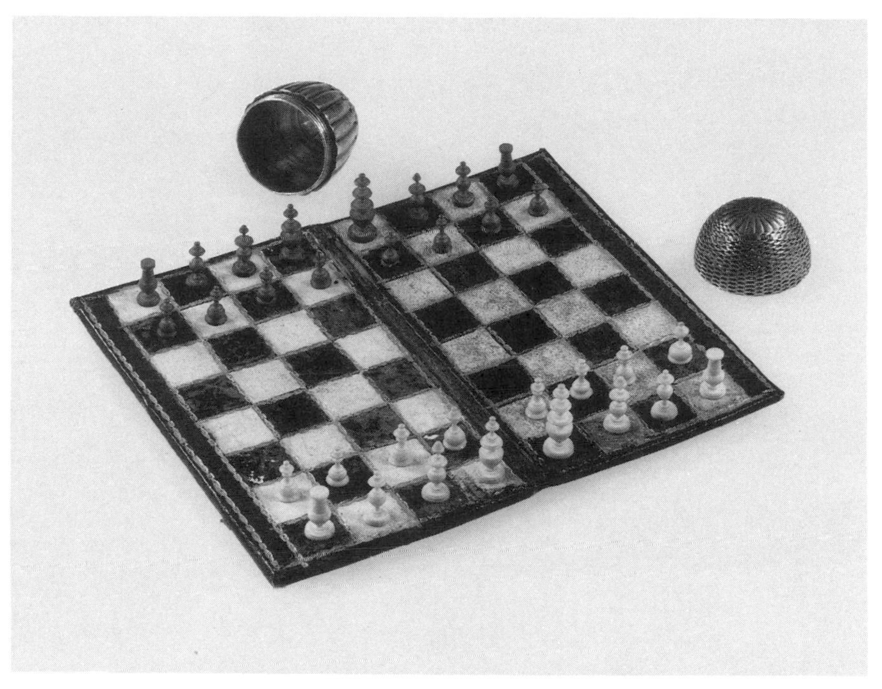

Benjamin Franklin's Chess Set

Franklin's printer in Passy, in 1779.[6] Years later, when Carey and his fellow editors were soliciting contributions for the first issues of *The Columbian Magazine,* they naturally turned to their famous Philadelphia neighbor. Carey may have either procured a copy of "Morals" from the author in 1786, or else have published the essay from an imprint he had kept since his days in the Passy shop. Either way, Carey's text is certainly authoritative.

What little else we know about "The Morals of Chess" is from Franklin's own hand. He ought to dedicate the piece to Mme. Brillon, he told her, because its best advice was based on his observations of her generous and magnanimous way of playing.[7] He, on the other hand, was not famous in Passy for the courtesy and fairness advocated in this bagatelle. According to Chaumont family legend, he grew impatient at the slowness of his partners, was prone to rearranging the board when his opponent left the room, and, as Chaumont once pointedly remarked, often drummed his fingers on the table.[8]

Sir, [before June 28, 1779]

Playing at Chess, is the most ancient and the most universal game known among men; for its original is beyond the memory of history, and it has, for numberless ages, been the amusement of all the civilized nations of Asia, the Persians, the Indians, and the Chinese. Europe has had it above 1000 years; the Spaniards have spread it over their part of America, and it begins lately to make its appearance in these northern states. It is so interesting in itself, as not to need the view of gain to induce engaging in it; and thence it is never played for money. Those, therefore, who have leisure for such diversions, cannot find one that is more *innocent;* and the following piece, written with a view to correct (among a few young friends) some little improprieties in the practice of it, shows at the same time, that it may, in its effects on the mind, be not

6. Mathew Carey, "The Autobiography of Mathew Carey," *The New England Magazine,* v, p. 409; Le Ray de Chaumont, Jr., to WTF, Nov. 20, 1782, APS.

7. To Mme. Brillon, undated. APS.

8. At this, BF was said to have replied, "Mon cher, c'est une bagatelle, et ce n'est pas la peine d'en parler." Le Ray de Chaumont, *Souvenirs,* p. 7.

merely *innocent,* but *advantageous,* to the vanquished as well as to the victor.

The MORALS of CHESS.

The game of Chess is not merely an idle amusement. Several very valuable qualities of the mind, useful in the course of human life, are to be acquired or strengthened by it, so as to become habits, ready on all occasions. For life is a kind of chess, in which we have often points to gain, and competitors or adversaries to contend with, and in which there is a vast variety of good and ill events, that are, in some degree, the effects of prudence or the want of it. By playing at chess, then, we may learn:

1. *Foresight,* which looks a little into futurity, and considers the consequences that may attend an action: for it is continually occurring to the player, "If I move this piece, what will be the advantages[9] of my new situation? What use can my adversary make of it to annoy me? What other moves can I make to support it, and to defend myself from his attacks?

2. *Circumspection,* which surveys the whole chess-board, or scene of action, the relations of the several pieces and situations, the dangers they are respectively exposed to, the several possibilities of their aiding each other; the probabilities that the adversary may make this or that move, and attack this or the other piece; and what different means can be used to avoid his stroke, or turn its consequences against him.

3. *Caution,* not to make our moves too hastily. This habit is best acquired by observing strictly the laws of the game, such as, *if you touch a piece, you must move it somewhere; if you set it down, you must let it stand.* And it is therefore best that these rules should be observed, as the game thereby becomes more the image of human life, and particularly of war; in which, if you have incautiously put yourself into a bad and dangerous position, you cannot obtain your enemy's leave to withdraw your troops, and place them more securely; but you must abide all the consequences of your rashness.

9. Dubourg's copy follows this with, "or disadvantages".

And, *lastly,* we learn by chess the habit of *not being discouraged*[1] by *present* bad appearences in the state of our affairs, the habit of *hoping for a favourable change,* and that of *persevering in the search of resources.* The game is so full of events, there is such a variety of turns in it, the fortune of it is so subject to sudden vicissitudes, and one so frequently, after long contemplation, discovers the means of extricating one's self from a supposed insurmountable difficulty, that one is encouraged to continue the contest to the last, in hopes of victory by our own skill, or, at least, of giving a *stale mate,*[2] by the negligence of our adversary. And whoever considers, what in chess he often sees instances of, that particular pieces of[3] success are apt to produce *presumption,* and its consequent, inattention, by which more is afterwards lost than was gained by the preceding advantage; while misfortunes produce more care and attention, by which the loss may be recovered, will learn not to be too much discouraged by the present success of his adversary, nor to despair of final good fortune, upon every little check he receives in the pursuit of it.

That we may, therefore, be induced more frequently to chuse this beneficial amusement, in preference to others which are not attended with the same advantages, every circumstance, that may increase the pleasure of it, should be regarded; and every action or word that is unfair, disrespectful, or that in any way may give uneasiness, should be avoided, as contrary to the immediate intention of both the players,[4] which is to pass the time agreeably.

Therefore, 1*st.* If it is agreed to play according to the strict rules, then those rules are to be exactly observed by both parties; and should not be insisted on for one side, while deviated from by the other: for this is not equitable.

2. If it is agreed not to observe the rules exactly, but one

1. These and the subsequent italicized words in the paragraph were not italicized in Dubourg's copy.

2. "Of giving a *stale mate*" is not in Dubourg's copy.

3. "Particular pieces of" is not in Dubourg's copy.

4. The copy reads, "Parties".

party demands indulgencies, he should then be as willing to allow them to the other.

3. No false move should ever be made to extricate yourself out of a difficulty, or to gain an advantage. There can be no pleasure in playing with a person once detected in such unfair practice.

4. If your adversary is long in playing, you ought not to hurry him, or express any uneasiness at his delay. You should not sing, nor whistle, nor look at your watch, nor take up a book to read, nor make a tapping with your feet on the floor, or with your fingers on the table, nor do anything that may disturb his attention. For all these things displease. And they do not show your skill in playing, but your craftiness or your rudeness.

5. You ought not to endeavour to amuse and deceive your adversary, by pretending to have made bad moves, and saying you have now lost the game, in order to make him secure and careless, and inattentive to your schemes; for this is fraud, and deceit, not skill in the game.

6. You must not, when you have gained a victory, use any triumphing or insulting expression, nor show too much pleasure; but endeavour to console your adversary, and make him less dissatisfied with himself by every kind and civil expression, that may be used with truth, such as, You understand the game better than I, but you are a little inattentive; or, You play too fast; or, You had the best of the game but something happened to divert your thoughts, and that turned it in my favour.

7. If you are a spectator, while others play, observe the most perfect silence. For if you give advice, you offend both parties; him, against whom you give it, because it may cause the loss of his game; him, in whose favour you give it, because, though it be good, and he follows it, he loses the pleasure he might have had, if you had permitted him to think till it occurred to himself. Even after a move or moves, you must not, by replacing the pieces, shew how it might have been played better: for that displeases, and may occasion disputes or doubts about their true situation. All talking to the players, lessens or diverts their attention, and is therefore unpleasing; nor should you give the least hint to either party, by any kind of noise or

motion.— If you do, you are unworthy to be a spectator.— If you have a mind to exercise or show your judgments, do it in playing your own game when you have an opportunity, not in criticising or meddling with, or counselling, the play of others.

Lastly. If the game is not to be played rigorously, according to the rules above mentioned, then moderate your desire of victory over your adversary, and be pleased with one over yourself. Snatch not eagerly at every advantage offered by his unskilfulness or inattention; but point out to him kindly that by such a move he places or leaves a piece in danger and unsupported; that by another he will put his king in a dangerous situation, &c. By this generous civility (so opposite to the unfairness above forbidden) you may indeed happen to lose the game to your opponent, but you will win what is better, his esteem, his respect, and his affection; together with the silent approbation and good will of impartial spectators.

From Barbeu-Dubourg

ALS: American Philosophical Society

Mon cher Maitre ce 28e. juin 1779

J'ai l'honneur de vous renvoyer cy joint votre manuscrit sur la morale des echecs dont j'ai gardé copie, que j'enverrai au 1er. jour a imprimer dans le journal de Paris, si vous ne vous hâtez de me le defendre.[5] Et apres en avoir laissé gouter au public le plaisir pur, je pourrai bien le lendemain ou surlendemain le faire suivre de mes petites reflexions, car il m'en roule par la tête quelques unes à ce sujet;[6] et quand elles s'eloigneroient un peu de votre opinion, vous m'avez deja passé plus d'une fois de semblables ecarts qui ne peuvent porter aucune atteinte a l'inviolable attachement que je vous ai voué

DUBOURG

Notation: Dubourg Paris 28 juin 1779.

5. Dubourg would not live through the end of the year, and the essay never appeared in the *Jour. de Paris.*

6. He brought them to BF on July 3.

From Alexander Coffin ALS: American Philosophical Society

Sir Amsterdam 28th June 1779

I Refer your Excellency to Mr Sayers Letter Which he Says will apologize for my Addressing you:[7] Tho I am Conscious that a disposition to Render To Our Country, is always Sufficient ground for it. I have myself been made a Prisoner & it may Soon Be my Lot Again Consequntly I feel most Sensibly The Superiority of the English at Sea. It is Therfore With Great Plesure I have Examined A modle of A Ship Contrived By Mr Sayer, Which must hearafter if Adopted give us infinite Advantage in Our Commerce.[8]

But the Subject of this Letter is Chiefly to assure your Excellency That Mr Sayer Can Construct a Ship On A New princeble, Which Cannot, under any Circumstance Be Taken, Nor Can Any Ship in the Kings Navy escape Capture or resist her force many minutes, the plan is the most Simple & the Effects are the most Evedent of any Thing in Nature, I am Astonished that No man has heretofore Thought of it for I Will Venture to pronounce the Fleet of England good for Nothing, the moment America has Ten of those Ships: They are built for half the money & in half the time Necessary in the Old Construction. Do not Suppose me Carried away With Warmth of Imagination. I Know I am right a Child Would See the Effects.

Mr Sayer is going from here for America he may be made prisoner—[9] I hope for the Good of my Country you will in

7. Presumably Sayre's June 7 letter to BF, in which he cited the favorable opinions of his new ship design held by Coffin and another ship captain, Alexander Cordis.

8. Enclosed with the present letter was a one-page testimonial in Sayre's hand and signed by Cordis and Coffin stating that the proposed ship "would sail much faster, under any circumstances—would be safer in bad weather—must be vastly stronger—cheaper built—cheaper rigg'd—easier managed with the same hands, and more durable . . ." than any ship heretofore used.

9. Sayre did not return to America until 1783: John R. Alden, *Stephen Sayre, American Revolutionary Adventurer* (Baton Rouge and London, 1983), pp. 135–6.

that Case instantly Effect his Exchange. I Trust too your Excellency Will also think me of Some Consequence, being made acquainted With the principles Suggested Especially In Case of Mr Sayers death. He means to go Over With me.

I Congratulate your Excellency present good Appearances for Our Country & for the World at Large. & am most you Obedient Humble Sert. ALEXR. COFFIN

Addressed: A Son Excellence / Benj: Franklin Minr / Plenipotentiere / de le Etat Eunis de / Amerique / a Paris

Notation: Coffyn Alex: 28. Juin 1779

From Jean de Neufville & fils

ALS: American Philosophical Society

High Honourable Sir! Amsterdam the 28th. Júne 1779.

We hope yoúr Excellency may have approved of the plan of the Loan which we had the honoúr to convey by oúr last;[1] or that we may come to some alterations, which should prove agreable and practicable at the same time, bútt we heard the former loan should not you be shúre, before we should attempt to any further measúres this we should be glad to know exactly, how it stands, for certainly, this is not a mere cúriosity, bútt as we are persuaded Y E. herself will be convinced of, of the greatest conseqúence.

Now we begg annew the favoúr of the Speadiest expedition for the inclosed,[2] oút of the 8 Aman. vessells now in port we gott 4 to oúr consignment, in the futúre we may expect more to us in proportion, may we throúgh the means of YE. be usefúll likewise to the publicq. May we begg leave again to recomand oúr Selfs to her powerfúll inflúence!

This last brigg which arrived ús yesterday clear'd fr. St Eústatia, she comes fm. Boston, and tho' Known to be called Amsterdam She is the fast sailing and brave General Arnold now

1. Above, June 17.
2. Missing.

commanded by MacGee, we keep this with the utmost Secrecy.[3]

As we will pútt always the útmost reason for pride to be honourd With Any Commands from yoúr Excelle. We will be always with the útmost Regard and Veneration High Honourable Sir! Yoúr Excellencys most devoted and obedient servants. JOHN DE NEUFVILLE & SON.

Mr. John Tempel Esqr. did ús the honoúr to dine with ús he Came over by Capn. MacGee and desired his Compliments to Y E.[4]

Addressed: To his Excellencÿ / B: Franklin Esqr. / ambassador & Minister plenipotentiaire / of the thirteen united states of america / &a &a &ca / at Passi

Notation: Neufville John & Son 28. June 1779.

From Samuel Wharton

ALS: American Philosophical Society

Dear Sir Paris 28 June 1779

I send under Cover the News Paper, and learn by several Letters, which I received yesterday from London, That the Ministry and People were under very great Apprehensions of an Invasion, and the Destruction of their Commerce. One of our Friends writes me, That Orders were dispatched to Sir Charles Hardy to return immediately with the Fleet under his Command; and He wanted, of the proper Compliment for it, near four Thousand Men.[5] The same Gentleman informs

3. The brig *General Arnold,* commanded by James Magee, was wrecked off Plymouth, Mass., in December, 1778, with much loss of life: Mass. Hist. Soc. *Proc.*, 2nd ser., x (1895–6), 393; XII (1897–9), 199. Magee now commanded a brigantine named the *Amsterdam:* Allen, *Mass. Privateers,* p. 74; Claghorn, *Naval Officers,* pp. 192–3.

4. John Temple, the would-be peacemaker (XXIV, 300n), now hoping to convince the British Opposition of the hopelessness of continuing the war: Lewis Einstein, *Divided Loyalties: Americans in England during the War of Independence* (London, 1933), pp. 100–1.

5. Actually Hardy's orders, which did not arrive until after he set sail, were to put to sea immediately. See Wharton's letter of June 21 and Patterson, *The Other Armada,* p. 107. For his shortage of sailors see *ibid.*, p. 104.

Me,—That the Detachment, which was sent from New York, consisting of abt. 2400, and commanded by Colonel Mathews,—was return'd from his Expedition on the Coast of Virginie, after destroying some Craft,—making a few Prisoners, and bringing off some Plunder.—[6] My Son[7] & I will do ourselves the Honor of dining with You on the 5th. of July.— A Day ever memorable for the most glorious Revolution, That ever signalised a People! I am with the sincerest Respect Your Excellency's most obedt. & most humble Servt.

S. WHARTON

His Excellency Benjn. Franklin Esqr. &c &c &c—

Addressed: A Son Excellence / Monsieur / Monsieur Franklin / &c &c &c / Passy

Notation: S. Wharton Paris 28 juin 1779

From Jean de Neufville & fils

ALS: American Philosophical Society

High Honourable Sir! [after June 28, 1779][8]

Will yoúr Excellency give me leave to transcribe at the foot of the present the latest important news we gott here from the Continent if she knew it already, She will excúse ús Zeal from the pleasúre we natúrally felt on the Arrivall of two bottoms from oúr frends in those qúarters, we have seven Sail in oúr harboúr and some more are dayly expected; may we enjoy the protection and Kind influence of yoúr Excellency those connections will give ús—business equal up to oúr spirits, of

6. The expedition mentioned in Wharton's June 21 letter and in the annotation of Digges' June 11 letter; it was far more successful than this letter implies, capturing Portsmouth and Norfolk, burning Suffolk and destroying many supplies: Richard K. Showman *et al.*, eds., *The Papers of General Nathanael Greene* (5 vols. to date, Chapel Hill, 1976—), IV, 49–50n.

7. Joseph, who wrote BF on May 31.

8. Dated by the news from Boston, which appeared in the June 29 issue of the *Gaz. de Leyde* and presumably was brought by the ship mentioned in the firm's June 28 letter. That letter must have preceded this, as it clearly refers to its June 17 letter as being "our last."

which we may hope Y E. will be convinced; and So complimenting YE. on the Last declaration of the Coúrt of Spain in favoúr of the American Caúse we make bold to add that if oúr wishes and those of oúr Worthy Protector of this City are granted, we may soon see likewise the Knot fastly tied which we endeavourd to Lay between the Two Sister Republicks.[9]

May we begg the favoúr again to have the enclosed forwarded,[1] tho' we have occasion fr. writing we are ashamed to say our neighboúrs enjoy increased protection in the American trade, bútt we further we dare Say we will always if not Surpass them be equal to the most Zealoús Among them, in trúe affection for the Country Where Liberty resides.

May we begg once more for the Continúation of the powerfúll protection of yoúr excellency and so subscribe with the utmost Veneration and Regard High Honoúrable Sir! Yoúr Excellencys most devoted and Obedt Servants

John de Neufville & Son.

Extract of the providence Gazet of the 24th. of Aprill

Boston, 22 Apl. On friday last great joy was diffused through this town, by the Arrivall of the Continentall fregat Warren Jno. Hopkins Esqr. after a very Súccessfull crúise she sailed fm. hence some weeks ago accompanied with the queen of france fregat Capn. Olney and the ranger of 20 Gúnns Capn Simson in the Continentall service[2] they first took a privateer schooner of 14 Guns, from New York for which they gott intelligence of a fleet of provisions and stores bound fm that place to Georgia to a large Amoúnt for the supply of the brittish Army the fleet consisted in 9 Saill 7 of which have been taken, of the most considerable as

Kings ship Jason	Capn. Porterfield	20 Gúnns	150 men

9. A reference to a Dutch-American treaty de Neufville had negotiated with William Lee; see BF's letter to Dumas of March 12.

1. Not located.

2. For the cruise of the *Warren, Queen of France,* and *Ranger* see Gordon's letter of May 5.

ship Maria	16 Gunns	84 Men with 1800 Case of flour
privateer schooner the hibernia briggs patriot, Prince frederick, bachelor, john, and schooner Chance with stores. &ca.	8 Case Gúnn	45 men—

The jason Arrived on Saturday last the schooner Charlotte on friday at Rotterdam with oút the Valúes of the Vessells those prices [prizes] amoúnt far upward £80,000 stg. in Another paper it is Said fm. boston the 26 Apl. that all the Vessells had retúrnd safe and brought in the mentiond 8 prices.

This is probabily due to the Cautious advice we heard Some time ago given by great Generall Washington that Such a transport should be expected.[3]

Addressed: To his Excellencÿ / B: Franklin Esqr. / Ambassador Plenipotentiary of the / Thirteen United States of No America. / at Passi

Notation: Neufville John & *Son*

From Peter Amiel

ALS: American Philosophical Society

Honored Sir Nantes the 29 June 1779

Capt: Jones haveing granted me leave of absence for to *stay at L'Orient:* to settle my private Affairs;[4] since his departure, Monsieur De Chaumont has been so kind as to offer me appartements in his Chateau, this Sir is to beg it as perticular

3. In early March Washington had advised Congress of the convoy: Fitzpatrick, *Writings of Washington,* XIV, 206. He mentioned the capture in general orders: *ibid.*, XIV, 443.

4. For which see Jones's June 18 letter to BF.

favor that you'l be so kind as to extend my leave for his Place. I am Honored Sir your Respectfull Humble Servant

PETER AMIEL

To The Honorable B: Franklin Esqr:

Notation: Amiel Peter 29. June 1779.

From John Bondfield

ALS: American Philosophical Society

Sir Bordeaux 29 June 1779

Refering to what I had the honor to write you last post this serves only to advise you that in consiquence of my engagements that become due in the course of next month for the fifty six pieces of artillery I have drawn in favor of Messieurs Bory freres & Co[5] at four Months from this day for ninteen Thousand eight hundred Livres in the following Sums

29 June to Bory freres & Co at 4 Uzce.[6]

do	do	do. . .	3000 *l.t.*
do	do	do. . .	3200 *l.t.*
do	do	do. . .	3400 *l.t.*
do	do	do. . .	3600 *l.t.*
do	do	do. . .	3800 *l.t.*
do	do	do. . .	2800 *l.t.*
			19800

To which you will please to give due honor.

The Spanish Fleet from Contrary Winds are prevented from getting out of Port both at Corronna & Cadiz. I have the honor to be with due Respect Sr. your very hhb Servant

JOHN BONDFIELD

His Excellency B Franklin

Addressed: His Excellency B Franklin / Esq / Plenipotene des Etats Unies / a / Paris

5. Possibly brothers of the man Bondfield introduced in February: XXVIII, 549.

6. Uzance. A thirty-day delay in which to make payment.

From Alexander Gillon

ALS: American Philosophical Society

Sir Nantes 29th. June 1779

By Letters lately recd. from So. Carolina I am well acqd. with its Situation & therefore take the liberty to address your Excellency thereon requesting you will weigh how far America is Interested in that States success or misfortunes & that if the Object you have in view for the Continental Ships & Vessels of War in Europe is not superior to that of the relief of the Bleeding Inhabitants of So. Carolina & Georgia you will please to consider whether the Fleet I lately saw at L'orient might not to immediately proceed to the relief of them States.[7] I know the force of the Enemy there & know the Exact Force of the Fleet you had fitted out at L'Orient thus am Convinc'd it is equal to the purpose requird. You know I have wav'd every impediment to a proper Harmony subsisting between officers going on such an Expedition by preparing to go as a Volunteer on a former similar Expedition[8] & that my officers wou'd do the same but if it is thought that the Plan can be better Executed without any of the officers (presence) from that State we in such case wou'd be glad to point out the method we shou'd adopt was we to Command which your officer may accept or reject, I trust your Excellency will not judge me capable of attempting to dictate to you on this business. Far be such an Idea from me I only address you as the Superior Naval American officer in Europe fixd as such by the Laws of our Land & my Commission also as a Citizen to point out to you the danger of those States & the way to Shun it by the means you have at your Command, which I presume will be sooner prepar'd than any Vessels I cou'd Purchase or fit out for that Plan I therefore beseech your Excellency will be pleas'd to enable me to relieve that besieged Country by fur-

7. The squadron must have been John Paul Jones's. For the general mood of apprehension at this time in South Carolina about the British in Georgia see Ward, *War of the Revolution,* II, 684.

8. In June, 1778, against two privateers blockading Charleston harbor: D.E. Huger Smith, "Commodore Alexander Gillon and the Frigate South Carolina," *S.C. Hist. & Geneal. Mag.,* IX (1908), 193.

nishing me with the means now under your direction or that you will direct the commanding officer of Your Fleet to proceed as soon as possible to So. Carolina if your prefer the later I can furnish him with a pretty true list of the Ships & their Station on that Coast, they are so few that by my last advices frm there it was expected that if I arrd. with the three Frigates I was order'd to procure I shou'd be an equal force to the British Navigation there or in Savannah River— You know I have some money of the State here, that I also have a power to purchase or Build & therefore cou'd remove every difficulty of any of these Vessels being own'd here or of any part of them because I cou'd on the States acct. purchase out any Owner who may be concern'd that disapproves of this Expedition, but if any Such owner I think I could point out advantages that wou'd arise to him on such a Voyage that might Induce him to hold his concern, I have lately made such offers that I trust will be deem'd very beneficial thus I am not without some hopes of getting the three Frigates I was sent for, permit me to mention them to you for your opinion & that if you think proper you may mention it to Mr Chaumont or any of your friends that you think likely to hold A Share therein—it is to raise a sum not Exceeding 15 a Ls. [*l.t.*] 1,800000 by subscription throughout this Kingdom Holland &ca 12 a 1500,000 of which is for to Build three Frigates & is on acct & risque of the State conformable to my Powers, the Surplus of a 600,000 may be laid out in merchandise & 3 fast sailing Ships to carry them all on acct. & risque of the Subscribers with Vessels & Goods I promise to Convoy to the State of So. Carolina & to their Address, I also promise that the State will within six months after our arrival there Convoy the Vessels with the proceeds of these Goods to St. Domingo Martinico or Guardaloupe wherever there may be A French Convoy ready, or that the State will within 12 Months after my arrival there order me to Convoy the Sd Ships & Effects to any Port of Europe. I propos'd to pay Seven per Ct. Interest per annum for the advance made for the State to pay full & ample Commsons. to the House that Under took the business & to repay such advance in two & three years & to make it Still more beneficial I advice that half of the Nett proceeds of these

Goods should be put out at Interest of 7 per Ct. in the State & that if the owners chuse they may refit the Ships I Convoy to here & send these out again under my Convoy with very trifling Cargoes to bring home to here the such half that was at Interest, this divides the risk & I presume is one of the best Voyages any Speculators to our Continent can make from Europe.

In hopes of these proposals being accepted I am preparing to build here & in the Vicinity have therefore tho't proper to write to Mr. de Sartine to day to Craving he will Grant me permission to Build three Frigates in this Kingdom & to fit them out, in all of which I will rigidly adhere to the Laws of his Country, will you be pleas'd to support that request that I may be fav'd with A Speedy reply. I will thank you for yours hereto, directed to me under Cover to Messrs. H. L. Chaurand freres merchts. here,[9] & if you have or do receive any Letters for me I will Esteem it as a favour if you will please to send them to me as above, please present my respects to your worthy Grandson & assure yourself that I am with every Respect—

Your Excellencys Most Obedt. & most hble Servt.

A. GILLON

Commodore of the Navy of the State of South Carolina

His Exclly Benja Franklin Esqre Minister Plenepotentiary at the Court of Versailles Passé

Notation: A. Gillon Nantes 29. juin 1779.

From David Hartley

ALS:[1] American Philosophical Society; transcript: Library of Congress

My Dear friend June 29 1779

In the course of a negotiation lately on foot I had at one time entertained hopes of Success.[2] I am still inclined to hope that something is gained, perhaps in the minds of men, wch

9. XXVIII, 423.
1. Marked "Copy" by Hartley.
2. See Hartley's letter of April 10.

may hereafter serve as a reference to form some future basis of accommodation upon, when a more fortunate hour may come. You understand that neither of the parties is formally committed by what has passed. A private person being a well-wisher to peace & to the rights of mankind, has endeavored to offer a mediation, & to devise terms upon wch the parties might approximate to each other. Some recent events wch have just happened may for a time suspend propositions of peace, but the principles upon wch I have endeavored to mediate seem to me still to remain the same, & perhaps the time may come when those principles may be more favorably received. Whenever that time shall come, I shall be ever upon the watch to meet it; but be assured of this, that I will never be the instrument of any fallacious negotiation, if I have reason to suspect insincerity.— In our late business I did entertain considerable hopes of success at one time, & I am inclined to believe that many persons of high description on this side of the water, were well disposed to the terms proposed, & therefore I am at a loss to account for the sudden breaking off of the treaty. The suddenness of the delivery of the spanish rescript was a surprize to me, tho I had always taken account for a spanish interference in case of the continuance of the American & french wars. This event therefore does certainly suggest some conjectures to my thoughts & now that I have seen the spanish rescript itself, & find in it a declaration many months ago, that they wd certainly require a settlement of their own matters in dispute, before any final settlement of the then subsisting disturbances between the contending parties shd be suffered to take effect,[3] I can easily imagine that spain might think it necessary to accelerate its pace, if any idea had got abroad of any possible settlement between Great Britain & France and America being on the carpet. I can have no reason but mere suspicion to impute any such consideration as a ground of their conduct, but the appearance of the rescript

3. A paraphrase of a passage in Almodóvar's declaration; see Sir Francis Piggott and G. W. T. Omond, *Documentary History of the Armed Neutralities 1780 and 1800* (London, 1919), pp. 120–1.

itself does by no means seem to militate with such a conjecture, because that rescript does not proclaim or make good any justifiable or ostensible causes of war. It is a mere bundle of shallow and empty pretences importing only this; we will pick a quarrel with you because we will.

No man conversant in political life & events, need be surprized at such conduct, because I believe most European nations wd have done the same thing; but to me who keep in view at all times Peace with america as the polar star to steer by; I reason thus; that there seems to be nothing american in the motives of the Court of Spain, & consequently, that, the ground of any negotiation between GB. France & NA remains as it did respecting america. Whatever engagements America may have formed they will doubtless observe them most faithfully, nor wd I ever make a proposition to them to committ any breach of honour. But Peace & settlement are and ought to be their objects. There is no common sense in their entangling themselves in all the Gothic crusading follies of European nations amongst whom the only definition of man seems to be, a fighting animal, or the Gladiator of God's creation to mangle & to destroy his works.— I have said it, & repeat it again to keep clear of the suspicion of tampering; Engagements ought to be most religiously observed, but those being religiously fulfilled, nations ought to look to the permanent interests of their respective communities. The argument is very fair & avowable from America to the H. of Bourbon, thus; we will perform any engagements according to the obligation contracted to your full & just content, But if France & Spain from seperate motives of their own, are bent upon war indefinitely with Great Britain, upon the memory of old resentments & jealousies, why shd we be dragged as parties thro such a war, if any opportunity shd occur to us of making terms satisfactory to ourselves, & consistent with our original views & engagements. Fight on & destroy each other if you think that either the laws of god or man can justify you in so doing, in the dregs of your old Gothic world. But leave the new world at peace, to encrease & to multiply, to subdue the Earth & to fertilize it. Withhold not your consent to our entering into a ten years neutrality[4] till your madness has spent itself.— In this argument you see that I conceal nothing. I wd avow it openly. The proposition is fair & equitable from America to the H of Bourbon, & if they shd withhold their consent, or grudgingly oppose such a proposition, if I were an American I shd not mark such conduct with the term of magnanimity. I have not by any means lost my hopes that the proposition just now alluded to of a neutrality for a sufficient length of term, for America, may be consented to at some future time. You may be assured that if I cd bring to effect such a sentiment & proposition, I shd do it not only with the most cordial inclination, but as the first of public duties. Here let matters rest between us for the present, only remembering that if ever I shd at any time herafter make any similar proposition to you, that I never mean to throw out any secret dishonorable suggestion, but what I now avow as being my settled principle of thinking & reasoning upon principles of national justice & honour. My only view for my own Country is this; To lay a foundation for an eventual national[5] reconciliation & good correspondence between Great Britain & North America. Peace and good will between us.—Yrs &c DH

To Dr Franklin

From Cradock Taylor[6]

ALS: American Philosophical Society

Sir Aix in Provance the 29th. 1779 June

I make no doubt but by this time Mr. Frazer has acquainted Your Excerlency in what Manner I came into the British Navy but for fear he Shod. not I take the liberty to Acquaint you that I was against my Inclination taken out of a Nuteral Vessel

4. Replaces "truce".

5. Replaces "a national".

6. Born in Orange County, Va. (*c.* 1754), Taylor attended school briefly with James Madison and knew Edmund Pendleton; both men were interested in helping Taylor procure his freedom. See William T. Hutchinson and William M.E. Rachal, *et al.*, eds., *The Papers of James Madison* (19 vols. to date, Chicago and London, 1962–), II, 262n, 307, 311.

& Compeld. to serve his Britanick Majesty.[7] I Now embrace this oppertunity of Returning to my Native Cuntry America an oppertunity I long have wished for I hope your Exerlency will take my case into Consideration as I have no Friends in this place (& what is still worse no Money) but have been Oblig'd to live upon my 12 Sols per. day tho not without Contracting some Small Depts now Sir if your Excerlency will be so kind as to obtain me my liberty to Return to my Native Cuntry (which I make no doubt but you can from the Aliance betweeen France & America) it will ever be esteemed as the greatest favour that could be conferd on your most obedient & greatly Obligd. Humbl. Servt. CRADOCK TAYLOR

[*In the margin:*] I have taken the liberty to send a copy of part of this letter to the French Minister—[8]

Addressed: aix / a Son Excellence / Monsieur Le Docteur Franklin / ambassadeur des Etat unis de / L'amerique, a la Cour de france, / à Paris.

Notation: Cradock Taylor, Aix in Provance, June 29. 79

From "Daniel Thomson"[9]

ALS: Historical Society of Pennsylvania

Sir London 29 June 1779

We natives of America, and, from one cause or other, residing in this city, have formed ourselves into a weekly society:

7. Frazer wrote Taylor on June 7. He had just learned that Taylor was among the British prisoners on parole at Aix. He remembered the young man well from King William County, Va., and encouraged him to leave the service he was in and return to America. He was confident BF could arrange things with the French minister. APS. See also Frazer's letter of June 26, above.

8. Presumably Sartine, whom BF wrote on Taylor's behalf on Nov. 17. Library of Congress. Taylor's plight was also the subject of an undated letter from John Penn to James Lovell asking him to interest BF in obtaining the young man's freedom. APS. Taylor's appeals for money and liberty will continue into vol. 30 and after.

9. BF was apparently as puzzled by this piece as we are. It may be the "very foolish paper" that Samuel Wharton, when asked for an opinion by

and as the result of our last meeting seems to us of great national importance; it was unanimously resolved, to have the whole that passed upon the subject, laid before your Excellency, as the proper channel for procuring the approbation of Congress.

At a meeting of the society held the 21st currnt, a member rose and addressed the Chairman as follows.

What I have Sir, to propose may at first seem shocking to every Gentleman present; because, I will venture to say, that there is not one of them who does not glory in the name of *American.* And indeed, 'till very lately, no man was more delighted with it than I; nor would I agree to give it up for any other, provided we had all America to ourselves: but this is not the case, Spain has vast territories there. The Dutch, French, and Portuguese have also Colonies there; and as for the Indians and Savages, they still possess, by far, the greatest part of that immense continent. Now Sir, As the inhabitants of all those countries are Americans as well as we; they are along with us, and on our account, branded with the epithets of *Unnatural Americans, Rebellious Americans* and such like: nor, however unfair, can it be otherwise while we continue under the same name with them: therefore, that none may be liable to reproach on our account, I move Sir, That the too general appellation of *Americans* be laid aside by us; and a name so thoroughly pointed be substituted in its stead, that either the glory, or disgrace that may attend our present conflict, or future actions, may be alone applicable to ourselves. This member being seated, another spoke thus.

Sir, I must confess I was very much startled with the commencement of the Gentlemans speech; but he has, so fully and

---

BF, dismissed as the work of a "Junto of American Tories" and returned with a letter which we tentatively date July 19, 1779. APS. We have been unable to trace "Daniel Thomson" and suspect, as Mary Beth Norton has kindly suggested, that this letter is actually a satire on the meetings of the London loyalist association formed in May, 1779. For the association see Mary Beth Norton, *The British Americans: the Loyalist Exiles in London* (Boston, 1972), pp. 162–6.

clearly, shown the necessity there is for giving up a name that includes the subjects of other Powers, that I am entirely of his opinion. Could they read our language, they must doubtless be exceedingly hurt at the illiberal aspersions bestowed by the English on the Americans at large. But exclusive of this Sir, it is now time for the inhabitants of that great Continent to be particularly distinguished. Americus Vespusius gave that country its present name; and had it continued in the intire possession of the native savages, that name might have done for them for ever: but now Sir, that it has been grasped by different European Powers, and cannot fail in time of being covered with Kingoms and Empires; it is equally improper to continue the name *American* to any one of its natives, as it would be to have no other name for a native of either Germany, Russia, France, Spain, &ca, than that of an *European.* I therefore, most cordially, approve of the motion. This Gentleman's speech being ended, a third person got up and spoke to this purpose.

Mr. Chairman, I do not rise up to differ in opinion from my worthy countrymen. I most sincerely wish for any name that may be less liable to load us and others with English abuse. The people of this country have, of late, taken a great dislike to our cause. The name *American* has I think become hateful to them all. I go no where without meeting with some disagreeable compliment or other as, I am not fond of an American.— The Americans are ungrateful monsters.— The Americans have imbibed the blood of their brethren the Savages; they tar and feather, and, like them, dance about the victim.— They seem to disregard the miseries of their fellow creatures, and so on. I say Sir, that for these and many other reasons, I certainly wish that it was possible to change our appellation. I hate to be inrolled under the same name with a Savage, but Sir, Should we fix upon a name that may be agreeable to all of us here; are we to suppose that the ruling Powers in North America will adopt that name? They are at present called the American Congress; I will not say that they are justly so called, for they certainly do not give laws to all America. But can we expect that they will stamp their deeds with the name we shall give them? Or are we weak enough to hope, that the British Parliament will, in their debates & decrees, fall in with that name? I have done. A fourth member got up and said

Sir, During the two first speeches, the same objections occurred to me that have been made by the worthy Gentleman who spoke last; but on recollecting that France had once no other name than Gaul, and Scotland than Caledonia; and that in this great Metropolis, what was called the other day Tyburn Road is now known only by the name of Oxford Street; I concluded, that it can be no difficult matter to fix a name on a people who, in fact, have had hitherto none by which they could be clearly distinguished from others. It indeed Sir, depends upon the propriety of the name given; if it be not quite descriptive and applicable it may fail; if otherwise, it will not only be immediately in every mouth, but be applied in all publications; and especially by the Editors of news papers who are, in general, men of great discernment, and who study to establish propriety. I do not say it will at once be made use of by the Legislative Bodies of either country; yet it will, from reason and necessity, make its way even among them, and that with such rapidity, that, I will venture to assert, the word *Americans* shall not, in a few years, be heard in any country, except to distinguish the American Indians from those in other parts of the world. And now Sir, I doubt not but this Society will approve of the motion; a motion for which, I think, the maker deserves not only our best thanks, but those of all our brethren wherever dispersed.

No other member offering to speak, the Chairman rose up and put the question; and tho the meeting consisted of forty two members, and many of these suspected of being but seeming friends to our cause, yet there was not one dissenting voice. He then proceeded thus.

Gentlemen, I must acknowledge that during the different speeches on this interesting motion, I felt a transporting pleasure within my breast. I have all along, since the commencement of our noble struggle for liberty, suffered exceedingly on account of others being included with us by name, either in our merit or demerit, I therefore wish success to the motion: but as one of the Gentlemen very judiciously observed, if the name given be not pointed and descriptive, our hopes may be defeated; to prevent which, I propose, that we determine nothing further 'till this day week; and in the interim, it is to be hoped every Gentleman present will employ his thoughts in finding out a name suitable to our Character, Dignity, and Growing Greatness. Upon which the Society broke up highly satisfied.

At a meeting held the 20th. there was a very full Society. The Chairman then opened the business, after which many names were proposed, and much pro and con past without giving apparent satisfaction. At length the venerable member who made the motion got up and addressed the Chair as follows

Sir, It must be allowed that any one of the names proposed, would clearly point us out as a peculiar people: but Sir, it strikes me, that by adopting either of them, our origin may, in future ages, be intirely lost. Britain seems to be upon the decline and may not recover; but be that as it may, Britannia has made the world tremble to such a degree, that her fame is, and must be great in the annals of history. The knowledge therefore of being sprung from so dignified a mother, cannot fail to give courage and consequence to her children at any period of time, and wherever providence may place them. To preserve therefore this most essential knowledge, and also to include with us, our brethren in the Floridas, and Nova Scotia &ca, who, tho they have not yet joined us, may in time see their error: I propose Sir, that all the American Provinces that now are, or may hereafter be, under the dominion of the offspring of this Island may, for their general name, be henceforth called New Britain.

The Gentleman being seated, silence and a seeming astonishment took place for a considerable time. Then several members got up one after another; but as their speeches tended chiefly to illustrate the honours and advantages that must arise from so animating and proper a name; we shall defer troubling your Excellency with them for some days. When the Gentlemen who thought proper to deliver their sentiments had done, the Chairman arose; and after putting many names without effect, he last of all put New Britain, upon which every hand was up. He then wished us joy of our new name, which he said, seemed to have already dignified our countenances. After embracing each other as New Britons, we concluded the evening in drinking many loyal healths such as,— Prosperity to New Britain.— Valour to New Britain's sons and Love to her Daughters.— The New British Congress. &ca. &ca. We greet you well.

Signed by order of the Society — DANIEL THOMSON
Secretary

P.S. We have Sir resolved that a copy of this epistle be published in the news papers.[1] This resolution was taken from a belief, that our new name cannot be disliked by the Ruling Powers in either country, for the following reasons. First, It has nothing to do with the present contest. Again, It is equally honourable for both parent and children. And lastly, The propriety of it must be the same, whether we are, or are not again, connected with the mother country.

From Alexandre-Henry-Guillaume le Roberger de Vausenville[2]

ALS: American Philosophical Society

Monsieur — Paris ce 29 Juin 1779.

J'ai eu lhonneur de vous envoyer un exemplaire de mon ouvrage intitulé: Essai Physico-géomètrique sur la quadrature

1. *The Public Advertiser* printed the piece on July 16, 1779, prefaced by a note to the printer stating that the speeches and resolution of the Society had been transmitted to BF and that a subject so worthy of public attention ought to find a place in the newspaper.

2. An astronomer and former corresponding member of the Académie des sciences who became openly antagonistic to the institution after its decision in 1775 not to consider papers dealing with squaring the circle. (That decision is explained in *Histoire de l'académie royale des sciences,* MDCCLXXV (Paris, 1778), pp. 61–6.) Vausenville, a "quadrateur," felt that his 1774 paper on that subject entitled him to the 150,000 *l.t.* being offered by the Académie as a prize for a paper relating to longitude at sea. Now, as he indicates in this letter, he was suing the institution. His challenges brought the debate into the public view; the astronomer Joseph-Jérôme le Français de Lalande (XVII, 307n; XXVI, 408) was forced to answer Vausenville by a letter in the *Jour. de Paris,* July 8, 1779. For an account of Vausenville and his lawsuit see Roger Hahn, *The Anatomy of a Scientific*

du cercle dont le texte imprimé est ci-joint.[3] C'est M. le Roux au colege de boncourt[4] a qui je lai remis & qui s'est chargé de vous le faire parvenir. Jespere qu'il s'en sera acquitté; mais sil l'avoit oublié, je me ferois un vrai plaisir de vous en envoyer un autre. Lacademie des sciences de paris à Gardé le Silence sur cet ouvrage quoi qu'expressement invitée par ma lettre du 20. Jer. der. [dernier] de l'approuver ou de le contester. Le s. Dalembert s'est absolument refusé d'y repondre. Les autres géomètres de lacademie également invités à le contester ont gardé le silence, excepté le S. de la lande qui ma dit des injures aulieu de me fournir des raisons. & les journalistes n'ont pas voulu réçevoir ma reponse. Ladessus j'ai pris le parti de faire sommer l'academie d'approuver ou de contester, & ce par exploit de lavasseur huissr. [huissier] audr. [auditeur] en la Prévôté de lhotel du roy en datte du 25. Juin, & de faire inserer son jugement dans les journaux. Sur le refus du s. d'alembert, je l'ai fait assigner au chatelet pr. voir dire que son refus vaudra approbation & qu'il sera debouté de l'oppon. [opposition] formèe en 1771. au rapport fait en ma faveur, à l'acade. des sciences, par M. Pingrè.[5]

A lègard des Srs. Jeaurat & Cousin,[6] je les ai fait sommer d'apporter raisons & moyens suffisants pour justifier la dénégation portée dans leur rapport fait à lacade. le 21. Jer. 1775. & au refus je les ai fait assigner au chatelet pr. voir dire que

---

Institution: the Paris Academy of Sciences, 1666–1803 (Berkeley, and London, 1971) pp. 145–7. See also Quérard, *France littéraire,* under Le Rohbergherr de Vausenville.

3. A printed prospectus of his *Essai physico-géométrique* (Paris, 1778), written under the name Le Rohberg-Herr de Vausenville, is at the APS. Vausenville also published a supplement to that essay in 1779: Hahn, *The Anatomy of a Scientific Institution,* p. 417.

4. Leroux was *maître-ès-arts,* and editor from 1768 to 1776 of the *Journal d'éducation:* Quérard, *France littéraire,* v, 208.

5. Alexandre-Guy Pingré (1711–96), an astronomer: *Index biographique des membres et correspondants de l'académie des sciences du 22 décembre 1668 au 12 novembre 1954* (Paris, 1954), p. 410.

6. They were the astronomer, Edme-Sébastien Jeaurat (1724–1803), and the mathematician Jacques-Antoine-Joseph Cousin (1739–1800): *ibid.*, pp. 262, 128.

leur rapport sera cassè coe. [comme] faux . . . &c. en conseqce. quils seront condamnés &c.

Je vais faire imprimer le tout & j'aurai lhonneur de vous en faire part si vous le trouvez bon. Je vous demande permission de vous faire passer un exemplaire, en vous suppliant de le faire parvenir à la societé de philadelphie par la 1ere. occasion.

J'ai lhonneur d'être avec les Sentimens de la plus parfaite Consideration Monsieur Votre très humble & très obeissant serviteur

DE VAUSENVILLE
rue & f. B. St. Denis

150.000. *l.t.* deposés aux mains de lacade. pr. cette decouverte, est la cause de sa resistance.

Addressed: A Monsieur / Monsieur Le Docteur franklin / en sa maison / *à Passy* / d.V.

Notation: Vausenville De 29. Juin 1779.—

From Jonathan Williams, Jr.: Two Letters

(I) Copy: Yale University Library; (II) ALS: American Philosophical Society

I.

Nantes June 29. 1779.

I herewith send you two Invoices—the first for Goods Shipped by your order on Acct & risque of Gr Green of Rhode island on board the three Friend. Capt Colman amounting to .... £936.12*s.*[7]

The Second for sundrys for Mrs Bache which you desired me to send with M De Luzernes Baggage (as the three Friends was taken up to Carry his Baggage & as my Cousin[8] went passenger in

7. See JW's letter of May 6 for Gov. Greene's request.

8. His cousin is Jonathan Williams III. For the goods to be sent to Sarah Bache see JW's letter of June 8.

that Ship I thought best not to trouble M De Luzerne & put it on board under my Cousins Care)	£ 316
	1252.12
I deduct from this sum fifteen Louis which you advanced to Mr Richard for me	360
	892.12

The Ballance £892.12*s.* I have this day drawn on you for in favr of Messrs Cottin & fils & Jauge at 15 days date which closes this affair.

Dr. Franklin—

II.

Dear & hond Sir.— Nantes June 29. 1779.—

Accept my most gratefull Thanks for your friendly Favour of the 17th Inst. I would immediately set off to see you, but that I have at length a number of Auditors to examine my Acct. and I expect to begin on them in a few Days, when this is done I shall immediately leave this Place.—[9]

I have written Billy all the news I can collect.—[1]

I am ever with the greatest Respect Dear & honoured Sir Your dutifull & affectionate Kinsman JONA WILLIAMS J

Addressed: His Excellency. / Doctor Franklin.

Notation: Williams Jona. June 29. 1779.

9. Schweighauser had by this time recovered sufficiently to become the fifth member of the committee (with Johnson, Nesbitt, Cuming, and Gridley). JW wrote these gentlemen a formal letter on June 30 giving background information, asking for a meeting, and informing them that their decision would be final, subject only to the revision of Congress. Yale University Library.

1. That letter, of the same date, quoted news from a letter of Capt. Green. Green himself wrote BF on June 25, above. A postscript to JW's letter to WTF gave an account of the *General Arnold*'s successful engagement with a letter of marque. APS.

To John Paul Jones

LS:[2] National Archives; copies: National Archives, Library of Congress

Dear sir, Passy 30. June 1779.

Being arrived at Grois, you are to make the best of your Way, with the Vessels under your Command, to the West of Ireland; and establish your Cruise on the Orcades, the Cape of Dirneus, and the Dogger Bank: in order to take the Ennimies Property in those Seas.[3]

The Prizes you may make, send to Dunkirk, Ostend, or Bergen in Norway: according to your Proximity to either of those Ports. Address them to the Persons M. De Chaumont shall indicate to you.[4]

About the 15th August, when you will have sufficiently cruised in these Seas, you are to make Route for the Texel, where you will meet my further Orders.[5]

If by any personal Accident you should be render'd unable to execute these Instructions, The Officer of your Squadron next in Rank, is to endeavour to put them in execution.

2. In WTF's hand. In a July 8 letter to Jones (National Archives) BF explained that the following instructions had been drafted in French by Sartine's ministry and brought to him by Chaumont. BF then had them translated into English.

3. The Orcades is another name for the Orkney Islands. Morison, *Jones*, p. 194, claims that the second reference point is the Cape of Lindesnes (also known as the Naze), the southern tip of Norway; another possibility is Cape Dennis (Dennis Head) at the northeast tip of the Orkneys: Thomas J. Schaeper, *John Paul Jones and the Battle off Flamborough Head: a Reconsideration* (New York, 1989), pp. 108–9. The Dogger Bank is one of the prime fishing grounds in the North Sea.

4. On June 30 Chaumont told Jones to send his prizes to the French consul at Bergen or, for prizes directed to Ostend or Dunkirk, to M. Calliez *père* (XXVIII, 560–1): Bradford, *Jones Papers,* reel 3, no. 660.

5. Shipping to and from Amsterdam generally passed through the channel south of the Texel, an island off the entrance to the Zuider Zee. Wood needed by the French navy had been accumulating at Amsterdam; see Dumas' letter of June 11. As the Dutch refused to convoy it to France, Jones's squadron, after completing its initial cruise, would be available to bring the timber ships safely through the English Channel: Dull, *French Navy,* pp. 174–6.

With best Wishes for your Prosperity, I am ever, Dear Sir, your affectionate Friend & humble Servant. B FRANKLIN

Honble Capt. Jones.

Endorsed: from his Excellency Doctor Franklin Passy June 30th. 1779 recd. L'Orient July. 6th. 1779. No. 11.

From Dumas

ALS: American Philosophical Society

Sir the Hague June 30th *1779*

My last of the 24th. inst. gives you an account of what passed the same day in the Assembly of Holland. The following day, they *resumed,* as they call it, the resolution, & confirmed it; which being done the States separated, & will not meet before the end of July, in ordinary meeting. My intention was to set out Sunday, but finding myself not very well, I have complied with my wifes desire to stay till sunday, being the happy 4th. of July, when I think to reach at least Rotterdam, & then to go on without losing time.

N—— persists in his ambitious schemes. He has received another American Vessel the Amsterdam, Cap. Mac Gee, with four american passengers adressed to him. I am very glad of it for him, & wish him great successes in this line: but I must repeat it, I think it not proper to confer to him, nor to any foreigner having his own business besides, such eminent powers as he asks for. After all I want still to see him perform his engagements with yr. Excy., as to the Loan.

As to the Bar—— C——, when I saw him at Amst. he intended to me a very high compliment, by telling me, Till he was convinced, as he was now, of my being so early a Servant to America, & not an uncalled one, his intention had been to get himself appointed Minister for America in his own Country, by the Interest of his great friends in America, & of his Correspondent there Mr. Erkelens a Dutch Mercht.: but now he would give it up, & not envy me a Coach and horses. I gave him to understand, I never had horses, but men & their Concerns, in my head, & therefore would not interfere, if he should apply for his horses to America. He wished I would concert with him what we had to write severally to Am———, & give one of my dispatches to his friend Lt. Col. Diriks, who is to return there: both which I declined.

I am happy in the expectation to be at Passy, as well as every where in the world, with a respectful attachment, Sir, yr. most humble & obedient servant D

I beg yr. indulgence for my English.

Yesterday at 4 o clock in the morning the G. Py. dispatched 6 Messengers to the other provinces, with the *Lettres circulaires* of this province.

Paris to his Exc. B. Franklin

Addressed: To his Excellency / B. Franklin Esqr. Min. Plen. / of the Un. St. &c. &c. / *Passy*./.

Notation: Dumas June 30. 79

From "Comte" Julius de Montfort de Prat[6]

ALS: American Philosophical Society

Monsieur a Passy le 30 juin 1779.

C'est avec la satisfaction la plus sensible que J'accepte L'invitation gratieuse de Votre Exçellence de célébrer avec Elle L'anniversaire De nôtre glorieuse et éternelle indépendance; J'ay L'honneur D'être avec un profond respect de vôtre Exçellence, Monsieur, Le très humble et très obéissant Serviteur

JULES CTE. DE MONTFORT

J'ose prendre la liberté De faire icy mille compliments à Monsieur Votre petit fils.

Addressed: à / Son Exçellence Le Docteur Franclin / Ministre plénipotentiaire Des Etats / unis de L'amerique, en son hotel / *A Passy.*

Notation: Jules Comte de Monfort Passy le 30e juin 1779.

6. A major in Pulaski's Legion who gave himself the title of "comte"; he was on leave in France: XXVIII, 481n.

From John Torris

ALS: American Philosophical Society

Sir Dunkerque 30th. June 1779

I have the honnour to address your Excellency a Copy of the Particulars of the Cruise of the Black Prince Cutter Capt. Stephen Marchant, per Letter from him dated Morlaix 23d. Inst., received yesterday—[7] The 21 Prisonners He put on shoare at the disposal of your Excellency in Morlaix, you'll be Please to order Immediatly what you are pleased to do with them. Mr. Marchant Ramsoned a Brigg,[8] & I beg your Excellency will write him at Morlaix, where he will wait for your Answer, how he shall manage the said Ramsomer & the Payment of the Ramson. He was forced to Ramson the said Brigg haveing not hands enough to man his 8. Prises, the 6. of which still expected to arrive, I hope I shall hear from, per the next mail, & god Send it![9]

If this Cutter the Black Prince, can Ramson, as we all apprehend she can, I beg of your Excellency to mention the Case to the Brave Capt. Marchant, who will do honnour to his Coulours, & how to manage his Ramsons.—

I sent Mr. Marchant the directions about the Pacquets Boats from Dover to Calais, your Excellency did me the honnour to send me the 18th. Inst. & I am sure he will strictly attend to them.

Mr. John Diot a Clark of my House is gone express to Morlaix to attend the Cutter and the Prises, & he has orders to advise your Excellency of all that Passes, & if any difficulty happens, to write also to M. De Sartine & to Mr. De Chardon Mre. des Requettes avocat Gnal du conseil des Prises, who are well inclined in my favour.

I shall obmit nothing to deserve the approbation of your Excellency & to give all satisfaction to my Employers.

I remain with respect Sir Your most obedient & most humble servant

J. Torris

Notation: Mr: Torris June 30. 1779

7. In fact Marchant wrote Torris twice on the 23rd; the letters, which generally parallel those he wrote BF on the same day, are at the APS.

8. The *Three Sisters;* see Marchant's first letter to BF of the 23rd.

9. The six prizes were recaptured by the British, as Marchant told BF.

Index

Compiled by Jonathan R. Dull and Barbara B. Oberg
(Semicolons separate subentries; colons separate divisions within subentries.)